The Minnesota Guide

Anne Gillespie Lewis

★

Fulcrum Publishing
Golden, Colorado

To my husband, Stephen Lewis, with love and thanks

The information in *The Minnesota Guide* is accurate as of June 1999. However, prices, hours of operation, addresses, phone numbers, websites, and other items change rapidly. If something in the book is incorrect or if you have ideas for the next edition, please write to the author at Fulcrum Publishing, 350 Indiana Street, Suite 350, Golden, Colorado 80401-5093.

The Minnesota Guide provides many safety tips about weather and travel, but good decision making and sound judgment are the responsibilty of the individual. Neither the publisher nor the author assumes any liability for injury that may arise from the use of this book.

Library of Congress Cataloging-in-Publication Data
Lewis, Anne Gillespie.
    The Minnesota guide / Anne Gillespie Lewis.
        p.   cm.
    Includes index.
   ISBN 1-55591-362-8 (pbk.)
   1. Minnesota Guidebooks.   I. Title.
   F604.3.L5   ,   1999
   917.7604'53—dc21   99-31529
                                                        CIP

Printed in Italy
0 9 8 7 6 5 4 3 2 1

Cover photograph: Gary Alan Nelson
Back cover photograph: Minneapolis skyline. Copyright © Minnesota Office of Tourism. Used by permission.
Cover and interior design: Michelle Taverniti
Maps: GrayMouse Graphics
Editorial: Daniel Forrest-Bank, Kris Fulsaas
Composition: Bill Spahr

Fulcrum Publishing
350 Indiana Street, Suite 350
Golden, Colorado 80401-5093
(800) 992-2908 • (303) 277-1623
www.fulcrum-books.com

Contents

Acknowledgments

It would not have been possible to complete this book without the help of my husband, Steve, who went along on many of the journeys, made editing suggestions and proofed the chapters. Thanks, honey! Thanks, also, to our kids—Alix and David.

Some of my friends—Anne Mooney McLoone, Margery Martin, Jeanne and Ron Matross, Anne Lynch-Skaw, Sabrina Loomis, Isabelle Eubanks and Jane Johnson roamed Minnesota with me. Others—Jan McElfish, Marita Karlisch, Pat Larson Ehlers, Kathy Emery, Karen Anderson, Becky Eaton, Joe and Renee Gillespie, Jenny Obst, Carole Bearon, Val and Phil Smith, Opal Ronning, Jean Ross (and her son, Rob), Jo Paul, Candy Magnuson, Jane Bartow, Marie Gery, Ella Rolvaag Tweet and her daughters Torild Homstad and Solveig Zempel and Nancy Peterson Hoyt—listened to me, laughed with me and gave good advice. Our kind neighbors, Greg and Barb Stacy and Teresa Clarkin, house- and cat-sat, and the guys at Dick's 66 in St. Anthony Village kept the old Toyota running.

I owe a huge debt of gratitude to the Department of Natural Resources' Carmen Diestler for help in writing about Minnesota's State Parks, and to Connie Hill, super librarian at the North East Branch of the Minneapolis Public Library, and her dedicated crew. Many staff members at the Minnesota History Center and the historic sites were helpful; a special thanks to Tom Ellig, who read the section on the U.S.–Dakota Conflict and made suggestions.

Thanks to my friend Dave Hansen and his parents, Henry and Charlotte, for hospitality and tales of Minnesota's forests. Many others, including my cousin Myrlie Peterson Altergott in Northwood, North Dakota, the McLoones in Waseca, and Kathie and Dave Gerber, in Iowa, welcomed me into their homes. Days spent at Aurora Haas's Perham cottage are fondly remembered.

Many thanks to Minnesota tourism representatives who answered questions and checked facts. Jeff Howard, Mary Somnis and others in the Northern Lights Tourism Alliance, Linda Fryer in Ely, Kathy Bittner Lee in Brainerd, Jean Friedl in St. Paul, Tim Ward in Detroit Lakes and Carroll Kukowski in Aitkin were especially generous with time and logistical support and Al Thurley of Winona has been—as always—cheerful and optimistic.

The staff members of the Minnesota State Parks—especially Al Sobek at Lake Shetek and Jim Cummings of Mille Lacs Kathio—have been very helpful. Thanks, too, to Joan Hummel, Chuck Lennon, Paul Stafford and others at the Minnesota Office of Tourism; the St. Croix Valley Tourism Alliance; Bill Gardiner, former naturalist at Voyageurs National Park; and the state of Wisconsin. Thanks to Vanessa Hanley for her fact-checking help. Despite all the help given me, any errors that remain are my own responsibility.

A final thanks and wave of farewell to the "Red Wing Girls," among them my great-grandmother Christine Anderson Peterson, my grandmother, Melissa Peterson Anderson, and my mother, Eleanor Anderson Gillespie. Their stories of Minnesota lingered long after they had gone and provided a starting point for this book.

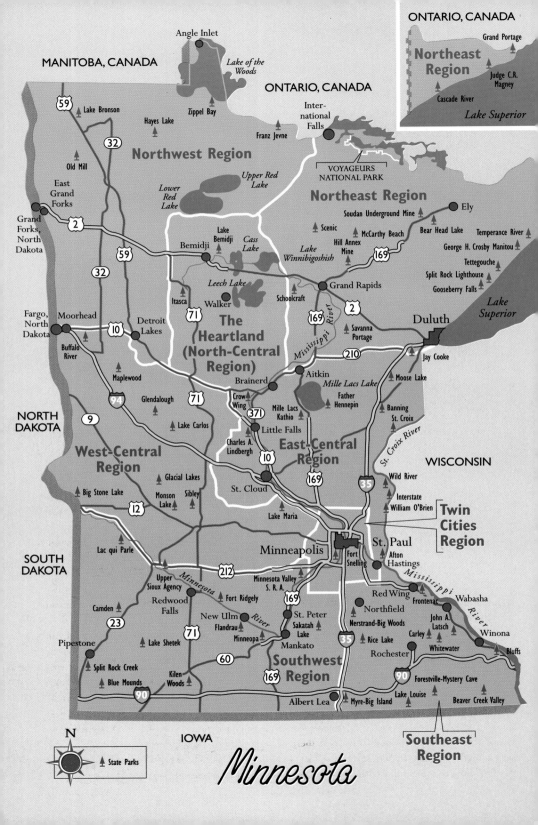

ONTARIO, CANADA

Northeast Region

Grand Portage

Judge C.R. Magney

Cascade River

Lake Superior

Angle Inlet

MANITOBA, CANADA

Lake of the Woods

ONTARIO, CANADA

59 Lake Bronson

Hayes Lake

Zippel Bay

Old Mill

32

Northwest Region

Franz Jevne

International Falls

VOYAGEURS NATIONAL PARK

East Grand Forks

Lower Red Lake

Upper Red Lake

Northeast Region

Grand Forks, North Dakota

2

59

32

Bemidji

Lake Bemidji

Cass Lake

Itasca

Walker

Leech Lake

Lake Winnibigoshish

Schoolcraft

Soudan Underground Mine

Ely

Scenic

McCarthy Beach

Hill Annex Mine

Bear Head Lake

Temperance River

George H. Crosby Manitou

Split Rock Lighthouse

Tettegouche

Gooseberry Falls

169

Grand Rapids

Fargo, North Dakota

Moorhead

10

Detroit Lakes

71

The Heartland (North-Central Region)

Brainerd

169

Mississippi River

Savanna Portage

2

Duluth

Lake Superior

Buffalo River

Maplewood

Crow Wing

Aitkin

Mille Lacs Lake

210

Jay Cooke

Moose Lake

94

Glendalough

71

Lake Carlos

Mille Lacs Kathio

Father Hennepin

Banning

St. Croix

NORTH DAKOTA

9

371

Little Falls

East-Central Region

St. Croix River

WISCONSIN

West-Central Region

Big Stone Lake

Glacial Lakes

Monson Lake

Sibley

Charles A. Lindbergh

10

169

St. Cloud

Wild River

Interstate

William O'Brien

Twin Cities Region

12

Lake Maria

Lac qui Parle

SOUTH DAKOTA

Camden

23

Pipestone

Upper Sioux Agency

Redwood Falls

212

Minnesota River

Fort Ridgely

New Ulm

Flandrau

Minneopa

71

Lake Shetek

60

Minneapolis

Minnesota Valley S.R.A.

169

St. Peter

Sakatah Lake

Mankato

Fort Snelling

St. Paul

Afton

Hastings

Mississippi

Red Wing

Northfield

Nerstrand-Big Woods

Rice Lake

Southwest Region

35

Frontenac

Wabasha

John A. Latsch

Carley

Whitewater

Winona

Rochester

90

Bluffs

Split Rock Creek

Blue Mounds

Kilen Woods

90

Albert Lea

Myre-Big Island

Forestville-Mystery Cave

Lake Louise

Beaver Creek Valley

Southeast Region

N

State Parks

IOWA

Minnesota

Introduction

Background Information

Why explore Minnesota? Well, why the heck not? We Minnesotans love it here, but we're a little shy about pushing it, because most of us—if we are true Minnesotans—were told by our mothers not to brag. On the other hand, there is plenty to brag about, from the stunning beauty of the northern lakes and the more subtle spell of the endless prairie to the abundant and fast-paced cultural life of the metropolitan area.

Our license plates proclaim that this is the land of 10,000 lakes. That, too, shows our modesty. There are actually about 15,000 lakes, and we're not just counting mud puddles. Of course, most of them are frozen a good part of the year, but that just means more time for ice fishing in them and snowmobiling and cross-country skiing across them. Water is a big factor in Minnesota. Even the name "Minnesota" is composed of two Dakota words that mean "cloudy" or "sky-tinted waters."

Some of the loveliest and most remote lakes are those near the Canadian border in the Boundary Waters Canoe Area Wilderness and in Voyageurs National Park, Minnesota's only national park. Red Lake is the largest lake totally within the boundaries of the state, but Lake Superior, which forms the northeast boundary of the state, is the largest inland lake (in area) in the world. Did I mention that the Mississippi River starts its life here? At its source, in Itasca State Park, visitors walk across it on stepping stones. In all, there are 25,000 miles of streams and rivers in Minnesota.

Outdoor recreation plays a big role in the lives of many Minnesotans. On Friday afternoons, lots of us head "up north" to "the lake," as if there were only one lake in the whole state, as historian William E. Lass says. At "the lake" is "the cabin," ranging from modest, one-room dwellings to out-and-out mansions, and 150,000 of us own one. The rest of us try hard to make friends with people who own a cabin so they'll invite us up. If that doesn't work, we spend a week at a resort—fishing, teaching the kids to water-ski, or just plain loafing—and visitors to Minnesota will also find plenty of opportunities for outdoor recreation.

Minnesota is a bit of a paradox, however. Though the outdoors figures strongly in the state's offerings, both the arts and sports—amateur as well as professional—play big roles here, too. The Twin Cities are second only to New York City in the number of theaters per capita. Music, dance, and the visual arts are well represented throughout the state; museums are among the best in the country; and many people's weekend plans include watching the Vikings play football or cheering on the University of Minnesota Gophers. And, of course, you can shop till you drop at the Mall of America.

Good old Minnesotans are even becoming a bit surprising. We just elected Jesse Ventura, a former Navy Seal, professional wrestler, and talk show host, to the governorship. He defeated the mayor of St. Paul and the Minnesota attorney general, son of the late Hubert Humphrey. Immediately, someone started selling bumper stickers and T-shirts that proclaim "Our governor can beat up your governor."

Also, the recent influx of immigrants from Southeast Asia, Africa, the former Soviet Union, and other distant locales has changed this traditional white-bread state into more of a multigrain loaf. And speaking of food, these same immigrants have vastly increased the number of ethnic restaurants, particularly in the Twin Cities.

So ignore what you've heard about the weather and take the public's favorite movies about Minnesota—*Grumpy Old Men* and *Fargo*—

with a grain of salt. Both are representative of narrow slices of Minnesota life. Ice fishing is popular but not universal, and not all Minnesotans sound like the actors in *Fargo*. But whether you're a Minnesotan or one of the 25 million visitors to the state each year, look around and decide for yourself.

Recommended Reading

Although it is difficult to pick one book about Minnesota and proclaim it the best book written about the state, there is one book that has endured for decades. It is the *WPA Guide to Minnesota,* a creation of the Federal Writers Project of FDR's Works Progress Administration. First published in 1938, it was republished by the Minnesota Historical Society in 1985. Although the state has changed greatly in more than 60 years, the essence of Minnesota can still be found within the pages of this minutely detailed and engagingly written book. For a humorous look at Minnesota, read Howard Mohr's *How to Talk Minnesotan: A Visitor's Guide* (Penguin Books, 1987) and Garrison Keillor's *Lake Wobegon Days* (Viking, 1985). And no, there is no Lake Wobegon in Minnesota.

History

Minnesota became the 32nd state on May 11, 1858, but its human history began thousands of years before that. Ancestors of today's American Indians roamed over the land that would become Minnesota thousands of years before the Dakota and the Ojibwe arrived; these early people left traces of their culture in a few small objects, such as the 9,000-year-old spear points found in what is now Mille Lacs Kathio State Park in central Minnesota. All around Minnesota, also, are thousands of burial mounds that attest to the presence of an ancient culture. Grand Mound near International Falls, the largest of these, is more than 100 feet long and more than 45 feet high.

The Dakota, or Sioux, as many people still refer to them, were the principal residents of Minnesota for centuries until the Ojibwe (Chippewa or Anishinabe) moved into northeast and central Minnesota from their traditional home at the eastern end of Lake Superior. The two

tribes clashed often, and a century-long, off-and-on series of fights began in 1736 and ended with the Dakota pushed into southern Minnesota.

The Dakota held sway when the first Europeans arrived in Minnesota. Exactly who these Europeans were is not certain. French explorers Pierre Radisson and his brother-in-law, Medard Chouart, Sieur des Groseilliers, were undoubtedly in Wisconsin in 1660 and may well have ventured into Minnesota, but they left no record. Nearly 20 years later, in 1679, Daniel Greysolon, Sieur Du Luth—for whom the city of Duluth was named—was definitely in Minnesota, claimed the land for the king of France, Louis XIV, and visited Dakota villages near Mille Lacs Lake.

A few months later, in 1680, Recollect Priest Louis Hennepin and two others were confronted by some Dakota while exploring the Mississippi below Lake Pepin. They were taken—perhaps unwillingly—to the Mille Lacs area, where Du Luth found them some six months later and took them back to New France (Canada).

After the first adventurers came the fur traders, looking for valuable beaver pelts to be made into hats worn by fashionable heads in Europe. The French presence in Minnesota lasted until they lost much of North America to Great Britain in 1763, but it has never really vanished. For proof, look at a map of Minnesota—many of the names of communities, streets, and bodies of water are in French. In Minneapolis, the main downtown streets are Nicollet, LaSalle, Hennepin, and Marquette. Most often the French names get mangled—Lake Le Homme Dieu near Alexandria comes out something like "Lahommadew"—and some are bashed beyond recognition— Riviere des Embarrasses somehow was transformed into "Zumbro" River.

After the Brits took over, the North West Company, a fur trade operation out of Montreal, became a dominant force, with the French-Canadian voyageurs doing the grunt work and paddling far into the interior. The post at Grand Portage was an important stopping place and rendezvous point for voyageurs, Indians, and company officials. There were other fur trade companies, too, including the American Fur Company.

In the aftermath of the American Revolution, the English skedaddled, leaving unresolved until the 20th century a pesky dispute about the boundary around Lake of the Woods. The resulting little splotch of land that sticks up on Minnesota's northern border—called the Northwest Angle—is actually north of part of Manitoba, Canada, and drivers must pass through Canadian customs to get to it.

After the Louisiana Purchase, Lieutenant Zebulon Pike was sent out by boat in 1805 to find a likely spot for a fort. After admiring the bluffs along the Mississippi near the current city of Winona, Pike and his crew arrived in what is now near the heart of the Twin Cities metro area. For the fort he picked the high ground where the Minnesota and Mississippi Rivers meet and persuaded the local Dakota to let the United States use it. The resulting complex—Fort Snelling—was finished in 1819 and still stands. It was the first European–American establishment of size in Minnesota. Across the Minnesota River from the fort was the limestone house of Henry Sibley, a fur trader who came to Minnesota in 1834 and later became the first governor of the state and a key figure in the U.S.–Dakota Conflict of 1862.

From the 1830s onward, the face of Minnesota changed rapidly. Missionaries arrived in what became Red Wing in the early 1830s, and the towering white and red pines started to fall, with the first sawmill in the state opened at Marine-on-St. Croix in 1839. Most of the new arrivals came by steamboats, which began swanning up and down both the Mississippi and Minnesota in the 1820s.

Almost inevitably, the government pressed the Ojibwe and the Dakota to relinquish their lands in return for promises. Treaties in 1837 with both tribes meant that nearly all land east of the Mississippi River was ceded to the United States and thus was available for settlement. The government continued to chip away at Indian land, until the treaties of 1851—perhaps the most decisive events in Minnesota history—took over most of southern Minnesota for the federal government, leaving the Dakota with a small strip of land along the Minnesota River.

After signing the treaty, the Dakota were incensed to discover that they had been fooled into signing an agreement giving tribal funds to fur traders owed money by individual tribal members. The Dakota who signed evidently thought they were signing yet another copy of the treaty, instead of the so-called "trader's paper."

The resentment on the part of the Dakota, the cramped reservation, the lack of promises kept, and the wretched poverty and hunger of the tribe all combined to cause the bloody U.S.–Dakota Conflict in 1862, which left about 500 white settlers and an unknown number of Dakota dead. The conflict, in the midst of the U.S. Civil War, resulted in the banishment of the Dakota and the execution of 38 Dakota the winter following the conflict. Many more would have been hung if Bishop Henry Whipple—whom the Indians called Straight Tongue—had not intervened with President Abraham Lincoln.

At the start of the Civil War, Minnesota Gov. Alexander Ramsey volunteered to send the first soldiers in the Union to the war. They acquitted themselves well, if with tragic results. On July 2, 1862, the 262 men of the First Minnesota Infantry charged the Rebels. They lost, through death or wounding, 215 of the 262, but their actions were crucial to the war effort.

The 1860s were busy years. In 1862 the Homestead Act lured thousands of immigrants and land seekers to the state. Settlers could get 160 acres of land if they agreed to build a dwelling place, live on the land for 5 years, and pay some closing costs. According to historian William E. Lass, 62,000 homestead claims were made by 1880.

Although the state's first European-American settlers tended to come from the East Coast, a huge influx of immigrants from northern Europe came in the mid- to late 1800s, giving Minnesota its predominantly Scandinavian and German mix, with a sprinkling of other ethnic groups thrown in. The largest single immigrant group were the Germans, but the immigrants from the various Scandinavian countries together outnumbered them.

The coming of the railroad in the 1860s and 1870s made travel easier in Minnesota and also saw the decline of steamboat traffic. The first towns to develop in the state were along the river routes, but the railroad's coming meant that communities throughout the state began to thrive. Lumbering continued to be important, though the heyday of the industry declined and most of the big pines were gone by the early 1900s. Mining was the next big thing, with iron ore found in northeastern Minnesota. There was even a brief, exciting gold rush in the 1890s, in what is now Voyageurs National Park.

Agriculture became increasingly important as the 19th century ended and the 20th dawned, with Minnesota one of the nation's chief producers of wheat. Flour mills soon sprang up to process the wheat, and great milling companies were born and still survive—Pillsbury and General Mills among them. Red Wing, on the Mississippi River, was once the leading grain-shipping community in the United States.

Minnesota has long been known as a center of medicine, and the whole world recognizes the name "Mayo Clinic." The clinic was started by frontier doctor William W. Mayo almost accidentally when he had to set up a pioneer "ER" in the aftermath of a tornado in 1883. His two sons, "Dr. Will" and "Dr. Charlie," greatly expanded the clinic and pioneered the concept of group practice.

Minnesota's 20th-century growing pains included ugly incidents and accusations toward German Americans during the First World War, and a bloody truckers' strike in 1934 that left several dead and Minnesota temporarily under martial law. The Great Depression of the 1930s was hard on Minnesotans, as it was on everyone. It was then that the Civilian Conservation Corps (CCC) and other FDR programs found work for unemployed young men, who carried out many civic projects, including building bridges, planting trees, and constructing many state park buildings.

Postwar years saw a gradual drift away from the traditional family farms, with farming operations growing larger and larger and rural dwellers headed for the city. During the 1980s, there was a severe farm crisis and many farmers had to sell out. Corn, soybeans, and sugar beets are among the principal crops, and there is a "dairy belt" running diagonally from the southeast to the west-central portion of the state. On the Iron Range, too, business declined after the war and only perked up again when the taconite mining process was introduced. The northern third of the state, especially in the northeast, is heavily forested with evergreens and birches, and logging and taconite mining are still important industries. The fortunes of the Iron Range fell again when many U.S. steel mills closed, and the area is now trying to diversify. The Twin Cities are home to many well-known companies, such as 3M and Honeywell. In addition, many high-tech and medical specialty firms are located in Minnesota.

Duluth became the farthest inland port when the St. Lawrence Seaway was completed in the 1950s, and now passenger cruise boats are beginning to visit the port. The resort and outdoor recreation industry, which began late in the 19th century, has grown steadily, and interest in both summer and winter recreation has made Minnesota a drawing card for those interested in outdoor sports. Recently, the completion of the mammoth Mall of America—the largest shopping mall in the country—has lured shoppers from around the world.

Visitors to Minnesota, especially those from other countries, are often eager to see American Indians, but often have outdated stereotypes about them. American Indians, who were the first humans to live in Minnesota, have always had a strong influence on the culture and history of the state, most recently in their establishment of popular casinos on reservations. However, American Indians who live in Minnesota—and in all of the United States, for that matter—lead the same kind of life and dress in the same way that anyone else does. Only at powwows—wonderful celebrations generally open to the public, with dancing, drumming, and singing—are visitors apt to see the traditional dress of the Ojibwe or Dakota on 1990s Indians. The American Indian Center in Minneapolis publishes a list of powwows in its monthly newspaper *The Circle*.

The 1990 census showed 49,909 American Indians living in Minnesota, though the Minnesota Indian Affairs Council now puts that number at more than 55,000. Nearly half live in the Twin Cities metro area, but a large percentage also live on the 11 Indian reservations scattered around the state. The reservations are nations-within-nations, on land that the Indians retained after ceding much of their land in return for rights and services guaranteed by 16 treaties and four agreements with the U.S. government.

St. Paul skyline. Copyright © Minnesota Office of Tourism. Used by permission.

Of these reservations, seven are home to Ojibwe and four are Dakota reservations. These latter are in the southern part of the state. The largest of the Ojibwe reservations—Red Lake—is in northern Minnesota and is roughly the size of the state of Rhode Island. Red Lake is one of only two closed reservations in the country (the other is in Oregon), with all land held in common by tribal members, as the tribe never signed it away. For information about Minnesota's Indians, treaties, and reservations, visit the website for the **Minnesota Indian Affairs Council** at **www.indians.state.mn.us.**

Those who want to learn about American Indian history and culture can visit the Minnesota History Center in St. Paul and the Mille Lacs Indian Museum in Onamia, a marvelous showcase of many aspects of historical and contemporary Ojibwe life. Some of the Indian-owned casinos also have cultural centers, and several museums, historic sites, and cultural centers in southwestern Minnesota focus on Dakota life and history.

Recommended Reading

The best short history of Minnesota may be William E. Lass's *Minnesota: A History,* first published in 1977 by Norton and later republished in a sec-

ond edition. Lass's book is a highly readable but also thorough walk through Minnesota history. Rhoda R. Gilman's *The Story of Minnesota's Past* (Minnesota Historical Society, 2nd ed., 1991), intended for younger readers, makes equally good reading for adults who want an overview of state history. Gilman's book is well illustrated with historic and current photos, art, and maps.

The history to end all histories of Minnesota is, of course, William Watts Folwell's *A History of Minnesota* (Minnesota Historical Society Press, 1969), four volumes of great detail on the history of the state, which the casual reader will probably find a little *too* detailed. *Father Louis Hennepin's Description of Louisiana—By Canoe to the Upper Mississippi in 1680* (University of Minnesota, 1938) gives an early look at what became the state of Minnesota and its Dakota inhabitants. Hennepin, a Recollect priest, was very opinionated, and his strong—not to say exasperating—personality is readily apparent to the reader. The translation was done by Marion E. Cross. Hennepin's description of Indian customs is particularly interesting. Peg Meier's *Bring Warm Clothes—Letters and Photos from Minnesota's Past* (Neighbors Publishing, 1981) is a treasure trove of Minnesota history, written by the high and mighty personages (such as Bishop Henry Whipple) and the obscure (such as the woman whose letter provided the title of the book). This is history at its most painless and entertaining, and the photos are great too.

William W. Warren's *History of the Ojibway People* (reprinted by the Minnesota Historical Society, 1984), though more than a century old, is still one of the standard resources on Ojibwe history and customs. For a contemporary view of Ojibwe life, read Jim Northup's alternately hilarious and poignant *Walking the Rez Road* (Voyageur Press, 1993) and *The Rez Road Follies* (Kodansha America International, 1997). Roy W. Meyer's revision of his 1967 *History of the Santee Sioux* (University of Nebraska, 1993) gives a detailed account of the Minnesota Dakota (Sioux) from their first encounter with French explorers and missionaries to the present time. In addition, there are several books about the U.S.-Dakota Conflict and individual Dakotas, particularly the fascinating Little Crow, who was a villain or hero, depending on your point of view.

Geography and Geology

Minnesota is in the north-central portion of the United States, with its northern border on two Canadian provinces, Manitoba and Ontario. Minnesota is a big place, more than 400 miles from north to south and ranging from almost 200 miles to just under 400 miles from east to west. It's the 12th largest state in the United States and the second largest east of the Rockies—Texas has Minnesota beat. The area was first surveyed by David Thompson in 1797; Thompson kept a meticulous diary (available in the library of the Minnesota History Center) of his work, the weather, and his companions.

The shape of Minnesota is kind of goofy. The southern border is a clean slice, dividing Minnesota from Iowa. On the eastern border, the Mississippi River and the St. Croix River zig and zag as they form part of the boundary with Wisconsin; the Arrowhead of northeastern Minnesota follows the north shore of Lake Superior. The western border, which Minnesota shares with North and South Dakota, runs fairly straight, except for a big bump about midway,

to accommodate a bend in the Minnesota River. The Red River—ordinarily a meek little stream, but which flooded with disastrous consequences for Grand Forks and East Grand Forks in 1997—separates Minnesota from North Dakota. In this book, some information is included on a few North Dakota and Wisconsin cities and towns that lie on the border of Minnesota and are frequently visited in conjunction with Minnesota places.

On the Canadian border, the Minnesota line follows a centuries-old route taken by the French-Canadian voyageurs, except—whoops—for the little toot that sticks up like a chimney on top of the state. That's the Northwest Angle—a surveyor's mistake, to make a long story short. You can only get to the Angle by boat on giant Lake of the Woods or by car, in which case you must drive in and out of Manitoba, Canada. Minnesota also shares its northern border on the east with Ontario.

The landscape of Minnesota was formed by fire and ice, not to mention wind and water. Once upon a Precambrian time, several billion years ago, Minnesota had mountains, which gradually eroded into the relatively flat state we see today. However, among the Precambrian rocks that remain evident are the granitelike, swirly-colored Morton Gneiss, found near Morton and Granite Falls in the Minnesota River Valley, and the Canadian Shield, which forms the picturesque, rocky landscape of northeastern Minnesota. The Morton Gneiss is approximately 3.5 billion years old, according to Constance Sansome, writing in *Minnesota Underfoot,* making it perhaps the oldest rock in the world. The Canadian Shield is about a billion years younger.

Then about 1,100 million years ago came periodic volcanic eruptions that laid down a deep layer of basalt over much of the state. Next, seas came and went in Minnesota, leaving proof that this was once an ocean state: the little sea critters that were left behind became fossilized, and massive amounts of limestone and sandstone were deposited. The coming and going of the seas, according to Sansome, is well illustrated in the strata that form Barn Bluff in Red Wing, in southeastern Minnesota.

However, the state as we see it today was primarily the work of the Ice Age, four major periods of glaciation with warmer periods sandwiched between. The periodic deep freezes began about two billion years ago and ended approximately 10,000 years ago, Sansome says. It was the last glacial period, called the Wisconsin Glaciation, that formed most elements of the current landscape in Minnesota. The glacier covered all but portions of southeastern and southwestern Minnesota, and in its slow retreat it sculpted the hills, valleys, and many lakes and streams of the state. The glacier left behind moraines that can clearly be identified if you know what you're looking for. Glacial Lakes State Park in western Minnesota and the nearby driving trail that traces glacial movement are good places to learn about effects of the glacier.

Remaining when the ice melted was massive Glacial Lake Agassiz, which once covered much of northwestern Minnesota. When it also disappeared, it left its flat lake basin as a legacy for the northwest. Postglacial meltwater produced lasting results. In Glacial River Warren in western Minnesota it left the broad Minnesota River Valley. In the St. Croix in the east, it created the world's deepest potholes.

In the middle of northern Minnesota, around Red Lake, is an area known as the big bog. The highest elevation is 2,300 feet at Eagle Mountain in northeastern Minnesota, and the lowest point is 600 feet above sea level, also in northeastern Minnesota. The Laurentian Divide, in northeastern Minnesota, sends water south to the Gulf of Mexico via the Mississippi River, east to Lake Superior, and west and north to Hudson Bay.

Recommended Reading

Constance J. Sansome's *Minnesota Underfoot* (Voyageur, 1983) is a detailed description of the geology of Minnesota, divided by areas. Sansome also includes advice about local recreation. John R. Tester's *Minnesota's Natural Heritage—An Ecological Perspective* (University of Minnesota, 1995) gives a comprehensive account of both the geography—including animal and plant populations within specific areas—and the geology of Minnesota, and has beautiful photos and useful charts

to boot. Bill Holm's latest book, *The Heart Can Be Filled Anywhere on Earth* (Milkweed Editions, 1996), and Paul Gruchow's books about the prairie—*Journal of a Prairie Year* (University of Minnesota, 1985) and *Grass Roots* (Milkweed Editions, 1995)—combine introspection with graceful observations of prairie country.

Flora and Fauna

Before settlement by European Americans began in earnest in the 19th century, Minnesota was characterized by a boreal coniferous forest in the north, a diagonal band of hardwoods (called the Big Woods) from the southeast through the middle, and tallgrass prairie in the south. Settlement changed all that, though remnants of all three exist. Minnesota has an area of 79,617 square miles, with 59 percent of total land area now agricultural.

Minnesota has a wide variety of flowers and other plant life, due to several distinct biosystems. The remaining and replanted tallgrass prairie areas, which stretched for mile upon mile in the western and southern part of the state before being mostly ripped up by the plow, have plants and grasses that are very different from those found in the evergreen and tamarack forests of the north and the remnants of the Big Woods hardwood forest of the southeast and central portions of Minnesota.

Prairie plants include cactus, early-blooming pasque flowers, blazing star, and many others. In the Big Woods near Northfield are the tiny dwarf trout lilies, known to grow only in Minnesota and only in a very limited area. In the north are found giant white and red pine trees that escaped the loggers. The red pine, also known as the Norway pine, is the state tree. Bogs and wetlands in Minnesota produce insectivorous sundews and pitcher plants as well as the state flower—the elegant pink-and-white showy lady slipper. An aquatic grass that has been a staple of the American Indian diet for centuries and now is a trendy side dish is wild rice, which grows in lakes in northern Minnesota. It is not rice, but a grass that grows in water, either lakes or flooded paddies.

Deer and raccoons are among the most commonly seen wild animals in Minnesota, and both

David L. Lewis of Minneapolis stands astride the Mississippi River as it begins in Itasca State Park in the Minnesota heartland region. Crossing the infant river on stepping stones is a favorite visitor activity in the park.

animals are hazards on the road. In northern Minnesota, there are black bears, moose, and even a couple of herds of elk; these are sometimes encountered. Heard but seldom seen are the gray wolves, once nearly vanished but now greatly increased in numbers since they became protected. They are now classified as "of special concern," rather than endangered or threatened. Farmers whose livestock are killed by wolves would like to see this protection cease, but so far the wolves still have the law on their side. Fox and coyotes are becoming increasingly evident, even in urban areas, and there are occasional sightings of mountain lions, also in the "of special concern" category.

Bald eagles are back now, after they nearly vanished from the state as the result of DDT and other poisons. They nest along the Mississippi River, and Wabasha in southeastern Minnesota has an eagle-watching center. Other birds of prey, including hawks and osprey, can be seen in Minnesota. Waterfowl, including the big and beautiful trumpeter and tundra swans, and many songbirds live or pass through Minnesota during migrations.

The Mississippi Flyway is a conduit for mass migrations of hawks and other birds. Hawk Ridge in Duluth is a lure for those who want to watch the hawk flights in fall. On a quiet night on a northern Minnesota lakeshore, listen and you may hear the haunting laugh of the common loon, Minnesota's state bird. Several birds in Minnesota—the piping plover, burrowing owl, and two kinds of sparrows—are among those categorized as endangered.

Recommended Reading

L. David Mech's books on wolves, including *Wolf,* first published by Doubleday in 1970 and reprinted by the University of Minnesota Press, provide a thorough introduction to Minnesota's loved and hated gray wolves. Robert B. Janssen's *Birds in Minnesota* (University of Minnesota Press for the James Ford Bell Museum of Natural History, 1987) is a helpful field guide to the some 400 species of birds found in Minnesota.

Climate

If visitors haven't already heard the old saw that Minnesota's climate is "ten months of winter and two months of rough sledding," they will almost certainly hear it before they leave this climatically dramatic state.

Winter we have. The coldest temperature ever recorded in Minnesota—a bone-chilling 60°F below zero—occurred in 1996 at Tower, in the northeastern corner of the state. But it gets cold in the Twin Cities, too: The record low there is minus 41°F, way back in 1888. The average date for the first fall freeze is October 13, and the average date for the last is April 20. The average snowfall annually is 42.3 inches, with 24.7 inches of rain tossed in, too. Most of the state has snow cover that lingers from mid-December to mid-March.

The windchill factor, always included in weather reports, should be heeded. It is true that exposed skin freezes quickly in subzero temperatures, and visitors are often unprepared for the extreme cold and wind.

Out-of-staters are often shocked at the heat and humidity of Minnesota summers. Temperatures in the 90s are not at all uncommon in July and August, and the mercury hit a record 114°F in Moorhead on July 6, 1936. Throughout the year, temperatures can vary by about 15°F from north to south. The coolest spot in summer is usually the north shore of Lake Superior, where a condition known as the "Lake Effect" moderates the temperature in both winter and summer.

Minnesotans have learned to be conscious of weather warnings, as they really can mean the difference between life and death sometimes. In winter, sudden blizzards—high winds and blowing snow—can cause whiteouts, a particularly dangerous situation for drivers on highways or those who strike out on foot. In winter, heed storm warnings and carry an emergency kit in your car—with food, water, candles, blanket, etc. In the spring, tornadoes are likely to whirl across the state. Again, listen to weather warnings broadcast on radio and TV and, if warning sirens sound, seek shelter at once in basements or windowless rooms. Note that the warning sirens are tested at 1:00 P.M. on the first Wednesday of each month throughout Minnesota.

Visitor Information

General Information

For those who want to visit Minnesota, and for state residents as well, the **Minnesota Office of Tourism** is the first place to contact. The administrative office is in St. Paul. Written queries should go to the **Fisher's Landing TIC, Rte. 1, Box 70A, Fisher, 56723; 800-657-3700 or 651-296-5029, fax 651-296-2800, 800-627-3529 for TTY service. Website: www.exploreminnesota.com.**

The tourism office also has 11 highway travel information centers that are open year-round: Thompson Hill off I-35 near Duluth; Anchor Lake near Eveleth in northeastern Minnesota; International Falls on the Canadian border; Fisher's Landing near Crookston in northwestern Minnesota; on I-94 at Moorhead, St. Cloud, and St. Croix; and on I-90 at Beaver Creek, Worthington, Albert Lea, and Dresbach. There is also an information center at Grand Portage, which is open from May to October.

There is an **Explore Minnesota USA** information center and store in the Mall of America. Visitors can buy state park permits, tick-

ets and season passes for state attractions, Minnesota gifts, and lodging gift certificates in addition to obtaining travel information.

Tips for Visitors

U.S.–Canadian Customs—Minnesota shares its northern border with Manitoba and Ontario in Canada. There are several entry points. Those open 24 hours are near Pembina, Warroad, Baudette, International Falls, and Grand Portage. U.S. citizens need only a driver's license or other form of state identification. Noncitizens should carry passports.

Drinking and Smoking—You must be 21 years old to drink alcohol in Minnesota. There is no smoking in public buildings in Minnesota; that's why you see little knots of people puffing away just outside the doors of public buildings, even in very cold weather.

Clothing—Dress appropriately if you're going to be doing outdoor adventuring in Minnesota. Winter recreation is wonderful if you are dressed for it, and miserable if you are not. Layer your clothes and be sure to wear a hat and gloves or mittens. Conversely, summer temperatures soar and the visitor who thinks Minnesota is never hot will have a rude and sweaty awakening unless—again—proper clothing is packed.

Highway Hazards—Every year, cars kill about 15,000 deer in Minnesota, 4,000 in the Twin Cities area. Signs on highways alert drivers to areas where deer cross frequently. Although moose are less often spotted, they can be deadly if they collide with a vehicle. Signs warn of moose along the western portion of U.S. Hwy. 2, which ends at East Grand Forks on the North Dakota border. Minnesota roads, especially the interstates and major highways, are usually in good shape. Heavy snow may slow traffic in winter. The **State Dept. of Transportation** gives information on road conditions and detours, **800-542-0220 or 651-405-6030.**

Mosquitoes and Ticks—Minnesotans like to tease visitors by telling them that the mosquito is our state bird. They do seem as big as birds when you're fighting off the buzzing menaces. Once the sun goes down, they go on a feeding frenzy. Be prepared by slapping on plenty of repellent. Both wood ticks and deer ticks are present in Minnesota, usually from spring until midsummer. Because of the deer tick–borne Lyme Disease, use special cautions—wear lightweight long-sleeved shirts and long pants, even in hot weather, tucking pant legs into socks, and avoid walking through tall grasses and underbrush in tick season. Tick repellents can also be used.

Telephones—Minnesota has five area codes, two introduced rather recently. In Minneapolis and surrounding suburbs, the area code is 612; although more area codes may be added for the suburbs, nothing was determined at press time. In St. Paul (except for the St. Paul campus, which shares a telephone system with its 612 Minneapolis campus) and southeastern Minnesota to just below Wabasha, the area code is 651. If you are calling St. Paul from Minneapolis, or vice versa, you must first dial the area code, although the call will not be charged at long-distance rates. The 320 area code is for the area around the Twin Cities north and west across the center of the state. Area code 507 is for the southeastern portion that includes Winona and Kellogg, as well as the south-central and southwest, and 218 is the area code for northern Minnesota.

Addresses—Many addresses in rural Minnesota have changed recently and more changes are scheduled—all to make it easier for emergency vehicles to locate properties when they need to. I have tried to verify all addresses, but some will have changed after this book goes to press.

Getting There
By Plane—The main airport, the **Minneapolis–St. Paul International Airport,** is located in Bloomington, a suburb south of Minneapolis. The airport is close to both Minneapolis and St. Paul and has direct connections to Europe and Asia, via Northwest Airlines, which is headquartered in Minnesota and also flies to destinations within the United States and Canada. Icelandic

Air flies directly to Iceland from Minneapolis–St. Paul and onward to European destinations; other carriers serve domestic and foreign destinations. There is also regularly scheduled air service to **Duluth, Fargo-Moorhead, Hibbing,** and **Rochester.**

By Train—As everywhere else, **Amtrak** service within Minnesota is limited. However, the train travels from the Twin Cities to Red Wing and Winona in the southeast, and also to Detroit Lakes and Fargo-Moorhead in the north. Call **800-872-7245** for national information and reservations or **651-644-6012** for St. Paul station information.

By Bus—There is **Greyhound** bus service, **800-231-2222,** to and from the Twin Cities to smaller population areas in Minnesota, and also throughout the United States and Canada.

By Car—All major car rental firms can be found in the bottom level of the Minneapolis–St. Paul International Airport. I-35 runs from the southern border of Minnesota north to Duluth. It is intersected by I-90, which is in southern Minnesota. I-94 enters Minnesota near the Twin Cities and follows a northwest course to Moorhead on Minnesota's western border.

Information for Disabled Visitors
Visitors who need lodging facilities that can accommodate wheelchairs can call the **Minnesota Office of Tourism, 800-657-3700, 651-296-5029,** or for **TTY service, 800-627-3529,** for help in finding them. The annual state parks guide (see Camping, below) has a category for campsites that are accessible for those with a physical disability. Often, state parks also have short trails that are wheelchair accessible. **Wilderness Inquiry,** a nonprofit group that began in 1978, has adventure trips (canoeing, dogsledding, skiing, fishing, etc.) for all, including persons with physical disabilities. Trips are in Minnesota and surrounding states and also range far beyond the Upper Midwest. **1313 Fifth St. SE, Minneapolis, 55414; 800-728-0719, 612-379-3858 for voice or TTY. Website: www.wildernessinquiry.org.**

How This Book Is Organized

The book is organized into eight regions—Twin Cities, Southeast, Southwest, West-Central, Northwest, Heartland, Northeast, and East-Central. Within these regions are 35 destinations (chapters), usually a city but sometimes a larger geographical area. Chapters begin with an overview and a history of each destination, with a boxed section on getting there. Next you might find listings for major attractions; a selection of festivals and events; outdoor activities with individual sections for biking, boating, hiking, swimming, and so on; sightseeing and museum-based attractions; suggestions for where to stay and where to eat; and, finally, services that may be helpful. The index will help you navigate your way around the specifics of what you want to see and do in Minnesota.

Major Attractions

Some of the destinations in this book include this category when the attraction is one of the main reasons people visit the place. For example, Itasca State Park, where the Mississippi River begins, is a major attraction in the Mississippi Headwaters chapter. Major attractions are listed in the order of their significance.

Festivals and Events

Within each chapter, festivals and other special events are listed in chronological sequence. Among the best-known festivals in Minnesota are the St. Paul Winter Carnival, the Minnesota State Fair, and the Minneapolis Aquatennial. Music festivals that draw crowds include the WE Fest in northwestern Minnesota.

In summer, nearly every community has a Fourth of July celebration. Many places also have summer festivals, usually involving a parade, perhaps a street dance, food booths, and sometimes ethnic dancing or festivities. July and August are the months when county fairs are held. Try to attend one for a look at a side of America that is fast disappearing. Late fall is the season for the lutefisk and meatball suppers in Lutheran churches all across the state. Many lovers of lutefisk (dried cod cured in lye and resurrected into a baked, quivery mass doused with melted butter) draw up a list and eat at as many suppers as they can manage. Traditionally, one of the first lutefisk suppers was at Faith Lutheran in Madison, close to the South Dakota border. Madison features a huge fiberglass fish honoring its lutefisk industry, plus several historic buildings now being renovated.

Recommended Reading

Blue Ribbon—A Social and Pictorial History of the Minnesota State Fair by Karal Ann Marling (Minnesota Historical Society, 1990) tells the story of Minnesota's beloved state get-together. It's all here—from the midway to the food to the butter sculptures of Princess Kay of the Milky Way.

Outdoor Activities

In Minnesota, outdoor activities, whether in winter or summer, are of primary interest to both locals and visitors. Winter brings the expected sports of skiing and snowmobiling, as well as snowshoeing, snow tubing, ice-skating, and even ice fishing. In summer, water-based activities

Pink and white lady slipper, Minnesota's state flower. Copyright © Minnesota Office of Tourism. Used by permission.

abound: boating (especially canoeing), fishing, swimming. Minnesota's abundance of lakes and rivers, including the headwaters of the Mississippi, entice thousands of visitors each year. Many of these activities take place in state and federal parks and forests, but Minnesota also has an abundance of local parks as well.

Within Minnesota are two national forests—Superior, in the northeast corner of the state, and Chippewa, in the north-central portion of Minnesota. The well-known Boundary Waters Canoe Area Wilderness (BWCAW) is part of Superior National Forest. Both forests have wonderful recreational opportunities—hiking, cross-country skiing and snowmobile trails, fishing, camping, etc. The BWCAW draws canoers from around the world to experience the solitude and beauty of the north woods. For **Chippewa National Forest** information, contact headquarters at **Rte. 3, Box 244, Cass Lake, 56633; 218-335-8600.** The **Superior National Forest** headquarters can be reached at **8901 Grand Ave. Pl., Duluth, 55808; 218-626-4300.**

There are 11 national wildlife refuges in Minnesota—Sherburne, Rice Lake, Agassiz, Tamarac, Sandstone, Rydell, Hamden Slough, Mille Lacs, Crane Meadows, Minnesota Valley, and Big Stone refuges, plus the Upper Mississippi National Wildlife and Fish Refuge, which extends to other states south of Minnesota. Some of the refuges are described in this book. For information on all, contact the **U.S. Fish and Wildlife Service**'s wildlife refuge offices. The eight-state district that includes Minnesota is located in Minneapolis, at **1 Federal Dr., BHW Federal Bldg., Fort Snelling, 55111; 612-713-5400.**

There are 66 state parks and four recreation areas in Minnesota, many of which are very popular with campers. Many of the state parks have sites of historic significance, as well as excellent recreation opportunities. The parks are scattered throughout the state and include various types of landscapes.

Minnesota has 57 state forests, mainly in the northeastern and north-central parts of the state, although Richard J. Dorer Memorial State Forest, an enormous tract of land that is divided into several units, is in southeastern Minnesota, close to the Mississippi River. Most state forests, which are working forests where trees are grown for harvest, have campgrounds and often contain lakes or rivers. Many have day-use areas, hiking trails, horseback riding trails, snowmobile trails, and trails for mountain bikes and off-road vehicles, but recreation is not organized as it is in the state parks. Entry into state forests is free, although some developed campgrounds charge a fee. A state parks guide and an overall guide to state forest day-use areas and campgrounds, and also maps of individual forests and sometimes units within forests, are available from the **Dept. of Natural Resources (DNR), 500 Lafayette Rd., St. Paul, 55155; 888-MINNDNR** (in Minnesota) or **651-296-6157.**

Recommended Reading

Listening Point by Sigurd Olson (Knopf, 1958) is a Minnesota classic. Olson, a pioneer conservationist/naturalist/writer, lived in Ely. A good general guide to outdoor pursuits in the state is Jim Umhoefer's *Guide to Minnesota Outdoors* (NorthWord Press, 1992). *Wild Minnesota* (NorthWord Press, 1993), with text by Greg Breining and gorgeous photography by Richard Hamilton Smith, deftly displays and describes the wonders of Minnesota. For armchair travel in Minnesota's great outdoors, read *Up North* (Pfeifer-Hamilton Publishers, 1987) or other books by Sam Cook, an outdoor writer for the Duluth daily paper. Cook writes thoughtful, philosophical essays about his outdoor adventures.

BIKING

Maps of state bicycle trails are available from the DNR (see Outdoor Activities, above). Currently, there are 15 state trails, not all suitable for touring bikes. Some are suitable for mountain bikes. A number of state parks and state forests have mountain bike trails. Also, many communities and counties have developed their own bike or multiuse trails, many connecting with state trails. Contact the tourism bureaus of specific areas to obtain trail information.

Recreational motor vehicles—all-terrain vehicles, off-highway vehicles, and off-road vehicles—are becoming more and more evident.

The Dept. of Natural Resources publishes a handbook of regulations for these vehicles and a map of trails for off-highway vehicles. For a copy of either, contact the DNR.

BOATING

The American Indians, who were the first residents of Minnesota, relied on birch-bark canoes for transport on lakes and rivers. Later, the voyageurs employed by the fur trade did the same. Now canoeing and its younger cousin, kayaking, are two of Minnesota's most popular recreational activities. It's not just a wilderness activity—witness the racks of canoes on the lakes in the Twin Cities, and the many cars driving through city streets adorned with a canoe on top. Though many people own their own canoes, they can be rented readily, sometimes at state parks. Minnesota has 24 designated canoe river routes. Some of the rivers are divided into segments, and separate maps are available on each segment. The Mississippi River is divided into 10 segments. Maps of these canoe routes and the Lake Superior kayak trail can be obtained from the DNR (see Outdoor Activities, above). The **Minnesota Canoe Association** holds classes and offers a variety of canoe trips; **P.O. Box 13567 Dinkytown Station, Minneapolis, 55414; 612-985-1111.** Motorboats and personal watercraft (more commonly known by the brand name Jet Ski) are also popular.

FISHING

Minnesotans love to fish, and it seems that they like talking about fishing almost as much. Not surprisingly, Minnesota ranks first in the country in the number of fishing licenses per capita, and a good share of Minnesotans are poised to sink their lines after midnight on a Friday in mid-May, when the season opens for walleye and northerns. There are 144 species of fish in Minnesota, but walleye is the state fish. It, along with northerns, muskies, and large- and smallmouth bass, are the chief quarries of anglers. For information on seasons and licenses, contact the **Dept. of Natural Resources, 500 Lafayette Rd., St. Paul, 55155; 888-MINNDNR** (in Minnesota) or **651-296-6157.**

Trout and salmon also are big draws; a separate trout stamp is required in addition to a Minnesota fishing license to catch trout. Licenses are available for a year and also for shorter periods. They can be purchased at many places, including bait shops.

Fishing isn't just a warm-weather activity in Minnesota. In winter, about 250,000 people drill holes in the ice and sit inside fish houses—basic or luxurious—waiting for a bite. On Mille Lacs Lake and other popular ice-fishing lakes, there are so many fish houses that it seems little towns have sprung up overnight. The houses must be off the ice by the end of February.

More and more, the catch-and-release regulations and attitude prevail. Nevertheless, the DNR estimates that 35 million pounds of sport fish are caught each year. The Minnesota Dept. of Health puts out an annual guide to fish consumption, telling readers how to trim and cook fish to get rid of contaminants and also telling about safe consumption levels. To obtain this guide, contact the DNR (see Outdoor Activities, above).

Recommended Reading

Shawn Perich's *Fishing Lake Superior* (Pfeifer-Hamilton, 1994) is a comprehensive guide to fishing on the lake, on the shore, and in the streams emptying into Superior.

GOLF

Even though Minnesota has a short golfing season, a recent study showed that there are more than 400 golf courses and 25 driving ranges in the state. Many of the top courses are in resort country, especially in the Brainerd area. Some of the courses have hosted top national tournaments. For information on golfing in Minnesota, contact the Minnesota Office of Tourism (see General Information, above).

HIKING

Hiking trails are numerous in Minnesota. The big one is the Superior Hiking Trail, which will eventually stretch from Duluth to the Canadian border. Most of it is completed now, and hikers are enthusiastic about its variety of terrain and difficulty levels. In addition, many of the biking trails (see Biking, above) are also used by hikers, and all but a few state parks have extensive hiking trails. State and national forests also have hiking trails, many in remote near-wilderness areas.

Recommended Reading

No hiker on the Superior Hiking Trail should be without the *Guide to the Superior Hiking Trail* (Ridgeline Press, 1993), which has detailed, mile-by-mile descriptions of the trail and its surroundings. Mary Jo and Jim Malach's *Walking Minnesota* (Voyageur Press, 1991) gives valuable walking tips, lists resources and organizations, and outlines both outdoor and indoor walks throughout Minnesota.

HUNTING

Hunting and trapping are popular activities in Minnesota. Each year, the Dept. of Natural Resources publishes a handbook of hunting and trapping regulations. Quarries include deer, bear, moose, wild turkey, and small game. There are approximately 800,000 deer in Minnesota, and hunters annually kill about one-quarter of the deer population. The hunting regulations and seasons are complex, and some of the hunting is by permit issued by lottery. Regulations change from year to year. The handbook is available from the DNR (see Outdoor Activities, above).

SKIING

Minnesota, with its usually abundant snow and long winters, is a great place for cross-country skiing. There are more than 2,800 miles of cross-country ski trails in the state, approximately 1,500 of them groomed. The Gunflint Trail in northeastern Minnesota is prime cross-country territory, as the season can last from November to April. Skate-skiing has been growing steadily in popularity, and about three dozen trails are groomed for skate-skiers. More than 50 state parks have cross-country trails, and don't forget that many downhill ski areas also have cross-country trails. Using public trails requires the purchase of a state ski pass, which is sold at state parks and other cross-country venues. Cross-country skiers who would like to join a club for organized trips, lessons, or tips should contact the **North Star Ski Touring Club, P.O. Box 4275, St. Paul, 55104.**

Minnesota does have downhill ski areas, though the state is certainly no threat to Colorado. Most mountainlike skiing can be found at Lutsen in northeast Minnesota, but there are also about a dozen other ski areas in the state. Contact the Minnesota Office of Tourism (see General Information, above) for more information.

SNOWMOBILING

Snowmobiling is one of the most popular winter sports, and several snowmobile makers are located in Minnesota. The state is crisscrossed by 20,000 miles of groomed and marked trails, often maintained by local snowmobile clubs. For a map of regional snowmobile trails or a copy of the snowmobile regulations, contact the DNR (see Outdoor Activities, above).

SNOWSHOEING

Some state parks offer snowshoe outings and even classes in making snowshoes, and 18 of them have snowshoes for rent.

Seeing and Doing

In each chapter, this section includes activities that may take place outdoors or indoors but that are generally less physically demanding than those listed in Outdoor Activities. Many of the things to do in this category involve visiting a commercial or public enterprise of some sort.

ART GALLERIES AND MUSEUMS

Under this heading, look for art museums, art and cultural centers, art galleries, and any other facility focused on fine art.

CHILDREN AND FAMILIES

A few chapters feature places to visit with little ones, including zoos. In most cases, however, the places listed in Seeing and Doing can be appropriate for families; if you're not sure, call the establishment to check.

GARDENS AND ARBORETA

Though a public garden may be designated a park, if its main feature is its gardens, you'll find it listed under this category.

MUSEUMS AND HISTORIC SITES

Most of the major museums are represented in this book, but not all county museums and other museums around the state are included. Readers should seek them out, however, particularly if they are interested in local history. Also included under this heading are historic places that may be open-air sites rather than actual museums.

PARKS

In this category, you will find state parks as well as smaller local parks, such as city and county parks, especially those that contain such facilities as public swimming pools, outdoor music facilities, and the like. Minneapolis, St. Paul, Duluth, and Rochester all have extensive municipal park systems. Larger parks that most people visit for outdoor activities are usually listed under those specific activities, with a brief listing under Parks that includes information on facilities and who to contact.

The jewel in the crown of Minnesota's 66 state parks and four recreation areas is generally conceded to be Itasca State Park in northern Minnesota, where the Mississippi River begins. In fact, many people think Itasca should be designated as a national park. Visitors should not neglect the other state parks, however, given their scenic, recreational, and historic attractions. Most of the parks have camping facilities, and nearly all have hiking and cross-country skiing or snowmobiling trails. There is a fee for entry, payable on a daily or annual basis and well worth the investment. State residents and longtime visitors may be interested in joining the hiking or passport clubs associated with the state parks. For a brochure and map giving locations and details on camping, trails, and rentals for all state parks, contact the DNR (see Outdoor Activities, above). For campsite reservations, call **The Connection** at **800–246-CAMP** or **612-922-9000.**

Voyageurs National Park is Minnesota's only national park and it is also the national park that encompasses the most water. Lying up against the Canadian border, the beautiful park is in territory once known as the "voyageurs highway." Pine-covered rocky islands dot the lakes of the park, and bears and eagles are among its inhabit-

The common loon, Minnesota's state bird. Copyright © Minnesota Office of Tourism. Used by permission.

ants. For details, see Voyageurs National Park Area in the Northeast Region.

Recommended Listening

Charlie Maguire, a Minneapolis folksinger and composer, wrote and sang 19 songs about Minnesota state parks and their history on *State Park Tapestry*, released for the state park centennial in 1991. The cassette and songbook are out of print, but available from the public libraries. However, some of the songs are available on Maguire's latest CD, *Harbour Lights: The Second Voyage* (Mello-Jamin Music, 1988). The songs—about brave Itasca State Park director Mary Gibbs and Ozawindib, who showed Henry Schoolcraft the source of the Mississippi River—are wonderful ways to learn about Minnesota history.

PERFORMING ARTS

Under this heading you might find listings for dance, classical music, opera, and various kinds of theater.

SCENIC DRIVES

Highway 38, north of Grand Rapids, was chosen as a U.S.-designated Scenic Highway a few years ago. It winds among lakes and is surrounded by a blaze of colorful trees in autumn. See the Grand Rapids chapter in the Northeast Region section for details. The federally designated Great River Road stretches from where the Mississippi River begins and meanders along it, over many roads.

The route is scenic and also of historic interest. A map of the Minnesota portion, and separate brochures on segments of the Great River Road in the state, are available (see below). Ten scenic byways—including the Great River Road—cover the state, providing drivers with a variety of scenery. The drives are posted with distinctive signs to help drivers follow them. Throughout the state are designated wildflower routes that take visitors past wildflowers blooming in season. One of the best known is Highway 11 from Baudette to Greenbush near the Canadian border in northwestern Minnesota. The showy lady slipper, Minnesota's state flower, blooms in profusion along this route. Also spectacular for prairie and other native flowers is the Shooting Star route, near the Iowa border. Information on the Great River Road and the state scenic byways is available from the **Minnesota Office of Tourism, 800-657-3700** or **651-296-5029. Website: www.byways.org.**

SHOPPING

Listings under this heading include places that purvey products unique to a region in Minnesota, or that really should be included in a visit, to experience a slice of Minnesota life.

TOURS

Tours included in this category are usually fee-required guided tours, such as boat tours and cave tours, but they can also be free, self-guided walking tours and the like. Most driving tours are listed under Scenic Drives.

Where to Stay

Minnesota has a wide number of choices for hotels and motels, from deluxe hotels to small mom-and-pop motels. Increasingly, visitors seem to enjoy staying at bed-and-breakfasts and small inns, and more and more of these open every year in Minnesota. Unique places to stay include a floating bed-and-breakfast anchored in downtown St. Paul, and a sod house on the prairie. For a true Minnesota vacation, stay at a resort on one of the state's 15,000 lakes. These accommodations range from the luxurious and modern to the rustic. Some visitors, indeed, prefer to seek out small resorts where they can hark back to the pioneer days, while others want every modern convenience and good fishing, too. For information, request a brochure on accommodations, bed-and-breakfasts and inns, and/or resorts from the Minnesota Office of Tourism (see General Information, above).

The following price guidelines have been included. Insofar as possible, prices are current. Price categories are for a double room or similar accommodation, which in a bed-and-breakfast includes breakfast. Prices change, so check before you make a reservation. Note that some prices, particularly for resorts, are not included, usually when a complicated price structure warrants calling the establishment itself.

$	Under $25
$$	$25 to $50
$$$	$50 to $100
$$$$	$100 and up

CAMPING

There are many private campgrounds in Minnesota, and in addition, many resorts also have spaces for RVs and sometimes tent camping. Each year, a guide to campgrounds is issued by the Minnesota Office of Tourism (see General Information, above).

Most counties have some campsites, and many have excellent, well-equipped campgrounds on beautiful sites. Towns and cities often also have campgrounds. Some of the sites are free. Contact counties or local tourism offices for information (see individual chapters).

Most of Minnesota's 70 state parks and recreation areas have camping facilities. The campsites may or may not have electricity and varying degrees of other amenities. Campsites are classified as drive-through, drive-in, walk-in, pack-in, cart-in, bike-in, or canoe- or kayak-in. The kayak-in sites are located along the north shore of Lake Superior. State parks with extensive horseback trails, such as Forestville in southern Minnesota, often have campgrounds specifically for horses and riders, with corrals for horses. Campsites nearly always have fire rings, picnic tables, and toilet and water facilities, and many have shower buildings. Winter camping is available at all state parks, but only a few have modern toilet facilities available year-round. However, all have rustic toilet facilities and water all year. Check with individual parks if you have questions about campsites or the services available.

In addition to tent and RV sites, there are camper cabins in state parks, and more and more are being built. Some of the camper cabins are for summer use only, but some are winterized. They are fairly bare-bones, but are a kind of halfway house for those who want to feel they are camping without actually putting up a tent. Some state parks also have additional accommodations, usually guest houses or cabins that were built before the area became a state park, including the cabins at Tettegouche State Park in northern Minnesota.

Reservations are advisable in summer, particularly in the most popular state parks, including Itasca and Whitewater. Call **The Connection** at **800-246-CAMP** or **612-922-9000.**

State forest campgrounds are often more secluded than state park campgrounds and are often closer to activities forbidden in state parks, including hunting in season. Some of the state forest campgrounds are very rustic, while others have many amenities. Entry into state forests is free, although some developed campgrounds usually charge a fee; the more rustic campsites are free. A map of state forests, which includes a list of campgrounds, is available from the DNR (see Outdoor Activities, above).

For information on camping in Voyageurs National Park, see the chapter on the park in the Northeast Region section of this book. For information on camping in Chippewa National Forest or Superior National Forest—including permits for camping in the Boundary Waters Canoe Area Wilderness, contact the forest headquarters (see Outdoor Activities, above).

Where to Eat

I have tried to include a wide range of eating establishments for each destination; however, my personal bias is probably apparent. I lean toward the small-town cafes and ethnic restaurants, although I have included many long-established restaurants both for their usually excellent food and for their popularity over the years. Although I don't disparage chain restaurants, everyone knows them and I think most visitors need no advice in finding them. I've tried to emphasize local specialties—in Minnesota, this often means fish and sometimes game. No restaurant has paid to be included in the book. The following price guidelines have been included. Insofar as possible, prices are current. Price categories are for the price of an entree—which can include a breakfast, lunch, or dinner entree—per person, not for an entire meal.

$	Under $5
$$	$5 to $10
$$$	$10 to $20
$$$$	$20 and up

Services

Each chapter concludes with a listing of chambers of commerce and other sources of local visitor information; some chapters also include a description of local transportation such as city bus service.

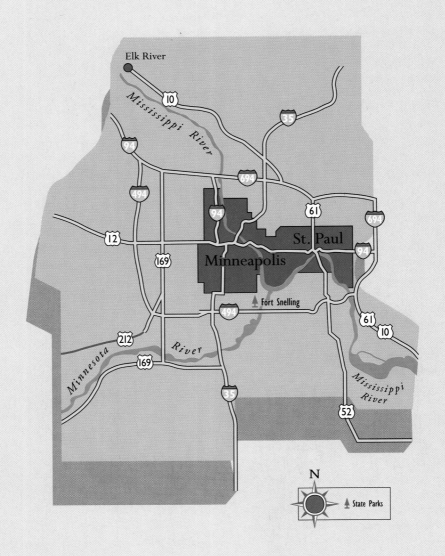

Twin Cities Region

Twin Cities Region

Adding color and texture to the Minneapolis skyline is one of the city's newest symbols: the Spoonbridge and Cherry Fountain in the sculpture garden adjacent to the Walker Art Museum, by sculptors Claes Oldenburg and Coosje van Bruggen.

(Spoonbridge and Cherry, 1987–88. Aluminum stainless steel paint. Collection Walker Arts Museum; gift of Frederick R. Weisman.) Photo courtesy of the Greater Minneapolis Convention and Visitors Association.

Minneapolis and St. Paul

Minneapolis and St. Paul are called the Twin Cities, but they are far from identical. Residents of each city—especially native Minneapolitans or St. Paulites—see them as very distinct, and it is almost a point of pride for some people to say they never go to the other city. Conventional wisdom has it that St. Paul is older and more conservative, more like Eastern cities in looks and attitude. Minneapolis, on the other hand, supposedly turns to the West, with shiny glass skyscrapers and considerably more flash. St. Paul has traditionally been thought of as Irish Catholic, and Minneapolis as Scandinavian Lutheran—a sort of Ole and Bridget combo instead of the Scandinavian Ole and Lena, as in the ever-present Scandinavian jokes.

Are all these cliches true? Yes and no: St. Paul is indeed the smaller and quieter of the two; the St. Paul Cathedral is in St. Paul, whereas the gigantic congregation of Mount Olivet Lutheran is in Minneapolis; and there are more tall, glittery buildings and more things to do at night in Minneapolis than in St. Paul. But that is painting each town with a very broad brush. Both are beautiful cities, clean and green and big on self-improvement. Is there sibling rivalry? Certainly, but that doesn't stop the cities from, on occasion, cooperating.

Without looking at a map, many people would say Minneapolis is west of the Mississippi River and St. Paul is east of the river, but a large chunk of Minneapolis is east of the river, too. On the map, Minneapolis and St. Paul are roughly the same size, but Minneapolis is a nearly vertical rectangle, whereas St. Paul has a horizontal shape. The two are connected by I-94, a modern umbilical cord uniting the Twin Cities, and the trip from one downtown to the other is about 11 miles. Downtown Minneapolis is set at an angle to the city's regular grid of streets, and the Mississippi River, though not far from downtown, doesn't yet play the prominent role that it does in St. Paul's center. Minneapolis turned its back to the river for decades and only recently has it become a popular recreational asset, with residents taking a brisk walk along the "Mississippi Mile" and over the old stone arch bridge in all seasons.

St. Paul has two parks in the heart of downtown. Rice Park, surrounded by the St. Paul Hotel, the Ordway Music Theatre, the Landmark Center, and the James J. Hill Library, functions as a modern town square. Mears Park anchors Lowertown, the older section of downtown. Minneapolis's most central park—Loring Park—is on the outskirts of downtown, but Nicollet Mall, which has a seasonal farmers market on Thursdays, serves some of the functions of a park. Out-of-town visitors are often surprised by the network of "skyways" connecting buildings in both downtowns. Built to protect downtown workers and visitors from the elements, the skyways soon developed into little cities within cities, with restaurants, shops, and services. Minneapolis and St. Paul each have about 5 miles of skyways. They connect to hotels and some apartment buildings, and it is possible to live, eat, bank, work, and shop without going into the open air.

History

The Dakota and Ojibwe Indians were both living around the site of the present Twin Cities when the first explorers recorded European settlers arrived. Among the first explorers was Father Louis Hennepin, who saw the falls that halted traffic up the Mississippi River in 1680, and named it after his patron saint, St. Anthony. The area was under several different flags—French, Spanish, British, and finally American—in the years when the Twin Cities began to develop. All the while, of course, the Indians considered the land as belonging to all.

Impetus for settlement came when Fort Snelling, at the junction of the Minnesota and Mississippi Rivers, was established in 1819. Fur trader and later governor Henry Sibley was just down the river, at Mendota. The first steamboat arrived at Fort Snelling in 1823, and treaties with the Ojibwe and Dakota in 1837 allowed European settlement in much of what is now the metropolitan area. Technically, both cities started in 1838. Minneapolis began when Franklin Steele made a claim near St. Anthony Falls (now Minneapolis); St. Paul had a rather unsavory start when an outcast named Pierre "Pig's eye" Parrant built a shack on the present city site.

Lumber and agriculture built the cities' economies, and agribusiness is still a vital part of Minneapolis. Flour milling was king in Minneapolis, and several food companies known worldwide, including Pillsbury and General Mills, have headquarters here. James J. Hill, whose Great Northern Railroad opened up the American West, lived and worked in St. Paul, as did several kingpins in the lumber industry.

Today, agribusiness and forestry industries have been joined by such technology-oriented giants as 3M and Honeywell. In addition, the Twin Cities have become important in advances in medicine: the heart pacemaker was invented and is still manufactured here. The Twin Cities are

---

Getting There

*Minnesota's principal airport, Minneapolis–St. Paul International Airport, is located in Bloomington, a suburb about 9 miles south of Minneapolis and St. Paul. The airport has connections to everywhere and direct flights—on homegrown Northwest Airlines—to the United Kingdom and to Asia. The busy airport also is used by about a dozen other major airlines as well as airlink services. Air traffic has grown so fast in recent years that it is hard for the parking ramps to keep up; yet another expansion of parking is now under way. **Amtrak** trains running between Chicago and Seattle stop in Minneapolis. The Amtrak station is located between the two cities, in St. Paul's Midway Area; **730 Transfer Rd., St. Paul, 55114; 651-644-1127. Greyhound Lines** operates from the Twin Cities to all areas of the United States, with connections to Canada. There are bus stations in both downtown areas; **800-231-2222.** Two major interstates slice through the Twin Cities: I-35, which runs north and south, and I-94, which connects the cities from east to west before it turns north and heads toward Fargo, North Dakota. I-35 splits into a west and an east section (through Minneapolis and St. Paul, respectively) far outside the city limits on both the north and south sides; be sure you know which one you want, 35-W or 35-E. The Twin Cities are a day's drive from Chicago and Winnipeg, Manitoba.*

---

financial centers for the region, and the giant University of Minnesota, with its two Twin Cities campuses, is also one of the area's largest employers.

The look of the residents of the Twin Cities has changed as well. Of late decades, the white-bread image of both cities has altered. There has always been an American Indian population and recently there has been considerable in-migration of other ethnic groups, including African

The Mall of America, the largest shopping mall in the United States, is a top tourist draw. Photo courtesy of the Mall of America.

Americans, Africans, Vietnamese, Hmong, and Hispanic Americans.

These days, the two cities cannot be discussed without including the inner, middle, and outer rings of suburbs that surround them. All in all, the metropolitan area has a population of about 2.7 million, more than half the state total of 4.4 million. However, the suburbs claim the largest share of the metro population, while Minneapolis's population is approximately 369,000 and St. Paul has about 272,000 residents.

Major Attractions

Mall of America

Well, they built it, and they came. More than 200 million people have visited the enormous Mall of America in Bloomington—the largest such mall in the United States—since it opened in 1992. In fact, the MOA (or the Megamall, as many people call it) outdraws visitors to Disney World, Graceland, and the Grand Canyon combined, ac-

cording to the MOA website. About 7 percent of the shoppers come from outside the United States.

The mall is anchored by four department stores in its four corners—Macy's, Bloomingdale's, Nordstrom, and Sears. But that's only four of the 500-plus stores in the mall. Tenants include more than two dozen shoe stores; a Chapel of Love, which has been the site of more than 1,500 marriages; seven sporting goods stores; dozens of clothing stores; 22 sit-down restaurants and 27 fast-food restaurants; a multistory amusement park; an enchanting Lego playland and store; a store that specializes in products dealing with the human anatomy; a bead store; four luggage stores; a comedy club; a store that carries farm toys; a couple of travel agencies; a separate walk-through aquarium in an underwater park; and a Minnesota Tourism office. Tired already? Try walking it: a circuit of each level is 0.57 mile. Speaking of walking, several thousand mall walkers show up to trek around the mall for exercise.

The four department stores at the corners of the mammoth building are connected by shopping "avenues." In the middle, accessible from all sides, is the three-story Knott's Camp Snoopy, a full-scale indoor amusement park that has a roller coaster, other breath-catching rides, and gentler rides for younger kids.

The fourth level of the mall is reserved for entertainment, including a 14-screen movie theater, and nightclubs/bars/restaurants such as America's Original Sports Bar, Knucklehead's Comedy Club, Planet Hollywood, and Fat Tuesday.

Buses run frequently from Minneapolis and St. Paul to the mall. In downtown Minneapolis, catch bus No. 80 on Nicollet Mall between Third and 12th Sts. In St. Paul, take bus No. 54, which leaves downtown on Sixth St. between Jackson and Kellogg Blvd. There are also taxi stands at the north entrance of the mall and at the transit station, located on the lower level of the east parking ramp. There is free parking in the spacious lots. The retail section of the MOA is open daily, though restaurants, nightclubs, and other attractions may have varying hours. Open Mon.–Sat., 10:00 A.M.–9:30 P.M.; Sun., 11:00 A.M.–7:00 P.M. Located at the **junction of I-494 and Hwy. 77**

(Cedar Ave. S.) in Bloomington; 612-883-8800. Website: www.mallofamerica.com.

Mystic Lake Casino

The second most popular tourist destination in Minnesota is Mystic Lake Casino in Prior Lake, the state's largest gaming spot. The casino is open around the clock and includes more than 125 blackjack tables and 2,200 slot, video poker, and keno machines. There is also a nonsmoking area in the casino. All this, and a hotel and top-class entertainment, too. The casino is owned by the Mdewakanton Sioux Community. **2400 Mystic Lake Blvd., Prior Lake, 55372; 800-262-7799 or 612-445-9000.**

Festivals and Events

St. Paul Winter Carnival

late Jan. to early Feb.

The grand old man of winter festivals, St. Paul's 10-day celebration began in 1886, as a rebuke to a newspaper reporter from the East Coast who accused St. Paul of being "another Siberia, unfit for human habitation." To this day, St. Paul proves him wrong by wallowing in winter, with Minnesotans lured out of their warm houses by two parades, baseball and golf played on ice and snow, giant ice slides, sleigh rides, a treasure hunt, and ice-carving and snow-sculpting contests. Occasionally, a glittering ice palace has been constructed. **651-223-4700.**

Taste of Minnesota

Fourth of July weekend

Munching and music—that's what the Taste of Minnesota in front of the Minnesota Capitol in St. Paul is all about. A huge crowd shows up for the weekend to sample food from area restaurants and listen to a variety of music on several different stages. As a finale on the Fourth, there is a spectacular fireworks display. Fee for food; the music is free. **651-772-9980.**

Minneapolis Aquatennial

mid-July

The Aquatennial originated in 1940 as a summer festival promoting Minneapolis and its lakes, and many of the most popular events—a race of boats

Mystic Lake Casino and Hotel at Prior Lake is among the state's leading tourist attractions, owned by the Mdewakanton Band of Dakota Indians. Photo courtesy of the Greater Minneapolis Convention and Visitors Association: Bob Perzel.

made entirely of milk cartons and a sand-sculpture contest—still take place on city lakes. But there are events on land as well during the 10-day event, including parades, a fireworks display, and a block party on Hennepin Ave. Admission by paid button for some events. **612-331-8371.**

Minnesota State Fair

late Aug. to Labor Day

Attendance at this 12-day "great Minnesota get-together" in St. Paul regularly tops one million. The fairgrounds—300 acres in all—includes space for animal barns; a coliseum for horse shows and rodeos; buildings devoted to crafts, 4-H projects, art, food, and horticulture; and a midway of rides and games of chance. Politicians stand ready to shake hands with passersby, and serious salespeople demonstrate their wares. But, to tell the truth, most Minnesotans go to the fair for the food. Yep, it's pig-out time every year. Particularly popular are the foods-on-a-stick. Don't miss the Olde Mill boat ride; tiny, greasy, sugared doughnuts (sold on several corners); the sculpture done in butter of Princess Kay of the Milky Way (the fair's annually chosen royalty); the church dinners; and the all-you-can-drink milk booth. Entertainment and fireworks nightly in the grandstand. Fee. Located in St. Paul; the **main entrance is off Snelling Ave. 651-642-2200.**

Renaissance Festival

weekends in Aug. and Sept.

Rascals and refined gentry from the 16th century, all correctly costumed, roam the grounds of the Renaissance Festival, jousting, playing music, interacting with visitors, and demonstrating and hawking crafts and food. Watch out or you may be waylaid by the festival's favorite comedy duo, Puke and Snot. Fee. Located southwest of Minneapolis, **4 miles south of Shakopee, off Hwy. 169. 612-445-7361.**

Holidazzle Parades

late Nov. through Dec.

Who cares if this is a ploy to draw people downtown to shop? It's fun to watch and livens up Minnesota's dark late afternoons in midwinter. The paraders and floats are aglow with lights and glitter as they march down Nicollet Mall every night when the sun sets. For information, call the Greater Minneapolis Convention and Visitors Bureau, **800-445-7412.**

Outdoor Activities

Biking

In St. Paul, there is a 1.75-mile biking trail around Lake Como and a 3-mile trail around Lake Phalen, which connects to the Willard Munger State Trail, plus trails along much of the Mississippi River. For information, call **651-266-6400.** Bikers have plenty of options in the metro area. In addition to the parks listed below, see Parks in Seeing and Doing.

Gateway State Trail

This 18.3-mile multiple-use trail starts in St. Paul and is level and accessible for wheelchairs. Users are surprised at the sometimes-rural nature of a trail in an urban area—the trail goes through parks, wetlands, and fields as well as urban territory. Biking, hiking, cross-country skiing, horseback riding, and in-line skating are permitted, but no motorized vehicles are allowed. For a map with trail features, contact the **Dept. of Natural Resources, 500 Lafayette Rd., St. Paul, 55155; 888-MINNDNR** (in Minnesota) or **651-296-6157.**

Grand Rounds Scenic Byway

A nearly complete tour of Minneapolis can be made by following the 53-mile Grand Rounds Scenic Byway by bike. The most scenic part of the byway is through Wirth Park and down through the string of lakes in the southwest portion of the city, then across on Minnehaha Parkway over to Minnehaha Park. Forty-three of the miles are designated bike trails. **612-661-4800.**

Luce Line State Trail

The 63-mile Luce Line, on an old railroad grade, stretches from Plymouth to Cosmos. From Plymouth to Winsted, the surface is limestone; for the rest of the trail, it is a natural surface. In the east, users can see remnants of the Big Woods here and there; in the west, there are remainders of the tallgrass prairie. Usage permitted includes biking, hiking, mountain biking, cross-country skiing, and snowmobiling. Snowmobiles are not permitted east of Stubb's Bay Rd. in the metro area. There is a parallel treadway for horses. For a trail map, showing trail features, contact the **DNR, 500 Lafayette Rd., St. Paul, 55155; 888-MINNDNR** (in Minnesota) or **651-296-6157.**

Minnesota Valley State Trail
See Minnesota Valley Recreation Area under Hiking, below.

Boating
Around the Twin Cities, cars with canoes on top are a common sight. Although most of these folks may be on their way farther north, many canoe right in town in city and county parks. A couple of favorites are Minnehaha Creek and Lake of the Isles. If you don't have your own canoe, many large parks rent them (see Parks in Seeing and Doing). For boating information, contact **Midwest Mountaineering, 309 Cedar Ave., Minneapolis, 55454; 612-339-3433.**

Fishing
Lakes in both cities, as well as the Mississippi River, draw anglers. Lake Como in Como Regional Park in St. Paul is stocked with walleye, largemouth bass, and bluegill, and has a fishing pier; boats with electric motors are allowed on the lake. Minneapolis's Lake Calhoun, another popular fishing spot, also has a fishing pier.

Golf
Minneapolis has five 18-hole golf courses for the public—Wirth Regional Park, Columbia, Hiawatha, Gross, and Fort Snelling—and St. Paul has three 18-hole courses, at Como Regional Park, Highland Park, and Phalen Regional Park. For information, call the parks (see Parks in Seeing and Doing). Suburban public courses include **Edinburgh USA Golf Course** in Brooklyn Park, which has hosted the LPGA Classic, **612-424-7060; Brookview** in Golden Valley, **612-544-8446;** the tough **Bunker Hills** course in Coon Rapids, **612-755-4141;** and **The Wilds**, in Prior Lake, **612-445-4455.** In addition, there are many wonderful private courses in the Twin

Cities, such as **Hazeltine National** in Chaska, **612-448-4500,** which has twice hosted the U.S. Open; check them for visitor privileges.

Hiking
It's easy to find hiking trails in the many parks in the Twin Cities area. In Fort Snelling State Park, the 3-mile hike to Pike Island gives visitors a nice view of both the Minnesota and Mississippi Rivers. In the fall, walk along the Gun Club Lake route to see migrating waterfowl. There are 18 miles of hiking trails and 5 miles of surfaced bike trails. Como Lake in St. Paul and Lake Harriet and Lake of the Isles have well-used walking paths around the lakes. The "Mississippi Mile" corridor along the river in downtown Minneapolis is popular with downtown workers at lunchtime. See Parks in Seeing and Doing for some other ideas.

Minnesota Valley Recreation Area
Part of the state park system, this recreation area has varying landscapes, from wetlands to floodplain forest to bluff tops and oak savanna. There are 4.5 miles of self-guided trails, nearly 70 miles of hiking along the Minnesota Valley State Trail, 6 miles of surfaced bike trails, and 35 miles of trails for mountain bikes and horseback riders. The recreation area stretches along six counties and is interwoven with the Minnesota Valley National Wildlife Refuge. Follow signs from Hwy. 282 and U.S. Hwy. 169 to enter the area. **19825 Park Blvd., Jordan, 55352; 612-492-6400.**

Skating

ICE-SKATING
Skating rinks have always been a part of Minnesota winters. Today, although outdoor skating is not as popular as it once was, many parks still have ice rinks.

Como Lake
Part of St. Paul's wonderful Como Park, Como Lake doubles as an outdoor rink in winter. It doesn't open until late Dec. or early Jan., depending on the weather. There are no rentals. Located on the lake at **Lexington Pkwy. N.; 651-487-9311.**

Holidazzle parades dazzle downtowners. Photo courtesy of the Greater Minneapolis Convention and Visitors Association.

John Rose Oval

Built as both a public rink and a practice rink for speed skaters, the Roseville rink gives recreational skaters a real workout. The oval, which opened in 1993, is the largest outdoor sheet of ice in the United States. It is 110,000 square feet and contains a 400-meter track for speed skating (and, later, in-line skating). Beginners are welcome, too. There are skates for rent. The season opens about Nov. 1 and closes in early Mar.; the oval is used for in-line skating in spring and summer. There is also an indoor rink at the same place. Skates can be rented. Fee. **2661 Civic Center Dr., Roseville, 55113; 651-415-2170.**

Lake of the Isles

One of the favorites is the rink on the northeast corner at Lake of the Isles in Minneapolis, on a serpentine lake in one of the city's choicest residential districts. There is a warming house, on the east side of the lake. From Hennepin Ave. S., follow W. Franklin to the lake. Free. No rentals. Call **612-376-4900** for details.

IN-LINE SKATING

You see in-line skaters everywhere, but Lake Calhoun in south Minneapolis, off W. Lake St., seems to be *the* place to skate in summer. In Roseville, the public John Rose Oval is used for in-line skaters in spring and summer (see Ice-Skating). In winter, skaters turn to the HHH Metrodome in downtown Minneapolis. In-line skates can be rented. Fee. Enter at gate D. Call for a schedule. Located at **900 S. Fifth St., Minneapolis, 55415; 612-825-3663. Website: www.roller-dome.com.**

Skiing

CROSS-COUNTRY

There are many cross-country ski trails, including trails for skate-skiing as well as diagonal skiing, in the seven-county metropolitan area. In winter, Fort Snelling State Park has 18 miles of cross-country ski trails, with 9 miles for skate-skiers. For a listing of metro trails, with length, general description of the trail, difficulty ratings, and phone numbers, contact the **DNR, 500 Lafayette Rd., St. Paul, 55155; 888-MINNDNR.** Although skiers must have a state ski pass, **612-522-4584,** there is generally no fee for skiing in metro parks; however, county and state parks charge admission fees. In Minneapolis, Theodore Wirth Regional Park on the city's western edge is a public golf course that is transformed to a skiers' wonderland with a coating of snow. There are about 6.5 miles of trails, varying from flat to quite steep. There is a warming house, and skis can be rented. Located at the **intersection of Glenwood and Theodore Wirth Pkwy.** Other public golf courses also double as cross-country ski venues in winter. In St. Paul, Como Regional Park has a cross-country ski center and more than 4 miles of groomed trails, some of which are lighted until 10:00 P.M. Skis can be rented. Located at **1431 Lexington Pkwy., St. Paul, 55103; 651-488-9673.** There are 5 miles of cross-country ski trails in Minnesota Valley Recreation Area (see Hiking).

DOWNHILL

Buck Hill

A cleared slope and a rope tow marked the beginning of Buck Hill ski area in 1954. Now the ski area boasts eight lifts, one of them a quad chair lift, and a dozen different runs. Its kids' and women's programs are well regarded. A snowboard park and equipment rental are available. The chalet has a cafeteria and an adults-only restaurant. Located **just off I-35 in Burnsville; 612-435-7174.**

Hyland Hills

Part of Hennepin County's Hyland Lake Park Reserve, Hyland Hills is the closest ski area for residents of the metropolitan area. The area has 14 runs served by three triple chair lifts. The ski school includes classes for those over 40 as well as children and women only. There is a half pipe for snowboarders. Equipment can be rented. The chalet has food service. **8800 Chalet Rd., Bloomington, 55438; 612-835-4604.**

Snowmobiling

The outer fringes of the metropolitan area have snowmobile trails, as do some of the regional parks (see Parks in Seeing and Doing). During winter in Minnesota Valley Recreation Area, snowmobiles rule—there are 35 miles of trails for them (see Hiking).

Swimming

Parks in both Minneapolis and St. Paul have swimming beaches at lakes and also at swimming pools; in addition, most county parks have swimming facilities. Main beaches in Minneapolis include **Lake Nokomis, 4965 E. Nokomis Pkwy.,** and **Wirth Lake, 3200 Glenwood Ave. N.** Neighborhood beaches (free; no bathhouse) are at **Cedar Lake, 3300 Cedar Lake Pkwy.; Harriet North, Lake Harriet Pkwy.;** and **Calhoun Thomas, W. Lake Calhoun Pkwy.** Minneapolis pools, which charge a fee, include **Rosacker, 1520 Johnson St. NE, 612-370-4937; Webber, 4300 Webber Pkwy., 612-370-4915;** and **North Commons Water Park, 1701 Golden Valley Rd., 612-370-4945.** For general information on swimming, call **612-661-4875.**

In St. Paul, **Como Pool** is open from early June until Labor Day. Fee. Call for hours. Located at **Horton Ave. and N. Lexington Pkwy.; 651-459-2811.** There is also a pool at **Highland Park, 1840 Edgecumbe Rd., 651-699-7968.** In addition, **Lake Phalen Regional Park** has a beautiful beach. Free. Open daily from

mid-June to Labor Day. Call for hours. Located **north of Wheelock Pkwy.** (the entrance is at Wheelock Pkwy. and Arcade); **651-776-9833.**

Seeing and Doing

Art Galleries and Museums

Both Minneapolis and St. Paul have "art crawls" of galleries in the cities. St. Paul does free self-guided "crawls" to studios and galleries of about 150 artists in **St. Paul's Lowertown.** Held in the spring and fall on Fri. and Sat. nights. For details, call **651-292-4373; Website: www.artcrawl.-org. Minneapolis's warehouse district** sponsors eight free self-guided tours of more than half a dozen artists' studios and galleries eight times a year. The first is the week after Labor Day; the crawls are held about every six weeks, on Sat. nights, 6:00–9:00 P.M. See local papers for listings.

Frederick R. Weisman Art Museum

Striking—some would say startling—in appearance, this oddly angled, shiny aluminum outer shell houses a splendid collection of contemporary art and imaginative temporary exhibitions, displayed in wonderfully light and airy rooms. It is part of the University of Minnesota and was designed by Frank Gehry. There's a great gift shop, too. Free. Open Tues., Wed., Fri., 10:00 A.M.–5:00 P.M.; Thurs., 10:00 A.M.–8:00 P.M.; Sat.–Sun., 11:00 A.M.–5:00 P.M. **333 E. River Rd., Minneapolis, 55455; 612-625-9494.**

Minneapolis Institute of Arts

The 'Tute, as it is known, recently had a complete makeover and added much more gallery space. Stone lions now guard the 24th St. entrance. The MIA, greatly respected among similar art museums, provides a comprehensive look at the fine arts, including several period rooms that are seasonally decorated for the holidays and part of a local house designed in 1908 by Frank Lloyd Wright. The imperial jade "mountain," an exquisitely carved sculpture that is part of the T. B. Walker jade collection, is one of the institute's best-known pieces. The MIA also has many excellent paintings, including Rembrandt's *Lucretia* and a collection of impressionism's best, including Van Gogh's *Olive Trees*. The institute's large and well-regarded Asian gallery includes a fine collection of Chinese bronzes. Also featured is art from Africa, Egypt, and Amerindia. The MIA has a restaurant and coffee shop. Free admission (except for special exhibits) and parking in a ramp behind the institute. Open Tues., Wed., Fri., Sat., 10:00 A.M.–5:00 P.M.; Thurs., 10:00 A.M.–9:00 P.M.; Sun., noon–5:00 P.M. **2400 Third Ave. S., Minneapolis, 55404; 612-870-3200** for recorded information, **888-MIA-ARTS** anywhere in the United States, **612-870-3131**. **Website: www.artsMIA.org.**

Minnesota Museum of American Art

Housed in a series of rooms ringing the inner court of the stately Landmark Center in St. Paul, the Minnesota Museum of American Art has paintings by well-known artists such as Grant Wood, Thomas Hart Benton, and Childe Hassam, plus traveling exhibits. Free. Closed on major holidays. Open Tues.–Wed. and Fri.–Sat., 11:00 A.M.–4:00 P.M.; Thurs., 11:00 A.M.–7:30 P.M.; Sun., 1:00–5:00 P.M. **75 W. Fifth St., St. Paul, 55102; 651-292-4355.**

Walker Art Center and
Minneapolis Sculpture Garden

The Walker, under the direction of Martin Friedman, established itself as one of the hippest contemporary art museums in the country. Friedman has moved on, but the Walker remains daring in its exhibitions and is quick to snare important traveling exhibitions. The Walker took another big step more than a decade ago when it opened the sculpture garden across from the museum proper. The centerpiece in the garden is the Spoonbridge and Cherry sculpture and fountain, by Claes Oldenburg and Coosje van Bruggen. To one side of the garden, which is divided into separate "rooms" by hedges, is a small conservatory, where a Frank Gehry–designed giant fish with scales of glass rests on its tail in a pond surrounded by orange trees. The conservatory is a most welcome spot on a cold day in January. In addition to art, the Walker also sponsors an ambitious pro-

gram of films, music, and special events. Fee for museum; sculpture garden and conservatory are free. Museum and conservatory open Tues., Wed., Fri., Sat., 10:00 A.M.–5:00 P.M. (10:00 A.M.–4:00 P.M. on second Fri. of each month); Thurs., 10:00 A.M.–8:00 P.M.; Sun., 11:00 A.M.–5:00 P.M. Sculpture garden open daily, 6:00 A.M.–midnight. **725 Vineland Pl., Minneapolis, 55403; 612-375-7600. Website: www.walkerart.org.**

Children and Families

Children's Theatre Company

What started as a tiny company years ago grew into a polished theater, presenting shows such as *The 500 Hats of Bartholomew Cubbins* and other well-known and -loved stories. Fee. **2400 Third Ave. S., Minneapolis, 55404; 612-874-0400.**

Como Zoo

The compact zoo, recently completely redone, has lions, tigers, and bears, and wolves, too. Kids of all ages love it. Go in summer (though the zoo is open year-round) to catch the antics of "Sparky the Seal" in a free show twice daily except Mon., at 11:00 A.M. and 2:00 P.M. During the holidays, the zoo is illuminated with thousands of twinkly lights. Best of all, it's free at all times. Open daily 10:00 A.M.–6:00 P.M. Apr.–Sept.; 10:00 A.M.–4:00 P.M. in winter. Located **between Hamline and Lexington Aves. on Midway in St. Paul; 651-487-8201** or **651-487-8200.**

Minnesota Children's Museum

This is child's play that adults will love, too. Shake a piece of flexible metal to make a booming peal of thunder, operate a crane, make it rain on a model village, or don an ant costume and crawl through a maze of pathways in a giant "anthill." It's hands-on all the way, and the excitement of the kids is contagious. Fee. Open year-round, Tues.–Wed. and Fri.–Sun., 9:00 A.M.–5:00 P.M.; Thurs., 9:00 A.M.–8:00 P.M. Also open Mon., 9:00 A.M.–5:00 P.M., Memorial Day–Labor Day and holidays. Closed Thanksgiving and Christmas Days. **10 W. Seventh St. (Seventh and Wabasha), St. Paul, 55102; 651-225-6000.**

Minnesota Zoo

Natural habitat is the emphasis in this vast zoo in Apple Valley. The animals are here, all right, but they often have wide-open spaces in which to roam, so be patient when looking for them. There is an indoor tropical forest, and a Minnesota Trail focuses on animals native to the state. A monorail runs through most of the zoo. Discovery Bay, the largest addition since the zoo first opened in 1978, houses dolphins, sharks, and other aquatic dwellers. Fee. Open daily, 9:00 A.M.–4:00 P.M. in winter; 9:00 A.M.–6:00 or 8:00 P.M. other times. Located south of the Twin Cities; follow Hwy. 77 (Cedar Ave. S.) and watch for signs. **13000 Zoo Blvd., Apple Valley, 55124; 800-366-7811 or 612-432-9000.**

Gardens and Arboreta

Como Park Conservatory and Ordway Memorial Japanese Garden

Outside it may be winter, but inside this glittery glass conservatory, it's a tropical paradise. Stroll among palms and lemon trees, walk amid a tame jungle of ferns, and gaze at the splashes of color in the seasonally changing flower shows in the sunken garden. The conservatory, which opened in 1915, was recently refurbished. Outside but near the conservatory is the Japanese garden, which opened in the early 1900s but—oddly—disappeared for years; after two renovations it was rededicated in 1992. It is a quiet, peaceful haven. The tea ceremony is performed on occasion in the teahouse. Fee for conservatory; Japanese garden is free. Conservatory open daily, Apr.–Sept., 10:00 A.M.–6:00 P.M.; Oct.–Mar., 10:00 A.M.–4:00 P.M. Japanese garden open daily Mother's Day–Labor Day or by appointment; call for hours. Como Park is located **between Hamline and Lexington Aves. on Midway, in St. Paul; 651-487-8200.**

Eloise Butler Wildflower Garden and Bird Sanctuary

Marsh marigolds, showy lady slippers, and shy violets are just a few of the many wildflowers that bloom in season in this serene, 14-acre sanctuary, which is the oldest public wildflower garden in the United States, begun in 1907. There are self-guided trails in both the shady woodland garden and the sunny prairie garden. A small interpretive building has exhibits and books about nature, including a biography of the garden founder, botanist and conservationist Eloise Butler. Guided tours and special programs—such as full-moon hikes and talks on medicinal plants—are offered on weekends. The tamarack bog is located across the parkway; ask for directions at the interpretive center. Free. Open daily, 7:30 A.M.–dusk, Apr. 1–Oct. 31. Located on the western edge of Minneapolis, in Theodore Wirth Regional Park. Entrance to the garden is **off Wirth Parkway, south of Hwy. 55; 612-370-4903.**

Lyndale Rose Garden and Rock Garden

On the northeast shore of Lake Harriet in Minneapolis is the beautiful Lyndale Rose Garden, sloping down toward the lake. The garden, which opened in 1907, is the second-oldest public rose garden in the country and is a favorite site for weddings. The roses bloom from mid-June to late Sept.; the garden season is extended by spring bulbs and perennials. Across from the rose garden is a rock garden, restored in recent years after the original had long since disappeared. Adjacent to the rock garden is the Roberts Bird Sanctuary. On Dupont Ave. S., turn west on 42nd St. to the gardens; there is parking nearby. **612-370-4838.**

Noerenberg Gardens

This lovely garden, on Lake Minnetonka's Crystal Bay in Orono, was once a private paradise and is now a Hennepin County park. It is many gardens in one: there is a collection of more than 1,000 daylily cultivars, a grape arbor, and an azalea collection as well as many perennials and annuals. Open in summer, Mon.–Fri., 7:00 A.M.–8:00 P.M., and Sat.–Sun., 8:00 A.M.–8:00 P.M.; in fall until Oct. 15, Mon.–Fri., 8:00 A.M.–3:30 P.M., and Sat.–Sun., 9:00 A.M.–5:00 P.M. **2840 N. Shore Dr., Wayzata, 55391; 612-475-0050.**

University of Minnesota Landscape Arboretum

Gardeners should not miss the arboretum, more than 900 rolling acres of gardens ranging from the very formal to delightfully informal. There is a garden for every taste—from herbs to roses to prairie flowers. True to its name, the arboretum is home to many kinds of trees as well. Walkers love roaming the garden paths, while those less able or with little time can drive slowly through the arboretum. There are many special events and classes. A tearoom serves lunchtime and teatime treats, and there is a garden-oriented gift shop. Fee. Open daily year-round, 8:00 A.M.–sunset in summer; 8:00 A.M.–5:30 P.M. in winter. Located on Hwy. 5, 9 miles west of Hwy. 494. **3675 Arboretum Dr., Chanhassen, 55318; 612-443-2460.**

Historic Sites

Alexander Ramsey House

Costumed "servants" show visitors around the Victorian home of Minnesota's first territorial governor, Alexander Ramsey. Cookies are included in the tour. Many of the furnishings in the house are original, and the table in the dining room is set for a sumptuous meal. The house is seasonally decorated during the holidays. The office is in the adjacent carriage house. Free for Minnesota Historical Society members; others

It's always 1827 at Historic Fort Snelling. Photo courtesy of the Greater Minneapolis Convention and Visitors Association.

pay a fee. Open daily May–late Nov.; call for holiday hours. Hours: Tues.–Sat., 10:00 A.M.–3:00 P.M.; Sun., 10:00 A.M.–3:00 P.M. Located near Irvine Park off W. Seventh St. in St. Paul. **265 S. Exchange St., St. Paul, 55102; 651-296-8760.**

Foshay Tower Museum

Minneapolis's Foshay Tower, built in 1929 and at 447 feet (32 stories) the tallest building in the Midwest for years, is now dwarfed by other skyscrapers, but it still offers the only good public birdseye view in the city. The open-air observation deck and museum are on the 31st floor of the tower. The museum collection includes photos, video, and the sheet music for the "Foshay Tower–Washington Memorial March," by John Phillip Sousa. Fee. Open Apr.–late Oct. depending on weather, Mon.–Fri., noon–4:00 P.M.; Sat., 11:00 A.M.–3:00 P.M. **821 Marquette Ave. S., Minneapolis, 55402; 612-359-3030.**

Historic Fort Snelling

The fort, completed in 1825, was built at the confluence of the Mississippi and Minnesota Rivers. The complex of buildings is fascinating to explore, and the history center in the reception area is also of interest. The stone barracks housed soldiers sleeping two to a bunk, and the sutler's store, sort of a post exchange of its day, sold items and served as a community center for the soldiers. Costumed interpreters tell of life in the 1820s in the wilderness fort, and exhibits give details of the soldiers, European-American civilians, and American Indians who lived in and around the fort. One of the buildings, the round tower, was built in about 1820 and is probably the oldest structure in Minnesota. The sights, sounds, and smells of frontier life surround visitors. This is living history at its best. The daily cannon shoot thrills kids. Free for members of the Minnesota Historical Society; others pay a fee. The fort is open May–Oct., Mon.–Sat., 10:00 A.M.–5:00 P.M.; Sun., noon–5:00 P.M. The history center, through which visitors pass to enter the fort, is open year-round, Mon.–Fri., 10:00 A.M.–5:00 P.M. Located **at the junction of Hwys. 5 and 55,** 1 mile east of Minneapolis–St. Paul International Airport; **612-726-1171.**

Designed by noted architect Cass Gilbert, the Minnesota State Capitol Building in St. Paul was built in 1905. Photo courtesy of the St. Paul Convention and Visitors Bureau.

James J. Hill House

Jim Hill thought big: big railroad, big house. His 1891 mansion was the largest in the Midwest. And it isn't just huge, it's amazingly detailed: a two-story art gallery, stained glass windows, carved leather wall coverings, and intricately carved woodwork are some of the eye-catchers. Admission is free for members of the Minnesota Historical Society; others pay a fee. Open year-round, Wed.–Sat., 10:00 A.M.– 3:30 P.M. **240 Summit Ave., St. Paul, 55411; 651-297-2555.**

Minnesota State Capitol

The gleaming-white State Capitol, with four prancing golden horses posed just below its dome, is a beautiful structure, designed by well-known local architect Cass Gilbert and built in 1905. A guided tour of the Capitol interior includes information on state government, some Minnesota history, and a description of its important role in the Civil War. Tours are given on the hour, with the last tour starting 1 hour before closing. Free. Open year-round, Mon.–Fri., 9:00 A.M.–5:00 P.M.; Sat., 10:00 A.M.–4:00 P.M.; Sun., 11:00 A.M.–4:00 P.M. **75 Constitution Ave., St. Paul, 55102; 651-296-2881.**

Murphy's Landing

Nineteenth-century pioneers live on at Murphy's Village, a collection of 40 buildings representing the homesteads of the many ethnic groups who settled in the Minnesota River Valley between 1840 and 1890. The village is on the banks of the river, and costumed interpreters demonstrate crafts and chat with visitors about daily life in the 19th century. Transportation through the village is on foot or by horse-drawn trolley. Daily music and entertainment, and also special events. Fee. Open Memorial Day–Labor Day, Tues.– Sun., 10:00 A.M.–5:00 P.M.; Sept. and Dec., Sat.– Sun., 10:00 A.M.–5:00 P.M. Located 1 mile east of Shakopee on Hwy. 101. **2187 E. Hwy. 101, Shakopee, 55379; 612-445-6900.**

Oliver H. Kelley Farm

Pick heirloom vegetables from the garden or watch farmhands plow fields with oxen and horses at the Kelley farm, where living-history interpreters demonstrate how farming was done in the 1860s. Visitors get a chance to try their hand at some farm chores and relax in this nice piece of Minnesota history. Animals on the farm are bred to have the characteristics of animals used in the 1860s. There is also a visitor center. The farm is open May–Oct., Mon.–Sat., 10:00 A.M.–5:00 P.M., and Sun., noon–5:00 P.M.; the visitor center is open year-round. Located **2.5 miles southeast of Elk River on Hwy. 10; 612-441-6896.**

Sibley Historic Site

Two limestone houses belonging to two men who had an active role in both the fur trade and the subsequent history of Minnesota are fascinating treasuries of a bygone life, including a life-size portrait of one family's pet wolfhound. Henry Sibley, a regional manager for the American Fur Company and later Minnesota's first governor, built one house in the mid-1830s, with the help of voyageurs and American Indians. His neighbor Jean Faribault, who had a trading post in the area, replaced his original log house with a limestone house a couple of years later. Tours include the 1843 cold-storage building for furs, which is furnished with furs, trading-post items, and a price list (muskrat pelts went for 8 cents each in 1843). The site also has special programs, including singing and drumming by descendants of the Dakota who occupied the land before European Americans. Fee. Open May–Oct., Tues.–Sat., 10:00 A.M.–5:00 P.M., and Sun., noon–5:00 P.M. Located on Hwy. 13 in Mendota Heights, a St. Paul suburb. **1357 Sibley Memorial Hwy., Mendota, 55150; 651-452-1596.**

Museums

American Swedish Institute

The fairy-tale "castle," with its towers, gargoyles, and elaborate ornamentation, is an American immigrant's dream. It was a dream that came true for Swan Turnblad, a poor Swedish immigrant who made his fortune with a Swedish-American newspaper and then built his castle. It was finished in 1908, but Turnblad lived in it only a short time. In 1929 he turned it over to his fellow Swedish Americans, to be used as a cultural center. The house was built and finished by old-fash-

ioned craftsmen with materials imported from Europe. Its 33 rooms are furnished with antiques and have elaborate wood carvings and plasterwork. In the music room, 52 cherubs are carved into the woodwork. Throughout the house are 11 ceramic-tile stoves. At Christmas, rooms are decorated as they would be in Scandinavia. The stunning staircase is a dramatic "stage" for the white-gowned chorus that sings traditional Swedish songs in the early morning of St. Lucia Day, Dec. 13.

The house is on the National Register of Historic Places. A permanent exhibition of Swedish life in the Twin Cities is on the top floor; temporary exhibits and a permanent exhibit of Swedish glassware occupy the second floor. The institute has a coffee shop, a gift shop, and a bookstore with items in English and all the Scandinavian languages. A monthly Swedish smorgasbord is open to the public. The ASI presents many special programs and concerts. Fee. Open Tues., Thurs.–Sat., noon–4:00 P.M.; Wed., noon–8:00 P.M.; Sun., 1:00–5:00 P.M. **2600 Park Ave., Minneapolis, 55407; 612-871-4907.**

Gibbs Farm Museum

Step back to the 19th century, when farms like this were common within what is now St. Paul and its suburbs. Costumed interpreters demonstrate what life was like then. The farm has a house, two barns, plenty of farm equipment, a schoolhouse where children can register for a day at school in summer, and fields with crops typical of the period. Fee. Open May–Oct., Tues.–Fri., 10:00 A.M.–4:00 P.M.; Sat.–Sun., noon–4:00 P.M. Located at **Cleveland and Larpenteur Aves. in Falcon Heights** (just across the border from the St. Paul city limits); **651-646-8629.**

James Ford Bell Museum of Natural History

Kids and adults as well love the touch-and-see room at this cozy museum, located on the University of Minnesota campus. In addition, there are fascinating dioramas of Minnesota's major habitats as they were 150 years ago, with lifelike animals and plants. Fee (free on Thurs.). Open Tues.–Fri., 9:00 A.M.–5:00 P.M.; Sat., 10:00 A.M.–5:00 P.M.; Sun., noon–5:00 P.M. **10 Church St., Minneapolis, 55455; 612-624-7083.**

Minnesota History Center

Even if you hated history in school, you'll love this place. The dramatic setting alone is worth the trip. Centered spectacularly through the long windows on the second floor is a view of the State Capitol. Inside the History Center, past times are alive and well. "Minnesota A to Z" will jog the memories of longtime residents and fascinate visitors, with exhibits such as the loon song under "L," the 37-foot birch-bark canoe under "C," and the videos of the Minnesota Twins World Series triumphs under "B" for baseball. Kids like climbing inside the full-size boxcar and the replica of a grain elevator, and learning about the ancient task of harvesting wild rice. Changing exhibits use interactive techniques, recordings, etc., to make history lessons painless. The center's restaurant is good enough to be a destination in itself. There is also a wonderful library for those who really want to dig into the past. The gift shops have reasonably priced souvenirs of Minnesota, all historically correct. Free. Open Mon. during summer only and Tues.–Sun. year-round. Hours: Mon., Wed.–Sat., 10:00 A.M.–5:00 P.M.; Tues., 10:00 A.M.–8:00 P.M.; Sun., noon–5 P.M. Hours are different for the library, which is closed Sun. The center is located on the **corner of Kellogg and John Ireland Blvds. in St. Paul,** near the intersection of I-94 and I-35 E; **800-657-3773, 651-296-6126,** or **651-296-1430** for a recorded message with directions and hours. **Website: www.mnhs.org.**

Science Museum of Minnesota

What to do with the kids or yourself on a rainy day, or even a sunny one? Head for the new science museum, built into the bluffs on the Mississippi River and opened in Dec. 1999. The building's 90-foot drop from Kellogg Blvd. to the river flats has been incorporated cleverly to give visitors dramatic river views in all directions. The museum's well-loved exhibits of dinosaurs and fossils, anthropology, and experiments are supplemented by a new hall of human biology and a large-screen theater. Outside, there are 10 acres of science parks. Fee. Located on **Kellogg Blvd. across from RiverCentre in St. Paul;** **651-221-9444.**

Nightlife

FILM

Stay awake for **Midnight Hong Kong Films**—these gems are shown at midnight Fri. and again at 11:00 A.M. Sat., at the **Riverview Theatre, 3800 42nd Ave. S., Minneapolis, 55406; 612-729-7369. Oak Street Cinema,** on the east bank of the University of Minnesota campus, presents obscure and popular classic films, including "lost" gems like Eisenstein's *Ivan the Terrible,* and mounts special series, such as a Fri.-night Hindi film festival. Gauge the kind of crowd from the fact that they sell coffee in addition to popcorn and soft drinks. Staffed by volunteers. **309 SE Oak St., Minneapolis, 55414; 612-331-3134.**

University Film Society

Al Milgrom was a graduate student in 1962 when he started the film society, in part to see the kind of movies no other local movie theater showed. Over the years, the society developed a sterling reputation for showing first-run movies that mattered—before anyone else not only in town, but in the whole country. Milgrom, director of the society, says hundreds of directors—including Jean-Luc Goddard and Abel Gance—have appeared to talk about their films before the screenings. The society hosts an international film festival in late Apr. and early May as well as several other smaller festivals. Films are shown in the **Bell Museum on the University of Minnesota campus, 17th and University Ave., Minneapolis; 612-627-4430** for film information and **612-627-4431** for the society office.

LIVE MUSIC

Whatever your favorite style of popular music, chances are you'll find it somewhere in the Twin Cities. There are bars by the dozen playing everything from ska to retro lounge-lizard favorites. The young and hip gravitate toward the Loring Bar and Cafe near Loring Park in Minneapolis (see Where to Eat). The Local, an upscale Irish pub, became an instant hit when it opened last year (see Where to Eat). For longevity and good fun, go to Nye's in northeast Minneapolis, which has a piano bar and Polish food that often draw out-of-town musicians looking for a breather. Consult *City Pages,* the Twin Cities' alternative newspaper, for a complete list of places to hear music, as venues and musical styles are constantly in flux.

Many of the places listed below offer a range of music, as well as their individual specialties. A few defy categorization, as they book the best, whatever the genre. You can hear anything at the **Fine Line Music Cafe,** from live disco to Sun. gospel brunches to a tribute to John Denver to lounge orchestras—the Fine Line serves them all up. **318 First Ave. N., Minneapolis, 55401; 612-335-8181. First Avenue and Seventh Street Entry,** a hulking former bus station, is the one place out-of-town music fans want to see. The Artist-Formerly-Known-as-Prince played here before he became well known, and exteriors for his movie *Purple Rain* were shot here. In addition to regular performances, First Avenue has all-age concerts and Sun.-night dances for the younger crowd. **701 First Ave. N., Minneapolis, 55403; 612-332-1775.** The Seventh Street Entry, on the same premises, presents up-and-coming local groups in a smaller room. And don't forget the **Target Center** in Minneapolis, which was the place to hear Garth Brooks for nine (count 'em—nine) consecutive nightly sellout performances in 1998. **600 First Ave. N., Minneapolis, 55403; 612-673-0900.**

Blues

Chicago's great bluesmen passed through the Twin Cities, creating affection for Chicago's urban-style blues. Most established of the blues clubs is the **Blues Saloon,** in St. Paul's Frogtown neighborhood, **601 N. Western, St. Paul, 55103; 651-228-9959. Famous Dave's BBQ and Blues,** at Hennepin and Lake in Calhoun Square, **3001 Hennepin, Minneapolis, 55408, 612-822-9900; Brew Bakers,** in the **McKnight 36 Plaza in North St. Paul** (take Hwy. 36 east to McKnight Rd.), **651-779-0243** or **651-773-5061;** and **Biscuits and Blues,** in the **Bandana Square Center in St. Paul, 651-644-BLUE,** serve stylish food and drink along with big names in blues. The **Blues Alley, 15 N. Glenwood, Minneapolis, 55403, 612-333-1327,** showcases local blues talents.

Bunker's, 716 N. Washington Ave., Minneapolis, 55401, 612-338-8188; The Cabooze, 917 Cedar Ave., Minneapolis, 55404, 612-338-6425; 5 Corners Saloon, 501 Cedar

The castlelike American Swedish Institute in Minneapolis was originally the home of Swan Turnblad, a poor Swedish immigrant who became the successful publisher of a Swedish-American newspaper. Photo courtesy of the American Swedish Institute.

Ave., Minneapolis, 55404, 612-338-6424; the **400 Bar, 400 Cedar Ave., Minneapolis, 55404, 612-332-2903;** and **Whiskey Junction, 901 Cedar Ave., Minneapolis, 55404, 612-338-9550,** are great spots to hear some rhythm and blues. All except Bunker's are clustered along Cedar Ave. in Minneapolis, on the west bank of the Mississippi and near the University of Minnesota.

Disco/Lounge

Ground Zero/The Front is a two-part club that advertises a "cool swanky atmosphere" featuring retro lounge music and disco. Some early hours for those under 21. **15 NE Fourth St., Minneapolis, 55413; 612-378-5115.**

Old piano pro Lou Snyder packs them in for sing-alongs Fri.–Sat. at **Nye's Polonaise Room,** an institution in northeast Minneapolis. You'll also find music of other kinds, plus good and filling Polish meals. Out-of-town entertainers show up often. **112 E. Hennepin Ave., Minneapolis, 55414; 612-379-2021.**

Folk/Ethnic

Lovers of pure folk music show up at **Cedar Cultural Center.** There is eclectic food to be had in the front room, but the big back room, with folding chairs set up in rows, is for listening only. The Cedar gets internationally acclaimed folk musicians, such as Martin Carthy and the Watersons from the United Kingdom, the hypnotic Finnish group Värtinnä, and Hawaiian slack-key guitarists. The nonprofit center is maintained by members who volunteer their time to keep it going. **416 Cedar Ave. S., Minneapolis, 55404; 612-338-2674.**

Kieran's Irish Pub, 330 Second Ave. S., Minneapolis, 55401, 612-339-4499, and the **Half Time Rec Irish Pub, 1013 Front Ave., St. Paul, 55103, 651-488-8245,** have a corner on Irish music. Kieran's usually has bands in the front bar and the back room and also has music for Sun. brunch. Kieran's, under the same ownership as the Local, also is noted for good Irish food.

Mayslack's, famous for its humongous roast beef sandwiches, has polka bands on Sun., a perfect match for this Polish-American neighborhood in northeast Minneapolis. Country, rock,

and blues are offered Thurs.–Sat. The building is among the city's oldest. **1428 Fourth St. NE, Minneapolis, 55413; 612-789-9862.**

Roam the globe at the **Blue Nile,** an Ethiopian restaurant (and good, too) that offers music from everywhere: there are reggae nights, African nights, Latin nights, etc. **2027 E. Franklin Ave., Minneapolis, 55404; 612-338-3000.** Another alternative rock/reggae/world beat venue is the **Red Sea Bar and Restaurant, 316 Cedar Ave., Minneapolis, 55404; 612-333-1644.**

Hard Rock

Fans of metal and/or hard rock gravitate to **O'Gara's Garage,** at **Snelling and Selby Aves. in St. Paul, 651-644-3333,** or **Ryan's,** at **Fourth and Sibley, in St. Paul's Lowertown, 651-298-1917.**

Jazz

The Twin Cities Jazz Society, an avid promoter of the local jazz scene, sponsors a **JAZZLINE, 651-633-0329**—updated weekly—of upcoming shows and publishes a monthly newsletter. The **Artist's Quarter**—the "A.Q.," as jazz fans call it—is the spot to hear good local players and occasionally out-of-town hotshots. Located downstairs in one of St. Paul's grand old buildings, the A.Q. is agreeably dark and cozy. There are generally two shows Thurs.–Sun., with a cover charge for the better-known names; poetry with jazz is on Wed. Drinks and a limited menu are available. **366 Jackson St., St. Paul, 55101; 651-292-1359.** *The* place for serious jazz, the elegant **Dakota Bar and Grill** has a triangular stage between the bar and the dining room (see Where to Eat). Intimate and acoustically correct, the little stage has held some of the biggest names in jazz, such as pianists McCoy Tyner and George Shearing, bass player Ray Brown, and drummer Elvin Jones. The crowd here comes mostly to listen to music, not to use it as background for chitchat. There is a separate bar menu. Located in Bandana Square, north of Energy Park Dr. and west of Lexington in St. Paul. **1021 E. Bandana Blvd., St. Paul, 55108; 651-642-1442.** At **Sophia,** sit up by the bar and let the music wash over you. Sophia has jazz—often with a vocalist—Wed.–Sat. in an intimate setting on the east bank of the Mississippi. **65 Main St. SE, Minneapolis, 55414; 612-379-1111.**

Rockabilly/Traditional Country

Lee's Liquor Bar was just a corner bar until it went rockabilly, hooking onto the revival of the real old-timey country music as well as kitschy lounge music. It draws a huge crowd of all ages to listen and, above all, to dance. It's stuck off by its lonesome (except it's anything but, these days), 3 blocks west of Hennepin at **101 Glenwood Ave. N., Minneapolis, 55403; 612-338-9491.**

Swing

Swing's the thing at many bars in the Twin Cities. Swing lessons are drawing hordes of people in their early 20s at places like **Mario's Keller Bar, 2300 University Ave. NE, Minneapolis, 55418, 612-781-3860,** and others.

Parks

The metro counties have remarkable regional parks, with recreational possibilities as diverse as archery, downhill skiing, horseback riding, and snowshoeing. The Metropolitan Council, which plans the regional parks, park reserves, and trails system, with the advice of the Metropolitan Parks and Open Space Commission, periodically publishes a comprehensive map and guide to both summer and winter activities in all regional parks in the metropolitan area. Addresses and phone numbers of county, state, and federal units mentioned are also given. To have a free copy mailed, call **651-602-1140.**

The lakes within Minneapolis are the pride of the city and well used by residents. Most of the lakes are in the southern half of the city. The most popular of these and also the largest are **Lakes Harriet and Calhoun.** Sailing, swimming, and fishing (summer and winter) are just a few of the activities. At Lake Harriet, a turreted bandstand is the venue for free nightly concerts during summer. During summer and on weekends in Sept., three renovated streetcars, with slippery wicker seats, chug along the 1-mile track between Harriet and Calhoun. **Cedar Lake,** a quieter place, has secluded picnic spots, a public beach,

and even a nude beach (find it yourselves!). Minnehaha Creek connects Lake Harriet with two lakes on the southeast side of the city, **Lakes Hiawatha and Nokomis,** which also have beaches and other water sports. Walkers, joggers, and bikers regularly circle the lakes. Canoes can be rented at Lakes Harriet and Nokomis.

East of Nokomis is one of the most visited spots in the Twin Cities: **Minnehaha Falls,** celebrated by poet Henry Wadsworth Longfellow (who never actually saw the falls). The falls, a rushing torrent if there has been a recent rain, can dwindle to a trickle in dry spells. **Minnehaha Park,** which contains the falls, recently underwent a major makeover. The park has been a popular spot for family and group picnics and celebrations for generations. You can get a good view of the falls from the top, but climb down the steps for a closer view. On the city's western edge is **Theodore Wirth Regional Park,** which has a lake, a wildflower garden (see Gardens and Arboreta), an unusual quaking tamarack bog, and hiking trails. It has a much wilder feel than other city parks. **Loring Park,** on the edge of downtown, is amid trendy cafes, bars, etc., and has weekly outdoor movies during summer. For information on Minneapolis parks, call **612-370-4900.**

Como Park is the oldest and best of St. Paul parks. Founded in 1872 on the shores of Como Lake, when it was outside the boundaries of St. Paul, the park remains a place where residents converge. In addition to the zoo (see Children and Families) and the conservatory (see Gardens and Arboreta), the park has a small amusement park (run by a private concessionaire), a swimming pool, cross-country ski trails and warming house, a golf course, a walkway/bikeway around the lake, and an open-air bandstand. Other St. Paul city parks include **Hidden Falls/Crosby Farm Regional Park,** which is long and narrow and follows a bend in the river; **Cherokee Park,** with wonderful views of the river; **Indian Mounds Park,** where there are 2,000-year-old burial mounds, which should be treated with utmost respect; and **Lake Phalen Regional Park,** with a sandy beach and a golf course. For information on St. Paul parks, call **651-266-6400.**

Fort Snelling State Park

Adjacent to Historic Fort Snelling, the state park is a great place for urban dwellers to "escape" to nature without leaving the metro area. The park is located at the confluence of the Minnesota and Mississippi Rivers. Before Europeans arrived, generations of the Mdewakantonwan Dakota who lived in the area believed the confluence of the mighty rivers was the place of origin, the center of the world. Much of the park is on the Minnesota River floodplain. Huge cottonwood trees, willow, ash, and silver maple are part of the park's scenery. The park has a swimming beach, an interpretive center with a year-round naturalist program, a new visitor center, and trails that are linked to Minnehaha Falls and the Minnesota Valley National Wildlife Refuge (see Wildlife Viewing). There are no camp-sites in the park. It's located near Minneapolis–St. Paul International Airport at **Hwy. 5 and the Post Rd., St. Paul; 612-725-2389.**

Valleyfair Family Amusement Park

Valleyfair is the typical summer amusement park—full of screams and thrills and good fun. The roller coaster is a real monster, and many of the other rides also scare visitors happy. There are tamer rides for smaller children or chicken-hearted adults. There is also a water park in the complex. Located near the Minnesota River. Open May–Sept. Fee. **One Valleyfair Dr., Shakopee, 55379; 800-FUN-RIDE or 612-445-7600. Website: www.valleyfair.com.**

Performing Arts

CLASSICAL MUSIC

Minnesota Orchestra

A respected orchestra worldwide, the Minnesota Orchestra—under the direction of Eiji Oue—has recently toured more than ever before. At home in Minneapolis's Orchestra Hall, the year's offerings include full-scale renditions of classical music, recitals by guest artists, and performances by popular favorites, including Rosemary Clooney and Marvin Hamlisch. The orchestra also sponsors "Sommerfest," which features the music of Vienna. During the festival in July–Aug., adjacent Peavey Plaza is turned into a market-place, with food, music, and dancing. **1111 Nicollet Mall, Minneapolis, 55403; 800-292-4141 or 612-371-5656.**

Plymouth Music Series

Hometown musical whiz-kid Philip Brunelle is the force behind this excellent, 30-year-old se-ries. Brunelle conducts a chorus and also a smaller ensemble group that tackle many obscure pieces by well-known composers, such as Leonard Bernstein's *White House Cantata,* as well as music by newcomers. The music is an eclectic mix of popular and classic. There are also guest artists. The series of half a dozen performances are given at area concert halls. **612-624-2345.**

St. Paul Chamber Orchestra

The orchestra, now under the direction of Hugh Wolf, presents varied programs of classical mu-sic. Bobby McFerrin, who had the hit song "Don't Worry, Be Happy" a few years ago, is the orchestra's creative chair. The orchestra usually plays at the Ordway Music Theatre in St. Paul, across from Rice Park. **651-291-1144.**

DANCE

Ethnic Dance Theater

One of just a handful of ethnic dance companies in the United States, the EDT presents programs featuring beautifully costumed dancers in meticu-lously researched and choreographed dances from around the world. Company director Donald LaCourse started dancing when he was just a few years old, following the example of his folk-danc-ing parents. The choreographing came early, too. "We have movies of when I was very little, and I was already telling my brother and sister what they should do," LaCourse laughs. The EDT—which has no stage of its own—performs locally and nation-ally and tours internationally. **2337 Central Ave. NE, Minneapolis, 55418; 612-782-3970.**

LIVE RADIO

A Prairie Home Companion

Public radio fans across the country know of Minnesota (and the mythic town of Lake Wobegon) from Garrison Keillor's Saturday show, a melange of music, monologues, and skits from the honey-toned Keillor, who is himself from a northern suburb of the Twin Cities rather than the prairie town he has spun yarns about for years. Fee. Broadcast live at 4:45 P.M. most Sats. from the Fitzgerald Theater, **on E. 10th and Exchange Sts. in St. Paul; 651-290-1221.**

THEATER

Minneapolis is second only to New York in the number of theaters per capita. This is a development of recent decades, spurred by the opening of the Tyrone Guthrie Repertory Theatre. The Guthrie, which is reportedly considering a move or expansion, is well respected nationally. The theaters are too numerous to give more than a sampling here.

Brave New Workshop

Dudley Riggs founded this hotbed of comedy and satire decades ago and it's now being run by workshop veterans. Not afraid to skewer anything and anybody, this troupe's recent offerings have included *VIAGRA: The Second Coming . . .* and *Saving Clinton's Privates, or Swallowing the Leader.* Performances Wed.–Sun. at **Calhoun Square, 3001 Hennepin Ave. S., Minneapolis, 55408; 612-332-6620.**

Chanhassen Dinner Theatres

The largest professional dinner theater in the country, the Chanhassen mounts productions of familiar fare such as *Brigadoon* and *State Fair.* Performances are Tues.–Sun. Located in Chanhassen, half an hour west of downtown Minneapolis, at the junction of Hwys. 5 and 101. **501 W. 78th St., Chanhassen, 55317; 612-934-1525.**

Great North American History Theater

Local history turned into drama (comedy, tragedy, or a combination of both) is what this unusual theater is all about. One of the 1998 productions was *Axel and His Dog,* a valentine to a much-loved kids' TV show from four decades ago; another was about the children sent out to the Midwest on the "Orphan Train." **30 E. 10th St., St. Paul, 55101; 651-292-4323.**

Guthrie Theatre

The Guthrie, founded in 1963 by Sir Tyrone Guthrie and now under the direction of Joe

Dowling, puts the actors practically in the laps of the audience. Over the years, the Guthrie has mounted many ambitious and successful productions, from musicals such as *Guys and Dolls* to a trilogy based on Greek tragedy. Shakespeare, Ibsen, and contemporary dramatists are well represented on the Guthrie stage. The season usually consists of six plays. Call to ask about the theatre's rush policy and tours. **725 Vineland Pl., Minneapolis, 55403; 612-377-2224.**

Historic State Theatre

This lavish testimony to Hollywood glamour was built in the early 1920s and restored to all its former glory—molded plaster cherubs, white-glazed terra-cotta facade, Corinthian pilasters, and all. The Ordway in St. Paul (see below) and the State—and the Orpheum, across the street from the State—in Minneapolis are the places to see touring shows and also catch one in tryouts that may become a big Broadway hit, such as *The Lion King.* **807 Hennepin Ave., Minneapolis, 55403; 612-339-7007.**

Old Log Theater

For more than half a century, the Old Log (yes, in an old log building) has been delighting audiences with Don Stoltz's versions of comedies from New York and London. Stoltz, himself an actor, founded the theater and has often appeared on stage. It's the oldest continuously running theater in the country. The theater complex also includes a bar and restaurant. Located in Excelsior, about 20 minutes west of Minneapolis. **5175 Meadville St., Excelsior, 55331; 612-474-5951.**

Ordway Music Theatre

Traveling versions of major musicals are presented at the Ordway, in St. Paul's downtown. These are big, lavish productions that are musts for lovers of musical theater. The Ordway is also the place to catch the St. Paul Chamber Orchestra and the Minnesota Opera. **345 Washington St. (across from Rice Park), St. Paul, 55102; 651-224-4222.**

Penumbra Theatre Company

The only professional black theater group in Minnesota, the Penumbra has presented premieres of several August Wilson plays and offers *Black Nativity* each holiday season. **270 N. Kent St., St. Paul, 55102; 651-224-3180.**

Scenic Drives
Lake Minnetonka

West of Minneapolis is beautiful Lake Minnetonka, once a weekend getaway from the cities, easily reached by a trip on the trains that connected the towns with the lake. Now ringed by beautiful homes, the lake is still a popular spot for day-trippers. Wayzata, with its pricey boutiques and array of eating places, is one of the largest communities. On the other side of the lake is the more raffish Excelsior. The restored steamboat *Minnehaha* sails between the two towns (see Boat Tours). The lake itself is a series of bays so distinct from one another as to seem merely interconnected lakes, not one huge body of water. Very little of the lakeshore is in public hands. Lake Minnetonka Regional Park to the southwest, Noerenberg Memorial Park to the north, and several other parcels are the only areas that give public access. For a look at the lake, follow Hwy. 12 west of Minneapolis. Drive south on either Hwy. 15, for a drive past some of the major bays, or on Hwy. 101, which takes a scenic route over the bridge between Gray's Bay and Wayzata Bay, and then turn west on Hwy. 7 to go to Excelsior.

Minneapolis Lakes

Visitors to Minneapolis are impressed by the large lakes within the city limits. Cruise around the lakes, starting in Theodore Wirth Park, south of Hwy. 55, and driving from the near north over Hwy. 12 to the chain of lakes—Cedar, Lake of the Isles, and Calhoun—then on to adjacent Lake Harriet. From Harriet, drive along Minnehaha Parkway past Lakes Nokomis and Hiawatha to Minnehaha Falls. Use a city map to plot your route. Be aware that the parkways around Lake Calhoun, Lake of the Isles, and Lake Harriet are one-way.

Summit Avenue

Magnificent Victorian mansions and statuesque shade trees line Summit Ave. in St. Paul. The governor's house is here, as is the house that James J. Hill built and the St. Paul Cathedral, modeled after St. Peter's in Rome. Not so palatial is the apartment building near Summit, at 481 Laurel Ave., where author F. Scott Fitzgerald was born in 1896. Many houses on and around

The Metrodome, home to Minnesota's beloved sports teams: the Vikings, the Twins, and University of Minnesota. Copyright © Minnesota Office of Tourism. Used by permission.

Summit are associated with Fitzgerald, principally the row houses at 593 and 599 Summit. In the latter, he finished *This Side of Paradise,* published in 1919. (A life-size statue of Fitzgerald, looking oddly small, is in Rice Park in downtown St. Paul.)

Recommended Reading
David Page and Jack Koblas have compiled a detailed look at local Fitzgerald hangouts, called *Toward the Summit—F. Scott Fitzgerald in Minnesota* (North Star Press of St. Cloud, 1996). Its maps and photos will please true Fitzgerald fans.

Shopping
There *are* shopping places other than the Mall of America (see Major Attractions), but the Bloomington behemoth is what out-of-towners make a beeline for. Downtown Minneapolis has **Dayton's,** between **Seventh and Eighth Sts. on Nicollet Mall.** Dayton's has long been the mainstay of local department stores. Downtown has a variety of other stores, including the upscale shops in **Gaviidae Center. Grand Ave. in St. Paul,** the **uptown area of Minneapolis (Lake and Hennepin),** and **50th and France in Edina,** just off the western edge of Minneapolis, have eclectic boutiques and specialty stores. In addition, there are "the Dales," other malls with anchor department stores—including **Ridgedale** in the western suburbs of Minneapolis, **Rosedale** in the northern St. Paul suburb of Roseville, and **Southdale** in Richfield. Southdale claimed to be the first indoor shopping mall in the country when it opened in the 1950s.

Although independent bookstores are feeling the pinch from the giants, they are still a force on the local book scene. The **Hungry Mind, 1648 Grand Ave., St. Paul, 55105,** specializes in books from small presses and university presses, but stocks a good general selection and also has a cool little cafe, the Table of Contents; **651-699-0587. Micawber's,** also in St. Paul, has a particularly good selection of regional books and children's books. It's in a little shopping area at Carter and Como Aves. that could double for a Dickensian village. **2238**

Carter Ave., St. Paul, 55108; 651-646-5506.

Often voted "best record store" in local polls, the **Electric Fetus** started out on the west bank of the Mississippi in 1968. It has moved and expanded and expanded, but it remains one of the best stores to find CDs and cassettes—new and used—in a wide range of music styles. The "Fetus" also carries some clothing and gift items, and the smell of incense will take you right back to the '60s. **2000 Fourth Ave. S., Minneapolis, 55404; 612-870-9300. Oar Folkjokeopus** (no, that's not a series of typos) carries a wide selection of new releases and also used LPs and 45s. **2557 Lyndale Ave. S., Minneapolis, 55405; 612-872-7400.** For vinyl lovers, there is **Hymie's Vintage Records, Etc.,** which is full of oldies; **3318 E. Lake St., Minneapolis, 55406; 612-729-8890.**

Sports

Minnesota Timberwolves
NBA basketball came back to Minnesota for the 1989–90 season after more than 40 years. The Wolves play from the first part of Nov. to mid-Apr. Single-ticket prices are $10–$35. **Target Center, 601 First Ave. N., Minneapolis, 55403; 612-337-3865.**

Minnesota Twins
The Twins play pro baseball in the HHH Metrodome in downtown Minneapolis, although there has been plenty of talk in recent years about their moving. The plaza in front of the dome has entertainment and food vendors before the games. Season is early Apr.–late Sept. Single-ticket prices are $4–$19. **612-33-TWINS.**

Minnesota Vikings
The days of the "Purple People Eaters," the Vikings' defensive line, are long gone, but the Vikes put up a good fight in 1998, missing another Super Bowl shot. Minnesota's NFL team plays in the HHH Metrodome in downtown Minneapolis, a blessing late in the season when the temperature plunges. The season is from early Sept. to late Dec. Single-ticket prices are $28–$53. **612-333-8828** or **612-989-5151.**

Minnesota Wild

Hockey fans who had been in mourning since the North Stars decamped for Texas were thrilled when plans for the Wild were announced. They'll play in St. Paul starting in 2000; call the St. Paul Visitors Bureau for details (see Services) and **(612) 333-PUCK** for ticket information.

St. Paul Saints

Fans who yearned for outdoor pro baseball were delighted when the Saints, of the independent Northern League, set up shop in St. Paul in 1993. The team isn't bad, and the pig that carries the balls onto the field is great. The Saints' foes include the Duluth Dukes. The Saints are bells-and-whistles baseball at its summertime best in sunshine or under lights at St. Paul's Midway Stadium. Single-ticket prices are $4–$7. Tickets are sometimes hard to come by; try calling a couple of weeks in advance. **651-644-6659.**

Tours

BOAT TOURS

Delta Queen Steamboat Company

The venerable *Delta Queen* steamboat and her younger siblings, the *Mississippi Queen* and the *American Queen,* make several 7- and 14-day cruises out of St. Paul in the summer and fall. The big boats tie up at **Lambert Landing at the foot of Jackson St. in St. Paul; 800-543-1949** or **504-586-0631.**

Padelford Packet Boat Company

This is tourism the easy way: climb aboard one of the five riverboats operating on the Mississippi River and see the sights. The boats depart from Harriet Island in St. Paul and Boom Island in Minneapolis. Cruises vary in length. The Minneapolis cruise includes "locking through" the No. 1 lock on the Mississippi; the St. Paul cruise goes up to Fort Snelling. Operates daily Memorial Day–Labor Day, with some cruises in Sept.–early Oct. There are cruises at noon and 2:00 P.M. from both docks and also dinner, lunch, and brunch cruises. Fee. Boom Island is near downtown Minneapolis; enter the parking lot from the east side of the Plymouth Ave. bridge (NE Eighth Ave. in

northeast Minneapolis). In St. Paul, cross the Wabasha bridge from downtown and follow the signs to Harriet Island. **651-227-1100.**

Steamboat Minnehaha

Back from a watery grave, the restored steamboat *Minnehaha* is as good as new and spruced up with a snazzy maroon-and-gold paint job. She's been making trips across Lake Minnetonka in her second life for several years now. Lake dwellers who want to shop at Wayzata without getting out their own boats are making good use of the little lady. She scoots between Excelsior and Wayzata. Call for hours. Fee. **612-474-4801.**

Wabasha Street Caves

In the 1930s, St. Paul was a haven for big-time gangsters, who hung out in caves created by sand mining. The caves, grandly renamed Castle Royale, were a pretty scary place, as bullet holes in the fireplace testify. Three of the cave "rooms" were lined with bricks and are now rented out for special events; two rooms have natural walls. Cave tours are given year-round at 11:00 A.M. Sat.; year-round gangster tours, which take visitors on a two-hour tour of sites with gangster associations, are at noon on Sat. Fee. **215 Wabasha St. S., St. Paul, 55107; 651-224-1191.**

WALKING TOURS

Minnesota Historical Society Walking Tours

Volunteers conduct tours on various topics involving the Mississippi River near St. Anthony Falls. Tours include bike rides (bring your own bike), a crime tour, a natural history hike, a tour of the west-bank milling district, etc. Most last 90 minutes and are free for MHS members. Reservations are advised; don't forget to browse in the MHS bookstore. The program office may move to the west bank, but now it is at **125 SE Main St., Minneapolis, 55414; 612-627-5433.**

St. Anthony Falls Heritage Walking Tour

This self-guided tour is a 1.8-mile trek along both banks of the Mississippi River near downtown Minneapolis, crossing the river on the stone arch bridge and the Hennepin Ave. bridge. A brochure gives a brief history of the river at St. Anthony

The Jonathan Padelford, a sternwheeler, offers passengers a fun way to explore the Mississippi River in downtown St. Paul. Photo courtesy of the St. Paul Convention and Visitors Bureau.

Falls, and kiosks along the riverbanks offer more information. Obtain the brochure from the St. Anthony Falls Program Office, **125 SE Main St., Minneapolis, 55414; 612-627-5433.**

Wildlife Viewing

Minnesota Valley National Wildlife Refuge

One of the few urban wildlife refuges in the country, the Minnesota Valley NWR offers visitors a rare chance to see wilderness on the edge of a metropolitan area. Land owned by the refuge is interspersed with parcels of land owned by the state Dept. of Natural Resources and other entities (see Minnesota Valley Recreation Area in Hiking). The valley has always provided habitat for many plants and animals, and the refuge preserves the characteristics that keep the habitats viable for plant and animal species. Consequently, patient visitors may spot or hear coyotes, bald eagles, beavers, and badgers, among the many animals that live in or visit the refuge. The 34-mile-long corridor, which follows the river, includes several different ecosystems. Stop at the visitor center first to orient yourself to the refuge. Later, take the 0.5-mile, self-guided bird-watching trail or strike out on a longer trip on foot or skis on the refuge's trails. The entrance to the refuge is near the intersection of I-494 and 34th Ave. S., close to the Humphrey Charter Terminal; follow the signs. The visitor center is at

3815 E. 80th St., Bloomington, 55425; 612-445-7714.

The Raptor Center

Eagles, hawks, owls, and other wild birds of prey are nursed back to health at this world-renowned center, on the St. Paul campus of the University of Minnesota. Volunteer members of the "flight crew" help recovered birds learn to fly again. Visitors can get a close view of the birds and a look at the center for free, or reserve a group presentation for a fee. There are about 30 resident birds, including an osprey, peregrine falcon, red-tailed hawk, and great horned owl, in addition to eagles. Open year-round Mon.–Fri., 9:00 A.M.–4:00 P.M., and Sat., 11:00 A.M.–4:00 P.M. **1920 Fitch Ave., St. Paul, 55108; 612-624-4745. Website: www.raptor.cvm.umn.edu.**

Where to Stay

Hotels, Motels, and Inns

Minneapolis and St. Paul have representatives of all the major motel and hotel chains, including the homegrown Radisson Hotels, and these are predictable and satisfactory for those who want the security of knowing exactly what they are booking, sight unseen. Hotels are in both downtown areas as well as clustered on the perimeter of the cities, many near Minneapolis–St. Paul International Airport. All are listed in national directories and also local phone books. Below are addresses and phone numbers of some of the major hotels in the Twin Cities area.

Days Inn at RiverCentre, 175 W. Seventh St., St. Paul, 55102; 800-DAYSINN or **651-292-8929.**

Embassy Suites—Bloomington, 2800 W. 80th St., Bloomington, 55431; 800-EMBASSY or **612-861-1000.**

Embassy Suites—St. Paul, 175 E. 10th St., St. Paul, 55101; 800-EMBASSY or **651-224-5400.**

Holiday Inn—Minneapolis Airport, 2700 Pilot Knob Rd., Eagan, 55121; 800-HOLIDAY or **651-454-3434.**

Hotel Sofitel Minneapolis, 5601 W. 78th St., Bloomington, 55439; 612-835-0211.

Hyatt Regency—Minneapolis, 1300 Nicollet Mall, Minneapolis, 55403; 800-370-1234 or 612-370-1234.

Marquette Hotel, 710 Marquette Ave., Minneapolis, 55402; 612-333-4545.

Minneapolis Hilton and Towers, 1001 Marquette Ave. S., Minneapolis, 55403; 800-445-8667 or 612-397-4840.

Minneapolis Marriott City Center, 30 S. Seventh St., Minneapolis, 55402; 800-228-9290 or 612-349-4068.

Minneapolis–St. Paul Airport Hilton, 3800 E. 80th St., Bloomington, 55424; 800-445-8667 or 612-854-2100.

Radisson Hotel Metrodome, 615 Washington Ave. SE, Minneapolis, 55414; 800-333-3333 or 612-379-8888.

Radisson Hotel St. Paul, 11 E. Kellogg Blvd., St. Paul, 55101; 800-333-3333 or 651-292-1900.

Radisson Hotel South, 7800 Normandale Blvd., Bloomington, 55439; 800-333-3333 or 612-893-8412.

Radisson Plaza Hotel Minneapolis, 35 S. Seventh St., Minneapolis, 55402; 800-333-3333 or 612-339-4900.

Sheraton Minneapolis Metrodome, 1330 Industrial Blvd., Minneapolis, 55416; 800-325-3535 or 612-331-1900.

In addition, there are many less expensive hotel chains around the periphery of the Twin Cities. For example, **Country Inns and Suites** are in Bloomington, Burnsville, Roseville, Plymouth, and many other suburbs; call **800-456-4000.** Also, there are **Super 8**s in Bloomington, Brooklyn Center, Crystal, Roseville, and Maplewood; call **800-800-8000** for details on all of them. Besides the chains, there are a few unusual hostelries, described below.

Covington Inn—$$$$

Talk about rocking gently to sleep—it's the river that sings the lullaby at the Covington, an inn in a boat right in the heart of downtown St. Paul. This most unusual bed-and-breakfast, anchored at Harriet Island across from downtown St. Paul,

opened in 1995 and has five units. There are three staterooms—all shipshape—with private baths, fireplaces, and all manner of land-lubberlike conveniences, and a wonderful two-story suite and a lower two-room suite with portholes. The upper part of the topside suite was the vessel's pilothouse; it is now a comfy sitting room, with windows on all four sides for a 360-degree view. Three of the five units have private decks also. One room, the Mate's Quarters, is wheelchair-accessible. One unit is in the former engine room. A snug salon for guests has books about the history of the river and related art. Breakfast, served year-round, is served in the adjacent No Wake Cafe mid-Mar.–mid-Nov. **Pier One, Harriet Island, 3B, St. Paul, 55107; 651-292-1411.**

Hyatt Whitney—$$$$

The Whitney started life as a flour mill on the banks of the Mississippi in 1879, though the lobby area, with its grand curving staircase, was added later. After the mill closed down, the building lived a rather murky existence until it was beautifully restored and opened as a hotel in 1985. The small hotel—there are 97 rooms, including 40 bi-level suites and a penthouse—has a decidedly European feel. All rooms are well equipped for business visitors and have irons, ironing boards, and bathrobes. Because the hotel was originally a mill, the rooms vary in height and somewhat in shape. All the ceilings are at least 14 feet high and the windows are correspondingly higher than most hotel windows. Because the walls are unusually thick, the windowsills are so deep as to seem almost like window seats. The two-story suites have spiral stairs connecting the living and sleeping rooms and they have a second bath and a wet bar. The penthouse, reserved by Elton John and many other celebrities as they come through town, has a fireplace, baby grand piano, terrace, and whirlpool bath. The hotel also has a restaurant, the Whitney Grille, and an outdoor garden seating area that is used in spring and summer. To ensure a riverside view, reserve an odd-numbered room. Guests are given complimentary transportation downtown, a few blocks from the hotel. Located near St. Anthony

Falls. **150 Portland Ave., Minneapolis, 55401; 612-339-9300.**

Nicollet Island Inn—$$$$

Though the Nicollet Island Inn is just a few minutes from busy downtown Minneapolis, it seems a world away. The sturdy, square limestone building, built in 1893 as a woodworking factory making doors and sashes, now offers guests a quiet haven in the place where the city began. The inn has 24 rooms, decorated with dainty floral-print wallpaper and period reproductions. Some rooms have brass beds or four-posters, and there are cookies and spring water awaiting guests. One nice touch: each room comes with an iron. The rooms have views of the city or the river. The pleasant lobby has a fireplace and cozy seating, with antiques such as the beautiful old Eastlake buffet adding to its charm. The carved bar, from a New Hampshire drugstore, is more than 150 years old. The restaurant is popular and offers good views of Nicollet Island. **95 Merriam St., Minneapolis, 55401; 612-331-1800.**

The Saint Paul Hotel—$$$$

Often considered the best hotel in the state, the Saint Paul Hotel has a long and glittering history. It was built in 1910, designed by the same firm responsible for New York's Grand Central Station, on a site where there had been a hotel of sorts since John Summers opened his house to travelers in 1856. Over the years, the hotel has welcomed those with famous names, such as Charles Lindbergh, F. Scott and Zelda Fitzgerald, and President William Taft, and also served as a gathering place during St. Paul events, such as the Winter Carnival and the annual high school hockey tournaments. The Saint Paul Hotel is the only Twin Cities hotel with membership in the National Trust's Historic Hotels of America program.

Despite its early and continued success for decades, the hotel went through hard times and closed in 1979. It was rescued by the St. Paul Companies and underwent a $20 million makeover. The lobby, with its antique chandeliers, potted palms, and cozy seating groups, combines elegance and a comfortable, intimate atmosphere.

The concierge staff, ensconced behind an antique desk, is very helpful. The 254 well-appointed rooms and suites are also fully equipped for businesspeople. The hotel has a rooftop exercise complex. Request a room overlooking Rice Park for a lovely view of central St. Paul, particularly during Winter Carnival, when ice sculptures and twinkly lights adorn the park. The hotel's restaurants are well regarded and very popular with local residents. Afternoon tea at the hotel is a meal in itself; call **651-228-3860** for tea reservations. **350 Market St., St. Paul, 55102; 800-292-9292 or 651-292-9292. Website: www.stpaulhotel.com.**

Camping

Dakotah Meadows Campground—$

Rent tent or RV sites next to Mystic Lake Casino. There are about 100 tent sites; RV sites have electric, water, and sewer hookups. There are also seven tepees for rent, with a fire ring inside each tepee. In addition, there are 24 cabinlike "park homes." Free shuttle to the casino. **2341 Park Pl., Prior Lake, 55372; 800-653-CAMP or 612-445-8800.**

Hennepin County Parks—$

Baker Park Reserve on Lake Independence in central Hennepin County has 210 campsites. **Carver Park Reserve** has 54 sites and two hike-in sites. Carver is west of Chanhassen, which is west of the Twin Cities. For reservations for both, call **612-472-4911.**

Where to Eat

Below are descriptions of popular restaurants in the Twin Cities, followed by longer entries for a variety of restaurants, chosen to represent a wide geographic, economic, and specialty range and also to highlight some of the places that the "locals" frequent that might otherwise escape the notice of visitors. The list isn't intended to be comprehensive, given the number of restaurants in the Twin Cities.

There are several areas in both cities that have clusters of restaurants. Adventurous visitors should head toward Nicollet Ave. in Minneapolis, between 24th and 29th Sts., for a United Nations of cafes, grocery stores, and markets. Banners on each side of the street proclaim it "Eats Street." Among the restaurants are the **Rainbow** (Chinese), **2739 Nicollet Ave., Minneapolis, 55408, 612-870-7084; Christos** (Greek), **2632 Nicollet Ave., Minneapolis, 55408, 612-871-2111;** the **Black Forest** (German), **1 E. 26th St., 55404, 612-872-0812;** and many Asian restaurants. Nicollet Ave. also has Asian markets.

In downtown Minneapolis, the area with the greatest concentration of eating places is the Warehouse District, north of Hennepin Ave. Two blocks south are trendy **Restaurant Aquavit** (Scandinavian), **on Seventh St.** and the **Nicollet Mall, 612-343-3333; The Local, an upscale Irish pub, 931 Nicollet Mall, 55402, 612-904-1000;** venerable places such as the **New French Cafe, 128 N. Fourth St., Minneapolis, 55401, 612-338-3790;** innovative restaurants such as the almost-vegetarian and justly celebrated **Cafe Brenda, 300 First Ave. N., Minneapolis, 55401, 612-342-9230;** and colorful places such as the Caribbean-inspired **Chez Bananas** (see below). **D'Amico Cucina,** which has won rave reviews from just about everyone, is also in the Warehouse District, in the Butler Square building; **100 N. Sixth St., Minneapolis, 55403, 612-338-2401.** Across from Loring Park is the trendy **Loring Bar and Cafe,** which has entertainment and outdoor seating; **1624 Harmon Pl., Minneapolis, 55403, 612-332-1617.**

In the Minneapolis uptown area (several blocks centered on Hennepin and Lake St.), there is a wide choice of restaurants, including **Figlio's,** in Calhoun Square, one of the most popular of the Twin Cities' raft of Italian restaurants, **3001 Hennepin Ave., Minneapolis, 55408, 612-822-1688;** and the **Bryant Lake Bowl and Theater,** which has—as its name implies— bowling, wacky theater, and meals all rolled into one, **810 W. Lake St., Minneapolis, 55408, 612-825-3737, 612-825-8949 for theater.**

St. Paul's uptown equivalent is Grand Ave., a long strip that parallels elegant Summit Ave. Here you'll find the well-regarded **Table of Con-**

tents, a small cafe tucked into the Hungry Mind bookstore (see Shopping).

The Twin Cities have a large Vietnamese population, and the number of Vietnamese restaurants continues to grow steadily. Many are located in St. Paul along University Ave., but they are tucked away in all corners of the city; try **Que-Viet Village House, 2211 NE Johnson St., Minneapolis, 55418, 612-781-4744.** Likewise, there are many Chinese restaurants and a growing number of other Asian restaurants. A student favorite of many years is the **Village Wok, 610 Washington Ave. SE** (near the University of Minnesota's Minneapolis campus), **Minneapolis, 55414, 612-331-9041.**

Also near the University of Minnesota's Minneapolis campus are two areas that serve students and area residents. "Dinkytown," adjacent to the University Ave. end of the campus, has old-timers such as **Annie's Parlour, 315 14th Ave. SE, 554J4, 612-379-0744,** and **Vescio's, 406 14th Ave. SE, 55414, 612-378-1747** (burgers and Italian specialties, respectively); minuscule **Al's Breakfast,** where hungry students and faculty line up waiting to grab a vacant stool by the counter, **413 14th Ave. SE, 55414, 612-331-9991;** and the **Espresso Royale Caffe,** a student haven, **411 14th Ave. SE, 55414, 612-623-8127.** On the Washington Ave. end of campus are several eating places, including the bar-and-burger standby of **Stub and Herb's, 227 SE Oak St., Minneapolis, 55414, 612-379-1880.**

The Mall of America has many restaurants, from fast-food places to trendy places such as **Planet Hollywood, 612-854-7827,** and the **Rainforest Cafe, 612-854-7500** (check out the real parrots in the front), to good, nongimmicky restaurants such as the **California Cafe, 612-854-2233.**

In St. Paul, **Forepaugh's,** in an 1870 Victorian mansion, serves elegant French fare just a couple of blocks off W. Seventh St. on the edge of downtown, **276 S. Exchange St., St. Paul, 55102, 651-224-5606,** while breezy, popular **Cossetta's** dispenses wonderful Italian food quickly (via a cafeteria line and Italian imports), **211 W. Seventh St., 55102, 651-222-3476.**

For lovers of juicy steaks, there is **Manny's Steakhouse,** a New York–style steakhouse, **1300 Nicollet Mall, Minneapolis, 55403, 612-339-9900;** and **Murray's, 26 S. Sixth St., Minneapolis, 55402, 612-339-0909,** in downtown Minneapolis. Murray's, one of the Twin Cities' oldest restaurants, also has wonderful garlic toast. If you are looking for ethnic food markets, try the small and super-friendly **Delmonico's** for Italian imports; **1112 NE Summer St., Minneapolis, 55413, 612-331-5466.** There are Mexican-American supermarkets on Lake St. in Minneapolis and also on Concord St. in St. Paul. A hybrid that works is **Morgan's Mexican-Lebanese Grocery,** on Robert St. in west St. Paul, **736 S. Robert St., 55207, 651-291-2955.** For those who hunger for dried mutton, lamb roll, and other Scandinavian delicacies, **Ingebretsen's, 1601 E. Lake St., Minneapolis, 55407, 612-729-9331,** is the place to shop. Several ethnic markets, including Indian, Middle Eastern, and Mexican, are on Central Ave. in northeast Minneapolis. And don't forget **Surdyk's Liquor Store and Cheese Shop** (at Hennepin and University Aves. in northeast Minneapolis), **303 E. Hennepin Ave., Minneapolis, 55414; 612-379-3232** (liquor store) or **612-379-9757** (cheese shop). The sheer number of wines and cheeses is staggering.

Dakota Bar and Grill—$$$ to $$$$

Regional cuisine has been a buzzword for years now, but Lowell Pickett was the pioneer among local restaurateurs in using home-produced foods. He opened the Dakota, a casually chic restaurant in Bandana Square, in 1985. Executive chef Ken Goff has been with the Dakota since it opened, and he continues to produce innovative and beautifully presented entrees. The Dakota has remained loyal to local products over the years and carries only American wine, including wines by nearby Bailly winery (see the St. Croix Valley chapter). The trout served as an entree come from a Wisconsin trout farm, and local pheasant, mushrooms, wild rice, and game are often on the menu. Desserts are also given a Minnesota accent—blueberries and maple syrup are used in some. The Dakota has also evolved into the best

place to hear nationally known jazz musicians in the state (see Nightlife). Open Mon.–Thurs., 5:30–9:30 P.M.; Fri.–Sat., 5:30–10:30 P.M.; Sun., 11:00 A.M.–2:30 P.M. and 5:00–9:00 P.M. From mid-May through summer, dinner hours are extended one hour. **1021 Bandana Blvd., St. Paul, 55108; 651-642-1442.**

Casper's Cherokee Sirloin Room—$$ to $$$$

One of the Casper family is usually on hand when you have lunch or dinner in this well-known and well-loved steakhouse in West St. Paul. In 1970, Bob and Dorothy Casper bought the Cherokee bar and small restaurant, which had opened in 1934, and their descendants have expanded it and started a second restaurant in the suburb of Eagan to keep up with the popularity. What's the secret? "I guess it's the personal touch," says Dan Casper. "We try to get around to each table twice during the meal. We have a lot of repeat customers," he adds. The entryway is lined with autographed photos of celebrities, and the dining room beyond is nicely and unobtrusively decorated; no gimmicks here, just a pleasant place for serious eating.

Steaks are the feature at the Cherokee: big steaks (32 ounces), little steaks (8 ounces), steaks with seafood, steak sandwiches, and steak as a topping for Caesar salad. There are other menu items, too: seafood, chicken, ribs, and pasta dishes, as well as burgers and sandwiches. The early-bird dinners Mon.–Thurs. until 6:00 P.M. are bargains. The original Cherokee is located at the intersection of Hwy. 13 and Smith Ave. From St. Paul, follow the High Bridge, west of the Wabasha Bridge, across the Mississippi. Open Mon.–Fri., 11:00 A.M.–3:30 P.M. and 5:00–10:00 P.M.; Sat., 11:00 A.M.–3:00 P.M. and 5:00–10:30 P.M.; Sun., 10:00 A.M.–2:00 P.M. and 3:00–9:00 P.M. **886 S. Smith Ave., West St. Paul, 55118; 651-457-2729.** The new Cherokee is located at Cedar Ave. at Cliff Rd. in Eagan. Open Mon.–Sat., 11:00 A.M.–10:00 P.M., and Sun., 10:00 A.M.–9:00 P.M. **4625 Nicols Rd. S., Eagan, 55122; 651-454-6744.**

The St. Paul Grill—$$ to $$$$

All of St. Paul seems to gather here for lunch,

and busy as it is, the frosted glass panels defining the seating areas give it an air of privacy. Lunch choices range from sandwiches and salads to heartier items such as roast beef hash topped with fried eggs. The Grill, which opened in 1990, is also popular at dinnertime. Although it does have lighter entrees, such as pastas, walleye, and chicken, the dinner menu features classic meaty fare, such as 24-ounce porterhouse steak, pork chops in a bourbon and brown sugar marinade, and veal chops with sauteed artichokes. The wine list is extensive. Open Mon., 11:30 A.M.–2:00 P.M. and 5:30–10:00 P.M.; Tues.–Sat., 11:30 A.M.–2:00 P.M. and 5:30–11:00 P.M.; Sun., 11:00 A.M.–2:00 P.M. and 5:00–10:00 P.M. **350 Market St., St. Paul, 55102; 651-292-9292.**

Birchwood Cafe—$$ to $$$

Off by its lonesome, in a part of town that needed a good restaurant, the Birchwood has an eclectic menu, with pastas, soups, and sandwiches all homemade and tasty. Trendy, too, as the pasta with roasted veggies in a savory balsamic vinegar–graced sauce testifies. Order at the counter and then take a seat in the commodious cafe. Service is very informal; patrons bus their own dishes and can linger without getting the evil eye from the staff. Open Tues.–Fri., 7:00 A.M.–8:00 P.M.; Sat., 8:00 A.M.–8:00 P.M.; Sun., 9:00 A.M.–2:00 P.M. **3311 E. 25th St., Minneapolis, 55406; 612-722-4474.**

Chez Bananas—$$ to $$$

Both the decor and the food will take you on a tour of the Caribbean faster than you can say "jerk chicken." Chez Bananas features entrees from many islands as well as a head-spinning selection of rums. A variety of peppers and fruits are used in most dishes, such as the Apple Chipotle Pork and Coco-Banana Shrimp. Located in the lively warehouse district. Open Sun.–Mon., 5:00–9:00 P.M.; Tues.–Fri., 11:00 A.M.–10:00 P.M.; Sat., 5:00–10:00 P.M. **129 N. Fourth St., Minneapolis, 55401; 612-340-0032.**

Market Bar-B-Que—$$ to $$$

For more than 50 years, the Market Bar-B-Que has been smoking ribs and chicken for hungry Twin Citians and a loyal following of out-of-towners, including Jay Leno. Leno once declared the Market's ribs the best in the world. His autographed photo and those of many other famous faces line the walls of the restaurant's big, noisy rooms. The atmosphere is informal—red-and-white-checked vinyl cloths cover the tables, and jukeboxes in the wooden booths get heavy use. Service is cheerful, the ribs are good, and everyone seems to have a good time. The ribs are pit-smoked and the Market's sauce, in regular and hot versions, is served on the side. The restaurant is still run by the original owners, according to Steve Polski, president of the restaurant and part of the founding family. The family may be the same, but the prices certainly have changed—a replica of the 1946 menu shows barbecued spareribs at $1.35. There are two locations. The downtown restaurant is open Mon.–Sat., 11:30 A.M.–2:30 A.M., and Sun., noon–midnight. **1414 Nicollet Ave., Minneapolis, 55403; 612-872-1111.** The Wayzata restaurant is open Mon.–Sat., 11:30 A.M.–midnight (1:00 A.M. for the bar), and Sun., noon–11:00 P.M. **15320 Wayzata Blvd., Wayzata, 55391; 612-475-1770.**

Sunsets on Wayzata Bay—$$ to $$$

Sunsets, on Lake Minnetonka in Wayzata, is a great place to enjoy a look at the lake, if you can get a lakeside seat. The popular restaurant offers lots of pasta and chicken dishes for both lunch and dinner, plus an enticing variety of generously sized salads. Several low-fat items are also on the menu. Have something slimming and you can pop for the Key Lime Pie for dessert. Open Mon.–Sat., 6:30 A.M.–11:00 P.M., and Sun., 9:30 A.M.–11:00 P.M. **700 E. Lake St., Wayzata, 55391; 612-473-5253.**

Key's Restaurants—$ to $$

It's worth the wait to have breakfast at the Key's Restaurants. The original restaurant, started by Barbara Hunn in 1973, seems to be always buzzing with customers. And someone's always having breakfast, 'cause the Key's serves it all day long. The usual breakfast standards are here, plus a few surprises, such as the Mexican Omelet and Bran Apple Walnut Pancakes. At lunch (the original Key's on Raymond does not serve dinner), meat loaf— as an entree or in a sandwich—roast beef, grilled pork chops, liver with onions and bacon, and other comfort foods make customers feel coddled. Open daily except Thanksgiving and Christmas, Mon.–Sat., 6:00 A.M.–3:00 P.M., and Sun., 7:00 A.M.–2:00 P.M. At last count, there were nine other Key's Restaurants, all run by Barbara Hunn's kids, in-laws, and grandchildren. The original is located at **767 Raymond Ave., St. Paul, 55114,** just off University Ave.; **651-646-5756.**

Mickey's Diner—$ to $$

Ya gotta eat at Mickey's when you go to St. Paul. The little red-and-yellow diner, one of only two diners in the country to be listed on the National Register of Historic Places, has served everyone from Arnold Schwartzenegger and Bill Murray to local politicians to down-and-outers since it opened in 1939. Yes, it opened 60 years ago, and it has stayed open every day since, 24 hours a day. You may have to wait: there are about a dozen and a half stools at the counter, and just a few booths in the back. Mickey's has a real lived-in look and the staff doesn't waste time with chitchat during the morning rush, but the food is good and swiftly produced. A quarter in the jukebox will get you music with your meal, but the songs listed are all at least 30 years old. Still, "Love Potion No. 9" is a cool accompaniment to an order of the "2s" (2 eggs, 2 pancakes, 2 pieces of bacon or sausage). Besides the buttermilk pancakes, the diner boasts of its baked beans, Mulligan stew, and bean soup, all made on the premises from prewar (that's World War II, folks) recipes. No checks accepted. Located on St. Peter and Seventh Sts., with 30-minute parking at the side. **P.O. Box 16368, St. Paul, 55116; 651-698-0259.**

Taste of Scandinavia—$ to $$

There are two "Tastes" in the metro area serving the same wonderful Scandinavian food and owned by Soile Anderson, a Finn who once ran one of St. Paul's most elegant restaurants. The new places are combination cafes and bakeries. Some of the offerings are authentically Scandinavian—Swedish meatballs, open-faced sandwiches, *lefse*—and other dishes are more American. Don't leave without tasting the Pulla, a Finnish coffee bread flavored with cardamom and cinnamon and dotted with raisins. The St. Anthony Park neighborhood location is open Mon.–Fri., 7:00 A.M.–6:00 P.M., and Sat., 7:00 A.M.–5:00 P.M. **2232 Carter Ave., St. Paul, 55108; 651-645-9181.** The North Oaks (an upscale northern suburb) location north of St. Paul is open Mon.–Fri., 7:00 A.M.–6:30 P.M., and Sat., 7:00 A.M.–5:00 P.M., **845 Village Center Dr., North Oaks, 55127; 651-482-8876.**

Matt's Bar—$

Matt's would be just another pleasant neighborhood bar if it weren't for Lucy. That's Lucy as in "Jucy Lucy," a succulent double hamburger patty, with cheese in between the patties, grilled until the cheese turns molten. Matt's reportedly sold 65,000 of the wonderfully oozy burgers in 1996. Lucys come wrapped up, rather than on a plate, and the waitress cautions those who have never before tackled a Lucy to wait a few minutes until she cools down. A basket of fries on the side is enough for two. Open Mon.–Wed., 11:00 A.M.–midnight; Thurs.–Sat., 11:00 A.M.–1:00 A.M.; Sun., noon–midnight. **3500 Cedar Ave., Minneapolis, 55407; 612-722-7072.**

Coffeehouses, Sweets, and Treats

Marissa's Bakery, 2750 Nicollet Ave., Minneapolis, 55408, 612-871-4519, has a wonderful array of Mexican pastries and cookies. **Cafe Latte, 850 Grand Ave., St. Paul, 55105, 651-224-5687,** practically invented caloric desserts. Many patrons think **Dunn Brothers Coffee House, 1569 Grand Ave., St. Paul, 55105, 651-698-0618,** serves the best coffee around.

Services

Local Visitor Information

Written or telephone information on Minneapolis is available from the **Greater Minneapolis Convention and Visitors Association, 4000 Multifoods Towers, 33 S. Sixth St., Minne-**

apolis, 55402; 800-445-7412. **Website: www.minneapolis.org.** Walk-in information is available at the **Minneapolis Information Center,** in city center on Seventh St., at the Nicollet Mall; Mon.–Fri., 10:00 A.M.–7:00 P.M.; Sat., 11:00 A.M.–6:00 P.M.; Sun., noon–6:00 P.M. **612-335-5827.**

Visitors can obtain information and brochures Mon.–Fri., 8:00 A.M.–5:00 P.M., from the **St. Paul Convention and Visitors Bureau, 175 W. Kellogg Blvd., St. Paul, 55102;** **800-627-6101** or **651-265-4900. Website: www.stpaulcvb.org.**

Transportation

There are local bus connections between St. Paul and Minneapolis and throughout both cities and suburbs. Basic fare is $1.50 during rush hours, $1 during other times. In both downtown zones, fares are 50 cents during rush hours and 25 cents at other times. **612-373-3333. Website: www.metrotransit.org.**

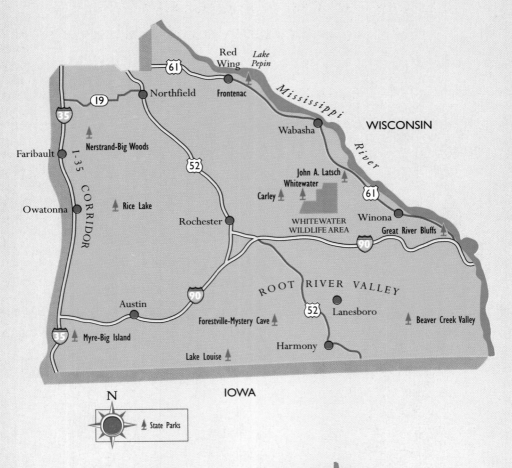

Red
Wing

*Lake
Pepin*

61

Northfield

Frontenac

19

Mississippi

35

WISCONSIN

Faribault

I-35

Nerstrand-Big Woods

Wabasha

River

52

John A. Latsch

CORRIDOR

Whitewater

61

Rice Lake

Carley

Owatonna

Rochester

WHITEWATER

Winona

WILDLIFE AREA

Great River Bluffs

90

ROOT   RIVER   VALLEY

Austin

90

52

Lanesboro

Beaver Creek Valley

35

Myre-Big Island

Forestville-Mystery Cave

Harmony

Lake Louise

N

IOWA

State Parks

Southeast Region

Southeast Region

Pastoral beauty graces Minnesota's southeast region. Copyright © Minnesota Office of Tourism. Used by permission.

Harmony

"We live in Harmony, in more ways than one," says business owner Joyce Jacobson, speaking of the tranquil Root River Valley town of Harmony, population 1,100. It is said that the town got its felicitous name during a meeting of rival ethnic groups, all of whom had their own ideas about names. Finally, legend says, after much bickering, one townsman raised his voice above the others and said, "Let us have harmony here!"—and so they did.

The town is a couple of miles north of the Iowa border in the southeast corner of Minnesota. The pace of the 20th century slows in Harmony, due partly to the usual unhurried style of small towns and partly to the presence of a colony of nearly 100 old-order Amish families who moved to the area from Indiana in 1974 and live on small farms around Harmony.

A chance to peek at the lives of the Amish, who drive slowly along the country roads in their horse-drawn buggies, combined with the pleasant countryside, is a magnet for tourists. Fall, when the foliage is at its most colorful, is one of the busiest times, and it's foolhardy to drive down for a fall weekend without reserving a place to stay.

History

Harmony is near the south fork of the Root River, whose branches flow through and unite the string of towns known as the bluff country. The southeast part of the state, unlike most of the rest of Minnesota, was not covered by glaciers, and this "driftless" region has extremely varied topography.

The Dakota were most likely the original American Indian residents. They were followed by other tribes, the last being the Winnebago, who moved from the area in 1848. European settlers—mainly from Norway, Germany, and Ireland—drawn by the rich soil and the cheap land, founded Greenfield Prairie, slightly southeast of present-day Harmony, in 1852.

The early years of European settlement were tough: the winters of 1855 and 1856 were so cold, according to the town's centennial history book, that the north sides of the log cabins didn't thaw out for 90 days. Later, in 1873, a blizzard killed 70 people. Greenfield Prairie gradually declined as the new town of Harmony developed, spurred by rumors of the coming railroad. The first train arrived in 1879, on narrow-gauge tracks.

Getting There

Harmony is about two and a half hours south of Minneapolis–St. Paul. For the most direct route from the Twin Cities, follow Hwy. 52 through Rochester into Harmony. Alternatively, take I-35 south from the metro area and go east on I-90, picking up Hwy. 52 south of Rochester, or drive along the Mississippi River on Hwy. 61, continuing west on I-90 north of LaCrescent.

Festivals and Events

Fall Foliage Festival
late Sept.

Colors are usually at their best during late Sept., and Harmony takes advantage of it with a festival that includes activities that change from year to year, including church dinners, a dance, community garage sales, and style shows. Contact the Harmony tourism office (see Services) for the exact date and a schedule of events.

Outdoor Activities

See the Lanesboro and the Root River Valley chapter in this section.

Seeing and Doing

Scenic Drives

The portion of Hwy. 52 from County Rd. 12 southeast of Preston to Prosper, just north of the Iowa border, is designated an Amish Buggy Byway. The horse-drawn buggies are a frequent sight, and slow-moving, so use care. Continuing east on Hwy. 44 after leaving Hwy. 52, the road runs along a high ridge, with sweeping views of the countryside.

Shopping

Austin's Angora Goats and Mohair

You can't miss the Austin's establishment; look for the color purple and plenty of it. Effervescent Ada Austin, with her husband, Jim, started the farm-and-shop enterprise with a truckload of angora goats, enthusiasm, and little experience; she is happy to show visitors her cuddly goat kids, who are born in the spring and remain cute through the summer. The silky goat hair is sheared and sent out to Ada's daughters and other home crafters, who turn it into gossamer sweaters and mittens, plus angels and Santas trimmed in the angora hair. Ada also sells goat's-milk soap and raw mohair. Austin's is **1 mile east of Harmony off Hwy.**

52. Take the first gravel road to the left for 1 mile; the farm is on the right. The Austins also have four primitive camping sites with fire rings, picnic tables, and a portable potty. Firewood for campfires is brought by Amish neighbors. **507-886-6731.**

Tours

Amish Community

Since 1974, when old-order Amish families began buying farms in the Harmony area, the non-Amish, or "English" as the Amish call them, have coexisted peacefully with their new neighbors. The Amish live a simplified life, without phones or electricity. They speak a German dialect among themselves, but they also speak English. Both sexes dress in dark clothes; Amish women wear prayer "kapps" on their heads and the men have beards but no mustaches. They use horses for farmwork and transportation, and Minnesota permits them to have their own schools.

The Amish live mainly east of Harmony, in farms along gravel roads. A clothesline bearing dark blue or black clothes flapping in the wind often signals an Amish farm. Their horse-drawn buggies are a frequent sight on the country roads and along Hwy. 52.

Although the Amish keep themselves apart from the "world," some families make products that they are happy to sell to non-Amish at local farmers markets in Harmony, Lanesboro, and other bluff country towns, and many also sell from their farms.

One word of caution: Amish with something to sell usually have a sign by the road advertising their wares. If there is no sign, assume that they do not wish to be disturbed. Those who are selling something often build a small shed specifically for that purpose. If the owner is not there, payment (including checks) can be put into a box designated for that purpose.

Although visitors can drive around the Amish community themselves, locally based tours of the area are popular and easier than navigating back roads. The tours do not operate on Sun. and observe the Amish "no photography" stricture. Two companies give most of the tours, which last several hours. Both are local and use knowledgeable

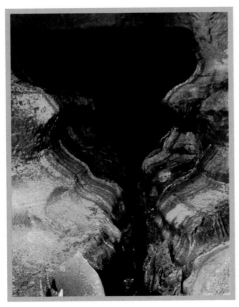

"The Last Room" in Niagara Cave. Photo courtesy Niagara Cave: Mark Bishop.

local "English" guides. Items for sale include a variety of baskets, baked goods, candies, and beautifully made rocking chairs and other pieces of furniture. Some tours also include a stop at the lovely little stone Lenora United Methodist Church Pioneer Center, begun in 1856 and rebuilt in 1865. In bygone years, circuit-riding preachers served the church, which is still open for special services.

Michel Amish Tours, 45 Main Ave., Harmony, 55939, 507-886-5392 or **800-752-6474,** the first to offer Amish tours, beginning in 1986, operates by car and bus year-round, weather permitting. Van tours are given by **Amish Country Tours, P.O. Box 906, Harmony, 55939, 800-278-8327** or **507-886-2303,** from Apr. until late fall, with car tours only the rest of the year. Both companies offer individual tours, with a guide riding along in the visitor's car, and step-on guides for van or bus tours. Step-on guide service for cars is $22–$25. Van tours are $10 for adults and $5 for children ages 5–12.

Niagara Cave

The disappearance of three little piggies in 1924 led to the discovery of the huge Niagara Cave.

Three boys, searching for the pigs, tracked them to an opening in the ground. The boys slid down and were amazed by the openings they spotted. They climbed out, pigs in hand, but adults paid little attention to their tale. It wasn't until 1934 that the cave became a tourist attraction. Some "rooms" in the cave are more than 100 feet deep, cut by underground streams that are still making fissures in the limestone.

A 60-foot waterfall is one of the cave's best-known features, and many stalactites and fossils can be seen. Hundreds of weddings have been held in the "Crystal Wedding Chapel," according to owner Mark Bishop. Bishop recently started a gemstone sluicing operation; visitors can buy bags of dirt salted with gemstones to wash in a sluice. All bags contain at least some gemstones. When touring the cave, walking shoes are recommended, and a light jacket should be worn year-round as the cave temperature is a constant 48°F. There are picnic grounds near the entrance. Hour-long guided tours are given daily May 1–Sept. 30, 8:30 A.M.–5:30 P.M.; on weekends Apr. and Oct., 8:30 A.M.–5:30 P.M.; and by appointment. Admission: $7 adults, $4 children ages 5–12. The cave is **2 miles south of Harmony.** Take Hwy. 139 to Niagara Rd., then go west 2 miles. **800-837-6606** or **507-886-6606. Website: www.niagaracave.com.**

Where to Stay

Hotels, Motels, and Inns

Country Lodge Motel—$$ to $$$

Once a creamery for local farmers, the Country Lodge Motel is a quiet oasis for travelers. Vestiges of the motel's former life can be seen in the high ceilings and pleasantly odd angles of some of the rooms, and guests drive in through the old delivery port. Joyce Jacobson, a teacher, and her husband, Murrell, a farmer, have decorated the 24 rooms and hallways with Amish patchwork wall hangings and oil paintings in browns, blues, and grays depicting Amish life. The motel has free coffee and cookies plus stacks of magazines. The continental breakfast, included in the price, features local jams and honey. The Jacobsons also offer guide services. **525 Main Ave. N. (Hwy. 52), Box 96B, Harmony, 55939; 800-870-1710** or **507-886-2515.**

Selvig House—$$ to $$$

Selvig House was built in 1910 by Dr. Carlus Selvig, a dentist and civic activist. The big, comfortable house near the center of Harmony is now owned by Carol and Ralph Beastrom, friendly and knowledgeable hosts. The house boasts original woodwork, wood floors, and beveled leaded glass. Two of the four bedrooms have private baths. "Doc's Room," on the main floor, is in the former library. The blue-and-white room and its bath are wheelchair-accessible. Upstairs, the "Selvig Room," with a green color scheme, has a cupboard full of dollhouse furniture and its own porch with a swing. It shares a bath with the "Amish Room," a beautifully spare space with white walls and blue woodwork. In the Amish tradition, the curtains are strung on a cord and fold back over nails pounded into the window frame. "Eleanor's Room," a small, predominantly rose-tinted room inhabited by teddy bears, has its own bath. Breakfast is included. **P.O. Box 132, 140 Center St. E., Harmony, 55939; 888-887-2922** or **507-886-2200.**

Judy's Lane Guest House—$$

When Bob and Judy Peters's kids were young, Judy constantly drove up and down the long, tree-lined lane from the house to the street. "I was up and down so often that Bob named it Judy's Lane," she laughs. The kids are grown up now, but Judy is still in motion, cosseting overnight guests. The Peterses (Dr. Bob is the local veterinarian) live on 35 acres of farmland within the town limits. They are hospitable folk, and the guest quarters, part of their own house, are comfortable and nicely decorated. Part of the house is more than 100 years old. Parents with kids may wish to rent the upstairs bedroom, with its two single beds, to tuck their children into while they take another room for privacy. The largest of the three bedrooms has striking tulip-patterned wallpaper, a private bath, and a private deck. Judy does not serve breakfast, but coffee is available and guests have the use of the refrigerator. There is cable TV in all rooms; VCRs and a wide selection of videos are offered. In addition, guests can play the baby grand piano in the living room. Downtown Harmony is within walking distance. Bike storage and rentals are offered, and the Peterses are happy to give touring advice. **710 Main Ave. S., Harmony, 55939; 507-886-4166.**

Where to Eat

Harmony House Restaurant—$ to $$

Harmony has just a few places to eat, and this informal cafe, on the main street, draws a crowd for its plain and hearty fare. Open Sun.–Thurs., 5:30 A.M.–8:00 P.M., and Fri.–Sat., 8:30 A.M.–9:00 P.M. The pies, rolls, and pastries are homemade. Located **on Main Ave. N.; 507-886-4612.**

Services

Harmony Tourist Information, P.O. Box 141E, Harmony, 55939; 800-247-MINN or **507-886-2469.**

Lake Pepin

Just below Red Wing, Minnesota, the Mississippi River, minding its own business on its way south, suddenly trips over the delta made by the mouth of Wisconsin's Chippewa River and swells until it is 3 miles across—the widest point in its entire length. The Mississippi doesn't slim down to its pre-Chippewa size until approximately 25 miles downstream. This wide spot in the river is called Lake Pepin. Local residents in the villages around the broadening of the river refer to it as a lake; it looks like a lake, and boaters and fishers say it acts like a lake.

It is a beautiful place, whether you choose to explore it from the Minnesota or the Wisconsin side (although this book is about Minnesota, in places like this we cross state boundaries to include the region as a whole). From either state, the bluffs and hills that surround the lake provide a pretty frame, golden in the sunlight and deep blue, purple, and rose at twilight.

Lake Pepin is a major winter nesting area for bald and golden eagles. Bird-watchers as well as other recreationists make the lake and the towns that are strung around it—like pearls on an oval necklace—popular tourist destinations. Lake City, the largest town, has a population of about 4,500. Stockholm, Wisconsin, the smallest, claims 89 souls on a sign on one side of town and 82 on another sign. Whatever—as they say in Minnesota. Several years ago, the 12 towns around the lake decided to market themselves as a single unit, with a brochure including information on the entire 85-mile drive around the lake. (Red Wing is now part of this unit, but it is treated separately in this guide.)

The towns in Minnesota, from north to south, are Frontenac, Lake City, Camp Lacupolis, Reads Landing, Wabasha, and Kellogg. On the Wisconsin side, going south, are Bay City, Maiden Rock, Stockholm, Pepin, Nelson, and Alma. Lake Pepin, like nearby Red Wing, is increasingly popular with visitors. When the leaves

peak in the fall, it is nearly impossible to find lodging without reservations.

History

Before European settlers arrived, the Dakota and Fox Indian tribes used Lake Pepin as a hunting and fishing ground. One of the first Europeans to explore this section of the Mississippi was the French priest Louis Hennepin, who passed through the region in 1680. In 1727 an expedition led by René Boucher of Montreal, in what was then called New France, landed near Frontenac and built a log stockade named Fort Beauharnois. Within the fort, two Jesuit missionaries created a mission that was probably the first church in Minnesota. The French left in 1736 after losing much of North America to Great Britain.

Activity around the lake gradually changed from fur trading to logging to agriculture pursuits. A once-thriving business around the lake was harvesting freshwater clams, for the occasional pearls but principally for making mother-of-pearl buttons. Well into the 20th century, heaps of discarded clamshells could be seen on the lakeshore. The lake, principally around Frontenac, also drew late-19th-century vacationers, and the village of Old Frontenac became a fashionable summer resort. Lake Pepin, then as now a dangerous place in a storm, was the scene of one of Minnesota's worst boating disasters when the excursion steamer *Sea Wing* capsized during a summer thunderstorm in 1890 and nearly 100 people died.

In recent years, the area has lured artists and craftspeople, and also those with an abiding interest in producing and preparing fine foods, such as the folks who run the Harbor View Cafe, in Pepin, Wisconsin.

Festivals and Events

Grumpy Old Men Days—Wabasha
Feb.
To celebrate the movie of the same name, even though it was not actually filmed in Wabasha, the city holds an ice-fishing contest, a dance, and a spaghetti-eating contest. **P.O. Box 105E, Wabasha, 55981; 800-565-4158 or 651-565-4158.**

85-Mile Garage Sale—All Around Lake Pepin
first weekend in May
Private homes and businesses all around the lake join in on this huge garage sale, basically dawn to dusk, that signals the start of the summer season on Lake Pepin. Call the Lake City Chamber of Commerce, **800-369-4123 or 651-345-4123.**

Water Ski Days—Lake City
last full weekend in June
Water-skiing was invented in 1922 by Lake City resident Ralph Samuelson. A pair of Samuelson's skis now hang on the wall of the town's Chamber of Commerce. The festival in Lake City draws thousands for water-ski shows, boat races some years, a parade, and bands. Contact the Lake City Chamber of Commerce, **800-369-4123 or 651-345-4123.**

Stockholm Art Fair—Stockholm
third Sat. in July
Stockholm is mobbed for this annual art fair. Artists and craftspeople from around the region have their creations for sale. Contact Amish Country, **715-442-2015.**

Laura Ingalls Wilder Days—Pepin
third weekend in Sept.
The beloved author of the "Little House" books, Laura Ingalls Wilder was born in a cabin north of Pepin, Wisconsin. The town celebrates its famous daughter with a Laura look-alike contest, a play about her life, a talent show, and old-fashioned crafts exhibits. Contact the Pepin Visitor Information Center, **P.O. Box 274, Pepin, WI 54759; 715-442-3011.**

Johnny Appleseed Days—Lake City
first weekend in Oct.
The area around Lake City is the largest apple-producing spot in the state. The festival includes a pie-baking contest, a toilet-racing contest, and other events. Contact the Lake City Chamber of Commerce, **800-369-4123 or 651-345-4123.**

Outdoor Activities

Birding
Frontenac State Park is on the Mississippi River Flyway and is a good place to watch migrating birds, including bald and golden eagles in winter. A great number of warblers can be seen there, including the far-ranging sanderling and ruddy turnstone warblers, which fly from South America to the Arctic and back each year. See Parks.

Getting There
To reach the Minnesota side of Lake Pepin, take Hwy. 61 to Red Wing and continue south on Hwy. 61. For Wisconsin towns, cross the Mississippi River at Red Wing and continue south on Hwy. 35.

The Mississippi River widens into Lake Pepin in southeast Minnesota. Copyright © Minnesota Office of Tourism. Used by permission.

Eagle Watch

Humans aren't the only creatures who endure Minnesota's long winters. When the bald eagles, once endangered because of toxic chemical use, recovered their numbers, they again became common sights in the Lake Pepin area. In 1989, Mary Rivers spurred the organization of an eagle observatory on Wabasha's city deck. The observatory is staffed by trained volunteers during prime eagle-sighting times—Nov.–Mar.—to help visitors learn about these magnificent birds. Open Sun., 1:00–3:00 P.M. A new visitor center is scheduled to open in January 2000. Contact the Wabasha Area Chamber of Commerce for information. **P.O. Box 105E, Wabasha, 55981; 800-565-4158 or 651-565-4158.**

Rieck's Lake Park

Each year, in late Oct. and early Nov., tundra swans fly from their summer home in Canada to winter nesting grounds. They stop for R and R along Lake Pepin. Many of them congregate on Rieck's Lake, north of Alma, Wisconsin. Each year, more and more people come to observe the big, beautiful, noisy white birds. A wildlife observation platform is staffed by volunteers during the migration. There are picnic and camping facilities. To join a guided "Swan Watch" tour, see the Winona chapter in this section.

Boating

Great River Houseboats

Just south of the southern end of Lake Pepin is the Wabasha Marina Boatyard, where Great River Houseboats operates a fleet of seven houseboats, which sleep 4–10 people. Each boat has a kitchen and bathroom with a shower. The houseboats can be rented by the week or weekend, and the smaller boats can be rented for 24 hours. Owner Russ Morgan usually spends up to two hours explaining the operation of the boats and the river to renters, but he says he'll stay with clients until they feel comfortable. Most people, Morgan says, head downriver to the miles of sandy beaches below Wabasha; because most of the land is public, it's easy to find a spot to tie up for the night. **1009 E. Main, Box 247, Wabasha, 55981; 651-565-3376.**

Lake Pepin

Lake Pepin is often studded with sails skimming

across the water. Many of them call the marina at Lake City—the largest small-boat marina on the Mississippi—home. Sailboats as well as other types of boats, canoes, pedal boats, bikes, and fishing gear can be rented at **Sail Away** in **Lake City; 651-345-5225.** For sailors with their own boats, overnight mooring can be rented at the **Lake City Marina, 651-345-4211,** which is municipally owned.

Zumbro River

The Zumbro River, which joins the Mississippi near Kellogg, is a popular canoeing river. Bring your own canoe or rent one. There are canoe access points at several places, including the Richard J. Dorer Memorial Hardwood State Forest (see Parks).

Fishing

People do fish in Lake Pepin, especially on the breakwater with its wheelchair-accessible ramp or at the pier, both at Lake City. Fish in the lake include walleye, northern pike, panfish, and channel catfish. However, due to the presence of PCB toxins, especially in carp, Dept. of Natural Resources literature recommends caution in eating fish caught in the lake. For pier fishing information, call **651-345-4211.** For fishing information call the **Area Fisheries Supervisor** in **Lake City, 651-345-3365.**

Hiking

The Kruger Unit of Richard J. Dorer Memorial Hardwood State Forest has three hiking trails, including a 0.75-mile, gently sloped paved trail accessible to wheelchairs, a more challenging 2-mile trail for hikers and ski touring, and a 5-mile trail—for nonmotorized uses—that hugs the bluffs and valleys along the Zumbro. See Parks.

Skiing

CROSS-COUNTRY

There is cross-country skiing in Frontenac State Park, which has 6 miles of trails, and in Lake City's Hok-Si-La Park, as well as the Kruger Unit of the Richard J. Dorer Memorial Hardwood State Forest, which has 1.5 miles of trails. See Parks.

DOWNHILL
Mount Frontenac

Mount Frontenac, on the river bluffs, is one of the few downhill ski places in southern Minnesota. There is a 420-foot vertical drop, with beginner, intermediate, and expert runs. One beginner run, "Easy Mile," starts at the top of the hill for a long, gentle glide. The runs are served by three double chair lifts. There is a chalet; equipment, including snowboards, is for rent. Call for hours. Between Red Wing and Lake City on Hwy. 61. **Box 119, Frontenac, 55026; 800-488-5826, 651-338-5826,** or **651-345-3504.**

Snowmobiling

The "Zumbrowatha" area, which ranges from Lake Pepin back into the Zumbro River Valley, is covered by trails developed by members of area snowmobile clubs. A map of the groomed snowmobile trails is available from Frontenac Honda, on Hwy. 61 in Frontenac, **651-388-5607,** and from other sponsors of the trails throughout the southeast area.

Seeing and Doing

Museums and Historic Sites

Arrowhead Bluffs Museum

Les Behrns and his son John have amassed an amazing collection of Winchester rifles and also stuffed big-game animals from all over, displayed in this museum overlooking Wabasha. The Winchester collection contains one of every kind of Winchester ever made from 1866 to 1982. The collection also includes American Indian and pioneer artifacts. Les also does hunting consulting and can tell spine-tingling tales of his own hunting trips. Open May–Dec. Fee. Located 2 miles west of Wabasha on Hwy. 60. Watch for signs. **R.R. 3, Box 7, Wabasha, 55981; 651-565-3829.**

Laura Ingalls Wilder Museum

Wilder's first book, *Little House in the Big Woods,* was set in Pepin, and each year thousands of visitors come to the town looking for traces of Laura. Most of them visit the museum, which has a quilt that belonged to Laura as well as other items pertaining to Wilder and Pepin history. Free. Open mid-May–mid-Oct. Call for hours. Located at **306 Third St. (Hwy. 35), Pepin, WI 54759;** contact the Pepin Visitor Information Center, **P.O. Box 274, Pepin, WI 54759; 715-442-3011.**

Little House Wayside

Little girls—and their mothers—who nostalgically love the "Little House" books of Laura Ingalls Wilder are enthralled to see the spot near Pepin, Wisconsin, where the author was born in 1867. Although the family's original cabin is long gone, a replica has been constructed. There are picnic tables and toilets, and the water pump really works. Snow may make the cabin inaccessible in winter. Free. From Pepin, take County Rd. CC for 7 miles. There is no phone at the site. Call the Pepin Visitor Information Center for site details; **715-442-3011.**

Stockholm Institute

A tiny white building that was the former Stockholm, Wisconsin, Post Office tells the story of the Swedes from Varmland who founded the town in 1854, making it the oldest Swedish settlement in western Wisconsin. Many photos document Stockholm's early days, and a selection of local history and Scandinavian history books are for sale. Open weekend afternoons, from spring through fall. It's near the corner of Hwy. 35 and County Rd. J in the middle of the little village, and has no phone. Call **Spirit of the River, 715-442-2900,** or **Stockholm Antiques, 715-442-2113,** for information.

Wabasha County Museum

In the days when lumbering was king, Read's Landing was one of the busiest towns along the lake. Now it is picturesque and quiet, but the Wabasha County Museum here houses many area artifacts, including those showing the history of American Indians and the logging and clamming industries that were so important locally. Open mid-May–Sept. Fee. Located 1 block west of Hwy. 61 S. in Read's Landing. The museum has no phone; for information and hours, call Carla Schuth, **651-565-4251.**

Other Sights

Lock and Dam No. 4

River rats love watching boats "lock through" at the Alma, Wisconsin, lock. There is an observation area on Alma's main street, Hwy. 35, where watchers can get a close view of the lock operation, and an adjacent parking lot is located on Hwy. 35. Boaters are admitted by pulling a cord, by radioing ahead, or by phoning **608-685-4421.**

Parks

Buena Vista Park

If ever a spot were well named, it is Buena Vista Park in Alma, Wisconsin. The view is terrific. Sit on a bluff top 500 feet above the Mississippi River and look down at the intricate river life below. The city park has toilets and picnic tables. To reach it, head south on Hwy. 35 past most of the business district in Alma, and turn left onto County Rd. E. Some of the turns on the way to the park are sharp and the road is steep. **608-685-3330.**

Frontenac State Park

Several spectacular lookouts over Lake Pepin are among the draws at Frontenac State Park, on the bluffs on the Minnesota side. The park surrounds the lovely community of Old Frontenac, with hiking trails to either side of the town. There are 15 miles of hiking trails in the park, as well as 8.4 miles of snowmobile trails and 6 miles of cross-country ski trails. The road upward leads to campgrounds, trails (including a self-guided nature trail), and the lookouts, several along what riverboaters traditionally referred to as "Point No Point." Along the bluffs near the group camp is In Yan Teopa, a rock with a hole in it traditionally considered sacred by American Indians. The park is also home to the timber rattler, which is of little danger to visitors but should be left alone. The park is between Red Wing and Lake City off Hwy. 61. Turn east on County Rd. 2 at the north end of the new village of Frontenac. For information, contact the park manager at **29223 County 28 Blvd., Frontenac, 55026; 651-345-3401.**

Richard J. Dorer Memorial Hardwood State Forest

Two units of the Richard J. Dorer Memorial Hardwood State Forest, the largest of Minnesota's 57 state forests, are near Lake Pepin. Hikers tend to gravitate to the Kruger Management Unit, while horseback riders usually stick to the Zumbro Bottoms Unit. Much of the Kruger Unit consists of steeps slopes above the Zumbro River 5 miles west of Wabasha. Near the entrance on County Rd. 81 are picnic tables and a campground. There is a fee for camping. The Zumbro Bottoms Unit has extensive trails for riding, and riders and hikers share some of the trails. Camping with horses is allowed in several areas. There is also a canoe camp area by the river. Use of the unit is sometimes restricted during wet and muddy weather. For information on either unit, contact the **Area Forest Supervisor** at **1801 S. Oak, Lake City, 55041; 651-345-3216.**

Performing Arts

THEATER

Lake Pepin Players

The Lake Pepin Players, a professional summer theater, set up shop in Pepin several years ago. The six-play season runs June–mid-Oct. The playhouse is at Second and Lake Sts. in Pepin, Wisconsin. **800-823-3577** or **715-442-3109.**

Seasonal Favorites

Pepin Heights

Nearly half a century ago, Gil Courtier decided that apples had a good chance of surviving Minnesota's brutal winters on the sheltered bluffs on the shores of Lake Pepin. Time has proven him right, as visitors to Pepin Heights's sales room just south of Lake City find. Samples of many apple varieties, as well as the Courtiers' own apple cider and sparkling apple cider, are available. The harvest is from early Aug. until approximately the end of Oct. On Hwy. 61, 1.5 miles south of Lake City. **1753 S. Hwy. 61, Lake City, 55041; 800-652-3779** or **651-345-2305.**

Rush River Produce

Picking blueberries in summer and raspberries in the fall are just two reasons to make the drive to Rush River Produce, near Maiden Rock, Wisconsin. The farm, run by the Cuddy family, sits on a hill somewhere near the top of the world. The views of the Rush River Valley and Lake Pepin below are awesome. The Cuddys won't object if you bring a picnic lunch. Open daily July–Sept. Call for availability. Take County Rd. A off Hwy. 35 near Maiden Rock. Turn left at 420th St. and turn right after 1 mile onto 200th Ave. The farm is at the end of the road. **W4098 200th Ave., Maiden Rock, WI 54750; 715-594-3648.**

Scenic Drives

Minnesota

Hwy. 61 on the Minnesota side of Lake Pepin is not as high as the Wisconsin side, and is closest to the lake at Lake City and Wabasha. Part of the Great River Road, it is always pretty.

Wisconsin

Hwy. 35, also part of the Great River Road, hugs the river along Lake Pepin, with several parking and picnic areas. Near Maiden Rock is a parking area with a plaque telling the legend of the young Indian girl who jumped to her death from one of the high bluffs rather than be married to a man she didn't love. Eagles and turkey buzzards soar above the bluffs here. Near Maiden Rock is a designated Rustic Road, AA or 120th Ave. In the spring, the road is lined with white trillium. At Pepin, turn onto County Rd. CC, which leads to Laura Ingalls Wilder's birthplace, past hilly farm country, continuing on to Lund, with historic Sabylund Lutheran Church, and follow County Rd. J back down to enter Stockholm through the woods behind it.

Shopping

L.A.R.K. Toys

A dragon at once fierce and cuddly, with a tiny wizard on its back, leads the parade of fantastic, beautifully carved animals and mythic creatures on the splendid carousel at L.A.R.K. Toys near Kellogg. The carousel, finished in 1997, draws children and all who are young at heart.

The dragon is trailed by such companions as a moose with a beaver on its back and a pelican with a bill full of fish. L.A.R.K is an acronym for Lost Arts Revival by Kreofsky, as in Donn Kreofsky, a former art professor who started it all by carving wooden toys in his garage. The complex also has a children's bookstore, a toy museum, an ice cream shop, and a refreshment stand. There is a fee for the carousel ride. Open daily; call for hours. North of the junction of Hwys. 61 and 42, turn west onto County Rd. 18 and into Lark Lane; **507-767-3387.**

Tours

Lake City Historic Walking Tour

A brochure guides visitors on a short walking tour past some of Lake City's oldest buildings, including the 1866 Lake Pepin Pearl Button building. Contact the Lake City Chamber of Commerce, **800-369-4123** or **651-345-4123.**

Where to Stay

Bed-and-Breakfasts

Bridgewaters Bed and Breakfast—$$$ to $$$$

In Bridgewaters Bed and Breakfast (near the bridge over the Mississippi in Wabasha), each of the five rooms is named for a bridge. The grandest room has a Jacuzzi, a fireplace, and a lovely old spoon-carved bed. Two rooms share a bath; the others have private full or half baths. The dining room, where breakfast is served, has exquisite wooden parquet work and a handsome built-in buffet. The gardens and porch are nice spots for relaxing. Owners Bill and Carole Moore are friendly and know the area well. **136 Bridge Ave., Wabasha, 55981; 651-565-4208.**

Eagles on the River—$$$ to $$$$

This striking contemporary b-and-b has a good view of the lake and—yes—there are often eagles on the river. The owners have taken advantage of the fact that *Grumpy Old Men* was set in Wabasha and named one of the rooms after the movie; the room has an outdoor and fishing theme. A second

Dragon and wizard on the L.A.R.K. carousel.

room has not only a double whirlpool bath but a private bath with a tub. Breakfast is included. **1000 Marina Dr., Wabasha, 55981; 800-684-6813 or 651-565-3509.**

Harrisburg Inn—$$$

"A view with four rooms" is the slogan of the Harrisburg Inn in Maiden Rock, Wisconsin. Perched on one of Lake Pepin's hills, the inn has beautiful lake views from all its rooms. There is even a panorama from the claw-foot tub in the bathroom of the Morning Glory room. Each room has its own bath; one has a sunny balcony and one a shady porch. Breakfasts may include locally made sausages and cheeses. In the spring, giant white trillium, along with many other wild-flowers, bloom near the house. **W3334 Hwy. 35, P.O. Box 15, Maiden Rock, WI 54750; 715-448-4500.**

Red Gables—$$$

Red Gables, surrounded by spacious grounds, is an 1865 melange of both the Italianate and Greek Revival styles. Current owners Mary and Doug DeRoos have restored it with wall coverings and trim that replicate the era of its heyday. Guests are welcome to play the piano in the parlor. All five rooms have private baths and are furnished with antiques. Several have brass or iron-and-brass beds. Breakfast is included. **403 N. High St., Lake City, 55041; 651-345-2605.**

Victorian Bed and Breakfast, Lake City—$$$

Every room in this elegant Victorian stick-style house, built in 1896 by a banker, has views of Lake Pepin. The three bedrooms are furnished with antiques—one has a canopy bed—and each has a feather bed. Two of the rooms have a full bath; the third has a half bath. Downstairs the golden, marvelously carved butternut woodwork is eye-catching, and the lovely stained glass is also original. Breakfast is included. **620 S. High St., Lake City, 55041; 651-345-2167.**

Hotels, Motels, and Inns

Anderson House—$$ to $$$$

At Wabasha's Anderson House, Minnesota's old-est operating hotel, the rooms come in all differ-ent sizes and color schemes, and so do the cats. Visitors have their choice of one of the dozen or so felines that wait patiently in their own glass-doored "cat houses" to share guests' rooms for the night. And yes, the cats come with their own food and litter boxes. The humans are well cared for, too, in the Anderson House's antique-filled rooms and especially in the hotel's marvelous restaurant (see Where to Eat). Some rooms have shared baths; others have their own. Suites have whirlpool baths. Time may not stand still at the Anderson House, but it moves at a slow and ex-ceedingly pleasant pace. The present owners are the fourth generation to run the red-brick hotel. The Anderson House is on the National Register of Historic Places. Children are welcome. **333 W. Main St., Wabasha, 55981; 800-535-5467 or 612-565-4524.**

Camp Lacupolis—$$ to $$$

In the mid-1800s, the road northbound ended at the camp's site, which is south of Lake City, owner B. Koch says. From that point, travelers had to take a boat. After the road was devel-oped around the high cliffs, the first fishing re-sort was established. Current owners Koch and her husband, Dick, have made it into a family fishing resort. Eleven of the cabins are older but comfortable, with modern conveniences and rustic appeal. Five upscale units, which stay open in winter, are in a splendid new log house. There is space with central plug-ins for 20 RVs, and also spaces for tents. Camp Lacupolis has always been a hot spot for fish, Koch says. It is situated a little below the south end of the lake, and channels in the river range from a few feet deep to one that is nearly 80 feet deep. A ledge between the deepest channel and a 20-footer is legendary for catching walleyes. Big fish that have come out at the camp include monster walleyes, a northern that topped 16 pounds, and a 38-pound catfish. There is a harbor for anglers to dock their own boats; bait and gas are sold, and boats and motors are rented. The Kochs also have a small coffee shop. **R.R. 4, CL 1, Camp Lacupolis, 55041; 651-565-4318. E-mail: lacupols@clear.lakes.com.**

Camping

In **Frontenac State Park,** there are 58 modern campsites, 19 of them with electricity. All have picnic tables and fire rings. Running water and showers are available. In addition, there are 6 rustic, all-season walk-in sites, plus a primitive group camp. For reservations, call **The Connection** at **800-246-CAMP** or **612-922-9000.** The **Richard J. Dorer Memorial Hardwood State Forest's Kruger Management Unit** has 19 campsites, all with fire rings and picnic tables. They are served by water pumps and outdoor toilets. There is a fee for camping. In the forest's **Zumbro Bottoms Unit,** visitors may camp with their horses at several places, including the North, West, and Main assembly areas. Near the river are canoe campsites. There is no fee for camping in Zumbro Bottoms. Call **651-345-3216** for information.

Hok-Si-La Campground—$

Lake City's municipal campground is in a park of the same name on Lake Pepin, just off Hwy. 61 on the north end of town. The park has hiking, cross-country ski, and nature trails, plus a swimming beach and a free public boat launch. The several dozen primitive campsites have water hookups and toilets. **651-345-3855.**

Village Campground—$

In Wisconsin, Stockholm's Village Campground has RV and tent campsites, a boat ramp, a beach, and picnic space, right along the sandy beach. The campground has electricity, a hand pump, and toilets. Open Apr.–Thanksgiving. Cross the railroad tracks on Spring St. and head toward the lake. **715-442-2023.**

Where to Eat

Harbor View—$$ to $$$$

Fans of the Harbor View drive an hour and a half down from the Twin Cities and then wait another hour or so (no reservations) to get into this excellent restaurant opposite Pepin's pretty marina. There is a printed menu for lunch, but all evening offerings change daily. Co-owner and chef Paul

Hinderlie drolly describes his cuisine as "Scandinavian with lots of garlic." He likes to use lamb, from a local producer, and venison. The setting is informal, and boaters in shorts and T-shirts are welcome. The homemade breads are crusty manna and the desserts are especially delicious. Closed from the Sunday before Thanksgiving through mid-Mar. Call for days and hours open. Located at **First and Main Sts.** in **Pepin, WI; 715-442-3893.**

Anderson House—$$ to $$$

Plan to lie down for a nap after you eat at the Anderson House. The splurge starts with the tray of homemade breads, continues with stick-to-the-ribs specialties such as beer and cheese soup, chicken with Dutch dumplings, and stuffed smoked pork chops with braised red cabbage, and finishes with a flourish of old-fashioned desserts, such as sour cream raisin pie, double Dutch fudge pie, and eggnog cake. Cookbooks featuring the restaurant's recipes sell well. The Anderson's Dutch Kitchens offers breakfast, lunch, and dinner, and Sun. brunch. Check out the early-bird dinner specials. From approximately Mar. 1 to Dec. 1, the restaurant is open daily, 8:00 A.M.–9:00 P.M. Call for winter hours. **333 W. Main St., Wabasha, 55981; 800-535-5467** or **651-565-4524.**

Star Cafe—$$ to $$$

A relative newcomer to Stockholm, Wisconsin, the Star quickly gained a fine reputation. The cafe features locally raised organic meats, vegetables, herbs, and fruits in its sophisticated offerings. A customer favorite is the chicken cashew salad with a curry dressing. The Star honors Stockholm's heritage with Swedish pancakes and lingonberries on Sun. Open from about mid-Apr. through Dec. Call for days and hours open. Located at the **intersection of Hwy. 35 and County Rd. J** in **Stockholm, Wisconsin; 715-442-2023.**

Chickadee Cottage Tea Room and Restaurant—$ to $$

Close your eyes and take a sip of tea and a bite of buttered scone heaped with jam at the Chickadee Cottage in Lake City, and you will think you are in England. The ladies at the Chickadee know the drill: tea is served in china pots, thank you very much, and the other yummy bits and pieces of an English tea—dainty sandwiches, strawberry jam, and Devonshire cream—are served with style, too. The Chickadee also serves breakfast and lunch, all in a warmly decorated old house on busy Hwy. 61 in Lake City. Teatime is 2:30–4:30 P.M. Tues.–Sun. Closed in winter. **317 N. Lakeshore Dr., Lake City, 55041; 651-345-5155.**

The Galley—$ to $$

If you need a quick lunch with good homemade soups, sandwiches, and pies, stop at The Galley. The spacious cafe (it seats 100) in downtown Lake City draws plenty of locals because it has friendly, fast service and the food is good, plentiful, and well prepared. Open Mon.–Thurs., 6:00 A.M.–7:00 P.M.; Fri.–Sat., 6:00 A.M.–8:00 P.M.; Sun., 7:00 A.M.–7:00 P.M. **110 Lyon Ave. E., Lake City, 55041; 651-345-9991.**

Ole's Bar—$ to $$

Ya gotta love Ole's in Maiden Rock. It's dark, it's right next to the railroad track, it's got friendly folks behind the bar, and it serves juicy buffalo burgers. Once, when about the tenth train in a row had zoomed by, owner Rick Baker said enthusiastically, "I love trains—every time one goes by, I just want to reach out and hug it." Ole's serves sandwiches, burgers, and the whole line of "Leinies," the local beer from Leinenkugels Brewery at Chippewa Falls, Wisconsin. Open Mon.–Tues., 10:00 A.M.–2:00 A.M.; Wed.–Fri.,

7:00 A.M.–2:00 A.M.; Sat.–Sun., 8:00 A.M.–2:30 A.M. **3515 Hwy. 35, Maiden Rock, WI 54750; 715-448-9231.**

The Root Beer Stand—$

Judy Lortscher just can't get away from The Root Beer Stand in Lake City. She and the stand were born in the same year, 1948. As a girl, she spent time at her grandmother's house a block away from the '50s-style drive-in. As a teenager, Judy worked in the stand's kitchen. When she grew up, Judy bought the place. The root beer, mixed on the spot, is a cool delight on a hot day. Carhops serve burgers and root beer. Judy tells about a Kansas City man who stopped his car when he spotted the stand and told her it was just like an imaginary root beer stand he had written a song about. To Judy's delight, he fetched his guitar and sang the song to her. Open daily Memorial Day–Labor Day, 11:00 A.M.–10:00 P.M.; Apr. 1–Memorial Day, Mon.–Fri., 3:30–9:00 P.M., and Sat.–Sun., 11:00 A.M.–9:00 P.M. **805 N. Lakeshore Dr., Lake City, 55041; 651-345-2124.**

Services

Lake City Chamber of Commerce, 212 S. Washington St., P.O. Box 150, Lake City, 55041; 800-369-4123 or 651-345-4123. Wabasha Chamber of Commerce, 800-565-4158.

Lanesboro and the Root River Valley

Lanesboro is a near-magical little town nestled in a ring of limestone bluffs that rise sharply up from the Root River. The Root River Valley is really a series of valleys, formed by the several branches of the Root River and numerous small creeks, all on their way to the Mississippi River. The area, which for tourism marketing calls itself "Historic Bluff Country," is bounded by I-90 to the north, the river to the east, and the Iowa border to the south; to the west it peters out where I-90 dips south to join Hwy. 218.

The variety of terrain within the valley, from broad, open land to steep hills and limestone bluffs, is due to the lack of glaciation during the last Ice Age. Where the limestone is close to the surface, rain percolating through the soft stone can make it as holey as Swiss cheese. These so-called sinkholes, especially prevalent near the town of Fountain, result in the somewhat disconcerting sight of treetops rising from farmers' fields; tree trunks are obscured by the "sink."

The Root River Valley is an outdoor-lover's paradise. Lanesboro is the center of the Root River State Trail, which is increasingly popular with bikers, in-line skaters, and cross-country skiers. The outdoor activities are balanced by the town's thriving cultural life, abetted by a recent influx of visual and performing artists. Add to this mix the fact that the downtown is on the National Register of Historic Places, plus the presence of old-order Amish, who sell produce and other wares at the Sat. market in summer, and it is clear why Lanesboro has become one of the state's most popular destinations.

Its popularity sometimes threatens to overwhelm the town, especially on July and Aug. weekends. Summer weekdays are much less crowded; off-season, the town is positively serene. Visitors aren't the only ones who like what Lanesboro has to offer. The Root River State Trail runs right through town, and it provides recreation of another sort for unofficial town historian Don Ward, a Lanesboro native who is half Norwegian and half Irish, and thus perfectly represents the town's original European settlers. Ward says drolly, "We don't have to go out of town for entertainment now. I just go sit on a bench and watch the tourists perform."

Lanesboro adroitly treads the fine line between small-town charm and warmth, and cultural sophistication. It may have a winery and a wonderful professional theater, but it still lacks a stoplight—and residents want to keep it that way.

History

Lanesboro is constantly being rediscovered. A succession of American Indian tribes were here before the Europeans—mostly Norwegian and Irish—settled the town in the 1860s, and many of them used the community as a base for settlement farther west, especially after the railroad came to town in 1868. In the 1870s the town was "discovered" again, by a New York company that saw it as a potential resort. The company bought up about 3,000 acres of land, built a four-story hotel, and dammed the river to form a recreational lake before it disbanded in about 1880, according to Ward.

Lanesboro's population reached approximately 2,000 near the end of the 19th century, but it's now less than half that. Lanesboro had another renaissance when the first bed-and-breakfast—Mrs. B's—opened in 1984 and paved the way for other lodging places and restaurants. The opening of the Root River State Trail encouraged still more tourist-oriented businesses.

Festivals and Events

Norske Vinter Fest
Presidents' Day weekend, Feb.
Winter is long and dark in Minnesota, so a mid-winter break is welcome. The fest includes a candlelight cross-country ski session and other events, which vary from year to year. For information on this and other Lanesboro festivals, call the Lanesboro Visitor Center, **800-944-2670** or **507-467-2696.**

Sykkle Tur
third weekend in May
Norwegian for "bicycle tour," this event starts the summer season. Recently, the Overland Inn in Whalan has organized a "stand-still" parade, in which the spectators parade around the floats, bands marching in place, and other parade units. There are festivities in other Root River State Trail towns, and restaurants and other businesses offer specials for bikers and hikers. Call the Lanesboro Visitor Center, **800-944-2670** or **507-467-2696.**

Buffalo Bill Days
weekend that includes first day of Aug.
William Cody, aka Buffalo Bill, was a Civil War pal of a local doctor, and when Cody visited Lanesboro in the early 1880s, according to Lanesboro historian Don Ward, the doctor organized an exhibition of riding and roping skills by

Root River State Trail, outside of Lanesboro. Photo courtesy of Southeastern Minnesota Historic Bluff Country.

local Winnebago Indians for Cody's benefit. Ward speculates that the Lanesboro shows inspired Cody's famous Wild West Show. At any rate, it's the story behind Buffalo Bill Days, whose events include a Sun. parade. Call the Lanesboro Visitor Center, **800-944-2670** or **507-467-2696.**

Western Days
second weekend in Aug.
A twilight trail ride, a street dance, a parade, a horse show, and band concerts are all part of Chatfield's 30-year-old festival in the "Chosen Valley." For details, call **507-867-3810.**

Oktober Fest
first Sat. in Oct.
The fall colors are usually at their best for this polka festival. The dancing goes on all day at the

---

Getting There
Lanesboro is a drive of slightly more than two hours from the Twin Cities, on Hwy. 52 to Fountain, and east on County Rd. 8. From the east, I-90 connects with Hwy. 16, a scenic road that leads to Lanesboro.

Lanesboro Community Center. Call the Lanesboro Visitor Center, **800-944-2670** or **507-467-2696.**

Outdoor Activities

Biking

Root River State Trail

The main portion of this multiple-use trail is a 36-mile stretch from Fountain to the Money Creek Forestry Unit. A 5.5-mile spur trail along the south branch of the Root River connects Preston to the main trail (Harmony–Preston Valley State Trail was to be extended from Preston to Harmony). Preston native Jimmilee Miller painted a mural of Preston's first train along the trailhead building. The trail is paved with asphalt and there is no use fee. Because it is developed along an abandoned railway grade, the trail is quite level, even wheelchair-accessible. The trail, nearly always within sight of the limestone bluffs, has 46 bridges and often goes through bucolic farmlands. In summer, several concerts are held at towns along the trail. Trail centers, with information, parking, rest rooms, and nearby camping facilities, are at Lanesboro and Rushford. Additional parking lots and rest rooms are at Fountain and Preston. Other campsites, parking areas, and picnic tables are scattered along the trail.

Rentals and Tours

This is a partial list of bike and other equipment rental places. **The Village Square** rents bicycles; **99 Main St., Fountain, 800-946-2676** or **507-268-4406. The Historic Scanlan House** rents bikes, canoes, and cross-country skis; **708 Parkway Ave. S., Lanesboro, 507-467-2158. Little River General Store** rents bikes, canoes, and cross-country skis; **104 Parkway Ave. N., Lanesboro, 800-944-2943** or **507-467-2943. Capron Hardware** rents bikes; **119 Parkway N., Lanesboro, 507-467-3714** or **800-726-5030. Brickhouse** rents bikes; **104 E. Main, Preston, 507-765-9820. Old Barn Resort** rents bikes and inner tubes; **R.R. 3, Box 57, Preston, 800-552-2512** or **507-467-2512.**

C&C Crossing, at the Preston trailhead, rents bikes; **507-765-2318.** In Whalan, the **Overland Inn and Touring Company** provides a trail shuttle; **618 Main, Whalan, 507-467-2623** or **800-240-4162.**

Birding

Bird-watchers love Beaver Creek Valley State Park (see Parks), as it is possible to sight birds not found elsewhere in the state. Wild turkeys are common sights.

Boating

Canoeing along the Root River is great for novices or for families. The river's Class I rapids are not hard to negotiate, except during high water. The stretch of river from Chatfield to the Mississippi is 90 miles, with hardwood forest, steep limestone bluffs, and wooded pastures along the way. For a map call **888-MINNDNR** or **651-296-6157.**

Fishing

Fish found in Lake Louise, one of very few lakes in the Southeast Region, are bass, crappie, bullheads, and carp. Because most of the Root River Valley's water is in the form of streams, fishing here is primarily for trout. Many of the rivers and streams in the valley, including Beaver Creek and the branches of the Root River, are trout hot spots. Beaver Creek, filled with many brown trout and also with wilier brook trout, winds merrily through Beaver Creek Valley State Park, topped here and there with a bright green carpet of watercress—which provides cover for the brookies and should not be picked. Considered one of the best trout streams in southeast Minnesota, Beaver Creek yields brown trout that reportedly top 16 inches. Habitat for brown trout is provided by the convergence of three spring-fed streams in Forestville State Park, making it a destination for trout trackers. See Parks. Call the Area Fisheries Supervisor in Lanesboro for seasons and license information, **507-467-2442.**

Hiking

The Root River State Trail (multiple-use) stretches 36 miles from Fountain to the Money

Creek Forestry Unit; see Biking. At Beaver Creek Valley State Park, the Beaver Creek Valley Trail is the favorite hike, according to Park Manager Bill Bellman. The steep Switch Back Trail is a contrast to the level valley hike and provides good views at the cliff top. In Forestville State Park, there are 16 miles of hiking trails. Big Spring Trail leads to the Big Spring, source for Canfield Creek. See Parks.

Hunting

White-tailed deer are abundant in the southeast part of Minnesota. Here, too, are flocks of wild turkeys. The Oak Ridge Unit of Richard J. Dorer Memorial Hardwood State Forest, near Houston, is open for public hunting during seasons. For seasons and license information, call the Dept. of Natural Resources Winona office, **507-453-2950.**

Skiing

CROSS-COUNTRY

Cross-country skiers flock to the level Root River State Trail (see Biking). Other trails in the area, including those in the Oak Ridge Unit of the Richard J. Dorer Memorial Hardwood State Forest and state parks, offer more challenging skiing as they are hillier. **Forestville State Park, 507-352-5111,** has 6.5 miles of ski trails. The **Oak Ridge Unit, 507-523-2183,** has an 8.8-mile trail for nonmotorized recreation, including cross-country skiing and snowshoeing; loops of the trail vary as much as 300 feet in elevation, providing for exciting skiing. A 2.2-mile portion of a Houston County snowmobile trail runs across the northern portion of the unit. See Parks.

Seeing and Doing

Art Galleries and Museums

Cornucopia Art Center

Part gallery, part showcase and shop for area artists and craftspeople, the art center—a nonprofit cooperative—is a great place to find wonderful things you didn't know you needed but will love. Among them are Frank Wright's wooden spoons.

They come in all shapes and sizes: there are swoony spoons, stand-up spoons, sexy spoons—even a series of "Roux Stir" spoons with the handle a stylized rooster's comb. Wright includes with each sale a spoon-care letter that urges buyers to "talk with your spoon." The gallery shows feature many kinds of art, including that of local artists, according to executive director Michaeljon Pease. Call for hours. Located on Parkway in the heart of Lanesboro. **P.O. Box 152, Lanesboro, 55949; 507-467-2446.**

Museums and Historic Sites

There are many museums in the blufflands area, including the 1876 **Methodist Church Museum** in Spring Valley, which has photos and artifacts describing author Laura Ingalls Wilder's family's stay in the town. Fee; call for hours; **221 W. Courtland St., Spring Valley, 55975, 507-346-2763** or **507-346-7659.** Call the **Lanesboro Historic Preservation Association and Museum** for its hours; **105 Parkway Ave. S., Lanesboro, 55949; 507-467-2177.** The **Fillmore County Historical Center,** in Fountain, is free; call for days and hours open. It's at the junction of Hwy. 52 and County Rd. 8; **507-268-4449.** The **Houston County Historical Society Museum** in Caledonia is free. Open year-round, Mon.–Wed., 10:00 A.M.–4:00 P.M.; June–Sept., it's also open Sat.–Sun., 1:00–4:00 P.M. **1212 E. Main St., Caledonia, 55921; 507-724-3884** or **507-896-2291.**

Historic Forestville

It's always 1899 in Forestville, a restored village that is run by the Minnesota Historical Society but is within the larger Forestville State Park. The little village, reached by a restored Victorian bridge across the Root River, includes the Meighen Store, which closed in 1910, leaving most of its wares on the shelves for visitors to see. The entire village is on the National Register of Historic Sites. Visitors need a state park entry permit to enter Historic Forestville. Although park visitors can walk around the village year-round, the building interiors can be toured only with costumed living-history guides. Tours are offered Memorial Day weekend–Labor Day,

The store at Historic Forestville in Forestville State Park. Photo courtesy of the Minnesota Historical Society.

Tues.–Sun., and in the fall, Sat.–Sun. Located 4 miles south of Hwy. 16 on County Hwy. 5 and 2 miles east on County Hwy. 12; **507-765-2785.**

Schech's Water Powered Mill

By the side of pretty little Beaver Creek is a three-story native-stone mill built in 1876. Michael J. Schech, a master miller from Bavaria, bought it in 1887 and his descendants still own and operate the mill. Once used to grind "Schech's Best Flour," the mill now grinds feed for farm animals. One caution: the mill and grounds are private property, not part of nearby Beaver Creek State Park. Owner Ivan Krugmire gives tours of the picturesque mill for a small fee. Call ahead for an appointment. Located 6 miles northwest of Caledonia, off County Rd. 10; **507-896-3481.**

Nature Centers

DNR Fish Hatchery

Visitors are welcome to take a sneak peek at the tiny trout that will be stocked in the area's streams. This state hatchery is open Mon.–Fri., 8:00 A.M.–4:30 P.M. Free. Located 1.5 miles west of Lanesboro off Hwy. 16; **507-467-3771.**

Eagle Bluff Environmental Learning Center

This private, nonprofit, member-supported center seeks to teach visitors of all ages how to appreciate natural resources and use them responsibly. The center is in the Richard J. Dorer Memorial Hardwood State Forest and has 11 miles of trails, including a self-guided interpretive trail, a limited-mobility trail, and groomed cross-country ski trails. Classes focus on the environment, including local geology, and on confidence- and team-building, using a "high ropes" course. Family events have included an annual canoe ramble and a cross-country ski get-together. Sun. brunch programs with a naturalist are popular, and many visitors come to learn about the shiitake mushroom-growing project or to buy fresh or dried shiitakes. Fee for courses and events. The center is 5 miles northwest of Lanesboro. Follow County Rd. 8 west for 2 miles, then County Rd. 21 for 1.2 miles to the township road leading to the center. **1991 Brightsdale Rd., Rte. 2, Box 156A, Lanesboro, 55949; 507-467-2437. Website: www.eagle-bluff.org.**

Other Sights

The Chatfield Brass Band Music Lending Library

The world's only music lending library is in Chatfield, at the northern edge of the Root River Valley, an area residents refer to as the "chosen valley." The library's aim is to preserve music—all kinds, not just band music—and lend it as needed. Carmen Narveson, a music teacher and library volunteer, says requests come in from around the world. The library has approximately 50,000 items available for loan, including a wall of marches. Visitors are welcome. Call for hours. **81 Library Lane, Box 578, Chatfield, 55923; 507-867-3275.**

Spring Grove Bottling Works

Since 1895, Spring Grove soda pop has slaked the thirst of southeast Minnesota. The soda pop, in eight flavors—including strawberry, creme soda, and black cherry—is produced in a small factory in Spring Grove. The pop is hard to find outside the area, so if you develop a taste for the fizzy stuff, stop by the factory for a few bottles—they will even sell single bottles. Call for hours. **215 Second Ave. NW, Spring Grove, 55974; 507-498-3424.**

Parks

Beaver Creek Valley State Park

A favorite camping spot for young families, Beaver Creek Valley State Park is one of the state's loveliest. The transition from open farm fields to the park's deep, forested domain happens quickly. The level country road into the park is soon surrounded by cliffs up to 250 feet high on either side. Beaver Creek must be forded at several points, although signs indicate the depth at which fording is dangerous during high water. After heavy rains, according to park information, flash flooding can be a problem in the canyonlike surroundings. Escape routes, via steps to the top of the cliffs, are clearly indicated. In a clearing near the campground, one of many springs in the park bubbles up from the base of a sheer rock wall. In the spring, the woods and bits of prairie are a wildflower lover's delight. A playground, with a wading pool set into a sand surround, keeps kids occupied. The timber rattlesnake also lives in the park, but is seldom sighted; it is protected and visitors who see one are urged not to harm it and instead to contact park staff. The park is 5 miles west of Caledonia on County Rd. 1 off Hwy. 76. Information: Beaver Creek Valley State Park, **Rte. 2, Box 57, Caledonia, 55921; 507-724-2107.**

Forestville State Park

Probably one of the state's most varied state parks, with Mystery Cave and Historic Forestville within its bounds, Forestville is the most heavily used by horseback riders. The 14 miles of scenic, hilly horse trails and the large number of horsecamp units (80) are big draws. Timber rattlers are present but seldom seen; birds are abundant. Located 4 miles south of Hwy. 16 on County Rd. 5, then 2 miles east on County Rd. 12. Forestville State Park, **Rte. 2, Box 128, Preston, 55965; 507-352-5111.**

Lake Louise State Park

Portions of the oak savanna, a prairie polka-dotted with trees, still survive in the park, which is in a transitional zone between the woodlands and the prairie. Just off the Shooting Star Wildflower and Historic Rte. (Hwy. 56), the park attracts wildflower seekers as well as families who like to swim and fish in Lake Louise, formed when the confluence of the Upper Iowa and Little Iowa Rivers was dammed. The level hiking trails are ideal for families with young children and with older people. The campsites include six horsecamp units. **Rte. 1, Box 184, LeRoy, 55951; 507-324-5249.**

Richard J. Dorer Memorial Hardwood State Forest

The Dorer State Forest, which covers much of the southeast portion of the state, has several recreation areas, including Wet Bark/Oak Ridge near Houston. The Oak Ridge Unit has an 8.8-mile trail for nonmotorized recreation, including cross-country skiing, snowshoeing, hiking, and horseback riding. Loops of the trail vary as much as 300 feet in elevation, providing for exciting skiing. A 2.2-mile portion of Houston County snowmobile trail runs across the northern portion of the unit. There are four campsites. Located 5 miles west of Houston on County Rd. 13. For information on area forest units, contact the area supervisor, **Box 278, Lewiston, 55952; 507-523-2183.**

Performing Arts

LIVE RADIO

"Over the Back Fence"

The St. Mane Theatre is the venue for Lanesboro's homegrown variety show "Over the Back Fence." The show is carried by KFIL in Preston (103.1

The Commonweal Theatre Company production of Room Service. *Photo courtesy of the Commonweal Theatre Company: Scott Prahl.*

FM), and a studio audience is welcome to the live show (arrive at 6:45 P.M.). May–Aug., Sun., 7:00–8:00 P.M. **206 Parkway N., Lanesboro, 55949; 800-657-7025** or **507-467-2525.**

OPERA

Ye Olde Opera House

Residents of Spring Grove, a hotbed of Norwegians just a stone's throw from Iowa, built a new stage in Ye Olde Opera House several years ago and now take part enthusiastically in summer and fall productions here. The Opera House is the Southeast Region's largest community theater. **155 W. Main St., Spring Grove, 55974; 507-498-5221** or **507-498-5859.**

THEATER

Commonweal Theatre Company

Look closely at the ticket taker and the usher at the lovely little St. Mane Theatre on Lanesboro's main street. Chances are, they will next appear on the stage of the former silent movie theater. The small, professional Commonweal Theatre Company was started in 1989 by Eric Lorentz Bunge and two other graduates of Denver's National Theatre Conservatory. The Commonweal, a nonprofit organization, puts on lively, well-acted performances of both classic and contemporary theater at the St. Mane. The season now stretches mid-Feb.–mid-Dec. **206 Parkway N., Lanes-boro, 55949; 800-657-7025** or **507-467-2525.**

Scenic Drives

Several towns in the bluff country have developed brochures or tapes for scenic and historic drives. Spring Grove has three cassettes that provide nuggets of history and geography as you drive along **three routes**—two cover the area and the third is a tour of early churches, almost all of them Lutheran in this Norwegian stronghold. Small fee for cassette rental. Contact the Ballard House in Spring Grove, **507-498-5434.** The Lanesboro Visitor Center, **800-944-2670,** has a brochure that offers a self-guided exterior tour of some of the town's **oldest private residences,** and another brochure detailing **two self-guided auto tours** of the surrounding

countryside. **Six drives,** covering all of the historic bluff territory, are featured in a brochure titled "Back Roads and Bluff Country Magic," available from local tourism offices or from the Historic Bluff Country office, **800-428-2030.** Follow almost any road in bluff country and it will be scenic. However, two are actually designated scenic routes: the Bluff Country Drive and Shooting Star Scenic Byway.

Bluff Country Drive

Bluff Country Drive, alias Hwy. 16, stretches from I-90 in the west to Hwy. 44 in the east, for a sweep across the main part of the historic bluff country. Traveling on Hwy. 16 takes riders from the open plains of the west through the lovely valley, hugging close to the Root River after Lanesboro.

Shooting Star Scenic Byway

The Shooting Star Scenic Byway, all on Hwy. 56, is a 26-mile route that begins at Hwy. 63 on its eastern edge and ends at I-90 in the west. For 17 miles, the road shares a right-of-way with an abandoned rail line, and between the road and the rail bed is a treasure trove of wildflowers, including the "shooting star," a wild primrose that grows nowhere else in the state. The drive also passes by the Taopi Prairie site, skirts Lake Louise State Park, and passes through several small towns with historic buildings. A wayside rest and interpretive kiosk is at the east end, and at Rose Creek near the west end are trails and picnic facilities at a city park.

Tours

Mystery Cave

A cool respite on a summer day is a tour through intriguing Mystery Cave, part of Forestville State Park but 5.5 miles away from the main park. The limestone cave is Minnesota's longest cave, with 12 miles of passages. The temperature in the cave year-round is 48°F. Two tours are given Memorial Day weekend–Labor Day. The one-hour historic tour, offered daily, has standard electric lighting and is fairly level, with ramped concrete walkways. This tour includes a look at beautiful and well-named Turquoise Lake. On weekends, there is a two-hour Minnesota Caverns Tour. It is not recommended for small children or people with heart problems or physical limitations, as it has numerous steps and gravel paths and is lit by handheld electric lanterns. Fee (state park permit needed). From Hwy. 16, follow County Rd. 5 south to the cave, along a gravel road. **507-937-3251** for cave or **507-352-5111** for main park.

Wineries

Scenic Valley Winery

Sampling the local fruit wines at the Scenic Valley Winery in Lanesboro is a popular pastime. The tasting is done in the sales room of the winery in downtown Lanesboro. The winery is open Apr.–Dec., Mon.–Sat., 10:00 A.M.–5:00 P.M., and Sun., noon–5:00 P.M. **101 Coffee St., Lanesboro, 55949; 507-467-2958.**

Where to Stay

Bed-and-Breakfasts

Cady-Hayes House—$$$ to $$$$

Peggy Hanson's century-old Queen Anne b-and-b, within walking distance of downtown Lanesboro, is a felicitous combination of restrained elegance and comfort. Windows are of ornately beveled glass, and the high walls in the house have beautifully stenciled borders. Guests can help themselves to sherry, play the restored Chickering grand piano, or settle down to play a board game. There are three bedrooms, all with private baths. The smallest has simple, Amish-style furniture; the Norwegian room, with its own sitting area, is decorated with Norwegian rosemaling and a wooden bed so huge it had to be assembled in the room; a two-room suite has a table and chairs tucked into a turret. Hanson can arrange for rental of recreation equipment. She and Lanesboro artist Frank Wright also offer a morel mushroom hunt for b-and-b guests who make a contribution to the Cornucopia Art Center (call for information). Breakfast is included

in your stay. **500 Calhoun Ave., Lanesboro, 55949; 507-467-2621.**

Historic Scanlan House Bed-and-Breakfast— $$$ to $$$$

Michael Scanlan, a poor Irish immigrant and one of Lanesboro's founders, left behind his rags-to-riches story and this ornate 1889 Queen Anne house, the first in town to be listed on the National Register of Historic Places. The house boasts an onion dome, a turret with its own balcony, many stained glass windows, and rare stamped leatherette wall covering in the dining room. Pleasant owner Kristen Mensing has decorated the five rooms lavishly in Victoriana, including both antique furniture and bric-a-brac. The Doll Room has a sleigh bed, a two-person whirlpool bath, and an antique doll collection. The Masquerade Suite has a two-person whirlpool bath, a fireplace, and the turret balcony. Breakfast is included. Bike rental can be arranged. **708 Parkway Ave. S., Lanesboro, 55949; 800-944-2158 or 507-467-2158.**

Mrs. B's Historic Lanesboro Inn and Restaurant—$$ to $$$

The current tourist craze for Lanesboro all began in this lovely little inn, also well known for its cuisine (see Where to Eat), on Lanesboro's main street. The narrow, 1872 limestone building has 10 charmingly and distinctively decorated rooms, including one with a Norwegian theme, and is smack-dab on the Root River State Trail. Some rooms have fireplaces and all have private baths. Full breakfast comes with the rooms. **Box 411, 101 Parkway, Lanesboro, 55949; 800-657-4710 or 507-467-2154.**

Hotels, Motels, and Inns

Green Gables Inn—$$$

Yes, this modern motel on the edge of Lanesboro does have green gables (the owner is a fan of the *Anne of Green Gables* books) and it also is a cut above most motels. There are 12 comfortably furnished rooms, four of them connecting suites with private decks. Some rooms are handicapped-accessible and all are smoke-free. **303 Sheridan**

St. W. (Hwy. 16), Lanesboro, 55949; 800-818-GABLES or 507-467-2936.

Cottage House Inn—$$ to $$$

Where's Waldo? Probably in the kitchen of this cozy inn, whipping up breakfast. Waldo and Marilyn Bunge had their son build this nine-room inn a few years ago, on Lanesboro's main street. The rooms offer quiet comfort and are furnished sparely and with care. One room has several pieces decorated with Norwegian rosemaling painting. In other rooms, there are nice touches such as china cabinets like your grandmother's, complete with bits of china. All rooms have full baths, but none has a television. There is a TV in the comfortable lounge, however, along with a supply of books and magazines, including all the *Waldo* books. Waldo makes guests delicious breakfasts for an extra charge. The Bunges, lifelong local residents, are good sources of information about the area. The inn is handicapped-accessible. **209 Parkway N., Lanesboro, 55949; 800-944-0099 or 507-467-2577.**

Val-A Lodge—$$ to $$$

New in 1996, this 12-room motel is conveniently located if you're headed south into the Root River Valley. The rooms are nicely furnished, and some have dry bars and microwave ovens. Mill Creek runs behind the motel, a bucolic change from busy Hwy. 52 in front. In the lobby are two lighted antique gas pumps, plus a collection of glass gas globes that used to top pumps, all in pristine condition. Orange juice, rolls, and coffee are served in the morning. **150 Hwy 30 W. (intersection of Hwys. 30 and 52), Chatfield, 55923; 507-867-3066.**

Camping

The Old Barn Resort—$

There really is an old barn, four stories high, built in 1884 and restored as the restaurant and headquarters of this big and busy camping/hostel/restaurant operation. Located right on the Root River, the resort has 130 developed campsites with water and electricity, half of which have sewer hookups, and also spaces for tent campers.

Although mainly a camping destination, the resort also has four large dorm rooms, housing 9–16 people in bunks, and a private room for one or two persons. Bedding and towels are included, and bathrooms are shared. The hostel has kitchen and laundry facilities and a game and recreation room. The heated pool is enclosed and usually full of tired bikers cooling off in summer. A fee is charged for those who wish to use only the pool. **Rte. 3, Box 57R, Preston, 55965; 800-552-2512 or 507-467-2512.**

State Parks—$

Beaver Creek Valley State Park has 42 drive-in sites, 16 with electricity, and 6 walk-in campsites. **Forestville State Park** has 73 drive-in sites, 23 with electricity; the park also has 60 horsecamp sites. **Lake Louise State Park** has 22 drive-in sites, half with electricity, and 6 horsecamp sites. For reservations, call **The Connection, 800-246-CAMP or 612-922-9000.**

Sylvan Park Campground—$

Lanesboro's municipal campground has 40 sites with water and electricity, and 60 sites for tent campers, with no reservations taken. The park is located off Kirkwood St. E. in the heart of Lanesboro; **507-467-3722.**

Root River Campsites—free

There are several free Dept. of Natural Resources primitive campsites along the Root River that can be used by canoe travelers. All refuse must be packed out. They are shown on the Root River Canoe and Boating Map, available from the **DNR, 888-MINNDNR or 651-296-6157.** In addition, there are developed campsites at several units of the Richard J. Dorer Memorial Hardwood State Forest close to the Root River; call **507-523-2183** for information on location and amenities.

Where to Eat

Mrs. B's Historic Lanesboro Inn—$$$

Dine in the lovely little dining room of Mrs. B's, perhaps piling on calories again after losing them biking the Root River State Trail. The multicourse dinners have drawn many visitors to Lanesboro in recent years. By reservation only. Call for days and hours open. **101 Parkway, Lanesboro, 55949; 800-657-4710 or 507-467-2154.**

The Victorian House—$$$

Chef Jean-Claude Venant, born and trained in France, offers an elegant evening meal in the well-regarded restaurant he and his wife, Sonja, opened in their Victorian white frame house. Dinner is served in a private dining room. Open year-round by reservation, for dinner only. Call for hours and days open. **709 Parkway S., Lanesboro, 55949; 507-467-3457.**

The Old Barn Resort—$ to $$$

Fare at the restaurant of this resort, a camping center on the Root River, ranges from burgers to prime rib. The restaurant is in the beautiful old barn. Dress informally, but come prepared to eat. Portions are large and prices are right. Open approximately Apr. 1–Nov. 1, Mon.–Fri., noon–8:00 P.M., and Sat.–Sun., noon–10:00 P.M. **Rte. 3, Box 57, Preston, 55965; 800-552-2512 or 507-467-2512.**

Bake Shoppe Cafe—$

The spacious cafe/bakery, with its wooden booths and photos of Spring Grove around the walls, is a nice place for lunch or coffee and a fresh-baked goody. Soups are made fresh daily by chef Paola Utecht. The cafe serves breakfast and lunch, and baked goods all day. Open year-round, Mon.–Sat., 7:00 A.M.–4:00 P.M. **131 Main St., Spring Grove, 55974; 507-498-5482.**

Chat 'n Chew—$

This is where the Lanesboro locals gather to—yes—chat and chew. The homey cafe serves hearty breakfasts and good, plain food such as meat loaf sandwiches—fast if you need it, slow if you can linger—amid saucy signs such as "Don't criticize the coffee, you may be old and weak someday." Open Mon.–Fri., 6:00 A.M.–3:00 P.M., and Sat.–Sun., 6:00 A.M.–2:00 P.M. Located at the **intersection of Hwy. 16 and Parkway Ave., Lanesboro; 507-467-3444.**

Overland Inn—$ for pie

Almost everyone who rides through Whalan on the Root River State Trail makes a stop at the Overland Inn for pie and maybe soup and a sandwich, too. But the pies are the drawing card. Owner Dave Harrenstein, who juggles college teaching with restaurant running, may have been only a trifle optimistic when he added to his inn sign the words "Home of World Famous Pies." The pies include cream pies, fruit pies, a sour cream raisin pie, and specialty pies such as chocolate fudge and maple walnut. Open seasonally; call for days and hours open. **Milepost 16 on Root River State Trail, Whalan, 55986; 800-240-4162 or 507-467-2623.**

Services

For information on all bluff country towns, contact **Historic Bluff Country, P.O. Box 609, 45 Center St. E., Harmony, 55939; 800-428-2030 or 507-886-2230.**

For Lanesboro information only, call the **Lanesboro Visitor Center, 800-944-2670 or 507-467-2696.**

For lodging opportunities, call **HBC Vacancy Service, 800-79-BLUFF.**

Northfield

"Northfield, City of Cows, Colleges and Contentment" reads the sign just outside the pretty little river town of Northfield. That's Northfield in a nutshell: the city of 16,000 is justly proud of its two well-regarded liberal arts colleges, St. Olaf and Carleton; there are indeed cows close by; and the residents seem pretty contented. Who wouldn't be happy to live in a town where civility and sophistication reign, the main street is a picture postcard, and the Cannon River burbles through the city, luring walkers along its paths and fisherfolk along its banks?

However, that's only part of the story. For most Minnesotans, the name "Northfield" is synonymous with the notorious outlaw Jesse James. The city fathers and mothers are probably too modest to add "We kicked Jesse's butt" to the sign, but that's what happened on a day in Sept. 1876. And the town has never forgotten, wearing the defeat of Jesse James in its otherwise bucolic history the way an upright businessman might sport a flashy tie.

History

Like most towns that grew up around a river, Northfield began as a milling town. The town was founded in 1855 by John North, a New England lawyer who soon convinced other East Coasters to join him. It wasn't long before the Cannon River was dammed to power the Ames flour mill, now restored and owned by Malt-O-Meal, a producer of breakfast cereals. North built a mill, had a general store, and founded both a reading room and the Northfield School, which later became Carleton College.

The town was prospering and minding its own business when Jesse and Frank James, the Younger brothers, and a few others rode into town on Sept. 7, 1876, intending to rob the First National Bank. The bank's acting cashier, Joseph Lee Heywood, refused to open the safe, and one of the gang shot him dead. After a shootout on the main street, two other members of Jesse's gang and Nicholas Gustafson, a Swedish immigrant who was a bystander, lay dead. The surviving outlaws galloped out of town, citizens in pursuit, fleeing along what is now called the Outlaw Trail. Part of the gang was apprehended, but Jesse and Frank escaped. Jesse was murdered a few years later in Missouri, but Frank was cleared of crimes and died an old man.

Aside from that one brush with notoriety, Northfield's history has been unremarkable. As the town grew, dairying replaced milling as the major occupation, but industry, including Malt-O-Meal and Sheldahl Inc., a firm producing flexible circuits and laminates, are now an important part of the town's economy. The colleges, of course, have always been vital in the town's economic as well as intellectual life. Northfield has a greater-than-average share of writers, artists, and others who live by their creative wits. Artist Mary Ericksen declares that Northfield is the best place in the world; she says the town's tolerance is what encourages the creativity.

Festivals and Events

Defeat of Jesse James Days
first weekend after Labor Day

Get in town early if you want to see the James gang and the townspeople shoot it out on Division St. at the end of this five-day celebration. The raid is reenacted several times Sat.–Sun. The festival draws the largest crowd—about 100,000—of any nonmetro festival in Minnesota. During the reenactment, the gang, on horseback wearing ankle-length white "duster" coats and bearing six-shooters, bursts into town along closed-off Division St. During the ensuing seven-minute shootout, blanks fire loudly, horses gallop up and down the street, and spectators in the front row can almost smell the sweat. Then the gang hightails it out of town and it's all over for another year. The festival also includes a parade, an arts fair, a carnival, and a professional rodeo. **800-658-2548** or **507-645-5604.**

Outdoor Activities

Biking

The Northfield Chamber of Commerce has a brochure with recommended biking tours of 10–30 miles; directions are very specific. There is an approximately 2-mile bike trail from Northfield to Dundas. Another 20- to 30-mile route goes to Nerstrand Big Woods State Park through rolling farmland. For a brochure, contact the chamber office (see Services).

Boating

The Cannon River in Northfield, and at Dundas a few miles south, is a good canoeing river and fairly placid, with few rapids. River access for canoes is at the Cannon River Wilderness Area (see Parks), Dundas City Park, and Sechler Park in Northfield. In Northfield, there is a dam between the Fourth and Fifth St. bridge with no developed portage; riprap and retaining walls around the dam make carrying canoes difficult. For a map call **888-MINNDNR** or **651-296-6157.**

Getting There
Northfield is 35 miles south of the Twin Cities. The fastest route is I-35 to Hwy. 19, then east to Northfield. Minneapolis–St. Paul International Airport is 30 minutes north of Northfield.

Fishing

In Northfield, the Cannon yields bluegills, bullheads, walleyes, northern pike, crappies, smallmouth bass, and carp. Call the Area Fisheries Supervisor, **651-345-3365,** for seasons and license information.

Hiking

Hiking trails abound in parks around Northfield. Nerstrand Big Woods State Park has 13 miles of hiking trails, 8 miles of cross-country ski trails, and 5 miles of snowmobile trails. For a sample of the hikes in that park, start behind the information center and follow the boardwalk, looking for trout lilies during the last two weeks in Apr. Stop at Hidden Falls, a sheer rock wall that wept into a stream below until heavy rains made it into more of a falls. Follow the Beaver Trail parallel to Prairie Creek, cross the oak bridge, and walk back along the Oak Ridge Trail, through steep and sometimes challenging terrain, to the information center—a total hike of about 1.5 miles. For more information, see Parks.

Seeing and Doing

Art Galleries and Museums

Mary Ericksen Studio and Gifts

Mary Ericksen's small combination studio and shop is overflowing with her whimsy and warmth. Ericksen, who works on her art in a tiny studio separated from the shop by a partly drawn white lace curtain, is a St. Olaf graduate and has been an artist-in-residence there as well as a children's book illustrator. Most of her work is done in pastels, such as her delightfully daffy

Jesse James Days. Courtesy of the Northfield Area Chamber of Commerce.

animals and happily lopsided stars. Some of these, in miniature, adorn pins and earrings, but larger originals are also available. Ericksen also sells works by other local artists. The studio/shop is tucked into the back of the Nutting Mall on Northfield's main street. Open Tues.–Sat., 11:00 A.M.–5:00 P.M.; sometimes also open Sun. or Mon. **220 Division St., Northfield, 55057; 507-645-9131.**

Northfield Arts Guild

A center for townspeople as well as tourists, the NAG is a nonprofit organization that showcases visual and performing arts. NAG has two sites: one at 411 W. Third St. is a performing space; the other is the Center for the Arts, at 304 Division St., where there is gallery space for shows by local and regional artists as well as a shop selling work by local artists and craftspeople. The guild also has classes. The building housing the Center for the Arts was one of the first Minnesota YMCAs outside the Twin Cities area, and it was visited by Mark Twain in 1886, who described himself in the guest book as a "Professional Tramp." Open year-round, Mon.–Wed. and Fri.–Sat., 10:00 A.M.–5:00 P.M.; Sat., 10:00 A.M.–9:00 P.M. **304 Division St., Northfield, 55057; 507-645-8877.**

Somers Studio and Gallery

Fred Somers does exquisitely detailed pastels and oils portraying the natural world. One person described Somers's art as "poetic realism," and the lovely, shimmering studies of the natural realm do capture both the real and the wished-for world. Call for hours. Located 5.5 miles south of Northfield on Hwy. 246. **9775 Dennison Blvd. S., Northfield, 55057; 507-645-5031.**

Gardens and Arboreta

Carleton College Arboretum

Nearly half of the college's acreage is devoted to the peaceful arboretum beside the Cannon River, where the public is welcome to walk or ski year-round. The "Arb" dates to the turn of the century and contains 10 miles of cross-country skiing and running trails as well as a 20-station fitness trail. The college also uses the arboretum for scientific and environmental studies. The aboretum, which has picnic facilities, is a few blocks from downtown. Maps are available at the **Carleton Bookstore, 1 N. College St., Northfield, 55057.** For information call the Carleton News Bureau, **507-646-4184.**

Museums and Historic Sites

Carleton College

Carleton College, founded in 1866, is just a few blocks from downtown Northfield. The campus is compact, and many of the buildings are Gothic in appearance. It is a few years older than cross-town rival St. Olaf, and its graduates include homegrown economist Thorstein Veblen. Many people—students and residents alike—swear they can tell the difference between the "Carls" and the "Oles" by their looks and their dress. In truth, not all Oles are blonde or Norwegian and not all Carls wear black. However, both colleges have fine national reputations. Visitors are welcome on campus. Several buildings are on the National Register of Historic Places. Ask the Carleton News Bureau about special public events at Goodsell Observatory or current art exhibits. To reach the campus coming east on Hwy. 19, turn left onto Hwy. 3 and then right onto Second St.; Carleton is on the left at the top of the hill. Maps are available from the Carleton News Bureau, **119 Leighton Hall, Northfield, 55057; 507-646-4184.**

Dundas

A tiny village 2 miles south of Northfield on Hwy. 3, Dundas has five buildings—a church, a store, a mill, and two houses—on the National Historic Registry and all were built by the Archibald family. The Episcopal Church of the Holy Cross looks like an English country church. Its benefactor, John S. Archibald, also built the mill and the Martin Oaks House, now a bed-and-breakfast. His brother Edward built the other historic house, and a cousin built the store. The Archibalds keep slightly apart from lesser mortals even in death. A family plot in the churchyard is fenced, and a wrought-iron figure of a weeping angel adorns the gate. (Dundas doesn't dwell on the past, however, and recently built a snazzy lighted ball field in the city park along the river to let fans root for the Dundas Dukes far into the summer nights.) For information, call the Northfield Area Chamber of Commerce and Convention and Visitors Bureau, **800-658-2548.**

Historic Northfield

Drive or walk past Northfield's points of interest and historic houses, using a brochure available from the Northfield Chamber of Commerce. Buildings described in detail include the 1855 YMCA, graced with a two-story bay window and the word "welcome" carved in stone above the door. Most of the buildings are downtown, but the tour also includes structures at both Carleton and St. Olaf Colleges and the home of Norwegian-American author O. E. Rolvaag. On a nice day, sit on a bench in Bridge Square in the heart of Northfield's downtown. An antique popcorn wagon sells snacks in season. On one side of the square is Division St., with its row of historic buildings. On the other side of the square is the Cannon River, with the lovely restored Ames Mill, and several bridges across the river. There is a stone walkway along the river. On Thurs. evenings during summer, a variety of activities—from concerts to ice cream socials to pie baking—are held in the square. For information contact the Northfield Area Chamber of Commerce and Convention and Visitors Bureau, **500 Water St. S., P.O. Box 198, Northfield, 55057; 800-658-2548.**

Northfield Historical Society's Bank Museum

The historical society has restored the First National Bank to the way it was when the James and Younger gang arrived to rob it in 1876. Visitors can see a teller's window and the safe. An interpretive center tells about the aborted robbery and displays artifacts from the gang. The society occasionally gives living-history portrayals of those involved in or close to the raid, including murdered bank cashier Joseph Lee Heywood and Zerelda James Samuels, Jesse James's mother. Jesse's mom, who offers a fierce defense of her son's character in the reenactment, is played convincingly by Marie Gery, who has done considerable research on the James family. (See also Festivals and Events for the raid reenactment.) Open Tues.–Sun., 10:00 A.M.–4:00 P.M. **408 Division St., Northfield, 55057; 507-645-9268.**

Norwegian-American Historical Association

If you are a Norwegian American, you may find information about your forebears in the association's extensive archives, housed in the basement of the St. Olaf College library. Most of the materials are in Norwegian, but some—particularly newspaper obituaries—are in English. There is no charge for the first half hour of research, and the staff is very helpful. Open year-round, Mon.–Fri., 10:00 A.M.–noon and 1:00–4:00 P.M. **1510 St. Olaf Ave., Northfield, 55057; 507-646-3221.**

Outlaw Trail

After Jesse James and his gang flubbed the bank robbery in Northfield, they beat it out of town, followed by irate townspeople. Their escape route as far as Hanska, where part of the gang was captured, has been well documented and there is a brochure for drivers wanting to trace the route. Guides are available for groups. For information call the Northfield Area Chamber of Commerce, **800-658-2548.**

St. Olaf College

Founded in 1874 by Norwegian immigrants, the pretty college "on the hill" on Northfield's west side once was so heritage-conscious that any student who was more than one-quarter Norwegian was required to study Norwegian. Today, Norwegian is still taught, but it's taken by choice. Most students choose to spend at least one semester abroad. O. E. Rolvaag, author of the classic Norwegian-American immigrant novel *Giants in the Earth,* taught here. The college's choirs are highly regarded. The campus is a lovely place to stroll, and the Steensland Art Gallery is open to the public. There are public restaurants in the student center. A campus map is available from the student center. To reach the campus coming east on Hwy. 19, turn left at the St. Olaf sign and follow the road up the hill. **507-646-2222** for college information, **507-646-3556** for Steensland gallery, or **507-646-3040** for upcoming events, including the Christmas smorgasbord.

Parks

Cannon River Wilderness Area

The 850-acre Cannon River Wilderness Area, a Rice County park, hugs the Cannon River 5 miles south of Northfield on Hwy. 3. It contains some of the big hardwood trees that were part of Minnesota's original "Big Woods." The park has hiking and cross-country ski trails and picnic areas. For information, call the Northfield Area Chamber of Commerce, **800-658-2548.**

Nerstrand Big Woods State Park

The towering trees that arch over walkers in Nerstrand Big Woods State Park are the remnants of a hardwood forest of about 5,000 acres that existed prior to the arrival of European settlers in the area. Major clear-cutting and small-woodlot activity whittled the Big Woods down to small pieces of the once-huge forest. Luckily, conservationists realized the significance of the remainder and established this state park in 1945. Besides the trees, there are more than 50 varieties of wildflowers on the forest floor, including the dwarf trout lily, a delicate spring flower on both the federal and state endangered species lists. A walk in late Apr. and early May reveals a carpet of wildflowers, including both the dwarf and the standard trout lily, plus anemone, sunny yellow marsh marigolds, and pink and white Dutchmen's breeches. The park is 11 miles southeast of Northfield. From Hwy. 3, follow Hwy. 246 out of Northfield, and follow signs to Nerstrand. **9700 170th St. E., Nerstrand, 55053; 507-334-8848.**

St. Olaf Nature Trail

A 3-mile nature trail at St. Olaf College begins by the Skoglund Center and winds through several patches of wetlands. Birds, including waterfowl, are often seen along the trail, which is open to the public. A map is available at the information booth in the student center (see Museums and Historic Sites).

Seasonal Favorites

Sogn Valley Orchard

The drive along County Rd. 9 in the scenic Sogn Valley is beautiful when the fall leaves are at their peak. Stop at the Sogn Valley Orchard, which sells many apple varieties as well as apple cider, pumpkins, and other good things. Open seasonally; call for hours. Located 1 mile west of Sogn on County Rd. 9, or 1 mile east of Hwy. 56 on County Rd. 9. **507-263-5750.**

Shopping

Jacobsen's

A real old-fashioned department store, Jacobsen's has a timelessly practical and friendly air. There are flannel shirts, long underwear, quilting supplies, and a good variety of fabrics. "You need it, we have it" is the store's slogan. Open Mon., Thurs., 8:00 A.M.–8:00 P.M.; Tues.–Wed., Fri.–Sat., 8:00 A.M.–5:30 P.M. **419 Division St., Northfield, 55057; 507-645-4672.**

Where to Stay

Bed-and-Breakfasts

Martin Oaks Bed-and-Breakfast—$$$

The splendid gardens, the magnificent feline bulk of Mrs. Waddleberry, or the spirited conversation of owners Frank and Marie Gery would be more than enough to draw visitors back to Martin Oaks Bed-and-Breakfast in the sleepy little village of Dundas. But the house itself, Martin Oaks, a Victorian Italianate mansion built in 1869, envelopes overnighters in luxury and comfort. The parlor, with a baby grand piano waiting for players, is filled with interesting bibelots and books, and the antique Victorian parlor suite is downright comfortable. Guests find treats in their rooms when they retire, and there is hot coffee waiting in the hallway in the morning before breakfast. Marie, a poet with a wickedly funny sense of the absurd, has a wide-ranging library, with books and magazines for all tastes. She's an inspired cook who serves creative and bountiful breakfasts. Though the house may be elegant, the Gerys are down to earth and helpful about suggesting tours. But it's not necessary to leave quickly once you are there. Stroll outside, inspect Marie's garden, try the swing hanging from the massive oak tree, go watch the Dundas Dukes play, or sit and listen to the gurgle of the three-tiered iron fountain. Book ahead for busy week-

ends at the colleges. **107 First St., Dundas, 55019; 507-645-4644.**

Hotels, Motels, and Inns

Archer House—$$ to $$$$

The red-painted Archer House, with its white-railed porches and mansard roof, is a Northfield landmark. It dates to 1877, but fell on hard times until the 1980s, when it was restored and an addition was built. It's popular with parents of students at St. Olaf or Carleton and as a weekend getaway. Some of the 36 units overlook the river. There are 19 suites with whirlpool baths. Some rooms have handmade quilts on the beds. The main floor contains shops and restaurants, as well as the hotel reception area. **212 Division St., Northfield, 55057; 507-645-5661** or (in Minnesota) **800-247-2235.**

Camping

At **Nerstrand Big Woods State Park** there are 61 semimodern campsites and 23 sites with electricity, along with 18 rustic pioneer campsites. For reservations, call **The Connection, 800-246-CAMP** or **612-922-9000.**

Where to Eat

The Tavern—$ to $$$

There is a tavern in this town—but the name is misleading. Although the Tavern does sell alcoholic beverages, it's better known as the place where parents treat their college kids. It's rustic and cozy, with friendly service. The menu is all over the globe, with Mexican and Greek specialties thrown in among more standard fare. The Greek-style potatoes, fried in olive oil, are scrumptious. Open year-round, Sun.–Thurs., 6:30 A.M.–10:00 P.M., and Fri.–Sat., 6:30 A.M.–11:00 P.M. **212 Division St., Northfield, 55057; 507-663-0342.**

J. Grundy's Rueb-n-Stein—$ to $$

Once two restaurants, this is now one big burger heaven, with Reuben sandwiches also a specialty along with imported beer. Open Mon.–Sat.,

11:00 A.M.–1:00 A.M., and Sun., 11:00 A.M.–midnight. **501 Division St., Northfield, 55057; 507-645-4405.**

The Ole Store—$ to $$

Yes, this is the home of the "Ole Roll," a cinnamon roll topped with a caramel glaze that is a dieter's downfall. If there are any Ole Rolls left, they are made into ORFT—Ole Roll French Toast. The cafe, just a couple of blocks from St. Olaf College, has several small rooms, all with Norwegian-inspired decor. The Ole Store isn't just for breakfast; lunches and dinners are good, too. There is an actual store on the other side of the cafe, with groceries, candies, and local jams and jellies for sale. Open Tues.–Wed., 6:30 A.M.–2:00 P.M.; Thurs.–Fri., 6:30 A.M.–2:00 P.M. and 5:00–8:00 P.M.; Sat., 8:00 A.M.–2:00 P.M. and 5:00–8:00 P.M.; Sun., 8:00 A.M.–2:00 P.M. **1011 St. Olaf Ave., Northfield, 55057; 507-645-5558.**

Hogan Brothers—$

Grab a booth or table before you get in the (usually) long line of students to order your hot or cold hoagie, pita pocket, or soup of the day. The service is fast and the food is fine and filling. All this, and sometimes acoustic music, too. Open Sun.–Mon., 11:00 A.M.–9:00 P.M.; Tues.–Thurs., 11:00 A.M.–10:00 P.M.; Fri.–Sat., 11:00 A.M.–11:00 P.M. **415 Division St., Northfield, 55057; 507-645-6653.**

Quality Bakery and Coffee Shop—$

The Quality Bakery has been around since 1903, and no wonder. Its baked goods are just the thing for a midmorning snack. Next to the bakery is the coffee shop, where breakfasts and lunches, as well and coffee and doughnuts and other Qual-

ity goods, are served. Open Mon.–Sat., 6:30 A.M.–5:30 P.M., and Sun., 6:30 A.M.–5:00 P.M. **410 Division St., Northfield, 55057; 507-645-8392.**

Coffeehouses, Sweets, and Treats

Brick Oven—$

Brick Oven's breads can vanish in a hurry, so get there early. The bakery uses fresh grains, stone-milled right on the spot, to make its specialty breads such as country wheat and sunflower, French herb bread, and oatmeal raisin. No additives, preservatives, or oils are in the breads, and honey, molasses, and maple syrup are the sweeteners. A tasting table lets customers sample before they choose. Open Tues.–Fri., 6:30 A.M.–6:30 P.M., and Sat., 6:30 A.M.–5:00 P.M. **960 Professional Dr., Northfield, 55057; 507-645-9517.**

Goodbye Blue Monday—$

The espresso and cappuccino here are fine, but the soft, comfy couches make this coffeehouse a home away from home. It's like a lived-in living room and always full of students, so it's a good place to play that perpetual Northfield guessing game of "who's a Carl and who's an Ole?" Open Mon.–Fri., 6:30 A.M.–1:00 A.M.; Sat., 7:00 A.M.–1:00 A.M.; Sun., 8:00 A.M.–1:00 A.M. **319 Division St., Northfield, 55057; 507-663-6188.**

Services

Northfield Area Chamber of Commerce and Convention and Visitors Bureau, 500 Water St. S., P.O. Box 198, Northfield, 55057; 800-658-2548 or 507-645-5604.

Red Wing

What's the prettiest town in Minnesota? Red Wing would get the vote of many people. It lies cradled among high bluffs, watching the Mississippi River go by. In winter, thousands of twinkling white lights on buildings and in parks warm up the frozen nights. In summer, hanging baskets of colorful flowers adorn Main St. and Levee Park, the riverside park where paddle wheelers, resembling floating white wedding cakes, still pay the pretty lady a call. As the boats approach Red Wing, their calliopes sometimes play "Pretty Red Wing," an old song about an Indian maiden's lost love.

In the song, pretty Red Wing is weeping, but not this Red Wing. The town, with a population of a little more than 15,000, is pretty, civically and historically aware, and prosperous, thanks to its status as a tourist destination and to a thriving industrial base. Red Wing Shoes, footwear of choice for many a working man and woman for decades, is a major employer. Red Wing Potteries, which made sturdy stoneware, massive crocks, and other pottery pieces now avidly collected, closed in 1969 but the old "pot shop" is now reborn as a warren of antique and other shops.

along the Minnesota River. Despite the treaty, Wacouta's band remained in the area even after a fire destroyed their village in 1853. They were finally forced to leave after the U.S.-Dakota Conflict of 1862.

Wacouta died in South Dakota, but gradually others in the band moved back to the Red Wing

History

There was a real Red Wing—three, in fact—but they were Dakota chiefs, not weeping maidens. For centuries, the site of Red Wing was a hunting ground and settlement for the Dakota Indians. For several generations, the chiefs of the band were called Red Wing, in addition to their tribal names.

The last of these chiefs, also called Wacouta, kept the band in the area after the treaty of 1851, which was signed between the U.S. government and other Dakota Indians and gave most of southern Minnesota to the government in exchange for moving all the Dakota to a small reservation

The Fall Festival of Arts in Red Wing takes place on the Main Street, which is blocked off during the fair. Photo courtesy of the City of Red Wing.

area, settling on Prairie Island, where many lived in poverty. Of late years, however, the band's economy has improved greatly with the advent of first bingo games and later the Treasure Island Resort and Casino complex.

The first European settlers in Red Wing were two Calvinist missionaries from Switzerland, who arrived in 1837, but extensive European settlement didn't come until the 1851 treaty was signed. Easterners were among the first settlers; Scandinavians and Germans followed.

The town prospered and on occasion tooted its horn a bit blatantly, as it did in this glowing description in the 1894 city directory: "Forty miles below St. Paul, nestled among bluffs, lies the city of Red Wing, bustling with life and activity on every hand, filled with cozy homes and happy, contented and intelligent people, who are here earnestly and faithfully doing the life work set apart for them."

Festivals and Events

Outdoor Concerts
Wed. evenings in July
The Red Wing Arts Association sponsors free concerts at Central Park in downtown Red Wing. The musical groups are an eclectic lot, ranging from brass bands to folk and rock. For information contact the association, **210 Bush St., Red Wing, 55066; 651-388-7569.**

River City Days
first full weekend in Aug.
Old Man River has seen plenty of boat traffic, but it took Red Wing to put dragon boats on the river. For nearly 10 years, the colorful dragon-boat races have been part of the annual River City Days festival, which began in 1983. Activities go on from Bay Point Park, next to the marina, to downtown's Levee Park. There is also a parade, fireworks, a craft show, and a car show. Contact the Chamber of Commerce (see Services).

Fall Festival of Arts
second week in Oct.
The Red Wing Arts Association started this outdoor art festival, which features juried art. The main street is blocked off and art rules for the weekend. For information, contact the association, **210 Bush St., Red Wing, 55066; 651-388-7569.**

Artists' Holiday Sale
Nov.–Dec.
The Red Wing Arts Association, formed about 50 years ago, holds an annual sale of members' work. Contact the association for exact dates and location; **210 Bush St., Red Wing, 55066; 651-388-7569.**

Outdoor Activities

Biking

Cannon Valley Trail
One of the most popular biking, hiking, and cross-country ski trails in the state, the Cannon Valley Trail runs 19.7 miles from Red Wing to Cannon Falls. The trail is fairly level, with a bit of a downhill gradient toward the Mississippi. Run jointly by the towns of Red Wing, Cannon Falls, and Welch, it was dedicated in 1986 on the former Chicago Great Western Railroad line paralleling the Cannon River. Trail manager Bruce Blair says, "Every quarter mile along the trail, there is something different as it gently twists and turns." Between Cannon Falls and the Anderson Memorial Rest Area, Blair adds, trail users find themselves

on a terrace—the result of a rock cut for the railroad—with the sheer bluffs high above and the river far below. About 3 miles from Red Wing, 90 feet above the trail itself, is the Red Wing Archaeological Preserve, where archaeological digs are conducted occasionally. At Welch, halfway along the trail, there is a rest stop with many facilities, including a trail station, camping, and phones. The trail station offers programs, including occasional musical events. On the first Sat. of each month during May–Sept., specialists in a topic from wildflowers to Native American culture are stationed along the trail to talk to visitors. Bikers or in-line skaters must buy a wheel pass for the trail, available at trailheads. Cross-country skiers must have a state ski pass. Contact the **Cannon Valley Trail Office, City Hall, 306 W. Mill St., Cannon Falls, 55009, 507-263-5843;** or the **Welch Station, 651-258-4141.** For biking maps, contact the **Red Wing Visitors and Convention Bureau, 800-498-3444.**

Rentals and Tours
Bike rentals can be found at **Ripley Rental and Sales, 3257 Industrial Park Rd., Red Wing, 55066; 651-388-5984** (seasonal). **Trail Station and Bicycle Works** rents, sells, and repairs bikes and also rents in-line skates; it may also rent cross-country skis and snowshoes, **214 Fourth St. N., Cannon Falls, 55009; 888-835-2453** or **507-263-5055. Welch General Store** also rents bikes, **14689 Welch Trail, Welch, 55089; 651-388-7494** (seasonal).

Boating

Cannon River
The Cannon River is approximately 80 miles long and has few rapids, a good river for canoeists. From open country in its upper reaches, the river flows into a wide gorge after it leaves Cannon Falls; the surrounding bluffs are up to 300 feet high. There are access points, toilets, and picnic tables at several points, including Hannah's Bend Park in Cannon Falls, which also has drinking water. The last takeout before the Mississippi is at the Cannon Bottom Rd. bridge near Red Wing.

Bring your own canoe or rent one (see below). Maps are available from the **Dept. of Natural Resources, 500 Lafayette Rd., St. Paul, 55155; 888-MINNDNR** or **651-296-6157.**

Rentals and Tours
If you don't have your own canoe, head for **Welch Mill Canoeing and Tubing,** which offers two canoe trips. A shuttle service takes canoes and customers upriver to put in at Cannon Falls for a 12-mile trip back to Welch; or you can put in at Trout Brook for a 5-mile journey. Ross Nelson, who lived in Welch, started his business 25 years ago after he tubed down the river. "We made fifty-two bucks on the first day and we spent it all on more tubes," he recalls. Since then, tubing the Cannon has become a popular cooldown on hot summer days. Large or small tubes can be rented. Open daily, late Apr.–early May. Welch is between Hastings and Red Wing off Hwy. 61 on the Welch Village Rd. **26389 County 7 Blvd., Rte. 1, Box 153, Welch, 55089; 800-657-6760** or **651-388-9857.**

Fishing
Trout are the big draw in the **Hay Creek Management Unit** of Richard J. Dorer Memorial Hardwood State Forest. Hay Creek winds through the unit and was opened for winter catch-and-release trout fishing several years ago. The winter season was quite successful, although plenty of trout seekers wait until warmer weather. **1801 South Oak St., Lake City, 55041; 651-345-3216.** Channel catfish can be caught in the Mississippi and in the lower reaches of the Cannon River, but caution should be used in eating the fish, due to possible PCB toxin content. For information on seasons, licenses, and consumption, call the Area Fisheries Supervisor, **651-345-3365.**

Golf

Elmdale Hills Golf Course
Hank and Pueblo are great caddies: they never talk, they don't expect a tip, and they won't snicker at your swing. One catch: they only work on Mon. and Tues.; otherwise, they are out to

pasture—Hank and Pueblo are llamas. The llamas are a lighthearted feature for Elmdale Hills,
a 27-hole course created in 1995 from owner
Bruce Brage's family farm. Brage, according to
his wife, Diane, was a casual golfer and she had
never played. Still, the Brages' brainstorm resulted in a hilly, scenic course set among trees.
From the clubhouse, you can see for several miles.
The toughest hole, according to Diane, is the par-
three seventh hole, which requires a very straight
shot over a gully to reach the green. Greens fees
are $20 for 18 holes. Clubs can be rented. Open
dawn–dusk, Apr. 1–Oct. 1. The course is 2 miles
from Miesville, which is between Hastings and
Red Wing. In Miesville, turn south onto Hwy. 91
(Nicolai Ave.). **26161 Nicolai Ave., Miesville,
55009; 888-487-6634 or 507-263-2507.**

Mississippi National Golf Links
This 36-hole public course, established in 1986,
is two 18-hole courses in one: many of the holes
in the Highlands course crown the bluff top, from
where there is a spectacular view. The par-three
eighth hole on the Highlands course is especially
difficult, as it has a 150-foot vertical drop. Many
of the holes on the course are edged by the bluff-
land forest. Features include a clubhouse with
food service, a bar, and a pro shop. In winter,
there are cross-country ski trails on the course.
Greens fees are $25.50 for 18 holes. Open dawn–
dusk, late Mar.–Oct. Located on the east side of
Hwy. 61. **409 Golf Links Dr., Red Wing,
55066; 651-388-1874.**

Skiing

CROSS-COUNTRY

Sorin's Bluff
Nearly 9 miles of cross-country ski trails—of
varying difficulty—extend from the Mississippi
National Golf Links up onto Sorin's Bluff. Maps
are available from the Red Wing Visitors and
Convention Bureau, **800-498-3444.**

DOWNHILL

Welch Village
Lee and Clem Nelson grew up skiing in the tiny
village of Welch, and established a ski operation

on the valley's wooded hills in 1965. The once-
modest operation now has the greatest area of
skiable terrain of any state area. Welch Village
has a vertical drop of 350 feet and 35 runs,
served by two quad chairs, five double chairs,
and one triple chair. There is a Mity Mite surface lift for kids enrolled in the learning center.
Daredevils like Welch's "Chicken" run, while
novices are happy with "Long Way Home," nearly
a mile long, or the gentle "Heidi's Hollow." Chalets have three food-service areas, plus an adults-
only section. Skis, snowboards, and short "sled
dogs" can be rented. Open daily except Christmas Day, early Dec.–mid-Mar. Take the Welch
Village Rd. from Hwy. 61. **Welch, 55089; 800-
421-0699, 651-258-4567,** or (toll-free within
the Twin Cities) **222-7079. Website:
www.welchvillage.com.**

Seeing and Doing

Antiquing
Red Wing is full of antique shops, particularly
around the old pottery works. Drive down Old
W. Main St., parallel to Hwy. 61, and be tempted.
There are also several antique shops within the
old Pottery Place itself (see Shopping). Collectors of Red Wing pottery will think they've died
and gone to heaven.

Museums and Historic Sites

Barn Bluff
You'll be following the footsteps of Henry David
Thoreau when you climb up Barn Bluff, the hulking 300-foot rock at the end of downtown Red
Wing. Thoreau, suffering from the tuberculosis
that killed him, spent time "botanizing" on the
bluff in June 1861. The published notes on his
trip are fragmentary, but his 17-year-old traveling companion, Horace Mann Jr., wrote descriptive and amusing letters to his mother, saying,
for instance, that mosquitoes in Minnesota
seemed as big as pigeons. The letters are included
in the book of Thoreau's notes. Barn Bluff consists of many different types of rock, including
limestone, sandstone, and shale—many laden

Barn Bluff.

with fossils. The bluff was once an island, but it now stands high and gives a sweeping view of the river. There are two routes to the top. The front trail, with steps all the way, faces the town and is much tamer than the back trail, which faces the river. Henry Sorensen, assistant public services director, was instrumental in developing the back trail about 20 years ago. "It's just like a mountain trail," he says. "It twists and turns, and you do have to watch where you are going." Both trails are reached from E. Fifth St., which passes under Hwy. 61. Park on either side of the street past the underpass.

Goodhue County Historical Museum

The museum gives an entertaining, educational, and complete look at Goodhue County history. Collectors of Red Wing pottery enjoy the collection of pottery pieces. There are also displays of the Dakota Indian village that preceded the city of Red Wing, as well as information on famous local residents, such as Eugenie Anderson, the first woman to be a U.S. ambassador; Frances Densmore, who collected Indian songs for the Smithsonian Institution; and A. P. Anderson, the inventor of puffed wheat and puffed rice (see also Other Sights). The museum, one of the best county museums in the state, also offers many programs, including lectures, and cosponsors archaeological field schools with the Minnesota Institute of Archaeology. The view of downtown Red Wing from the museum's bluff is spectacular. Fee. Open Tues.–Fri., 10:00 A.M.–5:00 P.M., and Sat.–Sun., 1:00–5:00 P.M. **1166 Oak St., Red Wing, 55066; 651-388-6024. Website: www.goodhistory.org.**

Other Sights

The Anderson Center

The Anderson Center for Interdisciplinary Studies provides short-term residencies for creative persons in all fields, including scientists, artists, writers, and humanists. In turn, the residents give lectures, give readings, or make school appearances. Some events, including arts workshops, are public. The nonprofit, privately funded center is located on the Tower View Estate, home of the late A. P. Anderson, the developer of puffed wheat and puffed rice. Call for hours. Located on Hwy. 61. **5354 Tower View Dr., P.O. Box 406, Red Wing, 55066; 651-388-2009. Website: www.pressenter.com/~acis.**

Parks

Red Wing City Parks

Barn Bluff (see Museums and Historic Sites) and Sorin's Bluff (see Scenic Drives) are part of the city park system, as is Levee Park, at Bush and Levee Sts. in downtown Red Wing. Drive along Levee St. to **Bay Point Park** to see the giant stylized tepee frame and a wonderful view of Red Wing. On one side of the park is the **Boathouse Village,** where boat storage houses ride up and down on anchoring "gin poles," automatically adjusting to the river's level. **Colvill Park,** east of downtown on Hwy. 61, is a good family park, with a swimming pool, playground, picnic tables, and a boat launch. Call the city park department, **651-385-3674.**

Richard J. Dorer Memorial Hardwood Forest, Hay Creek Management Unit

This forestry unit is hilly and contains nearly 25 miles of trails. Some trails are reserved for cross-country skiing and hiking. There are parking facilities and picnic tables, but no camping; a private campground (see Camping) is adjacent. Contact **1801 S. Oak St., Lake City, 55041; 651-345-3216.**

Performing Arts

THEATER

Sheldon Theatre

The first municipal theater in the country when it opened in 1904 and the pride of Red Wing, the Sheldon was restored in 1987 and now showcases national entertainment as well as homegrown talent. Tours and a multimedia program on Red Wing's history are given June–Oct., Thurs.–Sat., 1:00 P.M.; and Nov.–May, Sat., 1:00 P.M. **443 Third St., P.O. Box 34, Red Wing, 55066; 651-385-3667** or **800-899-5759.**

Scenic Drives

Sorin's Bluff

Sorin's Bluff can be hiked, but more often people drive to the top, on Skyline Dr., reached from E. Seventh St. At the top is Memorial Park, with its wonderful overview of the city of Red Wing. There are picnic tables and hiking and mountain bike trails.

Shopping

Josephson's

Step back in time at Josephson's, a men's clothing store in operation since 1878. The interior retains some original features, and the sales staff is uniformly courteous. Big and tall sizes are carried, as well as standard sizes. Open Mon.–Wed., Fri.–Sat., 9:00 A.M.–5:00 P.M., and Thurs., 9:00 A.M.–9:00 P.M. **215-217 Bush St., Red Wing, 55066; 651-388-4261.**

Pottery Place Outlet Center

Shoes, cookware, clothing, and leather goods are among the outlet stores in the Pottery Place. Open Mon.–Sat., 10:00 A.M.–6:00 P.M.; Sun., 11:00 A.M.–5:00 P.M. **2000 W. Main, Red Wing, 55066; 651-388-1428.**

Red Wing Stoneware Company

Watch pottery making while you shop at Red Wing Stoneware, just off Hwy. 61. The company bought the records and rights to the old Red Wing Pottery, and spoon rests are made from the original mold. Other items are similar to the original blue-and-gray stoneware. Potters can be seen through a window in the work room. Open Mon.–Fri., 9:00 A.M.–5:00 P.M.; Sat., 10:00 A.M.–5:00 P.M.; Sun., noon–5:00 P.M. **4909 Moundview Ave., Red Wing, 55066; 651-388-4610.**

Riverfront Centre/St. James Hotel Shopping Court

The Riverfront Centre and the St. James Hotel Shopping Court have a variety of shops, including a Red Wing shoe store, a bookstore, and gift shops. Both are open daily. On opposite sides of Bush St. on Main St. For information on the shopping court, call the St. James Hotel, **651-388-2846.** Hours vary at the Riverfront Centre; for information call its Red Wing Shoes store, **651-388-6233.**

Uffda Shop

Across the street from Riverfront Centre is the Uffda Shop, where you'll find the best of

Scandinavia, including Norwegian sweaters, pewter, wood carvings, glassware, and food items. Ask the staff what "Uffda" means. Open Mon.–Wed. and Fri.–Sat., 9:00 A.M.–5:00 P.M.; Thurs., 9:00 A.M.–8:00 P.M.; Sun., noon–5:00 P.M. Located on the **corner of Main and Bush Sts.; 651-388-8436** or **800-488-3332.**

Tours

Cannon Falls

A brochure describing self-guided 1-, 2-, and 3-mile walking tours of Cannon Falls is available from the Cannon Falls Chamber of Commerce (see Services).

Red Wing

Three walking/driving tours are popular attractions: one takes you through the downtown district, another along the historic mall district (where the Sheldon Theatre is located), and the third covers the West residential district, with many prime examples of beautifully kept mid-19th-century homes. Map and brochure are available from the Chamber of Commerce (see Services).

Wagering

Treasure Island Resort and Casino

Treasure Island is one of Minnesota's largest casinos, with lots of slots, blackjack tables, video games of chance, and bingo games. Big-name entertainers are on tap, too, and there are several restaurants and a cultural center. In addition, visitors can dock boats in the casino's marina or plug RVs into the hookups at the RV park. The casino also offers daily river excursions. Open 24 hours daily. Located **near Hastings off Hwys. 61 and 316** (watch for signs); **800-222-7077** (casino) or **800-883-8496** (marina and RV park).

Where to Stay

Red Wing has many motels, and seems to gain new bed-and-breakfast operations annually. Call the Chamber of Commerce (see Services) for more choices.

Bed-and-Breakfasts

Candlelight Inn—$$$ to $$$$

A well-stocked library with beautiful woodwork and a cozy fireplace are two of the features that makes the Candlelight memorable. The five bedrooms in the 1877 Victorian house are beautifully decorated and each has a private bath. Some have whirlpool baths and fireplaces. Owner Mary Jaeb loves to cook and proves it with her breakfasts. The house is close to downtown. **818 W. Third St., Red Wing, 55066; 651-388-8034. Website: www.candlelightinn-redwing.com.**

Hotels and Motels

Best Western Quiet House Suites— $$$ to $$$$

On the outskirts of Red Wing, the Best Western has "theme" suites such as the log cabin and the fur trader's home, all with up-to-date conveniences—11 of the suites have whirlpools. There is a heated indoor/outdoor pool, which attracts intrepid swimmers even in winter. **Hwy. 61 and Withers Harbor Dr., Red Wing, 55066; 800-528-1234** or **651-388-1577.**

St. James Hotel—$$$ to $$$$

Heartbeat of the city as well as a wonderful old hotel, the St. James was built in 1875 for the river traffic. The legendary Clara Lillyblad, a onetime waitress who became the grande dame of the St. James, ran the hotel in its middle years after her husband died. On special occasions, "Clara," played by a hotel employee, returns to meet and greet folks, resplendent in her bewitching black gown and an enormous, befeathered black hat. The hotel was restored to its Victorian splendor in 1977 by the Red Wing Shoe Company. The 60 rooms have yesterday's charm and today's conveniences. Some have whirlpool baths, and beautiful handmade quilts cover each bed. There are two restaurants and a leather-and-oak English-style pub, Jimmy's, on the fifth floor. Something is always happening at the St. James: jazz nights, "Noon at the Jimmy" concerts, and Christmas teas are a sample. A member of Historic Hotels of America, the hotel has shops and restaurants along its spacious entry and interior courtyard (see Shopping). **406 Main St., Red Wing, 55066; 800-252-1875, 651-388-2846,** or (within Minneapolis or St. Paul) **227-1800.** Website: **www.st-james.hotel.com.**

Camping

Hay Creek Valley Campground—$

Adjacent to a well-known trout stream in the Richard J. Dorer Memorial Hardwood State Forest, the wooded campground has 100 water and electricity hookups and also a few tent sites. Within the campground are a heated swimming pool and a restaurant. Open mid-Apr.–Oct. Located **6 miles south of Red Wing on Hwy. 58; 651-388-9922** or **651-388-3998.**

Hidden Valley—$

Right next to the Cannon Valley Trail and equidistant from Red Wing and Welch, Hidden Valley Campground is in an ideal location for those who want to bike the trail or tube down the Cannon River. In business for 35 years, the campground has 200 sites with electricity and water, and a tent area. Open May 1–Oct. 1. **27173 144th Ave. Way, Welch, 55089; 651-258-4550.**

Where to Eat

Port of Red Wing—$$ to $$$$

With their walls of rough limestone layers, the cozy rooms in the Port of Red Wing seem chiseled into the bluffs. The restaurant, in the lower level of the St. James Hotel, is particularly inviting on cold winter evenings, when the French onion soup is especially warming. Open daily year-round, 11:00 A.M.–2:00 P.M.; about Memorial Day–Dec., daily, 5:00–9:00 P.M. **406 Main St., Red Wing, 55066; 800-252-1875, 651-388-2846,** or (within Minneapolis or St. Paul) **227-1800.**

Staghead Coffee House—$$ to $$$

The Staghead has an ambitious menu, part nouvelle, part wide-ranging international, with such items as wild mushroom risotto; rainbow trout from the Star Prairie, Wisconsin, trout farm; and New York bagels. All-Italian, all-Mediterranean, and all–et cetera nights are a Staghead feature. The restaurant's wine list includes selections from the nearby Bailly Winery in Hastings. Open Mon., 10:00 A.M.–2:30 P.M., and Tues.–Sat., 10:00 A.M.–10:00 P.M. **219 Bush St., Red Wing, 55066; 651-388-6581.**

Veranda—$ to $$$

Get a seat near the window at the Veranda and watch the river traffic go by below this popular restaurant in the St. James Hotel. In fine weather, it's possible to sit outside, but there is an enclosed veranda as well as the restaurant proper. The restaurant is light and airy and well coordinated—the border on the china even matches the wallpaper border on the walls. A favorite lunchtime entree is the California salad, made with strips of chicken and a melange of fruit—bananas, oranges, and strawberries—served with a side of banana dressing. The dinner specials have included 99-cent hamburgers. Open Sun.–Tues., 6:30 A.M.–5:00 P.M., and Wed.–Sat., 6:30 A.M.–8:00 P.M. **406 Main St., Red Wing, 55066; 800-252-1875, 651-388-2846,** or (within Minneapolis or St. Paul) **651-227-1800.**

Bev's Cafe—$

Bev Langer has had her down-home cafe for 14 years, and that's a lot of mashed potatoes and pies! Langer is proud of her homemade mashed potatoes and hash browns and also makes her own soups and desserts. The cafe is always buzzing with a local crowd. Open Mon.–Fri., 6:00 A.M.–8:30 P.M., and Sat., 6:00 A.M.–4:00 P.M. **221 Bush St., Red Wing, 55066; 651-388-5227.**

King's Bar and Grill—$

There is an informal contest to identify the best hamburgers in Minnesota. My cousin Jean Ross of Red Wing, who has no connection whatever with King's, declares that they make the best burgers in the state. She may be right, although there are many other contenders. King's is a pleasant, pine-paneled tavern that welcomes families. There's nothing fancy about the burgers—they are just juicy, tender, and great tasting. King's is the perfect place to visit before or after seeing the Miesville Mudhens play, across the road from King's. Open Mon.–Thurs., 8:00 A.M.–11:00 P.M.; Fri.–Sat., 11:00 A.M.–midnight; Sun., noon–11:00 P.M. On Hwy. 61 between Hastings and Red Wing. **11460 240th St. E., Hastings, 55033; 651-437-1418.**

Lorentz Meats—$

At the Cannon Falls trailhead, Lorentz Meats sells sandwiches and also has a deck to eat them on if you can't wait for the trail. Located 1 block from the trail. Open Mon.–Fri., 7:30 A.M.–7:00 P.M.; Sat., 8:00 A.M.–4:00 P.M.; Sun., 11:00 A.M.–4:00 P.M. **305 W. Cannon, Cannon Falls, 55009; 800-535-6382 or 507-263-3617.**

Coffeehouses, Sweets, and Treats

Braschler's Bakery and Coffee Shop—$

If Bob Braschler were in France, he could hang a little sign on his bakery tooting his horn about his artisan bread. But this is Minnesota, so it's word of mouth that brings bread lovers in for a loaf or two of the 150 kinds of bread he bakes. A favorite is the Swedish limpa—rye bread with orange and fennel—available Fri. and Sat. He also makes full-flavored breads such as onion sourdough rye. "Bread's good for ya" is Braschler's credo. Try the breads in sandwiches for lunch at the bakery's coffee shop. The coffee shop is open Mon.–Fri., 7:00 A.M.–4:00 P.M., and Sat., 7:00 A.M.–3:00 P.M.; the bakery is open Mon.–Fri., 6:00 A.M.–5:00 P.M., and Sat., 6:00 A.M.–3:00 P.M. **410 W. Third St., Red Wing, 55066; 651-388-1589.**

Services

Cannon Falls Chamber of Commerce, 103 N. Fourth St., Cannon Falls, 55009; 507-263-2289.

Red Wing Chamber of Commerce, 420 Levee St., Red Wing, 55066; 612-388-4719. Red Wing Visitors and Convention Bureau, 800-498-3444 or 651-385-5934. Website: www.redwing.org.

Rochester

Rochester is probably the biggest little city in the country, due to Big Medicine and Big Blue. Each year, approximately 1.5 million visitors from around the globe flock to the city of 77,000. Most of them, including such familiar names as the late King Hussein of Jordan and—in earlier years—Presidents Johnson and Reagan, seek reassurance and healing at the hands of doctors at the Mayo Clinic, but many also come to do business at Rochester's IBM offices.

The cosmopolitan nature of Rochester is immediately evident. In the downtown streets, conversations are in many languages. In the shop windows, signs are sometimes written in Arabic. Visitors arriving by plane from outside the United States can now go through customs in Rochester's international airport.

Yes, Rochester plays in the big leagues, but it's still a family-centered town at heart. Long-time residents still tell stories of the Mayo family, and the town's residents bust their buttons when local sports teams make it to the state tournaments. It's a comfortable place for its citizens, with plenty of park space and abundant golf courses. Residents are especially proud that the city has been voted among the most livable cities in the United States in several polls.

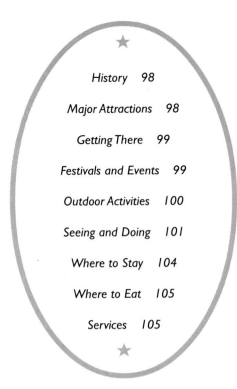

History

In Rochester, Indian bands lived in the area long before the arrival of European settlers in great numbers in the mid-1800s. It was settled in 1854 by George Head, who named it after his hometown of Rochester, New York. When W. W. Mayo came to Rochester to examine recruits for the Civil War in 1863, Rochester had only 3,000 residents. After that, much of the history of Rochester has been intertwined with the growth of the Mayo Medical Center (see Major Attractions).

Major Attractions

Mayo Medical Center

Known worldwide as a place of healing and research, the Mayo Medical Center started as a frontier emergency room, when a tornado devastated the town in Aug. 1883. At that time, the first Dr. Mayo, William Worrall Mayo, an English immigrant who had worked as a riverboatman, newspaper editor, and veterinarian before setting up a medical practice in Rochester, had been in the little town for more than 20 years. He was a well-regarded, energetic physician and surgeon who made house calls and operated in patients' homes.

When the tornado occurred, the number of people injured meant that temporary hospitals had to be set up and nursing care improvised. Dr. Mayo asked the Sisters of St. Francis to help with nursing. When the crisis was over, Mother Alfred of the order came to Dr. Mayo and offered to build a hospital if Mayo would staff it. The hospital opened in 1889 as St. Mary's Hospital, still an integral part of "the Clinic," as the medical center is known. It was W. W.'s sons, however, "Dr. Will and Dr. Charlie," who built the clinic into the medical behemoth it is today. They became innovative surgeons, who watched experimental surgical procedures and adapted them for use back in Rochester.

The Mayos are credited with starting group practice, begun when the Mayos asked other physicians to join their practice in 1892. Over the years, the Mayo Medical Center has been the site of many medical firsts, including the first hip replacement, the discovery of cortisone, and the first successful repairs of congenital heart defects. Several doctors on the Mayo staff have received Nobel Prizes for research efforts.

The innovative internal workings of the clinic's buildings and hospitals—including easily accessible medical records and a system of lifts and pneumatic tubes for swiftly transporting records and X rays throughout the clinic and hospitals—were the work of Mayo's all-around genius, Dr. Henry Plummer, who joined the clinic in 1901.

The Mayo brothers dissolved their partnership in 1919 and created the private, nonprofit Mayo Foundation, stipulating that profits go for education and research. Components of the foundation include the clinic, St. Mary's Hospital, and Rochester Methodist Hospital. An average of 1,300 new patients arrive daily at the medical center, with 138 admitted to the hospitals. On typical days, according to center data, 16,000 lab tests and 9,600 blood tests are given.

Both Mayo brothers died in 1939, and the last staff doctor to bear the Mayo name retired from the clinic in 1963, although several grandchildren and great-grandchildren have trained there. The center remains a vital force in medicine worldwide. The Mayo Medical School accepts only 42 of the nearly 4,000 applicants for each class, according to a history published by the Mayo Foundation. The clinic now has branches in Florida and Arizona as well as in the Upper Midwest.

Recommended Reading

The Doctors Mayo by Helen Clapesattle (University of Minnesota, 1941; 2nd ed., 1967) is an absorbing account of all the Mayos and of Rochester itself.

Getting There

*Rochester is approximately 90 miles south of the Twin Cities on Hwy. 52, and 353 miles from Chicago on I-90. The Rochester International Airport, on Hwy. 63, is served by several airlines. Rochester Transportation Systems, **507-282-2222**, has cabs and coaches to the airport. For those arriving in the Twin Cities, Rochester Direct (**507-280-9270 in Rochester and 612-725-0303**) and Rochester Express (**507-282-8673 or 800-479-7824**) schedule daily transportation between the Minneapolis–St. Paul International Airport and Rochester International Airport and vice versa.*

Festivals and Events

World Festival
Apr.

Rochester has a large international community, and the annual World Festival showcases the cultures and foods of 40–50 ethnic groups. The festival is held on a Fri. night and Sat. in Apr. Contact the Rochester International Association, **507-281-3900,** for details and time and location.

Courtyard adjacent to the Harwick Building at the Mayo Clinic. Photo used by permission of the Mayo Foundation.

Rochesterfest

last full week in June

Rochesterfest—a cheerful, noisy, nine-day blast—got its start in 1983 when Chuck Hazama, then the mayor, decided to have the city throw an annual party. Now more than 200,000 people show up for the festivities, which include the Midwest Lumberjack Championship, a parade, ethnic foods and entertainment, and a street dance. The festival ends with a drum and bugle corps competition, with all teams blasting together on the heart-thumping finale. Contact the Rochesterfest office, **507-285-8769.**

Outdoor Activities

Biking

Douglas State Trail

This level trail, built on an abandoned rail bed, runs 12.5 miles through agricultural scenery between Pine Island and Rochester. It has two separate paths: a paved path for bikers, hikers, and snowmobilers and an unpaved track for horseback riders and cross-country skiers. There are parking areas with picnic tables and toilets at the Pine Island and Rochester trailheads as well as at midpoint in the town of Douglas. For a trail map, call the **Dept. of Natural Resources, 888-MINNDNR** or **651-296-6157.**

Birding

Silver Lake

Approximately 30,000 Canada geese converge on or near Silver Lake in Rochester in Nov., most of them of the giant Canada goose subspecies. Many of them make a pit stop on their way south from Manitoba, but nearly half overwinter in Rochester. Some always nest in the same spot on the lakeshore, according to Jack Heather, DNR regional wildlife manager for southeast Minnesota. All but a small permanent flock of up to 300 geese start to leave in early Mar. and are gone by early Apr. Most residents coexist comfortably with the geese, Heather says, but some heartily dislike the mess the geese make. Visitors to the lake can buy corn for the geese at the park. Silver Lake, operated by the city park service, is located north of downtown, **between N. Broadway and 11th Ave. NE; 507-281-6160.**

Golf

The city of Rochester has three 18-hole golf courses—Eastwood, Northern Hills, and Soldiers Field, on which 150,000 rounds are played annually, according to parks spokesman Roy Sutherland.

Eastwood

This 18-hole public golf course has a restaurant and clubhouse facilities. Open approximately Apr.–Nov., daily, 7:00 A.M.–dusk. Greens fee for 18 holes is $20. Club rentals. **Eastwood Rd. SE, Rochester, 55904; 507-281-6173.**

Northern Hills

This 18-hole public golf course has a restaurant and clubhouse facilities. Open approximately Apr.–Nov., daily, 7:00 A.M.–dusk. Greens fee for 18 holes is $20. Club rentals. **4804 41st Ave. NW, Rochester, 55906; 507-281-6170.**

Rochester Golf and Country Club

Renowned golf course designer A. W. Chillinghast sculpted this hilly, 18-hole course, considered one of the best private courses in the state. Members can bring guests; members of other private clubs can also obtain reciprocal rights on weekends for greens fees of about $100. Open approximately early Apr.–Dec., Mon.–Fri., 8:00 A.M.–dusk, and Sat.–Sun., 7:00 A.M.–dusk. **3100 Country Club Rd., Rochester, 55902; 507-282-3170.**

Soldiers Field

This 18-hole public golf course has a restaurant and clubhouse facilities. Soldiers Field, more level than the other city-owned courses, is popular with seniors. Open approximately Apr.–Nov., daily, 7:00 A.M.–dusk. Greens fee for 18 holes is $20. Club rentals. **Third Ave. and Eighth St. SW, Rochester, 55902; 507-281-6176.**

Hiking

Whitewater State Park has hiking trails, as do Chester Woods County Park (11 miles) and

Carley State Park (6 miles); see Parks. The city of Rochester also has 8 miles of hiking trails. For information on city trails, call **507-281-6160.**

Skiing

CROSS-COUNTRY
In addition to the 12.5-mile Douglas State Trail (see Biking), there are cross-country ski trails in Carley (3 miles) and Whitewater State Parks (see Parks). Chester Woods County Park has 11 miles of trails. In Rochester, there are groomed trails at Eastwood Golf Course, Soldiers Field Golf Course (see Golf), and Quarry Hill Park. Eastwood and Quarry Hill rent skis. Contact the parks department, **403 E. Center St., Rochester, 55904; 507-281-6160.**

Seeing and Doing

Art Galleries and Museums

Rochester Art Center
For more than 50 years, the Rochester Art Center has brought art to the city. Two galleries display traveling regional, national, and international shows. The center has special events and classes. Free. Open Tues.–Sat., 10:00 A.M.–5:00 P.M., and Sun., noon–5:00 P.M. **320 E. Center St., Rochester, 55904; 507-282-8629.**

Southeast Minnesota Visual Arts
The Southeast Minnesota Visual Arts gallery features the work of local artists and gives visitors a chance to meet the artists who are members of the cooperative. Open Mon.–Wed., Fri.–Sat., 10:00 A.M.–6:00 P.M.; Thurs., 10:00 A.M.–9:00 P.M.; Sun., noon–4:00 P.M. **16 SW First St., Rochester, 55902; 507-281-4920.**

Museums and Historic Sites

Mantorville
Mantorville's downtown—a 12-block area—was listed on the National Register of Historic Places in 1975. Many buildings are constructed of the beautiful, local Mantorville limestone, and some frame structures date to the mid-1800s. The town is not a museum piece, however; visitors enjoy hissing villains at old-fashioned melodramas held on summer weekends at the Opera House, and they crowd the well-known Hubbell House restaurant. The 1865 Dodge County Courthouse is still used, as are most of the other historic structures. Mantorville, on the north branch of the middle fork of the Zumbro River, was settled in 1853 by brothers Peter and Riley Mantor. Limestone from the quarry was used throughout the country. Town and countryside tours are given by Irene Stussy-Felker, whose father once owned the quarry and the Hubbell House. Contact her at **P.O. Box 185, Mantorville, 55955; 507-635-3231.** Mantorville is 17 miles from Rochester—14 miles west on Hwy. 14, then 3 miles north on Hwy. 57. A visitors guide to historic buildings is available from the **Mantorville Chamber of Commerce, P.O. Box 358, Mantorville, 55955.** For town information, call **507-635-2331** or **507-635-2481.**

Mayowood
This 50-room mansion was home to three generations of the Mayo family and is filled with family mementos and festively decorated for the holidays. The Mayos gave the house to the Olmsted County Historical Society in 1965. Tours Apr.–Nov. Fee. Call for hours. **3720 Mayowood Rd. SW, Rochester, 55902; 507-287-8691** or **507-282-9447.**

Olmsted County Museum
The history of Rochester and other sites in Olmsted County such as Oronoco, which had a very brief gold rush in 1858, is depicted in rotating exhibits here. Open Tues.–Sat., 9:00 A.M.–noon and 1:00–5:00 P.M.; Sun., 1:00–4:00 P.M. **1195 County Rd. 22 SW, Rochester, 55902; 507-282-9447.**

Plummer House
Dr. Henry Plummer was the organizational and mechanical angel of the Mayo Clinic in its early days, and his own house, begun in 1917, contains many innovations, such as an intercom and a paging system, installed in his study. The house

Winter birding on Silver Lake. Photo courtesy of Jack W. Heather.

also had a central vacuum system, garage door openers, and the first gas furnace in the city. The 49-room house, which had 10 bathrooms, is now owned by the city of Rochester. Tours June–Aug., Wed., 1:00–7:00 P.M. Fee. The grounds are open from sunrise to sunset and include formal gardens, a bird trail, a quarry, and a water tower. **1091 Plummer Ln., Rochester, 55902.** Call the city Parks and Recreation Dept., **507-281-6160.**

Parks

Carley State Park

One of the smallest of the state parks, at 204 acres, quiet Carley is an alternative park for those who find Whitewater State Park (see Winona chapter) too crowded. Carley, located where the prairie and hardwood forest meet, has a 1-mile, self-guided trail plus 5 miles of hiking trails. In winter, there are 3 miles of cross-country ski trails. The north branch of the Whitewater River, a designated trout stream, flows through the park. The park is administered by Whitewater State Park. Take County Rd. 2 east of Rochester, jogging north on

Hwy. 42 before turning back to County Rd. 2, then go north on County Rd. 10. **Wabasha County Rd. 4, Plainview, 55964; 507-932-3007.**

Chester Woods County Park

Developed around a lake formed as a flood-control measure for Rochester, Chester Woods is a great getaway close to the city. The 1,332-acre park is hilly and has a swimming beach and a lake stocked with bass and panfish. There are 11 miles of combined horse and hiking trails, with more planned. Cross-country ski trails are groomed in winter. Canoes can be rented and there are 50 campsites. Fee. Located **6 miles east of Rochester on Hwy. 14; 507-285-7050.**

Rochester City Parks

Rochester's 72 city parks include golf courses, swimming pools, a park that is the permanent nesting ground of Canada geese, a nature center, and historic houses. The city's first, Central Park, dates to 1856, and the park board itself is nearly a century old. For information, contact the Parks and Recreation Dept., **507-281-6160.**

Performing Arts

MUSIC

Rochester Carillon

Several times each week, the Rochester Carillon's 56 bells ring out. For 40 years, the bell master has been Dean Robinson, who plays a wide variety of tunes. Concerts are Mon., 7:00 P.M., and Wed. and Fri., noon. The carillon located is in the ornate tower on top of the Plummer Building, **Second Ave. and Second St. SW,** across from the Mayo Building in downtown Rochester; **507-284-2511.**

Rochester Civic Music

Go "Down by the Riverside" in July and Aug. to hear the community band and summer festival choir. The concerts are presented by Rochester Civic Music, part of the city government since 1936. Summer concerts are held in Mayo Park behind the Mayo Civic Center on the Zumbro River. Free. Sun., 7:00 P.M. Contact the department at **Suite 170, 201 Fourth St. SE, Rochester, 55904; 507-285-8076.**

THEATER

Rochester Civic Theatre

The Civic Theatre, which got its start in the early '50s, puts on seven plays and two children's programs between Sept. and July each year, including a holiday production of Dickens's *A Christmas Carol,* and offers classes. Fees vary. **220 E. Center St., Rochester, 55904; 507-282-8481.**

Rochester Repertory Theatre

The Rep is a volunteer community theater offering six issue-oriented contemporary productions each season, usually Aug.–May. Call for ticket prices. **314½ S. Broadway, Rochester, 55904; 507-289-7800.**

Shopping

Barnes and Noble

Some Rochester residents get nostalgic when they visit the Barnes and Noble Superstore. This is a chain bookstore, yes, but squint your eyes and look around at the walls, with the fantastically lighted outlines of castles at twilight, and you may think you are back at the Sat.-afternoon movie matinees at the Chateau. Barnes and Noble had the smarts to save the interior of this marvelous old movie house, restoring it carefully. Plenty of books to buy, too! It's connected to the Centerplace Galleria Mall and across from the Rochester Marriott Hotel. Open daily, 9:00 A.M.–11:00 P.M. **15 First St. SW, Rochester, 55902; 507-288-3848.**

Goose Poop Art

Rochester's giant Canada geese are lovely to look at, but big producers of goose droppings. Many residents hate the slippery stuff, but one guy has actually taken the goose poop and made art out of it. Nearly 15 years ago, Gary Blum, a retired IBM worker, created a "picture" by sprinkling dried and ground-up goose droppings on an outline he had drawn and spread with glue. He gave the picture, as a joke, to a friend who was moving from Rochester and hated the geese. Word spread, and now Blum is a goose poop guru. He collects the droppings—which vary in color—in a bucket and gets to work in his garage. A typical comment, he says, is, "Hey, it doesn't look that bad." His subjects include geese and loons. Blum's pictures are matted and framed, and the droppings are odorless when they are dried. His wife, Pat, helps him with the assembly, all done in what Gary calls the "Casa de Caca." The art is sold at several places in Rochester. Contact Blum at **2626 Tuxedo Lane NW, Rochester, 55901; 507-289-5537.**

Tours

Mayo Clinic

Tours of the Mayo Clinic take in the offices of "Dr. Will" and "Dr. Charlie," preserved as they left them, with many autographed photos of celebrities. The 90-minute tours are given Mon.–Fri., 10:00 A.M., preceded by a short film. The Mayo art collection includes works by Joan Miro, Alexander Calder, Carl Milles, and Andy Warhol. Tours of the art collection are given Tues.–Thurs., 1:30 P.M. Both tours are free and advance registration is not necessary. Inquire at the information desk in the Mayo Building, which occupies a square block, between First and Second Sts. SW and Second and Third Aves. SW; Mayo's general phone number is **507-284-2511.**

Where to Stay

Rochester has thousands of hotel rooms. The downtown hotels, particularly the Kahler Grand and the Rochester Marriott, are crossroads of the world. A cacophony of languages can be heard in the lobbies, and elevator doors may open to reveal a Mayo patient in a wheelchair plus a whole ethnic retinue, all in national dress. A list of lodgings is available from the Convention and Visitors Bureau (see Services).

Bed-and-Breakfasts

Grand Old Mansion—$$ to $$$

Mantorville's Grand Old Mansion is nearing the century mark. The bed-and-breakfast is owned by Irene Stussy-Felker, a native of the Mantorville area whose dad owned the quarry and later saved the Hubbell House from being torn down. Stussy-Felker loved the mansion as a little girl. "It was always my dream house. When I was three or four, I pretended I was a fairy princess and lived in that house," she remembers. The large frame house, with a huge front porch that wraps around one side, has hand-carved woodwork and stained glass. There are four bedrooms. Many of the furnishings are antiques. On the grounds are two other units, an 1855 log cabin that has two bedrooms and an old schoolhouse that has three. Both have been completely modernized. Breakfast is included. **501 Clay St., Mantorville, 55955; 507-635-3231.**

Hotels, Motels, and Inns

Kahler Grand Hotel—$$$ to $$$$

The 706-room Kahler Grand Hotel has been a Rochester landmark for more than 75 years. It is in the heart of Rochester, between the Mayo Building and Rochester Methodist Hospital, with pedestrian subway access to both and also to the adjacent Rochester Marriott Hotel. The two-level lobby of the Kahler Grand is sedate and dignified, with a handsome vaulted ceiling. The Kahler Grand Hotel has wheelchairs available. There are three restaurants and a lounge. Rooms are comfortable and discounts are given to Mayo Clinic patients. The hotel's many shops and businesses include a pharmacy, an airline ticket office, and car rentals. **20 SW Second Ave., Rochester, 55902; 800-533-1655** or **507-282-2581. Website: www.kahler.com.**

Radisson Plaza Hotel Rochester—$$$$

Right in the heart of Rochester, the Radisson is new and sleek, with lots of dark wood and brass accents. The towering lobby has an intriguing open stairway. Work desks in each room have modem-access telephone lines for those in town on business. The hotel has a skyway to the Mayo Clinic. There are more than 200 rooms and suites, some with whirlpool baths. **150 S. Broadway, Rochester, 55904; 800-333-3333** or **507-281-8000.**

Rochester Marriott Hotel—$$$$

Formerly the Kahler Plaza, this is a favorite for clinic patients and their families. It has nearly 200 comfortable rooms, recently remodeled. The hotel is connected by tunnel to the Mayo Clinic and to shopping areas. **101 SW First Ave., Rochester, 55902; 800-228-9290** or **507-280-6000.**

Camping

Chester Woods County Park—$

This Olmsted County park, 6 miles east of Rochester on Hwy. 14, has 50 campsites, 34 of them with electricity. Reservations can be made in advance. **8378 Hwy. 14 E., Eyota, 55934; 507-285-7050.**

State Parks—$

There is camping at Carley and Whitewater State Parks, east of Rochester. Carley, the smaller of the two, has 20 sites, with no electricity available; Whitewater has 106 campsites, none with electricity, 32 accessible for handicapped campers. For reservations for either camp, call **800-**

246-CAMP or (in the Twin Cities area) call **The Connection, 612-922-9000.**

Where to Eat

The presence of the Mayo Medical Center has also had an influence on the city's restaurants: many of them advertise items for those on special diets and also offer meal delivery. The city has a variety of ethnic restaurants. Ask the Convention and Visitors Bureau (see Services) for a complete listing.

Michael's—$$ to $$$$

For nearly 50 years, under the ownership of four generations of the Pappas family, Michael's has been one of Rochester's most respected restaurants. Located in the heart of downtown, the restaurant, and its younger alter ego, adjacent the Pappageorge Taverna, serve many Greek specialties, such as grilled kabobs and a country Greek salad. The menus also offer steak, seafood, and chop entrees, making nods to regional specialties with such dishes as walleye pike and baked Minnesota pheasant served with wild rice. Open Mon.–Thurs., 11:00 A.M.–10:00 P.M., and Fri.–Sat., 11:00 A.M.–11:00 P.M. **15 S. Broadway, Rochester, 55905; 507-288-2020.**

Hubbell House—$$ to $$$

Everyone who was anybody seems to have come to the Hubbell House in Mantorville from the time it was a stagecoach stop in 1854 until the present. Placemats bear copies of famous signatures, from journalist Horace Greeley and violinist Ole Bull in the early days to such latter-day heros as Mickey Mantle, Dwight Eisenhower, and Roy Rogers. The interior of the restaurant consists of several separate dining rooms, all decorated in a Civil War–era style. The menu features steaks, seafood, and salads, with such comfort desserts as turtle pie and bread pudding. The Pappas family has owned the restaurant for more than 50 years. Open Tues.–Sat., 11:30 A.M.–2:00 P.M. and 5:00–9:00 P.M.; Sun., 11:30 A.M.–9:00 P.M. Located on Mantorville's main street, 17 miles from Rochester (Hwy. 14 to Kasson and Hwy. 57 to Mantorville); **507-635-2331.**

First Class—$ to $$$

Don't be surprised if your waiter or waitress suddenly appears on the stage at the First Class restaurant and belts out a show tune. All staff members, according to the manager, have to pass a vocal audition before they are put on the night wait shift. Between serving steaks, burgers, and seafood entrees, the staff sing for the customers. Open daily, 6:00 A.M.–10:00 P.M. **401 SW Sixth St., in the Soldiers Field Tower, Rochester, 55902; 507-288-2677.**

Services

Local Visitor Information

Rochester Convention and Visitors Bureau, 150 S. Broadway, Suite A, Rochester, 55904; 800-634-8277 or **507-288-4331.** Website: www.rochestercvb.org.

Transportation

Pedestrian subways and overhead skyways connect several of the Mayo Medical Center buildings with other downtown buildings. A map of the subways, skyways, and parking facilities is available from the Rochester Convention and Visitors Bureau (see above). **Rochester City Lines, 507-288-4353,** has bus transportation throughout the city; **Rochester Transportation Systems, 507-282-2222,** has cab service, limousine service, and a wheelchair and stretcher service. The Rochester Convention and Visitors Bureau has a list of car rental companies.

Winona

Winona is the perfect base for lovers of the outdoors. The city of 27,000, near the southeast tip of Minnesota and right on the Mississippi River, is near five state parks (two of them across the river in Wisconsin) and the Richard J. Dorer Memorial Hardwood State Forest. The river itself offers many recreational opportunities, from bird-watching to canoeing in the secluded channels. For a bird's-eye view, bicycle up to Garvin Heights and admire the spectacular view of the river valley. Winona is a local business center, with many young residents due to its colleges. It has also become a weekend destination for Twin Cities residents.

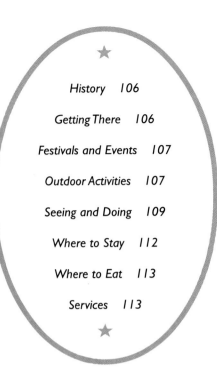

History

Winona is a city shaped by the Mississippi River, and the histories of the two are as intertwined as the channels in the river. The rock Sugar Loaf, Winona's best-known geographical feature, rises some 85 feet above the 500-foot bluff it sits on, making it 585 feet above the river. The unusual formation was a landmark for river travelers long before the town was born in 1851. In 1805 the explorer Zebulon Pike climbed one of Winona's bluffs and recorded that the view was "a most sublime and beautiful prospect." Pike's description could be made by today's visitors:

Getting There

Winona is 119 miles south of the Twin Cities. For the scenic route, take Hwy. 61 along the Mississippi River; alternatively, follow I-35 south and I-90 east, cutting onto Hwy. 43 for the last few miles. Winona is 304 miles from Chicago, via I-90. Amtrak services Winona via Chicago and the Twin Cities.

On the right, we saw the mountains we had passed in the morning, with the prairie behind like distant clouds. On the left and at our feet was the valley through which the Mississippi wound itself by numerous channels, forming beautiful islands as far as the eye could embrace the scene. It was altogether so variegated and romantic that a man may scarcely expect to enjoy such a view but twice or thrice in the course of his life.

Fittingly, it was a riverboat captain, Orrin Smith, who claimed the land that later became the city of Winona in 1851, after the Dakota had signed most of southern Minnesota over to the U.S. government. By 1858 the population was 800. Wheat and lumber fueled the local economy, and by 1868 Winona was the nation's fourth-largest wheat market and a rich town. A fire destroyed most of the downtown area in 1862, but the city soon rose again. A building boom in the late 1800s resulted in a spate of beautiful homes and commercial buildings. The riverboat traffic was heavy in its heyday, and so was the traffic in and out of Winona's many bars and houses of ill repute. The last madam was routed in a raid during World War II, and Winona's racy reputation soon quieted down. Today, the beautiful old buildings remain a tribute to Winona's past, while the industrial base supports a solid present. And all the while, the river just keeps rolling along.

Festivals and Events

Eagle Watch
first weekend in Mar.
In recent years, bald eagles have again been a common sight along the Mississippi. This two-day event starts with an educational program indoors and moves outside the next day for a bus trip, with expert commentary, to observe migrating eagles. The city of Winona sponsors the event, with the cooperation of Whitewater State Park and the Upper Mississippi River National Wildlife and Fish Refuge. Fee. For reservations, call the Winona Convention and Visitors Bureau (see Services).

Summer Band Concerts
Wed. evenings June–Aug.
Take a summer-evening picnic, spread a blanket out in front of the Lake Park Bandshell (there are benches, too), and wait for the music to start at 8:00 P.M. The concerts are played by the Winona Municipal Concert Band, the oldest continuously performing musical group west of the Mississippi. **507-452-2272.**

Steamboat Days
week of July Fourth
This good, old-fashioned Fourth of July bash features a carnival, fishing contest, two parades, an outdoor art fair, and fireworks. Begun as an event to honor old river captains and crew in 1947, the festival is now being held once again in downtown Winona. It's sponsored by the Winona Area Jaycees, **P.O. Box 308, Winona, 55987; 507-452-2272.**

Victorian Fair
last weekend in Sept.
Victorian crafts live again during this fall weekend, with demonstrations by costumed craftspeople, special events, food, and period music. Contact

The Julius C. Wilkie Steamboat Center is rich in riverboat lore. Courtesy of the Winona Convention and Visitors Bureau.

the Winona County Historical Society, **160 Johnson St., Winona, 55987; 507-454-2723.**

Swan Watch
first weekend in Nov.
Each fall, thousands of tundra swans—big, beautiful white birds—stop along the Mississippi River near Winona to rest before continuing their migration. The sight of so many wild creatures together—to say nothing of the noise they make—is unforgettable. The swan watch, like the eagle watch, consists of a lecture one evening and a bus trip to swan resting grounds the next day. Coffee and cookies are provided. Small fee. Contact the Winona Convention and Visitors Bureau (see Services).

Outdoor Activities

Biking
Several bike routes, varying in length and difficulty, are suggested in Winona's bicycling and

canoeing brochure. For a family, a **5-mile circuit around Lake Winona** is scenic and safe, as there is only one crossing with car traffic. Then there is the taxing ride **up Garvin Heights,** in which bikers climb 540 feet in just 1.15 miles. Tour de France winner Greg LeMond trained on it for the big race. The brochure is available from the Winona Convention and Visitors Bureau (see Services). The **6.5-mile Bronk Plowline Trail,** in Richard J. Dorer Memorial Hardwood State Forest, is popular with mountain bikers (see Hiking). A portion of the **Great River State Trail** for biking is within the Trempealeau National Wildlife Refuge, but biking is permitted on all roads (see Birding).

Birding

More than 280 kinds of birds visit Winona annually. The Winona Convention and Visitors Bureau (see Services) has a brochure with photos of some, from the huge bald eagle to the tiny Henslow's sparrow, plus eight suggested bird-watching tour maps. See also Eagle Watch and Swan Watch in Festivals and Events.

Trempealeau National Wildlife Refuge

Smaller and more intimate in feel than the Upper Mississippi Refuge (see Wildlife Viewing), the Trempealeau Refuge was created in 1936 as a refuge and breeding ground for migratory birds and wildlife. Great blue herons and pelicans are among the birds seen here. A 5-mile wildlife drive on a gravel road takes visitors through different habitats, with the best chance of seeing wildlife the early morning or evening. Free. The main entrance is off U.S. Hwy. 35, the Great River Rd. in Wisconsin, on West Prairie Rd. **W28488 Refuge Rd., Trempealeau, WI 54661; 608-539-2311.**

Boating

The Winona combined biking/canoeing brochure gives suggestions for trips that vary from placid Lake Winona to more challenging paddles on the Mississippi and in nearby rivers. The brochure is available from the Winona Convention and Visitors Bureau (see Services). Canoe route maps of two specific areas in the Mississippi are available from the Upper Mississippi River National Wildlife and Fish Refuge (see Wildlife Viewing).

Fishing

The Whitewater River, once silted up from the poor conservation practices of area farmers, was rejuvenated, and trout can now be found in it again. Fishing in the Mississippi is good, especially below the dams and in channels and sloughs, but state fish consumption guidelines should be followed. Eric Nelson, wildlife biologist for the Upper Mississippi River National Wildlife and Fish Refuge, cautions that smaller fish are safer to eat than larger ones, and says as much fat as possible should be removed either by trimming it off the fish or by cooking it off. In Richard J. Dorer Memorial Hardwood State Forest, Snake Creek, 4 miles south of Kellogg, has a designated trout stream running through the bottom of the deep valley; and Trout Valley, off Hwy. 61, has a spring-fed trout stream. In Trempealeau National Wildlife Refuge, fishing and hunting are by special permit.

Hiking

Hiking trails abound in and around Winona. In addition to the parks listed below, there is hiking on nature trails in Trempealeau National Wildlife Refuge (see Birding). See Parks for shorter trails.

Great River Bluffs State Park

Larger than the nearby John A. Latsch State Park, this park also has spectacular views of the Mississippi far below. At twilight, seen from one of the park's lofty lookouts, the bluffs and hills on the Wisconsin side of the river melt into rose and violet shadows, and the river reflects the colors and adds a silver shimmer of its own. The twin bluffs in the park are called King's and Queen's Bluffs. A self-guided nature trail runs a little more than a mile on King's Bluff. There are more than 5 additional miles of hiking trails. The park is 20 miles southeast of Winona at the junction of I-90 and U.S. 61. Exit I-90 at Hwy. 12, then take Hwy. 3 to the park. **Rte. 4, Winona, 55987; 507-643-6849.**

Richard J. Dorer Memorial Hardwood State Forest

The same Richard J. Dorer who saved the Whitewater Valley from eroding away continued his fight for conservation until his death in 1974.

The state forest, which he had helped establish, was renamed in his honor. Extending over much of southeast Minnesota, four of the management units are close to Winona. **Snake Creek,** 4 miles south of Kellogg, has trails for hikers, skiers, and horseback riders. In **Trout Valley,** off Hwy. 61, there is free camping in the parking lot, but there are no facilities available. During wild turkey season, hunters flock to Trout Valley. The Bronk Plowline Trail, a 6.5-mile trail on a ridge between **Stockton Valley** and the Mississippi River, is for nonmotorized use only and has scenic overlooks in both directions. It's popular with mountain bikers. The **Reno Unit,** near the Iowa border, is on dramatic bluffs along the Mississippi River, and its 13.3-mile trail—for hiking, riding, and snowmobiling—has a 500-foot rise, with wonderful views. There are two campgrounds with parking and picnic facilities, plus four walk-in campgrounds. Take Hwy. 26 west through Reno and follow the gravel township road to the trailhead. For more information on these units, including maps, contact the **Dept. of Natural Resources, 500 Lafayette Rd., St. Paul, 55155; 888-MINNDNR or 651-296-6157.**

Whitewater State Park

One of the most popular of all Minnesota's state parks, Whitewater is busy year-round. It was established in 1919 to halt the deterioration of the valley due to agricultural practices that resulted in widespread erosion, silting of rivers and creeks, and flooding. Stringent conservation practices, led by Richard J. Dorer of the Minnesota Dept. of Conservation, revived the valley and also encouraged the return of the brown and brook trout. The 2,800-acre park is part of the driftless region of the state, and 200-foot bluffs rise on either side of the valley. The park staff proudly proclaims that there are virtually no mosquitoes in the park, since the running waters of the park offer no breeding places. There is also solitude to be found here. Follow the 2-mile Trout Run Creek self-guided trail, on the valley bottom. Walk quietly and stop to observe—you may see a beaver gliding silently under the surface near a just-built dam in a creek. The hike up to Chimney Rock—a chimneylike rock with a hole through it—is tough going, but the long views of the valley below make it worthwhile. Six other trails vary from under a mile to 4.2 miles in length. The self-guided Meadow Trail takes only half an hour to walk and is perfect for young or beginning hikers, as it is level. The park's interpretive programs sell out quickly; act fast to secure a spot for special events, such as trout-fishing lessons and sleigh rides. The park has two interpretive centers, a swimming beach near the Chimney Rock Trail, two picnic grounds, and several separate campgrounds. Located west of Winona and 3 miles south of Elba on Hwy. 74. **Rte. 1, Box 256, Altura, 55910; 507-932-3007.**

Skiing

CROSS-COUNTRY

The city of Winona, state parks, and state forest units all have cross-country ski trails (see Hiking, and Parks). Great River Bluffs State Park has nearly 9 miles of groomed cross-country ski trails. Whitewater State Park has five trails that are used for cross-country skiing in winter. Ask for the cross-country ski guide from the Winona Convention and Visitors Bureau (see Services).

Snowmobiling

There are hundreds of miles of trails in southeast Minnesota; obtain a trail map from the Winona Convention and Visitors Bureau (see Services). A 7-mile groomed snowmobile/ATV trail zooms from Trout Valley to the ridge top in Richard J. Dorer Memorial Hardwood State Forest (see Hiking).

Seeing and Doing

Historic Sites

Pickwick Mill

The little village of Pickwick, with the old mill, waterfall, and millpond, is a charming sight. The six-story mill, completed in 1858, ran day and night during the Civil War to grind flour for the Union soldiers. After a devastating flood nearly destroyed it in 1980, the limestone mill was recently restored, and the restoration is continuing. Open June–Aug., Wed.–Sun., noon–5:00 P.M.; May and Sept.–Oct. 15, Sat.–Sun., noon–5:00 P.M.; and by appointment. Fee. An annual "mill day" is held on the second Sat. in Sept. Pickwick is south of Winona. Take Hwy. 61 to County Rd 7. **507-457-0499** or **507-452-9658.**

Museums

Julius C. Wilkie Steamboat Center
Steamboat run aground? No, it's a replica of the riverboat *Julius C. Wilkie* that sits on the flood-control dike. A museum on the first deck has plenty of riverboat lore. Guided tours are offered. Fee. Open May–mid-Oct., Mon.–Sat., 10:00 A.M.–5:00 P.M., and Sun., 1:00–5:00 P.M. **Levee Park, P.O. Box 733, Winona, 55987; 507-454-1254.**

Polish Cultural Institute/
Cultural Institute of Winona
Winona once had a large Polish population, as attested by the enormous Polish Catholic church St. Stanislaus Kostka, and the Polish Cultural In-

stitute. The institute has a fascinating collection of Polish folk art, family treasures, and artifacts from the Kashubian region of Poland. Open May–Nov., Mon.–Fri., 10:00 A.M.–3:00 P.M., and Sun., 1:00–3:00 P.M. **102 Liberty St., Winona, 55987; 507-454-3431.**

Watkins
Remember the Watkins man who sold vanilla door to door? It all began more than a century ago in Winona when Joseph R. Watkins got the bright idea to sell liniment from house to house, thus beginning the direct-sales business. Watkins widened his line to include home remedies, household products, and food items. The Watkins headquarters has a spectacular art glass window depicting Sugar Loaf Mountain in Winona, and may be toured by appointment; **150 Liberty St., Winona, 55987, 507-457-3300.** The Watkins home, built in the 1920s and lavishly decorated, also may be toured by appointment; **175 E. Wabasha St., Winona, 55987, 507-454-4670.** The museum (free) and store are open Mon.–Sat., 10:00 A.M.–3:45 P.M. Located at **E. Third St. between Chestnut and Liberty Sts.; 507-457-6095.**

Winona County Historical Society
The historical society runs the downtown Armory Museum, which has changing exhibits, special children's exhibits, and a permanent exhibit of beautiful stained glass. Fee. Open Mon.–Fri., 9:00 A.M.–5:00 P.M., and Sat.–Sun., noon–4:00 P.M. The historical society also has two other museums. The Bunnell House, south of Winona, is on the National Register of Historic Places; it tells the story of early settlers and is open seasonally (call for hours). The Arches Museum, west of Winona, highlights agricultural activities; call for hours. The society also sponsors an annual quilt show and the Victorian Fair (see Festivals and Events). **160 Johnson, Winona, 55987; 507-454-2723.**

Parks
Winona has a good park system. **Prairie Island,** on the Mississippi, has a deer park, a nature trail, camping and picnic facilities, boat launches, and

Fall colors in Winona. Photo courtesy of the Winona Convention and Visitors Bureau.

playgrounds. Nearby is **Levee Park,** where the *Delta Queen, American Queen,* and *Mississippi Queen* dock several times a summer. At the other end of the city, where Winonans head for a relaxing time, is **Lake Park,** with its beautiful rose garden, bandshell for summer concerts, and 5.5-mile trail for biking, jogging, or walking. There are picnic tables, playgrounds, an 18-hole Frisbee golf course, and volleyball sandpits. In addition to the Minnesota state parks near Winona, two Wisconsin state parks are nearby; **Merrick** and **Trempealeau** are 10 and 13 miles, respectively, from Winona.

John A. Latsch State Park

Known for its panoramic view of the river valley, John Latsch is a small, unpromising-looking park—until you take the steep path up to its summit. Riverboat pilots relied on the three tall bluffs in the park—Mounts Faith, Hope, and Charity—as landmarks. Tote a picnic lunch up the trail and enjoy a meal with a view. Located 12 miles northwest of Winona on Hwy. 61. The park is administered by Whitewater State Park, **507-932-3007.**

Downtown Winona from a bird's-eye view, looking up the Mississippi River. Photo courtesy of the Winona Convention and Visitors Bureau.

Garvin Heights

Everyone drives up to Garvin Heights to gasp at the Mississippi Valley below. The drive is easy; follow Huff St. across Hwy. 61 and wind up Garvin Heights Rd. and the High Rd. to the breathtaking lookout over the valley.

Performing Arts

THEATER

Winona State University's theater productions are open to the public; **507-457-5000.**

Scenic Drives

Apple Blossom Drive

A beautiful drive anytime along a ridge overlooking the Mississippi, the 17-mile Apple Blossom Drive is especially pretty when the trees bloom in May. In the fall, stop to buy apples from some of the dozen or so orchards. Or take a tea and apple dessert break at the **Apple on Main tea shop, 329 Main, 507-895-1995,** in the little town of LaCrescent. The drive, a state-designated scenic byway marked with apple blossom signs, is reached from Hwy. 61 by turning onto County Rd. 12 at Dakota and following it up to County Rd. 1. LaCrescent holds an apple festival the third weekend in Sept. Contact the LaCrescent Chamber of Commerce (see Services).

Tours

Historic Downtown Walking Tour

A number of Winona's downtown buildings are described in a brochure detailing a self-guided walking tour. A variety of architectural styles are represented, and some of the buildings are listed on the National Register of Historic Places. Oldest of the buildings is the **Winona Candy Company, 79 E. Second St.** It was built in approximately 1858 and may be the only structure to survive the 1862 fire. The brochure is available from the Winona Convention and Visitors Bureau (see Services).

Stained Glass

Winona is noted for the numerous beautiful examples of various styles of stained glass in its buildings and churches. A brochure, available from the Winona Convention and Visitors Bureau (see Services), lets visitors take their own tour through commercial buildings during business hours. Churches can usually be seen by appointment, and the brochure lists phone numbers for each church. In addition, **Conway Universal Studios, 507-452-9209,** and **Cathedral Crafts Studios of Stained Glass, 507-454-4079,** offer group tours by appointment.

Wildlife Viewing

Upper Mississippi River National Wildlife and Fish Refuge

The 284-mile-long refuge, which begins just south of Wabasha, is an aquatic paradise that annually beckons three million visitors who want to fish, watch birds, or canoe. The refuge, established in 1924, is headquartered at Winona and its holdings consist of braided channels of the Mississippi, marshland, and wooded islands. In secluded spots, it is easy to imagine that the area has not changed since European settlers first explored it. Wisconsin, Iowa, and Illinois are also part of the refuge, which harbors 270 bird species as well as 113 species of fish. The refuge bottomlands are anywhere from 2 to 5 miles wide. The sandbars in the refuge are perfect for picnicking, and pleasure boating is popular. Brochures on refuge fish, birds, reptiles, and amphibians are available, as are maps of the various pools of the refuge (Winona is adjacent to Pools 5A and 6), with harbors, lights, buoys, hazards, and other data noted. Two maps of canoe routes are similarly detailed. To obtain information, contact the refuge office, **51 E. Fourth St., Winona, 55987; 507-452-4232. Website: www.emtc.nbs.-gov/umr_refuge.html.**

Where to Stay

Bed-and-Breakfasts

Carriage House—$$$ to $$$$

Lumber baron Conrad Bohn built a three-story carriage house behind his own elegant house in 1870. The carriage house had a hayloft and rooms for the stable boys. Now Don and Deb Salyards live in the big house, and the carriage house is a long-established bed-and-breakfast with four rooms, all with private baths. In the Toy Room, for-

merly the stable boys' room, antique toys and teddy bears add a whimsical touch. In the Loft Room is a racy Winona memento: a claw-foot tub that was part of the notorious Madame Dupont's house of ill repute. The Salyards have single and tandem bikes available for guests. Breakfast is included. **420 Main St., Winona, 55987; 507-452-8256. Website: www.chbb.com.**

Hotels, Motels, and Inns

Americinn—$$$ to $$$$

The Americinn has 46 units, some with Jacuzzis. A two-story "lighthouse" suite, with a wonderful view of the Mississippi, is the favorite unit. The corner suite, looking like a little lighthouse from the outside, has a bedroom with a Jacuzzi on the lower floor and a sitting room on the upper, connected by a spiral staircase. Outside, a balcony gives a 360-degree view of the river and the town. **60 Riverview Dr., Winona, 55987; 800-634-3444 or 507-457-0249.**

Best Western Riverport Inn and Suites—$$$ to $$$$

Bring popcorn when you check into the Riverport, then hop into the '57 Chevy and watch an indoor "movie" on a large-screen TV through the windshield. The classic car doubles as a bed. Other fantasy suites in the hotel are a Roman bath and early American honeymoon suite. There are standard rooms and suites as well. **900 Bruski Dr., Winona, 55987; 800-595-0606** (reservations only) or **507-452-0606** (information).

Historic Trempealeau Hotel—$$

This great old hotel was built in 1871. It's known for its concerts in summer, and has eight basic, clean rooms, with shared bath. Light-sleeper alert: frequent trains on the adjacent tracks provide more than a little *Nachtmusik*. **150 Main St., Trempealeau, WI 54661; 608-534-6898.**

Camping

Prairie Island Park—$

In this city park is a campground with 80 electrical and 115 nonelectrical sites. It includes a convenience store, firewood sales, a central shower building, canoes for rent, and organized children's activities on weekends. Pets are allowed. Open Apr.–Nov. Located 2 miles north of Winona on **Prairie Island Rd., Winona, 55987; 507-452-4501.**

State Forests—$

Camping is permitted in some units of the state forests but not in others. There are designated campgrounds at the Reno Unit south of Winona, and camping is permitted (free) at Trout Valley in the parking lot, but there are no facilities. For more information on these units, including maps, contact the **Dept. of Natural Resources, 500 Lafayette Rd., St. Paul, 55155; 888-MINNDNR or 651-296-6157.**

State Parks—$

Whitewater State Park has 106 campsites, none with electricity, and also 4 walk-in sites and a group campground; 32 campsites are accessible to handicapped campers. At **Great River Bluffs State Park** there are 31 campsites, all of them handicapped-accessible, plus five sites that are bike-in and one group campsite. **John Latsch State Park,** upriver from Great River Bluffs, has 10 walk-in campsites. For reservations, call **The Connection, 800-246-CAMP or 612-922-9000.**

Where to Eat

Hot Fish Shop—$$ to $$$

The Hot Fish Shop *is* Winona to many visitors. The wonderful fish restaurant, in business since heck was a hush puppy (1931) features walleye dinners and all manner of seafood. The restaurant is casual in feel and loaded with memorabilia; kindly waitresses take good care of customers. Open Tues.–Sun., 6:00–11:00 A.M. and 11:30 A.M.–10:00 P.M.; Sun., 11:30 A.M.–8:00 P.M. Located at the **junction of Hwys. 14 and 61; 507-452-5002.**

Historic Trempealeau Hotel—$ to $$$

Over the river and round the bluffs is the funky Historic Trempealeau Hotel, established in 1871 and home to hip summer music events. The restaurant serves homemade soups and desserts. Entrees range from burgers to Italian and Mexican specialties to vegetarian dishes. The screened porch makes a pleasant place to sit on a hot day. Call for hours. **150 Main St., Trempealeau, WI 54661; 608-534-6898.**

Acoustic Cafe—$

A casual cafe, with live music on weekends, the Acoustic Cafe is right downtown. Sit outdoors in good weather. Hot hoagies, soups, espresso drinks, and beer and wine are some of the offerings. Open Mon.–Thurs., 7:30 A.M.–10:00 P.M.; Fri.–Sat., 9:30 A.M.–midnight; Sun., 9:30 A.M.–9:00 P.M. Corner of Second and Lafayette. **507-453-0394.**

Coffeehouses, Sweets, and Treats

Bloedow's Bakery—$

Locals rave about the huge loaves of country-style white bread—so big, a slice won't fit in a toaster—and doughnuts at Bloedow's, which has been in the same family since 1924. The line to get in sometimes stretches out the door and down the sidewalk. Open year-round, Mon.–Fri., 7:30 A.M.–5:30 P.M., and Sat., 7:30 A.M.–3:00 P.M. **451 E. Broadway, Winona, 55987; 507-452-3682.**

Services

LaCrescent Chamber of Commerce, P.O. Box 132, LaCrescent, 55947; 507-895-2800.

Winona Convention and Visitors Bureau, 67 Main St., P.O. Box 870, Winona, 55987; 800-657-4972 or 507-452-2272. E-mail: altwncvb@luminet.net. Website: www.visitwinona.com.

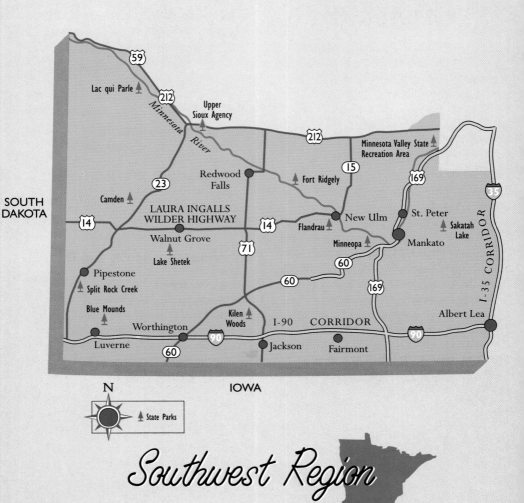

59

Lac qui Parle 🌲

212

Upper
Sioux Agency 🌲

Minnesota River

212

Minnesota Valley State 🌲
Recreation Area

15

Redwood
Falls

🌲 Fort Ridgely

169

23

Camden 🌲

I-35

SOUTH
DAKOTA

LAURA INGALLS
WILDER HIGHWAY

14

Flandrau 🌲 New Ulm

St. Peter

🌲 Sakatah
Lake

14

Walnut Grove

71

Minneopa 🌲

Mankato

● Pipestone

🌲 Split Rock Creek

60

60

169

I-35 CORRIDOR

Blue Mounds
🌲

Kilen 🌲
Woods

I-90   CORRIDOR

Albert Lea ●

● Worthington

90

90

Luverne

60

● Jackson

Fairmont

IOWA

N
🌲 State Parks

Southwest Region

Southwest Region

Native Prairie grasses are preserved at Blue Mounds State Park.
Copyright © Minnesota office of Tourism. Used by permission.

I-35 Corridor

Cities along the southern portion of I-35, which runs north and south nearly the length of Minnesota, are sometimes ignored by travelers in their haste to get "up north." Some of these communities grew because of the railroad, while others, such as Faribault, have a longer history.

Albert Lea, the first town that visitors enter coming north from Iowa, is an agricultural center, and emphasizes its central industry with farm tours for visitors. Austin will forever be known as Spamtown because it is the headquarters of the Spam-producing Hormel Company. Owatonna is proud of its stately bank, designed by classic prairie school architect Louis Sullivan. Faribault offers a melange of history, bargain shopping, and Brando (yes, as in Marlon).

On the other side of the interstate, Montgomery, Lonsdale, and New Prague are known for their Czech heritage; Hwy. 13 from Montgomery to New Prague was even designated the Czech Memorial Hwy. Waseca is an agricultural center, graced with a beautiful lake and home of the Waseca County Horse Thieves Detectives, founded in 1864 and still going strong (though they lean more to picnics these days).

History

Various Indian tribes lived and hunted along what is now the I-35 corridor before the European influx. One of the important figures in state history, Alexander Faribault, was a fur trader who united the two cultures—he was half Dakota and half European. In 1826 he set up a trading post in the town that now bears his name and his was the only business in that area for about 25 years. In the early 1850s, after the treaties of Traverse des Sioux granted most of southern Minnesota to the United States, wholesale settlement began. Another major historical figure, Bishop Henry Whipple, moved to Faribault in 1860. He started Indian missions and was the first Episcopal bishop in Minnesota. The land paralleling what is now I-35 proved to be wonderful farmland, and agriculture is still a major factor in the local economy.

Festivals and Events

Stories from the Heartland
Feb.
Master storytellers from across the country converge on Albert Lea for workshops, concerts, and just plain stories during this weekend. Call the Convention and Visitors Bureau for date and place (see Services).

Getting There
I-35 drops south from the Twin Cities to the Iowa border, a distance of about 115 miles.

Kolacky Days
fourth full weekend in July

Kolacky—a delectable fruit-filled bun—provide a great excuse for this festival in Montgomery, which is proud of its Czech heritage. Events include a Kolacky-eating contest, Czech music and dancing, a bun-run, parade, and queen coronation. This is one of the state's oldest street festivals; it started in 1929. Call the Montgomery Chamber of Commerce, **507-364-5577.**

Hot Air Balloon Rally and Air-O-Rama
second weekend in Sept.

Several dozen balloons take to the sky above the Faribault Airport. Also on tap are antique airplanes. Balloon rides can be purchased. Free. Call the Faribault Chamber of Commerce for information (see Services).

Big Island Rendezvous
first weekend in Oct.

A reenactment of the fur trade camps of the early 1800s, when various factions of the companies met each year to exhange furs, tally earnings, and have a good time, is held in Albert Lea's Bancroft Park. Costumed reenactors camp for the weekend. Music and crafts are also part of the festival. Fee. Contact the Albert Lea Convention and Visitors Bureau, **800-345-8414** or **507-373-3938.**

Outdoor Activities

Biking

Helmer Myre–Big Island State Park has 8 miles of mountain bike trails. There are 3 miles of surfaced bike trails at Sakatah Lake State Park. See Parks.

The Blazing Star Trail

This 21-mile, multipurpose paved trail will link Albert Lea with Austin, where it will join the Shooting Star Trail. The Blazing Star Trail is flat and easygoing in the west, hillier in the east. Part of it is on an old stagecoach trail. Access is near the memorial to hometown rock star Eddie Cochran. Look for wildflowers along the way.

Contact the Albert Lea Convention and Visitors Bureau, **800-345-8414** or **507-373-3938.**

Rentals and Tours

Ride around Albert Lea on a neon green bike. A deposit of a driver's license, credit card, or $20—all refundable—is all you need. Call the Albert Lea Convention and Visitors Bureau, **800-345-8414** or **507-373-3938,** for bike locations.

Birding

Helmer Myre–Big Island State Park has a marsh with an observation blind; among the park's many birds are white pelicans, which have a wing span of 6 feet. Thousands of these big birds can be seen during the fall migration. See Parks.

Rice Lake State Park

Rice Lake is noted as a wonderful place to spot migrating waterfowl and songbirds. The glacial lake for which the park is named, and the natural communities around it, are the focus of interpretive programs. The park's marshes offer good habitat for many kinds of birds. Located 8 miles east of Owatonna. From I-35, take Exit 42A (Hoffman Dr.) to E. Rose and turn left on County Rd. 19 to park. **8485 Rose St., Owatonna, 55060; 507-455-5871.**

Fishing

Although most people head "up north" to fish, there are plenty of fish to be caught in southern Minnesota lakes and rivers. The area around Waseca, in fact, is known as the Southern Lakes, and many visitors go there to fish. Sakatah Lake State Park, which has a handicapped-accessible fishing pier, contains walleye, largemouth and white bass, northerns, and panfish. For more information on seasons and licenses, call the Area Fisheries Supervisor in Waterville, **507-362-4223.**

Hiking

Helmer Myre–Big Island State Park has 16 miles of hiking trails, including a self-guided trail around the glacial esker. At Sakatah Lake there are 5 miles of combined hiking and cross-country ski trails. See Parks.

Skiing

CROSS-COUNTRY

State parks and the Sakatah Hills Trail are used by cross-country skiers. Sakatah Lake State Park has 5 miles of trails; Helmer Myre–Big Island State Park has 8 miles of cross-country ski trails. See Parks. In addition, many communities have groomed trails.

Snowmobiling

Sakatah Lake State Park has 3 miles of snowmobile trails. Contact area chambers for information (see Services).

Swimming

Many parks in the area, including Clear Lake in Waseca, have swimming beaches. Contact the local chambers for information (see Services).

Seeing and Doing

Museums and Historic Sites

Alexander Faribault House

The frame house of the fur trader Alexander Faribault, built close to the Cannon River in the town that bears his name, is open to visitors Apr.–Oct. Call the Rice County Historical Museum for hours and tour appointments. Fee. **12 First Ave. NE, Faribault, 55021; 507-332-2121.**

Sod root cellar at Farmamerica.

Farmamerica

Officially called Minnesota's Agricultural Interpretive Center, this is a living testimony to the state's agricultural past and present. Time Lane Rd., which can be driven or walked, takes visitors past buildings that reflect various eras in Minnesota farming, from the sod dugout of the pioneer days to the log cabins of a slightly later vintage, to the substantial farmsteads of the 20th century. For special events, which are held monthly, costumed volunteers are on hand to talk with visitors. In addition to the buildings and farm machinery, there are historically correct gardens and lovely prairie areas. A new visitor center was under construction as this book went to press. Call for hours. Farmamerica is located west of Waseca at the intersection of County Rds. 2 and 17. Fee. **P.O. Box 111, Waseca, 56093; 507-835-8000** (recorded message) or **507-835-2052.**

Louis Sullivan Bank

It isn't only architecture buffs who like the looks of Owatonna's pride and joy—the bank designed by noted architect Louis Sullivan. Built in 1907, the terra-cotta-trimmed bank has murals and stained glass in the interior. It is now Norwest Bank and is open Mon.–Fri., 8:00 A.M.–5:30 P.M., and Sat., 8:00 A.M.–noon. **101 N. Cedar Ave., Owatonna, 55060; 507-451-5670.**

Shattuck–St. Mary's

Marlon Brando spent time here, at the nearest thing to an old-style English public school Minnesota has. He was eventually asked to leave; in his recent autobiography, *Brando: Songs My Mother Taught Me* (Random House, 1994), he tells of his time at Shattuck in Faribault. The campus of the school, pushing 150 years old, once an Episcopal military academy for boys and now a coed school, is open to drive-through visitors. Go slowly to admire the wonderful old buildings, especially the Chapel of the Good Shepard. Much of the campus is part of the Shattuck Historic District, which is on the National Register of Historic Places. Many Faribault buildings, including those of the State School for the Deaf, have that historic classification. **1000 Shumway Ave., Faribault, 55021; 800-421-2724** or **507-332-5618.**

Story Lady Doll and Toy Museum

Hundreds of dolls, from the exquisite German and French dolls of the 19th century to dear old Raggedy Ann, will charm little and big kids. Fee. Open Tues.–Sun., noon–4:00 P.M. **131 N. Broadway Ave., Albert Lea, 56007; 507-377-1820.**

Waseca County Historical Society

Located in a former church, with beautiful stained glass windows, the museum has exhibits on American Indians who lived in the area and also on European settlers, with a separate exhibit on the railroad's impact on Waseca. Open Memorial Day–Labor Day, Mon.–Sat., and by appointment at other times. Call for hours. **315 Second Ave. SE, Waseca, 56093; 507-835-7700.**

Nature Centers

Riverbend Nature Center

At Faribault's Riverbend Nature Center, the ineptly named Straight River nearly ties itself in a knot, and in the oxbow it forms is a rock-strewn sandbar; many of the rocks have fossils imbedded in them. In the springtime, rare trout lilies bloom on the riverbanks. A pretty, nearly hidden waterfall is here, and a spring bubbles up under tall cedar trees. The center's 10 miles of trails are popular with local residents. The center, which is private, nonprofit, and member-supported, has interpretive programs. Open daily, 7:00 A.M.–10:00 P.M. (interpretive center has shorter hours; call). Located east of Faribault on Rustad Rd. **Box 186, Faribault, 55021; 507-332-7151.**

Parks

Albert Lea Parks

Don't let the "strip" approach off the interstate into Albert Lea fool you; there is a pretty town at the end of the strip, with Fountain Lake—which has walking paths on its shore—right downtown. On the edge of town is the huge Albert Lea Lake, bisected by I-35. Cruises of varying length are offered on the *Pelican Breeze,* a boat that is docked at Front and Frank Sts., op-

White-tailed deer. Copyright © Minnesota Office of Tourism. Used by permission.

posite the city pool. Fee. Contact the Albert Lea Convention and Visitors Bureau, **800-345-8414** or **507-373-3938.**

Helmer Myre–Big Island State Park

This park is a cool oasis in the midst of agricultural land. It began with a big (116 acres) wooded island on a big lake, and spilled over onto the mainland. Most of it is along Albert Lea Lake, which has 20 miles of shoreline. The park is a major recreation spot for southern Minnesotans. Highlights include an interpretive center with one of the state's largest collections of prehistoric artifacts, and picnicking on the big island. Located 3 miles southeast of Albert Lea on County Hwy. 38. Take exit 11 off I-35 and follow the signs. **Rte. 3, Box 33, Albert Lea, 56007; 507-379-3403.**

Sakatah Lake State Park

The Dakota Indians who once lived where the park now is called the area *Sakatah,* or "singing hills," and the name has persisted. The park, atop a glacial moraine, has a variety of habitats, which means that many animals—including deer, muskrat, raccoon, rabbit, mink, and red fox—can often be spotted. The lake within the park—also called Sakatah—is really a widening of the Cannon River. Boats and canoes are for rent. The lake has no swimming beach. The Sakatah State Trail runs through the park. There is a warming house in winter and a year-round naturalist. It is 1 mile east of Waterville on Hwy. 60. **Rte. 2, Box 19, Waterville, 56096; 507-362-4438.**

Performing Arts

THEATER

Minnesota Festival Theatre

The Minnesota Festival Theatre in Albert Lea, which is a professional summer theater, stages several productions each summer. Members of the company stay in local homes. For information, contact **P.O. Box 1134, Albert Lea, 56007; 800-944-5260 or (after June 1) 507-377-4371.**

Shopping

Even people in a hurry to get up or down the interstate stop to check out the discounts at the Medford Outlet Mall, located between Owatonna and Faribault, on the west side of I-35.

Faribault Woolen Mill Store

No visit to Faribault would be complete without a visit to the Faribault Woolen Mill Store, where the beautiful and warm blankets that have cuddled generations of customers can be bought at bargain prices. Some are first quality; some have minor flaws. Other items, including clothing, are also for sale. Open Mon.–Sat., 9:00 A.M.–5:30 P.M., and Sun., noon–5:00 P.M. **P.O. Box 369, 1819 NW Second Ave., Faribault, 55021; 800-448-9665 or 507-334-1644.**

Tours

Albert Lea is prime farm country, and the Convention and Visitors Bureau guessed right when it thought visitors might like to tour area farms. Most tours are geared to groups, but some farms

may arrange tours for family groups. Some of the farms that have tours raise potatoes and other vegetables, bees, buffalo, dairy cattle, sheep, miniature horses, ostriches and emus, and Christmas trees, in addition to having traditional grain operations. For information, call the Albert Lea Convention and Visitors Bureau, **800-345-8414** or **507-373-3938.**

DRIVING TOURS

Towns and villages all have stories to tell. Drive out east of Albert Lea on Hwy. 46 for a look at Hayward, noticing the **Burma-Shave signs,** the only ones of the once-abundant signs to still grace a road. The four signs, spaced just far enough apart for easy reading from a car, say: "Spring has sprung / The grass is riz / Where last year's / Careless driver is." The Odell family of Minnesota were the originators of the Burma-Shave signs. The first appeared in 1925, and the rhyming signs—cautionary or amusing and sometimes both—could be seen in 43 states for decades.

Hayward is the little town with the big-time meat market—Nick's. Owner Nick Schermer took over the **local butcher shop,** in business since 1898, more than 30 years ago and has been turning out award-winning sausages ever since. His summer sausage has taken the national grand championship ribbon in the meat trade for years. Nick also makes Czech liver sausage, head cheese, and Norwegian *rollepolse.*

Hayward also has an **old-time hardware store,** with high ceilings and an amazing assortment of hardware. It's been operating since 1900. Across the way is **Julio's,** a popular bar.

Hollandale, northeast of Albert Lea on Hwy. 251, east of I-35, is a testament to Dutch determination. Hollandale is the youngest settlement in Minnesota, according to Al Reynen, retired potato farmer and former mayor. About 400 families, many from the Dutch settlement of Pella, Iowa, moved onto small farms in the rich, drained peat lands in the early 1920s. Hollandale's story is told in the charming little museum called the **Hollandale Heritage Huis,** started by Al's wife, Doris. For information and hours, call the Albert Lea Convention and Visitors Bureau, **800-345-8414** or **507-373-3938.**

Where to Stay

Hotels, Motels, and Inns

All the cities and towns along I-35 have the usual chain hotels and motels. Bed-and-breakfasts and other types of accommodations are not nearly as plentiful here as in the rest of the state.

Schumacher's New Prague Hotel—$$$$

Schumacher's is a bit of Europe in southern Minnesota. A hotel since 1898, it was taken over in 1974 by the Schumachers, who have crafted it into a splendidly romantic destination, replete with wooden wainscoting and stained glass. The 11 rooms are all decorated distinctively, each with hand-painted folk-art details by Pipka, a Bavarian folk artist. European antiques, lace curtains, Austrian linens, and eider-down comforters are just some of the niceties at the hotel. Some of the rooms have gas fireplaces. The restaurant in the hotel is very well regarded and there is a gift shop. **212 W. Main St., New Prague, 56071; 800-283-2049 or 612-758-2133.**

The Victorian Rose Inn—$$ to $$$

The setting sun makes a visual poem of the stained glass window on the staircase of the elegant Victorian Rose Inn in Albert Lea. Built in the Queen Anne style, at a time when intricate wooden "gingerbread" trim was all the rage, the inn has three double rooms and a single. All but the single have private baths. The Kensington Suite has a lace-bedecked turret, and Queen Victoria's namesake room has a marble fireplace. **609 W. Fountain St., Albert Lea, 56007; 800-252-6558 or 507-373-7602.**

Camping

There are many private campgrounds along the I-35 corridor. Request a list from Albert Lea, Faribault, or Owatonna information offices (see Services).

State Parks—$

Helmer Myre–Big Island State Park has 99 campsites, 32 of which have electricity. At Rice Lake State Park, 16 of the 42 campsites have electric-ity. Both parks have a few canoe-in campsites. Sakatah Lake State Park has 62 drive-in sites, 14 with electricity, 4 bike-in sites, and a camper cabin. For reservations, call **The Connection, 800-246-CAMP or 612-922-9000.**

Where to Eat

Schumacher's New Prague Hotel—$$ to $$$$

John Schumacher has garnered a wonderful reputation for the food served in the dining room at the hotel. The latest in the Schumacher repertoire is a five-course elk tenderloin dinner. Game is a specialty here, as are mittel-European specialties such as Wiener schnitzel and sauerbraten. Leave room for the linzer torte and apfel strudel, too. Don't overlook the cozy bar, which has German and Czech beers. Open daily, 11:30 A.M.–4:00 P.M. (lunch) and 4:00–8:30 P.M. (dinner). **212 W. Main St., New Prague, 56071; 800-283-2049 or 612-758-2133.**

Lavender Inn—$ to $$$$

Travelers have been known to time their trips so that they wind up at the Lavender Inn restaurant in Faribault at mealtime. The restaurant, inside and out—including waitresses' uniforms—is lavish lavender, but somehow it isn't overdone and the dining areas are nicely, if eclectically, decorated. The color scheme may be a draw, but the food keeps 'em coming. It all started in 1960 as a drive-in run by Gaylen and Bebe Jensen. The Jensens' house was lavender, so they carried the color over to the drive-in, according to their daughter Gay Jensen-Paquin. The first indoor dining room was built in 1963, and the business has grown to include an art gallery and gift shop. The dinner menu includes seafood items such as frog legs and lobster tails as well as steaks, chops, and broasted chicken. Open daily, 11:00 A.M.–10:00 P.M. **2424 Lyndale Ave. N., Faribault, 55021; 507-334-3500.**

Trumble's—$ to $$$

Trumble's is the kind of family-oriented place, with satisfying food and plenty of it, that travelers hope to find. Try the homemade pie. Open

Sun.–Mon., 6:00 A.M.–10:00 P.M., and Tues.–Sat., 6:00 A.M.–11:00 P.M. **1811 E. Main, Albert Lea, 56007; 507-373-2638.**

Wimpy's—$ to $$

Pie's the thing at Wimpy's. Waitresses rattle off a long list of each day's homemade pies, and it's hard to say no—even after one of Wimpy's buffalo burgers or hearty dinners. Pictures of Wimpy's in the 1950s are on the walls in the main room, but there are several other rooms, too. Open daily, 5:00 A.M.–11:00 P.M. **520 Central Ave., Faribault, 55021; 507-334-4996.**

Coffeehouses, Sweets, and Treats

Franke's Bakery—$

Stop at Franke's for a couple dozen Kolacky, the tender, fruit-filled buns that are the delight of this Czech community. There are a few tables, if you can't wait to eat these marvels. Open Tues.–Fri., 6:15 A.M.–5:30 P.M.; Sat., 6:15 A.M.–3:00 P.M. **200 First St. S., Montgomery, 55069; 507-364-5025.**

Services

Albert Lea Convention and Visitors Bureau, 202 N. Broadway Ave., Albert Lea, 56007; 800-345-8414 or 507-373-3938.

Faribault Chamber of Commerce and Tourism Bureau, 530 Wilson Ave., P.O. Box 434, Faribault, 55021; 800-658-2354 or 507-334-4381.

Montgomery Chamber of Commerce, 507-364-5577.

New Prague Chamber of Commerce, 101 E. Main St., New Prague, 56071; 612-758-4360.

Owatonna Convention and Visitors Bureau, P.O. Box 331, 320 Hoffman Dr., Owatonna, 55060-0331; 800-423-6466 or 507-451-7970.

I-90 Corridor

I-90 slashes across the prairies of southwestern Minnesota, bound for South Dakota. If you're headed for the Black Hills, take a little time to explore the towns and country along the interstate.

Fairmont is a sparkling-clean little city, with five lakes within its limits and a wonderfully restored opera house. Jackson, according to a local booster, is the home of "the happiest people in the world." Worthington is where the Southwest shops. Luverne, with many buildings made from the beautiful, rosy Sioux quartzite, has Blue Mounds State Park in its backyard.

History

The earliest people in the area along what is now I-90 may have passed through as long as 12,000 years ago, although the first evidence of human habitation was of the late Archaic community about 5,000 years ago. They were followed by Woodland Indians and then by Iowa, Cheyenne, Arapahoe, and Dakota Indians, according to Tom Sanders, site manager for the Jeffers Petroglyphs. French explorers and traders were probably the first Europeans, although settlement didn't start in earnest until the railroad came through in the 1870s. Farming was—and still is—the principal business here. Much of the "Prairie-Lake" landscape was too wet to farm until it was drained.

Festivals and Events

Fridays in the Park
Memorial Day to early Aug.
Try to arrive in Fairmont on a Fri. in summer to enjoy free entertainment, a bargain lunch from a local restaurant (they take turns), and free popcorn at the gazebo in the downtown plaza. Lunch is 11:00 A.M.–1:00 P.M.; the entertainment begins at 12:15 P.M. Contact the Fairmont Area Chamber of Commerce, **507-235-5547.**

Buffalo Days
first weekend in June
How's your aim? Can you toss a dried buffalo chip (courtesy of the herd at nearby Blue Mounds State Park) into a toilet bowl? How about chowing down on a free buffalo burger or watching an antique tractor pull? These events and more go on at Luverne's celebration. Contact the Luverne Chamber of Commerce, **507-283-4061.**

Reenactment of a wagon train at Blue Mounds State Park. Photo courtesy of the Minnesota Department of Natural Resources.

Interlaken Heritage Days
second weekend in June

There was once a wonderful amusement park in Fairmont called Interlaken. It's long gone, but the spirit lives on each June when the citizens remember it with a parade, water-ski show, games, and food booths. For information, contact the Fairmont Area Chamber of Commerce, **507-235-5547.**

King Turkey Day
second weekend after Labor Day

King Turkey Day is very nearly the king of Minnesota festivals. It began in 1939 and was interrupted only by World War II. Events include the "Great Gobbler Gallop," a race whose entrants are real turkeys, and a parade with turkeys in the lead spot. Past visitors include Lyndon Johnson, Richard Nixon, and Jesse Jackson. Contact the Worthington Convention and Visitors Bureau, **800-279-2919** or **507-372-2919.**

Outdoor Activities

Birding
Bird-watchers can spot nesting blue grosbeaks, meadowlarks, and other birds of the tallgrass prairie at Blue Mounds State Park.

Boating
Fairmont's five lakes—four of them connected—form the straight backbone of the city and are perfect for spending a day boating or enjoying the scenery. The lakes all have access points for boaters. In Worthington, giant Lake Okabena dominates the city and provides a focus for recreation at several parks along the shore; activities include swimming, camping, and Wed.-night band concerts in summer by the long-lived city band, which first organized in 1893.

Rentals and Tours
Zanke's in Fairmont rents canoes and paddleboats; **445 Lake Ave., Fairmont, 56031; 507-235-6931.**

Fishing
Fairmont's five lakes have good fishing. Worthington's Lake Okabena has fishing from a dock. There is fishing in the river at Kilen Woods State Park. **Zanke's** in Fairmont is a bait shop and issues fishing and hunting licenses; **445 Lake Ave., Fairmont, 56031; 507-235-6931.**

Hiking
There are 13 miles of hiking trails in Blue Mounds State Park. Kilen Woods State Park has 5 miles of hiking trails. See Parks.

Snowmobiling
The flat prairie land makes for good snowmobiling, and many clubs in the I-90 area groom trails. Martin County's Blizzard Snowmobile Club—in the Fairmont area—maintains 100 miles of groomed trails. Contact the Fairmont Area Chamber of Commerce, **507-235-5547.** Luverne and Worthington also have active snowmobiling groups, and Luverne is surrounded by trails that go through the beautiful Blue Mounds State Park, which has 7 miles of trails for snowmobiles. Call the Luverne Chamber of Commerce, **507-283-4061,** or Worthington Convention and Visitors Bureau, **800-279-2919** or **507-312-2919.**

Seeing and Doing

Museums and Historic Sites

Cottonwood County Historical Society
The museum's big addition includes an art gallery, which will be used to display the work of local artists and also traveling shows. The late Robert Renick, who was trained as an artist but worked as a dairy farmer, donated his works—primarily abstracts—to the museum. Other exhibits in the museum center on the area's agricultural heritage, although there are some dating from the

pre-European era. Call for hours. **812 Fourth Ave., Windom, 56101; 507-831-1134.**

Fairmont Opera House

The Fairmont Opera House is a jewel that is getting plenty of use. The restored opera house, built in 1901 and listed on the National Register of Historic Places, is the venue for visiting entertainers as well as local theater groups. **P.O. Box 226, Fairmont, 56031; 507-238-4900.**

Parks

Blue Mounds State Park

Buffalo, cactus, and a mysterious line of rocks are all part of Blue Mounds. The park is named for the cliff of Sioux quartzite, nearly 100 feet high and 1.5 miles long, on its eastern boundary. To settlers headed west, the cliff appeared blue. The park is a remnant of the tallgrass prairie. Prickly pear cactus bloom in late June and early July, and wildflowers present a colorful late-summer show. By that time, the big bluestem prairie grass is 7 feet high. On the park's southern end is a 1,250-foot line of rocks, which align with the sun on the first day of spring and fall. No one knows who laid the rock "marker" or why. A big favorite with visitors is the buffalo herd at the northern end of the park. Even with the viewing platform and scopes, it may be difficult to see them if they are at the far end of the range. The campground, shaded by many trees, is along Upper Mound Lake, formed when Mound Creek was dammed; there is a swimming beach at Lower Mound Lake. The dam itself is built of rosy Sioux quartzite, and outcrops of the stone occur throughout the park. Don't miss the striking quartzite interpretive center, the former home of local author Frederick Manfred. The park is 3 miles north of Luverne, off U.S. Hwy. 75. **R.R. 1, Box 52, Luverne, 56156; 507-283-1307.**

Kilen Woods State Park

One of the smallest state parks, Kilen Woods is on the Des Moines River, amid the prairie. It has interpretive information on how the river valley was formed. In winter, kids enjoy the sliding hill and warming house. Go north on Hwy. 86 from I-90, passing through Lakefield and turning east onto County Hwy. 24. **County Hwy. 24, Lakefield, 56150; 507-662-6258.**

Performing Arts

THEATER

Both Fairmont and Luverne have active local theater groups. Fairmont's productions are at the Opera House, **507-238-4900** (see Museums and Historic Sites). The Luverne group, the Green Earth Players, performs at the venerable Palace Theatre, **104 E. Main, Luverne, 56156; 507-283-8526.**

Tours

Luverne, like Pipestone, has many beautiful old buildings made of the locally quarried Sioux quartzite. A brochure with a suggested walking tour is available from the Luverne Chamber of Commerce, **507-283-4061.** The tour includes the Palace Theatre, with its movie memorabilia museum; the quartzite Masonic building, which houses the Rock County Museum; the stone lion–guarded Hinkly House; the stately Rock County Courthouse; and the Carnegie Cultural Center. In addition to the buildings seen on this tour, many private homes were built of quartzite.

Where to Stay

Hotels, Motels, and Inns

Chain motels and some locally owned units abound along I-90. Inquire at the local Chambers of Commerce (see Services).

The Old Railroad Inn—$$ to $$$

This really was an inn for railroad workers for nearly a century, ending in 1970. The owner grew up in it, got to know many of the regulars, and turned it into a bed-and-breakfast when she returned some years later. There are lots of railroad memorabilia, and each of the four rooms is named for a different railroad company. Children are welcome. **219 Moore St., Jackson, 56143; 888-844-5348 or 507-847-5348.**

A buffalo herd in Blue Mounds State Park. Copyright © Minnesota Office of Tourism. Used by permission.

Camping

Blue Mounds State Park has 73 campsites, 40 with electricity, and also 14 walk-in sites. Kilen Woods State Park has 33 sites, 11 with electricity, plus three boat-in sites and four walk-in sites. For reservations, call **The Connection, 800-246-CAMP** or **612-922-9000.**

Where to Eat

Channel Inn—$ to $$

A Channel Burger—topped with cheese, bacon, and a fried egg—is a big seller at the informal cafe on the end of the channel that connects Budd and Hall Lakes in Fairmont. Boaters are welcome; there are places for docking. The inn, going strong for more than 40 years, is open daily, 11:00 A.M.– 1:00 A.M. **330 W. Lair Rd., Fairmont, 56031; 507-238-9700.**

Services

Fairmont Area Chamber of Commerce, 206 N. State St., P.O. Box 826, Fairmont, 56031; 507-235-5547.

Luverne Chamber of Commerce, 102 E. Main, Luverne, 56156; 507-283-4061.

Worthington Convention and Visitors Bureau, 1018 Fourth Ave., Box 608, Worthington, 56187; 800-279-2919 or **507-372-2919.**

Laura Ingalls Wilder Highway

The area along Hwy. 14—renamed the Laura Ingalls Wilder Highway—is wide-open prairie country. It is tamer in these days—although winter blizzards are a reminder of its ferocity—but it was a formidable opponent to early white settlers. The tall grass hampered travel and the deep-rooted prairie sod made plowing up the virgin land difficult indeed.

There are prairie lovers and prairie haters. Some revel in its open, unobstructed view, blazing sunsets, and wildflowers. Others find it empty and mournful, with a ceaseless wind whistling a melancholy chorus. Much has been written about the prairie and its people. One of the most powerful of prairie books is among the oldest: O. E. Rolvaag's *Giants in the Earth*, a 1927 novel of Norwegian immigrants who homesteaded on the South Dakota–Minnesota border.

Rolvaag's prairie seems friendly at first, with the sun shining and the grasses rippling around the wagons making their way ever westward. However, in the book's final chapter, titled "The Great Plain Drinks the Blood of Christian Men and Is Satisfied," he writes of the darker side of the prairie:

> . . . the strange spell of sadness which the un-broken solitude cast upon the minds of some. Many took their own lives; asylum after asylum was filled with disordered beings who had once been human. It is hard for the eye to wander from sky line to sky line, year in and year out, without finding a resting place!

Today, time and tractors have nearly conquered Rolvaag's prairie demons, and visitors seeking the gentler prairie of Laura Ingalls Wilder's books will find it. Summer shows the prairie in its green-and-gold glory, but winter snows can still make roads impassible. Summer is time for small pleasures—seeking out stars at night or trying on a sunbonnet in a re-created sod house. Summer is the best time for seeing the beauty, not the beast, in the undulating landscape.

Young tourists sample what life on the prairie was like for Laura Ingalls Wilder.

Getting There

Hwy. 14 stretches across the state, but the portion described here is the western half, with most of the sites roughly 150–200 miles from the Twin Cities. From New Ulm, follow Hwy. 14 west.

Recommended Reading

O. E. Rolvaag's *Giants in the Earth* (Harper and Row, 1927) is a novel of the struggle of Norwegian immigrants to homestead on the prairie. A sequel published two years later, *Peder Victorious* (Harper and Row, 1929), describes the transition from lonely homesteaders to growing communities, and the transformation of the prairie into farmland with roads and villages. Laura Ingalls Wilder's books about her childhood, especially the one describing her time in Walnut Grove, *On the Banks of Plum Creek* (Harper and Row, 1932), give an entertaining picture of frontier life. A current voice from the prairie, booming out of the tiny town of Minneota, is that of Bill Holm, descendant of Icelanders, world traveler, and baker of brown bread. Holm's books, the latest of which is *The Heart Can Be Filled Anywhere on Earth* (Minneapolis: Milkweed Editions, 1996) are moving and amusing, and full of true prairie tales even when they are set in China.

History

Archaeological evidence shows that for 8,000 years people have descended into the Redwood River Valley—site of Camden State Park—to hunt and fish. In the 1830s the American Fur Company established a trading post in the valley, though European-American settlers didn't start coming until the late 1850s. Until white settlers streamed into the southwestern part of Minnesota in the 19th century, the prairie was hunting country for the American Indians. After the U.S.–Dakota Conflict in 1862, the Dakota were removed and did not return for many years.

The area around Hwy. 14 has a string of small towns, each claiming different European heritage, including Norwegian, Danish, Polish, English,

and Icelandic. Even now, after much intermarriage, these towns celebrate their beginnings with festivals and ethnic foods. Marshall, the area's largest city, makes a convenient overnight stop but is not a tourist destination.

Major Attractions

Jeffers Petroglyphs

A very old story is told in 2,000 carvings incised on hard rock that juts out of the prairie in southwestern Minnesota. These petroglyphs were made by American Indians. Dating the carvings, which were made by using hammer stones to strike hard stone or antler chisels on the Sioux quartzite rock, is difficult, but the oldest may have been made around 3000 B.C. The petroglyphs—a Minnesota Historical Society (MHS) site—depict shamans, other humans, and various animals including deer, elk, buffalo, and turtles. Thunderbirds and arrows are among the figures carved into the rocks, which sit like islands among the prairie grasses. Some carvings are faint; visibility may be best on overcast days or from certain angles and at various times of the day. There is a new interpretive center located 3 miles east of Hwy. 71 on County Rd. 10, then 1 mile south on County Rd. 2. Open Memorial Day–Labor Day, Mon.–Sat., 10:00 A.M.–6:00 P.M., and Sun., noon–6:00 P.M.; May and Sept., Fri.–Sat., 10:00 A.M.–5:00 P.M., and Sun., noon–5:00 P.M. Fee (free to MHS members). **R.R. 1, Box 141, Comfrey, 56019; 507-628-5591.**

Tracing Laura Ingalls Wilder

Charles "Pa" Ingalls, father of beloved children's author Laura Ingalls Wilder, moved his family often, starting out in Wisconsin, and going on to Minnesota, Iowa, and South Dakota. The places are recalled by Wilder in the *Little House* series. The Ingalls moved to Walnut Grove, Minnesota, near the South Dakota border, in 1874. They first lived in a sod dugout on the banks of Plum Creek, and Laura's life there is recorded in *On the Banks of Plum Creek*. The TV series was based on the books. The town of Walnut Grove is a destination for Wilder fans. The site of the sod dugout can be seen on the banks of Plum Creek. A sign designates the site, which is on private land, and a small donation is requested of visitors. Ask for a map at the Laura Ingalls Wilder Museum in Walnut Grove (see Museums and Historic Sites). The museum is a "must" stop for Wilder fans, as it has Ingalls memorabilia, including a quilt Laura and her daughter made. Actors from the television series have visited the museum. The museum also has an 1898 depot, a replica of an 1880s school, a chapel, and a turn-of-the-century house, with period furnishings. You may be greeted at the museum by its director, Shirley Knakmuhs, alias Mrs. Oleson. Knakmuhs has played the testy Mrs. O. for nearly two decades of performances in "Fragments of a Dream," the outdoor pageant about the Wilder family (see Festivals and Events). As Mrs. Oleson, Knakmuhs has taken a whipped-cream pie in the face each night of the pageant, and she's had half a dozen "husbands."

Festivals and Events

Saddle Horse Holiday
Father's Day in June
Since 1947 the community of Lake Benton has been saddling up in mid-June for a trail ride in the hills around the town, ending with a parade and two-ring horse show. Hundreds of horses and riders—from preschoolers to octogenarians—show up, according to Jean Carr, who is one of the original planners. Visiting riders are welcome. Registration is at Hole-in-the-Mountain County Park (see Parks) on the day of the ride. Fee. Contact Carr at **507-368-4519.**

Ableskiver Days
weekend after Father's Day in June
Ableskiver, a round Danish doughnut, is a good excuse for this annual party, during which the doughnuts, along with Danish open-faced sandwiches, are for sale. Danish folk dancers perform and there is a community dance. Contact the Tyler Chamber of Commerce, **P.O. Box 445, Tyler, 56178; 507-247-3905.**

Jeffers Petroglyphs. Copyright © Minnesota Office of Tourism. Used by permission.

"Fragments of a Dream" Pageant
first three weekends in July
Relive Laura Ingalls Wilder's life and times during the open-air "Fragments of a Dream" pageant, set on the banks of Plum Creek. More than 100 Walnut Creek residents volunteer each year to put on the nine performances. In addition to costumed actors, there are real animals, pies, and a (tightly controlled) prairie fire. The performances are at 9:00 P.M. Some seats are reserved; others are first-come, first-served. Bring a wrap; it can get chilly. Fee. The site is 1 mile west of Walnut Grove off County Rd. 20. **P.O. Box 313T, Walnut Grove, 56180; 507-859-2174. E-mail: wpageant@rconnect.com. Website: www.walnutgrove.org.**

Outdoor Activities

Biking

Currie–Lake Shetek Trail
A 6-mile paved loop, along open, flat terrain, connects Lake Shetek State Park with the End-O-Line Park in Currie. The trail is for both bikes and pedestrians; no snowmobiles or horses are allowed. See Parks.

Rentals and Tours
Bikes can be rented at the **Mill Street Mercantile** in Currie, **507-763-1555** or **800-WINBORN.** Near End-O-Line Park is the **Trail's Edge Store,** a handy stop for thirsty bikers.

MOUNTAIN BIKING

Camden State Park, one of 13 state parks that permit mountain biking, has 4.2 miles of trail over hilly terrain, for which a map is available (see Parks).

Birding

A number of songbirds, including the bluebird, are found in Camden State Park. A self-guided trail at Lake Shetek State Park takes visitors around Loon Island, a bird sanctuary connected to the mainland by a short causeway. Park marshlands give glimpses of bird and pond life. A spotting scope is near Eastlick Marsh. Birds in the park include the pelican, for whom the lake is named (*shetek* is the Ojibwe word for "pelican"). See Parks.

Fishing

Lake Shetek, Brawner Lake (in Camden State Park), Lake Benton, eight other lakes in Lincoln County, and a few rivers have good fishing. Lake Shetek is a good walleye lake, according to Al Sobek, assistant park manager. Lake Shetek State Park also has two fish ponds stocked with crappies, sunfish, and perch. In Camden State Park, the Redwood River is stocked with German brown trout, and Brawner Lake contains bass and bluegill. For season and license information, call the Area Fisheries Supervisor in Windom, **507-831-2919.**

Hiking

Camden State Park has nearly 15 miles of hiking trails. At the top of the gradual hike up Dakota Valley Trail, hikers can see as far as 10 miles away. Hole-in-the-Mountain County Park has 5 miles of hiking trails. Lake Shetek State Park has 8 miles of hiking trails. See Parks.

Hunting

Pheasant hunting is a draw here, but whitetail deer are also abundant. For season and license information, call the Dept. of Natural Resources in Marshall, **507-537-6250.**

Skiing

CROSS-COUNTRY

There is cross-country skiing at Lake Shetek and Camden State Parks as well as other parks, including Lake Benton's Hole-in-the-Mountain County Park, which has 5 miles of cross-country ski trails. Camden State Park has 6 miles of cross-country ski trails, with an additional skate-ski trail of 1.3 miles. Lake Shetek State Park has 3 miles of cross-country ski trails. See Parks.

DOWNHILL

The downhill ski area at Hole-in-the-Mountain County Park in Lake Benton—a surprise for those who think southwestern Minnesota is completely flat—has two lifts and rents equipment. There is a small ski hill, with a vertical drop of 134 feet, served by a rope tow and a handle lift. See Parks.

Snowmobiling

The Southwest Ridge Runners Club maintains, among the many snowmobile trails in this part of the state, a trail leading from the southeast side of Marshall, near the intersection of Hwys. 23 and 59, south to Garvin. Camden State Park has 7.6 miles of trails for snowmobilers; Hole-in-the-Mountain County Park has 5 miles of trails; and Lake Shetek State Park has 5 miles of trails for snowmobilers. See Parks.

Seeing and Doing

Museums and Historic Sites

Danebod Historic Complex

The Danes who came to Minnesota were far outnumbered by the Norwegians and the Swedes, but there are a number of Danish settlements, including Tyler, where a historic complex called Danebod runs cultural camps and folk-arts workshops. The group of buildings includes a church with a sailing ship suspended from the ceiling, a stone hall on the National Register of Historic Places, a folk school, and a gym. Tours can be arranged. Contact the Tyler Chamber of Commerce, **P.O. Box 445, Tyler, 56178; 507-247-3905.**

End-O-Line Park

Minnesota's only remaining manually operated railroad turntable, still in its original site and still operating, is at Currie's End-O-Line Park. Visitors can hitch a ride for half a turn and children can ride on the miniature train. The park grew out of a 4-H project in 1972, when the railroad still came to Currie. The park also has a water tower, depot, foreman's house, roundhouse, and caboose switcher, plus a renovated general store and schoolhouse. Open Memorial Day–Labor Day, Mon.–Fri., 10:00 A.M.–noon and 1:00–5:00 P.M.; Sat.–Sun., 1:00–5:00 P.M. Also by appointment. Fee. Located just off Mill St. and south of the Des Moines River in Currie. **Rte. 1, Box 42, Currie, 56123; 507-763-3708.**

Lake Benton Opera House

Lake Benton Opera House, built in 1896 after a fire destroyed the first one, was scheduled for demolition in 1970, but a group of local citizens rescued it. Now, fully restored down to the horseshoe-shaped balcony, the Opera House is on the National Register of Historic Places and is used for community theater and special performances. **P.O. Box 1, Lake Benton, 56149; 507-368-4620.**

Laura Ingalls Wilder Museum

Those seeking traces of Walnut Creek's beloved author find plenty here. In addition to items from the Ingalls family, there are donations from the actors who played the family on the television series. One of the latest acquisitions is a facsimile of the rifle Michael Landon (Pa Ingalls) used on the series. See Major Attractions for more details. Fee. **330 Eighth St., P.O. Box 58, Walnut Grove, 56180; 507-859-2358 or 507-859-2155.**

McCone Sod Houses

Stan McCone, whose ancestors homesteaded on the prairie, built two sod houses from virgin prairie sod cut near his farm in Sanborn in the 1980s. One, a little dugout soddy, is quite primitive, while the other, larger sod house is called the "rich man's soddy" by Stan and his wife, Virginia. The larger house has whitewashed walls and is nicely furnished and used as a unique bed-and-breakfast (see Where to Stay). There is a trapper's cabin—with traps, skins, and American Indian artifacts—near the sod houses. McCone has also lovingly restored the prairie grasses and flowers. Tours Apr.–Oct. Fee. Located 1 mile east and 0.25 mile south of Hwys. 14 and 71. **12598 Magnolia Ave., Sanborn, 56083; 507-723-5138.**

Parks

Camden State Park

The prairie sky is wide and high and beastly hot in summer, so the wooded oasis of Camden State Park provides a welcome respite. Families are happy with the spring-fed swimming hole in the park. Springs are common in the park, according to park manager Paul Otto, who says there are 15 springs identified in a 5-mile stretch of the Redwood River. Along the river near the swimming hole are picnic tables. Canoes can be rented. One caution: in some spots, the river is subject to flooding; visitors should be alert for mud slides down the valley walls. Camden has a horsecamp (see Where to Stay) and 10.2 miles of horse trails. Wildflower fans like Camden because they can see both woodland and prairie flowers. The park is 10 miles southwest of Marshall, off Hwy. 23. **1897 County Rd. 68, Lynd, 56157; 507-865-4530.**

Hole-in-the-Mountain County Park

The Coteau des Prairies, called Buffalo Ridge by locals, stretches for miles across southwestern Minnesota. Near Lake Benton, there is a break in Buffalo Ridge—a hole in the mountain—and that's where this excellent county park is located, at the bottom of the surrounding bowl of hills. Located in saddle horse country, the park has 5 miles of riding and hiking trails, as well as campsites (see Where to Stay). Contact the Lincoln County Parks, **Hwy. 14 W., Lake Benton, 56149; 507-368-9350.**

Hole-in-the-Mountain Prairie

This prairie preserve is alive with butterflies—including the rare Dakota skipper—which love the grasses and the 200 species of wildflowers, including the small white lady slipper. The 775-acre prairie is owned by The Nature Conservancy.

One of the two McCone sod houses.

The preserve is 1.5 miles south of Lake Benton on U.S. Hwy. 75. There is parking on the west side of the highway. Call the Minnesota branch of **The Nature Conservancy, 612-331-0750.**

Lake Shetek State Park

Lake Shetek State Park can be enjoyed for its scenery and wildlife, for its recreational and fishing opportunities, and for its place in Minnesota history. On the southeast shore of the largest lake in southwestern Minnesota, the area is noted for its beauty as well as its tragic past. The area was long an American Indian settlement and bison hunting ground, but that changed when the first white settlers came in 1856. The little settlement ended abruptly on Aug. 20, 1862, when Dakota braves involved in the Dakota Conflict attacked Shetek and killed 15 settlers. A brochure guides visitors on a tour of the restored Koch cabin and four other cabin sites. Those who were killed are memorialized by a tall granite obelisk in the park. A second self-guided trail takes visitors around Loon Island; the hiking loop around the island

turns into an easy cross-country ski trail in winter. There is a sandy swimming beach on Lake Shetek, a wooded waterside campground, and one camping cabin. Rowboats and canoes can be rented and there are picnic tables. A paved bike trail begins at the park (see Biking). The park is 14 miles northeast of Slayton; take County Rd. 38 out of Currie and follow signs. **163 State Park Rd., Currie, 56123; 507-763-3256.**

Tours

North and south of Lake Benton are dozens of skinny, high-tech **wind turbines,** which make a fascinating sight to see as you drive along the back roads. A good view can be had from County Rd. 9 south of the city of Lake Benton.

DRIVING TOURS

Of five self-guided driving tours of the Southwest Region (all circle tours), two of them are in the Hwy. 14 area: one encompasses the "Little Europe" collection of towns of various heritage—Danish, English, Icelandic, Norwegian, and Polish—near South Dakota; the other includes railroad heritage, the McCone sod houses (see Museums and Historic Sites), and the Jeffers Petroglyphs (see Major Attractions). The tours are described in a brochure available from Travel Southwest Minnesota, **800-279-2919.**

Where to Stay

Bed-and-Breakfasts

Weaver's Haus Bed-and-Breakfast—$$$

Weavers or "wannabe weavers" are enchanted by this loom-lover's lair (there are five looms in Jeanette Hauschild's studio and plenty of examples of wonderful hand-weaving around the contemporary house). "I'm loom-crazy," says Jeanette. The b-and-b is conveniently located in a quiet town. The two comfortably furnished guest bedrooms have private baths. **315 E. George St., Ivanhoe, 56142; 507-694-1637.**

Sod House Bed-and-Breakfast—$$ to $$$$

Here are answers to your questions about staying overnight in a sod house: yes, it really is a sod house; yes, it really is comfortable; yes, I have stayed there myself—twice—and can hardly wait to stay again. Minnesota's most unusual bed-and-breakfast is also one of its most relaxing. The "soddy" is generously sized, with comfortable furniture. The whitewashed walls are sparkling-clean and give no hint of their earthen nature. The walls of the house are 2 feet thick, making it cool in summer and warm in winter, when a woodstove heats the little house on the prairie. A curtain separates the two double beds. There are old books to peruse, an antique fainting couch to recline on, old clothes to try on, and kerosene lamps to light. After a restful night (no traffic sounds, just the whisper of the wind and the prairie), wake to look out the window onto a sea of waving prairie grasses. Then make a quick trip to the sod outhouse and use the basin and ewer to wash. Next, it's time for Virginia McCone to come bearing baskets containing a hearty breakfast. That's living well—no matter what century we're talking about. Located 1 mile east and 0.25 mile south of Hwys. 14 and 71. **12598 Magnolia Ave., Sanborn, 56083; 507-723-5138.**

Triple L Farm Bed-and-Breakfast—$$ to $$$

You'll get a warm welcome at Lanford and Joan Larson's working farm just east of South Dakota. The Larsons, both former teachers, run a corn and soybean operation, and part of their land is in a conservation reserve program in which pheasant and deer abound. There is a hay-filled feed-sack swing hanging from a big tree, and there may be young farm animals around. The four rooms have cozy quilts and furnishings that include a handmade oak bed and a white iron bedstead. The largest room has a private bath; the other rooms share a bath. There is a separate smoking-allowed bunkhouse that has four bunks and a hide-a-bed, plus a small refrigerator, hot plate, and microwave, but no water or bathroom (there is an outhouse nearby). Hunting privileges can be arranged. Triple L is 3 miles south of Hendricks on Hwy. 271 and 1 mile west on Hwy. 19. **Rte. 1, Box 141, Hendricks, 56136; 507-275-3740.**

Camping

Hole-in-the-Mountain County Park—$

This county park has 50 campsites, all with electricity and some with water. All sites have picnic tables and fireplaces. There are some campsites for riders in the hills across the highway; the horsecamps fill up fast. Located on the edge of the city of Lake Benton. Contact the Lincoln County Parks Dept., **Hwy. 14 W., Lake Benton, 56149; 507-368-9350.**

State Parks—$

Lake Shetek and **Camden State Parks** both have campgrounds; Lake Shetek also has a camper cabin. At Lake Shetek, there are 98 drive-in campsites, 67 with electricity. In addition, there are 10 walk-in sites and the camping cabin. Camden State Park has 80 drive-in sites, 29 with electricity. The park also has 12 horsecamp sites, with a maximum capacity of 50. For reservations, call **The Connection, 800-246-CAMP** or **612-922-9000.**

Where to Eat

Southwestern Minnesota is cafe and supper club country, where you usually get good home cooking, but not gourmet fare. Among places recommended by local residents are the **Chalet, E. College Dr., Marshall, 55304; 507-532-4491,** and the **Valhalla Steak House,** 8 miles north and 1 mile east of Slayton on Lake Shetek; **507-763-3749.**

Mike's Cafe—$ to $$

Mike's in Marshall serves an excellent, cheap breakfast. It's known for homemade caramel and cinnamon rolls and other baked goods. Lunch and dinner are served, too. The place is plain, pleasant, and crowded; it's been in business for decades. Open Mon.–Fri., 6:00 A.M.–8:00 P.M., and Sat.–Sun., 6:00 A.M.–2:00 P.M. **203 E. College Dr., Marshall, 56258; 507-532-5477.**

Victorian Gardens—$ to $$

If your little "Laura" longs to carry her lunch in a

pail like Laura Ingalls Wilder did, order a "Laura's Lunch" from Victorian Gardens, a restaurant in Springfield. The lunch, packed in a galvanized pail with "Laura's Lunch" stenciled on it, consists of a homemade bun filled with ham, as well as chips, pickles, hard candy, a homemade cake doughnut, and a choice of beverage. The restaurant also has eat-in meals including pasta salads, homemade soup, sandwiches, and desserts and coffee specialties. Open Mon.–Thurs., 7:00 A.M.–6:00 P.M.; Fri., 7:00 A.M.–7:00 P.M.; Sat., 8:00 A.M.–4:00 P.M.; Sun., 9:00 A.M.–1:00 P.M. **8 W. Central, Springfield, 56087; 507-723-6594.**

Services

Lincoln County Promotion and Tourism (Ivanhoe, Lake Benton, Tyler, Hendricks), **315 E. George, Ivanhoe, 56142; 507-694-1138.**

Marshall Area Chamber of Commerce, 1210 E. College Dr., Suite 200, Marshall, 56258; 507-532-4484.

For Walnut Grove, contact the **Laura Ingalls Wilder Museum, 330 Eighth St., P.O. Box 58, Walnut Grove, 56180; 507-859-2358** or **507-859-2155.**

Mankato and St. Peter

On a map of the state, the Minnesota River looks like a giant, flexed arm. In the arm's "elbow" is Mankato; a bit downstream is St. Peter. In Mankato, the Blue Earth River joins the Minnesota River. The Minnesota River tries mightily to climb over its banks at times. The river towns, settled largely after the Dakota ceded their land in the treaty of 1851 (see below), are both home to educational institutions and both played crucial roles in state history. Mankato and North Mankato have a population of 41,570, more than four times St. Peter's 9,421. St. Peter is on its way to recovery after a tornado in 1998 devastated the town.

History

Many early explorers passed through St. Peter and Mankato. One, Pierre Le Sueur, came seeking the blue-colored earth—which he thought might be copper—that the Dakota used as face paint. The soil was not copper, but later Europeans found riches in the fertility of the soil.

It was in St. Peter, at a river crossing called the Traverse des Sioux, that the signing of the first of two treaties of 1851, perhaps the most crucial events in Minnesota history, took place. Treaty terms permitted mass settlement of former Dakota land by Europeans. Eleven years after the treaty was signed, the short but bloody U.S.–Dakota Conflict erupted. Many settlers and Indians lost their lives.

What began in St. Peter ended just 12 miles away in Mankato, when 38 Dakota were hanged in the largest mass hanging in U.S. history. In recent years, the two factions have held formal reconciliation events.

Mankato's first settlers, in 1852, were Henry Jackson and Parsons K. Johnson. The two formed a town-site development company. One of the earliest industries in town was a limestone quarry; milling and agriculture-related industries followed. Today Mankato is a regional trade center. St. Peter was founded just a year after Mankato, in 1853, by Captain William Dodd.

Festivals and Events

Minnesota Viking Training Camp
late July–early Aug.
Football fans show up on the hottest summer days to watch the training camp of the Minnesota Vikings, Minnesota's NFL team. Sessions are twice a day, six days a week at Blakeslee Field at Mankato State University. Practices are free; fee for scrimmages. Call the Mankato Area Chamber and Convention Bureau, **800-657-4733.**

Getting There
Mankato is approximately 80 miles from the Twin Cities; St. Peter is 12 miles north of Mankato. From the Twin Cities, take U.S. Hwy. 169 south to both.

A Minnesota Viking greets fans at training camp. Photo courtesy of the Minnesota Vikings: Rick A. Kolodziei.

Mankato Mdewakanton PowWow
mid-Sept.

Native Americans come from across the country for this powwow, held at Mankato's Land of Memories Park. There is dancing, along with traditional music and foods. Contact the Mankato Area Chamber and Convention Bureau, **800-657-4733.**

Nobel Conference
first Tues. and Wed. in Oct.

Nobel laureates are among the speakers during Gustavus Adolphus College's annual Nobel Conference. The conference, begun in 1965, is open to the public and is the only such gathering in the United States that is sanctioned by Sweden's Nobel Foundation. **507-933-7520.**

Celebration of Lights
Thanksgiving–New Year's Day

During the holidays, Mankato and North Mankato residences sparkle with thousands of lights. A map is available from the Mankato Area Chamber and Convention Bureau, **800-657-4733.**

Outdoor Activities

Biking

A map of area bike trails is available from the Mankato Area Chamber and Convention Bureau, **800-657-4733.**

Red Jacket Trail

A little more than 2 miles long, this scenic trail begins at Mankato's Rasmussen Park and ends at Rapidan, going over a railroad trestle at one point.

Sakatah Hills State Trail

A 39-mile multipurpose trail that stretches from Mankato to Faribault, the Sakatah Hills State Trail is on an abandoned railroad bed. The paved trail is quite level; some of the scenery is pastoral farmland. The trail runs through Sakatah Lake State Park. There are picnic sites along the trail and campsites at Bray Park in Madison Lake and at Sakatah Lake in Waterville. The parking lot at the west end of the trail is north of Mankato, off Hwy. 22. At Faribault, park in the lot on the north side of Hwy. 60, east of I-35.

Rentals and Tours

Rent bikes for the Sakatah Hills State Trail at **Pit Stop 60, Box 368, Elysian, 56028, 507-267-4560** or **800-WINBORN,** May–Oct.; and at **Ron's Hardware Hank, 229 E. Main, Waterville, 56096, 507-362-4308,** year-round.

MOUNTAIN BIKING

Mount Kato Mountain Bike Trails

During the off-season, mountain bikes take over the Mount Kato downhill ski runs, with 7-plus miles of trails. Rental bikes are available. May–Oct. Located 1 mile south of Mankato, off Hwy. 66 S. **800-668-5286** or **507-625-3363.**

Boating

The Minnesota, a designated canoe river, offers a gentle ride suitable for families. From Mankato downriver to Le Sueur, there are several campsites and access points. Maps of the river from Fort Ridgely to Le Sueur are available from the **Dept. of Natural Resources Information Center, 500 Lafayette Rd., St. Paul, 55155; 888-MINNDNR** or **651-296-6157.**

Hiking

The 39-mile Sakatah Hills State Trail (see Biking) is also used for hiking. Minneopa State Park (see Parks) has 4.5 miles of hiking trails. Many local parks, such as Sibley Park and Land of Memories Park, both in Mankato, also have hiking trails (see Parks).

Skiing

CROSS-COUNTRY

Minneopa State Park has about 4 miles of cross-country ski trails, and some Mankato city parks have groomed trails (see Parks). For other local trails call the Mankato Area Chamber and Convention Bureau, **800-657-4733.**

DOWNHILL

Mount Kato has 18 trails, served by five quad and three double chair lifts, plus three handle tows. Lessons and rental equipment are available; the two-level chalet has food service and a bar. There is also snow tubing. Located 1 mile south of Mankato, off Hwy. 66 S. Open daily in winter (except Christmas Day), Mon.–Tues., Thurs., Sat., 9:30 A.M.–10:00 P.M.; Wed., 9:30 A.M.–4:30 P.M.; Sun., 9:30 A.M.–9:30 P.M. **800-668-5286** or **507-625-3363.**

Seeing and Doing

Gardens and Arboreta

Linnaeus Arboretum

Replanted and tidied up after the 1998 tornado did much damage, Gustavus Adolphus College's Linnaeus Arboretum is a 55-acre oasis with plants representing Minnesota's three major natural divisions—the northern evergreen forest, the prairie, and the hardwood forest between the two. The arboretum also has a white garden, a lilac grove, and an 1866 Swedish pioneer cabin. Free. Located on the college campus (see Historic Sites for directions). **507-933-7003.**

Historic Sites

Blue Earth County Heritage Center

Among the exhibits are a section on the Dakota Conflict and artifacts from various groups represented in Blue Earth County history. The collection includes everyday items such as housedresses and sunbonnets. Fee. Open year-round, Tues.– Sat., 10:00 A.M.–noon and 1:00–4:00 P.M. **415 Cherry St., Mankato, 56002; 507-345-5566.**

Homes in Mankato and North Mankato are awash in lights during the holidays. Photo courtesy of the Mankato Area Chamber and Convention Bureau.

Dakota Execution Site

As a result of the U.S.–Dakota Conflict in 1862, 38 Dakota were hanged in Mankato that same year, near the site of what is now the Minnesota Valley Regional Library. Originally, 303 Dakota were condemned to death by a military court, but according to historian William E. Lass, all but the 38 were pardoned by President Lincoln through the intervention of Faribault's Bishop Henry B. Whipple, whom the Indians called "Straight Tongue." The city has recently completed Reconciliation Park at the site, where a plaque, a statue titled *Winter Warrior,* and a sculpture of a buffalo commemorate the Dakota. Each year a memorial run ending at the statue is held in their honor.

Gustavus Adolphus College

Founded in 1862 by Swedish immigrants, the college's pretty campus on a hill above central St. Peter is graced with sculptures by spacy professor emeritus Paul Granlund, who has a campus studio. A brochure and map help visitors locate the sculptures. The college's modernistic Christ Chapel contains many of his works. The college is nearly recovered from the devastation wrought by the tornado in 1998. There has been a movement to bring back the nickel cup of coffee to the campus—ask about it! The main college entrance is on College Ave., intersecting with U.S. Hwy. 169. Visitors can pick up a map for a self-guided tour of the campus from the office of public affairs, in the Carlson Administration Building; guided tours can be arranged by calling the office, **507-933-7550.**

Hubbard House

R. D. Hubbard was a prominent Mankato mill owner who built a sumptuous home that is now owned by the city of Mankato and operated by the Blue Earth County Historical Society. The R. D. Hubbard House has three marble fireplaces, cherry woodwork, a signed Tiffany lampshade, and wall coverings of silk. The 1871 mansion is on the National Register of Historic Places. Fee. Open spring through fall (call for exact dates), Sat.–Sun., 1:00–4:00 P.M. **606 S. Broad St., Mankato, 56002; 507-345-4154.**

On the Trail of Betsy, Tacy, Tib, and Maud

Several generations have read and loved the "Betsy-Tacy" books, about three little girls who lived in "Deep Valley," as author Maud Hart Lovelace called her hometown of Mankato. The 10 books were written between 1940 and 1955. They follow the girls as they grow up. Maud (who is "Betsy" in the series) and many other characters lived near downtown Mankato. Betsy was the leader of the trio. The early books chronicle the everyday joys of childhood—climbing trees, going to see grandparents, messing up their mothers' kitchens, etc. The later books show the girls attending school, falling in love, and getting married. Some of the houses described, including Betsy's and Tacy's houses, are still standing, but the original bench that stood at the foot of the hill on Center St.—where Betsy and Tacy met to plan their gentle adventures, such as climbing "the big hill"—disappeared. Shirley Lieske and her daughter Denise took on the task of raising money for a new bench, which is now in place. Lieske conducts tours of Betsy-Tacy landmarks on request; visitors can also use a self-guided brochure, available from the Minnesota Valley Re-

gional Library and the Mankato Area Chamber and Convention Bureau (see Services). The library's wing dedicated to Lovelace has a mural depicting events in her life. Contact Lieske at the North Mankato Public Library, **507-345-5120.** The Betsy-Tacy Society, **507-345-8103,** in Mankato has purchased "Tacy's" house and is restoring it.

Recommended Reading

Betsy-Tacy fans may find *Betsy-Tacy in Deep Valley* by Carlienne A. Frisch (Mankato: Friends of the Minnesota Valley Regional Library, 1985) and the longer *Betsy-Tacy Companion* by Sharla Scannell Whalen (Whitehall, Pa.: Portalington Press, 1995) helpful in identifying the real people and places in Maud Lovelace's series.

Treaty Site History Center

In July and Aug. 1851, chiefs of four bands of Dakota Indians signed away most of southern Minnesota in exchange for promises by the U.S. government, many of which later went unfulfilled. According to accounts of events leading up to the treaties, many of the chiefs felt that they had no choice because of the greater number of the whites, and they hoped, in exchange, to salvage money, goods, and reservations. The Treaty Site Museum, part of the Nicollet County Historical Society, has changing exhibits about aspects of the treaty and those involved in it, a collection of original colored engravings by Seth Eastman, and archives. Fee. Open Apr. 1–Sept. 30, Mon.–Sat., 10:00 A.M.–4:00 P.M., and Oct.–Mar., Mon.–Sat., 1:00–4:00 P.M. **1851 N. Minnesota Ave., St. Peter, 56082; 507-931-2160.** The historical society also operates the Cox house, which was built in a carpenter Gothic/Italianate style in 1871 and has period Victorian furniture. Fee. Open year-round, Mon.–Sat., 10:00 A.M.–4:00 P.M., and Sun., 1:00–4:00 P.M. **500 N. Washington Ave., St. Peter, 56082; 507-931-2160.**

W. W. Mayo House

Long before he started the Mayo Clinic in Rochester, the first doctor Mayo, William Worrall Mayo, lived in this small white frame house with his wife, Louise, and young family. Later, the Cosgroves, founders of the Green Giant Company, lived in the house, now owned by the Minnesota Historical Society and furnished in 1860s style. Fee. Open Memorial Day–Labor Day, Tues.–Sun., 1:00–4:30 P.M., and Labor Day–Oct. 15, Sat.–Sun. and holidays, 1:00–4:30 P.M. Tours by appointment. **118 N. Main St., Le Sueur, 56058; 507-665-3250.**

Parks

Mankato Parks

Among Mankato parks are two adjoining facilities where the Minnesota and Blue Earth Rivers meet. Sibley Park, on the east side of the Blue Earth, has a petting zoo, flower gardens, and a fountain for summer enjoyment, and ice skating and sledding in the winter. On the west side of the river is the Land of Memories Park, with its campground and cross-country ski trails. Both parks have paved riverside hiking/biking trails that connect with the Sakatah Hills State Trail and the Red Jacket Trail. The parks are located off S. River Front Dr. (Hwys. 60 and 169) in southwest Mankato. Call the Mankato Parks and Forestry Division, **507-387-8649.**

Minneopa State Park

The double waterfall is the star of Minneopa State Park. The horseshoe-shaped upper falls is like a miniature Niagara; the narrower lower falls cascades into a pool, where visitors sometimes wade (signs warn when it is dangerous to do so). The falls, in a steep, wooded glen, are separated by a pedestrian bridge that provides a good view of the upper falls; at the far side is a viewpoint from which both falls can be seen. In the northwest corner of the park stands an old stone windmill—sans sails—built in 1864. On the prairie are strewn "glacial erratics," rocks—some the size of cars—that are isolated relics of the long-gone glacier; work is under way to reestablish prairie areas within the park. There are hiking trails in the park and cross-country ski trails. It is located 5 miles west of Mankato, at the junction of Hwy. 68 and U.S. Hwy. 169. **Rte. 9, Box 143, Mankato, 56001; 507-389-5464.**

Performing Arts

For information on arts groups, contact the Mankato Area Chamber and Convention Bureau (see Services).

THEATER

Mankato is a lively arts center, thanks in part to Minnesota State University Mankato, which has public music and theater events. The university's Highland Summer Theatre offers a season of drama, comedy, and musicals. Contact the theater at **MSU, Box 8400, Mankato, 56002; 507-389-2118.**

Where to Stay

Mankato has a wide choice of motels. Contact the Mankato Area Chamber and Convention Bureau for a listing (see Services).

Bed-and-Breakfasts

Butler House Bed-and-Breakfast—$$$ to $$$$

This stately, turn-of-the-century house is often used for weddings and other special occasions. The public rooms are beautifully decorated and the fumed oak and cypress woodwork is formidable. Don't miss the mural on the dining room wall. Guests can play the Steinway grand piano or relax and read in one of the house's cozy window seats. There are five rooms, three of them suites, all with private baths. Breakfast is included. **704 S. Broad St., Mankato, 56001; 507-387-5055.**

Camping

Land of Memories Campground—$

This popular campground is at the confluence of the Minnesota and Blue Earth Rivers, near the center of Mankato. It's first-come, first-served at Land of Memories' 42 shaded sites, all of which have electricity. Good fishing here, but no swimming. Open May–Oct. Off Hwy. 169 S. on Hawley St. **P.O. Box 3368, Mankato, 56002; 507-387-8649.**

Minneopa State Park—$

Minneopa, just outside Mankato, has 62 campsites, only 6 of them with electricity. For reservations, call **The Connection, 800-246-CAMP** or **612-922-9000.**

Where to Eat

The Chestnut Tree Cafe—$ to $$

The Chestnut Tree, in a high-ceilinged building in downtown St. Peter, has good food and a wide choice of coffees. The atmosphere is relaxed and friendly and draws all ages, especially students from Gustavus Adolphus College. The cafe has live music and art exhibits; on the first Thurs. of each month, there is an open mike. The cafe has sandwiches, pizza, and an ever-changing lot of baked goods and desserts. The malts and shakes—sized either normal or huge—come in chocolate raspberry, chocolate peanut butter, and chocolate-covered espresso bean. Open Tues.–Thurs., 8:00 A.M.–10:30 P.M.; Fri., 8:00 A.M.–11:30 P.M.; Sat., 10:00 A.M.–11:30 P.M.; Sun., 10:00 A.M.–10:30 P.M. **410 S. Third St., St. Peter, 56082; 507-931-0106.**

Services

Le Sueur Area Chamber of Commerce, 500 N. Main St., No. 106, Le Sueur, 56058; 507-665-2501.

Mankato Area Chamber and Convention Bureau, P.O. Box 999, Mankato, 56002; 800-657-4733 or 507-345-4519.

St. Peter Chamber of Commerce, 101 S. Front St., St. Peter, 56082; 800-473-3404 or 507-931-3400.

New Ulm

What nationality predominates in New Ulm? Think about the city's name, watch the little figures nipping in and out of the glockenspiel downtown, taste the schnitzel, and *trink der gut* Schell beer in restaurants around town. *Ja, das ist ein* German town—founded by Germans and still pretty *Deutsch* overall.

Although Minnesota residents with Scandinavian roots outnumber the Germans, the largest single immigrant group was from Germany, and Germans are still the largest ethnic group. Nowhere is this more evident than in New Ulm, a city of some 13,000 on the Minnesota River. The city's architecture shows German influence, and local restaurants offer hearty German fare, especially during the festivals the New Ulmers love. And what would a German city be without a good brewery? In its time, there were five breweries.

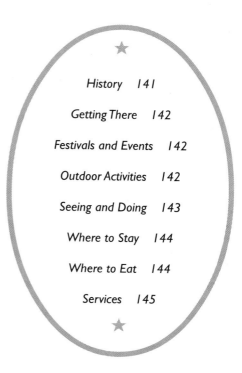

The house of the owners of the August Schell Brewery in New Ulm. Copyright © Minnesota Office of Tourism. Used by permission.

The August Schell Brewery is the only one remaining, and it is one of the town's biggest tourist draws.

Speaking of big—look up and notice the statue looming above town. It looks a bit like the Jolly Green Giant girded for battle, but up close it's Hermann, considered the father of German independence. Some people call him "Hermann the German." He's kept watch over the city from his hill since 1897.

Today New Ulm is a regional trade center with a thriving downtown. The ties with the old country have loosened with time and intermarriage. However, Germans are still the dominant ethnic group; although the language is fading as the old-timers die, *Danke Schön* ("thank you kindly") and other expressions can still be heard.

History

A group of German immigrants in Chicago formed the "Chicago Land Society" in 1853 and went to southern Minnesota in 1854 to select the New Ulm site. It was named for Ulm, Germany, and streets were laid out in an even grid; 100 years later, it's still easy to find any place in town. Land bought by the society, as elsewhere in southern Minnesota, was ceded by the Dakota Indians in the 1851 treaty. New Ulm was a busy place from its inception. Until the railroads came, steamboats on the Minnesota River brought both freight and passengers.

In Aug. 1862, during the U.S.–Dakota Conflict, New Ulm was attacked twice (see the Redwood Falls chapter in this section). Nature attacked the city, too. In 1870 a plague of grasshoppers brought near-starvation, and in 1881 a cyclone battered the city.

New Ulm's German heritage, a point of pride in early days as well as now, was a problem during World War I, when there was much anti-German sentiment. According to Rhoda R. Gilman, writing in *The Story of Minnesota's Past,* German-Americans in New Ulm in 1917 asked the U.S. government to excuse young German-Americans from fighting Germans. Angered, the governor of Minnesota yanked the mayor from office, and state newspapers called the New Ulm people traitors. Ironically, New Ulm was the site of a German prisoner-of-war camp during World War II.

Festivals and Events

Fasching and Bock Beer Festival
Sat. before Ash Wed. in Mar.
Fasching is the German version of Mardi Gras—a chance to thumb noses at winter and whoop it up before Lent. New Ulm's Fasching is indoors at Turner Hall, **102 S. State St.,** and features food, beer, entertainment, and a costume contest. Fee. Meanwhile, at Schell Brewery, the out-

door part of the festival is held on the brewery grounds. The bock festival is a magnet for college students. Contact the New Ulm Area Chamber of Commerce, **888-4NEWULM.**

Heritagefest
second and third weekend in July
There is entertainment on five separate stages, and a Kinderfest area for the youngsters, during New Ulm's celebration of heritage. European groups are among those performing songs and dances for an audience totaling about 40,000. The festival, which began in 1974, features the locally brewed Schell's beer and German food. Held at the Brown County Fairgrounds. Fee. Contact the New Ulm Area Chamber of Commerce, **888-4NEWULM.**

Oktoberfest
first and second weekend in Oct.
The leaves are at their flaming best during Oktoberfest, when New Ulm celebrates the harvest with beer, music and other entertainment, oodles of strudel, and other German food. The festival is in two venues: **Turner Hall, 102 S. State St.,** and the **Holiday Inn, 2101 S. Broadway,** with shuttle bus connections. On Sat., horse-drawn trolleys meander past some of the historic houses in town. Fee. Contact the New Ulm Area Chamber of Commerce, **888-4NEWULM.**

Outdoor Activities

Boating
Canoeing is possible on the Minnesota and Cottonwood Rivers. Maps of the canoe route on the Minnesota from Le Sueur to Fort Ridgely (including New Ulm) show access points, campsites, and rest areas. The map also shows Cottonwood River canoe access points. The Minnesota twists and turns between its low banks in the stretch covered by the map. Usually gentle, it can be a tyrant in flood, as it was in 1997. For a map, contact the **Dept. of Natural Resources Information Center, 500 Lafayette Rd., St. Paul, 55155; 888-MINNDNR** or **651-296-6157.**

Rentals and Tours

Canoes and bikes can be rented at the **Bicycle Peddler, 304 N. Minnesota St., New Ulm, 56073; 507-354-4646.**

Fishing

Due to agricultural runoff, fish caught in the Minnesota River should be eaten with care. For more information, call the Regional Fisheries Manager in New Ulm, **507-539-6000.**

Hiking

Trails within Flandrau State Park include a short, steep hike up to Indian Point, a riverside trail, and a trail to the group camp and also to the World War II German POW barracks; ask for the barracks key and directions at the park office. There are 8 miles of hiking trails, 8 miles of cross-country ski trails, and 1.3 miles of trails for snowmobiles. See Parks.

Seeing and Doing

Museums and Historic Sites

Harkin Store and Brown County Museum

The Harkin Store, all that's left of the community of West Newton, was started in 1870 by Alexander Harkin and closed in 1901. Now, with its costumed guides and amply stocked shelves, it gives visitors a glimpse into the past. About 40 percent of the stock is original, including the checkerboard. In cool weather, visitors gather around the wood-burning stove. The store is owned by the Minnesota Historical Society but is administered by the Brown County Historical Society, which also has a Brown County Museum in New Ulm. Fee. The store is open May, Sat.–Sun., 10:00 A.M.–5:00 P.M.; June–Aug., Tues.–Sun., 10:00 A.M.–5:00 P.M.; Sept.–Oct. 15, Fri.–Sun. (and holiday Mon.), 10:00 A.M.–5:00 P.M. Located 8 miles northwest of New Ulm on County Rd. 21. The Brown County Museum is open Mon.–Fri., 10:00 A.M.–5:00 P.M., and Sat.–Sun., 1:00–5:00 P.M. Fee. Located at Center and Broadway in New Ulm. Phone for both is **507-354-2016.**

Hermann Monument

Wherever you go in New Ulm, Hermann—the 102-foot statue in Hermann Heights Park—seems to loom over you. Climb up to the base of the century-old statue for a wonderful view of the city and the Minnesota River Valley. Fee. Picnic tables in the park. Located at **Center and Monument Sts.**

Wanda Gag House

Millions of children love Wanda Gag's wonderful prose and pictures in such books as *Millions of Cats* and *The Funny Thing.* Gag, who grew up in this turreted house, was an internationally known artist who struggled to get an art school education after her parents died, leaving her and six younger siblings behind. The house is on the National Register of Historic Places; borders in the house's rooms, painted by Wanda's artist father, have been restored. The house tour includes snippets of Gag lore, such as how the Gag children liked to lure the hurdy-gurdy player's monkey up into the tower and not let him down until the man played all his tunes. Call for hours. Free. **226 N. Washington St., New Ulm, 56073; 507-35WANDA.**

Other Sights

New Ulm Glockenspiel

A freestanding carillon clock tower whose two tons of bells play daily and chime the hour, the glockenspiel adds to New Ulm's charm. The bells play programmed musical pieces at noon, 3:00 P.M., and 5:00 P.M. Animated figures depict the city's history. Located at the **corner of Minnesota St. and Fourth N.**

Parks

Flandrau State Park

Flandrau is unique among the Minnesota state parks because it lies partly within an urban area. "Yes," says former park and current DNR employee Brenda Black, "this is the only state park where you can order a pizza and have it delivered." Still, Flandrau is far from citified, even if it's not in the wilderness. The Cottonwood River, a hunting ground for the Indians who preceded

The Harkin Store. Photo courtesy of the Minnesota Historical Society.

the European settlers, winds through the park. Gradually the river cut through 100–200 feet of glacial drift to the underlying sandstone, to form the park's valley. Buffalo bones can still sometimes be found in fresh gravel deposits along the riverbanks. The terrain of the park varies from oak-shaded bluffs along the river to marshland in the river bends. A hit with children and adults alike is the sand-bottomed, well-fed swimming pool. The park includes a playground, volleyball and horseshoe areas, and 60 picnic sites, in addition to campsites. Flandrau is several blocks southwest of Hwy. 15. From downtown, follow S. 10th St. to Summit Ave. and take a left to the park entrance. **1300 Summit Ave., New Ulm, 56073; 507-354-3519.**

Scenic Drives

Minnesota River Valley Scenic Byway

Watch for an eagle imposed on a sun—that's the sign for the Minnesota River Valley Scenic Byway. The byway crisscrosses the river, not always on the same road. From New Ulm toward Mankato, the byway is on Hwy 68. Northwest of New Ulm, take County Rds. 21 and 29 to Fort Ridgely. The scenery is pleasantly rural, with history around every bend in the river.

Tours

August Schell Brewery

August Schell created a little bit of Germany when he opened his brewery in 1860, later add-

ing an imposing house, formal gardens, and a deer park. Today, visitors can lap up history and sample Schell's beer, too, with a short brewery tour ending with generous tots of Schell's brews. The brewery escaped the destruction during the U.S.-Dakota Conflict of 1862 because of Schell's friendship with the Dakota, according to brewery information. Once one of five breweries in New Ulm, Schell's is the only one left. Until World War II, the brewery delivered beer to homes. The fifth generation of the family now runs the brewery. The house is not open, but the formal garden is. Exotic touches are the Edelweiss plants and the peacocks. Gift shop. Tours are given Memorial Day–Labor Day and during Oktoberfest. Call for hours. Fee for tour but not for the grounds. Located on the outskirts of New Ulm; go south on Broadway, then turn west on 18th S. and follow the signs; **507-354-5528.**

Where to Stay

New Ulm has several chain motels; contact the Chamber of Commerce (see Services) for a listing.

Camping

Flandrau State Park—$

Flandrau State Park, right in town, has 90 drive-in sites, 35 with electricity. For reservations, call **The Connection, 800-246-CAMP** or **612-922-9000.**

Where to Eat

Veigel's Kaiserhoff—$$ to $$$

Veigel's Kaiserhoff, a sprawling, informal downtown restaurant, has served German specialties for more than 50 years. Portions are more than ample. Even the appetizers have a German accent, with sauerkraut balls and marinated herring livening up the usual fare. Entrees include Wiener schnitzel, sauerkraut and braised ribs, and bratwurst or landjaeger (smoked pork and beef sausage) with hot German potato salad. Save room for the strudel. The restaurant is known for barbecue ribs and homemade sauce. Order a Schell's beer for a real New Ulm meal. Open Sun.–Thurs., 11:00 A.M.–9:00 P.M., and Fri.– Sat., 11:00 A.M.–10:00 P.M. **221 N. Minnesota, New Ulm, 56073; 507-359-2071.**

Lyle's Cafe—$

Winthrop, 16 miles north of New Ulm on Hwy. 15, is better known as the home of Lyle's Cafe. Some years ago, pie maker Mina Peterson was making pies by the dozens, when she was "discovered" by Dave Wood, a Minneapolis reporter. Mina's story appeared in *The Pie Lady of Winthrop and Other Minnesota Tales* (Neighbors Publishing, 1981), by Wood and Peg Meier. Mina's gone but two pie makers carry on. Lyle's has cream pies, berry pies, fruit pies, and nut pies. Have two pieces and order a third for the road. Lyle's has other food, too. Open Mon.–Fri., 6:00 A.M.– 8:00 P.M.; Sat., 7:00 A.M.–2:00 P.M.; Sun., 10:00 A.M.–2:00 P.M. **102 E. Fourth St., Winthrop, 55396; 507-647-9949.**

Services

New Ulm Area Chamber of Commerce/ Visitors Information Center, 1 N. Minnesota St., P.O. Box 384 VG, New Ulm, 56073; 888-4NEWULM or 507-233-4300.

Pipestone

Pipestone, which calls itself "the red stone city on the prairie," seems hyperactive in summer, when visitors pour into town to see Pipestone National Monument, take in an open-air performance of Longfellow's *Song of Hiawatha,* or make a pit stop on their way to or from the Black Hills in South Dakota. In other seasons, the city is far more tranquil and easier to appreciate.

Built out on what was the tallgrass prairie, Pipestone is atop the Coteau des Prairies—a flat-topped ridge that extends northward from Iowa. The ridge—which locals call Buffalo Ridge—is buoyed up nearly 1,000 feet by glacial drift and various types of rocks, including the Sioux quartzite of Pipestone National Monument. Pipestone has a population of 4,554. Its downtown, which some people miss if they only visit the monument, is beautiful, with many of its buildings constructed in the late 19th and early 20th centuries from the rosy Sioux quartzite quarried locally.

History

A succession of American Indian tribes lived around what is now the city of Pipestone, and Indians from across the continent visited the Pipestone quarry to obtain the red stone for making bowls of ceremonial "peace" pipes and other objects. The last to live here were the Dakota, who were here when the first European fur traders arrived.

The quarry first became well known among European Americans in the 19th century when artist George Catlin visited and sketched the quarry in 1836. Public interest in American Indian stories and places was stimulated when the poet Henry Wadsworth Longfellow, who never did visit Minnesota, scrambled several American Indian legends and sites together in his long poem *The Song of Hiawatha,* published in 1855. Early in

the poem the quarry is mentioned. The poem gained a huge following, with schoolchildren as far away as England learning it. It is the basis for Pipestone's annual open-air "Song of Hiawatha" pageant, held near the quarry.

The city's first European settlers were Charles Bennett and Daniel Sweet, who founded the city in 1876. The little settlement survived blizzards, grasshoppers, and prairie fires and became almost a boomtown by 1890, when the town was served by four railroads.

Major Attractions

Pipestone National Monument
Imagine the flat prairie slashed open with a sharp knife, revealing a secret world of waterfalls, wooded paths, and glowing red stone among harder, glittering quartzite—that is Pipestone National Monument. The quarry was used for centuries before it was protected as a national monument. Bowls for ceremonial American Indian

pipes are carved from the soft stone—officially called Catlinite. According to Chuck Derby, a Santee Dakota who once worked for the monument, carbon dating has shown that quarrying at Pipestone dates back to A.D. 900. The quarry was always a place of intertribal peace, Derby says. In addition, each person wishing to quarry the pipestone had to perform four ceremonies before reaching the quarry and working the layer of softer Catlinite out from between the layers of harder quartzite.

The monument, now 282 acres, was established in 1937. All people of American Indian ancestry can quarry the pipestone, provided they have tribal membership proof when they apply for a permit at the monument office. A 0.75-mile paved self-guided path accessible to wheelchairs takes visitors through rock formations to cool and pleasant Winnewissa waterfall. American Indians work at the monument, quarrying and working the stone into beautiful pipes, jewelry, and other works of art, some of which are for sale in the visitor center. A slide show and exhibits at the center present the culture and history of the area. There is a picnic area near the monument. The monument is open daily except for Christmas and New Year's Day. Fee. Located just north of Pipestone; follow signs from U.S. Hwy. 75 or Hwys. 23 or 30. For information: Pipestone National Monument, **36 Reservation Ave., Pipestone, 56164; 507-825-5464.**

Festivals and Events

Watertower Festival
last weekend in June
Pipestone's handsome stone and concrete water tower, which stands out on the flat prairie like a coastal lighthouse, is one of only two in the country; the other is in Brainerd. When the tower was restored in 1990, the city created "Watertower Festival," with a parade, street dance, and crafts fair and sales. The festival outgrew its original water-tower site and is now near the courthouse. Contact the Pipestone Area Chamber of Commerce and Convention and Visitors Bureau, **800-336-6125.**

"The Song of Hiawatha" Pageant
last two weekends in July, first weekend in Aug.

An abbreviated version of Longfellow's *The Song of Hiawatha,* with a cast of 200 from the community, has been presented each summer since the late '40s. The setting for the pageant is a natural amphitheater near the monument. Glacial boulders—called the Three Maidens—provide a backdrop. Fee. Parking off Hiawatha Ave. north of Main St. Call the Pipestone Area Chamber of Commerce and Convention and Visitors Bureau, **800-336-6125.**

Civil War Reenactment
mid-Aug., even-numbered years

Although no Civil War battles were fought in Minnesota, the Blue and the Gray go at it all over again every two years in a reenactment of other Civil War battles. Visitors can stroll through the historically correct encampment. Fee. Contact the Pipestone County Historical Museum (see Museums and Historic Sites) for details.

The Civil War Days Encampment, held every even-numbered year in Pipestone, draws 250 to 350 reenactors. Photo courtesy of the Pipestone Chamber of Commerce.

Getting There

Pipestone is approximately 190 miles southwest of the Twin Cities. Take Hwy. 212 west from Minneapolis, then Hwy. 23 south to Pipestone.

Outdoor Activities

Fishing

Bass, catfish, and northerns are in Split Rock Creek State Park's lake, the county's only lake. The lake is artificial, formed when Split Rock Creek was dammed in 1939. The lake is stocked with bass, catfish, and northerns and has a fishing pier (see Parks). For seasons and license information, call the Area Fisheries Supervisor in Windom, **507-831-2919.**

Hunting

Pheasants love to fatten up on the corn and soybean fields around Pipestone. Deer are also plentiful, as are ducks, to a lesser degree. Contact the Dept. of Natural Resources field office at Slayton, **507-836-6919.**

Snowmobiling

Pipestone County has nearly 100 miles of groomed snowmobile trails, including the popular 9-mile Casey Jones Trail from Pipestone to Woodstock. Access it at the junction of Hwys. 23 and 75 N. Contact the Pipestone Area Chamber of Commerce and Convention and Visitors Bureau, **800-336-6125.**

Seeing and Doing

Museums and Historic Sites

Little Feather Interpretive Center

Chuck Derby (Running Elk) is a jovial guy who uses humor and his storytelling skill to introduce audiences to Dakota history and culture. Derby, a Santee Dakota elder who worked at Pipestone National Monument for years, presents cultural

awareness programs on Dakota life at the center or off-site. The center has traveling and permanent exhibits on Dakota culture and sells beadwork, jewelry, pipes, and other objects made from pipestone, and books on Dakota history and life. Call for days and hours open, and for program charges. **317 Fourth St. NE, Pipestone, 56164; 507-825-3579.**

Pipestone County Historical Museum

The museum is housed in the former city hall, which was built of the beautiful local Sioux quartzite in 1896. It is a "must" stop for anyone interested in Minnesota, or for Kevin Costner fans. Exhibits include a Native American Gallery, with clothing, beadwork, peace pipes, weapons, and artifacts, most of which are of Dakota origin. In addition, there is a model of a sweat lodge. Kids and movie fans are delighted by the foam-and-fiber "buffaloid," one of 24 used for the four-minute buffalo hunt in Costner's film *Dances with Wolves.* The museum also has exhibits on artist George Catlin, early European settlement, and pioneer life. Catlin prints are sold in the gift shop. Fee. Open daily, 10:00 A.M.–5:00 P.M. **113 S. Hiawatha Ave., Pipestone, 56164; 507-825-2563. E-mail: pipctmu@rconnect.com.**

Parks

Harmon Park

Pipestone Family Aquatic Center, an outdoor pool complex in Harmon Park, has a water slide, drop slide, tanning hill, deck, and sand playground. The pool has "zero-depth" entry, so children get used to the gradually sloping pool as they would a natural beach. The park has a new playground, ball fields, and a sand volleyball court. Located at the intersection of Hwys. 30, 23, and 75 in Pipestone. For pool information, call **507-825-SWIM.**

Split Rock Creek State Park

The park has a swimming lake (formed when the creek was dammed in 1939) with a sandy beach; there are lakeside picnic tables. In summer the campground fills up often. Quartzite outcrops add interest to the park, which is set amid prairie farmland. Recent acquisitions will double park size. There is a 4.5-mile self-guided trail. Winter visitors slide, cross-country ski, or snowmobile. Boats, canoes, and paddleboats are for rent. Located 7 miles south of Pipestone on Hwy. 23. **R.R. 2, Jasper, 56144; 507-348-7908.**

Shopping

Monk's Second Hand

Rummage for treasures through the 23,000 square feet at Monk's. In business for decades, Monk's has antiques, furniture, and all kinds of doodads. Stuffed critters adorn the walls. Open Mon.–Sat., 9:00 A.M.–5:00 P.M., and Sun., 1:00–5:00 P.M. **504 Eighth Ave. SE, Pipestone, 56164; 507-825-5719.**

Sports

Ewert Recreation Center

The center has a small swimming pool, whirlpool, weight and exercise room, steam room, gym, and handball and racquetball courts. Visitors are welcome. Fee. Open daily year-round. Call for hours. **115 N. Hiawatha, Pipestone, 56164; 507-825-5834.**

Tours

WALKING TOURS

The entire historic district of Pipestone, consisting largely of rose-red, hand-hewn quartzite buildings, is on the National Register of Historic Places. The Moore block, on the southeast corner at the intersection of Hiawatha and Main Sts., is adorned with amazing and amusing gargoyles carved out of sandstone. A tour brochure is available from the Pipestone Area Chamber of Commerce and Convention and Visitors Bureau, **800-336-6125.**

Where to Stay

Hotels, Motels, and Inns

Historic Calumet Inn—$$$

Completed in 1888, the hotel has been redone

and is a wonderful getaway. The exterior is grayish pink quartzite, trimmed in red quartzite. A two-story wall of the red stone is inside the entry. Some of the 38 rooms have modern decor, but many are furnished in Victorian antiques, including claw-foot tubs. It's the best of both worlds; all rooms have cable TV and private baths. A hefty continental breakfast is included. **104 W. Main, Pipestone, 56164; 800-535-7610** or **507-825-5871.**

Camping

Pipestone RV Campground—$ to $$

The campground, across from the pageant grounds, is one of the few campgrounds to rent tepees. Two tepees, with carpeted floor and each holding up to six adults, are for rent, as are 55 RV sites and 13 tent sites. The campground has a heated swimming pool, playground, and horseshoe pitch. Reservations are a must during pageant weekends. A gift shop and grocery store are also on-site. **919 N. Hiawatha, Pipestone, 56164; 507-825-2455.**

Split Rock Creek State Park—$

The park has 28 campsites, two of them handicapped-accessible, 19 with electricity. For reservations, call **The Connection, 800-246-CAMP** or **612-922-9000.**

Where to Eat

Historic Calumet Inn—$$ to $$$

The hotel's country-style dining room offers standards and some surprises, such as steak tournedos topped with onions, peppers, garlic, and béarnaise sauce. The crusty buns are made fresh for each meal. Open Mon.–Thurs., 9:00 A.M.–9:00 P.M.; Fri., 9:00 A.M.–10:00 P.M.; Sat., 7:30 A.M.–10:00 P.M.; Sun., 7:30 A.M.–9:00 P.M. **104 W. Main, Pipestone, 56164; 800-535-7610** or **507-825-5871.**

Lange's Cafe—$ to $$

When the late Les Lange opened his cafe more than 40 years ago, he declared it would always be open, and buried the key beneath the con-

A waterfall in Pipestone National Monument. Copyright © Minnesota Office of Tourism. Used by permission.

crete to back up his pledge. Les kept his promise: the cafe, a magnet for folks who like good home cooking and wonderful pie, has never closed. His son Steve keeps the cafe open 24 hours a day, 365 days a year. It's a busy place at mealtimes, with tasty food served fast and efficiently. About a dozen kinds of pies are available every day; favorites, according to the staff, are banana cream, coconut cream, and sour cream raisin. Located on the eastern end of Pipestone, **on Hwy. 75 south of Hwy. 23; 507-825-4488.**

Services

Pipestone Area Chamber of Commerce and Convention and Visitors Bureau, 117 Eighth Ave. SE, P.O. Box 8, Pipestone, 56164; 800-336-6125 or 507-825-3316.

Redwood Falls

Redwood Falls, a thriving city of about 5,000 on the Minnesota River, is amid some of Minnesota's most productive farmland. A regional agricultural and trade center, it's ideal for exploring the Upper Minnesota River Valley, which is rich in history and in natural beauty.

Recent human history, specifically the 1862 U.S.-Dakota Conflict, has forever marked the Upper Minnesota Valley, but the natural history of the valley is also compelling. Local outcrops of rock termed Morton Gneiss (pronounced "nice") are a whopping 3.5 billion years old, according to Constance Jefferson Sansome's *Minnesota Underfoot,* making them perhaps the oldest rocks in the world. The multicolored swirled gneiss, found near Morton and other valley areas, is similar to granite in composition and is gray, red, and black. The broad Minnesota River Valley was formed by the Glacial River Warren, flowing out of Glacial Lake Agassiz 9,000–12,000 years ago. The current Minnesota River—except when it's flooding—is dwarfed by the size of its valley.

History

The Dakota Indians were the latest in a series of people who lived in the Upper Minnesota Valley, and it was along the Minnesota River that the U.S.–Dakota Conflict took place in 1862. The U.S.–Dakota Conflict, a term now preferred to the more inflammatory "Sioux Uprising," was a bloody six weeks that left about 500 white settlers and an unknown number of Dakota killed. It precipitated a 30-year period of war between the U.S. government and the Dakota that ranged far beyond Minnesota.

The trouble had been brewing since the treaty of 1851, in which four Dakota bands ceded most of southern Minnesota in return for a reservation along the Upper Minnesota, and another treaty in 1858, which took away about half of that reservation land. Treaty terms promised the Dakota money and food, but the government—immersed in the Civil War—was often late in paying and had not paid in the summer of 1862, when the Dakota were starving because the 1861 crop had failed and the new crop was not yet ready.

The conflict that resulted from the broken promises wasn't just a clear-cut case of whites vs. Dakota. The Dakota were in a state of flux: the government attempted to change traditional Dakota culture, convincing some Dakota to cut their hair, turn to farming instead of hunting, and adopt the ways of the whites. Some of the Dakota, such as Chief Little Crow (Taoyateduta)—later reviled by whites as the leader of the attacking Dakota—attempted to coexist peacefully with the white settlers, traders, and government officials while still keeping their traditional ways. The "blanket" Dakota and the "cut hair" Dakota were often scornful of each other. In addition, there was another faction: many Dakota were of mixed blood, and their allegiances varied greatly.

Chronology of the Conflict

There were some immediate catalysts for the start

of the conflict: the Dakota were insulted by Andrew Myrick, a white trader at the Lower Sioux Agency, who made an infamous remark—"let them eat grass or their own dung"—to the hungry Dakota, who had demanded their promised food. And, in the first actual bloodshed, four Dakota braves—in anger, in frustration, or on a dare—killed five white settlers near Acton on Aug. 17, 1862.

Between the two events, some of the Dakota decided they had nothing to lose and enlisted Little Crow, against his better judgment, in their cause. After some of the braves accused him of cowardice, he made an eloquent speech, related by his son later. He defended himself and warned of the inexhaustible number of whites, but cast his lot with the Dakota nonetheless, ending with a prediction and a promise:

You are fools … you will die like the rabbits when the hungry wolves hunt them in the Hard Moon. Taoyateduta is not a coward: he will die with you.

The Mdewakanton Dakotas attacked the Lower Sioux Agency on Aug. 18; one of the first whites to die was Myrick, found with grass stuffed in his mouth in retaliation for his remark. The fighting ended after six weeks and several battles between the Dakotas and government forces, plus raids in which settlers were attacked. Little Crow and others fled, but many other Dakota were captured; 38 were hanged (see the Mankato and St. Peter chapter in this section). Little Crow was killed in 1863—as he was picking raspberries—by a settler who had no idea he was killing a major figure in Minnesota history. The Dakota were turned out of their reservation after the conflict, and began returning about 20 years later.

Recommended Reading

The best general account of the conflict is still Kenneth Carley's *The Sioux Uprising of 1862* (Minnesota Historical Society, 1976). *Little Crow—Spokesman for the Sioux* (Minnesota Historical Society, 1986) is a biography of the complex Dakota leader by Gary C. Anderson, who is co-author, with Alan Woolworth, of *Through Dakota Eyes—Narrative Accounts of the Minnesota Indian War of 1862* (Minnesota Historical Society, 1988). The

latter provides accounts by Dakota and people of mixed heritage who were involved in or witnessed the conflict. Fiction lovers may enjoy Frederick Manfred's bloody, sexy, and compelling *Scarlet Plume* (Trident Press, 1964).

Major Attractions

U.S.–Dakota Conflict

The reasons for the U.S.-Dakota Conflict are complex, according to Tom Ellig, director of historic sites for the southern district of the Minnesota Historical Society. "It was a clash of cultures," says Ellig. "If there had been an attempt at greater understanding, perhaps things would have been different. Here [at the Lower Sioux Agency] we try to focus not so much on events, but on the cause and effects."

Lower Sioux Agency

The Lower Sioux Agency, site of the first major event of the conflict, is a good place to begin in trying to understand the U.S.–Dakota Conflict. On Aug. 18, 1862, the Dakota attacked and destroyed Agency buildings, took food, and killed some of the people living near the Agency. A stone warehouse being restored is all that remains of the once-thriving Agency of 1862. An exhibit and slide show introduce events in Dakota history that led to the conflict. The museum shop has books on Dakota life and history, as well as Dakota handmade items. Outside, a footpath leads to the Redwood Ferry site, where the Dakota fought troops from Fort Ridgely. The Agency, a Minnesota Historical Society site, is open May 1–Labor Day, Mon.–Sat., 10:00 A.M.–5:00 P.M., and Sun., noon–5:00 P.M.; Labor Day–Oct., daily, 1:00–5:00 P.M. Fee. Located 9 miles east of Redwood Falls, on County Hwy. 2. Contact the Agency at **32469 County Hwy. 2, Morton, 56270; 507-697-6321.**

Birch Coulee Battlefield

The battle of Birch Coulee, a major clash between the Dakota and U.S. troops, lasted approximately 36 hours. There is a trail to the battlefield and an interpretive kiosk. Recent changes include a new parking lot and improved access road. The battlefield is about 2 miles north of Morton off Hwy.

71; turn east onto County Rd. 2. Contact the Lower Sioux Agency, **507-697-6321.**

Fort Ridgely

Fort Ridgely, built in 1853 as a frontier peace-keeping station, tells the story of the Dakota Conflict. Inside the fort's restored stone commissary is a video, a scale model of the fort, and exhibits. The fort was attacked twice by the Dakota, on Aug. 20 and 22, 1862. Outside, foundations of buildings within the fort's boundaries have been reconstructed and interpretive markers placed. Near the fort is a cemetery where many involved in the conflict—including Eliza Muller, who both nursed the wounded and took an active part in the fort's defense—are buried. Entrance is free, but visitors need a state park admission sticker. Open May–Labor Day, Tues.–Sat., 10:00 A.M.–5:00 P.M.; Sun. (and holiday Mon.), 1:00–5:00 P.M. Located 7 miles south of Fairfax off Hwy. 4. Contact the fort at **R.R. 1, Box 65A, Fairfax, 55332; 507-426-7888** or **507-697-6321.**

Upper Sioux Agency

The Upper Sioux Agency was attacked on the evening of Aug. 18, 1862, and John Other Day, a Dakota friendly to the settlers, hid residents from the Indians. The Agency played a key role in the start of the conflict. Today the Agency is within Upper Sioux Agency State Park. There are interpretive markers describing the site's history. At the site is a brick duplex (not open), which housed Agency workers, and the faintly discernible foundations of other buildings. The Minnesota Historical Society owns the site, but there is no on-site staff. Contact the Lower Sioux Agency, **507-697-6321.**

Festivals and Events

Minnesota Inventors Congress
second full Fri.–Sun. in June

In one of the state's most unusual events, inventors—about 100 adults and even more young inventors—exhibit their inventions, sometimes to a crowd of 10,000. The inventions run the gamut from those that become household names—such as NordicTrack—to ideas that die quickly. The congress, first held in 1958, is the

Getting There
Redwood Falls is approximately 125 miles from the Twin Cities, via U.S. Hwys. 212 and 71; an alternate route is Hwy. 169 to Hwy. 19 west.

oldest continuously operating inventors convention in the world, according to congress staff. It's held at the Redwood Valley School. Fee. The office is open year-round, **507-637-2344.**

Lower Sioux Wacipi (Dance)
second full weekend in June

For more than 20 years, the Mdewakanton Dakota community has held an annual traditional *Wacipi* (dance), with drumming, dancing, and traditional singers, at the Lower Sioux Community in Morton, 6 miles east of Redwood Falls. Participants and visitors come from all over the United States and Canada. The Wacipi also has craft and food stands. Fee. For information, call the Redwood Area Chamber of Commerce and Tourism (see Services).

Corn Capital Days
Wed.–Sun., last week of July

There *is* such a thing as a free lunch. It's a sweet-corn feed, with beans and watermelon thrown in. The corn feed, which lures several thousand, uses 4,000 cobs of corn. The five-day festival includes a crafts fair, parade, and games for kids; the corn feed is on Sat., 11:00 A.M.–1:00 P.M. Held at Nester Park in Olivia, at the intersection of Hwys. 212 and 71. Call the Olivia Chamber of Commerce, **320-523-1350** or **888-265-2676.**

Farmfest
first Tues.–Thurs. in Aug.

Farmfest is an agricultural trade show with trimmings. The three-day fest, with representatives of 400 companies spread over 50 acres, lets farmers see agricultural products and equipment up close and test drive some of the machines. The show also features antique farm machinery, a crafts fair and toy show, food stands, and country music. Up to 60,000 people attend. Fee. Held at the Gilfillan Estate (see Museums and Historic Sites), on Hwy. 67 between Redwood Falls and Morton. **800-347-5863.**

Outdoor Activities

Birding

Lac qui Parle State Park, located at the southern end of the "lake" (actually the upper reaches of the Minnesota River), offers prime waterfowl- and bird-watching. Many visitors come to watch migrating geese and swans pass through the area in fall and spring, and pelicans nest on a small island in the area. Upper Sioux Agency State Park is also a bird-watcher's paradise; they'll find here blue herons, pelicans, belted kingfishers, shore-birds, and raptors such as red-tailed hawks. See Parks.

Boating

The Minnesota River is a popular canoeing river, and a good choice for neophytes as it is relatively calm, with light rapids above and below Granite Falls. Maps, with access points, campsites, and other information, are available from the **Dept. of Natural Resources, 500 Lafayette Rd., St. Paul, 55155; 888-MINNDNR or 651-296-6157.**

Fishing

The Minnesota River, now on its way to recovery from contamination, offers some good fishing, especially in Lac qui Parle Lake. Ramsey Creek in Redwood Falls is stocked annually with German brown trout. The Yellow Medicine River, in part of Upper Sioux State Park, has smallmouth bass, and the Minnesota River has walleyes, northerns, catfish, bullheads, and carp. Consult the state fish consumption advisories for safety suggestions in eating bottom feeders. For information on season, licenses, and attaining a fish consumption guide, call the **DNR, 888-MINNDNR or 651-296-6157.**

Golf

Golfers like Fort Ridgely State Park's hilly and wooded nine-hole golf course with artificial grass greens, which are slated for replacement. The course was built in 1925 and has very narrow fairways. Clubs can be rented. Greens fees are $6–$9. Open approximately Apr. 1–mid-Oct., dusk to dawn. **507-426-7840.**

Redwood Falls Golf Club

Next to spectacular Alexander Ramsey Park, this nine-hole, 36-par course has a sweeping view of the valley. Deer and other wildlife are frequent course visitors. Regulars say the third hole, be-tween the river and the woods, is the toughest. Visitors can obtain playing privileges at the private club. Rental clubs and lessons are available. Greens fees for 18 holes are $20 Mon.–Fri., $22 Sat.–Sun. Open Apr.–Oct., dusk to dawn. **107 E. Oak, Redwood Falls, 56283; 507-637-8901.**

Hiking

There are no state hiking (or biking) trails in the area, but there are hiking trails in state parks as well as in Ramsey Park, the Lower Sioux Agency, and Lac qui Parle Wildlife Management Area (see Hunting). Fort Ridgely State Park has 11 miles for hiking. Lac qui Parle State Park has 6 miles of hiking trails. In Upper Sioux Agency State Park, hikers have 16 miles of trails as well as two 0.75-mile river trails. See Parks.

Hunting

Hunters come to the Redwood Falls area for the abundant waterfowl and for partridge, pheasant, ruffed grouse, and deer. For information, call the DNR office in Redwood Falls, **507-637-4076.**

Lac qui Parle Wildlife Management Area

Stretching over a four-county area, the wildlife management area consists of more than 48 square miles of water and land. Within it are two huge lakes—Lac qui Parle Lake and Marsh Lake—and varying habitats, including wetlands, woodlands, and prairie, perfect for waterfowl and other birds, as well as animals and fish. Hikers as well as hunt-ers and trappers come to the area. A controlled goose hunt is held in designated hunting stations; those interested in hunting and trapping should contact the management headquarters. Camping is not permitted, nor is trespassing within the wild-life sanctuary area Sept. 20–Dec. 1 (but fishing is allowed on Lac qui Parle Lake following the goose hunt). Headquarters is on the northeast side of Lac qui Parle Lake between Watson and Milan, off U.S. Hwy. 59 on County Rd. 32. **14047 20th St. NW, Watson, 56295; 320-734-4451.**

Snowmobiling

Many local snowmobile clubs along the Minnesota River Valley maintain groomed trails. Fort Ridgely State Park has 9 miles of snowmobile trails. Upper Sioux Agency State Park has 16 miles of trails. Contact the Redwood Area Chamber of Commerce and Tourism (see Services).

Seeing and Doing

Museums and Historic Sites

Gilfillan Estate

The Gilfillan mansion and estate southeast of Redwood Falls testify to one man's dream. Charles D. Gilfillan, who made his money with a water system for St. Paul, bought 13,000 acres of prairie near Redwood Falls in 1882 and built a big house, offices, water tower, grain elevator, stockyard, and tenant homes. The estate was eventually subdivided and the farm site given to the Redwood County Historical Society. It's been restored and furnished in period style and can be seen Memorial Day–Labor Day, Sat.–Sun., 1:00–5:00 P.M. Fee. Located **8 miles east of Redwood Falls on Hwy. 67; 507-644-2490 or 507-249-3451.**

Lac qui Parle Mission

Joseph Renville, half Dakota and half French, was an explorer and fur trader who built a trading post on the shore of Lac qui Parle Lake and invited missionaries—who built the mission, one of the state's first churches—to the area. Renville was the link between the missionaries and the Dakota, and helped translate the Bible and hymns into the Dakota language. A wooden chapel, on the site of the original adobe church, has exhibits on the mission, the Dakota, and Renville. Up the hill overlooking the lake are missionary cabin sites. The chapel is open Memorial Day–Labor Day, but visitors can see the sites anytime. Free. There is no on-site staff. Located northwest of Montevideo, the mission is reached by going north on U.S. Hwy. 59 for 6 miles, then west on Hwy. 13 for 2.2 miles and right at the corner. The site, owned by the Minnesota Historical Society, is operated by the

Chippewa County Historical Society, **P.O. Box 303, Montevideo, 56265; 320-269-7636.**

Redwood County Museum

Once the county poor farm, the 30-room Redwood County Museum has many artifacts showing what middle-class life was like in the late 19th and early 20th centuries. The museum also has an exhibit of rare birds and a collection of antique machinery. A special exhibit contains information about the 46 inventors in the Minnesota Inventors Hall of Fame. A one-room schoolhouse is on the museum grounds. Open May 1–Sept. 30, Thurs.–Sun., 1:00–5:00 P.M. Located on **Hwy. 19 west of town; 507-637-3329.**

Parks

Alexander Ramsey Park

This park surprises first-time visitors driving into what appears to be flat Redwood Falls. The park, the largest municipal park in Minnesota, is in a deep and scenic valley formed by the Redwood River and Ramsey Creek. It was once part of the state park system, and a piece of music, "The Ramsey Park March," was composed for it in 1919. The city bought the park from the state in 1957 for $1. It's a local jewel, and free. Among the attractions of the 217-acre haven are two spectacular waterfalls—Ramsey Falls and Redwood Falls. Ramsey Falls is a rushing tumble in summer and an ice palace in winter. It is possible to drive fairly close, with a short walk to an observation deck. A hiking trail leads across the creek and behind the falls. Redwood Falls, on the Redwood River, is accessible only on foot. There is also a good view from a public terrace on Bridge St., above the park. The park has a popular zoo, 3.5 miles of hiking trails, and a 28-unit campground. It's on the northwest end of town; turn north on Lincoln St. and follow the signs. For information, call the Redwood Area Chamber of Commerce and Tourism, **800-657-7070 or 507-637-2828.**

Fort Ridgely State Park

This is a park of great diversity. The fort itself was the site of one of the major battles of the U.S.–Dakota Conflict (see History, and Major Attractions). There are also traditional pastimes. In winter, there is a sliding hill—with a warming house—as well as 4 miles for cross-country skiing. In summer, there are 9 miles of riding trails, a golf course, and picnic areas. The 584-acre park lies on the north bluff of the Minnesota River Valley, with wooded ravines as well as the open, riverside bluffs, where prairie wildflowers and grasses make a grand display in summer and fall. The park is 6 miles south of Fairfax on Hwy. 4, with the park entrance off Hwy. 29. **Rte. 1, Box 65, Fairfax, 55332; 507-426-7840.**

Lac qui Parle State Park

In the upper reaches of the Minnesota River, deltas formed where tributaries join it, causing it to balloon out to form areas like Lac qui Parle. The Dakota who lived there called it the "lake that talks." Early French explorers translated the name verbatim. A narrow strip of the park is on the lake's western shore, and it has picnic facilities, a boat launch area, and a natural sand beach, the only area of the lakeshore that is not rocky. The 570-acre park has 6 miles of hiking trails, 5 miles of which are used for horseback riding, and 5 miles of cross-country ski trails. A federal dam and recreation area with picnic tables is at the east end of the park, south of County Rds. 13 and 33. The park is 12 miles northwest of Montevideo off County Rd. 33. **Rte. 5, Box 74A, Montevideo, 56265; 320-752-4736.**

Upper Sioux Agency State Park

The Minnesota River and its wily little brother, the Yellow Medicine River, run roughly parallel for a time, until the Yellow Medicine swings sharply up to join the Minnesota. In this hilly "tongue" of land, made up of wooded slopes, river bluffs, and prairie, lies Upper Sioux Agency State Park and the old Upper Sioux Agency. Butterflies, and the prairie flowers they love, are abundant in summer. The grasslands are dotted with ancient, spreading bur oaks. High up in the park are lookouts over both rivers. A picnic area is near the historic site. Horses, hikers, and, in winter, snowmobilers share 16 miles of trails, and there are two 0.75-mile river trails, with brochures available from the park office. In winter, the park has a sliding hill and a warming

house. Visitors can also rent snowshoes. The park is 8 miles southeast of Granite Falls. **Rte. 2, Box 92, Granite Falls, 56241; 320-564-4777.**

Performing Arts

DANCE

Dakota Dance Troupe

Cansa'yapi Oyate, a traditional Dakota dance group, performs at places such as the Lower Sioux Agency and can be booked for educational performances and Dakota culture programs. Contact Michael and Kateri Lucio, **P.O. Box 247, Morton, 56270; 507-697-6431.**

Scenic Drives

Minnesota River Valley Scenic Byway

Meander along the Minnesota River Valley's scenic byway, but go slowly on the gravel section between Fort Ridgely and Granite Falls. Turn right from Fort Ridgely State Park to get on the byway, and follow the distinctive signs—an eagle superimposed on a sun.

Shopping

Birch Coulee Pottery

Dennis McLaughlin is a potter with a strong sense of place. McLaughlin, raised close to his current studio and home near Morton, says his stoneware pottery "is a reflection of who I am. I see myself as a prairie person and I am strongly influenced by my environment. I look at the natural forms here, such as Morton Gneiss [see chapter introduction], and try to recapture that rock in my work." The result of McLaughlin's efforts are sturdy stoneware pottery pieces in various finishes, including a celadon glaze and a wood ash glaze. He makes baking and serving pieces, as well as candle lanterns with cutouts to let the flame glow through, and dinnerware on commission. Visitors are welcome in his studio and adjacent showroom. Located next to the Birch Coulee Battlefield, 1.5 miles north of Morton; turn east onto County Rd. 2 from Hwy. 71. Contact him at **68634 County Rd. 18, Morton, 56270; 507-697-6372.**

Wagering

Jackpot Junction Casino Hotel

Gaming is a Dakota tradition, and Jackpot Junction is gaming gone big-time and nonstop—with more than 1,000 loose slots, 48 blackjack tables, bingo, and pull tabs. The complex includes entertainment with big-name stars and several restaurants. The casino has its own hotel and RV park but also offers shuttle service from hotels in the area. The casino is in the Lower Sioux Community at Morton, on **County Rd. 24, just off U.S. Hwy. 71 and Hwy. 19; 800-WIN-CASH.**

Where to Stay

Hotels, Motels, and Inns

Redwood Falls and its surrounding area have several motels in addition to the hotel at Jackpot Junction. Ask the Redwood Area Chamber of Commerce and Tourism (see Services) for a listing.

Lower Sioux Lodge—$$$ to $$$$

The lodge, at one end of the sprawling Jackpot Junction Casino Hotel complex (see Wagering), has 168 rooms and suites, all with computer modem hookups, as well as an indoor heated pool and spa, a sauna, and a workout center. If you don't want to leave the premises, the complex has three restaurants and four bars. On County Rd. 24, just off U.S. Hwy. 71 and Hwy. 19. For information or reservations: **Box 420, Morton, 56270; 507-644-4000.**

Camping

Alexander Ramsey Park—$

It's first-come, first-served here. There are 28 campsites, some with electricity. Showers are available. The park is on the northwest side of the city; follow Lincoln St. north, and take a left on Oak St. to the park. **507-637-5755.**

Jackpot Junction RV Park—$

A 40-unit RV park, with sewer and electrical hookups, is located in back of the casino (see Wagering). Ask about memberships that give discounts for the park and the casino. Located in Morton, on County Rd. 24, just off U.S. Hwy. 71 and Hwy. 19. **800-538-8379.**

State Parks—$

Fort Ridgely State Park near Fairfax has 39 drive-in sites, eight with electricity, and also three walk-in sites and 20 horsecamp sites, with a capacity of 80. **Upper Sioux Agency State Park** close to Granite Falls has 45 drive-in sites, 14 with electricity, and also two walk-in campsites and 45 horsecamp sites. **Lac qui Parle State Park,** near Madison and Montevideo, suffered damage during the floods of 1997. Check with the park before heading there; **320-752-4736.** Before the flood, there were 41 drive-in sites, 21 with electricity, 11 walk-in sites, and five horsecamp sites, with a capacity of 50. For state park camping reservations, call **The Connection, 800-246-CAMP** or **612-922-9000.**

Where to Eat

Valley Supper Club—$ to $$$

Redwood Falls' Valley Supper Club serves as a local meeting place as well as a restaurant, according to owner Karen Ness. The Nesses bought the supper club in 1986, and it is a popular place for lunch and dinner. The supper menu consists mainly of the basics—steaks, seafood, and ribs—with huge popovers a specialty. The Nesses also feature homemade soups. Open Mon.–Thurs., 11:00 A.M.–1:30 P.M. and 5:00–9:00 P.M.; Fri., 11:00 A.M.–1:30 P.M. and 5:00–10:00 P.M.; Sat., 5:00–10:00 P.M.; Sun., 11:00 A.M.–1:30 P.M. Located 1.5 miles north of Redwood Falls, in what used to be North Redwood. **110 Front St., Redwood Falls, 56283; 507-637-5541.**

Services

Redwood Area Chamber of Commerce and Tourism, 610 E. Bridge St., Redwood Falls, 56283; 800-657-7070 or **507-637-2828.**

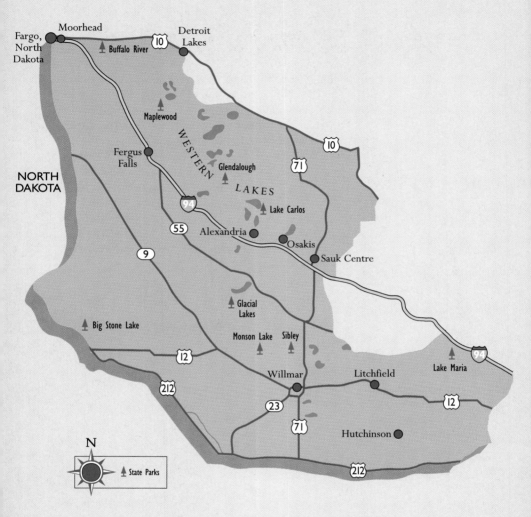

Moorhead

Fargo,
North
Dakota

Buffalo River

Detroit
Lakes

10

Maplewood

WESTERN

NORTH
DAKOTA

Fergus
Falls

Glendalough

LAKES

10

71

94

Lake Carlos

55

Alexandria

Osakis

9

Sauk Centre

Glacial
Lakes

Big Stone Lake

Monson Lake

Sibley

12

Litchfield

Lake Maria

94

Willmar

212

23

12

71

Hutchinson

212

N

State Parks

West-Central Region

West-Central Region

Boating on a Minnesota lake's glasslike surface provides quiet solitude. Copyright © Minnesota Office of Tourism. Used by permission.

Fargo-Moorhead

These are the other Twin Cities you might hear about in Minnesota. Moorhead, the smaller, has 34,000 residents, while Fargo, across the Red River in North Dakota, outdoes its sister city with 83,000 inhabitants. The two cities together form a metropolitan area that dominates the west and northwest sector of Minnesota and eastern North Dakota. (Because these cities are as linked as Minneapolis and St. Paul, this book includes Fargo, though it's not in Minnesota.)

Fargo-Moorhead is home to several colleges: Concordia College and Moorhead State University are in Moorhead, while North Dakota State University is across the river in Fargo, North Dakota. All three have thriving arts programs that are open to the public (see Performing Arts); Concordia is particularly well known for its music, including its annual Christmas concert.

Does Fargo the city bear any resemblance to *Fargo*, the award-winning Coen brothers' movie? Yes and no. There's plenty of snow and ice and lots of Scandinavians in Fargo, North Dakota, but the movie was set mostly in Brainerd, Minnesota, where (yup) you can also find snow, ice, and Scandinavians.

Fargo-Moorhead is a world away from Hollywood. Located in the Red River Valley, the cities are economic and shopping centers for a good portion of northwestern Minnesota and eastern North Dakota. The cities still retain separate identities, but cooperate on many things, including a single convention and visitors bureau. Neither city is a great beauty overall, though both have extensive and attractive park systems. There is an active arts community in each, partly due to the presence of the colleges.

History

One of Fargo's main streets is called N.P. (Northern Pacific) Ave., which suggests the importance

of the railroad to the early days of the city and of Moorhead across the river. The railroad came through in the early 1870s, and it was then that a riptide of settlers came in, seeking homesteads on the rich black soil of the Red River Valley. From 1879 to 1886, more than 100,000 European settlers came to settle in what was then the Dakota Territory, though American Indians were the first inhabitants.

The new farmers grew wheat, barley, and flax and later added sunflowers and sugar beets to the string of principal crops. The harvests were gratifying, except for the drought years of the 1930s. So much wheat was produced there that others took to calling the Red River Valley "the breadbasket of the world." Much of the research to create new varieties of grains was and still is done at North Dakota State University in Fargo. All this agricultural activity benefited the nearby cities and they are dependent on it to this day.

Even before the wholesale European settlement, there was considerable traffic along the Red River, both by American Indians who lived in the area and by Red River oxcarts, making their way from Winnipeg, Manitoba, down to St. Paul. The

Red River, a docile sight most of the year, can swell alarmingly, most recently in the terrible flood of 1997. Although Fargo was affected by the flood, it was the area to the north, especially around Grand Forks, that bore the brunt of the disaster.

Festivals and Events

Scandinavian Hjemkomst Festival
third or fourth weekend in June
Celebrate the ethnic contributions of the Nordic nations at this festival, on the grounds of the Heritage Hjemkomst Interpretive Center in Moorhead and also at Trollwood Park in Fargo. The festival includes dancing, entertainment, workshops, crafts, and Nordic foods. Free. **218-233-8484.**

Jazz in the Park
late July or early Aug.
You can hear jazz morning (well, almost), noon, and night during Fargo's River Jazz festival, sponsored by KDSU, the public radio station at North Dakota State University. Most events during the festival are outdoors and free, and all genres of jazz are represented, played in as many as 20 sessions by jazz musicians of regional and national note. The festival lasts sometimes just a weekend, and sometimes a week long, depending on the station's budget. **KDSU, 701-241-6900.**

Pioneer Days
third weekend in Aug.
The pioneer past comes alive at Bonanzaville USA in West Fargo with demonstrations of bygone skills and crafts such as weaving and candle dipping by costumed volunteers. Other events include a country market, singing, and dancing. All are held at Bonanzaville USA in West Fargo. Fee. **1351 W. Main Ave., West Fargo, ND 58078; 800-700-5317** or **701-282-2822.**

Western Minnesota Steam Threshers Reunion
Labor Day weekend
See how farming was done in the old days at the Threshers Reunion in Rollag, 45 minutes

---

Getting There
There is an airport in Fargo. For drivers, Fargo-Moorhead is about a five-hour trip from Minneapolis–St. Paul on I-94. Fargo, North Dakota, is right across the Red River from Moorhead, Minnesota.

from Fargo-Moorhead. The demonstrations of steam engines, horse-drawn machinery, and old-fashioned crafts on 230 acres of land draw thousands of spectators each year, making the Steam Threshers Reunion one of the largest events of its kind in the country. There are parades at 10:00 A.M. and 2:00 P.M. All this is done to the accompaniment of many musical groups. From Fargo-Moorhead, take I-94 east, then go east on County Rd. 10 and jog onto Hwy. 32. For information, call Virgil Gunnarson, **218-438-3215.**

Outdoor Activities

Birding
In Buffalo River State Park (see Parks) there are many kinds of birds, including the greater prairie chicken, sandhill crane, bobolink, and eastern meadowlark. In the spring, visitors to Bluestem Prairie Scientific and Natural Area (see Parks) can observe the "booming" (courtship activity) of the greater prairie chicken from blinds in the preserve; reservations—made through the office in March—are necessary.

Hiking
Buffalo River State Park has 12 miles of hiking trails. A 2.1-mile trail provides a good look at the prairie, and two self-guided interpretive trails, each about 0.5 mile long, point out park features. See Parks.

Skiing

CROSS-COUNTRY
There are 6 miles of groomed trails at Buffalo River State Park, plus a warming house to get out of the cold wind; ask at the Fargo-Moorhead

The Viking ship Hjemkomst, *in Moorhead. Copyright © Minnesota Office of Tourism. Used by permission.*

Convention and Visitors Bureau (see Services) for other trails in the area.

Snowmobiling

There are no snowmobile trails in Buffalo River State Park. Inquire at the Fargo-Moorhead Convention and Visitors Bureau (see Services) for a map of other areas.

Seeing and Doing

Art Galleries and Museums

Plains Art Museum

Recently moved into larger quarters in a historic building in downtown Fargo, the Plains Art Museum has a large collection of regional art and also art and artifacts—including baskets and clothing—from Plains and Woodland American Indian cultures. In addition, there is a collection of East African art. The museum, a nonprofit organization that is not state supported, has a restaurant and museum store. Open Wed., Fri., and Sat., 10:00 A.M.–6:00 P.M.; Tues. and Thurs., 10:00 A.M.–8:00 P.M.; Sun.,

noon–6:00 P.M. **704 First Ave. N., Fargo, ND 58102; 701-232-3821.**

Rourke Art Gallery and Museum

Brothers and artists James O'Rourke and the late Orland Rourke started their gallery, which showcases regional artists, in 1960. In 1975 they added a museum, with a permanent collection of art. Focus of the museum is contemporary art, much of it done by Midwestern artists, and American Indian and African art. There are a number of shows annually at both the gallery and museum. Among the gallery's recent shows has been art done by brothers, including the O'Rourke-Rourke brothers. Both the gallery and museum are open Fri.–Sun., 1:00–5:00 P.M. The museum is housed in the historic 1913 Moorhead post office, **521 Main Ave.,** and the gallery is in one of Moorhead's historic houses, at **523 Fourth St. S., Moorhead, 56560; 218-236-8861.**

Museums and Historic Sites

Bonanzaville USA

Named for the so-called bonanza farms—large wheat-producing farms to the west of Fargo—

Bonanzaville USA offers a peek at the area's past, with a sod house, log cabin, church, and other buildings transported to the 15-acre site. There are exhibits of antique cars, airplanes, and farm equipment and interpretive services by costumed living-history staff. Bonanzaville is part of the Cass County Historical Society, whose indoor museum and offices are at the same site. Bonanzaville is open June–Oct., daily, 9:00 A.M.–5:00 P.M.; the Cass County Historical Society is open year-round, Mon.–Fri., 9:00 A.M.–5:00 P.M. Fee. **1351 W. Main Ave., West Fargo, ND 58078; 800-700-5317 or 701-282-2822.**

Comstock House

The Comstock House, a stately Victorian frame house shaded by huge elms and surrounded by a lovely green lawn, old-fashioned hollyhocks, and roses, is a treasure trove of the past. Built by Solomon Comstock, the house still contains the Comstock family furniture, china and crystal, hundreds of books, and clothing belonging to family members. Ada Comstock, daughter of Solomon, went on to become the first dean of women at the University of Minnesota and was later president of Radcliffe College. Many of Ada Comstock's mementos are in the house, including her 1897 Smith College yearbook and an invitation to the White House from President Herbert Hoover. Open Memorial Day–Sept. 30, Sat.–Sun., 1:00–4:30 P.M., and by appointment. Fee. Located 0.5 mile north of the Hwy. 75 exit off I-94. **506 Eighth St. S., Moorhead, 56560; 218-233-0848.**

Heritage Hjemkomst Interpretive Center

Robert Asp dreamed of building a Viking ship and sailing it to Norway, the country of his ancestors. Asp, who was a school counselor, did build his dream boat, a 76-foot replica of a Viking ship, in nearby Hawley, but died before he could sail it. His children and other crew members took over where he left off and sailed the *Hjemkomst* (Homecoming) from Duluth through the Great Lakes, down the St. Lawrence Seaway, and across the Atlantic to Bergen, Norway, a distance of 6,000 miles, arriving in Bergen in 1982. Now back home in Minnesota, the *Hjemkomst* sits in a hall of honor in a building that mimics billowing white sails. A video describes the quest and journey. In June 1998 a replica of a Norwegian stave church also became part of the Hjemkomst center. Fee. In addition to the ship and church, the complex includes the Clay County Museum, depicting the history of the county, and temporary exhibits in the Heritage Hall. Both are open Mon.–Wed. and Fri.–Sat., 9:00 A.M.–5:00 P.M.; Thurs., 9:00 A.M.–9:00 P.M.; Sun., noon–5:00 P.M. **202 First Ave. N., Moorhead, 56560; 218-233-5604.**

Roger Maris Museum

Fargo's homegrown baseball hero has his own museum-in-a-hall in West Acres shopping mall. Maris, the Yankee slugger who broke the Babe's record when he hit 61 home runs in the 1961 season, helped the American Legion members select the photos, awards, and mementos displayed in glass cases along the hallway walls; Maris died in 1985. There is also a video that shows his 61st home run; Maris's record stood for nearly 40 years. The mall is open Mon.–Sat., 10:00 A.M.–9:00 P.M., and Sun., noon–6:00 P.M. Located at the **intersection of I-29 and 13th Ave.** For information, call the mall office, **701-282-2222.**

Parks

Bluestem Prairie Scientific and Natural Area

Adjacent to Buffalo River State Park, the 3,258-acre prairie offers visitors a chance to see what the land looked like before settlement. Walk into the preserve to get a sense of the wide expanse

The Comstock House in Moorhead. Photo courtesy of the Minnesota Historical Society.

of prairie grass that early settlers saw. Owned by The Nature Conservancy, the prairie has more than 300 kinds of plants, 70 bird species, and 20 kinds of butterflies. To reach the prairie, drive 14 miles east of Moorhead on Hwy. 10, south on Hwy. 9 for 1.5 miles, then east on a gravel road, continuing for 1.5 miles to a parking lot. **R.R. 2, Box 240, Glyndon, 56547; 218-498-2679.**

Buffalo River State Park

When Buffalo River State Park was created in 1937, it was intended for recreation. It still fulfills that function well: there are picnic tables and a swimming pond, as well as camping and hiking. The Buffalo River winds through the park, and the trees along its banks provide welcome shady areas under the hot summer sun. The fact that the park contained native prairie land was not of primary importance to the founders, but now it is considered an incalculable treasure. The park and surrounding preserved prairies make up a total area of more than 4,600 acres of tallgrass prairie, one of the largest areas like it in the country. Before settlement, the prairie grasses stretched as far as the eye could see. At Buffalo River and adjacent Bluestem Prairie Scientific and Natural Area, owned by The Nature Conservancy, visitors can get a sense of the vast expanse of years ago. The park contains more than 250 species of grasses and wildflowers. Sharp-eyed visitors may spot seldom-seen butterflies, such as the Dakota skipper and the regal fritillary. Located 14 miles east of Moorhead, off Hwy. 10. Contact the park at **R. R. 2, Box 256, Glyndon, 56547; 218-498-2124.**

Performing Arts

THEATER

Visitors to Fargo and Moorhead have several live theaters to choose from. Moorhead State University's Straw Hat Players are into their third decade of summer theater at the **Roland Dille Center for the Arts, at Ninth Ave. and 14th St. S. in Moorhead, 218-236-2271.** North Dakota State University's **Little Country Theatre,** begun in 1914, offers several productions Oct.–Apr.; **701-231-7969.** The **Fargo-Moorhead Community Theatre** stages five productions,

plus a children's play and a senior musical review, annually, Sept.–June; **333 Fourth St., Fargo, ND 58103; 701-235-6778 or 701-235-1901.**

Where to Stay

Fargo has a number of hotel and motel accommodations, and Moorhead also has a few. The choice is much larger in Fargo, however. There is a range of prices from budget motels to upscale hotels. Contact the Fargo-Moorhead Convention and Visitors Bureau (see Services) for a complete listing.

Camping

Buffalo River State Park—$

Many campers head for Buffalo River State Park in Moorhead, which has 44 campsites, 8 with electrical hookups. For reservations at all state parks, call **The Connection, 800-246-CAMP** or **612-922-9000.**

Where to Eat

In addition to middle-American cuisine at most restaurants and cafes in the Red River Valley, look for several Mexican restaurants in the Fargo-Moorhead area, reflecting the many Hispanic residents, who first came to help with the harvest and later made permanent homes here.

The Grainery—$$ to $$$

Black Angus beef is the specialty at this good, solid, locally owned restaurant tucked to one side of Fargo's West Acres shopping mall. It's a quiet, comfortable place at the end (or the middle) of the day, with reliable food. Try the beer cheese soup. Open Mon.–Sat., 11:00 A.M.–10:00 P.M., and Sun., 11:00 A.M.–6:00 P.M. West Acres is located at the **intersection of I-29 and 13th Ave. S. in Fargo, ND; 701-282-6262.**

Coffeehouses, Sweets, and Treats

Quality Bakery & Pastry Shop—$

Can tourists live on bread and pie alone? Sure, if

it's from the Quality Bakery. The bakery has two locations, one in Fargo and one in Moorhead. These bakers were turning out an amazing assortment of specialty breads before others caught on. Some of the breads include wild rice, nine-grain, Black Forest rye, and flax bread. There are lots of specials. During a visit one July, the bakery had declared it pie month, and I and my fellow travelers were tempted to spend our whole vacation hanging out in the bakery, scarfing down pieces of such tempting pies as toffee bar crunch, banana fudge, and chocolate peanut butter. Both locations are open Mon.–Fri., 6:00 A.M.–6:00 P.M., and Sat., 6:00 A.M.–3:00 P.M. **2532 S. University Dr., Fargo, ND 58103; 701-237-9326;** and **720 Main Ave., Moorhead, 56560; 218-233-6942.**

Services

Housed in a handsome version of a grain elevator, which some have called "cathedrals of the plains," the **Fargo-Moorhead Convention and Visitors Bureau** has information on both cities. **2001 44th St. SW, Fargo, ND 58107; 800-235-7654. Website: fargomoorhead.org.**

Highway 12

When Hwy. 394, which streaks west from downtown Minneapolis, reverts back to its original number and becomes Hwy. 12 again, rural scenery soon starts and a string of small towns appear. The highway meanders west, with a little tilt to the north, through prime farmland. The communities along the way and to the immediate north and south are on the small side, with the exception of Willmar (18,688) and Hutchinson (13,500).

Although not far enough north to be true lake and resort country, the route has sights that are well worth seeing. The late vice president Hubert H. Humphrey, who was a U.S. senator from Minnesota and mayor of Minneapolis before being tapped as Lyndon Johnson's running mate, lived on the lake at Waverly, and a Humphrey museum is in the works.

The eastern end of the district is fairly flat, but toward the west, the ice ages left a legacy of steep hills and deep lakes. Near the South Dakota border, the land flattens out again, a harbinger of the true plains.

History

After the treaties of 1851 were signed, European settlers poured into the area. A good portion of them were from Norway, Sweden, and Finland. Even today, many of the communities regard themselves as being one of those three ethnic groups. But the Scandinavians were far from the only settlers. One of the most unusual groups of founders was the Hutchinson Family, a singing group from New England, who started (you guessed it) Hutchinson in 1855. The Hutchinson settlement was ahead of its time; women were given an equal voice in local affairs from the start. The events in the 1862 U.S.–Dakota Conflict came full circle in the area around Hwy. 12. Although most of the action took place south of the present highway, the clash was set off when several Dakota killed white settlers at Acton. A year after the conflict ended, Chief Little Crow, who reluctantly led the Dakota in battle, was killed while picking raspberries near Hutchinson by a settler who had no idea whom he was shooting.

Festivals and Events

Little Crow Water Ski Team
Fri. in June–Aug.
Everything that can be done on water skis can be seen in this weekly summer-evening performance on the wide expanse of the Middle Fork of the Crow River in New London, north of Willmar. The prize-winning Little Crow Water Ski Team does synchronized skiing, daring acrobatic stunts, barefoot skiing, and a little clowning around during each performance. Held at Neer Park on the river in New London at 7:30 P.M. in June and July, and at 7:00 P.M. in Aug. Fee. **800-845-TRIP.**

Music in the Park
Mon. early June–Aug.
Free Monday-night concerts have been part of

Hutchinson's summer scene for nearly 20 years. The concerts—of a variety of musical styles—take place in the Library Square's Bandstand. Grab a blanket and come on down. Contact the Hutchinson Area Convention and Visitors Bureau (see Services).

New London–New Brighton Antique Car Run
second Sat. in Aug.

There's a crowd of early risers every year watching the 70 or so antique cars start their engines at 7:00 A.M. in New London, bound for New Brighton 120 miles away. Finishers get a medallion. At about 20 miles per hour, it takes all day for the autos, none built after 1915, to make the trip. There are rest stops along the way and the route is mainly on county roads, though it goes down 42nd Ave. N. in Minneapolis and over the Camden Bridge, to Long Lake Park in New Brighton. Entrants, often dressed in period costume, come from as far afield as Florida. The night before, there is a parade through New London at 5:30 P.M., followed by a community steak fry. New London City Hall, **320-354-2444.**

Fiddlers Festival
last Sun. in Sept.

Fiddlers from preschoolers to octogenarians enter the annual Fiddlers Festival at the Terrace Mill, in the tiny community of Terrace. Approximately 30 fiddlers from Minnesota and surrounding states vie for prizes, hold classes, and end with a fiddlers-all jamboree. Terrace Mill Foundation, **Old Mill Rd., Terrace, 56334; 320-278-3728.**

Outdoor Activities

Biking

Glacial Lakes State Trail

Bikers, hikers, in-line skaters, and those who use wheelchairs find it an easy glide from Willmar to New London on the multipurpose Glacial Lakes State Trail. The trail, on an old railroad bed, is paved with asphalt for those 12

miles and there is a parallel grass treadway for horseback riders. From New London to Hawick, the trail surface is crushed granite. Farther on, for the 18 miles from between Hawick to Richmond, the trail is undeveloped and paved with the original stones. There are rest rooms, parking areas, and scenic stops marked along the developed portion. There is parking opposite the Willmar Civic Center at the southern end of the trail. A paved-shoulder bike path connects Sibley State Park to the Glacial Lakes State Trail. Snowmobiles are allowed on the paved section in winter; check for restrictions on snowmobile tires with metal studs. Kandiyohi County information, **800-845-TRIP.**

Luce Line State Trail

The Luce Line, a 97-mile state multipurpose trail, starts in the Minneapolis suburb of Plymouth and runs through several parks in Hutchinson, alongside the Crow River, and beyond. Bikers, snowmobilers, cross-country skiers, and hikers are welcome on the trail, which is built on a railroad bed. A portion of the trail through Hutchinson is paved. For more information, call the Hutchinson Area Convention and Visitors Bureau, **800-572-6689** or **320-587-5252.**

Birding

In Monson Lake State Park, watch for white pelicans, herons, Western grebes, and songbirds on the lake and in the park. There is excellent birdwatching in Big Stone Lake State Park. Pelicans and cormorants are among the bird species in Sibley State Park. See Parks.

Boating

CANOEING
At Sibley State Park, canoers can put in at Swan

Lake (where there is a parking lot) and glide through that lake to Henschien Lake to Lake Andrew, with short portages linking each lake. See Parks.

North Fork of the Crow River

The North Fork of the Crow, a popular canoeing river, flows out of Lake Koronis; near the lake are 43 Indian mounds in two sites. The North Fork of the Crow is gentler in its lower reaches, and families can easily manage it downstream 'from Kingston. Upriver there are some rapids, and snags may be a problem. The maple-basswood Big Woods once lined the banks, but the area is now largely agricultural. The Dept. of Natural Resources canoe route map of the North Fork shows access points, campsites, rest areas, and points of interest. **DNR Information Center, 500 Lafayette Rd., St. Paul, 55155; 888-MINNDNR or 651-296-6157.**

Fishing

Although this part of the state is not known for trophy fish, anglers can still find respectable catches of walleye, panfish, bass, and northern in the many lakes. Big Stone Lake contains walleyes, northerns, and bluegills. Near the entrance to Glacial Lakes State Park is a spring-fed, landlocked lake whose clear waters yield a wide variety of fish, from northerns to sunnies. Fishing in the park at Mountain Lake is a quiet experience, as only electric motors are allowed. There are several fishing docks on the lake, as well as a boat launch. Monson Lake (in Monson Lake State Park) appeals to those who come to fish for walleye, northern, bass, and sunfish. The lake—relatively deep for this part of the state at 22 feet in some spots—is adjacent to the quiet, wooded campground. There are bass, northern, walleye, and panfish in Swan Lake at Sibley State Park. See Parks.

Hiking

With all the state parks around, not to mention the Glacial Lakes State Trail, it's easy to find a good hike in this area. In Glacial Lakes State Park, there are 16 miles of hiking trails, and one 0.5-mile self-guided interpretive trail. There are hiking trails in both portions of Big Stone Lake State Park. In Lake Maria State Park, there is a 300-foot self-guided trail along a boardwalk, as well as 14 miles of hiking trails. Altogether, Sibley State Park has 18 miles of hiking trails, two of them handicapped-accessible. See Parks.

Skiing

CROSS-COUNTRY

Although it is primarily a snowmobile trail, the Glacial Lakes State Trail (see Biking) provides a good, level workout, but it's not groomed. In Lake Maria State Park, 14 miles of trails are reserved for traditional cross-country skiing and 3.5 miles for skate-skiing. Cross-country skiers have 10 miles of trail (2 miles of which are for skate-skiers) at Sibley State Park. See Parks.

Snowmobiling

The Willmar–New London section of the Glacial Lakes State Trail connects with other area snowmobile trails. In winter, 11 miles of trails in Glacial Lakes State Park are used by snowmobilers. In Sibley State Park, snowmobilers have 6 miles of trail. Ask the tourist bureaus (see Services) for snowmobiling maps.

Seeing and Doing

Museums and Historic Sites

Gust Akerlund Photo Studio and Cokato Museum

Akerlund was the town photographer in Cokato for nearly half a century, and his studio and many of the thousands of photographs taken by this Swedish immigrant have fortunately been preserved. Entering Akerlund's studio is like stepping into a period Ingmar Bergman film. Akerlund's big old camera faces a canvas-painted backdrop, and natural light streams in from the skylight. Atop the camera is an endearingly worn dog puppet that Akerlund used to coax a smile from children. Part of the studio, which is on the National Register of Historic Places, contains an exhibition on the history of photography.

Akerlund's tiny 1930s apartment can also be seen. Adjacent to the studio is the city museum, which is also well worth spending some time in. Don't miss the mural on the museum's side, painted by Lance Albers; it depicts five Akerlund prints. Open year-round Mon.–Fri., 9:00 A.M.–4:30 P.M., and Sat.–Sun., 1:00–4:00 P.M. Located at Fourth St. W. and Millard Ave. in Cokato. **P.O. Box 686, Cokato, 55321; 320-286-2427. Website: www.cokato.mn.us/cmhs/.**

Kandiyohi County Historical Society and Museum

Kids and adults both like to climb up to the cab of the enormous Great Northern steam engine, now resting on the grounds of the county museum. The engine, built in the 1920s, symbolizes the days when Willmar was a railroad center. Inside the museum are historic artifacts and a new research center. Museum holdings off the grounds include a nearby field, plowed each spring with Belgian horses using antique agricultural implements; Sperry House, a family farmhouse with 1890s furnishings; and the Guri Endreson Cabin, where pioneers were saved during the U.S.-Dakota Conflict in 1862. For hours of the Sperry House and the cabin, contact the museum. The museum is open year-round Mon.–Fri., 9:00 A.M.–5:00 P.M.; plus during summer, Sat.–Sun., 1:00–5:00 P.M., and Thanksgiving Day–New Year's Day, Sun., 2:00–5:00 P.M. **610 Hwy. 71 NE, Willmar, 56201; 320-235-1881.**

Litchfield Grand Army of the Republic Hall

The Litchfield G.A.R. Hall, a fortlike yellow brick structure built in 1885, once was the site of weekly gatherings of local Civil War veterans, who convened in a large hall surrounded by photos of comrades and the words "We Are the Boys of '61" written in Gothic script on one wall. They sang, talked, heard speakers, and reminisced. The "Boys of '61" have long since died, but the hall remains a magnificent reminder of their service at such bloody battles as Gettysburg and Missionary Ridge in Tennessee. Visitors can see the hall, which is on the National Register of Historic Places, and many artifacts from the war, as well as books from the era. Behind the hall is the

Meeker County Museum, whose exhibits include a model of an early settler's cabin. The G.A.R. Hall and museum are both open Tues.–Sun., noon–4:00 P.M. **308 N. Marshall, Litchfield, 55355; 320-693-8911.**

McLeod County Heritage and Cultural Center

The work of late local wildlife-artist-made-good Les Kouba is well represented in this center. A gallery contains approximately 200 of his prints, many of his awards, and hundreds of arrowheads Kouba and his wife collected. The center also has exhibits on pioneer life, the Civil War, and agriculture. Open year-round Mon.–Fri., 10:00 A.M.–4:30 P.M., and Sat.–Sun., 1:00–4:00 P.M. **380 School Rd. N., Hutchinson, 55350; 320-587-2109.**

Terrace Mill

Although the first mill on this site was built in 1870, the present mill, spruced up recently with dark red paint, was opened in 1903 and operated as a mill until the late 1940s. Inside are exhibits of local arts, including a display of Norwegian rosemaling, a painting style carried to the United States by immigrants. The Terrace Mill Foundation sponsors many events, including a fiddlers contest (see Festivals and Events), rosemaling classes, a heritage festival in June, and a concert in August. In addition to the mill, which is on the National Register of Historic Places, the foundation's holdings include a stone bridge, a dam, a log cabin and cottage, and a miller's home. The mill is southeast of Glenwood on Hwy. 104. It's open for tours in summer Tues.–Sat., 9:00 A.M.–6:00 P.M., and Sun., noon–6:00 P.M. **Old Mill Rd., Terrace, 56334; 320-278-3728.**

Twine Ball

That's not just a big ball of twine behind the glass in Darwin—it was the biggest ball of twine in the world at one time, enshrined in the Guinness Book of Records of 1991. It all started in 1950, when a local farmer, Frances Johnson, picked up the bits of twine littering his farmyard and started to roll them into a neat little ball, according to his nephew Harlan Johnson. The little twine ball slowly became a big twine ball and finally was 11 feet tall, 40 feet around, and 11 tons in weight. Frances Johnson died in 1989, but the twine ball is displayed in its own center in Darwin, just off Hwy. 12. Harlan Johnson's wife, Arlene, offers tours of Meeker County that include a look at the twine ball as well as stops at historic sites such as the G.A.R. Hall (see above) and sites associated with the U.S.-Dakota Conflict of 1862. Contact her at **66009 305th St., Litchfield, 55355.**

Parks

Big Stone Lake State Park

Located along the eastern shore of 30-mile-long Big Stone Lake, which forms the border between Minnesota and South Dakota, the park is divided into two sections. The northern part, called the Bonanza Area, has a picnic area, swimming beach, boat launch, and group camp, as well as the Big Stone Lake Environmental Education Center. The Meadowbrook Area is 8 miles south of that, and has a campground, picnic tables, and a playground. There are plots of virgin prairie within the park. Around the park are granite and gneiss quarries,

The G.A.R. Hall in Litchfield provides the backdrop to a "living history" Civil War reenactment. Photo courtesy of the Meeker County Historical Society.

and fossilized shark's teeth—another reminder that the lake and its surroundings formed the southern end of ice-age Lake Agassiz—can be seen in the rock outcrops. Located 6 miles northwest of Ortonville on Hwy. 7. **R.R. 1, Box 153, Ortonville, 56278; 320-839-3663.**

Glacial Lakes State Park

This is one state park you won't soon forget. The retreat of the last glacier 10,000 years ago created roller-coaster scenery in West-Central Minnesota. These so-called Leaf Hills are a band of hills 10–19 miles wide that extend from Detroit Lakes southeasterly to Willmar. The entire area shows evidence of glacial formation, but Glacial Lakes State Park is probably the best visible example of what happens when tons of ice press down on the earth. The park terrain swoops up and down—here a hill that is a double for a camel's hump, there a high ridge that makes hikers feel they are on top of the world. Areas of the park have never been touched by the settler's plow, and these plots of virgin prairie support a wonderful variety of wildflowers and two rare butterfly species—the Dakota skipper and the Powesheik, small flutters of pale blue that may be seen by patient hikers. The park is a nice mix of heavily wooded areas and wide-open spaces, with glorious views. The park has an oak-shaded campground and a horsecamp area. For horseback riders, there are 11 miles of trails. Boats, canoes, and snowshoes can be rented. There is a swimming beach. The park is located 5 miles south of Starbuck; entry is from Hwy. 41. **25022 County Rd. 41, Starbuck, 56381; 320-239-2860.**

Hutchinson Parks

The far-sighted Hutchinson family, who founded Hutchinson, set aside 15 acres of land for parks in 1855, making Hutchinson's parks the second-oldest chartered park system; only New York's is older. Today, most of the city's 430 acres of parkland hug the Crow River, which runs through the community. Robert's and Masonic/West River Parks have boat landings, and Masonic offers camping for tents and RVs. At Ehiem Park is a bronze statue of Little Crow, leader of the Dakota during the U.S.–Dakota Conflict of 1862.

Camper cabin at Lake Maria State Park. Photo courtesy of the Minnesota Department of Natural Resources.

The statue was created by well-known Minnesota artist Les Kouba, who grew up in the area (see McLeod County Heritage and Cultural Center in Museums and Historic Sites). For information on the parks, call **320-587-2975.**

Lake Maria State Park

Lake Maria State Park is the perfect place for Twin Cities residents looking for a wilderness break without driving hundreds of miles. Geared to hikers, backpackers, and horseback riders, rather than those who like motorized recreation, the park prohibits boat motors of more than 20 horsepower. There is a drive-up group camp, but other campsites and the camper cabin are pack-in. In the park are remnants of the Big Woods, a maple-basswood forest that covered much of southeast Minnesota at one time, and pockets of wetlands with a wide variety of wildlife, including many reptiles and more than 200 bird species. Stop for the turtle crossing signs, as the park is home to the rare Blanding's turtle, with its bright yellow spots on the shell. There are 8 miles of horseback trails. There is also a sledding hill. The park is 9 miles west of Monticello. Follow Hwy. 39 west, and turn right on County Rd. 111.

The park address is **11411 Clementa Ave. NW, Monticello, 55362; 612-878-2325.**

Monson Lake State Park

One of the smallest state parks, and one of several in the area that are located along the Glacial Ridge Trail (a network of roads that follow the path of retreating glaciers), Monson Lake State Park was created in 1923 as a memorial to the members of the Broberg and Lundbergh families who were killed during the U.S.–Dakota Conflict of 1862. A chilling account of the attack, written by Anna Stina Broberg Peterson, a survivor, is available from the park office. Visitors may have the park all to themselves on some days. The park has a 1-mile hiking trail. There are 20 campsites. Enter the park south of Sunburg off Hwy. 9 via County Rd. 95 S. The park address is **1690 15th St. NE, Sunburg, 56289; 320-366-3797.**

Sibley State Park

One of the most popular state parks in Minnesota, Sibley seems to have something for everyone. Most visitors climb up to the top of Mount Tom, a hill made of glacial drift material that rises 1,375 feet above sea level. It's one of the highest points in western Minnesota, and the short, rather steep climb is well worth the view. Interpretive signs on the observation tower at the top tell the park's story. In addition to being part of the Alexandria Moraine formed by the last glacier, Sibley is in a transition zone between the prairie and the hardwood forest, so there is great diversity in animal and bird life, and 11 of the 19 amphibian species found in Minnesota live in the park. Take the easy, 0.75-mile Pondview interpretive trail around a wetland and watch for birds overhead, ducks and other waterfowl in the water, and frogs hopping around.

For horseback riders, there are 9.2 miles of trails. There are 5 miles of surfaced bike trails, and bikes as well as boats and canoes can be rented at the park. Lake Andrew has a swimming beach, handicapped-accessible fishing pier, and boat launch. In the spring, look for pasqueflowers blooming in the park's prairie parcels. In winter, the sliding hill and nearby warming house are popular with families. Camping is a favorite activity at Sibley. The park has a year-round naturalist and many scheduled activities. The interpretive center is a good place to watch small birds at the feeders and look out over the prairie pothole to the picturesque stone barn foundation beyond it. Much of the work in building the park and its handsome, solid buildings was done by the Veterans Conservation Corps, whose membership was made up of World War I veterans. The park is 15 miles north of Willmar, off Hwy. 71. **800 Sibley Park Rd. NE, New London, 56273; 320-354-2055.**

Performing Arts

THEATER

The Barn Theatre

Six shows a year in two seasons—summer and winter—are staged by the volunteer cast of the Barn Theatre, in downtown Willmar. **321 Fourth St. SW, Willmar, 56201; 320-235-9500.**

Scenic Drives

Glacial Ridge Trail

Drive along the 220-mile Glacial Ridge Trail, over the backbone of Minnesota, and you will have a sense of how the landscape was formed. Thousands of years ago, a lobe of the last ice-age glacier gave up the ghost here in western Minnesota, melting and depositing its load of loam and gravel and leaving little blocks of ice to melt into the steep-sided "ice-block" lakes in Kandiyohi County. The trail, recently named a Minnesota Scenic Byway, follows the ridge formed by the glacier, and it meanders delightfully on back roads and around lakes, through pastoral countryside. Follow the black-and-red signs carefully. There are several state parks and historic sites along the way. The trail stretches from Willmar at its southern end to a bit north of Alexandria. Maps are available from the Kandiyohi County Tourist Information Center (see Services).

Shopping

Mr. B. Chocolatier

Willmar used to be known as the coffee town, but Mr. B.'s (that's Dwight Barnes) luxurious Belgian-inspired chocolates is fast changing that. Barnes, who calls himself a "country photographer," operates a chocolate-shop-cum-photo-studio in Willmar. He shot pictures long before he got the chocolate bug, and went first to Switzerland and then to Antwerp, Belgium, to learn the chocolate trade. He imports the chocolate from Belgium ("the best chocolate in the world," he avers) and many of the other ingredients are also from Europe. The chocolates are as beautiful as they are delicious, with some molded in the shape of half a walnut, then topped with a real walnut half. If you have difficulty finding the shop, follow his directions; Barnes says, "It is right off Highway 12; go past the depot and it's the first turn to the right." Open Mon.–Fri., 9:00 A.M.–5:00 P.M., and Sat., 9:00 A.M.–1:00 P.M. **540 Benson Ave. W., Willmar, 56201; 320-235-1313.**

Where to Stay

There is no shortage of chain motels and hotels in the towns along Hwy. 12; ask the tourist bureaus (see Services) for help in locating them.

Bed-and-Breakfasts

Prairie Farm Bed-and-Breakfast—$$$

This big house on the prairie lets visitors unwind and listen to the silence. The house, nearly a century old, has two comfortable, nicely decorated rooms and one suite. There are private and shared baths. The house sits amid an 80-acre farm, and a trail leads to the nearby Crow River. In back, the owners have an antique car and truck collection that visitors are welcome to see. A hearty breakfast is served. **2334 175th St., Lester Prairie, 55354; 320-395-2055** or **612-470-1846.**

Camping

Hutchinson—$

Masonic/West River Park has campsites for RVs and tents; nine have full hookups and 20 sites have just electrical hookups. Located just off Hwy. 7 on the Crow River. **320-587-2975.**

State Parks—$

Big Stone Lake has 37 campsites, 10 with electrical hookups. Glacial Lakes has 39 campsites in an oak-shaded campground, four walk-in sites, and a horsecamp area. Lake Maria has 16 pack-in campsites and three year-round camper cabins. At Sibley, there are 134 campsites, 53 with electricity, plus a horsecamp with five sites. For reservations at all state parks, call **The Connection, 800-246-CAMP** or **612-922-9000.**

Where to Eat

Bavarian Haus—$ to $$$

Sauerbraten, Wiener schnitzel, all kinds of tortes, more than 50 varieties of German beer—is this *Himmel,* or what? Woody and Doris Lamprecht (she's from Mannheim, Germany) have been serving authentic German food and drink since 1992 on Hutchinson's main street. If you can't stop for lunch or dinner, at least pop in for a sinful piece of torte and good strong coffee. Nicely decorated, too, with a very European feel. Open for coffee, lunch, and dinner Mon.–Wed., 10:30 A.M.–8:00 P.M., and Thurs.–Sat., 10:30 A.M.–9:00 P.M. **36 N. Main St., Hutchinson, 55350; 320-587-4560.**

Main St. Cafe—$

The food is good, the price is right, and the big old cafe—a restaurant for 30 years— is dripping with history. Sit down and have a cup of coffee while you read the newspaper/menu, full of historical anecdotes about Litchfield, interspersed with lighthearted comments. Breakfast is served all day and there are daily lunch specials. The cafe offers the usual sandwiches and burgers, with an occasional surprise, such as the grilled fish melt with two cheeses on rye. Don't forget the pie. Open Mon.–Fri., 6:00 A.M.–4:00 P.M.; Sat., 6:00 A.M.–2:00 P.M.; Sun., 7:00 A.M.–2:00 P.M.; with a coffee and cake "happy hour" Mon.–Fri., 2:00–4:00 P.M. **226 N. Sibley Ave., Litchfield, 55355; 320-693-9067.**

Services

Hutchinson Area Convention and Visitors Bureau, 206 Main St. N., Hutchinson, 55350; 800-572-6689 or **320-587-5252.**

Kandiyohi County Tourist Information Center, 2104 Hwy. 12 E., Willmar, 56201; 800-845-TRIP.

Litchfield Chamber of Commerce, 219 Sibley St., Litchfield, 55355; 320-693-8184.

Western Lakes

Alexandria is the center of the Western Lakes area, with Fergus Falls anchoring the northwest edge of the lakes and Sauk Centre the southeastern end. Although Fergus Falls is the larger city, with 12,362 residents, it is primarily a business center that is near lakes, whereas Alexandria ("Alex" for short), with a population of nearly 8,300, is a destination for tourists, as it is in the midst of a chain of popular lakes. The area is bursting with lakes. Otter Tail County, which contains Fergus Falls, claims 1,048 lakes—more than any other county in the state. The much smaller Douglas County, where Alex is located, has 300 lakes. Settled mainly by Scandinavians, who are now outnumbered in total by those of German ancestry, the area still has a strong sense of heritage, and a sense of humor about it: ask anyone for the latest Ole and Lena jokes.

History

Alexandria is a city that was twice born. Its first round came in 1858, when five men settled in Douglas County; two—the Kinkead brothers—claimed land at Lakes Agnes and Winona, in the heart of present-day Alexandria. The town is named for one brother, Alexander Kinkead. In the summer of that year, a trail was cut by the U.S. Army to the border of the Dakota Territory, and settlers soon traveled by stage along the trail, starting communities in the county.

During the U.S.–Dakota Conflict of 1862, all settlers were asked to leave for more protected areas, and not all returned when settlement resumed. After the Civil War ended, the Fort Alexandria stockade was built. William Hicks, an entrepreneur who had a newspaper and a store, bought the town site in 1867 and most later settlers bought land from him.

In the late 1870s the railroad came through, bringing many more settlers in its wake. Alex's wide main street—the aptly named Broadway—was designed to prevent the wooden buildings from catching fire.

Fergus Falls, located on the Otter Tail River, owes its growth in part to the river's resources. George B. Wright built a dam on the river in 1871, a year before the city of Fergus Falls was incorporated, and industry grew up along that source of energy. The St. Paul and Pacific Railroad (later known as the Northern Pacific) reached Fergus Falls in 1879, and the little town grew rapidly, with a telephone system as early as 1882.

Sauk Centre, on the eastern edge of the lakes area, was a quiet farming center until red-haired Sinclair Lewis boldly parodied the town in his classic *Main Street*. Many of the townspeople took offense at the book, but now the entire main street of Sauk Centre has been renamed "the Original Main Street" and one section is on the National Register of Historic Places.

Recommended Reading

Sinclair Lewis grew up in Sauk Centre, the real "Gopher Prairie" depicted in his 1920 novel *Main*

Street. Though the novel now seems dated in many respects, it is still worth reading. First published by Harcourt, Brace and World, it has gone through many subsequent editions. For further reading on Lewis and *Main Street,* read *Main Street—The Revolt of Carol Kennicott,* by English professor and Lewis scholar Martin Bucco (Twayne Publishers, 1993).

Festivals and Events

Syttende Mai Parade
May 17
Dust off your *bunad* (Norwegian regional folk costume) and line up for the parade on Norway's Constitution Day. Alexandria's parade is always on May 17, starts at 1:30 P.M., and lasts 20 minutes or so. Before and after the parade, there is an open house, with Norwegian food such as *kransekake* and *rømmegraut,* and lots of coffee, at the Scandinavian Gift Shop (see Shopping). For more information call **320-763-6363.**

Ole Oppe Festival
third or fourth weekend in May
Big Ole, the 28-foot, four-ton Viking that greets visitors to Alexandria, first stood guarding the Kensington Runestone at the 1965 World's Fair in New York. Ole came home and now lends his name to this festival, which includes a street dance, a "Taste of Alexandria," and fireworks. For information, contact the Alexandria Lakes Area Chamber of Commerce (see Services).

SummerFest
second Sat. in June
This started out as "Scandinavian Days," but the other ethnic groups felt left out, so the name was changed several years ago. Fergus Falls' main street is blocked off for the festival, which includes a parade and crafts show. For details, contact the Fergus Falls Area Chamber of Commerce (see Services).

Vikingland Band Festival
fourth weekend in June
About two dozen marching bands and eight drum

and bugle corps compete in this festival that is Alexandria's largest, drawing thousands of spectators. There is a fee to attend the competition on Sat., but the parade on Sun. is free and great, noisy fun. Contact the Alexandria Lakes Area Chamber of Commerce for information (see Services).

Phelps Mill Festival
second weekend in July
Music and family entertainment—magicians, dancers, etc.—plus arts and crafts draw thousands to Phelps Mill County Park at the height of summer. The crowd has grown so large that there is shuttle service from several remote parking areas. Bring a blanket (all the events are outdoors) and a picnic lunch or buy food from vendors. The park is 15 miles east of Fergus Falls on Hwy. 1. For information, contact the Fergus Falls Area Chamber of Commerce (see Services).

Alexandria is home to Ole the Viking. Copyright © Minnesota Office of Tourism. Used by permission.

Spruce Hill Church Swedish Hymn Sing
fourth Sun. in July
Swedish immigrants built this church, and the Swedish heritage is honored each summer with a medley of Swedish hymns. The program begins at 2:00 P.M. at the church, which is part of the Douglas County Historical Society. Call the society (see Museums and Historic Sites) for directions to the church.

Resorters Golf Tournament
first full week in Aug.

One of the oldest golf tournaments in the state, the Resorters, played at the Alexandria Golf Course, draws hundreds of entrants in many different categories, and a huge gallery as well. The 18-hole course includes the notorious seventh hole, with a green in the shape of Minnesota that is surrounded by a moat. Gallery space is free for the tournament. The course is semiprivate; visitors pay a greens fee. **2300 N. Nokomis NE, Alexandria, 56308; 320-763-3604.**

Festival of the Lakes
first two weeks in Aug.

A series of chamber music concerts and master classes are the focus of this summer event. The concerts are broadcast over Minnesota and National Public Radio. **320-762-5666.**

Outdoor Activities

Biking

While there is no designated state trail in the Western Lakes area, both Alexandria and Fergus Falls have bike paths within the city, which are indicated on city maps (see the chambers of commerce in Services). Bikers also ride along the abandoned rail bed from Fergus Falls to Sauk Centre, about 70 miles.

Birding

Canada geese abound in Glendalough State Park, and bird-watchers will be pleased at the many other kinds of waterfowl that can be seen during spring and fall migrations. See Parks.

Fishing

With all the lakes in the West-Central region, it's no wonder that it is one of the state's prime fishing destinations. Many varieties of fish are here, including the prized walleye. Lake Carlos is an all-around fishing lake (catches include walleye, northern pike, bass, and crappie) that is 150 feet deep in spots. Both lakes in Maplewood State Park contain walleye, northern, and panfish. Beers Lake, according to park staff, also has some big bass and elusive muskies that can reach nearly 50 inches long. Rainbow trout are found in little Bass Lake, and Cow Lake contains bass and northern. See Parks. Ask the area chambers of commerce (see Services) or local resorts for more information.

A key component of Glendalough State Park is a unique plan of use for **Annie Battle Lake,** larger of the park's two fishing lakes. The lake was declared a Heritage Fishery, both in terms of how it is fished and how its fish will be conserved. Because the lakes were not overfished, some of the sunfish, in particular, grew quite large. To encourage the presence of these big sunnies and also other fish, the following restrictions are in effect on Annie Battle Lake: no motors or electric fish-finding devices are allowed; any canoes and boats must be carried in, as there is no launch; northerns and bass are catch-and-release; and there is a limit of five sunfish. At the park's other fishing lake, which is not subject to the restrictions of Annie Battle Lake, there is a boat launch.

Hiking

The many state parks in the area have excellent hiking trails, and plans are proceeding for funds to improve the railroad bed from Fergus Falls to Osakis as a multiuse trail. In Lake Carlos State Park, hiking trails include one that skirts Lake Carlos and goes around tiny Hidden Lake, where there is carry-in boating access to the lake. There are two self-guided trails: the Maple-Basswood Trail is 1.3 miles long, and on the park's eastern edge is the Wetlands Overlook Trail, a hiking/horseback trail of which more than 0.5 mile is a self-guided trail. There are 13 miles of hiking trails in all. Glendalough State Park has 8 miles of hiking trails; Maplewood State Park has 25 miles. See Parks.

Autumn at Maplewood State Park. Copyright © Minnesota Office of Tourism. Used by permission.

Inspiration Peak

A steep, but mercifully short, blacktopped trail up from the parking lot at this state wayside takes climbers to a panoramic view of the surrounding countryside. The peak, part of a glacial moraine, is the highest spot in western Minnesota and the second-highest point in the state. Author Sinclair Lewis loved it here and helped persuade authorities to preserve it. There are benches along the way if you need to rest. At the top, there is a view of nine lakes and three counties. Picnic tables are at the bottom of the hill. Free. Located 10 miles south of Clitherall. Follow Hwy. 5 south, then go east on County Rd. 5 and follow the signs. For information about the site, call the Fergus Falls Area Chamber of Commerce (see Services).

Skiing

CROSS-COUNTRY

Maplewood State Park's 13 miles of trails are a favorite with cross-country skiers, but other parks—state and county—in the area have good trails, too. Glendalough State Park has 8 miles of trails; Lake Carlos State Park has 5 miles. See Parks.

Spidahl Ski Gard

Veteran skier Walt "Speedy" Spidahl, who instructed soldiers in the art of cross-country skiing during World War II, began this day-use ski touring center, which has 12 miles of groomed trails. His son and daughter-in-law recently took it over and have continued to rent and sell skis in addition to running the touring center. There is a warming house with a small snack bar. Located northeast of Fergus Falls, just off Hwy. 22. Contact the Spidahls at **R.R. 1, Box 107, Erhard, 56534; 218-736-5097.**

Snowmobiling

State parks such as Lake Carlos (9 miles of trails) and Maplewood (15 miles of trails) have snowmobiling in winter. See Parks. In addition, maps of the snowmobile trails in the area are available from the area chambers of commerce (see Services).

Seeing and Doing

Antiquing

Alexandria and Osakis are particularly rich fields for antique seekers. The **Now & Then Antique**

Mall, 601 Broadway in Alexandria, has three floors of antiques and stays open all year; **320-763-6467.** Down the block at **517 Broadway** is **Yesterday's,** a secondhand and antique store so large (9,000 square feet) you could get lost in it—it also is open year-round; **320-762-8990.** Osakis, east of Alexandria, is also home to several antique stores, including the 25-dealer **Antiques Osakis, 26 W. Main, 320-859-3200,** open Memorial Day–Sept. 30 and again in mid-Oct. for a Christmas sale.

Museums and Historic Sites

Douglas County Historical Society
The historical society is located in the serene and beautiful home of Knute Nelson, a Norwegian immigrant who became Minnesota's first foreign-born governor and later served in the U.S. Senate for 28 years. The white frame house has period furniture, including a marble table brought back from a 19th-century European tour by an early Alexandria resident. In the basement of the house, staff and volunteers help visitors do research in area newspapers dating to 1875, census records, and family history files. The historical society, directed by the indefatigable Barbara Grover, also has collections of photos and vintage clothing and uniforms. Open year-round, Mon.–Fri., 8:00 A.M.–5:00 P.M., with house tours 9:00 A.M.–4:00 P.M. Free.

The historical society also sponsors bus tours of historic places in Douglas County and organizes the three annual services at the Spruce Hill Church (see Festivals and Events), built by Swedish immigrants in 1902 and now under the care of the historical society. One outstanding feature of the little church, which was used until 1967, is the beautifully carved and gilded pulpit, which depicts scenes from the Bible and has carved verses in Swedish. Call the historical society for directions to the church. The historical society is located at **1219 Nokomis St., Alexandria, 56308-3712; 320-762-0382.**

Otter Tail County Historical Museum
Take a stroll down Main St. inside the county museum to see what life was like in Otter Tail County around 1916. The permanent exhibit holds a wealth of artifacts that fascinate visitors. The museum also has exhibits on the presence of American Indians in area history and on recent county history. In front of the museum is a wonderful heritage garden, with flowers, vegetables, and herbs from yesteryear. Visitors can taste produce from the garden at a fall garden fair. The museum also has a library for those interested in family or local history. Open year-round, Mon.–Fri., 9:00 A.M.–5:00 P.M., and Sat.–Sun., 1:00–4:00 P.M. **1110 W. Lincoln Ave., Fergus Falls, 56537; 218-736-6038.**

Phelps Mill County Park
The Phelps Mill, one of the most photographed sites in the state, raises its stately white bulk at the side of the Otter Tail River near the village of Phelps. The mill, the site of the annual Phelps Mill Festival (see Festivals and Events), is on the National Register of Historic Places. The mill was restored and is administered by the Friends of the Phelps Mill, which is allied with the Otter Tail County Historical Society. The picturesque mill is the backdrop for many weddings; there are also picnic facilities. Visitors can see the mill's interior, with all the equipment intact but not working, during the summer. Signs give details about the mill works. Call for hours. Located 15 miles east of Fergus Falls, just off Hwy. 1. For more information call the Otter Tail County Historical Museum, **218-736-6038.**

Runestone Museum
True or false: Did Vikings visit Minnesota in 1362? For a century now, historians, runic experts, and plain old Minnesotans have been arguing about the authenticity of the rock found by Swedish farmer Olaf Ohman near Alexandria in 1898. The Old Norse runic inscription, translated by Norwegian scholar H. R. Holand of Wisconsin, reads:

8 Goths and 22 Norwegians on exploration journey from Vinland over the West. We had camp by skerries one days journey north from this stone. We were and fished one day After we came home found 10 men red with blood and dead Ave Maria Save from evil

On the stone's side, Holand deciphered another inscription as:

Have 10 of our party by the sea to look after our ships 14 days from this island Year 1362.

The stone, which is of native rock, is 31 inches long and weighs 202 pounds. Over the years, its authenticity has been questioned and defended again and again. Tour the museum, which also includes a video and a section on Viking history as well as the stone itself, and decide for yourself whether Ohman was an innocent discoverer of a historic find or the biggest jokester in state history. In back of the museum is a replica of Fort Alexandria, with several buildings inside the stockade, including a general store, church, and school. Fee. Open May 15–Oct., Mon.–Fri., 9:00 A.M.–5:00 P.M.; Sat., 9:00 A.M.–4:00 P.M.; Sun., 11:00 A.M.–4:00 P.M. Open Nov.–May 14, Mon.–Sat., 9:00 A.M.–5:00 P.M.; Sat., 9:00 A.M.–3:00 P.M. **206 Broadway, Alexandria, 56308; 320-763-3160.**

Sinclair Lewis's Boyhood Home

Sinclair Lewis, who affronted his hometown of Sauk Centre with the publication in 1920 of *Main Street*—which neatly skewered small-town life—grew up in this gray clapboard house not far from downtown. Much of the furniture is from the Lewis family and there is a gift shop in the kitchen. Joyce Lynd, a lifelong Sauk Centre resident and a guide in the house, says opinion in the town is still divided about Lewis. "Some like him and some don't," she says. Lewis, who was born in the house across the street, lived at the house from the time he was four until he graduated from high school. The house has no house number; look for the flags outside. Open Memorial Day–Labor Day, Mon.–Sat., 9:30 A.M.–5:00 P.M., and Sun., 10:30 A.M.–5:00 P.M.; call for Sept. weekend hours. Fee. **810 Sinclair Lewis Ave., Sauk Centre, 56378; 320-352-5201.**

Sinclair Lewis Interpretive Center

At the rest stop just off I-94 is the Sinclair Lewis Interpretive Center. It contains many bits of Lewis memorabilia, plus copies of photos of him and important people in his life. Free. Open Memorial Day–Labor Day, Mon.–Fri., 8:30 A.M.–5:00 P.M., and Sat.–Sun., 9:00 A.M.–5:00 P.M.; the rest of the year, open Mon.–Fri., 8:30 A.M.–4:30 P.M. Call the Sauk Centre Area Chamber of Commerce for information, **320-352-5201.**

Nature Centers

Prairie Wetlands Learning Center

Learn about the prairie wetland environment at the center, a 325-acre site containing 27 wetlands and 19 acres of virgin prairie, plus another 175 acres of restored prairie. An interpretive center opened in 1998. The center, which will serve as a residential environmental learning center for school groups, is also open to the public daily (call for hours). There are several miles of self-guided hiking trails and observation points from which to view a variety of waterfowl and prairie birds. A number of waterfowl species breed here in June. Eventually, there will be weekend programs for children and adults. The wetland center is the first residential environmental center in the United States run by the federal government. It is part of the U.S. Fish and Wildlife Service. Located next to the Otter Tail County Fairgrounds, 1 mile north of I-94, off the Hwy. 210E. bypass in Fergus Falls. **Hwy. 210E., Fergus Falls, 56537; 218-739-2291.**

Parks

Douglas County Parks

The five county parks offer visitors all kinds of recreation possibilities, from picnic tables to swimming in summer to cross-country skiing and tobogganing in winter. Runestone Park has the most complete slate of activities. A map of the parks is available; call the Douglas County Parks Division, **320-763-6001.**

Glendalough State Park

For 85 years before it became one of Minnesota's newest state parks, the parkland was used as a game farm and corporate retreat, thus preserving the land in a more original state than has been the case in many other state parks. The state worked with the public to shape how Glendalough would be used. The result is a more primitive state park than many others. The park's features include a boardwalk out into a beaver pond and 8 miles of hiking/cross-country ski trails, but no snowmobile trails. There are many deer in the park. The park has adopted a heritage approach to fishing (see Fishing). The park's 22 campsites and four camper cabins provide campers with a more traditional experience. All are "cart-in" sites, with campers wheeling their equipment to the site in a handcart. There are no electrical hookups, of course. The camper cabins are seasonal, but may be winterized later. The campground has showers and flush toilets—so it isn't a really primitive experience. Located 1 mile north of Annie Battle Lake on Hwy. 78 and 1 mile east on County Rd. 16. **R.R. 3, Box 28E, Battle Lake, 56515; 218-864-0110.**

Lake Carlos State Park

Located 10 miles north of Alexandria, Lake Carlos is a popular state park for water-based recreation, not a park for those who want to get away from it all. Boaters and anglers love Lake Carlos. The park wraps around the northern end of huge Lake Carlos, with coveted lakeside campsites filling up fast. A swimming beach with a bathhouse is adjacent to the group camp on the lakeshore. Watercraft can be rented at a nearby marina. Up from the lake is a horsecamp, with 8 miles of horseback riding trails in the park. In winter, 9 miles are used by snowmobiles and 5 miles by cross-country skiers. Located just west of Hwy. 59. **2601 County Rd. 38 NE, Carlos, 56319; 320-852-7200.**

Maplewood State Park

Maplewood, aptly named for the number of maples as well as other hardwoods, is a recreational paradise, with more than 20 lakes, many with very good fishing. The maples provide a vivid show of color in the autumn. The undulating terrain—swooping hills (some about 1,600 feet high) and shallow valleys—was formed by glacial action, with hills within the park dipping down into small, lake-filled hollows. Beers Lake and the south arm of Lake Lida (the north arm is just outside the park) both have boat launches, and rentals include boats and canoes at Beers Lake

and boats on Bass Lake. Lake Lida has a swimming beach and lakeside picnic tables.

The self-guided trail around Grass Lake teaches walkers about the geology and natural succession in the park; there is also a shorter, self-guided trail around the forest demonstration area. Drive slowly around the park on the 5-mile, two-way drive to get the lay of the land, stopping at some of the overlooks. In summer, there are 25 miles of hiking trails and 20 miles for horseback riders; winter visitors find 13 miles for cross-country skiing and 15 miles for snowmobiling. Maplewood also has a horsecamp, 3 walk-in campsites (2 can be used as canoe-in sites), and 60 regular campsites on the shore of Grass Lake, 32 with electrical hookups. Located 7 miles east of Pelican Rapids, on Hwy. 108. **Rte. 3, Box 422, Pelican Rapids, 56572; 218-863-8383.**

Performing Arts

THEATER

AAAA Theatre

This renovated theater is used for a variety of cultural events, including performances by touring groups, locally produced plays, and master classes by well-known musicians. Located right **on Broadway in downtown Alexandria; 320-762-8300.**

Theatre L'Homme Dieu

This professional summer theater, edging toward the big four-oh, stages a variety of classics, comedies, and musicals during its season mid-June–early Aug. The theater is **on the shores of Lake Le Homme Dieu.** Forget your French, incidentally, when you tackle that name: Minnesotans have transformed it into something that sounds like *la homma dew*. **320-846-3150.**

Scenic Drives

Otter Trail Scenic Byway

The Otter Trail takes drivers around both state and county roads, twisting and turning so that it passes by many of the county's lakes, Glendalough and Maplewood State Parks, and Inspiration Peak. Follow the cheerful otter-in-the-water signs or ask at the Fergus Falls Chamber of Commerce (see Services) for a county map showing the trail.

Shopping

Amundson Violin

Ken Amundson is the third generation of his family to repair violins. In the shop, violins hang neatly overhead in a row. His artistry is well known, and he repairs violins of musicians who play in major orchestras. Violins come in for first aid from all over the country and from foreign countries as well. Amundson also sells violins. Open year-round, Tues.–Fri., 10:00 A.M.–5:00 P.M., and Sat., 10:00 A.M.–3:00 P.M. **601 Broadway, Alexandria, 56308; 320-763-9096.**

Just Like Grandma's

If it's cute, you'll probably find it in one of the shops at Just Like Grandma's in Osakis. The shops are in back of the tearoom (see Where to Eat), and the handmade, high-quality crafts, clothing, and items for the home or cabin range from whimsical to practical. Some are made by local craftspeople. Open Memorial Day–Labor Day, daily, 10:00 A.M.–5:00 P.M.; Sept., Sat.–Sun.; and mid-Oct. for the Christmas boutique. Call for fall hours. **113 W. Main St., Osakis, 56360; 320-859-3823.**

Rolled Oats Pottery

Jane Schwarzwalter makes sturdy, attractive, and very functional stoneware in her studio/shop in Fergus Falls. A native of Fergus Falls, Schwarzwalter said she made mud pies a lot as a child "and I'm still doing it." Her lines include blue-and-white stoneware favored by area Scandinavians and another that features a stylized swoosh of an evergreen. Jackie, her sheltie, keeps her company in the studio, and barks to let Schwarzwalter know visitors are coming. Look sharp for the shop, as it is tucked into a small strip mall a bit off the street. Call for hours. **1217 N. Union, Fergus Falls, 56537; 218-736-6215.**

Scandinavian Gift Shop

If it's made in Scandinavia, you'll find it at the Scandinavian Gift Shop in Alex. It's Valhalla for those with longings for the Nordic countries and their wares. The shop carries Norwegian wool sweaters, needlework kits and supplies, traditional Christmas decorations, special baking equipment, and a good selection of books—yes, including Norwegian joke books. Several times a year, coffee and Scandinavian goodies are offered to shoppers. On Dec. 13, Santa Lucia Day in Sweden, a white-gowned "Lucia" serves Lucia buns and coffee. Open year-round, Mon.–Fri., 9:00 A.M.–5:30 P.M., and Sat., 9:00 A.M.–5:00 P.M. **604 Broadway, Alexandria, 56308; 320-763-6363.**

Victor Lundeen Company

This rambling shop is the grand old man of Fergus Falls retail businesses. The stationery shop, which began in 1914, has a wonderful assortment of stationery, greeting cards, postcards, books about the region, and odds and ends that you didn't know you needed, including cards with prints you'll want to save and frame. Those who love stationery will drool over the wide assortment. Open year-round, Mon.–Wed. and Fri., 8:00 A.M.–5:30 P.M.; Thurs., 8:00 A.M.–8:00 P.M.; Sat., 9:00 A.M.–5:00 P.M. **126-128 W. Lincoln, Fergus Falls, 56537; 218-736-5433.**

Sports

Garden Center

Alexandria is not just a resort town, it's a bowler's heaven, as the Garden Center has 34 lanes. Now run by the second generation, the center attracts lots of tournament bowling. There is a snack bar and lounge at the center. **503 Hawthorne, Alexandria, 56308; 320-763-6565.**

Tours

WALKING TOURS

Fergus Falls River Walk

The Otter Tail River winds through Fergus Falls, and residents take advantage of it with the pleasant, 5-block river walk through downtown. There are picnic tables beside the river, and it's easy to pick up lunch and mosey on down for a shaded retreat in summer. Access is at several points, including the Fergus Falls Area Chamber of Commerce (see Services).

Where to Stay

Bed-and-Breakfasts and Hotels

Cedar Rose Inn—$$$ to $$$$

All five rooms (one is a suite) at the Cedar Rose, a big, square Tudor revival built in 1903, are nicely furnished and comfortable, but animal lovers may favor the room with the veterinarian mementos. Florian and Aggie Ledermann own the house, and it's veterinarian Florian's own well-worn boots that you'll see in this room. Yorkshire's beloved James Herriot's books are here, too. The house has original molded plaster decorations, plus beautiful woodwork and stained glass. Four rooms have private baths. Breakfast is included. Convenient to downtown. **422 Seventh Ave. W., Alexandria, 56308; 888-203-5333 or 320-762-8430.**

Just Like Grandma's Bed-and-Breakfast—$$$

The three rooms over Just Like Grandma's tearoom are large and airy, with handmade quilts on the beds, just enough antiques furnishing the rooms, and peace and quiet after the tea takers leave. Handy to Lake Osakis and other area lakes. Owner Carol Mihalchick shows off part of her grandma's button collection in a framed display hanging proudly in the hall—just one of many ways in which Carol has made her house "Just Like Grandma's." Breakfast is served in the tearoom downstairs. Open seasonally (see Where to Eat). **113 W. Main St., Osakis, 56360; 320-859-4504.**

Palmer House Hotel—$$$

Sinclair Lewis would feel right at home walking into the commodious lobby of the restored Palmer House Hotel—the beautiful woodwork and the lovely old wooden furniture, grouped invitingly for conversations, are straight out of the early 1900s in Sauk Centre. For years, the hotel—built in 1901—went downhill, but it's been tastefully redone. There are 22 rooms—the spacious suite has a whirlpool. The restaurant on the first floor is popular with guests and local people alike; it's open daily for all three meals and has nightly dinner specials. **288 Original Main St., Sauk Centre, 56378; 888-222-3431 or 320-352-3431.**

Resorts

Radisson Arrowwood Resort—$$$ to $$$$

Arrowwood is a luxurious, year-round playground, with scads of activities. Located on Lake Darling, just outside Alexandria, the resort's rooms are decorated in a comfortable, country theme. The 450-acre resort has its own 18-hole golf course, a marina with all manner of watercraft, a 30-horse stable with trails and a riding ring, indoor and outdoor tennis, and supervised activities for children. Whoops, almost forgot about the lake, where visitors can swim, fish, and boat to their heart's content. In winter, there are sleigh rides, snowmobiles for rent, sledding hills, skating, and cross-country ski trails. Arrowwood has it all, including several restaurants. **2100 Arrowwood Ln., P.O. Box 639, Alexandria, 56308; 800-333-3333 or 320-762-1124.**

Geneva Beach Resort and Marina—call for rates

The area's first resort hotel north of the Twin Cities was built on Lake Geneva in 1883. It's long gone, but resorts have been thriving in the Alexandria area ever since. One of the smaller resorts is Geneva Beach, which has 12 units, varying in size, all of which have lake views. Bring towels; everything else is supplied. The resort is pleasant and great for families, with the grounds mowed and sloping gently down to the lake and its sandy beach. Boats and water toys (paddleboats, fun bugs, canoes, etc.) can be rented. The resort has a game room, and a piano is available for guests to play. Don't forget marshmallows to roast around the nightly bonfires. Baby-sitting is available. Geneva is at the end of the chain of lakes in and around Alexandria. Open June–Aug. **105 Linden Ave., Alexandria, 56308; 320-763-3200. E-mail: geneva@rea-alp.com. Website: www.rea-alp.com/~geneva.**

Camping

Many area resorts have RV and/or tent spaces for rent. Contact the chambers of commerce (see Services) for a listing of resorts.

State Parks—$

Glendalough has 22 campsites and four camper cabins. All are "cart-in" sites, with no electrical hookups. The seasonal camper cabins may be winterized later. There are handicapped-accessible showers and flush toilets. **Lake Carlos** has 124 drive-in sites, 81 with electricity, two walk-in sites, and a horsecamp with six campsites. **Maplewood** has a 20-site horsecamp, three walk-in campsites, and 59 regular campsites, 32 with electrical hookups, and one camper cabin. Lake Carlos and Maplewood also have handicapped-accessible showers and toilets. For reservations at all state parks, call **The Connection, 800-246-CAMP** or **612-922-9000.**

Where to Eat

Old Broadway—$$ to $$$$

Alexandrians flock to Old Broadway for upscale lunches and dinners. The restaurant, formerly a large private home, was enlarged still more for its current guise. There are several rooms, with ample seating. Lunch specialties include a variety of sandwiches and salads, while the dinner menu features prime rib in three sizes and seafood including Minnesota walleye and Alaska king crab legs. All soups and sauces are made from scratch. Open daily, 11:00 A.M.–10:00 P.M. **319 Broadway, Alexandria, 56308; 320-763-3999.**

Just Like Grandma's—$ to $$

Carol Mihalchick's grandma would no doubt be dazzled at what her granddaughter has wrought in her name. Carol accompanied a friend to Osakis a few years ago just for fun, and she left with the idea for Just Like Grandma's, a charming tearoom/gift shop/ice cream parlor/bed-and-breakfast, all rolled up into one rambling white Victorian house, gazebo, and outbuildings in the little village of Osakis. Customers line up on busy summer days, so it pays to make a reservation. The menu includes innovative and tasty salads, sandwiches, soups, and yummy desserts, served on dainty china plates in one of several rooms. Try the wild rice salad, a combination of wild rice, turkey, water chestnuts, cashews, and grapes in a mayonnaise dressing. A quiche and soup of the day are standard fare. Several cookbooks with the tea shop's recipes are sold here. Check out Grandma's Undergrounds, Carol's new basement coffee shop. Open Memorial Day–Labor Day, daily, 10:00 A.M.–5:00 P.M.; Sept., Sat.–Sun.; and mid-Oct. for the Christmas boutique. Call for fall hours. **113 W. Main St., Osakis, 56360; 320-859-4504.**

Traveler's Inn—$ to $$

For more than 70 years, Traveler's Inn has been a mainstay of Alexandria. The large restaurant does a brisk breakfast trade and serves sandwiches, burgers, and old-fashioned food such as hot turkey, beef or chicken sandwiches, liver and onions, and breaded veal cutlet. A local favorite for dessert is the sour cream raisin pie. Open daily, Sun.–Wed., 6:00 A.M.–8:00 P.M., and Thurs.–Sat., 6:00 A.M.–9:00 P.M. **511 Broadway, Alexandria, 56308; 320-763-4000.**

Viking Cafe—$ to $$

This is the kind of cafe Minnesotans cherish. It has wooden booths, the ceilings are high, the folks are local, and the pie is awesome. Everything is homemade at this Fergus Falls institution. Open daily, Mon.–Fri., 5:30 A.M.–7:00 P.M.; Sat., 5:30 A.M.–6:00 P.M.; Sun., 7:00 A.M.–2:00 P.M. Located in **downtown Fergus Falls; 218-736-6660.**

Services

Alexandria Lakes Area Chamber of Commerce is located in the same building as the Runestone Museum. **206 Broadway, Alexandria, 56308; 800-235-9441. Website: www.alexandriamn.org.**

Fergus Falls Area Chamber of Commerce is the place to go for tourism information. **202 S. Court St., Fergus Falls, 56537; 218-736-6951.** The city also has a convention and visitors bureau, tucked away in City Hall, but it is not as well equipped to deal with individual tourists as the chamber is.

Ask the **Sauk Centre Area Chamber of Commerce** about Sinclair Lewis sites. **1220 S. Main St., Box 22, Sauk Centre, 56378; 320-352-5201.**

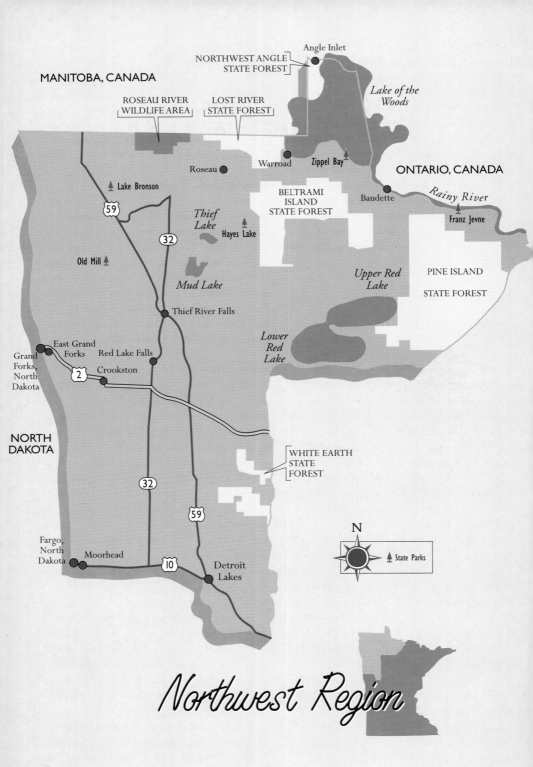

NORTHWEST ANGLE
STATE FOREST

Angle Inlet

MANITOBA, CANADA

Lake of the Woods

ROSEAU RIVER
WILDLIFE AREA

LOST RIVER
STATE FOREST

Warroad

Zippel Bay

ONTARIO, CANADA

Roseau

Rainy River

Lake Bronson

Baudette

59

Franz Jevne

32

Thief Lake

Hayes Lake

BELTRAMI
ISLAND
STATE FOREST

Old Mill

PINE ISLAND

Upper Red Lake

STATE FOREST

Mud Lake

Thief River Falls

Lower Red Lake

East Grand Forks

Red Lake Falls

Grand Forks, North Dakota

2

Crookston

NORTH DAKOTA

WHITE EARTH
STATE
FOREST

32

59

Fargo, North Dakota

Moorhead

10

Detroit Lakes

N

State Parks

Northwest Region

Northwest Region

A glorious sunset makes for a memorable close to a perfect day on the lake.
Copyright © Minnesota Office of Tourism. Used by permission.

Detroit Lakes

Detroit Lakes is the last big splash before the drier plains to the west. A longtime summer vacation spot, especially for residents of Fargo-Moorhead 50 miles away, Detroit Lakes is also a thriving city year-round. The Fourth of July in "D.L.," as the locals call it, is the highlight of the summer for many people. And so, even though the traffic may be slow-and-go around Little Detroit Lake in July, relax and enjoy summer at its best.

Two of the 412 lakes within a 25-mile radius of Detroit Lakes are in the city proper, and the city takes excellent advantage of them, especially a spectacular sandy beach along Little Detroit Lake. Winter sports are also making it big in D.L., with snowmobiling and cross-country skiing drawing visitors as well as local residents.

History

Much of Minnesota was named by intrepid French priests, and Detroit Lakes is no exception. Originally it was only called Detroit (for the strait, or *detroit,* between Big and Little Detroit Lakes), but in 1926 residents of the young city voted to tack the "Lakes" on, to avoid further confusion with the larger Detroit in Michigan. European settlement of the area began in earnest when the railroad came through in 1871. Prior to that, one of three branches of the Red River Ox Cart Trail went right through the little village of Detroit from the 1830s to the 1860s. One of the first large businesses in the area was the Fargo-Detroit Ice Company, which provided the ice for the Northern Pacific Railroad.

Festivals and Events

Polar Fest
usually third weekend in Feb.
Polar Fest celebrates every possible winter event, from dogsled and horse-drawn sleigh rides to candlelight sledding and cross-country skiing to a kids' ice-fishing derby. You can warm up at the chili cook-off or "freeze your buns off" in the race/walk of the same name. A popular event is the polar plunge—with intrepid folks leaping through a hole in the ice on Little Detroit Lake, all in the name of charity. A festival schedule is available from the Detroit Lakes Regional Chamber of Commerce (see Services).

Perham Turtle Races
every Wed. Memorial Day–Labor Day
The Wed.-morning turtle races draw kids from all over, and even some visiting from other countries. Turtleless kids can borrow one for the races, held on a paved track in the city park in the center of Perham. The fun starts at 10:30 A.M. (registration begins an hour earlier). For information, contact the Perham Area Chamber of Commerce, **155 E. Main St., P.O. Box 234, Perham, 56573; 800-634-6112 or 218-346-7710.**

Great American Think-Off
Sat. before Father's Day in June
An essay contest in which entrants ponder questions such as "Does God exist?" culminates in a

debate between four finalists before an audience. The Think-Off, one of many innovative programs sponsored by the New York Mills Regional Cultural Center, draws a couple hundred attendees, who vote on the winner. Held at the New York Mills Sports Center. Fee. Contact the cultural center for details (see Other Sights).

Northwest Water Carnival

first full weekend after Fourth of July weekend
A senior citizen of summer festivals, the annual event began more than 60 years ago and is still going strong. Events include boat races, a water fight between local fire departments and other teams, a sand castle–building contest, a street dance, and all manner of sports competitions. The Detroit Lakes Regional Chamber of Commerce (see Services) has schedules of events.

WE Fest

first full weekend in Aug.
Country music stars and camping are combined in the WE Fest weekend, which draws tens of thousands of fans. Stars who have performed at the fest range from old standbys such as Willie Nelson and Tanya Tucker to newcomers such as Deana Carter. Order tickets and reserve camping early, as this is a very popular summer event; latecomers with no camping or accommodations reservations will be disappointed. Information on the WE Fest campgrounds (i.e., location, recommended age groups) is available. Food vendors are on the festival grounds. Fee. **The Soo Pass Ranch, P.O. Box 1227, Detroit Lakes, 56502; 800-493-3378** or **218-847-1681. E-mail: wefest@tekstar.com. Website: www.wefest.com.**

Finn Creek Folk Festival

usually last weekend in Aug.
Finns settled the area around New York Mills in great number, and many of their descendants show up for the annual festival, held on the grounds of Finn Creek Museum near Detroit Lakes. The festival includes entertainment, Finnish singing lessons, Finnish soul food such as flat bread, horse-drawn wagon rides, demonstrations and crafts, plus tours of the farmstead. Finn Creek Museum is located 3 miles east of New York Mills

---

Getting There

Detroit Lakes is an hour from Fargo, North Dakota, and Moorhead, Minnesota, and 200 miles northwest of Minneapolis– St. Paul. Hwy. 10 connects either metropolitan area with Detroit Lakes.

---

on Hwy. 10, south 2.5 miles on Hwy. 106, then 0.5 mile west on a gravel road. **218-385-2233.**

Outdoor Activities

Birding

Tamarac National Wildlife Refuge

More than 200 species of birds have been sighted at this lovely, secluded refuge, and the most spectacular of these is the bald eagle. There are approximately 20 eagle nests and the big birds are a common sight. Rarer sights are the moose and the timber wolves in the refuge, which has an area of 43,000 acres, including more than a dozen lakes. Although the refuge can be seen by car, it's more rewarding to get out, binoculars in hand, and take your time looking for wildlife or walking along an old Indian trail. The Ojibwe Indians in the White Earth Reservation (which includes part of the refuge) harvest wild rice on refuge lakes each fall. Non-Indians can obtain a ricing permit; contact refuge authorities for details. The refuge allows day use only. Free. Maps are available from refuge headquarters; open Mon.–Fri., except federal holidays, 7:30 A.M.–4:00 P.M. **35704 County Hwy. 26, Rochert, 56578; 218-847-2641.**

Boating

Rentals and Tours

The gentle, twisting Otter Tail River is perfect for a family canoe trip. **Third Crossing Trading Company** can design a trip, supply the canoe, and arrange transport. Trips can be of any length and can include paddling through the lakes connected by the river. Located 10 minutes east of Detroit Lakes in Frazee on Hwy. 10. **119 E. Main St., Frazee, 56544; 218-334-2268.**

Taking the "polar plunge" at Detroit Lakes' winter carnival. Photo courtesy of the Detroit Lakes Regional Chamber of Commerce and Tourism Bureau: Tim Ward.

The Otter Tail, a fairly placid stream, has several tubing enterprises. Tubing draws a young and sometimes boisterous crowd. **Charlie's Otter Tail Tubing,** in business since 1984, offers a two- to three-hour trip down the Otter Tail. The few rapids are gentle, Charlie says. Located **7 miles east of Detroit Lakes on Hwy. 34; 218-847-1480.**

Fishing

Fishing is a hot pursuit—winter and summer—in D.L. Walleyes, northerns, and panfish lurk in the lakes, but not usually in the trophy size encountered in more northerly lakes. Fishing is allowed in Tamarac National Wildlife Refuge (see Birding), with launching ramps at several lakes. Fish present in the lakes include northerns, walleye, black bass, and panfish.

Rentals and Tours

For ice house rental, call **M & M Rentals** in Detroit Lakes, **218-847-5827.**

Golf

Detroit Country Club

Detroit Lakes has 11 golf courses nearby, but the best known of them is the Detroit Country Club, where the Pine-to-Palm tournament is held each Aug. The club has two 18-hole courses, both open to the public; the par-3–4 executive course is shorter. Rental equipment and lessons are available. Greens fees: main course, $30 Mon.–Fri. and $35 Sat.–Sun.; executive course, $22. Open Apr.–mid-Oct., daily, 7:00 A.M.–dusk. Located **5 miles south of Detroit Lakes on Hwy. 59; 218-847-8942.**

Skiing

CROSS-COUNTRY

Nearly 25 miles of trails—divided into loops for short as well as long jaunts—around Detroit Lakes are maintained by the Becker County Winter Trails Association. A map is available from the Detroit Lakes Regional Chamber of Commerce (see Services). In addition, there is skiing available for day users at Maplelag resort for a small fee; meals are not available for day users, however, although coffee and cookies are offered on weekdays (see Resorts).

DOWNHILL

Detroit Mountain has 15 runs, several served by a triple chair. Snowboarders have a separate area. Open Thanksgiving–mid-Mar., Thurs.–Sun. Located 2 miles east of Detroit Lakes on Hwy. 34, then 1 mile south. **218-847-1661.**

Snowmobiling

Detroit Lakes is in the center of the Winter Wonderland snowmobile trail system. More than 200 miles of groomed trails interconnect with other systems, such as Itasca West. City streets (except for those downtown) can be used to access the trails and the lake. Maps are available from the Detroit Lakes Regional Chamber of Commerce (see Services). For 24-hour reports on snow conditions, call **800-433-1888.**

Rentals and Tours

Snowmobiles can be rented at **Okeson Off-trail Sales** in Detroit Lakes, **218-847-9304.**

Swimming

With more than 400 lakes in the region, visitors have no trouble finding a swimming hole. One of the most spectacular spots is the mile-long city beach in Detroit Lakes, on W. Lake Dr. Lifeguards are on duty by the Pavilion in summer, daily, 11:00 A.M.–8:00 P.M. **218-847-4418.**

Rentals and Tours

Fairyland Cottages, across from the Detroit Lakes city beach, rents Jet Skis, paddleboats, tubes, and pontoons (see Resorts).

Seeing and Doing

Museums

Becker County Museum and Historical Society

A replica of the world's smallest gas station (a mere 4 feet by 5 feet), as documented in *Ripley's Believe It or Not,* is one of the museum's exhibits. The original station stood along Hwy. 10 in Detroit Lakes. Among other items in the museum's two stories are ice-cutting equipment from Detroit Lakes' heyday as an ice producer for the railroad, many American Indian artifacts, and an early snowmobile, called a snow scooter back in 1964. Open year-round, Mon.–Fri., 8:30 A.M.–5:00 P.M., and Sat., noon–4:00 P.M. Located on the **corner of Summit Ave. and W. Front St.; 218-847-2938.**

Finn Creek Museum

Among the many Finns who settled in this area were Siffert and Wilhelmiina Tapio, who homesteaded 80 acres in 1900. Today, their farmstead is an open-air museum, with the original house and sauna restored and joined by other buildings, including a blacksmith shop and barns. Open Memorial Day–Labor Day, daily, noon–5:00 P.M. Located 3 miles east of New York Mills on Hwy. 10, south 2.5 miles on Hwy. 106, then 0.5 mile west on a gravel road. **218-385-2233.**

Other Sights

New York Mills Regional Cultural Center

The oldest building in the little town of New York Mills houses a remarkable institution—the New York Mills Regional Cultural Center. The center sponsors many innovative programs, such as the Great American Think-Off (see Festivals and Events) and an Aug. music and film festival. In addition, there are musical, theatrical, and literary events, educational classes, and gallery exhibits. Open year-round, Tues.–Sat., 10:00 A.M.–5:00 P.M.; Apr.–Sept., Sun., 1:00–5:00 P.M. **24 N. Main Ave., New York Mills, 56567; 218-385-3339. Website: www.Kulcher.org.**

Scenic Drives

Fall Color Tour

Enjoy the brilliant fall foliage around Detroit Lakes on one of three mapped driving tours—all passing through or near state parks or wildlife refuges and meandering past many lakes. Driving time for each is from one to one and a half hours. Maps are available from the Detroit Lakes Regional Chamber of Commerce (see Services).

Shopping

Neegii/Friends as One

The Ojibwe who live in and around White Earth Reservation have historically gone ricing every fall for the nutty-tasting wild rice that has been an important part of their diet. Now served in the finest restaurants, wild rice was originally a staple for Ojibwe families. Members of the White Earth Band sell their harvested and processed rice, as well as beaded jewelry and crafts made from birch bark, through this retail store in Detroit Lakes. The store also sells dream catchers, the woven nets that Ojibwe parents traditionally hang over their children's beds to catch the bad dreams and let the good ones filter through. Open year-round, Mon.–Fri., 10:00 A.M.–5:00 P.M., and Sat., 10:00 A.M.–3:00 P.M. **525 Washington Ave., Detroit Lakes, 56501; 218-846-9463.**

Wagering

Shooting Star Casino

Shooting Star is a big casino, with several restaurants and a hotel in addition to hundreds of slots and 32 blackjack tables. The swimming pool complex is very inviting. Live entertainment is featured. Located on the White Earth Reservation, 30 minutes north of Detroit Lakes on Hwy. 59 in Mahnomen. **218-935-2701.**

Where to Stay

Bed-and-Breakfasts

The Log House and Homestead—$$$ to $$$$

Yvonne and Lyle Tweten have created the perfect romantic hideaway, and honored their families' history at the same time. As a child, Lyle Tweten lived in the little log house that visitors now stay in; it was moved to the site after a perilous four-county journey. The house, built by his great-grandparents, Danish immigrants Peter and Anna Jensen, sits high on a prairie hill overlooking Spirit Lake. The common room, with its comfortable wicker furniture and restfully soft blue paint, is a perfect place to relax and play one of the many board games kept for guests. The two bedrooms each have cozy goosedown comforters on the antique beds; one room contains a Norwegian immigrant trunk and the other room has Peter Jensen's own immigrant trunk. Two porches—one lakeside, one hillside—encourage sitting and enjoying nature.

Across the meadow from the log house is a three-bedroom homestead built in 1902 by Swedish immigrant Gust Fredholm. Yvonne Tweten's father had a fishing shack on land leased from the Fredholms, and Yvonne grew up spending summer weekends there. In 1978 the Twetens bought the entire 115-acre farmstead and the idea for an inn blossomed. The homestead now contains two rooms and a suite, all with balconies overlooking the lake and all with whirlpool baths and fireplaces. Antiques are judiciously used and luxury abounds. Full breakfasts are served in both the log house and the homestead. Take time to chat with the Twetens, both about their wonderful place and about their well-traveled lives. Call for directions. **P.O. Box 130, Vergas, 56587; 800-342-2318 or 218-342-2318. Website: www.loghousebb.com.**

Hotels, Motels, and Inns

Best Western Holland House and Suites—$$$

This clean motel, decorated with a Scandinavian motif, pleases families with kids as it has the only indoor water slide in motel accommodations in Minnesota, according to motel staff. The twisty, 133-foot-long slide is part of a pool complex. Centrally located; **615 Hwy. 10 E., Detroit Lakes, 56501; 800-33-TULIP or 218-847-4483. Website: www.Detroitlakes.com/bestwestern.**

Resorts

Fairyland Cottages—call for daily rates

Once upon a time in 1938, a charming row of cottages, each with a tiny porch and a tiny front yard, was built across from the beach at Little Detroit Lake. Several generations later the cottages are still going strong, sparkling with white paint and red trim and white-painted rocks outlining each minuscule yard. Cottages are named after the seven dwarfs or Snow White herself, with a wooden cutout of the namesake attached to the cottage. This is a place to play happily ever after, with the lake just across the street and plenty of activities available. Completely modernized, the cottages also come fully furnished with linens, bedding, and cookware. Mostly rented by the week. Only one cottage is winterized. Boats and other water-sport equipment can be rented. **410 W. Lake Dr., Detroit Lakes, 56501; 218-847-9991.**

Maplelag—call for rates

There are so many things going on at Maplelag, it's hard to find time to sneak in some cross-country skiing, the resort's reason for existing. Skiing on the more than 30 miles of trails that swoop through the maple woods and around frozen lakes is a big part of the total Maplelag experience, but so is jumping in the large outdoor hot tub when the temperature is 15° below, trying out the saunas (both a suit and a no-suit sauna are here), jumping through a hole in the ice into the lake (also known as "taking the plunge"), dancing up a storm, or chatting with newfound friends over one of Maplelag's innovative meals, served family style at long tables in the main building (rates include meals). Did I forget to mention the 24-hour cookie jars and the collections of stained glass windows, skis, and railroad memorabilia, all of which are handsomely displayed throughout Maplelag by owners Jim and Mary Richards?

The eclectic accommodations are also a big draw. They include real railroad cabooses as well as several very old and carefully restored log cabins, one of which has a sod roof. There are also more conventional accommodations in several buildings—some with very interesting histories—clustered around the main building. Bring a sleeping bag or rent linens. Maplelag rents skis and snowshoes and has skates available for guests to use. The Richards, along with their son Jay and daughter-in-law Jonell, manage it all with great verve. Reserve early for long weekends. Maplelag also offers "theme" weekends, such as the Chinese weekend. Maplelag is 20 miles northeast of Detroit Lakes. Call for directions. **30501 Maplelag Rd., Callaway, 56521; 800-654-7711 or 218-375-4466. Website: www.maplelag.com.**

Camping

Many resorts in the Detroit Lakes area have campgrounds for RVs and tents; contact the Detroit Lakes Regional Chamber of Commerce (see Services) for a list.

Where to Eat

Fireside Restaurant and Bar—$$ to $$$

At this long-established restaurant, you'll find a great view of Big Detroit, great sunsets, and really great ribs. The older crowd gathers here, and when they flee to warmer climes in the fall, the restful lakeside restaurant closes. Watch your dinner grilled on an open fire and don't forget to pick up some barbecue sauce to take home. Open Memorial Day–Labor Day, daily, from 5:30 A.M. (closing time varies); in spring and fall, call for days and

hours. **1462 E. Shore Dr., Detroit Lakes, 56501; 218-847-8192.**

Hotel Shoreham—$ to $$$

One of the oldest restaurants in the area (established in 1910) and undoubtedly the funkiest, the Hotel Shoreham sits on the channel that connects popular Lakes Sallie and Melissa. Inside, a huge moose head gazes down on diners, and old photos and college-sports memorabilia crowd the walls in the restaurant and bar. On the high bar ceiling are dollar (and larger) bills, shot up there in a method that the owner will explain only if you part with a dollar, too. A mural of a younger Hotel Shoreham, done by Chuck Merry, a local art teacher, is on one wall of the bar. And hey, let's not forget the food. The Shoreham is known for its walleye and homemade pizza, and also features 11-ounce ribeyes, cut from lean, organically raised Limousin cattle. Open from third Fri. in Apr.–late Sept., daily, 5:00 P.M.–1:00 A.M. Located 6 miles south of D.L. on Hwy. 59, then west 1 mile on County Rd. 22 in Shoreham on Lake Sallie. **218-847-9913.**

Main Street Restaurant—$ to $$

This is it, the Main Street Restaurant (actually it's on Washington Ave., but that *is* the main drag in D.L.)—complete with hot beef and pork sandwiches and homemade pie, and filling breakfasts. It's always busy with lots of local diners, and the food is good cafe cooking. Open year-round, Mon.–Sat., 7:00 A.M.–5:00 P.M., and Sun., 8:00 A.M.–2:00 P.M. **900 Washington Ave., Detroit Lakes, 56501; 218-847-3344.**

Services

Detroit Lakes Regional Chamber of Commerce and Tourism Bureau, 700 Washington Ave., Detroit Lakes, 56501; 800-542-3992 or 218-847-9202. Website: www.visitdetroitlakes.com.

Perham Area Chamber of Commerce, 155 E. Main St., P.O. Box 234, Perham, 56573; 800-634-6112 or 218-346-7710.

Lake of the Woods

Lake of the Woods, an enormous stretch of water that both Minnesota and Canada can claim, has about 65,000 miles of shoreline and some 14,000 islands. The lake dominates both the culture and the economy of the area, and is responsible for Minnesota's most abiding geographic anomaly—the little extra knob of land on the northern border.

Surrounded on three sides by Canada—making it necessary to drive through Canada to get back to Minnesota for those coming by car—this "Northwest Angle" is particularly beloved by fishers. Electricity and phone lines, not to mention the road, all came to the Angle within the last 20 years, according to Chamber of Commerce President Joan Undahl, who with her husband owns Norm's Resort. The Angle has fought hard and successfully to keep its one-room schoolhouse. Its post office, staffed by George Risser for nearly 30 years, is the most northerly zip code in the Lower 48 states.

The largest towns near the lake are Warroad and Baudette. Baudette is actually on the Rainy River, while Warroad is on the Warroad River. Warroad is 6 miles from Manitoba, Canada; Baudette is just across the Rainy River from the province of Ontario. While Baudette was named for an early settler, Warroad, originally War Road, took its name from the path west of the city that the Dakota and Ojibwe Indians often traveled on their way to fight each other. In addition to Baudette and Warroad, Roseau, west of the lake, is the third in the trio of area centers. All are hockey-crazed towns, and their high school teams have been regular contenders in the state hockey tournament. The outdoor life in and around the lake is a big attraction for both residents and visitors alike.

History

Although there is much evidence of prehistoric humans present after the great Glacial Lake Agassiz receded thousands of years ago, the first

European to see the still-massive remnant of the glacial lake was Jacques De Noyon, who arrived in 1688, according to a history written by the Lake of the Woods County Historical Society. More than 40 years later, Pierre La Vérendrye, the far-ranging French Canadian who explored much of western Canada, came to Lake of the Woods in 1732 and found several different tribes of American Indians settled here, including Dakota, Assiniboine, Cree, and Monsonis; the Ojibwe who now live in the area had not pushed so far west in La Vérendrye's time. He built Fort St. Charles on an island off the Northwest Angle on the lake, and used it as a base for his explorations. Lake of the Woods was part of the corridor for travels of the voyageurs working for the fur trade. During the heyday of the fur-trading industry, several rival fur-trading companies had posts on the lakeshore.

This Northwest Angle portion of Minnesota exists because of a boundary dispute begun in 1823 between the U.S. and British surveyors trying to ascertain the northwest point of the lake according to treaty terms. The result, finally settled in the 1920s, was that Minnesota retained the bit of land called the Northwest Angle, which is completely separated from the rest of the Lower 48 states.

The area went through several booms after the fur trade dwindled, including logging, commercial fishing, and, finally, tourism. Today, tourists and sport fishers often find their way—by car, boat, or plane—to "the Angle."

Major Attractions

Lake of the Woods

Shared by the United States and Canada, Lake of the Woods is the largest freshwater lake in the United States after the Great Lakes. There are more than 14,000 islands in the lake, which has an area of more than 2,000 square miles. The depth of the lake varies from several feet in the southern end to more than 150 feet in the north. Pristine white-sand beaches ring the south end of the lake, and stretches of the shore are nearly obscured by the rushes, while the rocky Canadian shield—granite outcrops that are among the world's oldest rocks—pokes through in the north. At the lake, once home to many commercial fisheries, most fishing now is done for sport. Famous for its walleye, the lake also harbors northern pike, muskie, sauger (a smaller relative of walleye), large- and smallmouth bass, sturgeon, crappie, and perch. Anglers flock to the lake summer and winter; most resorts along the lake offer guide and launch service. See Resorts.

Festivals and Events

International Series of Champions 500

last weekend in Jan.

Hundreds of crack snowmobilers start their engines in Warroad in this event and then race 500 miles over prepared tracks. Between the snowmobilers and the spectators, attendance can get close to 7,000, according to the Warroad Area Chamber of Commerce. Free. For details, contact the chamber (see Services).

Jack pines at Hayes Lake State Park. Photo courtesy of the Minnesota Department of Natural Resources.

Willie Walleye Day

first Sat. in June

Baudette, home of the 9,500-pound Willie the Walleye statue, celebrates the catch that Lake of the Woods and Rainy River are known for with a day that includes, naturally, a walleye fry. Other events are a street dance, kids' activities, and a craft sale. Contact the Lake of the Woods Tourism Bureau in Baudette (see Services).

Traditional Powwow

first weekend in June

Dancers, singers, and drummers in ornate dress from several tribes participate in the annual powwow, held at "the point" at the end of Lake St. on the beach in Warroad. For details, contact the Warroad Area Chamber of Commerce (see Services).

Wildflower Celebration

usually mid-June

The showy lady slipper—the lovely orchid that is the state flower of Minnesota—and its more modest cousins love this corner of Minnesota,

Getting There

Towns along the southern edge of the Lake of the Woods are slightly more than 300 miles from the Twin Cities, although the extra distance up to the Angle adds more than 75 miles. Hwy. 71/72 north from Bemidji provides the straightest shot north. There are international airports for charter and private planes at Warroad and Baudette, a landing strip at Angle Inlet, as well as float plane service from both Baudette and Warroad. Contact the Lake of the Woods Tourism Bureau in Baudette (see Services) for specifics.

and bloom profusely during June. Although they can be found along many county and back roads, those along Hwy. 11 are the most visible, which persuaded the late Gov. Rudy Perpich to declare Hwy. 11 a state wildflower route. Flower lovers recently fought the widening of the highway, and when their efforts failed, they recruited volunteers to dig up orchids and transplant them to a temporary "home" awaiting the end of the highway work. Most were replanted by spring 1999. The profusion of wildflowers is celebrated each June with a daylong event in Williams that includes a lunch, program, and maps for a self-guided tour of nearby sites showcasing 45 varieties of wildflowers. Call or write Celeste LaValla, owner of The Rustic Planter and one of the organizers of the save-the-orchids effort, for information on the celebration or on the orchid restoration effort. The celebration is free. **Rte. 3, Box 14, Warroad, 56763; 218-386-2744.**

Blueberry Festival and Chili Cookoff
first weekend in Aug.

This is usually peak time for blueberries on both the mainland and the islands. All the restaurants and cafes on the Northwest Angle and islands put blueberries on the menu this weekend, and there are other blueberry-oriented events. Visitors are welcome to pick their own; ask someone local first if it's a bad "bear year"; if so, better stay away

from island picking. For festival details, contact the Northwest Angle and Islands Chamber of Commerce, **800-434-8531.**

Run to the Lake Car Show
second weekend in Aug.

Dozens of lovingly cared-for antique cars parade through Warroad twice during this event, beginning from their places on the parking lot of the Patch Motel and ending up on the shore of Lake of the Woods. Live music and other events are part of the celebration. Ask the Warroad Area Chamber of Commerce (see Services) for details.

Oktoberfest
last weekend in Sept.

It's nonstop music of all kinds (polka, country, and big band) when Baudette puts on its annual Oktoberfest. Bands play from the afternoon until the wee hours for the three-day festival. There is a wooden dance floor under a huge tent. German food is available. Fee. Obtain details from the Lake of the Woods Tourism Bureau in Baudette (see Services).

Outdoor Activities

Birding

Birds are plentiful in Hayes Lake State Park—look for eagles, osprey, loons, herons, grebes, belted kingfishers, and other birds along the lakeshore in early morning and evening. Also in the park are sandhill cranes, cedar waxwings, magpies, and gray jays. At Zippel Bay State Park, bird-watchers are thrilled by such "big-lake" residents as white pelicans, double-crested cormorants, several kinds of gulls and terns, plus eagles and osprey. Greater sandhill cranes nest in the marsh north of the bay, and the piping plover, an endangered species, nests close by. See Parks.

Fishing

A lot of the fish stories you hear from those who have tried Lake of the Woods are true, not exaggerations. Ed Arnesen, part of the family that owns Arnesen's Rocky Point (see Resorts), says sturgeons that top 200 pounds have been caught. Once in a while, he adds, someone will get a 14-pound walleye or 30-pound northern. Arnesen reports that ice fishing has boomed in the last decade, probably due to greater interest in winter sports in general. As for the numbers, Arnesen says, "There are just as many fish in the lake now as there ever were." Fish in Hayes Lake (State Park) include crappie, sunfish, and northern (see Parks). Besides the excellent lake fishing, many people show up in the early spring for the superb walleye fishing on the Rainy River, when it is the only place in the state for open-water walleye fishing. There is good fishing at Franz Jevne State Park, on the Rainy River. For seasons and license information, call the Area Fisheries Supervisor in International Falls, **218-286-5220.**

Golf

Country Club

Golfers who like a challenge will find it in the nine-hole course in the Northwest Angle at the Country Club. Each hole is par 3–4, but it's the greens that provide the challenge: they are old-fashioned sand greens. And, since the Minnesota Pollution Control Agency decreed that sand greens can no longer be oiled, they can make for tough putting, according to course owner George Risser. The course is open to the public. Greens fees are $7. Clubs can be rented. Open about mid-May–mid-Sept., daily, daylight hours. Located **on County Rd. 333 in the heart of the town of Angle Inlet; 218-223-8001.**

Hiking

Hayes Lake State Park has 13 miles of hiking trails in all. In Zippel Bay State Park, there are 6 miles of hiking trails. See Parks.

Hunting

Beltrami Island State Forest (see Museums and Historic Sites) provides good habitat for ruffed grouse and attracts many grouse hunters. There is also good duck and goose hunting in the area, and deer abound in the Northwest Region, too. For season and license information, call the Dept.

of Natural Resources field office in Bemidji, **218-755-2964.**

Skiing

CROSS-COUNTRY

There are groomed cross-country ski trails at Hayes Lake (6 miles' worth) and Zippel Bay State Parks (see Parks), but the Lake of the Woods area is most definitely snowmobile country.

Snowmobiling

Around Lake of the Woods, snowmobile engines rev up after the first snowfall and don't quit until spring. Snowmobilers have more than 1,000 miles of trails to choose from. In Beltrami Island State Forest (see Museums and Historic Sites), south and west of Warroad, there are 58 miles of groomed trail, connecting with the 52.5-mile Baudette/Norris Trail, and that's just two of the trails. Snowmobile trail maps are available from the Lake of the Woods Tourism Bureau in Baudette (see Services). Winter visitors to Hayes Lake State Park find another 6 miles of snowmobile trails (see Parks).

Seeing and Doing

Museums and Historic Sites

Beltrami Island State Forest/Red Lake Wildlife Management Area

This 669,000-acre state forest, the second largest in the state, is an agreeable mix of sandy ridges loved by blueberries, plus tamarac- and spruce-dotted bogs, silvery streams, and a generous shot of history. Those who drive along its 250 miles of forest roads are surprised to learn that what appears to be a forest primeval was once a settlement. In the earlier 1900s, more than 1,600 farmers settled here, only to find later that the sandy, boggy land would not support them. Many moved out on their own, and the federal government, with the help of the Works Progress Administration (WPA) and the Resettlement Administration, later moved the rest out in the 1930s. Some went willingly; others protested—

The beach at Zippel Bay State Park. Copyright © Minnesota Office of Tourism. Used by permission.

but in the end, everyone departed. Their descendants return on the last Sun. of June for a picnic at the forest's picnic area. Many signs of the settlement, including cemeteries and foundations of houses, remain, as do about a dozen buildings of the Norris Civilian Conservation Corps (CCC) Camp, a depression-era program to help young unemployed men. The workers in the 1930s engaged in construction, planting trees, digging wells, etc. The camp buildings are now on the National Register of Historic Places and the camp is still in use as the headquarters of the Red Lake Wildlife Management Area, which shares land with the state forest. If staff have the time, they are happy to show visitors around the camp, but there is no formal tour. There are several small campgrounds on the state forest. The Bemis Hill campsite has good hunting and blueberry picking close by. The Minnesota state flower, the showy lady slipper, and other members of the orchid family can be seen growing along forest roads and are particularly prolific near Norris Camp. No charge for forest entry. Red Lake WMA, **P.O. Box 100, Roosevelt, 56673; 218-783-6861.**

Fort St. Charles

The restored fort, built in 1732 by explorer Pierre La Vérendrye, is located on Magnusson's Island just off Young's Bay in the Northwest Angle. In 1736 his son, Jean-Baptiste La Vérendrye, and a Jesuit priest, Father Jean Pierre Aulneau, along with 19 other men, were killed by a Dakota party about 20 miles from the fort. Their bodies were buried within the fort, and it was abandoned a few years later, after Pierre La Vérendrye's death in 1749. The fort fell into disuse and was nearly forgotten until 1908, when it was rediscovered and the bodies were removed. The stockade and corner bastions were restored, the sites of the buildings within the fort and the former gravesites were marked, and a memorial chapel was built—all through the efforts of the Minnesota Fourth Degree Knights of Columbus. There is no interpreter on site, but entry is free. For those without a boat, inquire at local resorts for transportation to the island (see Resorts, and Services).

Lake of the Woods County Museum

Lake of the Woods enthusiasts enjoy the bird's-eye view of the islands and shore of the lake provided by the museum's aerial slide-tape show. There are also exhibitions on the lake's geological and natural history, prehistoric human settlements, commercial fishing, logging, the devastating forest fire of 1910 (which killed 42 people), and the agricultural and pharmaceutical industries in the area. The museum, part of the Lake of the Woods Historical Society, is open May–Sept., Tues.–Sat., 10:00 A.M.–4:00 P.M., and Sun., 1:00–5:00 P.M. Free. **119 Eighth Ave. SE, East Baudette, 56623; 218-634-1200.**

Parks

Blueberry Hill

This DNR campground, also a day-use park, is a couple of miles west of Williams on one of the highest points in Lake of the Woods County. It is not really a hill by most standards, but is nonetheless well and truly named. In late July or early Aug., depending on the weather, it is covered with blueberries, free to the pickers. The park also has picnic sites and a campground. **218-634-2172.**

Hayes Lake State Park

Take a picnic down to the edge of Hayes Lake on a quiet day, and marvel at the stillness and beauty of the pristine water and the shoreline fringed with trees. If there is a place that is "away from it all," it must be Hayes Lake. The lake itself, surprisingly, has not been here for eons but was created when the North Fork of the Roseau River was dammed in 1973. Only electric motors are allowed on the lake, which keeps the noise down and perpetuates the wilderness atmosphere. Commonly seen animals are deer, fox, raccoon, and beaver, while black bears, moose, otters, and wolves are less frequent sights. Birding and fishing are good here, too. The 0.5-mile Pine Ridge nature trail hugs the lakeshore from the campground to the sandy beach. A second self-guided trail, 1.5 miles long, takes visitors through the homestead area in the park's western section; maps for both self-guided trails are available at the park headquarters. On the eastern edge of the park is a boardwalk over muskeg and bog areas, where rare plants can be spotted; ask for viewing advice at park headquarters. The park has 5 miles of unpaved trails for mountain bikes and 7 miles for horseback riders. Camping is permitted, and there are two seasonal camper cabins. The park is 22 miles southeast of Roseau

off County State Aid Hwy. 4. **HC4, Box 84, Roseau, 56751; 218-425-7504.**

Zippel Bay State Park

Lying on the fine white-sand beach dotted with driftwood, watching the waves approach the shore, it may seem that you have arrived on a tropical island paradise. But no—this is indeed a state park in northern Minnesota. The 2-mile beach is on Zippel Bay of the oceanlike Lake of the Woods, and the surrounding woods are jack pine, birch, and aspen—not a palm tree in sight. If you can stir from the beach, drive (through a golden tunnel of overhanging birch leaves in the fall) to the stone jetty on placid Zippel Bay itself. Picnic, fish from the pier, launch your boat, or climb the big rocks by the boat harbor for a super view of the moody lake. The park is worth a winter visit, too, as the shoreline and rocks are festooned with natural ice "sculptures." Slow to freeze because of its size, the lake also thaws slowly. Deer are common in the park, with timber wolves, black bears, coyotes, fisher, otter, moose, and the rare pine marten spotted more seldom. The berry picking is great, with blueberries, juneberries, chokecherries, and cranberries among the offerings. There are 6 miles of hiking trails and 12 miles of horse trails. The park, which has camping, is located 11 miles northeast of Williams; from Hwy. 11, go north 5 miles on County Rd. 2, then east on County Rd. 8 for 5 miles. **Hwy. 8, HC2, Box 25, Williams, 56686; 218-783-6252.**

Scenic Drives

Borderland State Wildflower Route

Hwy. 11 is a designated wildflower route, as the edges of the highway, from Baudette westward as far as Greenbush, are lined with flowers including Minnesota's state flower, the showy lady slipper. Widening of the highway (see Festivals and Events) may reduce their numbers.

Wilderness Drive, Beltrami Island State Forest

A wonderful map, with easy-to-follow routes and plenty of historical information, outlines five separate drives, including a spectacular fall color drive, almost entirely within the boundaries of the state forest. Only one warning: start with a full gas tank and allow plenty of time, as these roads are not meant for speeding and it is indeed dark in the forest at night. Maps are available from the Lake of the Woods Tourism Bureau (see Services).

Tours

Christian Brothers Hockey Sticks

The Christian brothers—Bill and Roger—were super hockey players and were on the 1960 U.S. Olympic teams that pulled off a stunning upset over the former U.S.S.R. to win the gold medal. Tours of this hockey-stick manufacturing plant last either 20 or 30 minutes and are given year-round, Mon.–Fri., 10:30 A.M. and 3:00 P.M. Located **in Warroad; 218-386-1111.**

Marvin Windows

This well-known window manufacturer, a huge place with Warroad roots going back nearly a century, offers one-hour tours of the factory for either walk-in visitors or by reservation. Located **in Warroad; 218-386-1430.**

Polaris Snowmobiles

Tours of the snowmobile factory, lasting 30–45 minutes, are given Mon.–Fri., 2:00 P.M. The factory is located **just south of Roseau, on the west side of Hwy. 89; 218-463-2312.**

BOAT TOURS

Island Cruises and Passenger Service

Charlie McKeever runs sightseeing cruises on Lake of the Woods; prices depend on the number in the party and the distance involved. He also ferries tourists from the mainland of the Angle out to the islands and drops them off to look at Fort St. Charles. McKeever was born on the Northwest Angle and is still there more than 70 years later; he was in the resort business and tried to retire, but he's still providing island passenger service. Charlie doesn't have a set schedule. The season runs about May 15–Nov. 1. His three boats are **docked at Young's Bay Resort,** now run by his son (everyone up here is related, it seems). **218-386-1128** or **218-223-8261.**

Rainy River Cruise and Shore Lunch

Take a leisurely cruise on the *Leonard C.,* a two-decker riverboat, down the Rainy River to Pine Island in the Lake of the Woods for a shore lunch of fried walleye, fried potatoes, and beans. The two-hour cruise and the all-you-can-eat lunch together cost $18 (1998 price). May–Sept., daily. Leaves **from the Sportsman's Lodge in Baudette; 800-862-8602.**

Wagering

Lake of the Woods Casino

Smaller than many of the state's casinos, Lake of the Woods Casino in Warroad has 250 slot machines, plus blackjack and keeno. Open Wed.–Sun., 24 hours, and Mon.–Tues., 8:00 A.M.–1:00 A.M. **1012 E. Lake St., Warroad, 56763; 218-386-3381.**

Where to Stay

Lake of the Woods has been a destination for tourists—mainly avid anglers—for nearly a century. There are many resorts to choose from, plus a few motels. For a complete listing, contact the Lake of the Woods Tourism Bureau, and the chambers of commerce at Warroad, the Northwest Angle, and Roseau (see Services). Below, in listings for which price ranges are not given, consult the resort; many have a variety of packages, which can include meals, ice-house rentals, etc.

Bed-and-Breakfasts

Hospital Bay Bed-and-Breakfast—$$$

Built as a private home in 1905, this building became Warroad's first hospital in the 1920s. After doing much restoration work on it, Harvey and Mary Corneliusen, who formerly farmed in the area, opened their four-room b-and-b. The rooms, decorated with Victorian-era furnishings, have private baths. A book-lined fireplace room off the dining room is inviting. There is dockage for those arriving by water, and a paddleboat and canoe for guests. The house is on the Warroad

River, just 0.25 mile from the lake itself. **620 Lake St. NE, Warroad, 56763; 800-568-6028 or 218-386-2627.**

Hotels, Motels, and Inns

The Patch Motel—$$
The Patch is a sprawling white motel in Warroad. The 80 rooms are comfortable, and the motel includes a pool and whirlpool, but the best part about staying here is the Patch Restaurant (see Where to Eat) just across the parking lot. If saving money is a concern, ask if any of the singles (actually a room with one, not the usual two, double beds) is available for a few dollars less. The Patch is very convenient for those doing business in Warroad. Located on Hwy. 11 W. in Warroad. **Box N, Warroad, 56736; 800-288-2753, fax 218-386-2723.**

Resorts

Angle Outpost—call for rates
The Angle Outpost has 12 cabins and is oriented to adults, rather than families with children. Many of the cabins have fireplaces. The central lodge has a nice dining room and a small store. Guide service is available. Open year-round, with heated ice houses for rent and transportation via track vehicles. **Box 36, Angle Inlet, 56711; 800-441-5014** (reservations only) or **218-223-8101.**

Arnesen's Rocky Point Resort—call for rates
Ed Arnesen's grandfather started his commercial fishing business, the first lake enterprise, in 1897. His son gradually got into the resort business after World War II, and Ed and his relatives have turned those few cabins into the thriving Arnesen's Rocky Point Resort. The 17 cabins are very comfortable and modern, with linens supplied. The wood-paneled restaurant/lounge has a massive stone fireplace; the house specialty—natch—is walleye. The resort setting, true to its name, is on a scenic rocky point on Lake of the Woods' south side, although there are sandy beaches close by. For a beautiful view of the lake, walk along the stone jetty that protects the marina. In winter, Arnesen's has 45 ice houses for rent; some have sleeping accommodations. Transportation is by track van with flotation devices for extra safety. Many packages are available. **R.R. 2, Box 816, Roosevelt, 56673; 800-535-7585.**

Carlson's Cabins—call for rates
Rick Carlson built these three showplace log cabins with his own hands, with loving attention to detail. They each have two bedrooms on the first floor, plus a loft bedroom, and can sleep up to eight. There are deer trophies on the walls, which are faced with half-round logs, and verandas from which to admire the view. The Lake of the Woods around Carlson's is very open, with few trees. Walleyes, muskies, northerns, jumbo perch, and large- and smallmouth bass are waiting to be caught here. Open year-round. A sod airstrip is next to the cabins. Families are welcomed by Rick and Beth Carlson, who have young children themselves. Two-night minimum stay. **P.O. Box 65, Angle Inlet, 56711; 800-735-8961 or 218-223-8961.**

Zippel Bay Resort—call for rates
Right next to the magnificent Zippel Bay State Park, the resort has 10 cabins and a pleasant dining room, cocktail lounge, and game room. The floating gazebo is the perfect place to sit and relax. There is good walleye and sauger fishing, and Zippel Bay provides excellent hunting for bluebill and mallard in the fall. Ask about packages available. **HC2, Box 51, Williams, 56686; 800-222-2537 or 218-783-6235.**

Camping

Many of the resorts in the area also have space for RVs and for tent campers; ask for a listing from area chambers of commerce and tourism bureaus (see Services). There is also camping in Beltrami Island State Forest (see Museums and Historic Sites).

State Parks—$
Hayes Lake and Zippel Bay State Parks have modern campsites, some with electrical hookups. There are 35 campsites at Hayes Lake, nine with electricity; Zippel Bay has 57 campsites. To

reserve, call **The Connection, 800-246-CAMP** or **612-922-9000.**

Where to Eat

Many of the resorts in the area have excellent restaurants and they are open to the public. This is walleye country and local restaurants often have it on the menu.

The Patch—$ to $$$$

Located across the parking lot from the popular Patch Motel, this bright and friendly restaurant features—not surprisingly—walleye, either on its own or with a steak. The rest of the menu consists of chicken, ribs, and all manner of sandwiches and burgers, including buffalo burgers. Tuck into a piece of homemade pie for dessert. Open Mon.–Thurs. and Sun., 6:00 A.M.–9:00 P.M., and Fri.–Sat., 9:00 A.M.–10:00 P.M. Located **across from the Patch Motel on Hwy. 11 W. in Warroad; 218-386-2082.**

Ralph and Randy's—$

Although this is a supermarket, rather than a cafe, it's easy to buy a picnic lunch at the well-stocked deli counter and take it to the many picnic places that are around Baudette or farther afield. Alternatively, eat at one of several tables in the supermarket; they have a super view of Baudette Bay. Located **right on Hwy. 11; 218-634-3130.**

Services

For information on Lake of the Woods County, contact the **Lake of the Woods Tourism Bureau, P.O. Box 518, Baudette, 56623; 800-382-FISH. Website: www.lakeofthewoodsmn.com.**

Northwest Angle and Islands Chamber of Commerce, P.O. Box 68, Angle Inlet, 56711; 800-434-8531.

Roseau Civic and Commerce, City Hall, 100 Second Ave. NE, Roseau, 56751; 218-463-1542.

Warroad Area Chamber of Commerce, P.O. Box 551, Warroad, 56763; 800-328-4455 or **218-386-3543.**

Upper Northwest

West of the forests and north of the lake country, the far northwest corner of Minnesota is a flat, sugar beet–planted expanse of prairie. It's not a traditional tourist destination, but that doesn't mean there isn't plenty to do, particularly if visitors are hardy outdoors fans or history buffs. Crookston, East Grand Forks, Red Lake Falls, and Thief River Falls are the largest towns in the area in Minnesota, while Grand Forks, North Dakota, at nearly 52,000, is the biggest town in the region. (Because East Grand Forks and Grand Forks cannot really be considered separately, Grand Forks, North Dakota, is included in this book on Minnesota.)

The deceptively small-seeming Red River flooded with disastrous consequences in the spring of 1997, causing particular havoc in the greater Grand Forks area, where the whole town of Grand Forks had to be evacuated. The residents are back now, most of the damage has been repaired, and tourist-oriented businesses such as motels and restaurants have long since been ready for visitors.

History

American Indians lived in the upper northwest before the first European settlers came; after the treaty of Old Crossing in 1863, the rich soil of the Red River Valley was opened for settlement. In earlier years, this was fur-trading country and Red Lake Falls was the site of a North West Company fur trading post in 1798. The area still has a French influence, due to the pockets of French-speaking Canadians who settled in towns such as Red Lake Falls and Gentilly, according to Virgil Benoit, whose French ancestry led him to form—with others—the Association of the French of the North (AFRAN).

Squeaky oxcarts, wooden wheels making their iron axles shriek with excruciating noise, traversed the trails that ran roughly in a line from St. Paul to Winnipeg, Manitoba, and beyond. The heyday of oxcart traffic transporting goods and people was in the mid-1800s. The railroad came through in 1871 and European settlement started in earnest then. Steamboat transport on the Red Lake River, and the Red River itself, had a few years of glory, too. Agriculture is still the basis for the area's economy.

Larson Cabin at Old Mill State Park.

Getting There

The Upper Northwest is approximately 300 miles northwest of Minneapolis and St. Paul. In Minnesota, Hwy. 59 runs through the middle of the Upper Northwest. In North Dakota, I-29 scoots along the eastern edge of the state, giving access to towns in the Upper Northwest. There is a major airport in Grand Forks, North Dakota.

Festivals and Events

Creameries Picnic
last Sun. in July
From 1928 until the mid-1950s, creameries in each local community usually held picnics in what is now Old Mill State Park. The park celebrates those memories with a picnic for all comers, with free ice cream. Picnickers must provide their own food, however. See Historic Sites. Held in the park picnic area, 1:00–5:00 P.M. **218-437-8174.**

International Woodcarvers Festival
first full weekend in Aug.
This festival has grown from a demonstration by one carver to a showcase of about 40 wood artists from the United States and Canada. Onlookers vote for their favorite carver. Wares are for sale as well. The festival is sponsored by Lake Bronson State Park, where the event is held, Sat.–Sun., 10:00 A.M.–5:00 P.M. See Parks. **218-754-2200.**

Heritage Days
third weekend in Aug.
The East Grand Forks Heritage Center, next to the Technical College on Hwy. 220 N., is the site of this annual back-to-yesteryear festival, featuring steam threshing, a country breakfast and dinner, a sawmill demonstration, storytelling, a pioneer village, dancing, and music. **218-773-7481.**

Ox Cart Days
third weekend in Aug.
This is a bang-up community festival in Crookston, where oxcarts used to wend their noisy way. Today's festival is short on oxcarts, but long on entertainment, with a torchlight parade, street dance, duck race, and art in the park. **218-281-4320.**

Catfish Days
usually last weekend in Aug.
There is a fishing contest for big channel cats lurking in the Red River during Catfish Days, of course, but events also include a frog-kissing contest (bring your own frog) and a fat-cat competition (bring your own chubby feline), as well as a catfish feed with farm-raised catfish. All events are located along the Red River, the weekend before the University of North Dakota begins its fall quarter. Fee. Call the East Grand Forks Chamber of Commerce, **218-773-7481.**

French Chautauqua and Arts Festival and Encampment
usually fourth weekend in Aug.
The French ancestors of many upper northwest residents are remembered each Aug. in this festival sponsored by the Association of the French of the North (AFRAN). The Chautauqua portion of the festival includes educational and entertaining lessons in local history, told in various forms, such as plays and living-history "reappearances" of such historical characters as Red Lake Falls founder and Métis leader Pierre Bottineau. Performing-arts events reflect the entire heritage of the upper northwest. The food, however, has a definite French flavor, with meat pie (*tourtiere*), pea soup, and baked beans among the foods sold. An encampment reenacting the 1840s is also part of the festival, which is at the Old Treaty Crossing Park in Huot, west of Red Lake Falls. Fee. For information, call Virgil Benoit, **218-253-2270.**

Grinding Day
last Sun. in Aug. before Labor Day
Each year, the Marshall County Historical Society fires up the old steam engine, and the grist mill at Old Mill State Park grinds flour once again.

Best of all, the flour is sold, too. Grinding Day brings back to life the milling days in the park, which go back to mills built by the Larson family, who homesteaded the land in 1882 and later built several mills. See Historic Sites. **218-437-8174.**

First Night Greater Grand Forks
Dec. 31

Residents on both sides of the Red River take part in this annual family-oriented celebration of winter. Shuttle buses—with step-aboard entertainers—take revelers from one venue to another. Events include concerts, theatrical performances (the 1997 event boasted an English pantomime), and outdoor fun. Fee. For information, contact the Greater Grand Forks Convention and Visitors Bureau (see Services).

Outdoor Activities

Biking

Lake Bronson State Park has 5 miles of bike trails; see Parks. **218-754-2200.**

Agassiz Recreation Trail

This 32-mile trail stretches from Fertile to Ulen, skirting the pleasant community of Twin Valley. This is a multiuse trail, so bikers share it with hikers, horseback riders, and, in winter, cross-country skiers, dog sledders, and snowmobilers; all are welcome on the twin 10-foot-wide treadways. **218-584-5169.**

Bottineau Trail

Volunteers converted an abandoned railroad bed in Red Lake Falls into the paved Bottineau Trail for bikers and hikers in summer. The trail, nearly 4 miles long, runs past the historic courthouse in Red Lake Falls and through several city parks before ending at County Rd. 11. (In winter, it's used for skiing and snowmobiling.) **800-832-5187.**

Birding

Birders are drawn to upper northwest Minnesota, rich in bird species because it is at the junction of three ecosystems—prairie, boreal forest, and aspen parkland. In addition, much of the land

is public, providing good habitat for various species. Spring and summer bird migrations bring many species (including warblers, finches, and hawks) to Old Mill State Park, adding to the already abundant bird life. Several kinds of owls—including the great gray owl, boreal owl, and yellow owl—have been seen regularly in the upper northwest area. Obtain a brochure from the Thief River Falls Chamber of Commerce (see Services) detailing seven auto routes of varying lengths for bird-watching in wildlife refuges and other public sites.

Agassiz National Wildlife Refuge

Nearly two-thirds of the Agassiz National Wildlife Refuge's 61,500 acres are wetlands, making the area a waterfowl paradise. About half of the 280 species spotted in the refuge nest there. Among the birds that can be seen are great blue herons, Franklin's gulls, great egrets, double-crested cormorants, and western grebes, as well as many ducks and Canada geese. Many songbirds also pass through during migration periods. **218-449-4415.**

Boating

RIVER TUBING

Rentals and Tours

On hot summer days, there are long lines of young people and a smattering of the older crowd waiting for the shuttle buses to take them to the start of the two- to three-hour float down the Red Lake River. The river flows past some high, eroded cliffs and wooded banks, and there are several islands in it where tubers can stop for a rest. **Voyageur's View**'s daily tube rental includes unlimited float trips. There is a campground adjacent to the tubing office. Open Memorial Day–Labor Day, daily. Located 1 mile north of Red Lake Falls on County Rd. 13. **Box 48B, Red Lake Falls, 56750; 218-253-2031** or **218-253-4329.**

Fishing

Lake Bronson is a likely spot for game fish such as northerns, walleyes, largemouth bass, and crappie. There are huge channel catfish—up to 20 pounds—lurking in the Red River; most people don't eat the cats, however, as these bottom feeders may contain unhealthy levels of contaminants. For information on seasons and licenses, call the Area Fisheries Supervisor, **218-847-1579.**

Hiking

Lake Bronson State Park has 14 miles of hiking trails (see Parks). In Old Mill State Park, there are 7 miles of hiking trails (see Historic Sites). There is also hiking on the 32-mile Agassiz Recreation Trail and the 4-mile Bottineau Trail (see Biking). In Fertile Sand Hills Nature Center, there are 10 miles of hiking trails (see Nature Centers).

Skiing

CROSS-COUNTRY

There are trails in Lake Bronson and Old Mill State Parks (6.5 miles in the latter—see Parks); in Red Lake Falls and Thief River Falls, residents often take to the frozen riverbeds to ski. Red Lake Falls also has the Bottineau Trail, a nearly 4-mile-long stretch along a reclaimed railroad bed, a multipurpose trail used for skiing and snowmobiling in winter; Agassiz Recreation Trail offers 32 miles of trail in winter (see Biking). Fertile Sand Hills Nature Center has 10 miles of trails (see Nature Centers).

Snowmobiling

The flat expanses in upper northwest Minnesota were made for snowmobiling, and the trails are certainly here in abundance. The 32-mile Agassiz Recreation Trail is open to snowmobilers in winter, as is the 4-mile Bottineau Trail (see Biking). Lake Bronson (see Parks) and Old Mill State Parks (see Historic Sites) also have trails available. In the upper northwest, there are approximately 1,300 miles of groomed trails, maintained by local snowmobile clubs, with 500 miles in the vicinity of Thief River Falls. For trail information in the Thief River Falls area, call **218-681-3720.**

Seeing and Doing

Art Galleries and Museums

North Dakota Art Museum

The University of North Dakota houses the North Dakota Museum of Art, but the museum is not part of the university. Basically a museum of contemporary art, its permanent collection includes works by regional as well as national and international artists. Open Mon.–Fri., 9:00 A.M.–5:00 P.M., and Sat.–Sun., 1:00–5:00 P.M. Located **on Centennial Dr.; 701-777-4195.**

Twin Valley Heritage Museum and Art Gallery

Artist Gene Lysaker, born and raised in Twin Valley and back after decades away in the advertising business, is so well regarded by the town that it built a gallery onto its museum just to show his work, which is more or less this gallery's permanent exhibit. Lysaker draws on memories of his boyhood in the town where Norwegian was commonly spoken until mid-century. Even now, Lysaker says, there are many who speak the language of their ancestors. Lysaker's lively Americana paintings celebrate the glories of small towns. Lysaker also does many wildlife studies, and recently has branched into computerized art. The gallery and museum, which contain pioneer artifacts and clothing among other things, are both worthwhile, and tourist information is available in the new building. Call for hours. Located **on Hwy. 32 in Twin Valley; 218-584-5658.** Lysaker's work can also be seen at his studio/workshop, **107 Norman Ave. NW,** just a block from the gallery; call first to be sure he's home; **218-584-8110.**

Historic Sites

Old Mill State Park

A cool oasis in the hot summer, Old Mill State Park includes both forested river land and some prairie, plus the two old mills that gave the park its name. Near the park, on an ancient beach ridge that is a remnant of Glacial Lake Agassiz, is the Pembina Trail, used by noisy oxcarts during the middle decades of the 1800s. In 1882 Lars Larson homesteaded what is now parkland, and in 1886 built the first mill on the Middle River. The Larson family built several successive mills in later years. The surviving mills, and a restored log cabin, are of great historical interest in the park; interpretive signs and an audiotape explain them in detail. The park is also a recreational draw, as the swimming pond, which has an artesian well as its source, is a perfect way to cool down in July and Aug. Near the pond are several beautiful stone and wood buildings and bridges built by the Works Progress Administration (WPA). Moose, wolves, bear, deer, and otter use the river valley as a travel corridor. A summer naturalist offers programs, and a short, self-guided trail leaves from the parking lot. In winter, children love the park's sliding hill and skating rink, and there are cross-country ski trails and 1.5 miles for snowmobilers. The park has camping. Located 13 miles east of Argyle, off County State Aid Hwy. 4. **Rte. 1, Box 43, Argyle, 56713; 218-437-8174.**

Museums

Peder Englestad Pioneer Village

Behind a stockade in Thief River Falls is the Pennington County historical museum featuring 19 buildings, including a church, depot, log houses, and stores. The buildings are filled with period artifacts. Open Memorial Day–Labor Day, daily, 1:00–5:00 P.M. Located **on Oakland Park Rd.; 218-681-5767.**

Nature Centers

Fertile Sand Hills Nature Center

The city of Fertile sponsors the Sand Hills Nature Center, where nature and arts programs are conducted throughout the year. There is a self-guided nature trail, 10 miles of hiking and cross-country ski trails, and a picnic area. Trail maps of the center (and of other wildlife management areas within 15 miles of Fertile) are available at the nature center and the Fertile Community Center. The nature center building, staffed by volunteers, is open year-round, often daily, 2:00–5:00 P.M. Located in the rolling sand hills 1 mile east of town. **P.O. Box 388, Fertile, 56540; 218-945-3129 or 218-945-6503.**

Parks

Agassiz Dunes

Glacial Lake Agassiz is long gone, but the sand dunes that were deposited 9,000–12,000 years ago along its eastern shore remain to delight visitors. The 435-acre dune field includes high sand dunes covered with prairie clover and dotted with ancient bur oaks. In the spring there is a lovely display of the pasqueflower. There is a walking trail threading through the fragile dunes and a parking area at the north end. Located 2 miles southwest of Fertile; after leaving Fertile on Hwy. 32, turn right on the gravel road 0.6 mile after crossing the Sand Hill River; continue for 0.5 mile, then turn left onto a dirt road. The dunes are owned by The Nature Conservancy and leased to the Minnesota Dept. of Natural Resources. **218-945-3129.**

Lake Bronson State Park

Users of this large state park can thank the dry 1930s for this prime recreation spot, containing the only sizable lake in the upper northwest. Drought during the '30s spurred the construction of a WPA-built dam on the Two Rivers River, creating 313-acre Lake Bronson. The lake has a popular sandy swimming beach, with a concession stand, and is also used for boating. Boats and canoes can be rented. Another legacy from those lean decades is the wood-and-stone "castle," as children call it, built by the WPA crew as a water tower but now used to give visitors a good view of the park. A summer naturalist leads many programs, including some given on the lake in a park boat. The flat landscape of the park was formed by Glacial Lake Agassiz, a massive body of water that covered the area, and one of the ancient beaches formed by its final retreat can be seen in the park. The 1.5-mile self-guided High Bank interpretive trail acquaints hikers with several aspects of the park, including Lake Agassiz. Moose are frequent park visitors, as are many bird species; deer, occasionally black bears, and many amphibians can also be spotted. In winter, there are snowmobile and cross-country ski trails. The park offers camping. The park staff may also have a large tent for rent, with cots, stove, and cooler available. Inquire at the park about the tent rental; for other reservations, see Camping. Located 1 mile east of the town of Lake Bronson, with access from Hwy. 28. **Box 9, Lake Bronson, 56734; 218-754-2200.**

Tours

Arctic Cat, Inc.

See how snowmobiles are assembled during a tour at the Arctic Cat plant in Thief River Falls. Tours are given Mon.–Fri., 1:00 P.M. **600 Brooks Ave. S., Thief River Falls, 56701; 218-681-8558.**

WALKING TOURS

Thief River Falls' 7.3-mile river walk takes pedestrians along the two rivers that meet in the city—the Thief River and the Red Lake River. The walk winds through six city parks and along two forest trails; pictographs along the route show what each river view was like years ago. A brochure with a walking map is available from the Thief River Falls Chamber of Commerce (see Services).

Wildlife Viewing

Agassiz National Wildlife Refuge is home to moose, plus one of the two resident wolf packs in national wildlife refuges in the Lower 48 states; the other lives in the nearby Tamarac National Wildlife Refuge (see the Detroit Lakes chapter in this section). A 4-mile self-guided auto tour may grant visitors a moose sighting (best times are early morning and late afternoon, when the moose feed near willow thickets). It's always advisable to check in with headquarters for tips on wildlife viewing, and permission for observation points not normally open to visitors may be given if conditions permit. Refuge staff also have the key to the former fire tower, 100 feet high, that can be climbed, but only during office hours, Mon.–Fri., 7:30 A.M.–4:00 P.M. Check with refuge staff about occasional public programs as well. Headquarters are 11 miles east of Holt on County Rd. 7. **Rte. 1, Box 74, Middle River, 56737; 218-449-4115.**

Where to Stay

Hotels, Motels, and Inns

The *Northwest Minnesota Visitor and Recreation Guide* (see Services) has a complete listing of accommodations available. For accommodations in Grand Forks, North Dakota, call the Greater Grand Forks Convention and Visitors Bureau (see Services).

C'Mon Inn—$$$

Part of a small chain of inns, this attractive new motel has all the amenities travelers have come to expect, at moderate prices. The pool area is particularly inviting after a long day. **1586 Hwy. 59 S., Thief River Falls, 56701; 218-681-3000.**

Chateau Motel—$$ to $$$

The Chateau is just what you want to find when you're on the road—a clean, modern motel with folks at the desk (often owners George and Joyce Nelson) who know the area. The chateau's 16 units more than fulfill these requirements. Located **north of Red Lake Falls; 218-253-4144.**

Camping

The *Northwest Minnesota Visitor and Recreation Guide* (see Services) lists campgrounds by community and also campgrounds in parks and recreational areas, including state forests. There is primitive camping in Heiberg Park north of Twin Valley on Hwy. 32. There are no facilities, but there is an outdoor toilet. No reservations. Free. No phone.

State Parks—$

Lake Bronson State Park has 194 campsites, 35 of them with electricity, and Old Mill State Park has 26 campsites, 10 with electrical hookups. To reserve a site, call **The Connection, 800-246-CAMP** or **612-922-9000.**

Thief River Falls City Tent and Trailer Park—$

Thief River Falls has 51 campsites, with full hookups, at its City Tent and Trailer Park, May 15–Oct. 1. No reservations. Located **on Oakland Park Rd.; 218-681-2519.**

Where to Eat

RBJ's—$ to $$

Tongue-in-cheek sightings of "bigfoot" in the Crookston area may be bogus, but RBJ's is playing the game. A hairy statue of bigfoot himself stands in the restaurant entry, and frosted ginger cookies in the shape of a big foot go quickly. The restaurant has walleye on the menu as well as a bigfoot burger (one-third pound of hamburger with everything, and fries) and homemade sweet rolls. Open year-round, Mon.–Sat., 6:00 A.M.–9:00 P.M., and Sun., 7:00 A.M.–9:00 P.M. **1601 University Ave., Crookston, 56716; 218-281-3636.**

Carol's Cafe—$ to $$

Friday is all-you-can-eat night at Carol's, a pleasant, airy cafe in downtown Thief River Falls. Carol's has good home cooking and excellent breakfasts. Open year-round (may be closed some holidays), Mon.–Fri., 4:30 A.M.–7:00 P.M.; Sat., 5:30 A.M.–6:00 P.M.; Sun., 6:00 A.M.–3:00 P.M. **118 N. Main St., Thief River Falls, 56701; 218-681-5420.**

Services

Perhaps the best visitor guide published by any region in the state is the *Northwest Minnesota Visitor and Recreation Guide,* published annually by the Northwest Regional Development Commission. It's all here: museums, outdoor recreation, motels, and restaurants. Get a copy at **115 S. Main, Warren, 56762; 218-745-6733.**

Crookston Area Chamber of Commerce, 1915 University Ave., Suite 2, Crookston, 56716; 800-809-5997 or 218-281-4320.

East Grand Forks Chamber of Commerce, 218-773-7481.

Greater Grand Forks Convention and Visitors Bureau, 4251 Gateway Dr., Grand Forks, ND 58203; 800-866-4566 or 701-746-0444.

Thief River Falls Chamber of Commerce, 2017 Hwy. 59 SE, Thief River Falls, 56701; 218-681-3720.

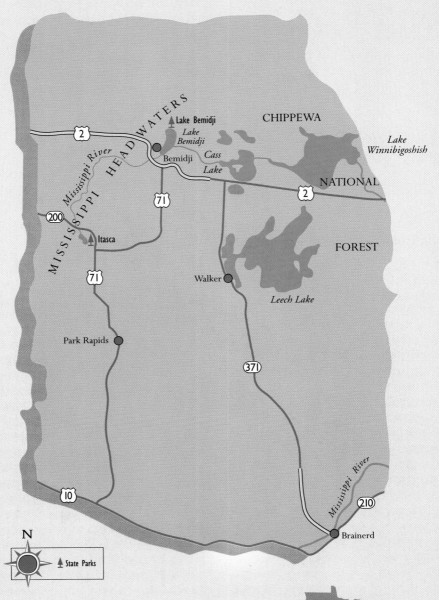

The Heartland
(North-Central Region)

The Heartland
(North-Central Region)

A nesting loon heralds a Minnesota spring.
Copyright © Minnesota Office of Tourism. Used by permission.

Brainerd

Brainerd and its surrounding lakes are synonymous with summer vacations for a great many Minnesotans, though the area was first important as a logging community and it still encourages the tall tales of legendary logger Paul Bunyan. Although many communities in the state claim Paul Bunyan as their own, kids know that he actually lives in Brainerd because Paul is their buddy—the seated giant in the red-and-black lumberjack shirt (at the Paul Bunyan Amusement Center) has called them by name and, like Santa, he knows where they live.

Lately, however, Paul is taking a back seat to Brainerd's claim to fame as the setting for *Fargo,* the quirky film that is a send-up of both mysteries and Minnesota. *Fargo* won 1997 Oscars for best original screenplay and best actress (Frances McDormand). The movie, made by Minnesotans Joel and Ethan Coen, may be named for the biggest city in North Dakota, but takes place mainly in Brainerd, even to the Brainerd logo on the police cars. When the movie first came out, the chamber of commerce got many calls from *Fargo* fans asking about points in the movie. Interest from outsiders has died down, but some residents still throw *Fargo* parties of their own, wearing big winter hats and "walking around acting stupid," as one local woman put it. Is Brainerd just as it's depicted in *Fargo*? Hey—see the movie, visit Brainerd, see for yourself (and don't forget to say hi to Paul).

Brainerd, with more than 12,000 residents, is the largest and best known of several communities in the area, including Brainerd's twin community, Baxter, as well as Nisswa, Pequot Lakes, Pine River, and Crosslake. Vacationers are drawn to the area for the 465 lakes within a 30-mile radius, some of the grandest resorts in Minnesota, and the multitude of activities for the whole family. Winter vacations are on the upswing, too, but summer is still the prime season in the Brainerd Lakes area.

History

Prehistoric Indian tribes left evidence of their lives in the burial mounds found near Gull Lake. Later, the Dakota and the Ojibwe battled, with the Ojibwe finally triumphing and driving the Dakota south. Much of the American Indian history as well as early European history of the area took place in what is now Crow Wing State Park, south of Brainerd. The French built a fort on the island at the confluence of the Crow Wing and Mississippi Rivers in 1752, and abandoned it a year later due to Dakota–Ojibwe fighting.

Half a century later, William Morrison came to the area, followed by his brother Allan, who established a trading post on the island in 1823 and later, in 1843, became the first permanent European settler in the county. The town of Crow Wing waxed and waned, the logging industry peaked, and, finally, in the 20th century the vacationing boom began, with visitors roughing it at first in tents, then renting rustic cabins from local people.

Now the Brainerd Lakes area has the largest concentration of major resorts in the state, and the area is still growing. Brainerd itself, as it is the county seat, remains important regionally as well as embodying the region "up north" that is the summer goal of so many Minnesota residents.

Festivals and Events

Fishing Opener for Walleyes and Northerns

mid-May

All the towns around Brainerd feel the excitement of the annual fishing opener. Whether it's cold and wet or warm and sunny, the anglers show up, ready to load up at the bait shops (some are open around the clock) and be out on the water poised to make the first cast at 12:01 A.M. Several communities have a special event for the opener. Nisswa Chamber of Commerce members serve coffee and doughnuts on the shore of Gull Lake in a modern version of a wanigan, the cook shack used during the lumbering days. For seasons and license information, call the Regional Fisheries Manager in Brainerd, **218-828-2624.**

Turtle Races

Wed. mid-June to mid-Aug.

Nisswa has held turtle races every Wed. afternoon in summer for more than 30 years. Kids can bring their own turtle or rent one at the races. Races, which have drawn nearly 400 entrants some days, start at 2:00 P.M. behind the Chamber of Commerce office in Nisswa. Call the chamber for details (see Services).

Bean Hole Days

Tues. and Wed. after Fourth of July

More than 2,000 bean lovers sometimes show up for Pequot Lakes' Bean Hole Days. On the first day, six huge, cast-iron bean pots, containing 150 gallons of beans, are buried atop pit fires to bake for a goodly number of hours. The next day, beans, buns, and lemonade are served at Bobberland Wayside Park in Pequot Lakes, from noon until the beans are gone. The festival is more than 60 years old. Contact the Pequot Lakes Chamber of Commerce (see Services).

> ### Getting There
> Brainerd is approximately 150 miles north of the Twin Cities. Take I-94 to St. Cloud, then go north on Hwy. 371 to Brainerd; alternatively, take U.S. Hwy. 10 to Hwy. 371. Brainerd also has an airport, with commuter flights from the Twin Cities.

Outdoor Activities

Biking

Paul Bunyan Trail

One of the newest state trails, the Paul Bunyan is 100 miles long. It starts in Brainerd/Baxter and ends at Bemidji, where it connects with the Blue Ox Trail; the two together are 210 miles long, one of the country's longest roadbed trails. The fairly level trail is perfect for family bike rides and is wheelchair-accessible. The trail is asphalt from Baxter to Hackensack and also asphalt for a small portion north of Lake Bemidji State Park. The trail goes past lakes and marshlands in some places. The Paul Bunyan and Heartland Trails share a short stretch around Walker. Access is at several towns along the way, including Pequot Lakes, Hackensack, Backus, and Walker. The Hackensack trailhead, on a lake, has rest rooms, a fishing pier, and picnic tables. It's a favorite of snowmobilers in winter. Trail maps are available from the Brainerd Lakes Area Chamber of Commerce, **800-450-2838,** or the Dept. of Natural Resources, **500 Lafayette Rd., St. Paul, 55155, 888-MINNDNR** or **651-296-6157.**

Rentals and Tours

Rent bikes at several places along the Paul Bunyan Trail, including **Easy Riders Bicycle and Sportshop, 415 Washington St., Brainerd, 56401; 218-829-5516.**

Boating

The Crow Wing, Pine, Gull, and Mississippi Rivers are all state-designated canoe rivers, with campsites, toilets, and rest stops along the way.

Golf is a popular sport in Brainerd. Photo courtesy of the Brainerd Lakes Area Chamber of Commerce.

All four are Class I rivers, meaning easy canoeing with a few, if any, gentle rapids. The **Pine River,** rising out of Pine Mountain Lake near Backus, flows through the Whitefish chain of lakes and meets the **Mississippi** 20 miles upstream from Brainerd. The Pine, whose shores are quite undeveloped, is a fairly gentle river, but use care when going through the Whitefish chain. The **Gull River** begins in Gull Lake and eventually joins the Crow Wing. The **Crow Wing,** also a good river for family canoeists, flows through marshy land at first, followed by jack-pine forests. Wildlife is abundant, and there are many campsites. Maps are available from the Dept. of Natural Resources, **500 Lafayette Rd., St. Paul, 55155, 888-MINNDNR** or **651-296-6157,** and the Brainerd Lakes Area Chamber of Commerce, **800-450-2838.**

Fishing

Brainerd draws a lot of anglers, but many of them also come with families, instead of making fishing the only object of their vacation. Here, as elsewhere, walleye and northern are probably the most-fished-for species, but most anglers are happy with panfish, too. Anticipation for the fishing season starts long before the walleye and northern season opens in mid-May (see Festivals and Events), with anglers getting their boats in shape and hanging around bait shops months in advance.

Rentals and Tours

Marv Koep started an association of fishing guides in the Nisswa area in 1961. In 1992, Dave Fischer (yup, that's his real name) bought it and named it Nisswa Professional Guides; 17 guides, including Koep, work for the association and they give individual service for up to three anglers per boat, all equipment (including boat and motor) and bait provided. Trips of various lengths are available. A couple of guides still do shore lunches, by reservation, on daylong trips, Fischer says. Contact Fischer at Koep's **Nisswa Bait and Tackle, 301 Smiley Rd., Box 349, Nisswa, 56468; 218-963-2547.**

Golf

What's the best place in the state to go for a golf vacation? Many golfers would say "Brainerd" without a second thought. There are nearly 30 courses in the area, several of them considered among the finest in the Upper Midwest. Most of the courses are associated with one of the large resorts (see Where to Stay). Many of the courses were designed by the biggest names in golf-course architecture, such as Robert Trent Jones II, Arnold Palmer, and Joel Goldstrand. The resorts offer areawide accommodations and golfing packages. Among the best-known courses are the following.

Breezy Point Resort

The **Traditional,** whose front nine goes back to the '20s, is a shotmaker's course. It's challenging for several reasons—the greens are undulating and many of the holes are doglegs, so powerful hitters have to take care not to overdo it. The back nine has two holes (15 and 16) that are absolutely L-shaped. There are rentals available. Greens fees: $25–$28 for 18 holes. Season is usually Apr.–Oct., dawn–dusk. **800-432-3777.**

Breezy's **Whitebirch** 18-hole course has several long par-4 holes and 5 holes in which water is a factor to contend with. The 16th hole skirts a lake in a swampy area that has beaver dams. The clubhouse has rental equipment. Greens fees: $35–$49 for 18 holes. Season is approximately Apr.–Oct., daily, dawn–dusk. **800-432-3777.**

Cragun's

Cragun's resort has 27 championship holes and a new nine-hole, par-3 executive course. The courses, according to Cragun's, are designed to meet the standards of an Audubon Signature Sanctuary course, blending golf with preservation of the environment. Existing water and wetlands provide an extra challenge for golfers. Rentals are available. Greens fees: $75–$105 for 18 holes. Season is approximately last week in Apr.–mid-Oct., dawn–dusk. **800-272-4867.**

Grand View Lodge

For all the courses at this resort, rentals are available; the season is May–Oct., 7:30 A.M.–dusk; call **888-437-4637** for information.

The **Pines,** a rolling 27-hole course, has at least four trees on every hole. These and other natural hazards make the Pines lovely to look at and a challenge to play. The Pines has also been named one of North America's best upscale courses by *Golf Digest*. Greens fees: $53.50–$63.50 for 18 holes.

The **Preserve,** which debuted in 1996, is an 18-hole course whose 75 feet of elevation change is just one of the things that make it challenging. The Preserve incorporates 40 acres of wetlands and 36 sand traps, and has bent-grass greens, tees, and fairways. In addition, there are 14 downhill tee shots. Greens fees: $45.50–$53.50 for 18 holes.

The **Garden** at Grand View is a nine-hole warm-up course that is a scenic delight, with flowers everywhere. Greens fees: $20.25 for 9 holes.

New in 1999 is the 18-hole **Deacon's Lodge** course, designed by Arnold Palmer. Greens fees: $90 for 18 holes, cart included.

Madden's

Madden's resort has 63 holes in all, headed by the 18-hole **Classic,** which has garnered honors, including being named third-best new upscale public course in North America in 1997 by *Golf Digest* magazine. The course, which has many changes in elevation, has water on nearly every hole and is very scenic. Greens fees: $85–$100. Caddies are available. Season is June 1–Labor Day. **800-642-5363.**

What a catch! Photo courtesy of the Brainerd Lakes Area Chamber of Commerce.

Madden's twin 18-hole **Pine Beach courses, East and West,** are old favorites. The West course is rolling and wooded, while the more open East 18 has one of the longest holes in the state—a 618-yard par-6. Greens fees: $35 for 18 holes. There is a nine-hole social course adjacent to Pine Beach East. Season is mid-Apr.– mid-Oct., 8:00 A.M.–dusk. **800-642-5363.**

Hiking

Many of Crow Wing State Park's 18 miles of hiking trails are near the Crow Wing and Mississippi Rivers (see Museums and Historic Sites). Pillsbury State Forest's 27 miles of multipurpose trails draw many hikers (see Parks).

Horseback Riding

Riders with their own horses favor the 27 miles of multipurpose wooded trails in Pillsbury State Forest (see Parks). There are also several stables that rent horses around Brainerd. Contact the Brainerd Lakes Area Chamber of Commerce (see Services).

Hunting

Wild Acres Game Farm

Duck and upland game hunters are pleased to discover the 500-acre shooting preserve that Mary Ebnet and her family run north of Brainerd. Mary, a champion breaker of target clays (can you break 98 out of 100 clays?), has bright blue eyes that sparkle as she tells her story. She built the game farm up as a single mother with a big family through her iron determination and lots of talks around the kitchen table. The result is impressive, with rows of food crops, such as sunflowers and sorghum, separated by neat paths through the rolling landscape. Nonhunters as well enjoy visiting the game farm and taking home some of the dressed game birds that are for sale. The Ebnets have dogs on hand to go out with the hunters, who may bring back mallards, pheasants, wild turkeys, quail, and partridge. The birds are hatched and raised by the Ebnets before they are released for hunters, sold wholesale to many Twin Cities restaurants, or sold retail at the farm or by mail. Tours can be arranged, and the Ebnets

also offer sleigh rides, lodging and meals by reservation in a rustic log lodge with a magnificent stone fireplace, a sporting clay range of 50 targets, trap shooting, and kennel facilities. Fee for use of facilities and tours. Open Aug.–Mar., shooting hours 8:00 A.M.–sundown. Reserve well in advance for hunting in Sept. and Oct. The farm is north of Pequot Lakes on Hwy. 371, east 1.25 miles on County Rd. 16, then watch for signs for the game farm. **HC 83, Box 108, Pequot Lakes, 56472; 218-568-5024 or 218-568-5748.**

Skiing

CROSS-COUNTRY

The Brainerd Lakes area has approximately 165 miles of cross-country ski trails, including both groomed and ungroomed trails. For ski touring away from it all, try the trails in Pillsbury State Forest. However, there is wonderful skiing right in Brainerd at the Northland Arboretum. The "Arb," which charges a small fee, has 12 miles of groomed trails of varying difficulty, with separate skate-only trails—set in a 600-acre preserve. One trail is lighted and there is a warming house. Stop at the gatehouse first. Located on NW Seventh St. in Brainerd (see Gardens and Arboreta). Also check out the state forest ski trails and Crow Wing State Park (6 miles of trails), south of Brainerd. Many of the resorts also have their own groomed trails.

Rentals and Tours

Rent cross-country skis at several places, including **Easy Riders Bicycle and Sportshop.** The shop also rents alpine skis, snowboards, and ice skates. **415 Washington St., Brainerd, 56401; 218-829-5516.**

DOWNHILL

Ski Gull

Ski Gull, which has a vertical drop of 205 feet, has 14 runs, most of which are accessed by a triple chair lift. The longest run is about 3,000 feet. The area also has two rope tows. Ski and snowboard rentals are available. Open Mon. and Sat., 10:00 A.M.–8:00 P.M.; Thurs., 1:00–8:00 P.M.; Fri., 10:00 A.M.–9:00 P.M.; Sun., 10:00 A.M.–6:00

P.M.; call for Christmas break hours. Located on the west side of Gull Lake. **Box 612, Nisswa, 56468; 218-963-4353.**

Snowmobiling

It's snowmobile country around Brainerd, with approximately 1,200 miles of groomed trails that run across lakes, through forests, and also along the Paul Bunyan State Trail. In Crow Wing State Park, there are 6 miles of trails for snowmobilers. Pillsbury's 27 miles of multipurpose trails draw snowmobilers in winter. Many of the resorts have snowmobiles and trails or access to them. Get current information on snow conditions and also a map of local trails from the Brainerd Lakes Area Chamber of Commerce (see Services).

Seeing and Doing

Children and Families

Nisswa Family Fun Center

This Nisswa complex has a 400-foot water slide, a hot tub, an in-line skating track and hockey rink (with equipment rentals), a video arcade, and a sand volleyball court. Fee. Open Memorial Day–Labor Day, daily, 11:00 A.M.–varying closing times. Located **on Hwy. 371 and County Rd. 77 N.; 218-963-3545.**

Paul Bunyan Amusement Center

One of a Minnesota kid's greatest thrills is walking up to the huge, seated Paul Bunyan and having Paul address you by name, as in, "Hi, Annie from Minneapolis." It's magic (with the help of a name whispered to the ticket taker) and makes Brainerd forever a place of fond memories. Paul, who is 26 feet high sitting down and has a 150-inch waist, is just one of the attractions at the amusement park. There are midway rides and also helicopter flights that zoom over the surrounding lakes. Fee. Open Memorial Day–Labor Day, daily, 10:00 A.M.–varying closing times. Located at the **junction of Hwys. 210 and 371; 218-829-6342.**

Rolling Thunder

Take your choice of several kinds of go-carts at this track at Brainerd/Baxter. Fee. Open Memorial Day–Labor day, daily, 10:00 A.M.–varying closing times. Located **on Hwy. 371, 2 miles north of the Paul Bunyan Amusement Center; 218-825-0933.**

Gardens and Arboreta

Northland Arboretum

You don't have to go to France to see Monet's garden at Giverny. The "Arb" in Brainerd has built a copy of the arched bridge over a stream, with Monet-like gardens surrounding it. The Arb also has 12 miles of hiking and unpaved biking paths through the 600-acre preserve, and is a serene spot for an afternoon stroll. Register at the gatehouse. Fee. Open daily, 8:00 A.M.–sunset. Located **on NW Seventh St. in Brainerd; 218-829-8770.**

Museums and Historic Sites

Crow Wing County Historical Society Museum

The Crow Wing County Museum is a well-documented look at life in the county, as well as a more intimate peek at the life of the county sheriff and his family who lived in the 1917 building that is now the museum. The sheriff's family lived in three stories in the front of the building; the jail was at the rear. Kids especially enjoy being able to step into the jail. Adults, on the other hand, are impressed by the living quarters, which are beautifully preserved and filled with donated period antique furniture and a collection of 180 dolls. Other exhibits include impressive examples of Indian beadwork and well-laid-out displays of local industry, including logging displays. There is also a section about the Milford Mine disaster, in which 41 miners perished on Feb. 5, 1924, in a mine east of Brainerd. Space is also given to recounting the career of Charles A. ("Chief") Bender, a local guy who played for the Philadelphia Athletics and who is the only American Indian in the Baseball Hall of Fame. Fee. Open year-round, Sat., 9:00 A.M.–1:00 P.M.; Memorial Day–Labor Day, Mon.–Fri., 9:00 A.M.–5:00 P.M.; Labor Day–Memorial Day, Mon.–Fri.,

Sunset over the Brainerd Lakes. Photo courtesy of the Brainerd Lakes Area Chamber of Commerce.

1:00–5:00 P.M. **320 Laurel Ave., Brainerd, 56401; 218-829-3268.**

Crow Wing State Park

It's quiet now in Crow Wing State Park, south of Brainerd, where the Crow Wing River threads gracefully through the heavily wooded park to join the Mississippi River. However, Crow Wing was not always the tranquil spot it is today. In 1768, according to historian William Warren, Crow Wing was the site of a major clash between the Dakota and the Ojibwe and was also the home of some of the greatest Ojibwe leaders, including Bug-o-na-ge-shig (Hole-in-the-Day). Later the fur traders came, with Allan Morrison establishing a post in Crow Wing in 1823. He was followed by missionaries, Red River oxcart drivers on their way to and from St. Paul, and settlers. Crow Wing became a thriving community of 700 souls at its largest. It was the northernmost European settlement on the Mississippi. Then, in 1868 came the decision to site the railroad elsewhere, and Crow Wing vanished, leaving only the Clement Beaulieu House—which is now being restored—a few gravestones and foundation

mounds, and the memories of a busier time. Interpretive signs identify some of the buildings, etc., in the Old Crow Wing town site. A recently constructed, 600-foot-long wheelchair-accessible trail leads to the Beaulieu House from the parking lot. Interpretive exhibits explain the natural and human history of the Crow Wing area, and a self-guided trail tells about the natural and historic features of the park. Boats and canoes can be rented at the park; the Crow Wing River is a state-designated canoe route and it is easy canoeing here. A woodland wildflower garden is across from the park office. There is camping and one camper cabin, with another cabin to be added. Located 9 miles south of Brainerd on Hwy. 371. **7100 State Park Rd. SW, Brainerd, 56401; 218-829-8022.**

Minnesota Resort Museum

See how the resorts were "in the olden days" in this two-story display of items including early resort furnishings, antique kitchen equipment and pottery, fishing gear, an ice house, a wooden rowboat, and an ancient Evinrude motor. The museum is housed in its own building at Driftwood Resort. Many of the old photos of resort life were taken by Frank Kamberling, who started the resort in 1900. There are also displays of the geological formation of the lakes as well as of the logging industry. Fee. Open Memorial Day–Labor Day, daily, 10:00 A.M.–5:00 P.M. Located on Whitefish Lake. **Rte. 1, Box 104, Pine River, 56474; 218-568-4221.**

Parks

Pillsbury State Forest

The forest, about 10 miles northwest of Brainerd, was one of the first areas logged in Minnesota, in the late 1880s. Subsequently, the state established the Pillsbury Forest Reserve here in 1900, with the state's first forest tree nursery started here in 1903. The forest, nearly 15,000 acres of northern hardwoods and evergreens, with many small ponds and lakes, is a great recreational resource. For a map, contact the Dept. of Natural Resource, **500 Lafayette Rd., St. Paul, 55155, 888-MINNDNR** or **651-296-6157,** or the Brainerd Lakes Area Chamber of Commerce, **800-450-2838.**

U.S. Army Corps of Engineers Recreation Areas

Families like the Corps Recreation Areas, as they usually have plenty of things to keep kids busy and are not wilderness areas. In the Brainerd Lakes area, the corps has two recreation areas; both have dams that were built in the 1880s to help regulate navigation on the Mississippi River, plus campgrounds, swimming beaches, picnic areas, and playgrounds. There is a fee for day use of the areas, such as swimming.

The **Gull Lake Recreation Area,** on the east side of Gull Lake near Brainerd, has a self-guided interpretive trail around a prehistoric Woodland Indian burial mound and also trails on hilly Government Point that provide a nice overlook of the lake. **8896 E. Gull Lake Dr. NW, Brainerd, 56401; 218-829-3334.**

The **Cross Lake Recreation Area,** just south of the town of Crosslake, has fishing seminars and other fishing programs, including a fishing derby for kids in July and weekly interpretive programs. Cross Lake is just south of the town of Crosslake. **Box 36, Crosslake, 56442; 218-692-2025.**

Shopping

Just up the highway from Brainerd is the town of Nisswa, whose Main St. is full of shops to lure vacationers. Kids love the **Totem Pole,** a fixture in lake life, with souvenirs galore; **P.O. Box 391, Nisswa, 56468, 218-963-3450. Zaiser's Gift and Souvenirs** claims to have the largest selection of moccasins in the state; **P.O. Box 122, Nisswa, 56468, 218-963-2404.** The **Adirondack Espresso Bar and Specialty Shops,** with its lovely pine interior and massive stone fireplace, is in the old Hotel Nisswa, built in 1923, and rescued by a renovation in 1995; **P. O. Box 601, Nisswa, 56468, 218-963-3421.** For more information, call the Nisswa Chamber of Commerce, **800-950-9610.**

Kinzie Candles

Watch candles being made, and shop for them, too. In addition to the wide variety of perfect, pretty candles of all shapes and sizes, there are sometimes a few "seconds" for sale at a bargain price. Tours by appointment. Retail store is open Mon.–Sat., 9:00 A.M.–5:00 P.M., and Sun., 10:00 A.M.–3:00 P.M. **201 County Rd. 11, Pequot Lakes, 56472; 218-568-8828.**

The Swedish Timber House

Outfit your family from head to toe—with the Norwegian skirts and sweaters, Swedish clogs, hats and mittens, and jewelry from all the Scandinavian countries sold here at this gift shop. Keep some money aside for crystal, porcelain, Christmas ornaments, and Scandinavian foods. The building itself was built of spruce logs in Leksand, in Dalarna, Sweden, then dismantled, numbered, and shipped to the west shore of Gull Lake, where it was reassembled in 1970. Open early May–late Oct., daily, 10:00 A.M.–5:00 P.M.; Dec., Sun. (until Christmas—call for hours). Located 12 miles north of Brainerd on Hwy. 371, then left 5 miles on County Rd. 77. **7678 Interlachen Rd., Nisswa, 56468; 218-963-7897.**

Sports

Colonel's Brainerd International Raceway
Top fuel drag races, motorcycle races, and National Hot Rod Assocation races are held May–Sept. Advance tickets available. Located **north of Brainerd on Hwy. 371; 612-475-1500.**

Where to Stay

Resorts
Brainerd has the largest confluence of Minnesota's traditional summer resorts, many of them run by successive generations of the same families. The large resorts all do a brisk business in conferences as well as family vacations. Most have packages in the Modified American Plan or American Plan in addition to European Plan (no meals included).

Manhattan Beach Lodge—$$$ to $$$$
Daydream about a haven in the north woods—comfortable yet rustic, with plenty to do and wonderful food to indulge in—and you might imagine something like Manhattan Beach Lodge. The historic building, built on Big Trout Lake in 1928, had been host to—as the owners put it—"Hollywood's famous and Chicago's infamous." Notorious bad guy John Dillinger had a summer place nearby and gambling was a constant activity in the lodge basement. But the glory days faded and the lodge was not in good shape when John and Mary Zesbaugh took it on. They drove in from their previous home in the East, Mary reading *Professional Dining Room Management* along the way to prepare for turning their love of fine food into running a dining room. The Zesbaughs completely redid the Manhattan Beach Lodge and reopened it in 1995, having made it into a wonderfully intimate getaway, furnished with pine pieces made locally and with many of the amenities of larger resorts without the anonymity. The 10 bedrooms are warmly decorated with pieced quilts, rocking chairs, and a view of the wonderful sunset over the lake. One room is wheelchair-accessible. The room rate includes a continental breakfast. The dining room (see Where to Eat) is excellent. Fish or boat

in the lake in summer, go leaf peeping in the fall, snowshoe or cross-country ski in winter. Located 3 miles north of Crosslake on County Rd. 66. **P.O. Box 719, Manhattan Beach, 56442; 800-399-4360 or 218-692-3381.**

Breezy Point Resort—call for rates
When Capt. Billy Fawcett, the flamboyant publisher of the risque *Whiz Bang Joke Book,* put $500 down on property and a few cabins on the shore of Pelican Lake north of Brainerd in 1921, even he could not have imagined what he was starting. The small resort that Fawcett bought grew and grew, even after his death and through several changes in ownership, until it became the enormous Breezy Point Resort of today. Visitors to the resort stay in a variety of accommodations ranging from basic to luxurious, from the beautiful log house that Fawcett built for his own use to condominiums, apartments, houses, and rooms. Some of the accommodations have fireplaces and Jacuzzis. Activities at Breezy Point include golf (see Golf); swimming, in two indoor pools or in the lake; fun on the lake in boats, canoes, and all kinds of smaller watercraft; tennis; and special activities. In winter, Breezy hosts an annual Ice Fest in January, but anytime in winter guests can go skating on lighted rinks, cross-country skiing, or snowmobiling. The resort has live entertainment and a dining room. Breezy Point's new restaurant, Antlers (see Where to Eat), is a short distance from the resort itself, on the side of one of the resort's golf courses. Open year-round. **HCR 2, Box 70, Breezy Point, 56472; 800-432-3777. Website: www.breezypt.com.**

Cragun's—call for rates
Don't leave Cragun's without talking to Merrill "Dutch" Cragun, the amiable host of this sprawling kingdom-by-the-lake. Cragun and his wife, Irma, run their resort—the largest in the state that does not have separately owned condos and time-shares—so effortlessly that it is as friendly and intimate as if it were a small ma-and-pa setup. Dutch was in it from the very beginning, helping his dad survey the property when he was just a little shaver of eight years. His dad, also named

Merrill Cragun, coined Minnesota's slogan, "Land of 10,000 Lakes," and is responsible for really popularizing the Paul Bunyan legend, rewriting the tall tales and copyrighting the name Paul Bunyan Playgrounds as a gimmick to draw visitors to fledgling resorts in the northland in the 1930s. The senior Cragun started the resort on a small scale in 1940, and signed a mortgage on the day Pearl Harbor was bombed. Dutch eventually took over, but his dad remained an active adviser until he died. "He loved the lake and he loved the business," says Dutch. In the last couple of decades the resort has grown dramatically. Cragun's was the first large resort to open year-round, according to Dutch, and aims at having activities for the whole family. Things to do at Cragun's include golf (see Golf), swimming in indoor and outdoor pools and in Gull Lake, visiting a sports center that has a golf simulator, fishing, other water sports, and tennis. Children have their own activity schedule at "Camp Cragun's." In winter, rent a snowmobile from Cragun's big fleet, or go ice-skating or cross-country skiing. Horse-drawn hayrides are another attraction. The resort has nearly 300 units, many in the lodge that hugs the shoreline, plus apartments and cabins. Rooms are nicely decorated, many with fireplaces and some with lovely paintings by Dutch's aunt, Cornelia Smith, who was painting well into her 90s. One section of the resort has lakeside rooms with Bavarian-style balconies from which guests can watch the sunrises. There are several eating places in the resort. **2001 Pine Beach Rd., Brainerd, 56401; 800-CRAGUNS. Website: www.craguns.com.**

Driftwood Resort and Golf—call for rates

Uffda, but there's a lot to do at Driftwood. Get up and ride a pony in front of the lodge every morning, play the nine-hole par-3 course, pig out at the Scandinavian smorgasbord every Fri. night, or laugh and applaud at the Mon.-night staff talent shows. Ya, you can fish, too, but mostly the resort considers itself a vacation place, says Tim Leagjeld, one of the owners. Nearly all the guests choose the meal plan. "One woman said to me, 'When we go away and I cook, that's a trip; when we go somewhere and someone else cooks, now

that's a vacation,'" laughs Leagjeld. The resort, which began in 1902, has been run by the Leagjeld clan—parents Ted and Sue, sons Tim and Dan, and Dan's wife, Donna—since 1959. They are good Norwegians, as you can tell from the Norwegian flags at the resort and the golf course. The 24 cabins, with carpeting and full baths in all, range from one to four bedrooms. The resort has a sandy beach, a pool, lots of kids' activities, and cruises on the lakes; the dining room is open to the public. Open approximately Memorial Day–Labor Day. Located on Whitefish Lake north of Brainerd. **Rte. 1, Box 404, Pine River, 56474; 218-568-4221 or 800-950-3540.**

Grand View Lodge—call for rates

The imposing Grand View Lodge, set amid 15,000 flowers and tall trees, has been welcoming guests for more than 80 years. The lodge was built by Marvin V. Baker on a site where there had been previous resort businesses. The rooms are charming, and the dining room on the first level has a beautiful log interior; check out the arty tabletops, too. Now the lodge, which is on the National Register of Historic Places, has been joined by other types of accommodations, including townhomes, clubhouse suites, and cottages. Activities in addition to golf (see Golf) include tennis, swimming (indoor pool and lake), boating, and a children's program. Although some of the accommodations are open year-round, the lodge is only open late Apr.–late Oct. Located north of Brainerd on Hwy. 371, then west on County Rd. 77. **S. 134 Nokomis, Nisswa, 56468; 800-432-3788. Website: www.grandviewlodge.com.**

Madden's—call for rates

Madden's is another of the classic names in Minnesota resorts. The resort, on a peninsula in Gull Lake, opened in 1929 and is still owned by the Madden family. Guests are housed in three separate areas, each with its own distinctive style. The Madden Inn and Golf Club lodging facilities, decorated in soft colors and contemporary furnishings, include some cottages fronting on the golf course (see Golf). The Madden Lodge, with a Colonial feel and decor, is where the resort began. Pine Portage, as its name suggests, has some accommodations with stone, wood-burning fireplaces and knotty pine woodwork. Golf is the big draw at Madden's, but there is an abundance of other activities, from swimming, boating, fishing, and tennis to such less-common pastimes as croquet and lawn bowling. The resort has a sod landing strip for private planes. There are several restaurants and a charming pub, loaded with dark wood and atmosphere. The resort has a variety of packages for theme vacations. Open mid-Apr.–Oct. **8001 Pine Beach Peninsula, Brainerd, 56401; 800-642-5363** or **218-829-2811. E-mail: maddens@uslink.net.**

Camping

Cross Lake Recreation Area—$

Just south of Crosslake, the recreation area run by the U.S. Army Corps of Engineers has 120 campsites on Cross Lake, part of the Whitefish Chain. There are 50 nonelectric sites for tents; the other 70 sites have electricity. The campground has showers and two dumping stations. The campground is family oriented, with three playgrounds to keep kids occupied. Space is usually available before schools let out for the summer. To reserve, call the recreation area. Located just south of Crosslake on Hwy. 3. **Box 36, Crosslake, 56442; 218-692-2025.**

Crow Wing State Park—$

There are 61 campsites in Crow Wing State Park, 12 with electricity, plus one canoe-in campsite and one camper cabin. **7100 State Park Rd. SW, Brainerd, 56401.** For reservations, call **The Connection, 800-246-CAMP** or **612-922-9000.**

Gull Lake Recreation Area—$

On the east side of Gull Lake, this U.S. Army Corps of Engineers campground has 39 sites, nine of them without electricity. Showers are available from the fishing opener (mid-May) to the third week of Sept., but the campground is officially open year-round. Close to Brainerd and its attractions, this campground fills up fast. Reserve early. **8896 E. Gull Lake Dr., Brainerd, 56401; 218-829-3334.**

Pillsbury State Forest—$

Rock Lake Campground in Pillsbury State Forest has a swimming beach and boat launch in addition to the 25 campsites, which have water available. There is also camping in Crow Wing State Forest north of Brainerd. Rock Lake is located 0.5 mile west of Pillager on Hwy. 371 W., then north 6 miles on County Rd. 1, then west along the lake road to the campground. **218-828-2565.**

Where to Eat

Many of Brainerd's resorts have wonderful dining facilities that are open to the public. Most of the big resorts operate on the American or Modified American Plan, but guests not staying at the resort can make dining reservations. Cragun's (see Where to Stay) is known for its Sun.-night poolside buffet. Brainerd is also a working town and the county seat, and there are many places to eat in the downtown area.

Antlers—$ to $$$

Breezy Point's restaurant is just down the road from the resort in the Whitebirch Club House, a beautiful log structure with a cathedral ceiling and a sweeping view. Look up at the ceiling and marvel at the lighting fixtures, intricate structures of antlers, with smaller versions on the walls. Dine inside or on the patio with a view of the golf course and ponds below. The menu is a nice mix of light and hearty fare, including steaks—a 14-ounce, bone-in ribeye stars here—ribs, pasta, and seafood. Pizzas and sandwiches are also available. Open year-round, daily, 11:30 A.M.–9:00 P.M. (to 10:00 P.M. in summer). **HCR 2, Box 70, Breezy Point, 56472; 218-562-7162. Website: www.breezypt.com.**

Manhattan Beach Lodge—$ to $$$

John and Mary Zesbaugh have made a successful marriage of sophisticated cuisine and north-woods standards. The two, who own the beautifully restored Manhattan Beach Lodge, serve walleye all right, but it may be a walleye-and-wild-rice cake, graced with lemon and remoulade, or walleye broiled in citrus butter and wine, or walleye deep-fried with a honey-pecan crust. The sandwiches, pastas, and entrees are equally delicious and innovative without trying too hard. Periodically, the menu may feature elk or other wild game. There are many specials, including a breakfast buffet and Bloody Mary bar on Sun. The comfortable dining room has an upscale rustic touch, with the original massive stone fireplace, and has terrific views of the lake sunsets. Open year-round; hours change seasonally. Located 3 miles north of Crosslake on County Rd. 66. **P.O. Box 719, Crosslake, 56442; 218-692-3381.**

Magic Skillet Cafe—$ to $$

What looks like an ordinary cafe in Brainerd is actually a magnet for rib lovers. Fans of the barbecued ribs drive a couple hundred miles for their treat, and have been known to order the sauce by the gallon to go. Only a few people know the secret sauce recipe, according to owner Cherrie Alholm. The original recipe for Soder's Smoky Bill ribs goes back at least 50 years, says Alholm. Take-out ribs, sauce, and Soder's baked beans are available, too. The cafe also does a brisk breakfast business (omelets are a feature) and offers breakfast all day. The lunch and dinner menu includes sandwiches, burgers, etc., as well as ribs. Open year-round, Mon.–Sat., 5:30 A.M.–7:30 P.M., and Sun., 5:30 A.M.–2:30 P.M. **123 NE Washington St., Brainerd, 56401; 218-829-5371.**

Morey's Fish House Seafood Cafe—$ to $$

A second location for the original Morey's, this one is larger and has seating space. Order your bagel and lox or smoked fish (whitefish, ciscoes, or trout are all good bets) to go or—if you can't wait—chow down at one of the tables. The walleye sandwich is a house specialty. Beer and wine are available. And—in a touch of "north woods meets the '90s"—they also have cappuccino, espresso, and lattes. Open year-round (closed major holidays), daily, 9:00 A.M.–6:00 P.M. Located **on Hwy. 371 N., 2 miles north of Hwy. 210; 218-829-8248.** Morey's original Fish House is located south of Brainerd, **on Hwy. 10 S. in Motley; 218-352-6345.**

Sibley Station—$ to $$

What's cooking? Lots of good stuff—from Hungarian mushroom soup to pesto pizza to a variety of subs and pitas. Try the delicious chili, made with molasses and beer, as well as the usual fixings. Many pastas are on the menu, including a vegetarian lasagna and chicken pesto (homemade pesto, of course). For dessert, try the yummy bread pudding or Swedish apple cake, topped with cinnamon ice cream. At Sibley Station—busy, casual, and friendly—the decor is eclectic, with old maps, *New Yorker* covers, an aquarium here and there, and, in the back room, a mural. Open Mon.–Thurs., 11:00 A.M.–9:00 P.M.; Fri.–Sat., 11:00 A.M.–10:00 P.M.; Sun., 10:00 A.M.–9:00 P.M. Located **in Pequot Lakes; 218-568-4177.**

Shamp's Meat Market—$

Bikers along the Paul Bunyan Trail often make a pit stop at Shamp's to get the makings for sandwiches. Shamp's is one of the few meat markets to sell elk. The Shamps (the third generation is now working at the market) also sell buffalo and raise their own beef and pork. The market offers many varieties of jerky and homemade sausages, including a wild rice summer sausage, that have won many awards. Open year-round, Mon.–Sat., 9:00 A.M.–5:30 P.M. Located **on Hwy. 371 S. in Pine River; 218-587-2228.**

Services

Located under the concrete water tower, which can be seen all over Brainerd, the **Brainerd Lakes Area Chamber of Commerce** has a wealth of information about this vacation draw. **P.O. Box 356, Brainerd, 56401; 800-450-2838, ext. 463,** or **218-829-2838. Website: www.brainerd.com.**

Nisswa Chamber of Commerce, 800-950-9610.

Look for Paul Bunyan's red-and-white bobber (actually Pequot Lakes' water tower), and the **Pequot Lakes Area Chamber of Commerce** office is just a cast away. **Box 208, Pequot Lakes, 56472; 800-950-0291** or **218-568-8911. Website: www.pequotlakes.com.**

Mississippi Headwaters

The mighty Mississippi River arises in the heart of northern Minnesota, surrounded by tall trees and the lonely cries of the loon. The area, dotted with lakes and thick with evergreens, birch, and aspen that turn to gold in the fall, is still sparsely settled. It's a land of vast forests and great beauty. For centuries before the tourists began coming for a respite from the hot cities, it lured explorers searching for the Mississippi's source. Visitors love to vacation here, but residents often have to scramble to make a living. Logging, always a mainstay of this area, is still important to the economy, as is tourism.

Bemidji, at the northern end of the Headwaters area, is the largest city, with a population of 11,000, and Park Rapids, south of Itasca State Park, has a population of a little fewer than 3,000. At the other end of the population scale is Dorset, which has a permanent head count of 12–20, depending on who's counting.

History

American Indians hunted and camped in the Headwaters area 8,000 years ago, and 500- to 900-year-old Indian mounds can be found here. The first European explorers mentioned that the Dakota lived here, but by the early 18th century, the Ojibwe had supplanted them. Many Ojibwe still live on reservations in the Headwaters region. French fur traders were the first Europeans to reach the area, and many European explorers vied for the honor of "discovering" the source of the Mississippi.

Though the native people were already well aware of the source of the Mississippi River, European explorers' search for it was noteworthy. Since 1541, when Fernando De Soto reached the southern portion of the Mississippi, finding its source became a goal for others. The first to see the upper Mississippi was the French missionary–explorer team of Jacques Marquette and Louis Jolliet, who reached it in 1673. A string of subsequent hopefuls—including Father Louis Hennepin, Zebulon Pike of Pike's Peak fame, and Italian Count Giacomo Beltrami—tried and failed to find the source. Finally an Ojibwe, Ozawindib, guided Henry R. Schoolcraft to the source in 1832. Schoolcraft dubbed the lake "Itasca," combining the Latin verITAS ("true") and CAput ("head") for "true source."

However, it is a legendary character who captured the public imagination. His name is Paul Bunyan, a giant born out of tall tales swapped by lumberjacks. How was the Mississippi formed? According to Bemidji tourism information, Paul did it: a huge water tank he was hauling sprang a leak, creating Lake Bemidji and Lake Itasca, with the rest of the water dribbling down to New Orleans as the Mississippi. Several communities claim Paul: Bemidji has statues of him and his pal Babe the Blue Ox; Brainerd has a seated, talking Paul;

Akeley has the tallest, nonmoving statue of Paul; and Hackensack put up a statue of Paul's girlfriend.

Major Attractions

Itasca State Park

Old Man River, the Mighty Mississippi, begins as a tiny stream flowing north out of Lake Itasca in what is now Itasca State Park. A marker at the source proclaims: "Here, 1,475 feet above the ocean, the mighty Mississippi begins to flow on its winding way 2,552 miles to the Gulf of Mexico." It's possible to hop across the infant stream on stepping stones here, and those who do it are usually photographed by their companions so they can show scoffers later that they did, indeed, walk across the Mississippi. The Headwaters is a busy place in summer, though quiet solitude is just a few paces away for those who wade around the first bend in the stream.

Glacial activity 20,000 years ago formed the "knob and kettle" topography of Itasca State Park, which lies in the Itasca moraine that fronted the glacier. Knobs—mounds of debris from the glacier—and kettles—depressions that became postglacial lakes—can be seen throughout the 32,000-acre park. Lake Itasca itself, with its two long and slender arms, owes its present shape to the Ice Age. The terrain is hilly, but not dramatically so. The highest point, in the south-central part of the park, is 1,700 feet. The park's jewels are the old-growth pine forests, a wondrous sight. (Although much of the forest was logged, areas of virgin pine remain.)

In the years between Henry Schoolcraft's "discovery" of Lake Itasca and the creation of Itasca State Park, Minnesota's first state park, logging began in earnest. After years of advocacy by people such as Jacob Brower, in 1891 the Minnesota Legislature passed, by one vote, a bill establishing the park. Considered the father of the park, Brower was its first—unsalaried—superintendent. However, much of the park's land remained privately held until 1918, and conservationists fought large-scale logging in the park until it ceased in 1919. One hero in the antilogging battle was 24-year-old Mary Gibbs, who in 1903 was the first

Getting There

Itasca State Park and the two largest towns in the area, Bemidji and Park Rapids, are within easy driving distance of each other. Bemidji, farthest north, is about 215 miles from the Twin Cities. If you're headed up here, take the advice of one local resort owner and get on the "Motley Express": Go north on U.S. Hwy. 10 to Motley, stopping for smoked fish at Morey's. Stay on Hwy. 10, then turn north on U.S. Hwy. 71 for Park Rapids and the park proper, or turn off Hwy. 10 and continue north on Hwy. 64 until you hit Hwy. 200. Follow Hwy. 200 west to U.S. Hwy. 71; turn north and it's a straight shot to Bemidji. Why take the Motley Express? You can avoid all the traffic going through Brainerd, a bottleneck in the summer as everyone heads "up to the lake." Alternatively, there is an airport at Bemidji, with commuter service from the Twin Cities.

woman in the country to be appointed a park superintendent. Gibbs faced down gun-toting lumber-company employees to get them to open the gates of a dam holding back the waters of the Mississippi.

The main (east) entrance to the park is 21 miles north of Park Rapids on U.S. Hwy. 71. The Headwaters area, which is located north and west of the east entrance off Park Dr., has parking for cars and bikes, a visitor center, a gift shop, and rest rooms. A short trail leads to the Headwaters. The 10-mile Wilderness Dr. starts at the Headwaters and is two-way until after the Ozawindib cabin turnoff. It skirts the Itasca Wilderness Sanctuary Scientific and Natural Area and then heads toward the east entrance. Along the way are several hikes, taking visitors to the state's tallest red pine and one of the tallest white pines, a 100-foot fire tower that can be climbed, a forest demonstration area, and an ancient bison kill site. The park has 33 miles of hiking trails, including self-guided nature trails and historic walking trails. There are also trails for biking,

Headwaters of the Mississippi River in Itasca State Park, as it begins its long, winding journey 2,552 miles to the Gulf of Mexico. Copyright © Minnesota Office of Tourism. Used by permission.

cross-country skiing, and snowmobiling. Year-round park programs include guided walks, children's programs, family campfires, evening lectures, narrated boat tours, and living-history presentations. The park rents bikes, boats, motors, canoes, and snowshoes. Itasca has sought-after lodging, plus camping. Douglas Lodge's dining room is beautiful and historic, and serves good Minnesota food, including walleye; Minnesota wines are also on the menu. **HCO5, Box 4, Lake Itasca, 56470; 218-266-2100** or **218-266-2114.**

Festivals and Events

Bemidji Polar Daze
third weekend in Jan.
Take all the events in a summer festival and hold them on ice and snow, and throw in dogsled races, and you have Bemidji Polar Daze. The weekend's events, held mostly on Lake Bemidji, include golf

on ice and "A Taste of Northern Minnesota" to sample local goodies. Contact the Bemidji Visitors and Convention Bureau (see Services).

St. Urho's Day
Mar. 16
Those Finns up in Menahga get a one-day jump on the Irish each year with St. Urho's Day, a tongue-in-cheek event that celebrates the hero who drove all the grasshoppers out of Finland. A statue of the saintly Finn in Menahga is the focal point for the mayor's annual proclamation of St. Urho's Day. Some wear St. Urho's colors, an unlovely combination of purple and green, for the day. Festivities begin with a breakfast put on by the Finnish-American Society, go on to a golf-on-ice competition, a parade, more food (including *Mojakka*—Finnish beef stew—and Finnish flat bread), and conclude with a dance and maybe a drink or two. The cocktail of choice? Why, Grasshoppers, of course. Free except for the food. For information, write to the Menahga Civic and Commerce, **Menahga, 56464** (no phone).

International Days at Concordia Language Villages
first Fri. in July and second Fri. in Aug.
Rub elbows with the world at the two international days sponsored by Concordia College's 10 language villages. More than 5,000 campers attend the summer sessions in the villages, which began in 1969. Campers exhibit their language and culture skills in songs and dances, and booths display the crafts of each country. An international buffet is available for a charge, but entry to the event is free. It's held at "Waldsee," the German village north of Bemidji on County Rd. 20; shuttle buses transport visitors from a parking lot. Call the Bemidji Visitors and Convention Bureau for directions (see Services) and the Concordia Language Villages for information, **800-222-4750** or (in Minnesota) **800-247-1044.**

Headwaters of the Mississippi Rodeo
Fourth of July weekend
Rodeo fans have been flocking to this annual event for more than 20 years. The officially sanctioned

rodeo features professionals who travel the circuit. Fee. Contact the Park Rapids Area Chamber of Commerce (see Services).

Sawdust Dayz
third weekend in July (July Fourth for the town's 1999 centennial)
Tiny Shevlin (population 157) remembers its logging heyday with the two-day lumberjack (and -jill) competition. Up to 3,000 spectators watch the lumberjacks saw, chop, roll logs, and throw axes. There are tamer events—such as horseshoe pitching—for nonlumberjacks. Shevlin is approximately 18 miles west of Bemidji on Hwy. 2. For information, call Tom Norgaard, **218-785-2206,** or Harry Larson, **218-785-2458.**

A Taste of Dorset
first Sun. in Aug.
Once you've had a taste of Dorset, you'll be back for the annual Taste of Dorset. The tiny community claims to be the restaurant capital of the world (see Where to Eat), and this event lets Dorset fans nosh samples from all restaurants. There are also games, music, entertainment, and contests. Held noon–3:00 P.M.; parking at Froggy's or along Hwy. 218, where shuttle buses transfer tasters. Located 5 miles east of Park Rapids and 1 mile north of Hwy. 34 on County Rd. 218. Call Park Rapids Area Chamber of Commerce (see Services) for more information.

Outdoor Activities

Bemidji State University Outdoor Program
BSU's Outdoor Program makes the north woods accessible for the public as well as students and staff. Sign up for a free hour-long lunch cruise (bring your own lunch) on Lake Bemidji each Tues. during summer, or for the three-hour cruise on the Mississippi, held a couple of times during the summer. The program also offers canoeing and sailing clinics, runs tours, and rents canoes, kayaks, sailboats, sailboards, mountain bikes, cross-country skis, snowshoes, and camping equipment. BSU students get a break on prices.

The office is in the lower level of Hobson Student Union on the BSU campus; **218-755-2999.**

Biking
There are 16 miles of surfaced bike trail in Itasca State Park (see Major Attractions). Lake Bemidji State Park has a 1-mile paved bike trail, and 5 miles for mountain bikes (see Parks).

Heartland Trail
One of the first trails in the country to be built on an abandoned rail bed, the Heartland Trail is a popular 49-mile stretch between Park Rapids and Cass Lake. It's mostly level, save for 4 hilly miles north of Walker. Look for bald eagles and many other birds and animals, as well as some giant white pines, along the trail. The surface is asphalt from Park Rapids to Walker, with a grassy parallel treadway for horseback riders and mountain bikers. The remainder of the trail is gravel and railroad ballast, with some sandy sections. There is trail parking at Heartland County Park in Park Rapids, and also at Dorset, Nevis, Akeley, Walker, and Erikson's Landing north of Walker. Get maps from the Dept. of Natural Resources, **500 Lafayette Rd., St. Paul, 55155; 888-MINNDNR** or **651-296-6157.**

Boating
From its source to Bemidji, the Mississippi is a small wilderness river with few rapids, and can be canoed easily by novices. For a map of the state-designated canoe route, contact the Dept. of Natural Resources, **500 Lafayette Rd., St. Paul, 55155; 888-MINNDNR** or **651-296-6157.**

Rentals and Tours
Narrated boat tours on Lake Itasca leave from the Douglas Lodge pier, Memorial Day–Labor Day. The 10-mile tour lasts one and a half hours. Fee. See Major Attractions.

Fishing
Area lakes are generally good fishing, with walleye, northern, and bass among the species found, as well as the wily muskie. Lake Bemidji supports walleye, northern, and perch (see Parks). All but the muskie reproduce naturally. Muskie finger-

lings are stocked regularly, according to information from the Friends of Lake Bemidji, and muskies weighing 30–40 pounds have been caught (and usually released). For seasons and license information, call the Area Fisheries Supervisor in Bemidji, **218-755-2974.**

Golf

Bemidji Town and Country Club

Founded in 1916, this 18-hole course bordered by stately Norway pines has rolling terrain and four holes that incorporate water. Open to the public, it's the site of the annual Birchmont tournament. Club rentals and lessons are available. Greens fees vary (up to $45 for 18 holes Sat.–Sun.). Open Apr. 15–Oct. 15. Located on the north shore of Lake Bemidji, off County Rd. 20. **P.O. Box 622, Bemidji, 56601; 218-751-4535.** Website: www.bemidjigolf.com.

Hiking

Itasca State Park has 33 miles of hiking trails, especially lovely in the golden fall forest (see Major Attractions). Lake Bemidji State Park has 14 miles of hiking trails (see Parks).

Skiing

CROSS-COUNTRY

Itasca State Park has 31 miles of trails (see Major Attractions). Lake Bemidji State Park has 9 miles of cross-country ski trails, and three candlelight ski tours are held in winter, one coinciding with a full moon (see Parks). The Bemidji Cross-Country Ski Club issues a map of seven area trails, with comments on the terrain, history, etc. The maps are available at the Bemidji Visitors and Convention Bureau (see Services). For information on snow conditions, call **800-458-2223.** Cross-country skiers have 15 miles of challenging trails at Buena Vista Ski Area (see below), and Buena Vista is the site of the annual Finlandia cross-country race.

DOWNHILL

Buena Vista Ski Area

The land on which Buena Vista is located has been in the Dickinson family for more than a century. A family-oriented ski area, Buena Vista opened its first run in 1936. There are 15 runs—the longest of which is 2,000 feet—served by four chair lifts. The vertical drop is 230 feet. Open Thurs.–Fri., noon–9:00 P.M., and Sat.–Sun., 10:00 A.M.–9:00 P.M. (also during school vacations). Located **12 miles north of Bemidji on County Rd. 15; 800-777-7958** or **218-243-2231. E-mail: bvski@bvskiarea.com.**

Snowmobiling

The Mississippi Headwaters area has hundreds of miles of snowmobile trails, many of which are interconnected. Itasca State Park has 31 miles of trails (see Major Attractions). There are 3 miles of trails in Lake Bemidji State Park and in many state forest lands (see Parks). The whole 49-mile Heartland Trail is groomed for snowmobiles in winter (see Biking). For maps, contact the visitor centers (see Services).

Swimming

Swimming beaches are plentiful in this area, from the big beach in Itasca State Park and the many resort beaches to the lovely sugar-sand beach on Spirit Lake in Menahga and the sandy beach on Lake Bemidji.

Seeing and Doing

Museums and Historic Sites

Camp Rabideau CCC Camp

Six decades ago, Camp Rabideau Civilian Conservation Corps (CCC) Camp was bustling with scores of young men, who planted trees and did many other tasks during Franklin D. Roosevelt's New Deal. The young men joined the CCC—FDR's "tree army"—in return for a small salary, room and board, and training. Today, the deserted camp of weathered green buildings, on the National Register of Historic Places, is slowly being restored and waits patiently in the woods for returning CCC veterans and younger visitors alike. The camp was one of 2,650 built across the nation, and it is now one of just a few lingering camps; 15 of its original 25 buildings remain. There are picnic facilities. Visitors can walk around the grounds anytime. Free. The buildings are open only at certain times; contact the U.S. Forest Service about hours. **HC 3, Box 95, Blackduck, 56630; 218-835-4291.**

Paul Bunyan and Babe the Blue Ox

Few visitors to Bemidji can resist having their photos taken with the statues of legendary lumberjack Paul Bunyan and his faithful companion Babe the Blue Ox, symbols of Bemidji since 1937. Some people can't resist reaching up and holding Paul's hand for the photo. The 18-foot statues are by Lake Bemidji, across from the visitor bureau.

Rapid River Logging Camp

Everyone loves Rapid River, especially when the steam-powered sawmill runs, Tues. and Fri. Tuck into an all-you-can-eat lumberjack meal in a rustic dining hall, visit the museum, and walk along the nature trails. It's fun and educational, and sure fills you up. Fee for meals. Open Memorial Day–Labor Day, Mon.–Sat., 7:30 A.M.–9:00 P.M., and Sun. (call for hours). Take Hwy. 71 north of Park Rapids and follow the signs to County Rd. 18. **218-732-3444.**

Parks

For Chippewa National Forest, see the Walker chapter in this section.

Lake Bemidji State Park

Lake Bemidji is a great family park. Kids love the sandy swimming beach on Lake Bemidji, and everyone is fascinated by the 0.25-mile boardwalk into a spruce-tamarack peat bog, where visitors can glimpse insect-eating pitcher plants and sundews. From early June to early July, orchids bloom, including the showy lady slipper, Minnesota's state flower. Another short boardwalk extends into a small lake where there is a beaver dam. Naturalist John Fylpaa is on duty year-round and leads Fri.-morning fishing expeditions for kids as well as pontoon boat trips. Twice a summer or so, there are canoe trips along the Mississippi River, which flows through Lake Bemidji. Space is limited, so sign up in advance at the park

office. The park's popularity, especially with families, can be partly explained by its location 6 miles outside of Bemidji, Fylpaa says. There is a boat launch, and the park rents boats and snowshoes. Hiking and biking trails are here as well. There is camping in the park. Located 5 miles north of Bemidji on County Rd. 21, then 1.7 miles east on County State Aid Hwy. 20. **3401 State Park Rd. NE, Bemidji, 56601; 218-755-3843.**

Performing Arts

THEATER

Paul Bunyan Playhouse

The Playhouse is the oldest continuously running professional summer theater in the state, having begun in 1950. A variety of productions run early June–mid-Aug. **314 Beltrami Ave., Bemidji, 56601; 218-751-7270.**

Woodtick Musical Jamboree

It's good, clean fun and toe-tapping music in the two-hour musical smorgasbord at Akeley's Woodtick Musical Jamboree. A house band plays country, gospel, folk, and contemporary hits as the band and other performers sing along. Lena (an Ole-less Lena, since Ole went to seek his fortune in the Big Apple) jokes her way through the performance. Owners Mike and Cindy Chase are proud that the jamboree is suitable for families with kids. And why is it named the Woodtick? Chase has a snappy comeback: "'Cause it's a good name and it sticks to ya." Fee. Reservations advised. Performances mid-June–Aug., Wed.–Thurs., 3:00 P.M. and 8:00 P.M., and Fri.–Sat., 8:00 P.M. Located **in downtown Akeley; 218-652-4200.**

Scenic Drives

Great River Road

Follow the federally designated Great River Road from the Mississippi's start to Grand Rapids on a scenic, 100-mile drive. The route starts in Itasca State Park and meanders, along with the river, through forests and past lakes, cities, and Leech Lake Indian Reservation. A detailed brochure is available at many tourist organizations or from the Minnesota Travel Information Center, **800-**

328-1461, (in Minnesota) **800-652-9747,** or **651-296-5029.**

Shopping

Bemidji Woolen Mills Factory Store

Paul Bunyan wannabes shop here. The Bemidji Woolen Mills have made wool shirts (not all of them in the black-and-red lumberjack plaid) since 1920. The factory store carries sturdy, attractive clothing for all, including shirts, jackets, coats, hunting clothes, and fur-lined hats with ear flaps, plus wild rice and Hudson Bay blankets. Open Mon.–Sat., 8:00 A.M.–5:30 P.M., and Sun., 10:00 A.M.–5:00 P.M. Located at Third St. and Irvine Ave. **P.O. Box 277, Bemidji, 56619; 218-751-5166.**

Lady Slipper Designs Outlet Store

Lady Slipper Designs began in 1973 as a way to boost the area economy by encouraging cottage industries and selling them wholesale. Today, Lady Slipper Designs has become one of the largest cottage-industry distributors in the country. Birch-bark containers and jewelry, rustic wooden frames and birdhouses, and hollow eggs bearing delicate impressions of leaves are among the popular products. There are about 100 producers now, about one-fourth of them Ojibwe Indians who make traditional crafts. Many of the products—plus other lines—are available at Lady Slipper Designs Outlet Store in Bemidji. Open Memorial Day–Dec. 31, Mon.–Sat., 10:00 A.M.–5:30 P.M., and Sun., 11:00 A.M.–4:00 P.M. **315 Irvine Ave. NW, Bemidji, 56601; 218-751-7501.**

Sister Wolf Bookstore

Tucked amid the restaurants in tiny Dorset is Sister Wolf Bookstore, run by the congenial Mary Kay Watson. The range of stock is very complete and Mary Kay will order anything she doesn't have on the shelves. Many of the books are Minnesota-related, and many regional authors do readings at the store. Open May–Sept., daily, 10:00 A.M.–9:00 P.M. Located **in downtown Dorset** (you really can't miss it); **218-732-7565.**

Where to Stay

Bemidji and Park Rapids have many types of accommodations, from chain hotels and motels to fishing and family resorts to sleek motels on the lake. Contact the Visitors and Convention Bureau (see Services) for a complete listing.

Resorts

A Place in the Woods—$$$$

It's tempting to say, "Find your own place in the woods; this is ours," but that would be mean and selfish. So, do come to this place in the woods, north of Bemidji and the perfect getaway. It began in 1991, when John and Lynn Short left the cities for the country life on Turtle River Lake. The 11 cabins appear rustic, but have all the modern conveniences and then some. They vary in size from the one-bedroom honeymoon cabins (with a double Jacuzzi) to larger, four-bedroom cabins. All have wood-burning stoves and well-equipped kitchens; some have

The largest white pine in Minnesota is a hallmark of Itasca State Park, as well as one of the state's earliest industries. Photo courtesy of the Minnesota Department of Natural Resources.

lofts. The interior walls are of half-round logs. The central Eagles Nest lodge, a magnificent log structure, has a cathedral ceiling and a cozy fire, with the makings for s'mores available. There are plenty of books, games, and videos. Downstairs is a sauna and just outside is a hot tub. In summer, laze in a hammock or go fishing or boating on the lake. There are kids' activities, too. Winter is for cross-country skiing. In summer there's a three-day minimum; weekly rentals are available. Located north of Bemidji on U.S. Hwy. 71, then east on County Rd. 22. **11380 Turtle River Lake Rd., Bemidji, 56601; 800-676-4547 or 218-586-2345. Website: www.aplaceinthewoodsresort.com**

Don't miss Paul Bunyan and Babe the Blue Ox, while visiting Bemidji. Copyright © Minnesota Office of Tourism. Used by permission.

Douglas Lodge, Cabins and Motel Rooms— $$ to $$$$

Accommodations vary greatly in Itasca State Park, from recently renovated rooms and suites in the historic log Douglas Lodge, to five one-bedroom cabins (two are log cabins with a fireplace and screened porch), to larger cabins sans kitchens to housekeeping cabins to 18 units of basic motel accommodation. All fill up very fast: reserve by calling **The Connection, 800-246-2267 or 612-922-9000.**

Bert's Cabins—$$ to $$$

For 60 years, visitors to Itasca State Park have snuggled into these cozy cabins amid tall pines, just outside the park boundaries. There are 11 cabins now, all very clean, completely equipped for housekeeping, and fully modernized. Some are small and visitors feel like they're playing house; five are deluxe winterized cabins with decks, screened porches, and fireplaces. There is a heated outdoor swimming pool. Dave and Pat Evenwoll, a friendly couple, own the cabins; Pat's dad, the original Bert, started the business in 1939. Open Jan.–Feb. and May–Oct.; weekly rentals available. Located 1 mile west of the Mississippi Headwaters. **HC 5, Box 1, Lake Itasca, 56470; 218-266-3312.**

Mississippi Headwaters Hostel—$$ (for two, midweek)

Open year-round, the hostel is in a historic log building. Go midweek to beat the crowds. Multibunk rooms sleep 32 in all, with private rooms sometimes available. There's a lounge with a stone fireplace and a well-equipped kitchen. Prices are lower for AYH members. Open year-round (except off-season breaks); call first. Book through AYH Hosteling International; **HCO 5, Box 5A, Lake Itasca, 56470; 218-266-3415.**

Ruttger's Birchmont Lodge—call for rates

Ruttger's is a grand old name in Minnesota resorts. The first Ruttger's was a bit to the east of Bemidji, but it's been more than 60 years now since the family bought the Birchmont. Randy Ruttger is the fourth-generation Ruttger to run one of the family's resorts. He presides over one with a long history: the first cabins for tourists were built in 1913, and guests through the years have included such diverse personages as Mrs. Woodrow Wilson, Malcolm Forbes, Crystal Gale, and Dr. Joyce Brothers. Well-known or not, all visitors are impressed by the 1,700-foot sandy beach on Lake Bemidji and the many water-related activities, including swimming, boating, and fishing. Swimmers have a choice of the lake, an outdoor pool, and an indoor pool in a recreation center. The resort also has a free supervised children's play program, to let parents relax. The restaurants offer good, homemade food, with lightly breaded, pan-fried walleye a favorite entree. The lobby of the big white lodge, the oldest three-story lodge in northern Minnesota, has a magnificent stone fireplace, wicker furniture, and two moose heads adorning the walls. The lodge's 29 rooms have rustic, knotty pine walls and slick new baths. In addition, Ruttger's has four townhouses and 29 cabins, ranging from one to four bedrooms. The cabins are done in knotty pine, also, and most have stone fireplaces. Ruttger's rates include water-skiing and sailboat rides. Located 4 miles north of Bemidji on County Rd. 21. **530 Birchmont Beach Rd., Bemidji, 56601; 888-RUTTGER or 218-751-1630. Website: www.ruttger.com.**

Camping

Menahga Memorial Campground—$

This is a municipal campground in a wooded setting. There are 22 sites, 10 with electrical hookups. The city plans to double the number of sites soon. No reservations. It fills up fast in summer. Open May–Oct. Located just south of the city of Menahga on U.S. Hwy. 71. For more information, call the Menahga City Clerk's office, **218-564-4557.**

State Forests—$

Most of the Minnesota State Forest campgrounds are in northern Minnesota, along lakes or rivers. Some are free; others charge a minimum fee. Some of the state forest sites in the headwaters area are: **Hungry Men Lake**—14 campsites with water, picnic sites, and lake access; located 10 miles north of Park Rapids on Hwy. 71, west 1.5 miles on County Rd. 41, then north 1 mile; **218-732-3309. Mississippi River**—16 free rustic canoe campsites; located at Trails and Waterways, **6603 Bemidji Ave., Bemidji, 56601; 218-755-2265.** For a complete listing of state forest, county, and national forest campgrounds, contact the Dept. of Natural Resources, **500 Lafayette Rd., St. Paul, 55155, 888-MINNDNR or 651-296-6157,** or Chippewa National Forest, **Cass Lake, 56633, 218-335-2226.**

State Parks—$

Lake Bemidji State Park has 98 campsites, 43 with electrical hookups. Itasca State Park has 237 drive-in sites, 100 with electrical hookups, plus 11 backpack sites and 11 cart-in campsites. To reserve state park campsites, call **The Connection, 800-246-2267** or **612-922-9000.**

Where to Eat

Union Station—$$$

Take one railroad station, redo it, and add lots of pasta, steak, seafood, and buffalo wings, and you have Union Station. Many of the entrees are grilled over sugar-maple-wood fires. The "rings and fingers" appetizer translates into calamari rings and walleye fingers. There is a nice selection of wines by the glass. Open Mon.–Sat., 4:00–10:00 P.M.; Sun., 4:00–9:00 P.M.; lounge open until midnight. Located **at First and Beltrami Aves., in downtown Bemidji; 218-751-9261.**

Dorset Restaurants—$ to $$$

If you haven't dined in Dorset, your life is sadly lacking. Or at least that's what Dorset's restaurateurs kiddingly suggest. The self-styled "Restaurant Capital of the World" is a little village of fewer than 20 permanent residents. It's impossible to walk along the boardwalk in summer, seeing happy vacationers chow down in the rollicking restaurants and inhaling tantalizing cooking smells, and not want to eat. Dorset knows this, and Dorset is ready for you. Although the **Dorset Cafe, 218-732-4072,** is the only year-round eating place, it's joined in summer by the **Dorset House Eatery** (pizza, burgers), **218-732-5556; Companeros** (Mexican food), **218-732-7624; La Pasta Italian Eatery, 218-732-0275;** and **Woodstock North Gifts and Tea Room, 218-732-8457.** The crowds make Dorset look like the center of the universe on a warm summer evening, and the wait may be a couple of hours long (really). Dorset is located 5 miles east of Park Rapids and 1 mile north of Hwy. 34 on County Rd. 218. Call Park Rapids Area Chamber of Commerce for information (see Services).

Douglas Lodge—$ to $$$

Wild rice soup and other Minnesota staples, including walleye and Minnesota wines, are on the menu at the historic Douglas Lodge in Itasca State Park, which underwent a renovation early in 1998. Open the Fri. before Memorial Day–first week of Oct., daily, 8:00 A.M.–8:00 P.M. Located **near the east entrance of the park** (see Major Attractions); **218-266-2122.**

Tutto Bene—$ to $$$

Tutto Bene is a little bit of Italy in downtown Bemidji, billing itself as an "Italian ristorante and Espresso Bar." The dinner menu offers such classic Italian dishes as chicken marsala, chicken cacciatore, and veal scallopini, with antipasti including eggplant parmesan and bruschetta. There are also lunch specialties. The restaurant is bright and sleek, and the pasta is homemade; don't forget the espresso or cappuccino to round out your Italian excursion. Open Mon.–Thurs., 11:00 A.M.–9:00 P.M., Fri.–Sat., 11:00 A.M.–10:00 P.M. **300 Beltrami Ave. NW, Bemidji, 56601; 218-751-1100.**

Services

The recently built **Bemidji Chamber of Commerce and Visitors and Convention Bureau**'s tourist information center is right on Lake Bemidji. It's beautiful as well as efficient inside, with an impressive stone fireplace, whose stones and bricks hail from all over, including the U.S. Capitol and the Statue of Liberty. Look for Paul and Babe opposite it. **300 Bemidji Ave., Bemidji, 56601; 800-458-2223.**

The **Park Rapids Area Chamber of Commerce** is at the south end of town, on U.S. Hwy. 71. **P.O. Box 249E, Park Rapids, 56470; 800-247-0054** or **218-732-4111.**

Walker

Walker and the area around it are dominated by the presence of Leech Lake, the Chippewa National Forest, and also Leech Lake Reservation. Like Brainerd, Walker is a summer (and, increasingly, winter) tourist destination, but unlike Brainerd, it still does not have all the commercial hoopla and the crowds that come with it. Walker is the seat of Cass County, and even though the population is a shade less than 1,000, it looms large in county life.

Walker still draws the serious anglers who stalk walleye and northern in the many bays of Leech Lake. However, the main street of Walker is turning trendy with many shops, and in downtown Walker visitors are likely to find bait and cappuccino for sale in adjacent establishments. Hilly Fifth St. drops down to the lake and a public dock, where vacationers can tie up their boats if they come to town.

Although Walker has courted tourists since the first resort was built in the late 1890s, it is only in fairly recent years that it has been a big draw, both for long-term vacationers and weekenders, and also for the young people and retirees who have moved to Walker because they want to live in the north country. Many of these new residents have come with the skills and zeal to start new businesses or shore up existing ones. With its boundaries restricted by the lake, the forest, and the reservation, Walker has little room to move and is slowly expanding south along Hwy. 371.

History

American Indians and the ever-present fur traders roamed the Walker area before the permanent European settlement began. Logging was responsible for jump-starting what is now Cass County, back in 1847, when an agreement was signed with Ojibwe leader Hole-in-the-Day and

a logging camp was set up on the Crow Wing River in the southern part of Cass County. Later, T. B. Walker, whose name now graces the Walker Art Center in Minneapolis, bought up land in what is now Walker with the thought of headquartering lumber operations here. However, he wanted the saloons and bordellos closed, and the hard-working, hard-partying lumberjacks refused. P. H. McGarry then came to the area and bought up the land from Walker, but not before the town had permanently been christened "Walker." McGarry, who was a state senator, was the real mover behind the establishment of the town. He also built the first resort on Leech Lake, with many prominent people among the resort guests.

The railroad had come to Walker in the late 19th century, but the government land office for homesteaders didn't open until 1910, when settlement by Europeans began in earnest. Farming was never a big factor in the area's growth. Logging remained the chief industry and is still important, although now tourism is the county's chief income producer.

Paddlers skim along the Mississippi River near Lake Winnibigoshish. Copyright © Minnesota Office of Tourism. Used by permission.

Festivals and Events

International Eelpout festival
second weekend in Feb.

What to do when winter gets boring up Walker way? Celebrate the ugliest fish around—the eelpout—and do it with such razzle-dazzle that 4,000–5,000 folks come to join in. Catching eelpouts, which resemble eels with whiskers, is the object of the festival. Prize-winning 'pouts bring in thousands of dollars. Other events include golf on ice, hot tubbing on the lake, and the "Eelpout Peelout" (a 5-mile run, come snow or come cold). Contact the Leech Lake Area Chamber of Commerce (see Services).

Cass Lake Powwow
three-day weekend closest to Fourth of July

Several hundred dancers, singers, and drummers from surrounding states and Canada participate in the annual Cass Lake powwow. The public is welcome; entry is free. There are food vendors on the grounds. It's held on the Veterans Memorial Grounds, 3 miles northwest of Cass Lake on Bingo Palace Dr. **218-335-8289.**

Leech Lake Regatta
mid-Aug.

About 60 sailboats in several different classes compete in this annual regatta (usually held two weeks before Labor Day), one of the largest in the Upper Midwest. The race starts at Walker Bay, and many onlookers turn out to see the gala parade of sails until they vanish out onto the big lake. It takes place on a Sat., Sun., and Mon. The regatta celebrated its silver anniversary in 1996. Contact the Leech Lake Area Chamber of Commerce (see Services).

Ethnic Fest
second weekend in Sept.

Dancers, singers, and musicians from a variety of ethnic groups, from American Indian to Scandinavian to Polynesian to Asian, have been among the groups joining in the Ethnic Fest, a fairly new festival that grew big in just a few years. Foods from many nations can be purchased and there is a parade on Sat. Up to 3,000 people attend on each of the three days. Contact the Leech Lake Area Chamber of Commerce (see Services).

Getting There

Walker is an hour north of Brainerd, and 195 miles from the Twin Cities. Take U.S. Hwy. 10 to Hwy. 371. Hackensack, another vacation destination, is south of Walker on Hwy. 371, while Cass Lake (both the town and the lake) are northwest of Walker.

North Woods Marathon

third Sat. in Sept.

The course through the splendidly arrayed trees in the Chippewa National Forest is a favorite one for many runners. The event includes a full 26-mile marathon, a relay marathon with teams of two runners, and a 10K run and 10K walk. Contact the Leech Lake Area Chamber of Commerce (see Services).

Outdoor Activities

Biking

Chippewa National Forest

The forest is a great place for mountain bikers and also for families. Trails range from easy to difficult. Many are near campsites. The Forest Service publishes a guide to the 18 bike routes within the forest, with small maps of each. Order the guide from the supervisor's office (see Hiking).

Heartland Trail

The Heartland Trail is a 49-mile trail built on an abandoned railroad bed. It runs from Park Rapids to Cass Lake. See Biking, in the Mississippi Headwaters chapter in this section.

Boating

The marshlands through which the Mississippi River flows from Cass Lake to Deer River make for wonderful waterfowl- and eagle-viewing. Although the river takes some sharp turns, there are no rapids, so it is easy going for canoers, but caution should be used going through the large lakes. For a map of the state-designated canoe route, contact the Dept. of Natural Resources, **500 Lafayette Rd., St. Paul, 55155; 888-MINNDNR or 651-296-6157.**

Fishing

Leech Lake

Leech Lake is one of Minnesota's largest lakes and certainly one of the most popular with those who fish. The lake, surrounded by the Chippewa National Forest, is the third largest entirely within Minnesota, after Red Lake and Mille Lacs. It has 640 miles of shoreline, and its irregular shape creates a multitude of bays, some shallow, some deep. Depth of the lake varies greatly, although it is 150 feet deep in spots. It is a magnet for anglers, who are particularly avid to catch walleyes, northerns, and the occasional elusive muskie. Steamboat Bay, a shallow part of the lake, is known as a hot spot for northerns. In addition to the fish, the lake attracts many different kinds of wildlife. Residents say they have seen black bears taking a swim in the lake on occasion, and deer are a common sight. For information on fishing in the area, call the Area Fisheries Supervisor in Walker, **218-547-1683.**

Rentals and Tours

Many visitors hire a fishing guide to teach them the ins and outs of Leech Lake fishing. A couple of years ago, 13 of the guides formed the nonprofit **Leech Lake Guide Coalition,** which charges a standard price—$150 for two people for a half day or $225 for two for a whole day of guided fishing, with everything but rain gear provided. A central number, which Chip and Ineke Leer answer, is used by the coalition members, who take jobs on a rotation system. **800-241-1532.**

Catch the **City Dock Launch** at the bottom of the Fifth St. hill in Walker for a half- or all-day walleye trip. Bait and filleting are provided, and tackle can be rented if you've come without it. Half-day trips, which costs $30 per person (whole-day trips are $50) leave at 8:00 A.M. and 1:00 P.M. Vera Stewart and her late husband started the business in 1961, and their son and his wife now run it. Even nonanglers enjoy the trip for its scenery, says Stewart. The Stewarts also have cottages and motel units (see Where to Stay). **P.O. Box 544, Walker, 56484; 218-547-1662.**

Golf

Tianna Country Club

At Tianna Country Club, there are animal hazards as well as the usual ones. "A deer walked out just as one player made a shot, and it was deflected off the deer," reports Assistant Manager Carrie Johnson. What does a player do when he or she hits a deer with a golf ball? "Just play it as it lies," laughs Johnson. The 18-hole course, noted for the beautiful trees that surround it, has a tricky second hole. It's a 170-yard par-3, which calls for a shot between trees and over a pond. Several tournaments, including the North American Indian Association tournament, are held annually. The public is welcome at Tianna, which opened in 1925. Rental clubs are available. Greens fees: $30 for 18 holes. Open Apr. 15–Oct. 15, daily, 6:00 A.M.–7:00 P.M. Located **1 mile west of Walker on Hwy. 34; 218-547-1712.**

Hiking

Chippewa National Forest

The 1.6-million-acre Chippewa National Forest, the first national forest east of the Mississippi when it was established in 1908, is an immense haven of trees and lakes, and its boundaries also include state, county, and private land and the Leech Lake Reservation. The Chippewa contains 700 lakes, 920 miles of streams, many wetlands, and 160 miles of hiking trails. Hunting and fishing are also popular pastimes, as are canoeing, biking, and cross-country skiing. Flyers detailing various activities are available from the park headquarters and at many of the district offices. There is camping. The Chippewa is a working forest, with 1 percent of its trees harvested each year. Wildlife is abundant and the forest has the largest number of breeding bald eagles in the Lower 48 states. In addition to its many hiking trails, a 68-mile section of the North Country National Scenic Trail crosses the Chippewa. The North Country Trail, not yet complete, will be part of a 3,200-mile scenic trail from New York State to North Dakota, with links to the Appalachian, Lewis and Clark, and Pacific Crest Trails. The Chippewa portion is the only Minnesota section completed. Follow the trail signs. Request information from the supervisor's office, **Rte. 3, Box 244, Cass Lake, 56633; 218-335-8600.**

Hunting

The area around Leech Lake is good deer and grouse hunting territory, and the marshlands also draw breeding and migrating waterfowl, so duck hunters like it, too. For seasons and license information, call the Dept. of Natural Resources field office, **218-755-2964.**

Skiing

CROSS-COUNTRY

The hiking trails in Chippewa National Forest are ideal for cross-country skiing. Those that are groomed for cross-country skiing in winter (73 miles total) include Oak Point, Simpson Creek, Miller, Suomi, Trout Lake, Goose Lake, and Shingobee. Shingobee, near Walker, is popular also for its swooping sliding hill, and it has a CCC-built warming house at the base of the hill. See Hiking.

Snowmobiling

There are approximately 600 miles of snowmobile trails in the Cass County–Hubbard County area. Maps and information on snow conditions are available from the Leech Lake Area Chamber of Commerce (see Services).

Seeing and Doing

Museums and Historic Sites

Cass County Museum, Walker Wildlife and Indian Arts Museum, and Huset School

One small entry fee gets visitors into three adjacent museums worth seeing. They are all next to the Leech Lake Area Chamber of Commerce, in Walker. The **Walker Wildlife and Indian Arts Museum,** owned by the city of Walker, contains American Indian artifacts and examples of traditional crafts, including many beadwork items such as beaded bandolier bags and moccasins, plus a re-creation of an Ojibwe village that features a full-sized birch-bark canoe and a wigwam. The museum also has full-sized dioramas with wildlife, including black bears and deer. The **Huset School,** built in 1912, is a one-room log school moved 45 miles to its present site. The school is a "hands-on" exhibit, according to curator Renee Geving, and kids are allowed to sit at the desks and write on the slates. The **Cass County Museum**'s variety of exhibits detail aspects of county history, such as logging, tourism, the railroad heyday, and individuals important in county history. The museum also has a kitchen, parlor, and bedroom with period furniture. Open June 1–Sept., Mon.–Sat., 10:00 A.M.–5:00 P.M. Located at the intersection of Hwys. 371 and 200 and Second St. in Walker. **Box 505, Walker, 56484; 218-547-7251.**

Chippewa National Forest's Supervisor's Office

An immense red-pine log building, which some call "the Log Palace," was built by the Pike Bay Civilian Conservation Corps in Cass Lake in 1935. The interior is log. The massive 50-foot fireplace and chimney were constructed from 265 tons of glacial rock. Both the logs and the rock were obtained nearby. In the lobby are historical displays and photos of the area and its people. Information about the Chippewa National Forest is available here and there is also a bookstore selling natural history books. The building houses the Chippewa National Forest's Supervisor's Office and is open for tours during business hours. Open Mon.–Fri., 7:30 A.M.–4:30 P.M. Located **on Hwy. 371 and Second St. W. in Cass Lake; 218-335-8600.**

Parks

Moondance Ranch and Wildlife Park

If this place doesn't keep the kids happy, nothing will. There are trail rides, a wildlife park and petting zoo, a water slide and miniature golf, a trout pond, bonfires, a gift shop, and a restaurant. Special events include powwows and a music festival. The tame deer can be hand-fed. In the wildlife park are tigers, wolves, buffalo, jaguars, black bears, and other critters. Open Memorial Day–Labor Day, daily, 9:00 A.M.–9:00 P.M.; shorter hours rest of year. Located at the **junction of Hwys. 371 and 200, 5 miles south of Walker; 218-547-1055.**

Walker City Park

A nice spot for locals and visitors to stop is the Walker City Park, right on Leech Lake. The park has a swimming beach with lifeguards, public boat docks, lighted tennis courts, playground equipment, and fish-cleaning facilities. Located on the east end of town on the lake. For more information, call the Leech Lake Area Chamber of Commerce, **800-833-1118.**

Scenic Drives

Chippewa National Forest

Take a 50-mile self-guided tour of the Chippewa National Forest for an intimate view of the north woods and its past and present inhabitants. The tour begins at the forest supervisor's office in Cass Lake (see Museums and Historic Sites) and continues past many historic and natural features, including the Pike Bay CCC Camp, which is also the spot where Henry Schoolcraft asked Ojibwe Chief Ozawindib to guide him to the source of the Mississippi River (see History, in the Mississippi Headwaters chapter in this section). Also along the drive are the Norway Beach Visitor Center and a view of Star Island, an island within Cass Lake that has its own lake. The lake, Windigo, is featured in traditional Ojibwe stories. Knutson Dam, a prime habitat for eagles, loons, blue herons, and ospreys, is on the tour, as is Webster Lake, which has a 6-mile trail, including a boardwalk into a peat bog. Stop at Camp Rabideau, a CCC camp (see the Mississippi Headwaters chapter in this section), the Gilstead Lake fishing pier, and the Blackduck lookout tower. The brochure is available from the forest office, **218-335-8600.**

Shopping

Che-wa-ka-e-gon Gift Shop

The Leech Lake Reservation runs this gift shop,

which features locally made Ojibwe crafts, including dream catchers, beadwork, and birch-bark items. Open daily, 9:00 A.M.–6:00 P.M. Located **in the Che-wa-ka-e-gon Complex on the north side of the city of Cass Lake, next to the reservation office; 218-335-8312.**

Liten Hus

This "little house" has a big selection of gifts, clothing (including those beautiful Norwegian sweaters), jewelry, and other items from the Scandinavian countries. Open year-round, Mon.–Sat., 9:00 A.M.–5:30 P.M. Located **on Minnesota Ave. and Fifth St., in Walker; 218-547-3919.**

Lundrigan's Clothing

Since 1937, Lundrigan's has sold stylish, weekend clothing in Walker, first for men only and now for both men and women. Lundrigan's carries classic lines, including Pendleton and Woolrich. Open year-round, Mon.–Sat., 9:00 A.M.–5:30 P.M. Located **at Minnesota Ave. and Fifth St., in Walker; 218-547-1041.**

Northern Exposure

Locally made furniture, perfect for a northwoods cabin, is sold here, as are items made by American Indians and other gift items. The shop recently expanded. Open year-round, Mon.–Sat., 9:00 A.M.–5:30 P.M., and Sun., 11:00 A.M.–4:00 P.M. Located **on Minnesota Ave. and Fifth St., in Walker; 218-547-3440.**

Reed's Sporting Goods

Hunters and anglers are like kids in a candy store when they get into Reed's, Walker's fascinating outdoor store in business since 1952. Reed's has 30,000 square feet of space, filled with 3,000 guns, lots of electronic fishing devices, bait, boots and waders, water skis, and all kinds of fishing gear, camping equipment, and clothing ranging from no-nonsense outfits for serious outdoor types to stylish outdoor clothes for those who get their fish at the supermarket. Reed's also has how-to videos and cooking equipment, and sponsors many workshops on fishing and hunting. Call for a free catalog. Open year-round, Mon.–Sat., 8:00 A.M.–6:00 P.M., and Sun., 9:00 A.M.–5:00

P.M. Located at Main St. and Sixth, in Walker. **Box 490, Main St., Walker, 56484; 800-346-0019 or 218-547-1505.**

Wagering

Northern Lights

Owned and operated by the Leech Lake Ojibwe, with hundreds of slots, plus blackjack, entertainment, and restaurants. Northern Lights' restaurant is open 24 hours and there is a bar. Located **4 miles south of Walker at the junction of Hwys. 371 and 200; 800-252-PLAY.**

Palace Bingo and Casino

Owned and operated by the Leech Lake Ojibwe, with hundreds of slots, plus blackjack, entertainment, and restaurants; the Palace is alcohol-free. Located **2 miles west of Cass Lake, on Bingo Palace Dr.; 800-228-6676.**

Where to Stay

Resorts

There are approximately 70 resorts in the Leech Lake area. Check with the tourism bureaus (see Services) for a complete listing of resorts (as well as motels and bed-and-breakfasts).

Adventure North—$$$ to $$$$

Chip and Ineke Leer took over an existing resort on Leech Lake with the idea of letting the vacationers say what they want in advance and then making a customized vacation package for them. "We want them to feel they're really on vacation. When they arrive, we even unload their car for them, and we've made all their arrangements, whether they want to fish, go horseback riding, or anything else. We also let them determine how long they want to stay, rather than just renting all our cabins by the week," said Ineke. The six cabins, from one to five bedrooms, and the suite in the lodge have a north-woods theme, with knotty pine interiors and Hudson Bay–style blankets. There is a Jacuzzi in the lodge suite. Facilities include a game room, laundry, and playground. Adventure North offers gourmet breakfasts and dinner (by reservation) for guests. Ineke cooks one entree, such as rosemary chicken or beef Wellington, nightly. Chip Leer is also a fishing guide. The resort is on the southwest side of the lake, on Trading Post Bay. **4444 Point Landing Dr. NW, Walker, 56484; 800-294-1532 or 218-547-1532.**

City Dock Cottages—$$$

Right next to the City Dock Launch service, also run by the Stewart family, are three housekeeping cottages and 12 motel units in downtown Walker. The Stewarts have had launch trips since 1961 (see Fishing). The City Dock is at the end of Fifth St.; for cottages, contact **No. 1 City Dock, Box 544, Walker, 56484; 218-547-1662.**

Huddles—$$$

This resort, one of the oldest on the lake that is still in the same family, has 51 cabins with one to four bedrooms. The Huddle family has had the resort since 1928; it's now run by Roy and Kay Huddle. There are two lodges and two restaurants, a heated swimming pool, a sandy beach on the lake, and a playground. Guides and launch trips are available. **HCR84, Box 517, Walker, 56484; 800-358-5516.**

Cedar Bay Resort—call for rates

Fern Kahlson wanted to start a b-and-b; her daughter Kris wanted to own a north-woods resort. They compromised and in the early 1990s bought an existing resort near Hackensack and fixed it up so that it is a resort with such b-and-b-like touches as handmade quilts on the beds and extensive perennial flower beds. The five cabins vary in size, age, and interior decoration; four have modern baths, but there is one rustic cabin without plumbing for those who want an old-fashioned vacation. The beach is sandy, with a gradual slope. One cabin is open year-round; the others, early May–Oct. Located 10 miles east of Hackensack on Widow Lake. **3066 Cedar Shores Dr. NW, Hackensack, 56452; 218-682-2431.**

Hiawatha Beach Resort and Houseboat—call for rates

Do you want to vacation *at* the lake or *on* the lake? Take your choice at Hiawatha Beach Resort in Steamboat Bay on Leech Lake. The resort, one of the oldest on the lake still in the same family, has 19 housekeeping cabins, plus a 50-foot houseboat that sleeps 10 people. The boat, which comes with a Mercury motor, has electronic fish-finding equipment and is fully furnished for housekeeping. Neophytes get full instructions before they go off on their own. The resort has an indoor swimming pool, children's activities, and a restaurant. Owner Larry Jacobson and his wife, Sue, are the third generation of Jacobsons at the resort. **10930 Steamboat Loop, Walker, 56484; 800-442-3224.**

Camping

If you're interested in a campsite at one of the resorts near Leech Lake, ask the Leech Lake Area Chamber of Commerce (see Services) for a listing.

Chippewa National Forest

Some of the most beautiful campsites imaginable, tucked away amid trees overlooking hills and lakes, are in the Chippewa National Forest. The 26 developed sites (i.e., with water, toilet facilities, etc.) require a fee; the many undeveloped sites are free. Popular sites include Stony Point, Norway Beach on Cass Lake, and Webster Lake near Blackduck. **Stony Point,** 14 miles east of Walker, is on Leech Lake. There are 44 sites, boat access, two boat harbors, a swimming beach, and picnic tables. Showers and electrical hookups are available. The campground is fairly open and grassy, but it's surrounded by an old forest of maple, oak, elm, and ash. Some of the trees in the area are more than 200 years old. Campgrounds are usually open mid-May–mid-Sept. The undeveloped sites cannot be reserved. Space at developed sites may be reserved for a small fee by calling **800-280-CAMP.** See Hiking.

Where to Eat

Arthur's—$$ to $$$$

A new screened-in deck that seats 150 is packing them in at Arthur's, where diners face west on Ten-mile Lake and have a wonderful view of the setting sun. Specialties include Greek lamb chops (with oregano, garlic, and lemon), steaks, beef kabobs, and pasta. In summer, there is pitchfork fondue: 12-ounce steaks are impaled on a pitchfork and dunked in a cauldron of boiling oil set outside on the restaurant grounds. Arthur's also has a children's menu. No reservations taken. Open Tues.–Thurs. and Sun., 5:00–9:00 P.M., and Fri.–Sat., 5:00–10:00 P.M. Located **3 miles north of Hackensack on Hwy. 371; 218-675-6576.**

Ranch House Supper Club—$$ to $$$

Always a popular place with all ages, the Ranch House has a cheerful, informal atmosphere and great steaks, prime ribs, and barbecued ribs. Giant popovers are handed around soon after diners are seated. Kids are served half portions at half prices. All-you-can-eat nightly specials. Open year-round, Mon.–Wed., 5:00–8:30 P.M.; Thurs.–Sat., 5:00–10:00 P.M.; Sun., 5:00–9:00 P.M. Located **4 miles north of Walker on Hwy. 371; 218-547-1540.**

Outdoorsman Cafe—$

This is a great place for a hearty, filling breakfast, and it's right downtown in Walker. The cafe is crowded, especially during the tourist season, but the service is fast and friendly. There are daily breakfast specials. Open Mon.–Sat., 6:00 A.M.–4:00 P.M., and Sun., 6:00 A.M.–noon. Located **on Minnesota Ave. and Fifth St., in Walker; 218-547-3310.**

Services

Cass Lake Area Civic and Commerce Association, P.O. Box 548, Cass Lake, 56633; 800-356-8615.

Leech Lake Area Chamber of Commerce serves the whole Leech Lake area, not just Walker. **205 Minnesota Ave., P.O. Box 1089, Walker, 56484; 800-833-1118. Website: www.leech-lake.com.**

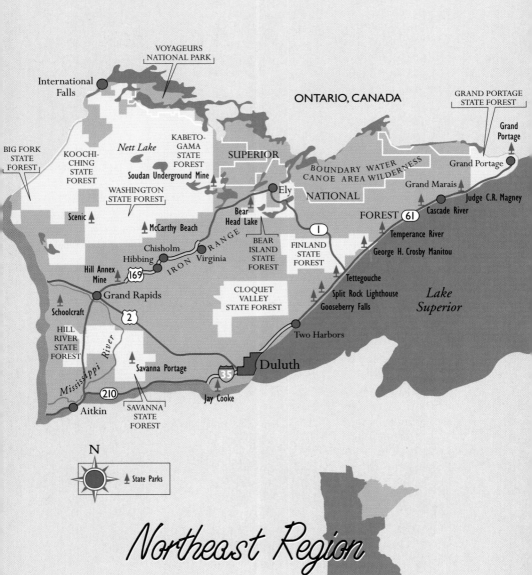

VOYAGEURS
NATIONAL PARK

International
Falls

ONTARIO, CANADA

GRAND PORTAGE
STATE FOREST

Grand
Portage

BIG FORK
STATE
FOREST

KOOCHI-
CHING
STATE
FOREST

Nett Lake

KABETO-
GAMA
STATE
FOREST

SUPERIOR

Grand Portage

BOUNDARY WATER
CANOE AREA WILDERNESS

Grand Marais

Soudan Underground Mine

WASHINGTON
STATE FOREST

Ely

NATIONAL

Judge C.R. Magney

Scenic

McCarthy Beach

Bear
Head
Lake

FOREST

61

Cascade River

Temperance River

Chisholm

BEAR
ISLAND
STATE
FOREST

FINLAND
STATE
FOREST

George H. Crosby Manitou

Hibbing

Virginia

IRON RANGE

Hill Annex
Mine

169

Grand Rapids

CLOQUET
VALLEY
STATE FOREST

Tettegouche

Split Rock Lighthouse

*Lake
Superior*

Schoolcraft

2

Gooseberry Falls

HILL
RIVER
STATE
FOREST

Mississippi River

Two Harbors

Savanna Portage

Duluth

35

210

Aitkin

SAVANNA
STATE
FOREST

Jay Cooke

N

State Parks

Northeast Region

Northeast Region

Shoreline camping is one of the highlights for paddlers in the Boundary Waters Canoe Area Wilderness. Copyright © Minnesota Office of Tourism. Used by permission.

Duluth

Duluth, long Minnesota's second city but a quiet and chilly one, has had a renaissance in recent years and is now a destination in itself, instead of being just the gateway to the North Shore of Lake Superior. Much of Duluth is perched on hills, with the cold waters of Lake Superior below. From the city's highest lookouts, the mammoth ore boats coming in and out of the harbor look like toy boats in a bathtub. A major port for ocean-going ships, Duluth is the western terminal of the St. Lawrence Seaway and the only port in North America so far from the sea.

Duluth has always been a working town, with industries as well as the port facilities, and a gritty, no-nonsense air remains in old neighborhoods despite the recent sprucing up of the harbor and the downtown area. It's an honest town, likable even in its shabby sections, and magnificent in its setting overlooking the largest of the Great Lakes.

Duluth has a population of approximately 86,000, while Superior, Wisconsin, just across the bridge, adds 27,000 more, and suburbs bring the total to more than 270,000 in the metropolitan area. Over the years, Duluth has had its economic ups and downs and the population has fluctuated but is now rising. Currently, tourism continues to climb, as does Seaway traffic. Duluth is the county seat of St. Louis County and is an important medical, educational, and financial hub for Northeast Minnesota.

History

Ojibwe Indians, many of whom still live in Duluth or on the nearby reservations, lived in the Duluth area (after succeeding the earlier Dakota) when the first Europeans came. Among the first were Pierre Radisson and Médard Chouart Des Groseilliers, in 1659, who later played a major part in the Hudson's Bay Company that opened up western Canada. However, it wasn't until 1679 that Daniel Greysolon, Sieur Du Luth (also written Dulhut), claimed the territory for France. The city later took its name from Du Luth. French voyageurs, acting for the North West Company and other fur-trading companies, including John Jacob Astor's American Fur Company, were active in the area until the beaver hat craze died and the fur trade ended.

European settlement began in the 1850s in Duluth and increased when the Soo Locks opened at Sault Ste. Marie, Ontario, in 1855. The railroad reached the new town in 1870 and the Duluth ship canal, which provided better access to the lake from the harbor, opened in 1871. Not until 1959, however, did the St. Lawrence Seaway's completion make Duluth the inland port that it is today.

Major Attractions

Lake Superior

Lake Superior is Duluth's chief drawing card for visitors. Superior is the biggest of the five Great Lakes, and the largest expanse of freshwater in the world. Superior is 350 miles from east to west and 160 miles north to south, with 2,980 miles of shoreline. It is famed for its beauty, feared for its dangerous storms and treacherous weather, and mourned for its shipwrecks and loss of life. The lake is visible from most places in Duluth—look down and there it is, stretching out to the horizon, speckled with a few dots here and there that become huge oceangoing ships as they come closer. Ships usually cross the lake in 24–36 hours. Duluth's international harbor, largest in area on the Great Lakes, is also the busiest bulk-cargo transshipment port. The port is iced in during the winter, but the ice-in, ice-out dates vary greatly, depending on the weather. Thus, the end of the 1997 season actually came in January 1998, when the last ship left. After a very mild winter, the first ship for the 1998 season came in during early March.

Although the lake can be enjoyed at most anyplace in Duluth and farther north, most visitors flock to the waterfront and Canal Park (see Parks). Ship watchers wave to the sailors aboard the huge vessels gliding through the canal, under the aerial lift bridge, which rises up 138 feet in 55 seconds to let ships through. Get updated information on ship comings and goings, and points of departure, for several days hence from the recorded message of the **Boatwatchers Hotline, 218-722-6489.** Note that times are approximate, as many factors can affect shipping.

Duluth Shipping News

The *Duluth Shipping News* is the brainchild of Kenneth Newhams, who figured rightly that visitors to Duluth would be as fascinated as he is with news about the ships visiting Duluth. The newletter, which comes out several times a week in summer and once a week in spring and fall, tells approximate arrival and departure times but also contains lots of nuggets of information about the ships and their crews. The *Shipping News* is also on the Internet; the website includes great color photos. The paper version is available at many places in Duluth, or contact Newhams, **218-722-3119. E-mail: knewhams@duluth-shippingnews.com. Website: www.-duluth-shippingnews.com.**

Seaway Port Authority of Duluth

The governing body of the Duluth-Superior Port keeps statistics and encourages the shipping busi-

> ### Getting There
>
> Duluth is about 150 miles from Minneapolis–St. Paul, halfway between the Twin Cities and the Canadian border. It's a straight but dull drive on I-35. There is airline service from the Twin Cities, Detroit, and Chicago, and bus service from Minneapolis and Thunder Bay, Ontario.

ness. Each year, according to the Port Authority, approximately 1,100 vessels visit the twin ports, carrying nearly 400 million metric tons of cargo. Ore is carried by half the ships, while 30 percent have coal and 10 percent carry grain. The Port Authority is also responsible for encouraging the renaissance of passenger ships to the port; 1997 was the first year in a long time that a cruise ship visited the port, and there may be more to come. **Website: www.duluthport.com.**

Festivals and Events

John Beargrease Race
usually first Sat. in Feb.

John Beargrease, an Ojibwe Indian and a North Shore mail carrier from 1887 to 1900, didn't let snow, ice, or frigid weather stop him from getting the mail through, with the help of his sled and team of dogs. His spirit lives on in the annual 300- to 500-mile John Beargrease Race. About 25 sled-dog teams race from Duluth along the North Shore—the finish varies from year to year—competing for prizes. Thousands of spectators show up for the start in Canal Park on Duluth's waterfront. Two shorter races are also part of the week, as are other events, such as a Musher's Banquet, also open to the public, and a "cutest puppy" contest. For details and changes in the event, contact Beargrease headquarters, **P.O. Box 500, Duluth, 55801; 218-722-7631. Website: www.beargrease.com.**

Grandma's Marathon
third weekend in June

Grandma's Marathon is a well-respected regular stop for runners who are trying for the Olympics, as well as for hundreds of other folks who enjoy the scenic run along Lake Superior's North Shore. In addition to the marathon proper, there are two shorter runs. Running isn't everything: marathon-related events include an all-you-can-eat spaghetti dinner, speakers, a health and fitness exposition, and entertainment. The marathon finishes at its namesake, Grandma's Restaurant in Canal Park. **218-727-0947.**

Bayfront Blues Festival
second weekend in Aug.

Duluth gets the blues big-time during the Bayfront Blues Festival. More than 20 jazz artists perform on two stages at Bayfront Park, and there are a slew of other jazz events during the weekend in local clubs, as well as movable jazz during a Moonlight Blues Cruise and a Blues Train excursion. This is one of the largest outdoor music festivals in the region. **715-394-6831.**

Outdoor Activities

University of Minnesota at Duluth's **Outdoor Center** sponsors many kinds of outdoor adventures as well as canoe and kayak classes and trips (see Boating). Rock-climbing sessions on an indoor climbing wall or at several places along the North Shore, hikes, bird-watching, and outdoor

Children chase the seagulls at Canal Park.
Copyright © Minnesota Office of Tourism. Used by permission.

education skills are also part of the program. Nonstudents are welcome. **121 SPHC, 10 University Dr., Duluth, 55812; 218-726-6533.**

Biking

Many of Duluth's city parks have bike trails. Perhaps the best combination biking-sightseeing trek is the trail along the Lakewalk, which wraps around the waterfront. For information, contact the Duluth Convention and Visitors Bureau (see Services). In Jay Cooke State Park, there are 5 miles of surfaced trails for bikers and 8 miles for mountain bikes (see Parks). The Boundary segment is an 80-mile natural-surface trail used mostly for snowmobiling, horseback riding, hiking, and mountain biking. It goes through heavily forested, sometimes impassable areas. Get maps from the Dept. of Natural Resources Information Center, **500 Lafayette Rd., St. Paul, 55155; 888-MINNDNR** or **651-296-6157.**

Willard Munger Trail

The last 3 miles of the 63-mile-long multipurpose Willard Munger Trail from Hinckley to Duluth were completed in 1998, making this the longest paved trail in the world. It is historic as well as scenic. From Hinckley, the trail is along the route taken by the train that saved many lives in the disastrous Hinckley fire of 1894. Farther on, the trail passes through state forests and near Moose Lake and Banning State Parks. At Carlton, there is a magnificent view of the St. Louis River from a railroad trestle, and the trail skirts the edge of spectacular Jay Cooke State Park sloping down to the west end of Duluth. The trail has many tent sites, and parking areas at Hinckley, Finlayson, Willow River, Moose Lake, Carlton, and Duluth. The main trail also connects with two other portions of the trail in Carlton. The 16-mile segment from Carlton to Gary–New Duluth is a combination of paved bike trail and the shoulders of highways. Call the Duluth Convention and Visitors Bureau, **800-4-DULUTH.**

Rentals and Tours

Bikes and in-line skates can be rented in Carlton at **Persnickety,** located **on Hwy. 210 W.; 800-730-8500** or **218-384-3367.**

Duluth harbor and aerial lift bridge. Copyright © Minnesota Office of Tourism. Used by permission.

Birding

Because Jay Cooke State Park has a variety of habitats, it has 173 bird species, both nesting and migratory. Look for warblers, pileated woodpeckers, marsh hawks, great blue herons, and migratory waterfowl. Ask at the park office for a birding checklist (see Parks).

Hawk Ridge Nature Reserve

Hawks and other birds, including such rarities as peregrine falcons and gyrfalcons, migrate southward each fall by the thousands along a corridor that passes over Duluth. The total of hawks varies annually, but in one record year—1991—more than 85,000 were observed. The birds hug the western tip of Lake Superior, riding updrafts created by the ridges running parallel to the lake. Peak time is mid-Sept.–late Oct. Greatest numbers occur when there is a westerly or northwesterly wind. At Hawk Ridge, 20 species of hawks have been observed. Anyone is welcome to watch and to take part in programs, or walk on the trails along the ridge above Duluth. The reserve is managed by the Duluth Audubon Society. Access to the reserve, above the east side of Duluth, is from the Skyline Parkway. For more information, call the Duluth Convention and Visitors Bureau, **800-4-DULUTH.**

Boating

CANOEING

The St. Louis River is a state-designated canoe route from the Iron Range to the city of Cloquet. The 92-mile route contains Class I and II rapids, a rating that indicates that the rapids are not difficult and easily portaged if need be. Scenery along the river varies from the wild to the domesticated. Wooded bluffs are in the northern portion of the river, while the middle section flattens out, with bogs and low woods along the banks. There are many campsites along the route. For a map, contact the Dept. of Natural Resources, **500 Lafayette Rd., St. Paul, 55155; 888-MINNDNR** or **651-296-6157.**

KAYAKING

Whitewater kayaking and canoeing instruction and trips are offered through the **Kayak and Canoe Institute,** which is part of the University of Minnesota at Duluth's (UMD) Outdoor Center (see above). Sea kayaking courses and trips on Lake Superior are also offered through the institute. There are three meeting places—the UMD campus, the Aquatic Center at the waterfront, and the Outpost Classroom/National Kayak and Canoe Center in Carlton, southwest of Duluth. For information, call **218-726-6533.**

Rentals and Tours

Superior Whitewater Raft Tours' two-and-a-half-hour trip down the tumbling St. Louis River on a raft provides plenty of thrills for novice and veteran rafters. The guided trips are run daily May–Sept. for those 12 and over. Shuttle service is included in the price. Located in Carlton, about 15 miles south of Duluth. **950 Chestnut Ave., Carlton, 55718; 218-384-4637.**

Fishing

Lake Superior is a big draw for sport fishers, but the St. Louis River draws those looking for walleye. The walleye swim upriver to spawn in the spring and come back down to the lake the morning after, so to speak. Those interested in charter fishing for lake trout and salmon on Lake Superior may want to book a half or full day's trip with one of the members of the **North Shore Charter Captain's Association.** Contact the Duluth Convention and Visitors Bureau (see Services) for members of the association. Anglers who like a challenge head for Jay Cooke State Park's (see Parks) 6-mile Silver Creek Trail and the spring-fed Silver Creek, which is stocked with brook trout.

Hiking

Duluth is a wonderful place for walkers and hikers; the city parks, including the lovely Lakewalk, offer good hiking and the nearby state parks have a variety of trails. For instance, Jay Cooke State Park (see Parks) has 50 miles of hiking trails. Its 4-mile CCC-Thompson loop was the road into the CCC camp in the 1930s. At the other end of that trail is the Pioneer Cemetery. Trillium and yellow lady slipper are among the spectacular wildflowers on display each spring along the 5.4-mile Grand Portage Trail.

Skiing

CROSS-COUNTRY

Duluth is a good central spot to try cross-country skiing in many different areas. State parks and forests, such as nearby Jay Cooke State Park (with 32 miles for traditional cross-country skiing) and Cloquet Valley State Forest, are excellent, as are the parks farther up the North Shore (see the two

North Shore chapters). The city of Duluth's parks also have cross-country trails—some lighted for night skiing—and Spirit Mountain ski area (see below) has more than 12 miles of groomed trails. Request information from the Duluth Convention and Visitors Bureau (see Services).

DOWNHILL

Spirit Mountain

Spirit Mountain is a big draw for alpine skiers from all over the Upper Midwest. With a vertical drop of 700 feet and a longest run of slightly more than a mile, Spirit Mountain offers a challenge to skiers of all abilities. The area has 23 runs—served by five chair lifts—plus three beginner areas, a snowboard and a freestyle area, a tubing hill, and cross-country trails. All this and a big chalet. Best of all, the area is just a few minutes from downtown Duluth. Many area hotels and motels offer ski packages. Lessons, ski clinics, and rentals are available. **9500 Spirit Mountain Pl., Duluth, 55810; 800-642-6377.**

Snowmobiling

Duluth is at one end of the 153-mile-long North Shore Trail that follows the shore of Lake Superior and has many rest areas and campsites. Within Duluth itself are 45 miles of groomed snowmobile trails. Snowmobile fans may want to visit Duluth over Thanksgiving weekend for the annual **Duluth National Snocross races.** For trail or race information, call **800-4-DULUTH** or **218-722-4011.** Jay Cooke State Park has 12 miles of trails for snowmobiles (see Parks).

Seeing and Doing

Art Galleries and Museums

Tweed Museum of Art

Upper Midwest artists such as George Morrison are represented in the Tweed collection, as are many members of the Hudson River Valley school, American impressionists, and also artists from earlier centuries in Europe. The museum is known for its ceramics collection and for its collection of Potlatch "Mountie" art. Fully half of the Tweed's collection consists of post-1950 art. Approximately 10 exhibits are presented annually. The Tweed is on the campus of the University of Minnesota at Duluth. Free. Open year-round (except university holidays), Tues., 9:00 A.M.–8:00 P.M.; Wed.–Fri., 9:00 A.M.–4:30 P.M.; Sat.–Sun., 1:00–5:00 P.M. **10 University Dr., Duluth, 55812; 218-726-8222. Website: www.d.u.edu/tma.**

Museums and Historic Sites

The Depot

The chateaulike Depot, built in 1892 and on the National Register of Historic Places, is a one-stop museum and arts shop, housing the Duluth Art Institute, the Duluth Children's Museum, the Lake Superior Railroad Museum, and the St. Louis County Historical Society. But that's not all. The Depot is also the home of the Minnesota Ballet, the Duluth Playhouse, the Duluth-Superior Symphony Orchestra, the Arrowhead Chorale, and Matinee Musicale. The historical society has many artifacts, including paintings, that tell the story of the many people—Ojibwe, missionaries, voyageurs, loggers, etc.—who played a part in the history of the county. Fee; one ticket provides entry to all four museums. All museums open May–Oct., daily, 10:00 A.M.–5:00 P.M.; Nov.–Apr., Mon.–Sat., 10:00 A.M.–5:00 P.M., and Sun., 1:00–5:00 P.M. **506 W. Michigan St., Duluth, 55802; 218-727-8025.**

Glensheen

Chester Congdon, a self-made man, had his version of a 17th-century Jacobean manor house built over a three-year period in the early 1900s. On the east end of Duluth, Congdon's 39-room house, called Glensheen, had all the trimmings of a country estate, including a bowling green, tennis court, boathouse, and gardener's cottage. Look closely at the intricate wood carving, done on the spot, and the "modern" bathroom fixtures. For all its luxury, the grand house has an unfortunate recent past: one of Congdon's descendants was murdered in an upstairs bedroom. Tour guides, out of respect for the family, won't discuss the murder. There are several different tours,

including a tour of the main house, a third-floor and attic tour, and a grounds tour. Fee. Open May 1–Oct. 31, daily, 9:30 A.M.–4:00 P.M.; Nov.–Apr., Sat.–Sun., 9:30 A.M.–4:00 P.M. **3300 London Rd., Duluth, 55804; 888-454-GLEN or 218-724-8864. Website: www.d.umn.edu/glen/.**

The Karpeles Manuscript Library

Some successful men buy professional sports teams with their fortunes; David Karpeles bought history with his money, and he's now letting everyone have a look at his treasures. Karpeles, a Californian who once lived in Duluth, collects manuscripts, including rarities such as the Magna Carta, the Gutenberg Bible, maps, and the sheet music written by Mozart, Bach, and Beethoven. The Duluth Library is one of six in the United States to display Karpeles's acquisitions in temperature-controlled conditions in rotating exhibitions. The libraries, in Karpeles's words, are "Dedicated to the Preservation of the Original Writings of the Great Authors, Scientists, Philosophers, Statesmen, Sovereigns and Leaders from All the Periods of World History." The Duluth Library, housed in a former church, also has Sun. musical programs. Free. Open year-round, Tues.–Sun., noon–4:00 P.M.; in summer, Mon. also. **902 E. First St., Duluth, 55805; 218-728-0630.**

Lake Superior Maritime Visitor Center

Peek into a fancy stateroom or cramped crew's quarters; shudder at the petrified remains of some sailor's long-ago breakfast, salvaged from one of the Lake Superior shipwrecks; admire the model ships; and take the wheel of a Great Lakes "ship," all in the fascinating Canal Park marine museum, run by the U.S. Army Corps of Engineers on the Duluth waterfront. Open Memorial Day–day before Labor Day, daily, 10:00 A.M.–9:00 P.M.; Apr.–Memorial Day and Labor Day–Oct., Sun.–Thurs., 10:00 A.M.–4:30 P.M., and Fri.–Sat., 10:00 A.M.–6:00 P.M.; Nov.–late Dec., daily, 10:00 A.M.–4:30 P.M.; late Dec.–Mar., Fri.–Sun., 10:00 A.M.–4:30 P.M. (closed major holidays). **600 Lake Ave S., Duluth, 55802; 218-727-2497.**

SS William A. Irvin

The SS *William A. Irvin*, the flagship of U.S. Steel's

Great Lakes fleet, carried ore and coal for 40 years before coming to a permanent rest in the Duluth-Superior Harbor. Visitors can go aboard the ship, which is berthed near the Aerial Lift Bridge on the Lakewalk. An hour-long tour of the 610-foot ship takes in everything from the cargo holds and engine room to the pilothouse, staterooms, guest galley, and dining room. Ticket price also includes a self-guided tour of the tugboat *Lake Superior*. Fee. Open Memorial Day–Labor Day, Sun.–Thurs., 9:00 A.M.–6:00 P.M., and Fri.–Sat., 9:00 A.M.–8:00 P.M.; Labor Day–mid-Oct., Sun.–Thurs., 10:00 A.M.–4:00 P.M., and Fri.–Sat., 10:00 A.M.–6:00 P.M. The ship is docked **on Duluth's waterfront, on Harbor Dr.; 218-722-7876** (during tour season).

Parks

Visitors and citizens alike take advantage of Duluth's extensive park system. Coming into Duluth from the north on Hwy. 61, it's convenient to stop at **Brighton Beach** to swim or have a picnic. Closer to downtown is **Leif Erickson Park,** with its Viking statue and gorgeous garden of 3,000 rosebushes in summer. **Enger Park,** perched high up, has beautiful gardens, the five-story stone Enger Tower, and a pleasant lookout from which to watch the ships going in and out of the harbor (bring binoculars!). **Canal Park,** adjacent to the canal leading into the harbor itself, has undergone a face-lift in recent years, with outdoor sculptures, new hotels, shops, and a wonderful marine museum (see Museums and Historic Sites). A boardwalk wrapping around the park and the walkway to the lighthouse are crowded in summer, with children and gulls crying out with equal frequency. One park often overlooked by visitors is **Park Point,** on the other side of the Aerial Lift Bridge. It's a park at the end of the long, skinny point that is separate from the rest of the city in actuality and in atmosphere. The point is edged with a 6-mile sand beach. The park itself has lots of amenities, but it is the sand dunes that surprise first-time visitors. There is also a trail to the end of the point. Bring a picnic lunch and a swimsuit and relax. For more information, call the Duluth Convention and Visitors Bureau (see Services).

Jay Cooke State Park

This is a park that has it all—wonderful rock formations, unlimited scenery, a suspension bridge over a rushing river, many interpretive programs, and a historic cemetery. Located on both sides of the churning St. Louis River near its outlet into Lake Superior, Jay Cooke has many trails for hikers, bikers, skiers, and horseback riders, some of which link up with the Willard Munger Trail (see Biking) on the north side of the park. The river, with its rapids and islands, is fascinating whether it's viewed from the slightly swaying bridge or from a high vantage point such as Oldenburg Point. In addition to the hiking trails, there are 6 miles of trails for horseback riders. Winter trails are almost as extensive, and snowshoes can be rented. Many white-tailed deer spend the winter in the park. Other large animals visitors may see are black bears, timber wolves, and coyotes. One of the largest of Minnesota's state parks at nearly 9,000 acres, Jay Cooke has a visitor center and a year-round naturalist, with many programs scheduled. There is camping at the park. Located 3 miles east of Carlton on Hwy. 210 E. **500 Hwy. 210 E., Carlton, 55718; 218-384-4610.**

Lake Superior Zoological Gardens

Among the zoo's 500 species of animals are such endangered ones as snow leopards, peregrine falcons, and bald eagles. Other zoo animals include Siberian tigers, kangaroos, and polar bears. It all started in 1923 when Burt E. Onsgard had a little bit of land to spare and a deer named Billy. The zoo is on the west end of town, with Kingsbury Creek winding by it. There is also a children's zoo. Fee. Open daily; Memorial Day–Labor Day, 9:00 A.M.–6:00 P.M.; Labor Day–Memorial Day, 10:00 A.M.–4:00 P.M. **7210 Fremont St., Duluth, 55807; 218-733-3777.**

Scenic Drives

A great bird's-eye view of Duluth can be had by driving along the 30-mile **Skyline Dr.,** 600 feet above Lake Superior. The drive begins on Hwy. 23 west of Duluth (watch for signs) and ends on the east side in Lester Park. In addition to the Skyline Dr. and the spectacular drive along the **North Shore,** the **Veterans Evergreen Memorial Hwy.** (a combination of Hwys. 210 and 23) offers spectacular scenery in a short distance.

Shopping

Duluth Tent and Awning

Campers have been buying Duluth packs for decades, but it is only in recent years that Duluth Tent and Awning, in business since 1911, has made such a wide variety of handbags, briefcases, and all manner of hold-alls, with the signature sturdy canvas material and buckles. The store, which also carries clothing, canoes and paddles, snowshoes, and gifts, is located in Canal Park. Open Mon.–Sat., 10:00 A.M.–8:00 P.M., and Sun., 10:00 A.M.–6:00 P.M. **365 Canal Park Dr., Duluth, 55802; 800-849-4489** or **218-722-1707. Website: www.duluthpacks.com.**

Northern Lights Books and Gifts

This pleasant shop in Canal Park specializes in Upper Midwest authors and also in subjects of regional interest. There is a large section on Great Lakes shipping. Open year-round, Sat., 9:00 A.M.–6:00 P.M., and Sun., 10:00 A.M.–6:00 P.M.; June–Labor Day, Mon.–Fri., 9:00 A.M.–8:00 P.M.; Labor Day–June, Mon.–Fri., 9:00 A.M.–6:00 P.M. **307 Canal Park Dr., Duluth, 55802; 218-722-5267.**

Superior Lake Gifts

This is not just another gift shop. Sandra Ettestad and her partner, Mark Marino, have created wearable works of art as well as mementos of the ships that clashed with the awesome power of Lake Superior. The T-shirts, sweatshirts, and other items are well made, and the designs are unique and sure to gain compliments for the wearers. The art based on ships is the result of research into the historic periods. Artwork made by Ettestad and Marino pays homage to ships such as the ill-fated *Mataafa,* which sank in 1905 with ine of its crew of 24 while within sight of thousands of Duluth residents, who were able to save only 15 crew members due to the intense storm. (Ettestad and Marino do double duty in the sum-

Jay Cooke State Park. Photo courtesy of the Minnesota Department of Natural Resources: Andrew Von Bank.

mer season, when they run the charming little malt shop next to the gift shop; the list of ingredients to put in the malts is seemingly endless, but perhaps could be computed if you are mathematically inclined.) Open year-round; call for hours. **716 E. Superior St., Duluth, 55802; 218-722-6998.**

Sports

Duluth-Superior Dukes

Part of baseball's Northern League, the Dukes won the league championship in 1997. This is baseball as it was meant to be—outdoors and fun. The Dukes play seven teams in the independent league, including the St. Paul Saints, May–Labor Day. **Wade Stadium, 34th Ave. W. and Grand Ave., Duluth, 55807; 218-727-4525. Website: www.dsdukes.com.**

Tours

Lake Superior and Mississippi Railroad

A 90-minute train ride along the scenic St. Louis River gives riders a chance to see wildlife as well as the river. The railroad, which uses historic equipment and also an open "safari car" for the excursions, is run by volunteers. The excursions are given mid-June–Aug., Sat.–Sun., 11:00 A.M. and 2:00 P.M. Fee. The train leaves from the Western Waterfront Trail parking lot at Grand Ave. and 71st Ave. W. (across from the zoo; see Parks). **506 W. Michigan St., Duluth, 55802; 218-624-7549.**

North Shore Scenic Railroad

The historic North Shore Scenic Railroad offers three tours—a short (one-and-a-half-hour) trip to Lester River, a six-hour excursion to Two Harbors and back, and an evening "Pizza Train" short trip. Other special trips are often scheduled. Fee. Operates May–Oct. Trains depart behind the Duluth depot and at the Two Harbors depot. **506 W. Michigan St., Duluth, 55802; 800-423-1273 or 218-722-1273.**

BOAT TOURS

Vista Fleet Harbor Cruises

A wide variety of cruises, from a narrated sightseeing trip to various lunch and dinner cruises, are offered by the Vista Fleet. The sightseeing cruise takes visitors under the Aerial Lift Bridge and also into the harbor. Operates mid-May–mid-Oct., daily. Located at the waterfront in Duluth. **218-722-6218** (information) or **218-722-1728** (reservations).

WALKING TOURS

Historic Tour of Old Duluth

An actor playing Dr. Thomas Preston Foster, a Duluth pioneer newspaperman, guides visitors on a walking tour of the old sections of Duluth; during summer, Sat., at 10:00 A.M. The starting point is the **intersection of Lake Ave. and Superior St. right downtown; 800-4-DULUTH.**

Wagering

Black Bear Casino and Hotel

The Fond du Lac Band of Lake Superior Chippewa owns this glittery casino, which is easily seen from I-35 on the way to Duluth. There are bingo, blackjack, and slots, plus entertainment and restaurants. Open 24 hours daily. The casino hotel is a convenient place to stay for access to many activities, as it is only 20 miles from Duluth. **1785-1789 Hwy. 210, Carlton, 55718; 888-771-0777 or 218-878-BEAR** (casino information), **800-553-0022** (hotel information from U.S. and Canada), or **218-878-7400.**

Fond-du-Luth Casino

Unusual in that it is located right in downtown Duluth, this casino has video slots, bingo, 16 blackjack tables, and other kinds of gaming. Open Mon.–Fri., 10:00 A.M.–2:00 A.M.; Sat.–Sun., 24 hours. **129 E. Superior St., Duluth, 55802; 800-873-0280 or 218-722-0280.**

Where to Stay

Bed-and-Breakfasts

The Olcott House Bed-and-Breakfast Inn— $$$ to $$$$

In the middle of the East End mansion district, the Olcott House is a gracious, pillared Georgian Colonial, with three luxurious bedrooms, all with private baths, and elegant common rooms, including a library, parlor, and music room. There is also accommodation in a separate carriage house. The Olcott House, built in 1904, is furnished with antiques. A candlelight breakfast is served. **2316 E. First St., Duluth, 55812; 800-715-1339 or 218-715-1339. Website: www.visitduluth.com/olcotthouse.**

Hotels, Motels, and Inns

Duluth has the usual hotel and motel chains, along with a few independent lodging spots. During the ski season, most accommodations offer packages that include lift tickets or free cross-country skiing.

Fitger's Inn—$$$ to $$$$

Fitger's Inn was a brewery from 1885 until 1972. Its 60 rooms and suites still bear traces of their original high ceilings (some approaching 20 feet in height) and walls their original exposed stone. Many rooms and suites have wonderful lakefront views and some also have fireplaces, skylights, balconies from which to watch the ships, and whirlpool baths. The lobby is quaint and comfy, and the shops and eating places (there is even a microbrewery on-site now) in the rest of the brewery complex are convenient. Located on the Lakewalk. **600 E. Superior St., Duluth, 55802; 888-FITGERS, 800-726-2982, or 218-722-8826. Website: www.fitgers.com.**

The Inn on Lake Superior—$$$ to $$$$

A new entry to the Duluth hotel pack, the inn lives up to its name: it really is right on the lake. Many of the light, airy rooms have balconies/porches that are just a long jump from the lake, and the continental breakfast is much more elaborate than most complimentary offerings. The inn is very convenient for exploring all of Duluth. **350 Canal Park Dr., Duluth, 55802; 888-668-4352 or 218-726-1111.**

Sundown Motel—$$

The rooms at the Sundown are very clean and comfortable, and have in-room TVs. The motel is right next to Spirit Mountain (see Downhill Skiing). All in all, the Sundown is a real bargain—a great choice for those on a budget. Book early. **5310 Thompson Hill Rd., Duluth, 55810; 218-628-3613.**

Camping

There are several campgrounds in and around Duluth, not including the wonderful camping opportunities in the state parks along the North Shore. Ask the Duluth Convention and Visitors Bureau (see Services) for a list.

Indian Point Campground—$

Located on the St. Louis River near the zoo (see Parks), the campground is owned by the city and operated by the University of Minnesota at Duluth. There are 50 sites, many with hookups. Open mid-May–beginning of Oct. In Duluth, turn left at Grand Ave. and 75th Ave. W. to the campground. **218-723-3337** or (when open) **218-624-5637.**

Jay Cooke State Park—$

In this wonderfully scenic park, there are 80 drive-in campsites, 21 with electricity. There are also four backpack and three walk-in campsites. A camper cabin was scheduled to open in fall 1999. For reservations, call **The Connection, 800-246-CAMP or 612-922-9000.**

Where to Eat

Pickwick—$$ to $$$$

The food is very good at Pickwick, but it's the cheerful, crowded, and historic restaurant itself that charms visitors. The Pickwick got its start as a saloon in 1888 and moved to its present site in 1914, going heavy on the Polish-German cooking that is still represented on its sandwich menu. Charcoal-grilled specialties, including steaks and chicken, are featured here. Appetizers include smoked whitefish from the lake and Polish sausage. Families feel at home, though Pickwick is also a place to celebrate an occasion. Rooms in the restaurant look like a mittel-European stage set, with beer steins everywhere. The beautiful white-oak woodwork was installed without any surface nails, and the paintings in the Dutch Room, done by F. W. Luertzer in 1893 for the old saloon and transported to its new location, show a conglomeration of images, including a smiling barmaid, a monk, and a grasshopper, to symbolize the grasshopper plague of 1893. Open Mon.–Sat., 11:00 A.M.–11:30 P.M. **508 E. Superior St., Duluth, 55802; 218-727-8901.**

Grandma's—$$ to $$$

Whether you're a runner carbo-loading on Grandma's signature Marathon Spaghetti or just another tourist looking for a good burger or a juicy steak, Grandma's has got what you need. This sprawling restaurant in Canal Park sparked the area's renewal and is probably the best-known tourist attraction, next to the harbor itself. It's always busy and friendly, with good solid food and plenty of eclectic bits and pieces to goggle at while you wait. Grandma's makes you feel young and hip, even after a hard day's sight-seeing. There are lots of wild rice specialties and several low-fat, low-cal specialties that sound good. Open year-round, Mon.–Thurs., 11:30 A.M.–9:00 P.M., and Fri.–Sun., 11:00 A.M.–10:30 P.M. **522 Lake Ave. S., Duluth, 55802; 218-727-4192.**

Amazing Grace Bakery and Cafe—$ to $$

Is this a bakery, a cafe, a coffeehouse, or a place to hear great music? Amazingly, it's all of these. Located in the Dewitt-Seitz Martketplace in Canal Park, the interior is dark, cozy, and spacious, with a pleasantly '60s feel. The breads and soups are made from scratch and are super. There are performances by nationally known acoustic folk and jazz musicians (cover charge for music). Go there—it's great. Open daily, 7:00 A.M.–11:00 P.M. **394 Lake Ave. S., Duluth, 55802; 218-723-0075.**

At Sarah's Table—$ to $$

A combination bookstore/coffeehouse, Sarah's has a few choice tables overlooking the lake. This is a nice place to relax with a cup of coffee and sandwich and browse among the books and music, chosen, according to the menu, to "honor the lives and creativity of women." The chefs are pretty creative, too: good salads, soups, and vegetarian specialties, plus daily specials. Located on the Lakewalk. Open Wed.–Mon., 8:00 A.M.–varying closing times. **728 E. Superior St., Duluth, 55802; 218-723-8569.**

Blue Note—$ to $$

The sandwiches are made to order, the coffee is strong and comes in assorted trendy guises, and the jazz (and other genres of music) is hot and cool at the same time in this comfy, friendly cafe in Canal Park. General Manager Andres Gonzalez tells a fascinating story about how he wound up in Duluth after growing up in South America. Open May–Oct., Sun.–Thurs., 9:00 A.M.–10:00 P.M., and Fri.–Sat., 9:00 A.M.–11:00 P.M.; Nov.–Apr., Sun.–Thurs., 10:00 A.M.–5:00 P.M., Fri., 10:00 A.M.–9:00 P.M., Sat., 9:00 A.M.–10:00 P.M. **457 Canal Park Dr., Duluth, 55802; 218-727-6549.**

Coffeehouses, Sweets, and Treats

European Bakery—$

Do not leave—repeat—do not leave Duluth without picking up some bread at the European Bakery, an outpost of Jewish grandmotherhood in downtown Duluth. Caraway rye bread is just one of the specialties made by the bakery for several generations. Other deli items are available in addition to the baked goods. Open Mon.–Fri., 8:00 A.M.–5:30 P.M., and Sat., 8:00 A.M.–3:00 P.M. **109 W. First St., Duluth, 55802; 218-722-2120.**

Hepzibah's Sweet Shoppe—$

Chocolate ore boats, just like the ones that ply Lake Superior, gladden the hearts of Lake Superior fans. The boats are said to be delicious, and the crunchy Lake Superior "rocks" that flank them in their packages are great for fooling friends. Open year-round, daily, 10:00 A.M.–9:00 P.M. **394 Lake Ave. S., Duluth, 55802; 218-722-5049.**

Services

Duluth Convention and Visitors Bureau, 100 Lake Place Dr., Duluth, 55802; 800-4-DULUTH or **218-722-4011. E-mail: cvb@-visit.duluth.mn.us. Website: www.visit-duluth.com.**

Don't forget to go to Superior, Wisconsin, when you visit Duluth; check out Duluth's sister city with information from the **Superior tourist center,** located at the junction of Hwys. 2 and 53. **305 Harbor View Pkwy., Superior, WI, 54880; 800-942-5313** or **715-392-2773. E-mail: supervisor@superior.com. Website: www.visitsuperior.com.**

Most visitors coming in from the south stop at the **Thompson Hill Tourist Information Center,** on I-35 at the Spirit Mountain Exit (follow the signs). This is not only open year-round, but has picnic tables outside and a splendid view; **218-723-4938.** There is also an **information center** at the Vista Dock on the waterfront May–Oct.; **218-722-6218.** At The Depot there is another year-round **information center, 506 W. Michigan St., Duluth, 55802; 218-727-8025.**

Ely

Ely has led two lives, the first—a life now past—as one of many mining towns in Northeast Minnesota, the second as a major gateway to the Boundary Waters Canoe Area Wilderness (see Major Attractions). Each summer, thousands of people hungry for the beauty of the woods and water use Ely as a jumping-off point, but the town itself has its own attractions.

Ely's most prominent booster was the late CBS-TV broadcaster Charles Kuralt, who fell in love with the place and bought the local, much-loved radio station (WELY 92.1 FM). Kuralt wrote glowingly about his adopted town, with testimonies such as: "I love this place! Anyone who has known the deep woods and the blue lakes for a week or a season puts themself to sleep ever afterward with memories of Ely"—and—"On the map, Ely appears to be the end of the road. For people who love the wilderness, beauty, and solitude, on the contrary, it's the center of the world."

Kuralt was not the first "escapee" from the faster-paced world to find solace in Ely. The area has long attracted those who sought not solitude, but the active, challenging outdoor life and the proximity to natural beauty. Among the first wave of those attracted by the natural setting were Dorothy Molter, a registered nurse from Chicago who lived in a remote cabin but welcomed a world of travelers, and writer-educator-conservationist Sigurd Olson, who moved to Ely from Wisconsin and wrote hauntingly of this northern paradise, inspiring many to make their own journey into the canoe country.

This influx of residents from Chicago, the Twin Cities, and points east continues. The newcomers have brought with them energy and a certain "big-city" sophistication that has not only made Ely a very cool small city but has occasionally raised the ire of longtime residents (and their young descendants) who probably think that their forebears came to work in the mines, not paddle

Canoers on Kawishiwi River. Copyright © Minnesota Office of Tourism. Used by permission.

around in canoes by day and sip lattes by night. One big bone of contention concerns the adjacent Boundary Waters Canoe Area Wilderness (BWCAW). While the issue doesn't strictly divide along these lines, many longtime Elyites want more motorized vehicles—both boats and snowmobiles—permitted there, while many of the residents-come-lately, as well as many of the vacationers who come up for canoe trips, support the ban on motors in most of the BWCAW. Check with the Ely Chamber of Commerce (see Services) or at BWCAW entry permit stations (see Major Attractions) to find out what the latest word is on motorized traffic.

A thriving city of 4,800, Ely is booming in winter as well as in summer and fall. Many visitors now plan winter vacations here, and cross-country skiing and snowmobiling are popular with residents also. Snowmobiles zip along side streets in winter, and cars and trucks carrying canoes are as common as mosquitoes during the other three seasons. Ely's main street is a busy thoroughfare with several shops offering locally made footwear and clothing. Happily, the city seems to have more than its fair share of artists and craftspeople, and those who like to shop in addition to spending time outdoors are not disappointed.

History

Ojibwe Indians inhabited the Ely area for centuries before the first Europeans—voyageurs seeking furs—showed up. After the fur trade faded in the early 1800s, a second wave of outsiders came in the mid-1800s, this time seeking gold. They found both fool's gold and the iron ore deposits that later became the economic lifeblood for all of Northeast Minnesota. The iron ore deposits were first found in 1883 in what is now the city of Ely, on the western shore of the present Miner's Lake.

The first load of ore from an Ely mine was shipped out from the Chandler, an open-pit mine, in 1888. Other mines, these going underground, were opened later. The underground mines required timbers for support and consequently a

---

> ## Getting There
>
> Ely is approximately 255 miles north of the Twin Cities. Take I-35 north to Duluth, then follow Hwy. 61 to Hwy. 1, which leads straight to Ely. An alternative route is to leave I-35 at Hwy. 33, which leads to U.S. Hwy. 53, and switch to U.S. Hwy. 169 north of Virginia, east to Ely. In the summer, there is air-link service from the Twin Cities to Ely. Contact the Ely Chamber of Commerce (see Services) for times.

flourishing logging and sawmill industry developed. The last mine near Ely closed in 1967, and by that time tourism, which had been around since the 20th century was in its teens, had begun to take off. Now canoers from around the world regularly show up for an Ely-based adventure.

Major Attractions

Boundary Waters Canoe Area Wilderness

Although Ely has its own attractions, most people who come here are headed beyond to the BWCAW, a vast, roadless expanse of lakes, forest, and sky that is the largest wilderness area east of the Rockies. More than 200,000 people visit the area annually. The BWCAW extends for about 150 miles just south of the Minnesota-Ontario border. On the Canadian side is Quetico Provincial Park. The remote, million-plus-acre wilderness area contains several thousand lakes and streams and more than 1,500 miles of water trails. Nearly all the lakes are reserved for nonmotorized craft. The federal Wilderness Act of 1964 established the BWCAW, and the area is all within the Superior National Forest.

In recent years, a permit system has been established to maintain an even distribution of canoers throughout the area and also to track usage. Permits are issued for one of more than 80 entry points and a specific day. Since many of the popular entry points are in demand, it's wise to reserve as early as possible because the number of permits for them is limited. The permits must be picked up by the person in whose name they are reserved. Summer (May 1–Sept. 30) quota permits for overnight stays and motorized day use can be reserved in advance by phone or mail. Send completed applications to **BWCAW Reservations, P.O. Box 450, Cumberland, MD 21502; 800-745-3399.** Self-issued permits for nonmotorized day use and for overnight stays the rest of the year can be obtained at entry points, at Superior National Forest offices, or by mail. **8901 Grand Ave. Pl., Duluth, 55808; 218-720-5324.**

Rentals and Tours

Many resorts in the Ely area also serve as outfitters and supply guides for those who want a canoe trip in the BWCAW but may not have the equipment or the experience to do it all on their own. Outfitters generally can also help visitors obtain entry permits. About two dozen of the local outfitters have formed the **Ely Outfitters Association.** Bob LaTourell Jr., a third-generation guide who runs LaTourell's Moose Lake Outfitters with his dad, Bob Sr., is president of the association. LaTourell can be reached at **800-365-4531** or **218-365-4531.**

Festivals and Events

Voyageur Festival
first weekend in Feb.

There are hot times in this cold town during the 10-day Voyageur Festival, what with the annual Mukluk Ball, in which ball goers dance up such a steamy storm that the windows have to be opened, even in subzero weather. The festival also includes a snow-sculpting contest, with teams coming from far afield to fashion sculptures from the huge blocks of snow in Ely's downtown. In addition, there are ski and snowmobile races, a "voyageur" encampment, and lots of arts and crafts. For information, call the Ely Chamber of Commerce (see Services).

Blueberry Arts Festival
last full weekend in July

It's not just the pies and other blueberry special-

ties that draw 25,000 people to the Blueberry Arts Festival—it's the art. The juried show of 250 artists and craftspeople coincides with the blueberry season in Ely, and the city celebrates both enthusiastically. The location is centered on Whiteside Park. Get your reservations for accommodations in early. Contact the Ely Chamber of Commerce (see Services).

Outdoor Activities

Biking

MOUNTAIN BIKING

Mountain bike enthusiasts can choose from 94 miles of mountain bike trails in five routes identified on a map distributed by the Kawishiwi Ranger District of the Superior National Forest. For a copy, contact the Ely Chamber of Commerce (see Services) or the district ranger office, **118 S. Fourth Ave. E., Ely, 55731; 218-365-7600.** Many mountain bikers also use the Taconite State Trail (see Hiking). No biking is allowed in the BWCAW.

Boating

In addition to canoeing in the BWCAW (see Major Attractions), many people canoe in the area just outside it, in the Superior National Forest and in state forests (see Parks).

Fishing

Sought-after walleye, northern, and bass lure anglers to Ely, but the area also harbors trout—lake trout, which are native to Ely lakes, and rainbow trout. Panfish also come big in the Ely area. Resort owners can tell visitors where to go to get their favorite catch (see Resorts). In the small, clear lakes of Bear Head Lake State Park there are trout, walleye, bass, and crappie as well, plus a handicapped-accessible fishing pier.

Hiking

The north woods are not just for canoers and anglers. Inside the **BWCAW** is the challenging, 38-mile Kekekabic Trail (an entry permit is needed for hiking it; see Major Attractions). There are campsites every 4–6 miles along the trail. The

Moose grazing in a pond. Photo courtesy of the Minnesota Department of Natural Resources.

western trailhead is east of Ely, near Snowbank Lake on Hwy. 18. Look for a sign a little more than 0.5 mile after crossing Snowbank Rd. In **Bear Head Lake State Park** there are 17 miles of hiking trails, with about 0.5 mile handicapped-accessible. Call the park at **218-365-7229.** In the **Kawishiwi Ranger District** of Superior National Forest, which is headquartered at Ely, there are 166 miles of hiking trails. The Superior National Forest office has trail information; **218-720-5324.**

Taconite State Trail

Hikers can use the 165-mile Taconite State Trail, which starts in Grand Rapids (see the Grand Rapids chapter in this section) among evidence of past mining and winds through state and national forests as it nears Ely. The terrain is a bit rugged and only the first 6 miles out of Grand Rapids are paved. The state trail has eight waysides and picnic sites. Hikers share the trail with horseback riders and mountain bikers. For information, call the Ely Chamber of Commerce, **800-777-7281.**

Hunting

Hunters flock to Ely for the deer, bear, moose, and grouse seasons. Contact the Ely Chamber of Commerce for details (see Services).

Skiing

CROSS-COUNTRY

There is good cross-country skiing right in Ely itself. Plenty of residents use their noon break to ski on the groomed Trezona Trail around Miner's Lake. The local cross-country ski club uses the 9 miles of groomed trails at Hidden Valley Recreation Area, and there are numerous other trails in the area, including some inside the BWCAW. In winter, Bear Head Lake State Park has 9 miles of cross-country ski trails. In Superior National Forest, there are 18 miles of groomed trails for cross-country skiers, plus 50 more miles of ungroomed trails. Skiers get a longer season up here, as the snow usually lasts until April. Skiers looking for another challenge may want to try "ski-joring," skimming along on skis pulled by a sled dog. Several local businesses offer ski-joring. Ask the Ely Chamber of Commerce for cross-country trail maps and ski-joring details (see Services).

Snowmobiling

Snowmobiles scooting along Ely streets are a common winter sight, but they are even more evident on the many snowmobile trails in the area, including the Taconite State Trail from Grand Rapids to Ely (see Hiking). In Northeast Minnesota, there are more than 3,500 miles of groomed trails, kept up by local snowmobile clubs. In Superior National Forest, snowmobiles can range over 110 miles of trails. In Bear Island State Forest there are nearly 30 miles of marked, groomed snowmobile trails. For information on snow conditions, a map of snowmobile routes in Ely, and maps of the Iron Trail and Northeast Minnesota snowmobile trails, contact the Ely Chamber of Commerce (see Services).

Seeing and Doing

Art Galleries and Museums

Brandenburg Gallery

Photographer Jim Brandenburg, who lives in Ely, takes stunning photos of the north country and its wildlife. His studies of wolves are wonderful. If you can't afford an original, posters are available, too. The gallery is upstairs of Piragis Northwoods Company (see Shopping) in Ely. Free. Open Memorial Day–Labor Day, daily, 6:00 A.M.–10:00 P.M.; Labor Day–Memorial Day, daily, 9:00 A.M.–6:00 P.M. **105 N. Central Ave., Ely, 55731; 218-365-6745.**

Museums and Historic Sites

Dorothy Molter Museum
Dorothy Molter, known to many as "the root beer lady," was a nurse from Chicago who made the north woods her home for decades. She lived alone but definitely was not lonesome, as the world came knocking at her cabin door for conversation and first aid as well as a cold drink of her home-brewed root beer. When she died, her cabin was dismantled and brought to Ely. The cabin, on E. Hwy. 169, is next to the International Wolf Center (see Wildlife Viewing). Open Memorial Day–Sept. 30, daily, 10:00 A.M.–6:00 P.M. **P.O. Box 391, Ely, 55731; 218-365-4451.**

Recommended Reading
Bob Carey's *The Root Beer Lady—The Story of Dorothy Molter* (Duluth: Pfeifer-Hamilton, 1993) gives a complete account of Molter's life.

Vermilion Interpretive History Center
While the history of the area—including Ojibwe, voyageur, logging, and mining—is covered well by the center, it also does a good job of presenting the story of Will Steger and Paul Schurke's expedition to the North Pole in 1986, the first unaided attempt to reach the pole by dogsled since 1909. One of the sleds is here, as well as many other artifacts and other material about the expedition. Fee. Open Memorial Day–Labor Day, daily, 10:00 A.M.–4:00 P.M. Located in the Vermilion Community College. **1900 E. Camp St., Ely, 55731; 218-365-3226.**

Recommended Reading
North to the Pole, by Will Steger and Paul Schurke (Times Books, 1987), is a detailed account of their 55-day journey to the North Pole.

Parks

Bear Head Lake State Park
Many state park employees, asked to name their favorite state park other than the one they work at, immediately say, "Bear Head Lake." Any visitor understands why. It's the felicitous combination of setting and nature-based activities. Located just south of the BWCAW, the park shares similar traits of wilderness quality and abundant wildlife. The bedrock of greenstone and granite was battered by glacial activity, which created the rugged and scenic terrain and formed Eagles Nest and Bear Head Lakes. Bear, moose, deer, wolves, and smaller animals frequent the park, while nesting eagles lead the list of birds that can be sighted. The park is heavily forested, with red and white pine, spruce, paper birch, and fir on the high grounds and tamarack, black spruce, and white cedar in the lowlands. The park also has several bogs. The park has a swimming beach. Interpretive programs are offered occasionally during the summer. Canoes and boats can be rented. There is camping in addition to a three-bedroom guest house for rent. The park is located 9 miles east of Tower on Hwy. 169, then 7 miles south on Hwy. 128. **9301 Bear Head Lake State Park Rd., Ely, 55731; 218-365-7229.**

Bear Island State Forest
The Taconite State Trail (see Hiking), a favorite of snowmobilers, runs through the forest, which is adjacent to Superior National Forest and the BWCAW. The terrain is steep in places, but outdoor enthusiasts like the many lakes and rivers. There is camping in several spots in the forest, including at Fall Lake, one of the entry points to the BWCAW. Principal access roads include U.S. Hwys. 169 and 1 and County Rd. 21. For a map, contact the Dept. of Natural Resources, **500 Lafayette Rd., St. Paul, 55155; 888-MINNDNR or 651-296-6157.**

Superior National Forest
The vast Superior National Forest, created by Teddy Roosevelt in 1909, covers much of the "Arrowhead" portion of Northeast Minnesota. The BWCAW is within its boundaries, but there

are many other recreational opportunities in the forest. There are four campgrounds within the district and numerous places to canoe. For more information, contact the district office, **118 S. Fourth Ave. E., Ely, 55731, 218-365-7600,** or the headquarters, **P.O. Box 338, Duluth, 55801, 218-720-5324.**

Shopping

Henry's Shoe Repair

Get a pair of Henry Held's moosehide choppers ("if they were any tougher, they'd rust" is his claim) and your hands will never be cold again. Check out the rustic custom-made furniture and knives, too. Oh yes, he also does shoe and camping equipment repair. Open Mon.–Fri., 9:00 A.M.–5:00 P.M. Located at 37 W. Sheridan St. Write Held at **Box 706, Ely, 55731;** after hours, call **218-365-4836.**

Mealey's Gift and Sauna Shop

Buy a sauna here or just a fragrant bar of sauna soap. All the Finnish immigrants in Ely made this sauna country, and Mealey's keeps the tradition going. The shop also has gifts from Minnesota. Open year-round, daily; call for hours. **124 Central Ave., Ely, 55731; 218-365-3639.**

Piragis Northwoods Company

If you can't find it at Piragis, you don't need it for your outdoor activities. The store in downtown Ely has everything from boots to canoes to books on nature, and also does outfitting and offers guided trips to the north woods and far beyond. Even if you're not an outdoorsperson, browsing at Piragis is fun. Open Memorial Day–Labor Day, daily, 6:00 A.M.–10:00 P.M.; Labor Day–Memorial Day, daily, 9:00 A.M.–6:00 P.M. **105 N. Central Ave., Ely, 55731; 800-223-6565.**

Steger Mukluks

Patti Steger Holmberg's Cree-style mukluks, fashioned from moosehide and soled with rubber, are warm and fashionable gear for cold winter weather. Patti's mukluks, which come in a variety of styles, have been worn on many expeditions, including treks to the North and South Poles. Open year-round, daily, 9:00 A.M.–6:00 P.M. **6 E. Sheridan St., Ely, 55731; 218-365-3322** or (for a catalog) **800-MUKLUKS.**

Wintergreen Northwoods Apparel

When Paul Schurke, Will Steger, Ann Bancroft, and several others made an unaided dogsled expedition to the North Pole in 1986, they all wore clothes made by Paul's wife, Susan. But you don't have to be a serious musher to have some of Sue Schurke's beautifully made clothes—including anoraks, windproof shirts and pants, and the signature fleece expedition hats—for outdoor chic as well as warmth. Open July–Labor Day, Mon.–Sat., 8:00 A.M.–8:00 P.M., and Sun., 8:00 A.M.–6:00 P.M.; Labor Day–July 1, Mon.–Fri., 8:00 A.M.–6:00 P.M., Sat., 9:00 A.M.–6:00 P.M., and Sun., 9:00 A.M.–5:00 P.M. **205 E. Sheridan St., Ely, 55731; 218-365-6602** or (for catalog orders) **800-584-9425.**

Tours

Heritage Homestead Tours

Finns settled in Embarrass, south of Ely, and built log structures that have endured so long that several are now on the National Register of Historic Places. A three-hour guided driving circle tour provides visitors with a look at the pioneer log buildings, including a 90-foot combination house and barn, plus saunas and farmsteads. Fee. Call the Ely Chamber of Commerce (see Services) for details.

BOAT TOURS

Emily's Burntside Heritage Tours

Emily Wahlberg, an Ely Finn who returned to the area after teaching in Chicago for many years, is enthusiastic about beautiful Burntside Lake and loves giving tours of it on her pontoon boat. The two-hour tour includes the historic sights, a look at the lake's 125 islands, and a view of Sigurd Olson's "Listening Point," which prompted the book of the same name. Fee. Tours—by reservation only—leave from Burntside Lodge. **2310 Passi Rd., Ely, 55731; 218-365-5445. E-mail: emilyw@northernnet.com.**

Gray wolf at the International Wolf Center. Copyright © Minnesota Office of Tourism. Used by permission.

Recommended Reading

Any book by the late naturalist/conservationist Sigurd Olson helps readers understand the lure of the north country. Particularly apt for Ely visits are *Listening Point* (Knopf, 1958) and *Open Horizons* (Knopf, 1969).

DOGSLED TOURS

Dogsledding is a popular pastime for Ely visitors in winter, and a number of places offer either short or long trips. **Paul Schurke,** who went to the North Pole by dogsled, runs tours from his resort, Wintergreen Lodge. Schurke's packages include lodge-to-lodge dogsled tours, dogsled camping in the BWCAW, international expeditions, and also overnight trips. Contact him at **800-584-9425** or **218-365-6022** for information and reservations. Others who provide "mushing" experiences include **White Wilderness,** which offers trips to remote cabins or lodge-to-lodge excursions; call **800-701-6238** or **218-365-6363; Website: www.northernnet.com/whitewld/. Greenstone Adventures** also features trips to cabins or tent cabins and can provide ice fishing, too; **218-365-6524** or **218-343-5840.**

Wildlife Viewing

International Wolf Center

Listen to recorded wolf howls, read about the lore and legends of wolves, watch the resident pack of wolves "wolf" down their supper of raw, red meat, and, finally, join an organized wolf "howl" at night (one of many guided field trips) to see if your group can make the real wolves howl back at you. It's all available at the wolf center, right in the heart of wolf country. Wolves have been known to appear in the city of Ely, and their presence and efforts to preserve them have been controversial, a topic that ties in with many of the historic aspects explored at the center. Fee. Open May–mid-Oct., daily, 9:30 A.M.–5:30 P.M.; mid-Oct.–May, Fri.–Sun., 10:00 A.M.–5:00 P.M. **1396 Hwy. 169, Ely, 55731; 800-ELY-WOLF. Website: www.wolf.org.**

Recommended Reading

L. David Mech, an internationally known wolf biologist, has written several books on wolves, including *The Way of the Wolf* (Stillwater: Voyageur Press, 1991). Mech, based in Minnesota, was the impetus behind the International Wolf Center, which opened in 1993.

Where to Stay

Bed-and-Breakfasts

Blue Heron Bed-and-Breakfast—$$$

The Blue Heron is not about Victoriana and lace—it's wilderness and old logs. The bed-and-breakfast, which claims it has "a million-acre front yard," is adjacent to the BWCAW. Of the three guest rooms in the lodge, two are in the original log cabin, which was part of a logging camp. The third room has windows on two sides from which to view wildlife. All three have lake views. A fourth "room" is a yurt, with bunk beds, a woodstove, and kerosene lanterns—comfortable even in temperatures of minus 35°F. A marsh nearby lures moose and there is a regular menagerie of animals in the area, from bear to otter to beaver and wolves. The b-and-b has canoes for guests to use. A hearty breakfast is included. Unlike most b-and-bs, the Blue Heron also offers dinners to the public; dinners include such dishes as pecan-crusted walleye and a meat loaf variation called buffa-loaf. A special series of dinners features the cuisines of the countries of the ancient Silk Road. Reserve dinner 24 hours ahead. **HCI3298 County Rd. 16, Ely, 55731; 218-365-4720. Website: www.blueheron-bnb.com.**

Finnish Heritage Homestead—$$$

Located on a working farm built by pioneer Finnish settlers, this b-and-b continues its Finnish heritage though its present owner, Buzz Schultz, has German forbears. Schultz is restoring the log homestead down to its original logs, and is happy to show guests the loom and fishing nets used by the homesteaders. The wood-fired Finnish sauna is part of the tradition, and the Schultzes serve some Finnish food as well. There are four rooms in the house, and several outbuildings date to the farm's establishment. Schultz is ready to tell guests about other historic sites in the Embarrass area as well as Finnish-oriented festivals and

activities, including a tour of pioneer log structures (see Tours). Breakfast is included. **4776 Waisanen Rd., Embarrass, 55732; 800-863-6545 or 218-984-3318.**

Hotels, Motels, and Inns

Holiday Inn Sunspree Resort—$$$

Yes, this is a Holiday Inn, but it's well worth staying in. Located right on Shagawa Lake in Ely, the resort is a handsome log structure, recently built. It has fishing, water sports, and hiking and snowmobile trails right on the hotel grounds. There's a good hotel restaurant, too, and an indoor pool. All 61 rooms and suites have a wet bar, refrigerator, coffee maker, and hair dryer. **400 N. Pioneer Rd., Ely, 55731; 218-365-6565.**

Paddle In—$$ to $$$

This locally owned motel is right in downtown Ely and open year-round. You can snowmobile up to the door in winter and there is a shuttle to the airport, as well as BWCAW packages that include shuttle service. Coffee is served all day. There are 15 units. You'll know the motel because of the big paddles on the sign. **1314 E. Sheridan St., Ely, 55731; 218-365-6036.**

Resorts

Ely has many resorts, some concentrating on the fishing trade and others catering more to families. Many people making a trip into the BWCAW stay for a night at a resort before and after their trip. Many resorts also provide outfitting service and guides for canoe trips. The Ely Chamber of Commerce (see Services) has a complete listing.

Burntside Lodge—$$$ to $$$$

The grand old man of Ely resorts, the Burntside was established in 1913 and sits ensconced amid the gray and green outcroppings of the Canadian Shield. It is a marvelous place to get away from it all, but is only 6 miles from Ely. The lodge has been owned by the LaMontagne family since 1941. The huge lodge has its original log furnishings and a large native stone fireplace. The restaurant, open to the public as well as guests, is in the lodge. The burnt orange paint (actually called

Red Cedar) used for the exterior of many of the 24 cabins contains pine needles and was specially formulated for Burntside Lodge. The cabins range from one to three bedrooms and also have many original furnishings. Two of the original lodge rooms were recently converted into a library and guest office. Located on the lake of the same name, Burntside has two swimming beaches, boat and canoe rental, playgrounds, and a hiking trail. Open Mother's Day–late Sept. **2755 Burntside Rd., Ely, 55731; 218-365-3894. Website: www.burntside.com.**

Big Lake Wilderness Lodge—call for rates

Yup, this is the last resort—the most remote resort you can reach by car in northern Minnesota. It's near the end of the Echo Trail, 23 miles from Ely's center. And what's at the end of the road? Some people think it's darn near paradise—a row of rust-colored log-sided cabins in a pine, maple, and aspen forest on the edge of an excellent walleye lake—all set in the rocky outcropping of the Canadian Shield. The lodge, which is more than 50 years old, is at an entry point for the BWCAW. The lodge has a naturalist (a beaver trapper by trade in the winter) who takes kids on guided walks in the woods. There are 13 cabins (four of them handicapped-accessible), plus two permanent tent sites on two islands that the lodge leases from the Forest Service. The cabins have no TVs or phones. "You don't want to come up here if you want to stay connected to the real world," laughs owner Sharon Schneider. The clean, neat housekeeping cabins all have baths with showers and tubs, and the lodge has some groceries for sale. All this and a sauna, too. Open from fishing opener–end of Oct., and sometimes through deer hunting season in Nov. **3012 Echo Trail, P.O. Box 359, Ely, 55731; 800-446-9080 or 218-365-2125. Website: www.northernnet.com/biglake.**

Camping

Most people headed up to Ely want to camp out in the BWCAW, for which a permit is needed (see Major Attractions). Many area resorts also have tent and RV campsites; ask the Ely Chamber of Commerce (see Services) for a listing.

Bear Head Lake State Park—$

There are 73 campsites, five backpack sites, and one boat-in campsite in the state park. In addition, Bear Head Lake has a three-bedroom guest house and a year-round camper cabin for rent. The park is located 9 miles east of Tower on Hwy. 169, then 7 miles south on Hwy. 128. For reservations, call **The Connection, 800-246-CAMP** or **612-922-9000.**

Superior National Forest—free

In the Kawishiwi District of the Superior National Forest that includes Ely, there are 65 campsites at 26 lakes. All have fire grates, tent pads, and latrines. Most have access to canoeing, boating, or hiking. Some are remote, while others are near resorts. The sites at Glacier Pond and Tofte Lakes are on designated trout lakes. Maps with campsites noted are available from the district forest office in Ely, **218-365-7600.**

Where to Eat

The Chocolate Moose—$ to $$$

An enormous mounted moosehead presides over the Chocolate Moose, housed in a stunning log building on Ely's main street. The Moose has daily breakfast specials that vary from Finnish pancakes to huevos rancheros, but pancakes (try the wild rice or blueberry varieties) and eggs are the mainstays. Buffalo burgers, sauteed walleye, and grilled meats are among the offerings for lunch and dinner. For dessert, just try to resist the homemade ice cream, which comes in more than 50 flavors. Open June–Aug., daily, 6:00 A.M.–9:00 P.M.; call for hours in May and Sept. **101 N. Central Ave., Ely, 55731; 218-365-6343.**

Shagawa Sam's—$ to $$$

Come on down to this cozy, crowded cafe for a hearty breakfast any time of the day, or for basic good stuff (half-pound burgers, steaks, walleye, and ribs on Wed. and Sat. nights) for lunch and supper. Homemade chili is a house specialty. The cafe and the cabins with pine interiors are on Shagawa Lake, but still right in the city. Open year-round, Sun., 8:00 A.M.–2:00 P.M.; Memorial Day–Labor Day, Mon.–Sat., 7:00 A.M.–9:00 P.M.; Labor Day–Memorial Day, Fri.–Sat., 7:00 A.M.–8:00 P.M. **60 Lakeview Ave., Ely, 55731; 218-365-6757.**

Vertin's Cafe, Pub and Supper Club—$ to $$$

This is old-time Ely. Vertin's has been in its present location since 1970, but it was a fixture at another location for several decades prior to that. House specialties are steak and walleye, but breakfast is served all day. There's a comfortable, hometown atmosphere. Open in summer, Sun.–Thurs., 6:00 A.M.–9:00 P.M., and Fri.–Sat., 6:00 A.M.–10:00 P.M.; in winter, Sun.–Thurs., 7:00 A.M.–8:00 P.M., and Fri.–Sat., 7:00 A.M.–10:00 P.M. Call for exact seasons. **145 E. Superior St., Ely, 55731; 218-365-4041.**

Minglewood's—$ to $$

One of Ely's newer restaurants, Minglewood's is in a big old house, with a great enclosed porch. There's a friendly, laid-back atmosphere and the food is very good. Whatever else you order, have Minglewood's homemade bread-and-butter pickles. There are many vegetarian entrees, although it is not a vegetarian restaurant per se. Pick up a box lunch (yes, it comes complete with the pickles) if you're planning a day on the water or snow. Minglewood's has ethnic specialties on various days of the week and a tempting array of baked goods for dessert. Open approximately Apr.–Sept., Mon.–Sat., 6:00 A.M.–3:00 P.M., and Sun., 6:00 A.M.–2:30 P.M. **528 E. Sheridan St., Ely, 55731; 218-365-3398.**

Services

The **Ely Chamber of Commerce** is located in a log cabin built in 1928 for the Wilderness Research Foundation. After the BWCAW was established in 1964, the cabin was dismantled and put back together in Ely. The chamber personnel are exceptionally well versed in local information. **1600 E. Sheridan St., Ely, 55731; 800-777-7281 or 218-365-6123. Website: www.Ely.org.**

Grand Rapids

Beyond Grand Rapids are the deep woods, and that's the way it's always been. The city on the Mississippi River was the head of navigation for steamboats in the 19th century, because it was at the foot of an impassable 3.5-mile line of rapids. Today it's a thriving county seat, still the regional center that it was at the height of the logging boom in the late 19th century. Scattered around Grand Rapids are 1,000 of Minnesota's 15,000 or so lakes. And of course there is the Mississippi, which helped create the town, along with the logging industry.

Today tourism is a mainstay of the city and area, with resorts peppered along the lakeshores. Many visitors from afar seek out Grand Rapids because it is the birthplace of Frances Gumm, better known as Judy Garland. Her restored birthplace may soon have its own yellow brick road.

History

The American Indians, as elsewhere in Minnesota, were the first humans in the area, and the first Europeans—explorers and missionaries—may have passed through the site of the present Grand Rapids as early as the late 1600s. In 1795 the North West Company established a fur-trading post at Leech Lake, to the west of Grand Rapids, and tradition says that Lieutenant Zebulon Pike must have passed through while exploring the Mississippi in 1806.

However, it was in the mid-1800s that the present Grand Rapids developed. This was the land of deep forests, and the sought-after giant white pine was the premium tree. Logging was going strong by the 1870s, and steamboats supplied the logging camps. Grand Rapids quickly became the center of logging operations, and the logging boom continued until the early years of the 20th century. The little town had plenty of saloons and rooms to accommodate the loggers who came out of the woods to spend their earnings. In 1872 the going wage for lumberjacks was $16–$18 monthly, according to *Logging Town: The Story of Grand Rapids, Minnesota*. Some of the "jacks" were legendary and went by descriptive "noms de axe," such as Pete-the-Porkie, Mosquito Ole, Paddy-the-Priest, and Pig-Eye Kelly.

In addition to logging, a mainstay of the Grand Rapids economy was the Mississippi River itself. Townspeople early on recognized the potential

A living-history portrayal of a 1930s forest ranger at the Forest History Center. Photo courtesy of the Minnesota Historical Society.

of powering a mill with water from the river, and in 1899 the Grand Rapids Water Power and Boom Company was established to construct mills and dams, according to *The Papermakers*. The first dam was built in 1902, and the Itasca Paper Company started milling operations the same year.

Charles K. Blandin, acting for the St. Paul newspaper, bought the mill in 1916 and later gained majority control. Blandin ran the mill for decades, and established his own foundation, to be run—as it is today—in Grand Rapids; the funds were to be "of material assistance in helping people to assist themselves," according to *The Papermakers*. The foundation, of which Blandin wrote he hoped would spread "at Christmas and throughout the year the spirit of Christmas," is unusual in that it is devoted to the welfare of residents of a city as small as Grand Rapids. Blandin died in 1958 and was buried across from the mill in his beloved adopted town.

Recommended Reading

Many of the original European settlers were alive when *Logging Town: The Story of Grand Rapids, Minnesota* was written in 1941 under the auspices of the Works Projects Administration. The book contains many lively anecdotes about the logging town in its early days. *The Papermakers—The Blandin Paper Company and Grand Rapids, Minnesota* (Grand Rapids: Charles K. Blandin Foundation, 1984) is not just another company history. Author Donald L. Boese gives a concise history of the town and a detailed look at the life and work of Charles K. Blandin, who ran the paper mill for decades and established the Blandin Foundation. Boese presents the bad as well as the good sides of Blandin, a self-made tycoon.

Festivals and Events

Judy Garland Festival
fourth weekend in June
Judy Garland spent her first years in Grand Rapids, and the city celebrates her every summer with a three-day festival. People connected with Garland are often celebrity guests, and some years the Munchkins from the movie cast of *The Wizard of Oz* appear. Events vary from year to year, but the theater in Grand Rapids always shows Garland's films during the festival. The event, nearly a quarter of a century old, is held at the Garland birthplace and also at the Children's Museum (see Museums and Historic Sites). Obtain details from the Garland birthplace, **800-664-5839.**

Mississippi Melodie Showboat
mid-July
Here comes the *Showboat!* The old paddle wheeler rounds the bend in the Mississippi, docks at the landing in Grand Rapids, and a cast of a couple of dozen pours out. The volunteer troupers—all local—sing, dance, and put on skits, then pile back on the boat and away they go. The festival, which started in 1955, celebrates the steamboat era in Grand Rapids's early days with several performances. Fee. For reserved seats, call **800-722-7814** or **218-327-1823.**

White Oak Rendezvous and Festival
early Aug.
More than a thousand historic characters, from voyageurs to fur company partners, in costume portraying the fur-trade era, flock to the White Oak Rendezvous and Festival, a three-day event that includes music, crafts, and food specialties from the fur-trade era of the late 18th through early 19th centuries. The rendezvous, organized by the White Oak Society in Deer River, also has RV campsites on the rendezvous grounds in Deer River. Fee. **800-472-6366** or **218-246-9393.**

Outdoor Activities

Biking
In Savanna Portage State Park there are 10 miles of mountain bike trails. Scenic State Park has a 2-mile paved bike path. See Parks.

Chippewa National Forest
North of Grand Rapids, on either side of scenic Hwy. 38, are five designated bike trails in the Chippewa National Forest. The routes range from

5 to 35 miles and vary greatly in difficulty, with the 10-mile Little Ruby loop, partly on a paved road, the easiest. For a map of the trails, contact the Marcell District Office, Chippewa National Forest, **49554 Hwy. 38, Marcell, 56657; 218-832-3161.**

Taconite State Trail

This 165-mile state trail from Grand Rapids to Ely is paved for the first 6 miles out of Grand Rapids. The multiuse trail, which goes past remains of mining operations near Grand Rapids and then winds through forests as it approaches Ely, is used by bikers, hikers, horseback riders, and snowmobilers. For information, contact the Grand Rapids Area Chamber of Commerce (see Services). See also Ely chapter.

Boating

North of Grand Rapids are canoe routes on the Bigfork, Rice, and Mississippi Rivers, all partly inside the Chippewa National Forest. Canoeing is easy on the Mississippi route (after the big lakes—Leech and Winnie are negotiated), but the Bigfork has some white water. The easy, 18-mile Rice River route is administered by the Forest Service, the other two by the Dept. of Natural Resources. For information, contact the Chippewa National Forest headquarters (see Parks).

Fishing

The multitude of lakes around Grand Rapids guarantee good fishing. Ask at resorts for the best lakes for fishing and the best spots to head for walleye, northern, and bass. In Chippewa National Forest, anglers are happy with the brown trout in Lucky Lake and the rainbows in Kremer Lake. In Savanna Portage State Park, fish in Lake Shumway include northern, bass, trout, and panfish. Both Coon and Sandwick Lakes in Scenic State Park have good fishing for northern, walleye, bass, and panfish. For information on seasons and licenses, call the Regional Fisheries Manager in Grand Rapids, **218-327-4430.**

Golf

The four 18-hole golf courses in the Grand Rapids area refer to themselves as the "Grand Slam."

Getting There
Grand Rapids is approximately 175 miles north of the Twin Cities, on U.S. Hwy. 169. There is bus service from the Twin Cities.

All four open in approximately mid-Apr. and usually close at the end of Oct. Two of the courses—**Wendigo Golf Club (750 Golf Crest Dr., Grand Rapids, 55744; 218-327-2211)** and **Sugarbrooke (P.O. Box 847, Grand Rapids, 55744; 800-450-4555 or 218-327-1462)** at Ruttger's Sugar Lake Lodge—were designed by famed course architect Joel Goldstrand. A third course, **Pokegama Golf Club,** which dates to 1926, is on the shore of beautiful Lake Pokegama; **3910 Golf Course Rd., Grand Rapids, 55744; 218-326-3444.** The fourth course, **Eagle Ridge Golf Course,** is north of Grand Rapids; **1 Green Way, Box 197, Coleraine, 55722; 218-245-2217.** It has large greens and wide fairways, and is on the edge of Trout Lake in the midst of splendid scenery. Greens fees for 18 holes at any of the four range from $20 to $30. All rent clubs. Several lodging facilities in Grand Rapids offer golf packages. Contact the Grand Rapids Area Chamber of Commerce for details (see Services), or the individual clubs.

Hiking

The state parks and the Chippewa National Forest near Grand Rapids offer excellent hiking trails. In the districts of the Chippewa closest to the city are half a dozen trails ranging from just a few miles to 21 miles. For information on the forest trails, contact the Chippewa National Forest office (see Parks). Park visitors can hike along the 6-mile portage in Savanna Portage State Park. It's not for the hiker who wants an easy time, however, as it is rugged and can be wet. There are 17 miles of hiking trails, and several boardwalks span wet or boggy ground. In Scenic State Park, the Chase Point Trail, which runs along a glacial ridge, gives a good view of the lakes, tiny leftovers of Glacial Lake Agassiz. The park has a

1-mile self-guided trail and 14 additional miles of hiking trails. See Parks.

Skiing

CROSS-COUNTRY

Cross-country skiers find hundreds of miles of skiing on 16 cross-country trails in and around Grand Rapids. In addition, there is good skiing at the North Central Experiment Station in town (see Other Sites), as well as at state parks, state forests, the Chippewa National Forest north of Grand Rapids, and Itasca County parks. The Suomi Hills Recreation Area in the Chippewa National Forest, about 15 miles north of Grand Rapids, has approximately 20 miles of groomed cross-country trails, for intermediate to advanced skiers, that wind around many small lakes in the forest. In winter, there are 17 miles of cross-country ski trails in Savanna Portage State Park. There are 7 miles of trails for cross-country skiers in Scenic State Park, plus a warming house. See Parks. For more information and snow conditions, call the Grand Rapids Area Chamber of Commerce (see Services).

Snowmobiling

In the vicinity of Grand Rapids are 18 groomed snowmobile trails that total more than 900 miles of trail. In Savanna Portage State Park, there are 40 miles of snowmobile trails. In winter, Scenic State Park has 12 miles of snowmobile trails plus a warming house. See Parks. The area snowmobiling clubs are very active. For a map of snowmobile trails and snow conditions, call the Grand Rapids Area Chamber of Commerce (see Services).

Seeing and Doing

Museums and Historic Sites

Forest History Center

This is a living-history re-creation so real that you'll practically pitch in and do some logging. The carefully reconstructed camp gives a fascinating glimpse of life in a logging camp circa 1900 and also the life of a Forest Service patrolman of the 1930s. The camp "cookie" doles out tall tales as well as food samples, and the big draft horses clomp along the dirt paths. On the river is a wanigan, complete with long underwear hanging from the rafters and food to feed the hungry loggers. There is also an interpretive center with videos, including a grainy film of the last big log drive in the 1930s and exhibitions. There are picnic facilities and nature trails, too, plus special interpretive activities. The Forest History Center is part of the Minnesota Historical Society. Fee (free for MHS members). Living-history features, interpretive building, and trails open Memorial Day–Oct. 15, Mon.–Sat., 10:00 A.M.–5:00 P.M., and Sun., noon–5:00 P.M.; interpretive center open Oct. 15–Memorial Day, Mon.–Sat., 8:00 A.M.–4:00 P.M. **2609 County Rd. 76, Grand Rapids, 55744; 218-327-4482.**

Itasca County Historical Society

Located in the restored old Central School, the Historical Society includes a county museum that traces the history of the Ojibwe Indians and showcases beautiful Ojibwe beadwork. It also presents information on the logging and papermaking industries as well as on Judy Garland and her career. There are five well-stocked period rooms and a research center. Open year-round, Mon.–Fri., 9:30 A.M.–5:00 P.M.; seasonally, Sat.–Sun., 9:30 A.M.–4:00 P.M. **10 Fifth St. NW, P.O. Box 664, Grand Rapids, 55744; 218-326-6431.**

Judy Garland's Birthplace

The little white house on the outskirts of Grand Rapids was the childhood home of a great big talent, singer Judy Garland. Garland, born Frances Gumm, lived in Grand Rapids during her early childhood. The house has been restored and some of the furnishings are original. A "Wizard of Oz" garden contains a field of poppies. Many activities of the annual Judy Garland Festival take place here (see Festivals and Events). Open May 1–Oct. 31, daily, 10:00 A.M.–5:00 P.M.; Nov.–Apr., by appointment. The **birthplace site** is located at **2727 Hwy. 169 S.** The **Judy Garland Children's Museum,** now in downtown Grand Rapids, will move to the Garland birth-

Logger with team of horses at the Forest History Center. Photo courtesy of the Minnesota Historical Society.

place site; the year 2000 is the scheduled completion date. Currently located at **19 NE Fourth St.** in Grand Rapids, the museum has lots of hands-on activities and an art and music room. Props from the movie *The Wizard of Oz* are among the exhibits. Contact both the birthplace site and the children's museum at **P.O. Box 724, Grand Rapids, 55744; 800-664-5839. Website: judygarland.com.**

Other Sites

North Central Experiment Station

For more than 100 years, the Experiment Station at Grand Rapids has been testing varieties of crops that are suited to the northern growing conditions, and it is well known for its cold-hardy blueberries and other small fruits. But the station is more than a research facility for agriculture and horticulture. The public is welcome to visit the plots that demonstrate annual all-American winners among flowers and vegetables. In addition, there are cross-country ski trails open to the public and a natural area of upland and lowland forest—including old-growth red and white pine—and bog areas. In the bog are pitcher plants, and in June, lady slippers bloom. Call to make sure grounds are open. Free. **1861 Hwy. 169 E., Grand Rapids, 55744; 218-327-4490.**

Parks

Chippewa National Forest

The Chippewa National Forest north of Grand Rapids is one of two national forests in Minnesota. Like Superior National Forest, the Chippewa provides plenty of recreational opportunities (see Boating, Hiking, Cross-Country Skiing). Among the forest highlights near Grand Rapids is the Suomi Hills Recreation Area, a remote, hilly, lake-speckled paradise for cross-country skiers, hikers, and bikers who like a bit of a challenge. Wildlife is abundant in Suomi Hills. East of Suomi Hills is the Trout Lake and Bluewater/Wabana Lakes area. Part of this district is classified as semiprimitive, with no motors allowed. The campsites along the chain of lakes are boat-in only. For information on the forest and maps for specific recreational pursuits, contact the **Marcell Ranger District,**

Chippewa National Forest, 49554 Hwy. 38, Marcell, 56657; 218-832-3161.

Savanna Portage State Park

Savanna Portage is an all-around state park, with plenty of recreational opportunities, lots of wildlife, areas of wilderness, and one big link to Minnesota history. The park takes its name from the historic 6-mile portage over the marshland (savanna) and woods that link the St. Louis River watershed (and thus Lake Superior) with the Mississippi watershed. American Indians used the path between the two river systems for centuries before the European explorers and fur traders started using it in the mid-1700s. The park, located southeast of Grand Rapids, is the state's third largest, at nearly 19,000 acres. Savanna Portage is a good park for family recreation. At Lake Shumway, campsites are right along the lake, and boats and canoes can be rented, but only electric motors are allowed. Kids enjoy the beautiful, pine-fringed swimming beach at Loon Lake, in addition to the lakeside campground. The park is 17 miles northeast of McGregor. Follow U.S. Hwy. 65 to County Hwys. 14/36 and follow that road to the park. **HCR 3, Box 591, McGregor, 55760; 218-426-3271.**

Scenic State Park

This park is well named: there are seven lakes, two with shorelines of virgin pine, which is amazing considering that Scenic is in the heart of logged-over country. However, local residents of Bigfork—the nearest community—started a movement to save the pines and birches around Coon and Sandwick Lakes, and their campaign resulted not only in the preservation of the trees but in the creation of Scenic State Park in 1921. Scenic's other lakes also have some virgin forest area, but only Coon and Sandwick are in their native state. Coon Lake has a swimming beach. There is no water-skiing on either lake, and boating speeds are restricted. A building constructed by the CCC houses the interpretive center and there is also a fire tower dating to the CCC era. Campsites are abundant here. The park is located 7 miles southeast of Bigfork on County Hwy. 7. **56956 Scenic Hwy. 7, Bigfork, 56628; 218-743-3362.**

Schoolcraft State Park

The 20th century does not intrude much at Schoolcraft State Park on the Upper Mississippi. The small (295-acre) park is in the midst of tall pines (one white pine is more than 300 years old) and provides a quiet spot to relax. This is not a park for families looking for a lot of activities. There is fishing in the river, however, and the Whisper Trail takes hikers through the virgin pine forest. The park is named for Henry Schoolcraft, who—with his Anishinabe (Ojibwe) guide, Ozawindib—charted the headwaters of the Mississippi River (see Mississippi Headwaters chapter in The Heartland section). Schoolcraft's diary indicates that he camped in the vicinity of the present park. There is camping in the park. To reach the park, go 8 miles west of Grand Rapids on U.S. Hwy. 2, 8 miles south on Hwy. 6, 2 miles west on County Rd. 28, another 2 miles west on County Rd. 65, and then 1 mile north on County Rd. 74. Address mail care of the Hill Annex Mine State Park, **P.O. Box 376, Calumet, 55716; 218-247-7215.**

Scenic Drives

Edge of the Wilderness
National Scenic Byway

A 47-mile stretch of Scenic Hwy. 38 was designated one of 20 National Scenic Byways in 1997. The highway meanders by many lakes and forests, including the Chippewa National Forest. The route is spectacular in the fall when the leaves turn. The Byway is between Grand Rapids and Effie. For more information, contact the Grand Rapids Area Chamber of Commerce, **800-472-6366.**

Great River Road

Historic as well as natural sights are part of the lure of the Great River Road that goes from Bena to Grand Rapids. In this area, the Ojibwe and the Dakota fought their last battle in northern Minnesota. The route is on various roads and highways. Hwy. 46—also known as the Avenue of the Pines—skirts the edge of Ball Club Lake (named for the club that the Ojibwe used in a game) and the town of Ball Club. The route crosses the Mississippi, and the changing channels of the river are evident along the route. For a brochure outlining the route, contact the Minnesota Office of Tourism, **800-657-3700** or **651-296-5029.**

Tours

Blandin Paper Mill

Retired workers lead tours at the Blandin Mill in Grand Rapids. See History for a description of the mill's past. The free 45-minute tours are restricted to those over 12 years old. Tours are given June–Aug.; call for days and hours. **218-327-6226.**

Where to Stay

Bed-and-Breakfasts

Seagren's Pokegama Lodge—$$$

Alan and Jean Seagren have turned a family resort on Pokegama Lake south of Grand Rapids into a bed-and-breakfast that truly feels like a home away from home. The b-and-b, which has five bedrooms, is right on the clear, beautiful lake. Inside, the Seagrens have a fascinating array of furnishings and divertissements, including a piano, a complete edition of the 1892 *Encyclopaedia Britannica,* puzzles, family antiques, and photos from Lapland. There is a library for guests and also an office with a fax and copier for those who can't stop working. All rooms have lake views. There are four baths for the rooms. There are also two housekeeping cabins. Jean often has cookies, pie, or some other goodie waiting for hungry guests to taste. The Seagrens' hearty "lumberjack" breakfasts are served on the resort's original 1920s china. The Seagrens are avid snowmobilers and a trail is right outside the door. **931 Crystal Springs Rd., Grand Rapids, 55744; 888-326-9040** or **218-326-9040.** E-mail: **seagrens@uslink.net.**

Hotels, Motels, and Inns

Country Inn—$$$

This clean and cheerful motel is part of a chain that provides homey touches, such as Tootsie Rolls

at the desk and cookies and apples for guests. Best of all for Judy Garland fans, it's right next to the Judy Garland birthplace (see Museums and Historic Sites). There is also direct access to the Taconite State Trail (see Biking), as well as in-room coffee and an indoor pool. **2601 S. Hwy. 169, Grand Rapids, 55744; 218-327-4960.**

Sawmill Inn—$$$

The Sawmill looks like the north woods, with its huge stone chimney and a saw perched on the roof. The lobby also has a woodsy feel to it. The spacious inn has 124 rooms and suites, and is very close to the Judy Garland birthplace (see Museums and Historic Sites). The inn, which dates back to the '30s, is a Grand Rapids institution with a big restaurant and lounge. Recreation facilities include a pool, saunas, and a whirlpool. **2301 Pokegama Ave. S. (Hwy. 169 S.), Grand Rapids, 55744; 800-667-7508.**

Resorts

Ruttger's Sugar Lake Lodge—$$$ to $$$$

Ruttger's is the oldest name in Minnesota resort history, but the Sugar Lake Lodge is a relative newcomer on the resort scene. The only resort on lovely Siseebakwet Lake (Sugar Lake), Ruttger's is a resort that has everything a family could want. There are free planned children's activities for kids ages four to 12 in summer and the usual lake activities—swimming, canoeing, boating, and fishing. Nonmotorized watercraft come free with lodging. Ruttger's 18-hole golf course is part of the four-course, 72-hole "Grand Slam" in the area (see Golf). In winter, the resort still goes strong, with snowmobiling, cross-country skiing, ice fishing, sleigh rides, and dogsled rides among the offerings. Snowmobiles can be rented at the resort. Those who don't want to do their own cooking can eat at Otis' Restaurant or Jack's Grill at the resort. Lodgings range from suites attached to the lodge to studios to larger cottages and villas along the golf course. Some have fireplaces and whirlpool baths and the larger ones have kitchens. Ruttger's is located 14 miles southwest of Grand Rapids. **P.O. Box 847, Grand Rapids, 55744;**

800-450-4555 or 218-327-1462. Website: www.ruttgerssl.com.

Camping

Itasca County Fairgrounds—$

The 25 electrical hookups are at a premium at this large public campground on the edge of Grand Rapids. Situated right on a lake ringed by tall pines, the campground has showers, picnic tables, etc. Recreation includes swimming, biking, and snowmobiling. **1336 Third Ave. NE, Grand Rapids, 55744; 218-326-6470.**

State Parks—$

Savanna Portage has 64 drive-in sites, 18 with electricity, as well as one canoe-in site and seven backpack sites. There is also an unheated camper cabin. A guest house that sleeps up to six is open year-round; it costs $60 per night, has a shower and toilet, and is furnished for housekeeping except for bedding and towels. **Scenic State Park** has 117 drive-in sites, 20 of them pull-through sites; 20 of the total sites have electricity. In addition, there are six backpack sites and four boat-in sites; two of the park sites are handicapped-accessible. **Schoolcraft State Park** has 30 campsites, none with electricity. There are also two canoe-in sites. For all state park camping reservations (including the camper cabins and guest houses), call **The Connection, 800-246-CAMP** or **612-922-9000.**

Chippewa National Forest—free or $

The Chippewa has a number of campsites, including boat-in-only sites north and west of Grand Rapids. Contact the Marcell Ranger District, Chippewa National Forest, **49554 Hwy. 38, Marcell, 56657; 218-832-3161.**

Where to Eat

Forest Lake—$ to $$$

The lakeside Forest Lake, right in Grand Rapids, is a two-story log restaurant. The top floor is lighter and airier; the ground floor steakhouse is more intimate. Both have coveted lakeside tables. Steaks, ribs, seafood, and buffalo (as in buffalo burgers) are the house specialties. There is a separate menu for the cozy bar. Upstairs dining room open in summer, daily, 7:00 A.M.–10:00 P.M.; in winter, Sun.–Thurs., 7:00 A.M.–9:00 P.M., and Fri.–Sat., 7:00 A.M.–10:00 P.M. Steakhouse open in summer, daily, 5:00–10:00 P.M.; in winter, Sun.–Thurs., 5:00–9:00 P.M., and Fri.–Sat., 5:00–10:00 P.M. Call for dates of seasons. **1201 NW Fourth St., Grand Rapids, 55744; 218-326-3423.**

The First Grade Restaurant—$ to $$

You'll rub your eyes and swear you are back in elementary school at the First Grade. Look around and you'll see old friends: the *Dick and Jane* readers and the alphabet cards. But the food in your old school was never like this. The restaurant, in a real school room with all the trimmings, serves wild rice salad, quiches, hearty breakfasts, and daily specials. If you really want to revert, have a peanut butter and jelly sandwich. Open year-round, Mon.–Sat., 7:00 A.M.–4:00 P.M., and Sun., 10:00 A.M.–2:00 P.M. **10 NW Fifth St. (Central School), Grand Rapids, 55744; 218-326-9361.**

Services

Grand Rapids Area Chamber of Commerce, 1 NW Third St., Grand Rapids, 55744; 800-472-6366. Website: www.grandmn.com.

Iron Range

There are three so-called iron ranges in Minnesota, but when people talk about "The Range," they mean the Mesabi Range, an ore-rich section of Northeast Minnesota that stretches from Hibbing on the western edge to Hoyt Lakes on the east, a distance that can be driven in less than an hour. The Iron Range contains the Laurentian Divide, which splits the watersheds between Hudson Bay and Lake Superior. Those who live on the Iron Range say that each of the communities has a different character, in part because of their patterns of ethnic settlement.

Immigrants from more than 40 countries came to work the mines, and they tended to seek out immigrants from their own countries. These days, intermarriage and movement in and out of the Range has altered traditional community makeup greatly, but pockets of original settlement still remain: in Virginia, on the east end of the Iron Range, for instance, Finlanders make up a big chunk of the population, while at the western edge of the Range, in Hibbing, Eastern Europeans are the

dominant ethnic group. "Rangers" are fiercely loyal to their communities, but once out of the Range, their loyalty transfers to the Range as a whole.

Hibbing, where Robert Zimmerman—known to the world as Bob Dylan—grew up, is the largest Iron Range community, with a population of ap-

Living-history portrayal by Gloria Anderson, who portrays a Swedish immigrant at Ironworld in Chisholm. Copyright © Minnesota Office of Tourism. Used by permission.

proximately 18,000, while the next-largest city, Virginia, is half as large, with about 9,400 inhabitants. Chisholm, with just over 5,000 people, and Eveleth, with about 4,000 people, are next in line. In all, there are about 45,500 residents in the communities that have banded together for promotion purposes to form the Iron Trail Region.

The communities were and remain mining towns, although taconite mining (crushing the lower-grade magnetic ore into powder, then pelletizing it for shipment to steel companies) has replaced "natural" ore mining, and abandoned natural-ore mines surround the towns. In many cases, nature has softened the minescapes, with vegetation gentling the steep walls and turquoise lakes at the bottom of the red pits. Dusty mine roads and hills of waste rock do remain.

Chisholm, with its flag-lined bridge spanning Longyear Lake within the city, is one of the most attractive of the communities, as is Eveleth, whose small downtown is flanked by "walls" of green hills. Each community has something to offer visitors and each retains an individual identity. Tourism is making inroads on the Iron Range now, and it's about time, as the area has many of the same outdoor recreational possibilities as the rest of northern Minnesota, plus the added attraction of the mines and their history.

History

The rich deposits of iron ore put the Iron Range on the map, but the geological and human history of the area go far beyond the mining boom years. The ores—hematite, taconite, and limonite—were deposited one to two million years ago, creating a band of ore about 120 miles long and 1–3 miles wide. The deposit is one of the richest in the world.

Before Europeans arrived, Ojibwe Indians inhabited the Iron Range. During the fur-trade era, a few French settlers came to the Range; the town of Embarrass testifies to their presence (the French word *embarrass* means "a barrier"). Later the short gold rush at Lake Vermilion brought prospectors in, but few settled. The present range towns sprang up after the discovery of iron ore in the late 19th century.

> ## Getting There
> Hibbing and Virginia are each about 190 miles north of the Twin Cities, and the drive takes about three and a half hours. The quickest route driving is probably up Hwy. 35 W. toward Duluth, branching off on Hwy. 33 through Cloquet and then north on Hwy. 53 to Virginia. Hibbing is west of Virginia on Hwy. 169, which links many Iron Range communities. There is air-link service to Hibbing from the Twin Cities.

Logging had already been big in areas of the Iron Range, particularly in Virginia, when the first ore was discovered, on Nov. 16, 1890, by the Merritt brothers in what is now the town of Mountain Iron. A cyclone in Aug. 1891 uprooted many trees on the Range and exposed more ore deposits. Miners from such places as Finland, Scandinavia, Serbia, Croatia, Italy, and Cornwall arrived in a steady stream throughout the 1890s to work in the mines and build the towns along the Range.

The big mining boom was largely over by the 1950s, with progressively lesser grades of ore being mined. Taconite mining lifted the Iron Range out of economic doldrums in the '60s and '70s, but the shift in the steel industries to imported ore caused another downturn. However, taconite mines continue to employ many local residents, and mining is still a major state industry. By diversifying the economic base of the Iron Range, including promoting tourism, the area hopes to retain its population.

Festivals and Events

Finnish Sliding Festival (Laskiainen)
first full weekend in Feb.
Kids and intrepid adults swoosh down ice slides onto the frozen lake beyond in this venerable Finnish festival, which started more than 60 years ago. Folklore said the family going the farthest on the slide would have the best crop of flax during the next growing season. Local residents work for weeks preparing the ice slides next to the

Birch trees reflected in McCarthy Beach State Park. Photo courtesy of the Minnesota Department of Natural Resources.

Loon Lake Community Center in the little town of Palo, south of Aurora. Inside the community center, Finnish foods are for sale and crafts such as spinning and weaving are demonstrated. Loon Lake Community Center, **218-638-2551.**

Land of the Loon Festival
third weekend in June

The many ethnic groups of the Iron Range are celebrated in this festival, which begins with a parade on Fri. Nearly two dozen ethnic food booths offer edible ancestral memories; ethnic dancing and music go on for the festival's two days. Arts and crafts booths and children's activities are also a big part of the festival, which takes place in Olcott Park in Virginia. **800-777-7395.**

International Polka Festival
last full weekend in June

Heading toward the quarter-century mark, the polka festival at Ironworld Discovery Center has drawn more than 7,000 musicians, dancers, and toe tappers during its annual four-day run. There are usually more than 25 bands, playing on several stages, for dancing and listening. Bands and fans have come from all over the United States and Canada and from several European countries as well. Fee. **800-372-6437** or **218-254-3321.**

Field of Dreams Festival
first two weeks in July

Field of Dreams was fiction, but one of its heroes, Dr. Archibald "Moonlight" Graham, was the real thing. Chisholm celebrates its ballplayer-turned-doctor with its festival including a ball game, parade, music, and food. For details, contact the Chisholm Chamber of Commerce, **218-254-3600. Website: www.chisholmchamber.com.**

Noel Sites and Northern Lights
early Dec.

Christmas lights twinkle Range-wide in this festival. Sleigh rides, costumed carolers, food, and festivities all week long help visitors get into the Christmas spirit. Past special events have included a buffet of ethnic foods, a treasure hunt, a musical, and an ice-skating program. For details, contact the Iron Trail Convention and Visitors Bureau (see Services).

Outdoor Activities

Biking

MOUNTAIN BIKING
The Iron Range offers excellent mountain biking, including the 50 miles of trails intended primarily

for intermediate to advanced bikers in the Giant's Ridge Recreation Area near Biwabik. In addition, there are trails in the Big Aspen area of the Superior National Forest north of Virginia. At McCarthy Beach State Park and along the Taconite State Trail (see Snowmobiling) that passes through the park, there are 17 miles of trails. For more information, contact the Iron Trail Convention and Visitors Bureau (see Services).

Mesabi Trail

When it is completed, the Mesabi Trail will stretch 132 miles from Grand Rapids to Ely. The multiuse trail is pieced together from rail beds, logging and mining roads, and existing bike trails. Several segments from Hibbing to Eveleth are completed. For information, contact the Iron Trail Convention and Visitors Bureau (see Services).

Rentals and Tours

Bikes can be rented at Giant's Ridge Golf and Ski Resort in Biwabik; **800-688-7669** or **218-865-4143.**

Birding

Bird-watching is popular at McCarthy Beach State Park, with more than 175 species visiting the park annually. See Parks.

Fishing

In addition to the usual fishing that northern Minnesota offers, many of the abandoned mine pits have been stocked with trout, mostly rainbows. Some of the pits are state-designated trout lakes, and special rules must be followed. For information on fishing for the area from Grand Rapids to Virginia, call the Area Fisheries Supervisor in Grand Rapids, **218-327-4430.** For the area to the east of Virginia, call the Area Fisheries Supervisor in Ely, **218-365-7280.** For a list of the stocked pits, contact the Iron Trail Convention and Visitors Bureau (see Services).

Golf

Giant's Ridge Golf and Ski Resort

One of the state's newest courses, the 18-hole course near the Giant's Ridge ski hill (see Downhill Skiing) opened in 1997, along the shore of

Wynne Lake. The par-72 public course has tree-lined fairways and two lakes, and is spiced by rock formations and outcroppings. Lessons are available and clubs can be rented. The greens fee of $60 per day includes a cart. Open approximately last week in Apr.–mid-Oct., dawn–dusk. **800-688-7669** or **218-865-4143.**

Hiking

There are 18 miles of hiking trails in McCarthy Beach State Park and 5 miles of hiking trails in the Soudon Underground Mine State Park. The Superior National Forest has a number of popular trails. Maps of the following trails and others are available from the Laurentian District office of the Superior National Forest (see Parks).

The **Pfeiffer Lake Trail,** next to the campground of the same name, is an easy trail of several miles, good for families with young children. One loop of the trail offers visitors self-guided interpretive signs that explain features such as a bog and wildflowers. Pfeiffer Lake is 30 miles north of Virginia off County Rd. 1 and Forest Rd. 256.

The **Laurentian Divide Fitness Trail,** a 1.5-mile trail, has 14 exercise stations and provides easy hiking. Also at the Laurentian Divide recreation area is the 15-mile **Lookout Mountain Trail,** where flaming maples in fall make it a perfect place to drink in autumn colors. In addition to the hikes, there are picnic tables for visitors. Located 4 miles north of Virginia on Hwy. 53.

The **North Dark River Trail** extends for 2 miles looking down into the North Dark River Gorge, which is a designated trout stream. A trail extension leads to the river. The trail is located 17 miles northwest of Virginia off County Rd. 688.

Skiing

CROSS-COUNTRY

There are approximately 180 miles of cross-country trails on the Range. In winter, McCarthy Beach State Park has 9 miles of cross-country ski trails. Giant's Ridge, well known for downhill skiing, is also a haven for cross-country skiers. The U.S. Olympic cross-country ski team trains here, which says a lot for the challenging expert trails. There are trails for skiers of lesser ability, too. For a detailed map of area trails and trail conditions, contact the Iron Trail Convention and Visitors Bureau (see Services) or the Laurentian District office of the Superior National Forest (see Parks).

DOWNHILL

Giant's Ridge Golf and Ski Resort
Giant's Ridge has a vertical drop of 500 feet, a lot for a Minnesota ski area. A double and a triple chair lift give access to the 34 runs. Snowboarding is also popular at Giant's Ridge. **800-655-7669** or **218-865-4143.**

Snowmobiling

The Iron Range is crisscrossed with snowmobile trails. There are more than 2,000 miles (yes, you read right) fanning out from the Iron Range, extending up to International Falls and northeast to Ely. McCarthy Beach State Park has 12 miles of snowmobile trails. For a map or trail conditions, call the Iron Trail Convention and Visitors Bureau (see Services).

Taconite State Trail
Though primarily used by snowmobilers, the 165-mile Taconite State Trail, which runs from Grand Rapids to Ely, is also used by hikers, horseback riders, and mountain bikers in summer. It's easy to see the impact of the mining industry along the trail north of Grand Rapids. The trail runs through McCarthy Beach State Park and connects to the Arrowhead Trail near Lake Vermilion. There are campsites and overlooks scattered along both trails. For a trail map, contact the Dept. of Natural Resources, **500 Lafayette Rd., St. Paul, 55155; 888-MINNDNR** or **651-296-6157.**

Seeing and Doing

Museums and Historic Sites

Greyhound Bus Origin Center
Have you ever gone Greyhound? This is where it all began. The photos and displays about the growth of the tiny company into the huge dog it became are interesting, but it is the old buses themselves that really hit the spot—on display are buses from 1914, the '30s, and the '40s, plus a 1956 Scenicruiser. It's adjacent to the Hibbing Historical Society Museum. Open mid-May–Sept., Mon.–Sat., 9:00 A.M.–5:00 P.M. Fee. Located **at Fifth Ave. and 23rd St., Hibbing; 218-263-5814.**

Hibbing Historical Society Museum
Hibbing, one of the main cities on the Iron Range, picked up and moved—lock, stock, and barrel—back in 1918, because the town was in a mineable area. The move is carefully documented in this museum, and visitors can also walk around the original town site, an eerie place with street signs, sidewalks, and steps leading to nothing but cleared ground. Open mid-May–Sept., Mon.–Sat., 9:00 A.M.–5:00 P.M.; call for winter hours. Fee. Located next to the bus museum, **at Fifth Ave. and 23rd St., Hibbing; 218-263-8522.**

Hull Rust Mahoning Mine
This mine was the first of the Mesabi Range's open-pit mines, and it is still engaged in taconite operations. The 3-mile-long pit and current operations can be seen from the observation deck at the mine, in Hibbing, on the north side of town. Follow Third Ave. E. to the observation platform. Free. For more information, call the Hibbing Area Chamber of Commerce, **218-262-3895.**

Ironworld Discovery Center
A statue of a huge miner signals the entrance to Ironworld, which celebrates the Iron Range and its cultures. The main building is the Iron Range Interpretive Center, which has exhibits on the ethnic groups who settled the Range and also on the iron mining industry. Part of Ironworld is like an open-air museum. Ride a trolley—a real one, which clangs and clatters—alongside the abandoned Glenn Mines to a restored depot. Once there, tour the restored house of a miner, and picnic among the trees. If you're lucky, you may hear one of the living-history guides sing "*Hälsa dem där hemma*" and other songs beloved by Swedish immigrants. Back at the main part of Ironworld, walk through the gardens at Festival Park, chat with other living-history guides about life among other ethnic groups and time periods, and watch demonstrators make ethnic crafts.

When you're hungry, grab a snack from one of the food stands or eat lunch at the Ironworld cafe, where cabbage rolls and pasties are among the offerings, and take in entertainment, which is regularly scheduled. Ironworld celebrates local immigrant groups with Ethnic Days, which features foods, craft demonstrations, dancing, music, and songs; ask for a schedule if you want to come on the day "your" ancestral group is spotlighted. Children like carousel rides, swooshing down a giant slide, and playing on the miniature golf course. For those interested in genealogy, there is the Iron Range Research Center, also located in Ironworld. Ironworld is open mid-June–mid-Sept., daily; Iron Range Research Center is open year-round, Mon.–Fri., 8:00 A.M.–4:30 P.M. (when Ironworld is open, the research center's hours are the same as Ironworld's). Fee. Located just off Hwy. 169 in Chisholm. **P.O. Box 392, Chisholm, 55719; 800-372-6437 or 218-254-3321.**

Mineview-in-the-Sky

Look down from this perch into a man-made canyon, nearly 3 miles long and about 0.5 mile wide, formed by open-pit mining. The Mineview, operated by the Virginia Chamber of Commerce, has picnic tables, a playground, panoramic viewers, and a display of mining equipment. Refreshments are available. The Mineview staff is very knowledgeable and has information on area attractions, including mine tours. Free. Open mid-May–Sept. 30, daily, 8:00 A.M.–7:00 P.M. The road to the Mineview is on the southeast edge of Virginia, off Hwy. 53. Virginia Chamber of Commerce, **218-741-2717.**

Minnesota Museum of Mining

Tour a replica of an underground mine and mining town or climb aboard some of the huge trucks and other machinery used in the mines. A video orients visitors to the story of mining on the Iron Range. In the Depot is a model steam train, with a background diorama painted by F. L. Jacques, a well-known Minnesota artist. Fee. Open end of May–mid-Sept., daily, 9:00 A.M.–6:00 P.M. Located **in Memorial Park, at the top of Main St., Chisholm; 218-254-5543.**

U.S. Hockey Hall of Fame

Many of the big names in U.S. hockey, including Eveleth's own John Mariucci, came from the Iron Range, and it is still a hockey hotbed. Hockey fans spend hours here, wandering among all the hockey paraphernalia, including videos of U.S. Olympic championship games in 1960, 1980, and 1998. Movie buffs like the original scoreboard from the "Mighty Ducks" movies. In the Great Hall are displays of the 100 players (all from the United States; Canadians are excluded) in the U.S. Hockey Hall of Fame. The first part of an ambitious renovation project was completed in 1998. Located **just off Hwy. 53 in Eveleth.** Stop in downtown Eveleth, too, and look at the world's largest hockey stick, which measures 107 feet long and weighs more than three tons. It faces a mural of a goalie on the side of a building. Open year-round, Mon.–Sat., 9:00 A.M.–5:00 P.M., and Sun., noon–5:00 P.M. (hours are subject to change). **800-443-7825 or 218-744-5167.**

Virginia Heritage Museum and Olcott Park Greenhouse

Virginia's logging history, once the world's largest white-pine industry, is portrayed in this museum. It's located in Olcott Park, which also houses a wonderful greenhouse, a great place to relax amid flowers and greenery, especially in the northern Minnesota winters. The museum is open May–Sept., Tues.–Sat., 11:00 A.M.–4:00 P.M.; Oct.–Apr., Thurs.–Sat., 11:00 A.M.–4:00 P.M. The greenhouse is open mid-June–third week in Aug., daily, 7:00 A.M.–7:00 P.M.; rest of year, Mon.–Fri., 7:00 A.M.–3:30 P.M., and Sat.–Sun., 7:00 A.M.–3:00 P.M. Free. Olcott Park is located **at Ninth St. and Ninth Ave., Virginia; 218-741-1136** (museum information) or **218-741-2149** (greenhouse).

Parks

McCarthy Beach State Park

This park is well named: the beach is super—it's long and sandy and slopes gently into shallow Sturgeon Lake. It's the perfect lake for a family swim. In addition to Sturgeon Lake, visitors can go boating in Side Lake, and in four connected lakes in the Sturgeon chain. The park also has a handicapped-accessible fishing pier. Boats, canoes, and motors can be rented. The lakes are surrounded by glacial moraines, and some of the park's trails, including 12 miles of horseback-riding trails, traverse the ridges on top of the moraines. There is camping in the park. Located north of Hibbing; take Hwy. 169 north to County Rd. 5, which is 16 miles from the park. **7622 McCarthy Beach Rd., Side Lake, 55781; 218-254-2411.**

Superior National Forest

Superior National Forest offers hiking, skiing, and snowmobile trails, as well as campgrounds, on the north side of the Iron Range. For information on activities in the forest, including campground details, contact the Laurentian District office, **318 Forestry Rd., Aurora, 55705; 218-229-8880.**

Scenic Drives

Leonidas Overlook

This is the highest point on the Iron Range, and it gives a great view of surrounding mines and also of current taconite operations. In Eveleth, on the west side, follow County Rd. 101 (Fayal Rd.) up to the top of the overlook.

Tours

Hibbing High School

Why tour a high school? This isn't just any old school, it's a vintage showplace, completed in 1923 at the cost of nearly $4 million. It was the talk of the state then and is still worth looking at. In the huge auditorium with its cut-glass chandeliers, even the door protecting the fire hose is a work of art: on a leaded green glass background are the words "for fire" worked in red stained glass. The seats in the auditorium are upholstered in gold velveteen. In the library is a huge mural depicting the ore-to-steel process and showing representatives of 16 of the Iron Range's ethnic groups. Tours begin in Rm. 126. Tours are given in summer, Mon.–Sat., 10:30 A.M., 11:30 A.M., 1:00 P.M., 2:00 P.M., and 3:00 P.M. Fee. Located at **Eighth Ave. E. and 21st St.; 219-263-3675.**

Hill Annex Mine State Park

With its beautiful blue-green lake surrounded by steep red-rock banks laced with greenery, the Hill Annex Mine State Park makes a colorful but serene picture. But for 65 years, the 500-foot-deep open pit was one of the state's most active mines, producing three million tons of ore from 1913 until it closed in 1978. Now visitors can tour the mine; there are interpretive exhibits in the mine clubhouse, but the park has no trails and there is no camping. The park is on the National Register of Historic Places. Next to the clubhouse is the old Calumet Depot, which has a gift shop and holds an annual "pie day" in June; it's worth checking to find out when. The one-and-a-half-hour tour winds partway down the roads of the mine in a gaily painted trolley, while a guide explains the mining process and points out buildings and equipment used for mining operations. Huge pieces of equipment are scattered around like toys forgotten by giant children. The rock exposed along the tour route is nearly two billion years old. The 90-minute tour starts from the mine clubhouse on the surface. Fee. Tours are given Memorial Day weekend–Labor Day, daily, starting at 10:00 A.M., and the last tour begins at 4:00 P.M. Located on the north edge of the town of Calumet. **P.O. Box 376, Calumet, 55716; 218-247-7215.**

Minntac Tour

Retired miners issue hard hats and take visitors on a tour of the taconite mine and the Minntac plant. The one-and-a-half-hour tour leaves by bus from the Mountain Iron Senior Citizen Center, Fri., 10:00 A.M. and 1:00 P.M. For information, contact the Iron Trail Convention and Visitors Bureau (see Services).

Soudan Underground Mine State Park

The Soudan was Minnesota's first underground mine, though it began as an open-pit mine, first shipping ore in 1884. The underground mine opened in the 1890s; the mine closed for good in 1963, and U.S. Steel Corp. donated the mine and surrounding land to the state. Now visitors can tour the mine. On the surface, visitors can see mine buildings and equipment. In addition, there are 5 miles of hiking trails, with a short, self-guided trail around the old open-pit mine. Visitors can fish in Lake Vermilion and picnic. In winter, there are 3 miles of snowmobile trails. The park has no campsites. For the tour, put on a hard hat, descend 0.5 mile into the earth in an elevator "cage," and climb aboard open cars in a mine train for a look at Soudan Mine. The one-and-a-half-hour tours are narrated by retired miners, who intersperse facts with stories of life in the "Cadillac of mines," as the Soudan was called for its excellent safety record. The mine has a constant temperature of about 50°F, so wear a coat or sweater and put on sturdy shoes for the bit of walking (including a 32-step spiral staircase) required. Fee. Tours are given Memorial Day–Labor Day, daily, starting at 9:30 A.M., and the last begins at 4:00 P.M. Located just a few blocks off Hwy. 169 in Soudan; follow directional signs. **1379 Stuntz Bay Rd., P.O. Box 335, Soudan, 55782; 218-753-2245.**

Wagering

Fortune Bay Casino

On the shore of Lake Vermilion, Fortune Bay Casino is owned by the Bois Forte Band of Ojibwe. It has the standard games of chance, plus a huge bingo hall. There is entertainment, plus a restaurant and a hotel right on the lakeshore. Visitors coming by boat can tie up at the casino dock. Open daily, 24 hours. **1430 Bois Forte Rd., Tower, 55790; 800-992-7529 or 218-753-6400.**

Where to Stay

Bed-and-Breakfasts

McNair's Bed-and-Breakfast—$$$$

Elegance among the pines is what you'll find at McNair's bed-and-breakfast. Both the bedroom and the suite in the main house are charmingly furnished with both antique and contemporary treasures. The suite includes a fireplace, kitchen, and living room. A separate carriage house is perfect for honeymooners. It has a fireplace flanked by white wicker rockers, plus a kitchen. All rooms are smoke-free. Breakfast is included. Located close to McCarthy Beach State Park,

McNair's is a good base for both summer and winter outdoor activities. **P.O. Box 155, 7694 Hwy. 5, Side Lake, 55781; 218-254-5878.**

Hotels, Motels, and Inns

Villas at Giant's Ridge—$$$ to $$$$

Right across from Giant's Ridge ski slopes, the Villas (formerly the Laurentian Resort) is a comfy place to relax after a day of winter sports or golf. Most of the approximately 40 units have fireplaces and kitchens and some also have saunas and Jacuzzis. The units are recently built and the decor is muted but pleasant. An outdoor swimming pool and tennis court are on-site. Units range in size from one to four bedrooms. **Box 350, Biwabik, 55708; 800-843-7434 or 218-865-4155.**

Hibbing Park Hotel—$$$

Hibbing's largest hotel, now locally owned, has 122 units, including three suites. The comfortable, recently renovated hotel has a spacious pool/recreation area. **1402 E. Howard, Hibbing, 55746; 800-262-3481 or 218-262-3481.**

Super 8—$$$

This is a super Super 8, thanks to the owner, who decorated it like an antique-filled country inn; splurged on a wonderful spa area, including a sauna-in-a-barrel and a huge hot tub; and then planted flowers all around the motel. All this and the rooms are fine, too. There are 54 rooms, some with Jacuzzis. The motel offers several recreational and dining packages. In addition, there is a ski-wax room. The Eveleth Super 8 regularly garners "excellent" ratings by the Super 8 administration. **P.O. Box 555, Eveleth, 55734; 800-800-8000 or 218-744-1661.**

Camping

State Parks—$

McCarthy Beach State Park has 86 drive-in sites, 18 with electricity, as well as three walk-in sites. There is no camping at either Soudan Mine or Hill Annex Mine State Park. All state park campsites can be reserved by calling **The Connection, 800-246-CAMP or 612-922-9000.**

Superior National Forest—$

There are three developed campgrounds in the forest. The largest, **Whiteface Reservoir,** has 53 campsites, about half with electrical hookups. The others, **Cadotte Lake** and **Pfeiffer Lake,** have 27 and 16 sites, respectively. Only about one-fourth of the sites are reservable. For more information, contact the Laurentian District office, **318 Forestry Rd., Aurora, 55705; 218-229-8880.**

Where to Eat

The Range is full of nice little cafes, where visitors can eat well and not pay too much. **Helen's Diner, on Lake St. in Chisholm, 218-254-7444,** is recommended, in addition to the places described below.

Valentini's Supper Club—$$ to $$$

Valentini's started out as a 24-hour cafe packing lunches for miners who dropped off their empty lunch pails and then picked them up before their shift started. What went in the pails? "Whatever the special was," says Mike Valentini, the third generation of his family to run the cozy supper club. Valentini's, as the name implies, serves American–Italian fare, and pastas are one of the house specialties. Open Mon.–Thurs., 11:00 A.M.–2:00 P.M. and 5:00–9:00 P.M.; Fri., 11:00 A.M.–2:00 P.M. and 5:00–10:00 P.M.; Sat., 5:00–10:00 P.M. Takeout service is also available. **31 W. Lake St., Chisholm, 55719; 218-254-2607.**

DeDe's Rainy Lake Saloon and Deli—$ to $$$

Before the mines opened, lumber was king in Virginia and this bustling deli honors the days of tall timber with logging memorabilia. The burgers and sandwiches are top-notch, and steaks and seafood, plus some Mexican dishes, fill out the menu. Wild rice is a featured accompaniment with many of the entrees. Open Sun.–Thurs., 11:00 A.M.–9:00 P.M., and Fri.–Sat., 11:00 A.M.–10:00 P.M. **209 Chestnut Ave., Virginia, 55792; 218-741-6247.**

K and B Drive-Inn—$ to $$

Everybody knows the K and B, a checkerboard beacon of red and white along Hwy. 53 just outside Eveleth. The K and B has old-fashioned car-hop service and equally good, old-fashioned food. Besides the usual burgers, the drive-in has broasted chicken and pasties, and many a homesick Ranger stops in for a pasty or two. Open Memorial Day–Labor Day, daily, 10:30 A.M.–10:00 P.M.; rest of the year, daily, 10:30 A.M.–8:00 P.M. Located **1.5 miles south of Eveleth on Hwy. 53; 218-744-2772.**

Coffeehouses, Sweets, and Treats

Food, particularly ethnic or old-fashioned specialties, is taken seriously on the Iron Range. If you have a hankering for *potica,* the sweet, honey-and-walnut pastry that is a Range favorite, it's available at many places, including the **Italian Bakery, 205 First St. S., Virginia, 55792, 218-741-3464,** and at the **Sunrise Bakery, 1813 Third Ave. E., Hibbing, 55746, 218-263-3544.** Both also do a brisk mail-order business for "expatriate" Rangers. Candy lovers can spend hours making choices at **Canelake's,** which makes its own mouth-watering confections and has an old-fashioned soda fountain, too. A local favorite at Canelake's is the "hot air," sponge candy that melts as soon as it hits your mouth. **414 Chestnut St., Virginia, 55792; 218-741-1557.** In business since 1905, Canelake's also mails its handmade, hand-dipped candies.

Services

Although individual cities on the Iron Range have separate information offices, information on all Range communities can be obtained from the **Iron Trail Convention and Visitors Bureau, 403 N. First St., Virginia, 55792; 800-777-8497** or **218-749-8161. Website: www.irontrail.org.**

Chisholm Chamber of Commerce, 218-254-3600. Website: www.chisholmmn-chamber.com.

Hibbing Area Chamber of Commerce, 218-262-3895.

Virginia Chamber of Commerce, 218-741-2717.

North Shore: Duluth to Tofte

The North Shore of Lake Superior in Minnesota is a rocky inland coast stretching 151 miles north and east of Duluth to Canada. Although the mileage count begins in downtown Duluth, most Minnesotans think the North Shore begins on the far side of the Lester River, on Duluth's eastern edge. Ojibwe Indians, fur traders, and immigrant Scandinavian fishermen have lived and worked on the North Shore. However, it became a prime tourist destination only when Hwy. 61—the one Bob Dylan immortalized in the song of the same name—was developed in the 1920s.

The highway hugs the lakeshore at many points, providing sweeping views of the largest of the Great Lakes. Lake Superior is a treacherous body of water, and many ships have been wrecked during sudden storms, when high waves swamped the ships or threw them against the unforgiving cliffs that line the lower portion of the North Shore. One spot, near Gooseberry Falls State Park, is named Castle Danger because of its shipwreck history.

On the other side of the road, at varying distances, is a high ridge of land running the length of the shore. As visitors drive north out of Two Harbors into northern Lake and Cook Counties, the "mountains" that unfold are called the Sawtooth Mountains, formed by an ancient lava flow that surged out from beneath what is now Lake Superior. Before you near the heart of the Sawtooths, there is a towering precipice—Silver Creek Cliff— where vehicles drive through a recently constructed tunnel in the ancient rock. This ridge and adjacent hills enhance a climatic quirk known as "the lake effect," acting as a barrier to trap warmer air coming off the lake in winter and cooler air in the summer. The 10°F or so temperature differences may be marginal but locals make the most of the "lake effect," jocularly calling the North Shore "the Scandinavian Riviera." The ridge also means that there is usually much less snow on the shore than there is back just a mile or two into the hills. Rivers and creeks rush down to the lake, providing excellent fishing and cool wading on hot summer days. Villages of a couple hundred residents are scattered along the North Shore. Two Harbors, with a population of about 3,600, is the largest settlement between Duluth and Tofte. In addition to tourism—now important in winter as well as summer—logging is still an important factor in the economy of much of the area.

Because the North Shore covers so much territory, this book divides it into two sections, Duluth to Tofte and Lutsen to Grand Portage. The Superior Hiking Trail, which eventually will parallel the entire North Shore, is described in this section, Duluth to Tofte. The Gunflint Trail is included in the Lutsen-to-Grand Portage section, which also includes Grand Marais.

History

The Ojibwe Indians were in the area when the first Europeans—probably the French explorers and, later, founders of the Hudson's Bay Company, Pierre Radisson and Médard Chouart, Sieur des Groseilliers—passed through, in 1660. Later came traders seeking furs to bring back to Europe.

Lake Superior was the liquid highway for the Indians, voyageurs, and, later, Scandinavians who made their living catching the abundant herring, just as they did in the old countries. Until the highway was developed in the 1920s, transport on the lake by steamer was much easier than transport on land. The area remained largely Scandinavian—those were the first languages children here learned—until the early decades of the 20th century had passed. Silver Bay, developed for the taconite industry, is the newest town in the lower part of the North Shore.

In the past decade or so, the North Shore has seen increasing development, and some longtime residents and newcomers alike, as well as tourists who want to get away from it all, don't especially welcome these new developments.

Split Rock Lighthouse. Copyright © Minnesota Office of Tourism. Used by permission.

Festivals and Events

John Schroeder Days
fourth weekend in June
The town of Schroeder honors its forefather with a logging festival, including logging contests, minnow races for the kids, and other summertime festival events. **888-616-6784.**

Outdoor Activities

Birding
Tettegouche State Park is prime bird-watching territory, as its diverse habitats mean that more than 140 varieties of birds have been seen there. See Parks.

Boating

KAYAKING
Sea kayaking on Lake Superior is becoming a popular sport. Paralleling the shore is the Lake Superior Water Trail pilot project, a "trail" of ap-

proximately 20 miles from Gooseberry Falls State Park to Tettegouche State Park that is intended mostly for sea kayakers. Some campsites at Split Rock Lighthouse State Park have been set aside for kayakers; no fires are allowed and there are no reservations taken. The first stage of the pro-

Getting There
From Duluth, which is approximately 150 miles from Minneapolis and St. Paul, continue north on Hwy. 61. You'll soon have to make a choice between the fast way to Two Harbors—the expressway—or the scenic route; the division is well marked. Don't miss the scenic route unless you are in a real hurry to get even farther north. There is air service to Duluth and bus service along the shore.

posed Lake Superior Water Trail is now "open." A map of the route includes campsites and access points. Copies of the trail map, noting outstanding features including shipwrecks, are available from the Dept. of Natural Resources Information Center, **500 Lafayette Rd., St. Paul, 55155; 888-MINNDNR or 651-296-6157.**

Diving

Scuba diving is popular along the North Shore. Underwater caves, shipwrecks, and remains from logging operations are among the things that divers can explore in Lake Superior. On a calm day, along the long breakwater at Two Harbors, visitors can see bobbing orange flags indicating divers below. Call the Lake County Visitor Information Center, **800-554-2116 or 218-834-4005.**

Rentals and Tours

The *Grampa Woo* (see Boat Tours) does scuba trips as well as scenic cruises. Trips are scheduled by other individuals, including **Jack Pendergrass** of St. Paul, who offers scuba dive trips in Lake Superior to suit divers of all skill levels; **612-484-4244.**

Fishing

On spring days, there may be a crowd of salmon fishers trying their luck at the outlet of many of the North Shore's rivers. Trout—several kinds—are also the goal of the river anglers. In Gooseberry Falls State Park, there's excellent trout fishing on the Gooseberry River and along the lakeshore. In Temperance River State Park, both the Cross and the Temperance Rivers are designated trout streams. Chinook salmon and steelhead are also found in the area. The four lakes in the original portion of Tettegouche State Park harbor northerns and walleye, while there can be good fishing for salmon and trout in the river and also in Lake Superior. There are trout in the two small lakes in Palisade Valley in Tettegouche State Park. Bensen Lake in Crosby-Manitou State Park has brown, rainbow, and brook trout, plus "splake," a combination of brook and lake trout. For seasons and licenses information, contact the Area Fisheries Supervisor, **218-723-4785.**

Rentals and Tours

Charter boats offer fishing trips on Lake Superior. The catch may include king and coho salmon and lake trout. Check with the tourism centers for information (see Services).

Hiking

Gooseberry Falls State Park has 18 miles of hiking trails, most of them heavily forested. In Split Rock Lighthouse State Park, most of the action is along the shore, with many of the park's 12 miles of hiking trails and 6 miles of self-guided trails winding around the bays. Trails on the other side of Hwy. 61 connect to the Superior Hiking Trail. In Temperance River State Park there are 22 miles of hiking trails. There are 23 miles of hiking trails in Tettegouche State Park, with 2 miles of self-guided trails. See Parks.

Crosby-Manitou State Park

Not a park for Sun. strollers, Crosby-Manitou is a rugged 3,320 acres of wilderness that showcases the cascading Manitou River and its gorge. The views of Lake Superior from the hills are spectacular. This park is for those who like the challenge of 24 miles of steep hiking trails (only a short trail around Bensen Lake is a flat, easy trek) and the possibility of seeing moose, deer, bear, and maybe even wolves. The 21 campsites are pack-in only, and only carry-in watercraft are allowed on the lake. The entrance is 7 miles north of Finland on County Rd. 7. Direct questions to Tettegouche State Park, **5702 Hwy. 61 E., Silver Bay, 55614; 218-226-6365.**

North Shore State Trail

Primarily a snowmobile trail, the North Shore State Trail stretches 146 miles from Duluth to Grand Marais. Because of possible standing water on the trail in the southern half, hikers may prefer the 70-mile portion from Finland to Grand Marais (see the North Shore: Lutsen to Grand Portage chapter in this section).

Superior Hiking Trail

The long-planned Superior Hiking Trail is now 220 miles long, from Two Harbors to Canada, with two gaps in it. The trail connects to seven state parks along the North Shore, sometimes with short spur trails. The narrow highline trail—meant for hiking only—is very scenic, often with panoramic views of Lake Superior. There is abundant wildlife along the trail and the fall colors are spectacular. The designated National Recreation Trail has received high praise by *Backpacker* magazine, which calls it one of the country's best trails and one of the top 25 in the world. Plans are to continue the trail until it stretches unbroken for about 300 miles from Duluth to the Canadian border.

There are many access points, making it easy for casual hikers to walk the trail for an afternoon and then take a shuttle back to their cars. For those who want to spend a longer time on the trail, there are campsites every 5–8 miles. The **shuttle,** running on a schedule like a bus, operates Fri.–Sun. from Castle Danger to Judge C. R. Magney State Park; **218-834-5511.** Alternatively, a program called Lodge to Lodge gives hikers a way to hike along the trail and have transportation back to their lodge, or on to another lodge to where their luggage has already been transported. Several resorts participate in this program (see Resorts).

The Superior Hiking Trail Association conducts guided hikes during spring, summer, and fall. Association membership supports trail development, which is done by volunteers, and includes newsletters with suggested hikes and special events. Maps of various sections of the trail, a trail guidebook, T-shirts, and other items are for sale at the Superior Hiking Trail Association office and store, **P.O. Box 4, 731 Seventh Ave., Two Harbors, 55616; 218-834-2700.**

Skiing

CROSS-COUNTRY

Cross-country skiers are in hog heaven on the North Shore, which has more than 245 miles of trails. The state parks are notable for their groomed trails. In Gooseberry Falls State Park, there are 12 miles of cross-country ski trails. Split Rock Lighthouse State Park's 12 miles of hiking trails double as cross-country ski trails in winter. In Temperance River State Park there are 17 miles of cross-country ski trails. Tettegouche State Park

has 12 miles for snowmobilers, plus 15.5 miles of traditional cross-country ski trails and 4 miles of skate-ski trails. See Parks. There are many other trails, including those in Superior National Forest (194 miles of groomed trails), at Pincushion Mountain, and around the Gunflint Trail. Many visitors participate in a lodge-to-lodge ski package called Nordic Ski Venture, in which nearly 30 resorts have cooperated. Skiers can go from one resort to another—or even stay in a Mongolian-style yurt—and their luggage is transported from one resort to the next (see Resorts).

Snowmobiling

The 146-mile North Shore State Trail (see Hiking), a favorite with snowmobilers, winds through forests behind the ridge that runs along the shore from Duluth to Grand Marais. The trail has a natural surface and is mostly through remote, near-wilderness areas. There is parking at Lester River, Tofte, and Cascade River State Park. The trail connects with many others. The North Shore has hundreds of miles of groomed snowmobile trails. Gooseberry Falls State Park has 3 miles of snowmobile trails. In Temperance River State Park there are 7 miles of snowmobile trails. Superior National Forest has 266 miles of trails. See Parks. A map of northeast snowmobile trails is available from the Dept. of Natural Resources Information Center, **500 Lafayette Rd., St. Paul, 55155; 800-766-6000 or 651-296-6157.** Call the local tourism centers (see Services) for information on snow conditions.

Seeing and Doing

Museums and Historic Sites

North Shore Commercial Fishing Museum

Until the 1920s, when the highway up from Duluth was developed, the North Shore was a little Scandinavia—with Norwegians at Tofte, Swedes at Lutsen, etc. The immigrants settled on the shore and fished for herring. The fishermen got the nickname "herring chokers," because they grabbed the netted herring and squeezed them hard to push them through the net. The old-timers

Gooseberry Falls State Park. Photo courtesy of the Minnesota Department of Natural Resources.

are gone, but the museum—housed in twin, red-painted replicas of the old fish houses—preserves their culture in artifacts, photos, and oral histories. Among the items are a fishing boat, a net winder, and a scarred fish-cleaning table, a few scales still clinging to its surface. Stories told in the museum also make visitors aware of the battle between the fishermen and the unforgiving lake. Fee. Open June–Oct., daily, 9:00 A.M.–7:00 P.M.; remainder of the year, daily, 9:00 A.M.–5:00 P.M. The museum also houses the Lutsen-Tofte Visitor Information Center; located at the **intersection of Hwy. 61 and the Sawbill Trail, Tofte; 888-616-6784.**

Recommended Reading

The heyday of the commercial fishing industry on the North Shore is recalled charmingly in the late Ted Tofte's book, *Wonderland of the Herring Chokers—Tales from the Early Days of Commercial Fishing on the North Shore of Lake Superior,* published in 1982 by Blackwater Press. The book is for sale at the museum.

Split Rock Lighthouse

To protect ships from what some people thought was the most hazardous body of water in the world—Lake Superior—the U.S. Coast Guard erected the Split Rock lighthouse, in response to the terrible storm of 1905 that endangered 29 ships on Lake Superior, two of which went aground here near the lighthouse site. Perched on a 130-foot cliff, the lighthouse is one of the best-known sights in Minnesota. The lighthouse was staffed until 1969, when modern navigational aids rendered it obsolete. The 25-acre site, now administered by the Minnesota Historical Society, includes the lighthouse, the keeper's house and two other houses, and the fog signal building. All the buildings are being restored to a pre-1924 state, when the lighthouse was accessible only by water. Open mid-May–mid-Oct., daily, 9:00 A.M.–5:00 P.M.; interpretive center only is open mid-Oct.–Nov. 30 and Jan.–mid-May, Fri.–Sun., noon–4:00 P.M. (closed most holidays). Fee. Located 22 miles northeast of Two Harbors. **2010 Hwy. 61 E., Two Harbors, 55616; 218-226-6372.**

The Tugboat "Edna G." and Two Harbors Lighthouse

The brightly painted little tug *Edna G.* bobs in the water at Two Harbors, dwarfed by the nearby ore docks. The tug used to pull ships in and out of the harbor, but now the *Edna G.*, more than a century old, is retired and owned by the city of Two Harbors. Visitors are welcome aboard for tours. Fee. The tug is docked at the waterfront in Two Harbors, close to the historic depot. For more information, contact the Lake County Visitor Information Center (see Services). While you are in Two Harbors, drive around to the other side of the harbor, to a long cement breakwater and the Two Harbors Lighthouse, which also has tours. Fee. Contact the Lake County Visitor Information Center (see Services).

Parks

Gooseberry Falls State Park

By far the most popular state park, Gooseberry Falls draws nearly a million visitors annually, compared to half that for the next most visited parks—Fort Snelling and Itasca. Its recent renovation—including a marvelous new visitor center—should draw even more visitors. Near the sprawling wood and stone center is a short path leading to the Lower Falls of the Gooseberry River, actually a series of three falls. Sit on a rock and eat your lunch, listening to the rush of water and looking for the lava flows from long-gone volcanoes. On the other side of Hwy. 61 is the Upper Falls—the fourth falls—and 0.75 mile upriver from it are the fifth falls. The Superior Hiking Trail dips into the park here and follows the river from a spot near the Upper Falls to the fifth falls. Near the Upper Falls is the old visitor center, a wonderful relic of the CCC days. The stone-and-wood building is one of several built in the park during the CCC camp stint constructing the park's buildings in the 1930s. The park has 10 miles of mountain biking trails and year-round naturalist programs. A favorite family activity is looking for agates among the pebbles on the beach at the mouth of the river. It takes patience, but the agates are there. White-tailed deer winter in the park and there are nesting colonies of herring gulls on the lakeshore. The area is also a wayside rest; those who use it only as a rest stop need not buy a state park permit. Located 13 miles northeast of Two Harbors on Hwy. 61. **3206 Hwy. 61 E., Two Harbors, 55616; 218-834-3855.**

Split Rock Lighthouse State Park

Adjacent to one of the most familiar Minnesota landmarks—Split Rock Lighthouse—is the state park of the same name. In 1998 the park was expanded to include Gold Rock Point, an 81-acre parcel of cliff lands and a rock-and-cobblestone beach that provides access to the *Madeira,* one of the most famous of Lake Superior shipwrecks. The *Madeira,* now on the National Register of Historic Places, went down, along with five other ships in the area, in a terrible storm in 1905. This disaster prompted the building of the Split Rock Lighthouse. Many of the hiking trails along the shore provide visitors with a wonderful view of the old lighthouse. The deeply indented shoreline has many nicely private picnic spots. There are also 6 miles of trails for mountain bikes. The park's nontraditional campsites include a kayak-in site, cart-in sites, winter sites, and combined backpack and kayak sites. Bear are seen in the park and there is a beaver colony in the Split Rock River. Located 20 miles north of Two Harbors. **3755 Split Rock Lighthouse Rd., Two Harbors, 55616; 218-226-6377.**

Superior National Forest

One of Minnesota's two national forests, the Superior National Forest occupies a big chunk of the North Shore. In the two districts closest to the shore (the Tofte and Gunflint Ranger Districts), there are hiking trails, naturalist programs, and 266 miles of trails for mountain bikes. Berry picking is permit-

Superior Hiking Trail. Copyright © Minnesota Office of Tourism. Used by permission.

ted in the forest (late July–early Aug. is usually blueberry season) and many people prefer to use the forest campgrounds, which are often less crowded than the state parks. There are eight campgrounds in the districts and 79 backcountry campsites. In the fall, drivers can follow four self-guided tours to see the autumn colors. Detailed maps of the forest and information on campgrounds, hikes, etc., are available from the Tofte Ranger District, **P.O. Box 2157, Tofte, 55615; 218-663-7280.**

Temperance River State Park

The narrow Temperance River Gorge, with its deep potholes scoured into the lava by the swirling action of the sand- and gravel-laden water over millennia, is a fascinating sight. The Cauldron Trail, just 0.25 mile long, is a self-guided trail that interprets the geologic and other features. Note the CCC stonework along the trail. The park is one of the state's smaller parks, but the adjacent Cross River State Wayside is much larger and also offers good hiking, recreation, and fishing. Recently annexed to the park is the Carlton Peak Addition. The peak, the highest along the North Shore, is 927 feet above Lake Superior. The Superior Hiking Trail connects the main part of Temperance State Park with the peak. Campers flock to Temperance, as it has the state park campground closest to Lake Superior. Park staff say the campground is about 98 percent full in July–Aug. Visitors often ask how the park got its name. Long ago, in the days when demon rum was fought by the temperance movement, some guy with a sense of humor noted that the river—unlike most North Shore rivers—had no (sand)bar at its mouth and so he tabbed it the Temperance River. Located just north of Schroeder, on Hwy. 61. **Box 33, Schroeder, 55613; 218-663-7476.**

Tettegouche State Park

This is a park that has it all—rivers, lakes, waterfalls, a Lake Superior shoreline, hikes that give visitors a good workout over semimountainous Sawtooth terrain, and a historic logging camp. Casual visitors can eat lunch in secluded picnic sites near the visitor center or take a short hike to spectacular Shovel Point. Farther south from the entrance, off the highway, is Palisade Head,

with a short trail leading to a lookout point 200 feet above Lake Superior. For a more active workout, drive up to the trailhead on the other side of the highway, where trails lead to inland lakes, many beautiful lookout points, and the towering Upper Falls on the Baptism River. The steep and rocky Palisade Valley, which is crossed by the Superior Hiking Trail, was added to the park in 1992, doubling its size; it has several walk-in campsites. On the shore of Mic Mac Lake is the rustic Tettegouche Camp, a haven of four log cabins, built by businessmen early in the 19th century. The camp is accessible only on foot, skis, snowshoes, or mountain bikes. The cabins can be rented. There is a 1.5-mile mountain bike trail. A campground is on the Baptism River and there is a kayak-in campsite on Lake Superior. Located 4.5 miles northeast of Silver Bay. **5702 Hwy. 61 E., Silver Bay, 55614; 218-226-6365.**

Shopping

Antilla's

If it's Scandinavian, Antilla's probably sells it, including Norwegian sweaters, practical Swedish plastic rugs, and Finnish sauna equipment and accessories. In Antilla's two shops, a variety of handmade wooden items, such as window boxes and bird feeders, are also for sale. Outdoors, the grounds are ablaze with red, yellow, and orange tuberous begonia, some of them 20 years old, according to shop owner Berdie Antilla. Open mid-May–early Oct., daily, 9:00 A.M.–5:00 P.M. **884 Hwy. 61 E., Little Marais, 55614; 800-839-5884 or 218-226-4884.**

Tours

North Shore Scenic Railroad

This train runs between Duluth and Two Harbors. See Tours in Duluth chapter; **800-423-1273 or 218-722-1273.**

BOAT TOURS

Grampa Woo III

See the North Shore from the other side with an afternoon cruise on the *Grampa Woo*, named after Capt. Dana Kollars's late father-in-law. On the two-and-a-half-hour cruise, sights can include Split Rock Lighthouse, Palisade Head, and Silver Cliff. Drinks and snacks are sold onboard. The boat can also be hired for charter fishing and other types of scenic cruises. Kollars also accommodates scuba diving groups, tailoring the trip to their specifics. Cruises are June–Sept., Thurs.–Fri. (from Two Harbors) and Mon.–Wed. (Beaver Bay), at noon. **218-236-4100** (fishing trips and cruises) or **218-226-4043** (scuba trips). Website: **www.grampawoo.com.**

Where to Stay

Bed-and-Breakfasts

Emily's Inn—$$$

Emily's Inn is a comfortable and genteel space over the restaurant and deli of the same name in the little community of Knife River. The b-and-b quarters are wonderfully spacious and very relaxing and private. There are great views of the Knife River. It's the perfect place for large families or two couples traveling together, as there are three bedrooms and a sizable living room. Because the bath and living area are shared, the whole upstairs is rented out either to one party or small groups, not to two parties that do not know each other. In the morning, go downstairs for the plentiful breakfast and learn a little about Emily herself from her granddaughter, the owner. Open year-round. **Box 174, Knife River, 55609; 218-834-5922.**

Hotels, Motels, and Inns

Flood Bay Motel—$$ to $$$

Clean, neat, and convenient, the Flood Bay Motel is right across from a cobblestone beach that is great for agate hunting. It's on the Superior Hiking Trail and just an agate's throw from Betty's Pies (see Where to Eat). What more could you ask? The motel is smoke-free and has homey decorative touches that you won't find in chain motels. Open mid-May–mid-Oct. Located 1 mile northeast of Two Harbors. **511 Hwy. 61, Two Harbors, 55616; 218-834-4076.**

Resorts

Bluefin Bay—$$ to $$$$

Bluefin Bay, a collection of peak-roofed, blue-gray properties containing 133 rental units, was designed to remind visitors of the coastal fishing villages that early Tofte residents left behind in their native Norway. These modern versions are pretty upscale fish houses, that's for sure—many of the units have windows that make the most of the up-close view of Lake Superior, and some units have fireplaces and Jacuzzis. The units vary greatly in size and amenities, but all guests can use the resort's recreational facilities, including saunas, indoor and outdoor pools, and a workout room. There are three restaurants, open to the public as well. **Bluefin Bay on Lake Superior, Tofte, 55615; 800-258-3346.**

Cobblestone Cabins—$$ to $$$

This is the North Shore—neat and functional cabins and a million-dollar view of Lake Superior. All that, and Jan and Kathy Horak's candlelit, wood-fired sauna, perched on the edge of the lake. Sluice yourself off between sauna sessions with buckets of cold water or go jump in the lake; it's good for ya. The resort began in 1926 and Jan Horak purchased it about 25 years ago. The Horaks have eight cabins with baths and kitchens, sleeping from two to 12 people; each has a fire ring for campfires. In winter, cabins are heated with wood-burning stoves, but only one cabin has running water. Winter visitors in the other cabins use an outhouse, bathe in the sauna, and get their water from five-gallon jugs. Cobblestone makes a great base for exploring the hundreds of miles of cross-country ski trails on the North Shore and inland. Cobblestone has two seasons: mid-May–Oct. and day after Christmas–Mar. **6660 W. Hwy. 61, Tofte, 55615; 218-663-7957.**

Camping

Lamb's Campgrounds and Cabins—$

A North Shore institution, Lamb's has been hosting visitors since 1922. The complex of 100 campsites and 15 log cabins is a popular place, and it is exceptionally clean and well landscaped. Electric-

*Sunrise over Lake Superior as viewed from Palisade Head near Tettegouche State Park. Copyright ©
Minnesota Office of Tourism. Used by permission.*

ity and sewer hookups are available for campers. Some of the campsites are on Lake Superior and the cabins, which have classic round-log interiors, are on the lake or the Cross River. The resort has showers and a sauna. Open May–late Oct. **P.O. Box 415, Schroeder, 55613; 218-663-7292.**

State Parks—$

Crosby-Manitou has 21 pack-in campsites; several are close to the parking lot on Bensen Lake, and the others are on the shore of the Manitou River. **Gooseberry Falls** has 70 drive-in campsites, none with electricity, and one kayak-in campsite. **Split Rock Lighthouse State Park** has five winter campsites, 20 cart-in sites, a kayak-in site, and four backpack or combined backpack/kayak sites. The popular **Temperance River** has 55 lakeshore drive-in campsites, 15 with electricity, and three cart-in sites. At **Tettegouche** the main campground, which is near the Baptism River, has 28 drive-in sites. There are also 13 cart-in and six walk-in sites in the park, plus one kayak-in site on Lake Superior. The four cabins of Tettegouche Camp, accessible on foot, bike, skis, or snowshoes, can also be rented. All state park campsites, with the exception of the kayak-in sites, which are first-come, first-served, can be reserved by calling **The Connection, 800-246-CAMP** or **612-922-9000.**

Superior National Forest—free or $

The national forest has backcountry camping as well as less-primitive campgrounds; for information on camping in the Tofte Ranger District, contact that office at **P.O. Box 2159, Tofte, 55615; 218-663-7280.**

Where to Eat

Scenic Cafe—$$ to $$$

Once a drive-in, this "cool little cafe," as the owners Polly and Charlie Merhar describe it in their Website, offers sophisticated and innovative fare, all served in a north-woods atmosphere. The menu has several popular vegetarian items, such as the Tempeh Reuben. Dinner entrees vary; walleye crusted with almonds in a sauce of shallots and blackberries is a good example of the Scenic's use of regional ingredients. Charlie Merhar says many customers come for the desserts, which always include pies such as raspberry rhubarb and chocolate pecan. The Scenic has great breakfasts, too. Open in summer, daily, 8:00 A.M.–9:00 P.M.; call for winter hours (reduced). Located 15 minutes north of Duluth, on the scenic route of Hwy. 61. **5461 North Shore Scenic Dr., Duluth, 55804; 218-525-6274.** Website: **www.sceniccafe.com.**

Rustic Inn—$ to $$$

Picture a little cafe on the North Shore of Lake Superior, and you know what the Rustic Inn is like. Built in 1930, the original part of the cafe has a log exterior and interior, and cheerful red-and-white-checked curtains. When highway work meant the cafe had to be moved three blocks, the owners also built an addition that more than doubled the size of the cafe. Crowded for the hearty breakfasts, the cafe also serves lunch and dinner. Specialties include pan- or deep-fried fresh herring from Lake Superior and homemade pies. Open in summer, daily, 8:00 A.M.–8:00 P.M.; call for winter hours. Located **2 miles south of Gooseberry Falls State Park on Hwy. 61; 218-834-2488.**

Betty's Pies—$ to $$

Betty's Pies is so famous that a schoolteacher in Two Harbors even wrote a musical about it; he called it, "I've Got My Eyes on Betty's Pies." For a while, most of Minnesota had its eyes on Betty's Pies, hoping that the little cafe, which opened in 1956, wouldn't disappear from the north-country scene. New owners took it over in 1998 and will be rebuilding farther back from the road in 1999. The old building will stay open until the new one is finished. The list of pies at the cafe is long, with a five-layer chocolate pie and blueberry pie among the top favorites. The new owners added pasties to the menu. There are a few outdoor tables. For many customers, a stop at Betty's is part of the North Shore experience. Open year-round, daily, 8:00 A.M.–8:00 P.M. **215 Hwy 61 E., Two Harbors, 55616; 218-834-3367.**

Emily's Deli—$ to $$

Local folks and tourists alike flock to Emily's for good home cooking in a relaxed atmosphere. House specialties include a smoked-trout salad, and a Fri.-night fish boil (from the second Fri. in Feb. to the third Fri. in Oct.). This is also a good place to order sandwiches to take out. It's a picturesque building, built in 1929 on the Knife River. The upstairs is rented out as a b-and-b (see Where to Stay). Open daily, Mon.–Thurs. and Sat.–Sun., 8:00 A.M.–4:00 P.M., and Fri., 8:00 A.M.–8:00 P.M. **Box 174, Knife River, 55609; 218-834-5922.**

Coffeehouses, Sweets, and Treats

Russ Kendall's Smoke House—$

Smoked-fish shops are scattered along the North Shore, but Russ Kendall's may be the oldest and best known. As you enter the small shop, the wonderfully smoky, fishy smell is so alluring that it is nearly impossible not to load up on smoked ciscoes and brown sugar trout and salmon. If you're lucky, Russ himself will help you, giving you samples to help you pick out your favorite. He started in the business as a boy, helping his dad sell smoked fish from the back of an REO Speedwagon. He opened the smokehouse in 1953. The shop also sells pop, cheese, pickles, and several kinds of crackers, for the makings of a wonderful picnic alongside Lake Superior. Open daily, 10:00 A.M.–6:00 P.M. Located **at Knife River, on the scenic portion of Hwy. 61; 218-834-5995.**

Services

Lake County Visitor Information Center is a wonderful combination: lots of tourism information and a relaxing rest stop as well. It's in the log cabin at the side of Hwy. 61, just north of Two Harbors. The staff is very helpful. Notice the hand-hewn totem pole on the grounds. Open mid-May–mid-Oct., Mon.–Sat., 9:00 A.M.–5:00 P.M.; Sun., 10:00 A.M–6:00 P.M.; in winter, Wed.–Sat., 9:00 A.M.–1:00 P.M. **800-554-2116** or **218-834-4005. Website: www.lakecnty.com.**

Lake Superior North Shore Association, at Lester River on the east side of Duluth, is a summer-only tourism information center. It's on the lake side of Hwy. 61 and has a few parking spaces in front. There is no phone.

Lutsen-Tofte Visitor Information Center, housed in the same building as the North Shore Commercial Fishing Museum (see Museums and Historic Sites), has very helpful staff for answering questions about the North Shore and providing information. Open June–approximately mid-Oct., daily, 9:00 A.M.–7:00 P.M.; rest of year, daily, 9:00 A.M.–5:00 P.M. Located at the **intersection of Hwy. 61 and the Sawbill Trail, Tofte; 888-616-6784** or **218-663-7804.**

North Shore: Lutsen to Grand Portage

The North Shore of Lake Superior in Minnesota stretches 151 miles north and eastward of Duluth to Canada. Opposite the lakeshore is a high ridge of land running the length of the shore. This ridge and adjacent hills are the closest thing to mountains Minnesota has.

Successive waves of people—Ojibwe Indians, fur traders, and immigrant Scandinavian fishermen—lived and worked on the North Shore and offshore on Isle Royale, which is part of Michigan, but culturally is part of the North Shore. In the 1920s Hwy. 61 was developed, and the North Shore became a prime tourist destination.

In addition to tourists, the North Shore has drawn permanent residents who want to get away from it all—retirees, artists and writers, and entrepreneurs anxious to cash in on the tourist business. During summer and fall the highway is crowded and it is almost impossible to find a room or camping spot on weekends without a reservation.

Along the North Shore are small towns. Grand Marais, with approximately 1,200 residents, is the largest settlement between Lutsen and Thunder Bay, Ontario. In addition to tourism—now important in winter as well as summer—logging is still an important factor in the economy of much of the area.

At Grand Marais, the Gunflint Trail begins. This federal forest road goes up over the ridge and into a wonderland of forests and lakes that are entry points for the Boundary Water Canoe Area Wilderness (see Ely chapter). Indians were the first to make the trail, followed by voyageurs, trappers, and miners. Now it draws tourists summer, fall, and winter. Although day-trippers come for cross-country skiing and hiking, many people stay at one of the Gunflint's resorts. Accommodations come in all types—from slick modern places to quintessential north-woods resorts to replicas of Mongolian yurts. The 55-mile road is paved and plowed in winter to make way for the school bus.

Because the North Shore covers so much territory, this book divides it into two sections, with the Gunflint Trail included in this chapter. The Superior Hiking Trail, which eventually will parallel the entire North Shore, is described in the North Shore: Duluth to Tofte chapter in this section.

History

The upper portion of the North Shore was on the voyageurs' route from Montreal to the Canadian Northwest. From Lake Superior they portaged the stretch along the Pigeon River to calmer waters farther west along what is called "the voyageurs highway." Grand Portage National

Monument is a reminder of the fur-trade heyday in the 18th and early 19th centuries, when the North West Company built its stockaded complex and the local Ojibwe were instrumental in carrying out the fur trade.

Until Hwy. 61 was developed in the 1920s, the area remained largely Scandinavian—with Norwegians at Tofte, Swedes at Lutsen, etc. The immigrants settled on the shore and fished for herring. Families spoke their native languages and had little contact with other cultures. Some fishermen—including the Nelsons at Lutsen—were the first to turn from netting herring to luring tourists.

Festivals and Events

Boreal Birding Festival
first weekend after Memorial Day
Birds—from warblers to hawks—are abundant along the Gunflint Trail, even if they are sometimes heard and not seen. The festival, new in 1998, is held during the nesting season when birds are very vocal. Events include field trips, seminars, and talks by birding experts. Call the Gunflint Trail Association, **800-338-6932.**

Fisherman's Picnic
first weekend in Aug.
The whole world seems to head to Grand Marais for the Fisherman's Picnic. There are many activities—including a parade, tennis tournament, loon-calling contest, fish toss, logging demonstrations and contests, and special events for children. Lots of people, however, show up for the traditional food—herring on a bun. The "Picnic" starts Thurs. and continues through Sun. It's sponsored by the Grand Marais Lions Club and held in downtown Grand Marais. Call Grand Marais Chamber of Commerce, **800-622-4014.**

Rendezvous Days and Pow Wow
second weekend in Aug.
These are two separate events—but with much in common—held on the same weekend at Grand Portage. Rendezvous Days, three days of re-created history of the fur-trade heyday, is held on

> ### Getting There
> Reach Lutsen from Duluth, which is approximately 150 miles from Minneapolis and St. Paul. From Lutsen, continue north on Hwy. 61. There is air service to Duluth and Thunder Bay, Ontario, and bus service along the shore.

the Grand Portage National Monument picnic grounds and also in the buildings enclosed within the stockade. There are costumed interpreters and activities that include blindfold canoe races, demonstrations of bread baking, and singing and dancing. Admission is free Sat., but there is an entry fee Fri. and Sun. Call Grand Portage Bay Travel Information Center, **218-475-2592.** Just up the road, near the Grand Portage Trading Post, are the Pow Wow Grounds, where the Grand Portage Band of Ojibwe sponsors the Pow Wow. Call the the Grand Portage Lodge and Casino, **800-543-1384.**

Outdoor Activities

Biking

MOUNTAIN BIKING
Mountain biking is an ever-growing sport on the North Shore, where the rugged terrain and areas of near-wilderness provide challenging conditions. At Lutsen, where there is downhill skiing in winter, mountain bikes rule at other times in their own Mountain Bike Park. Bikers can take the Gondola Skyride (see Tours) up to the base, rent a bike if they don't have one, and strike out on the park's 35 miles of trails over four mountains. Trails range from easy riding for beginners to those for experienced bikers, with the most challenging terrain including steep descents, exposed ledge rock, and wet areas. The Mountain Top Deli at the gondola summit has sandwiches, soups, beverages, and snacks. Serious bikers may want to rent a unit at Eagle Ridge at the Village Inn and Resort (see Where to Stay), which is right on the bike trails. Lodging and ride-pass pack-

Mountain bikers on a bridge overlooking Poplar River. Copyright © Minnesota Office of Tourism. Used by permission.

ages are available. The Mountain Bike Park is open June–mid-Oct., daily; May and late Oct., some weekends. From Hwy. 61, turn onto County Rd. 36, which leads to the parking lot at the gondola base. **218-663-7281.** Superior National Forest has several mountain bike trails. Maps of the areas are easy to read and contain comments on the individual trails. Contact the Tofte district ranger office, **218-663-7280,** or the Lutsen-Tofte Tourism Association (see Services) for maps.

Birding

There is plenty of bird life in Judge C. R. Magney State Park, with warblers nesting in summer and hawks migrating past the park in the fall (see Parks). See also Festivals and Events.

Boating

CANOEING

Boundary Waters Canoe Area Wilderness

The Gunflint Trail is one of two major entry areas for the Boundary Waters Canoe Area Wilder-

ness (BWCAW), a vast expanse of lakes, forest, and streams that attracts visitors from around the world. (Ely is the other major entry area.) BWCAW is part of the Superior National Forest. Permits are needed to camp in the BWCAW and also to make day trips into it while based at a resort or other accommodations (see Boating in the Ely chapter in this section; the BWCAW is described in greater detail there).

Rentals and Tours

There are many outfitters along the Gunflint Trail, at Tofte and Grand Marais. Among the outfitters is **Hungry Jack Outfitters,** run by Dave and Nancy Seaton, who are both experienced canoe guides. The Seatons—like most outfitters—do both full and partial outfitting, with either aluminum or Kevlar canoes. They make sure their clients are well prepared before they go, and map out routes suited to canoers of various levels of experience. The Seatons have bunk spaces for overnighting before and after BWCAW trips, and they also rent out two cabins to those who want a quiet vacation spot near the boundary waters. And don't forget the fish-kissing contest: give Dave and Nancy a picture of yourself kissing a fish you've caught and they'll put it on their real wall or their cyberwall. **318 S. Hungry Jack Rd., Grand Marais, 55604; 218-388-2275.** The Gunflint Trail Association has a list of outfitters; **Website: www.gunflint-trail.com.**

KAYAKING

Rentals and Tours

Cascade is one of several outfitters along the North Shore that rent equipment and also offer guided kayak trips. The two- to eight-day trips include jaunts to Isle Royale National Park (in Michigan) and along the Lake Superior Water Trail. **P.O. Box 141, Lutsen, 55612; 800-720-2809** or **218-387-2360. Website: cascade-kayaks@boreal.org.**

Golf

Superior National at Lutsen

The Poplar River winds through the spectacular 18-hole Superior National Golf Course, providing splendid scenery as well as an actual water hazard on several holes. The public course, one of the best regarded in Minnesota, opened in 1991. It is in Lutsen and lies between the Sawtooth Mountains and Lake Superior. Greens fees range from $21 to $43. Open May–Oct., dawn-dusk. **P.O. Box 117, Lutsen, 55612; 218-663-7195** (for tee-time reservations).

Hiking

In Cascade River State Park, a favorite though long hike is up to Lookout Mountain, which rises 600 feet above Lake Superior. Moose Mountain, on the other side of the river, is another popular hiking goal. There are 18 miles of hiking trails in the park. In Judge C. R. Magney State Park, there are 9 miles of hiking trails. See Parks.

Superior National Forest

In addition to all the hiking trails in the state parks, the Superior National Forest has many popular hikes, particularly in the Gunflint Trail area. **Eagle Mountain,** the highest point in Minnesota at 2,301 feet, gives wonderful views of the Superior National Forest and the Boundary Waters Canoe Area Wilderness. There is a 3.5-mile hiking trail to the summit, but be warned—the trail is steep and rocky. To reach the trailhead, go

north 3 miles from Grand Marais on the Gunflint Trail, west 6 miles on County Rd. 8, north 4 miles on County Rd. 27, west on Forest Rd. 170, and then proceed 5 miles to the trailhead. **Honeymoon Bluff,** overlooking Hungry Jack Lake, is a great place from which to watch the sunset. The 0.75-mile trail is short but very steep, and children should be well supervised. From Grand Marais, go 27 miles north on the Gunflint Trail, then east 3.5 miles to the parking area. The Gunflint Ranger District has maps of the hikes. **P.O. Box 790, Grand Marais, 55604; 218-387-1750.**

Skiing

CROSS-COUNTRY

The North Shore has a wealth of cross-country ski trails and businesses that cater to skiers. In Cascade River State Park, numerous cross-country skiers come for the 17 miles of trails, ranging from the easy lakeside trails to the nearly mountainous trails in the vicinity of Lookout and Moose Mountains. In Judge C. R. Magney State Park, there are 5 miles of trails for cross-country skiers. See Parks. The North Shore Mountains trails cover more than 120 miles and connect to many other trails in the area. The Gunflint Trail ski trails include the excellent Pincushion Mountain trails

Island off the Lake Superior shoreline. Photo courtesy of the Minnesota Department of Natural Resources: Andrew Von Bank.

just outside of Grand Marais and trails that extend all the way to the Gunflint Lodge. The lodge-to-lodge program, which involves many resorts and other lodging establishments on the North Shore and the Gunflint Trail, is an innovative way to ski and visit different lodgings, without the hassle of returning to retrieve your baggage at the end of the day. For information, call **800-322-8327.** Trail maps and reports on ski conditions are available from tourism centers (see Services).

DOWNHILL

Lutsen Mountains

This is as close to western skiing as you're gonna get in the Midwest. The four mountains that comprise the Lutsen ski area have a total of more than 50 runs. Moose Mountain, with a vertical rise of 800 feet, is the tallest of the four and also tops all others in the Midwest. Its runs are designated for intermediate and advanced skiers, and there is a new section designated for extreme skiers. Mystery and Eagle Mountains each have a 650-foot vertical rise and both have runs for skiers of all skill levels. Ullr Mountain is the baby of the group, with a vertical rise of 350 feet; that's where the beginner area is. There is also a snowboard park. Lutsen has a variety of lifts, including a gondola and double chair lifts. The ski area also includes 18 miles of cross-country ski trails, rentals, ski school, lodging, and restaurants. Active visitors enjoy the twisting alpine slide at Lutsen, accessible by a chair-lift ride to the top of Eagle Mountain. Lutsen is open mid-Nov.–early May. From Hwy. 61, turn onto County Rd. 36, which leads to the parking lot at the gondola base. **467 Ski Hill Rd., Box 129, Lutsen, 55612; 218-663-7281** or (for snow report) **800-260-SNOW.**

Snowmobiling

The 146-mile North Shore State Trail, a favorite with snowmobilers, winds through forests behind the ridge that runs along the shore from Duluth to Grand Marais. There are also snowmobile trails connecting with towns and resorts along the shore and Gunflint Trail. Contact tourism centers (see Services) for maps and also for reports on snow conditions.

Swimming

Lake Superior is too cold for swimming, so aside from inland lakes and the pools at resorts and motels, the place to go for a swim is the Grand Marais municipal indoor pool complex. In addition to the pool and diving board, you'll find a whirlpool, sauna, and wading pool. Open year-round. Fee. Located **on the harbor in Grand Marais; 218-387-1712.**

Seeing and Doing

Art Galleries and Museums

Johnson's Heritage Post and Gallery

Local artists—past and present—are represented in this gallery and museum. Open late spring–fall, daily, 10:30 A.M.–5:00 P.M.; Nov.–Apr., Fri.–Sun., noon–4:00 P.M. Free. **P.O. Box 35, 115 W. Wisconsin St., Grand Marais, 55604; 218-387-2314.**

Kah-Nee-Tah Gallery

Local and regional artists are featured in the gallery, a well-lighted, spacious place between Lutsen and Grand Marais. The excellent-quality works include paintings, sculpture, pottery, forged bronze and cast metal, baskets, dream catchers, and photography. Visitors are welcome, and all the art is for sale. Open in summer, daily, 10:00 A.M.–5:00 P.M.; in winter, daily, 10:00 A.M.–4:00 P.M. Gallery owners Jeanne Schlosser and Suellen Kruse also rent three cozy cabins, all with cobblestone fireplaces, decks, and views of the lake. Each cabin has a variety of books, and, if you leave before you finish a book, you are welcome to take it along! **4210 W. Hwy. 61, Lutsen, 55612; 800-216-2585** or **218-387-2585.**

Sivertson Gallery

The Sivertson family of Isle Royale was an old North Shore fishing family; now they're well known as a family of artists. Howard Sivertson's idyllic paintings depict a vanished life and chronicle North Shore history; his wife and daughters are also artists. Their work and that of other artists who capture the spirit of the north country—

including Inuit artists—are represented in the Sivertson Gallery (there are other Sivertson Galleries in Duluth and Bayfield, Wisconsin). Open in summer, daily, 9:00 A.M.–9:00 P.M.; call for winter hours. **12 Wisconsin St., Grand Marais, 55604; 888-880-4369 or 218-387-2491.**

Recommended Reading

Howard Sivertson's *Once Upon an Isle* (Mount Horeb, Wis.: Wisconsin Folk Museum, 1992) and *Tales of the Old North Shore* (Duluth: Lake Superior Port Cities, 1996) provide an enchanting glimpse of a vanished way of life on the North Shore.

Museums and Historic Sites

Cook County Historical Society Museum

The old lighthouse keeper's residence, built in 1896 and on the National Register of Historic Places, is home to thousands of artifacts connected with the history of Grand Marais and the surrounding Cook County. Open May–Oct., daily, 10:00 A.M.–4:00 P.M. Fee. **4 S. Broadway, Box 592, Grand Marais, 55604; 218-387-2883.**

Grand Portage National Monument

At the mouth of the Pigeon River is the Grand Portage, the "Great Carrying Place," of the American Indians and later the voyageurs. The Pigeon was not navigable near its end and canoes had to be portaged. At the start of the portage, inside a high wooden stockade, was the Great Lakes headquarters of the North West Company, a fur-trade establishment that was once the most profitable of the Great Lakes fur traders. The complex thrived—with the help of many of the local Ojibwe—until 1803, when it was abandoned because the company relocated to Canada. When the explorer and map maker David Thompson saw the site 20 years later, only clover-covered foundations remained. The buildings and the stockade were restored after the Grand Portage Band of Chippewa (Ojibwe) donated the site to the federal government in 1958. It was later declared a national monument, one of two in Minnesota.

The buildings within the stockade include an impressive great hall, a kitchen, a fur storage warehouse, and a lookout tower. An Ojibwe village is located on the grounds. The restored splendor of the Great Hall reflects the company's prosperity—the china and glassware on the long tables set for 1797 festivities are elegant, not what you would expect to see on the edge of the frontier. Near the Great Hall is a wonderful historic garden, tended by Margaret Plummer-Steen, a member of the Grand Portage Band of Ojibwe, who chats with visitors about the historic garden and explains the tradition of the "three sisters"—cornstalks twined with squash and beans—used by the Ojibwe as companion plants for centuries. The National Monument really comes alive during the annual Rendezvous Days (see Festivals and Events), when there are many costumed interpreters, but it is a wonderful place at any time. There are educational videos, walking tours, and interpretive programs. Open mid-May–mid-Oct., daily, 9:00 A.M.–5:00 P.M. Fee. Located on the waterfront in Grand Portage, but the superintendent's office is in Grand Marais, **P.O. Box 668, Grand Marais, 55604; 218-387-2788.**

Other Sights

Grand Marais has gradually become a magnet for both visual artists and writers. This is reflected in a disproportionate number of Grand Marais establishments devoted to teaching and exhibition (in museums and/or galleries) of these arts. The new Arrowhead Center for the Arts, which opened in 1998, is the newest example of community support of the arts. The city even has called a downtown peninsula "artist's point," as it is a favorite spot for artists to sketch and paint.

Arrowhead Center for the Arts

Housed in an addition to the local high school, the center provides state-of-the-art space for the Grand Marais Playhouse and also more studio and administrative space for the Grand Marais Art Colony. The playhouse, which began in 1971, now presents community theater year-round, instead of just during the summer. The art colony, which is more than 50 years old, offers summer weeklong classes in the visual arts and writing in two venues; in winter, dance companies use the space. The art colony classes, while open to all, are aimed at emerging artists who have some experience. Established artists teach "mentored" courses. The colony, which is not residential, also offers intergenerational classes. The Arrowhead Center for the Arts is also the performance site for the North Shore Music Association concerts and events. Fee. Open year-round. **P.O. Box 626, Grand Marais, 55604; 800-385-9585 or 218-387-1284.**

North House Folk School

Based on his own experience studying at a traditional folk school in Norway, Mark Hansen decided to start a school that would celebrate and teach the folk ways of all cultures. Courses run from half a day to several weeks, and vary from making a birch-bark canoe to Norwegian rosemaling (a type of floral painting) to beginning blacksmithing. The school is in a waterfront building, but attendees make their own arrangements for accommodations. The school is codirected by Hansen and Tom Healy. **P.O. Box 759, Grand Marais, 55604; 218-387-9762.**

Parks

Cascade River State Park

The Cascade River lives up to its name, careening down 900 feet in the last 3 miles of its journey to Lake Superior. Visitors get a good look at the river and its two falls on the portion of the Superior Hiking Trail that parallels the river. Both of the falls are not far from the trailhead. The river gorge is lush and beautiful, with moss, ferns, and wildflowers, such as dainty pink twinflowers, and shady spots providing a cool respite on hot days. Located 9 miles southwest of Grand Marais on Hwy. 61. **3481 Hwy. 61 W., Lutsen, 55612; 218-387-1543.**

Grand Portage State Park

The Ojibwe called the portage over the tallest falls in Minnesota (on the Pigeon River) Git-che-O-ni-ga-ming and the French named it Grand Portage, but both mean the same—"the long carrying place." Come to the park not only to see the falls, but—more importantly—to learn about the traditional Ojibwe (Chippewa) culture. Park staff, all of American Indian ancestry, teach visitors the old ways. "We want to show how the

Ojibwe lived in precontact days," says a park staff member, adding that the trails in the area, including the 9-mile "Grand Portage" used by the voyageurs, were in existence long before the fur trade began. The park is not owned by the state, as the land is leased from the Bureau of Indian Affairs, which holds it in trust for the Grand Portage Band of Chippewa (Ojibwe). It was established in 1989 and opened in 1994, through the joint efforts of the state and the Grand Portage Band. Naturalist activities include demonstrating how the Indians used the maple sap and classes in making traditional snowshoes. The 0.5-mile trail to the High Falls, which lives up to its name at 120 feet, is easy walking, and one of the three overlooks is handicapped-accessible. Middle Falls can be reached by a 3.5-mile trail, taking hikers over ridges and through dense forest. The High Falls is the culmination of 20 miles of waterfalls and rushing water on the Pigeon River, making it impassable and thus making a long portage necessary. There are picnic tables near the visitor center, but the small (300-acre) park has no camping facilities. Located at the eastern tip of Minnesota, 7 miles northeast of the village of Grand Portage **on Hwy. 61 W., Grand Portage, 55605; 218-475-2360.**

Isle Royale National Park

Isle Royale National Park, which has a resident wolf pack and moose, is an offshore nature paradise so well preserved that it has been declared an International Biosphere Reserve by the United Nations. The park, an island that is 45 miles long and only 9 miles wide, is in the midst of an archipelago of some 400 islands in Lake Superior. Although the island is much closer to Minnesota than Michigan, it is actually part of Michigan. However, the ferry from Minnesota is a much shorter trip than the Michigan ferry, and many tourists visit the park via Minnesota; the park seems to "belong" to the North Shore. Transportation to the island is by private boat or two boats that depart from Grand Portage. The *Wenonah* makes daily trips between Grand Portage and Windigo, on the island's near side, where passengers can get off to camp or stay on board for the return journey. The other boat, the *Voyageur II*, is both a passenger and mail boat that makes a trip around the island, overnighting at Rock Harbor. Reservations are necessary for the *Voyageur II,* and advisable for the *Wenonah. Voyageur II* runs May–Oct., several days a week, and *Wenonah* runs mid-June–mid-Sept., daily; both boats leave Grand Portage at 9:30 A.M. The mailing address is **1507 N. First. St., Superior, WI 54880; 715-392-2100** (reservations). The park has no roads, but 165 miles of hiking trails crisscross the island, connecting the 36 campgrounds. For information, contact park headquarters, **800 E. Lakeshore Dr., Houghton, MI 49931; 906-482-0984.** Website: www.nps.gov/isro/.

Judge C. R. Magney State Park

Is it magic or is it old Ma Nature? The Brule River, which rushes through C. R. Magney State Park, splits in two around a jutting rock. Half of the water drops down into a pool below; the other half is swallowed up in a huge pothole called the Devil's Kettle, where, according to local storytellers, it disappears forever. The trail up to the Devil's Kettle is 1.25 miles. There are picnic tables along the river. Before reaching the Kettle, the trail passes Upper Falls. Spring- and summertime visitors are enchanted by the wildflowers on display, including the tiny pink twinflower, wood anemone, marsh marigold, and moccasin flower. Named for the late Judge C. R. Magney, a Minnesota Supreme Court justice who was instrumental in establishing many of the North Shore state parks, the park is quieter than most of the other state parks farther south, in part because it has only 31 campsites, none with hookups. Located 14 miles northeast of Grand Marais on Hwy. 61. **4051 Hwy. 61 E., Grand Marais, 55604; 218-387-3039.**

Kadunce River

The Kadunce gorge is steep, with the Superior Hiking Trail running along it, but as Kadunce River empties into the lake, it calms down. There are picnic tables next to it and the cobblestone beach is a great place to pick up rocks, look for agates, and gaze out at the lake. Located south of Hovland on Hwy. 61. There is no on-site phone. In summer it is administered by Judge C. R. Magney State Park, **218-387-3039.**

Superior National Forest

The Superior National Forest occupies a big chunk of the North Shore. In the two districts closest to the shore (the Tofte and Gunflint Ranger Districts), there is a wide variety of recreational possibilities, including canoeing in the Boundary Waters Canoe Area Wilderness, which is part of the forest. (See the North Shore: Duluth to Tofte chapter in this section.) Detailed maps of the forest and information on campgrounds, hikes, etc., are available from the Gunflint district office, **P.O. Box 790, Grand Marais, 55604; 218-387-1750.** Website: www.gis.-umn.edu/snf.

Tours

AERIAL TOURS

The 2-mile Gondola Skyride whisks visitors up through the Poplar River Valley to the summit of Moose Mountain, 1,000 feet above Lake Superior. There is a deli at the mountaintop. Hiking and mountain bike trails start at the summit. From the ridgelines, you can see up to 100 miles over the lake and the forest. Open June–mid-Oct., daily; May and Oct., some weekends. From Hwy. 61, turn onto County Rd. 36, which leads to the parking lot. **218-663-7281.**

DOGSLED TOURS

Dogsledding goes back a long way on the North Shore. The best-known musher was John Beargrease, who delivered the mail along the Gunflint Trail and North Shore decades ago. Today, a dogsled race called the John Beargrease commemorates his "mail must go through" attitude (see Festivals and Events in the North Shore: Duluth to Tofte chapter in this section). For those who would like to try dogsledding, there are several outfitters that offer trips. Ted and Barbara Young, who have been Gunflint Trail residents for more than 20 years, offer many different adventure tours, including dogsled driving trips that vary in length from a day to much longer treks. The Youngs, who also arrange hiking, lodge-to-lodge, cross-country ski, snowshoe, and snowmobile trips, have built three Mongolian-style, canvas-covered yurts and also a secluded cabin to serve as lodging for visitors. The Youngs' company is **Boundary Country Trekking, 7925 Gunflint Trail, Grand Marais, 55604; 800-322-8327 or 218-388-4487.** The **Gunflint Lodge** also has dogsled driving lessons (see Resorts). Or check the **Gunflint Trail Association; Website: www.gunflint-trail.com.**

Wagering

Grand Portage Lodge and Casino

Right on Lake Superior, the casino offers blackjack, bingo, video slots, and other games of chance and has a 100-room lodge with rooms that overlook the lake or forest. The restaurant also has a view of the lake. There is a small campground with full hookups, plus an indoor pool and sauna. Special entertainment events have included a Bayou Boogie festival of Cajun music and food, and a country music festival. Open 24 hours. **P.O. Box 233, Grand Portage, 55605; 800-543-1384 or 218-475-2401.**

Where to Stay on the North Shore

Although lodging seems plentiful on the North Shore, especially in Grand Marais—which has many motels and cabins, plus the refurbished East Bay Hotel—rooms fill up fast on summer weekends and when there are special events. Check the list of Grand Marais lodgings on the **Website: www.grandmarais.com.**

Bed-and-Breakfasts

Dream Catcher Bed-and-Breakfast—$$$

Sue and Jack McDonnell ran an outfitting business on the Gunflint Trail until a few years ago, when they built their dream house and named it after a traditional Ojibwe custom. Dream catchers are fashioned of circles of ash wood laced with various materials to make a "web" and hung over the beds of children. It is said that the dream catcher captures the bad dreams of children and lets the good dreams through. Although dream catchers abound in the house, it's hard to imagine that guests would ever have bad dreams here. The three rooms are a comfortable mix of the old and new, and all have private baths. In the rooms are works by well-known local artists. The common areas are wonderfully designed: the dining room has a view of Lake Superior and the forest on three sides, and the large porch is perfect for summer evenings. A sauna and the fireplace in the living room help guests warm up after winter activities. The McDonnells are very active in their community and extremely knowledgeable about local recreational opportunities and history. Located about 5 miles south of Grand Marais on County Rd. 7. **2614 County Rd. 7, Grand Marais, 55604; 800-682-3119 or 218-387-2876. Website: www.dreamcatcherbb.com.**

Resorts

Thomsonite Beach Resort—$$$ to $$$$

Thomsonite is a gemstone found worldwide that is formed by crystallization of volcanic magma bubbles. The particular type of thomsonite with beautiful round "eyes," however, is found only on the North Shore. Former owner and expert thomsonite jewelry maker Tania Feigal sold the resort to Matt and Vicki Geretschlaeger early in 1998. They have done some remodeling and bought a collection of thomsonite gems and jewelry dating to 1942, which is on display at the resort. In addition, a supply of thomsonsite and jewelry made from it are for sale. The resort's 10 motel units, apartments, and guest houses, faced with hand-hewn log siding, are exceptionally well constructed and furnished; no flimsy walls or cut-rate curtains here. The furniture is custom-made. Some of the units have full kitchens. Three deluxe units have fireplaces, many of the units have porches or balconies, and one has a loft. In front of the resort is a nice lawn for relaxing and watching the waves on the lake. The resort prohibits smoking and pets. **2920 W. Hwy. 61, Lutsen, 55612; 888-387-1532 or 218-387-1532.**

Village Inn and Resort—$$$ to $$$$

This complex of 28 lodge rooms furnished in north-country style, and approximately 100 luxury condominiums and townhouses, is close to all of Lutsen's recreational facilities—skiing, hiking, mountain biking, golfing, and zipping down the alpine slide (see Downhill Skiing). At the day's end, relax in the swimming pools, whirlpools, and saunas. The two-story stone fireplace in the lobby/restaurant area is spectacular. **371 Ski Hill Rd., Lutsen, 55612; 800-642-6036 or 218-663-7241. Website: www.villageinnresort.com.**

Cascade Lodge—$$ to $$$$

The perfect base from which to ski on cross-country trails or explore the state parks along the North Shore, Cascade has 10 cabins, six of them made of logs, as well as 12 lodge rooms, a motel, and a three-bedroom house. Some of the units have whirlpool baths and fireplaces. It's right by the side of Hwy. 61 and is bordered on three sides by Cascade River State Park. The lodge restaurant is popular with guests and popular as a stopping place for those driving by. Open year-round. **3719 W. Hwy. 61, Lutsen, 55612; 800-322-9543 or 218-387-1112. Website: www.cascadelodgemn.com.**

Lutsen Resort—$$ to $$$$

This is the grand old man of Minnesota resorts. A Swedish immigrant fishing family named Nelson started taking in guests in the late 1800s. The hand-carved timber lodge, designed with Scandinavia in mind and built in 1952, has massive stone fireplaces and hand-hewed beams in both the lobby and the dining room. It is the North Shore dream come to life. The 32 lodge rooms are comfortable but not luxurious, which is somehow fitting. The resort has added Sea Villa townhomes, log cabins, and the 13-room Cliff House in addition to the lodge, for a total of 104 units. Amenities include an indoor pool, whirlpool, and sauna. Be sure to walk across the carved wooden bridge—surely one of the most romantic spots in the state. **5700 W. Hwy. 61, Lutsen, 55612; 800-258-8736 or 218-663-7212. Website: www.lutsenresort.com.**

Solbakken Resort—$$ to $$$$

Staying at Solbakken is about as close to Norway as you can get without crossing the Atlantic. Cabins perch on the rocky shore of Lake Superior, lodge rooms bear Norwegian names, and the wonderful common room—with its huge stone fireplace—is decorated with beautifully painted rosemaling in the Rogaland style, a type of floral painting common in Norway in past centuries. The log lodge was the old Sawbill Lodge, which was transported 35 miles down the Sawbill Trail to its present site. The six cabins are cozy and private. The resort also has six motel units, three lodge suites, and three homes with two or three bedrooms. The lounge has plenty of games and books for guests to peruse. Also, there is a combination bookstore and gift shop as well as a cross-country ski shop, including ski rentals. **4874 W. Hwy. 61, Lutsen, 55612; 800-435-3950 or 218-663-7566.**

Naniboujou Lodge and Restaurant—$$$

Even if you don't spend a night or have a meal at Naniboujou, you *must* stop to see it. The resort was built in the 1920s as a private club—with Babe Ruth, Jack Dempsey, and Ring Lardner among the charter members—but the club failed during the stock market crash and the lodge had a succession of owners afterward. Now on the National Register of Historic Places, the lodge has been restored to its heyday. In the large (30-by-80-foot) great hall, now used as a dining room, is Minnesota's largest native stone fireplace, weighing in at 200 tons. But it is the glowing and colorful geometric Cree Indian design painted on the ceiling and walls of the hall that immediately catches the visitor's eye. The 24 lodge rooms have been carefully restored, while modern conveniences have been added. Note, however, that there are no telephones or televisions in the rooms. That's historically correct, but also aids in the "away from it all" feel. Five of the rooms have wood-burning fireplaces. The restaurant has imaginative cuisine; no liquor is served and there is no smoking anywhere in the lodge. The restaurant is open daily, for afternoon tea and dinner; Mon.–Sat., for breakfast and lunch; and Sun., for brunch. The lodge is open mid-May–mid-Oct., daily; late Dec.–mid-Mar., Sat.–Sun. **20 Naniboujou Trail, Grand Marais, 55604; 218-387-2688. Website: www.naniboujou.com.**

Where to Stay on the Gunflint Trail

Bed-and-Breakfasts

Pincushion Bed-and-Breakfast—$$$ to $$$$

This comfortable and relaxing bed-and-breakfast was designed and built for cross-country skiers. That was back in 1986, when the cross-country craze was just gathering steam. It's a perfect setup: the four rooms decorated in a cozy country style have wood-paneled walls, private baths, and a signature pincushion on the bedside tables. The common area, where the hearty breakfasts are served, is beamed and has a fireplace. Guests can use the sauna. Skis and bikes can be rented in the ski-out shop downstairs, and the wonderful Pincushion Mountain ski trails are right outside. No smoking or snowmobiles. Open year-round. Located on the ridgeline of the Sawtooth Mountains. **968 Gunflint Trail, Grand Marais, 55604; 800-542-1226 or 218-387-1276.**

Resorts

Bearskin Lodge—$$$$

The sumptuous cabins at Bearskin—a resort since 1925—make guests want to move in for good. The log construction is meticulous and the finishing touches are just right: skylights in some cabins, braided rugs, handmade quilts, and screened porches for enjoying summer evenings without those pesky mosquitoes. The 11 cabins range in size from one to three bedrooms and they are spaced around the undulating shore of East Bearskin Lake. In addition, there are four two-story apartment suites in the elegantly rustic main lodge, with its handsome granite fireplace. The lower level of the lodge includes a sauna and a resting place for cross-country skiers who are passing through on the 34 miles of trails in the area. There is a children's program, with plenty of activities. Dinner, with hearty yet sophisticated fare, is available by reservation only. **124 E. Bearskin Rd., Grand Marais, 55604; 800-338-4170 or 218-388-2292. Website: www.bearskin.com.**

Gunflint Lodge—$$$$

For some visitors, the Gunflint Lodge is synony-mous with the Gunflint Trail, and the Kerfoot family members who own the lodge bear one of the best-known names in Northeast Minnesota. Justine Kerfoot, the family matriarch, came to the Gunflint more than 70 years ago. She turned 90 a couple of years ago, but wrote a newspaper column until 1998, and her books about life in the north woods make for fascinating reading. Her son Bruce and daughter-in-law Sue are the second generation to run the lodge, and the third generation is also involved. The lodge, paneled with wood that glows golden in the light from the stone fireplace, is the heart of the resort. Look around at the carved birds, the old photos, and other relics of bygone days, try a meal in the resort's renowned kitchen, and be sure to buy one of Justine's books in the well-stocked book corner. The 25 cabins beside Gunflint Lake range from one to four bedrooms. All have fireplaces in the living rooms, but not all have kitchens. Most cabins have whirlpool baths indoors and a few have large outdoor whirlpools. The resort has an ambitious program of activities, including those led by an on-staff naturalist, and offers several special-interest weekends, including weekends for women only. **143 S. Gunflint Lake, Grand Marais, 55604; 800-328-3325 or 218-388-2294. Website: www.gunflint.com**

Recommended Reading

Two books by Justine Kerfoot, *Gunflint: Reflections on the Trail* (Duluth: Pfeifer-Hamilton, 1991) and *Woman of the Boundary Waters* (Grand Marais: Women's Times Press, 1986), give a wonderful account of one woman's life in the wilderness.

Boundary Country Trekking (Yurts and Cabin)—$$$ to $$$$

Barbara and Ted Young run Boundary Country Trekking, which offers an array of adventure trips, many of them involving overnight stays in the Youngs' three canvas-covered Mongolian yurts or their remote cabin. However, all four lodging places can be rented on their own when they are not booked for trips. **7925 Gunflint Trail, Grand Marais, 55604; 800-322-8327 or 218-388-4487. Gunflint Trail Association Website: www.boundarycountry.com.**

Clearwater Lodge—$$$ to $$$$

Clearwater Lodge and Outfitters offers accommodations for every taste—from the charmingly old-fashioned, handcrafted rooms in the lodge to screen houses with wooden floors to a bunkhouse and even a tepee (rates are less for these accommodations). The lodge itself, built in 1926, is on the National Register of Historic Places and is the largest whole-log structure left standing in Northeast Minnesota. It was built with love and great skill by Charlie Boostrom, a Gunflint legend, who made the diamond willow furniture still used in the lodge. The mounted moose head and large stone fireplace, along with the unique furniture, capture a bygone time. There are three bed-and-breakfast rooms, with vertical "palisade" pine paneling and shared bath, and two housekeeping suites in the lodge. Clearwater also has cabins, plus full and partial outfitting for canoe trips. Open spring–fall. **774 Clearwater Rd., Grand Marais, 55604; 800-527-0554 or 218-388-2254. Website: www.canoe-bwca.com.**

Golden Eagle Lodge—$$$ to $$$$

Summer's nice at the Golden Eagle, but winter is when the resort comes into its own. Planned as a Nordic ski center, the lodge is surrounded by 37 miles of cross-country ski trails. Owners Dan and Teresa Baumann hang kerosene lanterns along a 1.5-mile loop twice a week in the evening for a romantic trek through the snow. There is also a skating rink. Two of the 11 units are barrier-free and all the two- to three-bedroom units offer year-round comfort, with whirlpool baths and fireplaces available in some. The main lodge is small and cozy, with a constantly filled cookie jar and lots of board games for guests. There is a tepee for kids to convene in during summer, with nature programs to keep them occupied. The tepee is a massive thing, with 32-foot poles making the frame. **468 Clearwater Rd., Grand Marais, 55604; 800-346-2203 or 218-388-2203. Website: www.golden-eagle.com.**

Heston's—$$$ to $$$$

A friendly and remote resort, Heston's has welcomed guests for more than 50 years on the upper reaches of the Gunflint Trail. Now the resort

Boundary Country Trekking's yurt on the Gunflint Trail. Copyright © Minnesota Office of Tourism. Used by permission.

is run by Greg and Barb Gecas (he's the grandson of the original owners) and their three children. Barb is a weaver and Greg brews English-type ale, which he is happy to have guests taste. The eight housekeeping cabins range from the rustic, which have no plumbing or running water, to elegant log cabins that have every modern convenience. In between are several older cabins. Why have cabins with no plumbing? Because, according to the Gecases, some people prefer to rough it and specifically request the no-frills cabins. There is a wood-burning sauna available. Heston's has a store for groceries for either cooking in the cabins or starting off on a trip to the adjacent Boundary Waters Canoe Area Wilderness. **579 S. Gunflint Lake, Grand Marais, 55604; 800-338-7230 or 218-388-2243. Website: www.gunflint-trail.com/hcs.html.**

Camping

Grand Marais Municipal Campground—$

This giant campground, right on Lake Superior, has more than 300 sites. There are 145 with full hookups, 103 with water and electricity, and 49 with no hookups. A playground, nature trail, softball diamond, and basketball hoop, in addition to the swimming pool complex, keep the kids occupied. Special activities include nature talks and programs presented by the U.S. Forest Service. For those who want to fish or go boating, there are marina facilities. Reservations are recommended. Open May 1–mid-Oct. Located on Hwy. 61 and Eighth Ave. W. **Box 820, Grand Marais, 55604; 800-998-0959** (reservations) or **218-387-1712** (general information).

State Parks—$

Cascade River State Park has 40 drive-in and five backpack campsites. **Judge C. R. Magney State Park** has 31 campsites, none with hookups. All state park campsites, with the exception of the kayak-in sites, which are first-come, first-served, can be reserved by calling **The Connection, 800-246-CAMP** or **612-922-9000.**

Superior National Forest—free or $

There are seven campgrounds in the Grand Marais Ranger District of the national forest, with 24 backcountry sites (which are free). The most popular campground is **Trails End,** which is at the end of the Gunflint Trail, next to the BWCAW. The campground is set between two lakes amid tall red and white pines; the rocky terrain is typical of the BWCAW scenery. The campground has 33 sites, some with water, but none with electricity. The campground is a good berry-picking spot and there is a self-guided nature trail at Seagull Lake. Visitors who intend to go into the BWCAW must have a permit for day use. Day-use permits for canoes are available on-site, but permits for motorboats (motor size is restricted) must be obtained through an outfitter or the forest offices. Most of the sites can be reserved; call the district office for more information, **218-387-1750. Website: www.gis.umn.edu/snf.**

Isle Royale National Park—free

Isle Royale, 17 miles southeast of Grand Portage and accessible by boat from there, has 36 campgrounds, many with space for only one to three tents, scattered the length of the 45-mile-long island. No reservations are taken for groups of fewer than six persons, and camping is first-come, first-served, though campers must obtain a free permit from park staff at Windigo or Rock Harbor. Groceries are available at both communities. See Parks.

Where to Eat

Lutsen Resort—$$ to $$$$

What to order here? Heck, take the herring or the Swedish meatballs—after all, you're on the Scandinavian Riviera now. This venerable restaurant, with its huge stone fireplace, rustic furniture, and grand views of Lake Superior, also offers good old standards like steak and chicken in addition to the fish. The desserts are great, too. Open year-round, daily, 7:30 A.M.–9:00 P.M. (reservations are recommended for dinner). Located in Lutsen by Lake Superior. **5700 Hwy. 61 W., Lutsen, 55612; 800-258-8736** or **218-663-7212. Website: www.lutsenresort.com.**

Black Bear Bar and Restaurant and Trail Center—$ to $$$$

Looking for the heart of the Gunflint Trail? Stop by the Black Bear—a combination grocery store/restaurant/resort and community center. Built in the 1930s for loggers, the Black Bear is a gathering place for residents as well as visitors. The store sells handmade quilts and animal pelts as well as provisions, fishing licenses, and bait. The bar and restaurant are busy all day. The steak marinated in a Jack Daniels sauce is a big favorite. Check out the wonderfully old-fashioned homemade desserts—apple dumpling, rice pudding, and bread pudding—as well as hearty breakfast dishes such as grilled oatmeal slices. The restaurant is casual and comfortable, with some north-woods antiques and lots of atmosphere. Open year-round, Sun.–Thurs., 8:00 A.M.–9:00 P.M., and Fri.–Sat., 8:00 A.M.–10:00 P.M. **7611 Gunflint Trail, Grand Marais, 55604; 218-388-2214.**

The Angry Trout—$$ to $$$

Yes, the Trout is a tiny bit trendy, but there is a reason restaurants become favorites—one look at the setting and the menu of the Angry Trout tells you why. The relatively new restaurant is practically in Lake Superior, with some lakeside tables outside as well as the many-windowed dining room inside. It is sheer joy to sit outside on a nice day and do a little lake watching and people watching while eating the Trout's good food.

Fresh fish, whether it be lake trout, herring, whitefish, or Alaskan salmon, is always on the menu. And that's fresh, as in never frozen, and most often caught by Lake Superior anglers. The fish is usually served with fettuccine, wild rice, or french fries and a green salad. There is also a grilled fresh-fish-of-the-day sandwich, served with a light sauce of tarragon, olive oil, and lime. Fish isn't all that's served, of course—pastas, chicken, and other entrees abound. Open May 1–Oct. 20, daily, 11:00 A.M.–8:30 P.M. Located at Grand Marais Harbor. **Box 973, Grand Marais, 55604; 218-387-1265.**

Sven and Ole's—$$ to $$$

If you've been in Minnesota for more than a few days, you've probably seen the blue-and-yellow bumper stickers for Sven and Ole's, a pizza place that is long on both pizzas and sass. The long menu of 'zahs includes a multitude of toppings (ever seen wild rice as a pizza topper?) and lots of blather—one of the menus had a whole list of the many meanings of *uffda,* that all-purpose Scandinavian exclamation. Do they really have a lutefisk pizza? Ask. Check out the Pickle Herring Club in the back. Open year-round, Fri.–Sat., 11:00 A.M.–10:00 P.M., and Sun.–Thurs., 11:00 A.M.–9:00 P.M. **9 W. Wisconsin St., Grand Marais, 55604; 218-387-1713.**

Gunflint Lodge—$ to $$$

Out in the woods in canoe country, visitors come to expect delicious shore lunches. At the Gunflint Lodge restaurant, you'll find a chef who's an expert at both the traditional angler's repast and at creating delicious and beautifully presented meals that make good use of local products. This paragon is Ron Berg, and any restaurant—in the woods or in the biggest of cities—would be lucky to have his talents. Berg started out as a teacher, worked as a fishing guide on the side, and has been head chef at this sophisticated restaurant since 1990. Fish—including beer-battered walleye with a sweet-and-sour mango sauce—is prominent on the menu, along with venison and other game. Berg uses the local berries and rhubarb to good effect in desserts and sauces, and

wild rice is paired with salmon in a chowder that is a variation of the usual Minnesota wild rice soup. Herbs are used liberally in the dishes and also as garnishes. Berg's recipes are in *The Gunflint Lodge Cookbook* (University of Minnesota Press, 1997). Open year-round, daily, 8:00 A.M.–9:30 P.M. **143 S. Gunflint Lake, Grand Marais, 55604; 800-328-3325 or 218-388-2294. Website: www.gunflint.com.**

Leng's Fountain Grill—$ to $$

This is an old-fashioned soda fountain and lunch counter that will take most visitors right back to their young days. You get quick service and good, plain food at Leng's. No chi-chi ambiance and hovering waitrons here—just darn good food. And it works; Leng's has been a Grand Marais staple since 1938. It did close briefly but re-opened with a new owner in 1998. Open year-round; call for hours. **5 W. Wisconsin St., Grand Marais, 55604; 218-387-2648.**

Services

Gunflint Trail Association has information on the Gunflint Trail, **800-338-6932** or **218-387-2870.** The **Website** for the Gunflint is wonderful, with quite a complete listing of lodging and outfitters and other businesses: **www.gunflint-trail.com.**

Grand Marais Chamber of Commerce, 800-622-4014.

Get information about Grand Marais and the surrounding area from the **Grand Marais Visitor and Information Center, 13 N. Broadway, P.O. Box 1048, Grand Marais, 55604; 888-922-5000** or **218-387-2524.**

Grand Portage Bay Travel Information Center, 218-475-2592.

Housed in the same building as the North Shore Commercial Fishing Museum, the **Lutsen-Tofte Tourism Association** is very helpful in answering questions about the North Shore and providing information. Located at the intersection of Hwy. 61 and the Sawbill Trail, in Tofte. **888-616-6784 and 218-663-7804.**

Voyageurs National Park Area

At the northern edge of Minnesota, the sky and the waters meld into a band of blue, with a fringe of evergreens and eons-old gray rock sandwiched in between. Looking at the serene and rugged vistas, visitors might think they have discovered a wilderness untouched by human history, but they would be mistaken. The land and lakes in and around Voyageurs National Park have served many peoples well for centuries. Indeed, the lakes and rivers formed one of the first "highways" in North America, the watery route traveled by the voyageurs in search of beaver pelts in the 1700s and early 1800s.

The park itself is the dominant feature of the area, but the towns and lakes that surround the park have many attractions also. International Falls—the inspiration for the "Frostbite Falls" of Bullwinkle and Rocky fame—is the largest of the communities, with a population of 10,000. Other communities in the area are Ash River, Lake Kabetogama, Crane Lake, Ranier, Orr, and Bigfork. The land, towns, and waters now draw tourists instead of fur trappers and gold seekers. Ranier is a tiny treasure of a town near the Rainy Lake Visitor Center of Voyageurs National Park, with a boardwalk, lakeside ice cream parlor, down-home cafe, Woody's "Fairly Reliable" (his words) guide service, a bookstore, and gift shops.

History

Approximately 4,000 years ago, the Archaic Indians lived in the Voyageurs area. They were followed by Laurel Indians—part of the Middle Woodland people—and a succession of others. Their lasting testimony is 17 miles west of International Falls—a huge, conical burial mound that rests in the dappled shade of green trees in sum-mer. Later residents included the Dakota and the Ojibwe. The Indians traversed the waters in their birch-bark canoes and introduced the craft—lightweight and waterproof when sealed correctly—to the French-Canadian voyageurs for whom the park is named.

The voyageurs—short, stocky, pipe-smoking men who carried hundreds of pounds on portages from lake to lake—paddled their way through the area in the fur-trade heyday of the late 18th and early 19th centuries in eight-man "North" canoes. Their journeys to gather beaver and other furs began in Montreal and stretched into the Canadian northwest. Both their strength and their high spirits became legendary, and their songs—sung to a brisk paddling rhythm—still survive. What North American schoolchild has not sung verse after verse of "Alouette, Gentille Alouette"? The fur-trade competition grew fierce at times and at one point there were several companies vying for the beaver pelts from which top hats were made. When the beaver-hat craze waned, the fur trade also died and the voyageurs became a distant memory.

Logging and commercial fishing took over in the 19th century. But the most glittering phase of the Voyageurs area's history came with the 1893 discovery of gold on Little American Island in Rainy Lake. The discovery caused a seven-year boom, as prospectors streamed in, mine shafts were sunk on several islands, and a whole town—Rainy Lake City—was born. The city was rough and ready, with 17 saloons for its several hundred residents. But the gold proved too costly to extract and mill, and the prospectors went on to the next field, the Yukon, leaving Rainy Lake City to die a quick death. Currently, the park is restoring a saloon that was built during a brief renaissance of the city in 1910.

The area's stark beauty, with its bountiful wildlife and fishing, has long attracted visitors. It is wilderness, yes, but a very accessible wilderness, with comfortable resorts at its edge. Resort owners, many of them second- or third-generation residents, are ready to help visitors learn the best way to enjoy this marvelous place.

Recommended Reading

Theodore C. Blegen's *The Voyageurs and Their Songs*, published in 1966 by the Minnesota Historical Society (see Museums and Historic Sites), is a

> ### Getting There
>
> *International Falls is approximately 300 miles north of the Twin Cities. It is served by air link from Minneapolis–St. Paul International Airport. For drivers, the area is a five-hour trek from the Twin Cities on I-35 and (through Duluth) Hwy. 53. The four entry points of Voyageurs National Park, as well as International Falls, are all off Hwy. 53. From Canada, the park is four hours from Winnipeg, Manitoba; three hours from Thunder Bay, Ontario; and, of course, just a hop, skip, and jump from Fort Frances, Ontario, across the international bridge from International Falls. Pedestrians can walk across at no charge; drivers are charged a fee.*

slim book that gives a concise history of the voyageurs and a fascinating glimpse of one aspect of their life—12 songs, with the original French words and an English summary. A tape of the songs, recorded by the male choir of the University of Moncton, New Brunswick, Canada, is also available.

Voyageurs National Park, Minnesota's only national park, was once a "highway" for fur trade voyageurs.
Copyright © Minnesota Office of Tourism. Used by permission.

Major Attractions

Voyageurs National Park

Voyageurs National Park, the only national park in Minnesota, stretches for 55 miles along the Canadian border. From the air, it is a vast patchwork of different shades of green and wide expanses of blue. One of the least used of the nation's national parks, Voyageurs is a water-lover's paradise. One-third of the park consists of water, and the main "routes" are the waterways used by the voyageurs during the fur trade. Glacial comings and goings over a million-year period scrubbed the area down to the stark gray rocks of the Canadian Shield, which is among the oldest rock in the world—approximately 2.7 billion years old.

Depressions left by the glaciers filled with water and formed the region's abundant lakes, which are liberally dotted with rocky islands. Many of the park's 500-plus islands are pine covered and have primitive campsites; others are bare, glaciated rocks. Some of the island namers had a sense of humor: "Your Island" and "My Island" are next to each other. About 30 lakes are within the park boundaries. Three of the largest—Rainy Lake, Sand Point Lake, and Namakan Lake—are sliced in two by the U.S.-Canadian border. A third large lake, Kabetogama, is entirely within the park. The Kabetogama Peninsula, a roadless expanse of trees, small lakes, and streams, lies between Rainy and Kabetogama Lakes.

Wildlife viewing varies by season. Birds in the park area include bald eagles, great blue herons, cormorants, and loons. Black bear and beaver are often seen, while river otter and moose are less frequently observed. Visitors may hear wolves howling, but rarely see one.

Boating

Unlike the similar-appearing and neighboring Boundary Waters Canoe Area Wilderness, Voyageurs National Park permits motorized vehicles—motorboats, including houseboats—on its four main lakes in summer and snowmobiles in part of the park in the winter. Most activities within the park involve water, so visitors need either their own boat or a hired one. They can rent boats, hire "water taxis," or take trips on cruise boats. Many resort owners rent boats and operate water taxis, while renting houseboats is a popular vacation for many visitors (see Where to Stay). Kayaking is becoming increasingly popular, and there are several canoe and kayak outfitters near the park (see Boating, in Outdoor Activities).

Park naturalists accompany many of the cruises by the park's two concession boats—the *Pride of Rainy Lake* in Rainy Lake and the *Sight-Sea-Er* on Lake Kabetogama, both of which have several different cruises, including jaunts to the historic Kettle Falls Hotel. Cruise boats offer trips to the old gold mines and other park highlights, including old fishing camps and the enchanting Ellsworth Rock Gardens, where a primitive sculpture garden and some hardy plants remain in a melancholy tribute to their creator. On the park's interpretive-program canoe trips, which leave from the Rainy Lake Visitor Center, a costumed volunteer "voyageur" teaches paddlers a traditional voyageur song. Call the Rainy Lake Center for details (see below).

Fishing and Berrying

Throughout the year, Voyageurs is a magnet for anglers. Kabetogama, according to one resort owner, is a "walleye factory." Area lakes also yield northern, muskies, smallmouth bass, crappie, and sauger. Fish aren't the only things visitors seek. Summer is berry time, and anyone is welcome to pick blueberries anywhere in the park.

Hiking

Hiking is popular, and visitors can get a real workout by boating to Kabetogama Peninsula, walking the rugged 2-mile Locator Lake Trail, unlocking a canoe or rowboat with a key obtained at the visitor center (reservations are necessary, but use of the boat is free), and then skimming across several beautiful small lakes. The boats and canoes are also available on several other lakes on the peninsula. Other popular hikes include the 9-mile Cruiser Lake Trail, which connects Rainy Lake with Lake Kabetogama. But it isn't necessary to walk the entire trail to appreciate the park. The 2.3-mile Echo Bay Trail, which wanders through forests and past beaver ponds, is accessed via the Northern Lights Rd. in the town of Kabetogama. Also worth doing is the 2.5-mile Blind Ash Bay Trail, which climbs up a rocky ridge above the visitor center and has wonderful views. The trailhead at Anderson Bay in Rainy Lake takes visitors high above the lake for sweeping views of the lake and its islands and wildlife, too.

Visitors to the Crane Lake area can hike the Vermilion Gorge and Falls Trails. The Vermilion River here tumbles wildly through the narrow cage of steep granite walls. The tamer, self-guiding Oberholtzer Trail, adjacent to the Rainy Lake Visitor Center, is 0.5 mile long, with the first 0.25 mile wheelchair-accessible. It is dedicated to Ernest Oberholtzer, a longtime area resident who co-founded the Wilderness Society and was an avid conservationist. "Obie's" vision of preserving the north country provided impetus for the creation of the park. Voyageurs National Park was created in 1975, making it one of the newest national parks.

Historic Sites

Little American Island, site of the gold discovery of 1893, has a small, surfaced trail to the mine. Also, Kettle Falls Hotel and its surroundings, including the dam, are interesting to explore. In a cartographic quirk, Canada lies south of the United States at that point. The hotel is reachable only by water in summer and snowmobile in winter. The popular hotel—white with a red roof and red-and-white striped awnings—was built in stages, beginning in 1910. All kinds of people have stayed at the hotel—trappers, lumberjacks, prostitutes, bootleggers, and prospectors. Many commercial fishermen lived nearby in the early days, and auctions of fish at the dock drew hundreds of people. During a complete restoration, the hotel bar's off-kilter wooden floor, whose middle is a foot higher than either side, was carefully redone. In the middle of the night, some guests have heard sprightly music from the bar. When they've come down to investigate, the hotel's current operator relates, the music stops. That's not the only mystery: Jack Ryan, a storekeeper, was murdered near the hotel, one of the park's two unsolved homicides.

Winter Sports

In winter, snowmobilers and cross-country skiers have the park nearly to themselves: there are more than 100 miles of groomed snowmobile trails and 10 miles of groomed ski trails. After the freeze-up, the only road into the park on which cars are permitted, the 7-mile Ice Rd. on Rainy Lake, becomes active.

Getting There

Currently, entry into Voyageurs National Park is free. However, that could change if Congress decides that all national parks must charge an entry fee. There are three visitor centers—at Rainy Lake, Lake Kabetogama, and Ash River—and an information center at Crane Lake. All three visitor centers show a short film on the park and have interpretive exhibits. The Lake States Interpretive Association sells maps, books, tapes, and some prints at the centers. Interpretive programs for visitors range from nature hikes, guided boat trips, and campfire programs to the canoe trips in a replica of a birch-bark "North" canoe used by the voyageurs 200 years ago (see Boating, above). The Rainy Lake Visitor Center, **218-286-5258,** is open year-round: early May–end of Sept., daily, 9:00 A.M.–5:00 P.M.; call to check winter hours. Lake Kabetogama, **218-875-2111,** and Ash River, **218-374-3221,** Visitor Centers are open early May–end of Sept., daily, 9:00 A.M.–5:00 P.M. Crane Lake Information Center, **218-993-2481,** has a shorter season; call for hours. The park headquarters is located in International Falls. **3131 Hwy. 53, International Falls, 56649; 218-283-9821. Website: www.nps.gov/voya.**

Recommended Reading

Lake State Interpretive Association has published several books about Voyageurs National Park that visitors will find useful. They include works on the park itself, such as *Voyageurs National Park,* written by Greg Breining, with beautiful photos by the late Arnold Bolz, published in 1987. The nonprofit association also has books on the gold rush in Rainy Lake and books on the historic Kettle Falls Hotel. The association's bookstores are at the visitor centers in the park and other venues.

Festivals and Events

Icebox Days
mid- to late Jan.

Revel in the coldest time of the year with a 10-day bash that includes lots of physical activities to warm visitors up, including softball on frozen Rainy Lake, a FreezeYer Gizzard Blizzard run, a moonlight ski, and a cross-country ski race. For information, contact the International Falls Area Chamber of Commerce, **800-FALLS-MN** or **218-283-9400**. **Website: www.rainylake.com.**

Lake Kabetogama Lady Slipper Festival
last weekend in June

Late June is prime time for viewing the lovely lady slippers in northern Minnesota. There is a patch of them right in front of the Lake Kabetogama Visitors Center at Voyageurs National Park, and they and other wildflowers are celebrated in this festival, which began in 1997. Events include a wildflower walk, tips on wildflower gardening, and boat trips to see the Ellsworth Gardens on the Kabetogama Peninsula. The festival also includes an arts and crafts fair. Contact the Lake Kabetogama Visitor Center, **218-875-2111.**

Orr Heritage Days
third weekend in July

Four different aspects of the town of Orr's heritage—the voyageur era, Native Americans, early settlers, and the railroad—are celebrated in this annual festival. Events vary from year to year, but may include such activities as "North" canoe rides, Ojibwe singers, and powwows. For information, contact the Orr Area Information Center, **800-357-9255.**

Outdoor Activities

Biking
MOUNTAIN BIKING

The Arrowhead State Trail, which extends for 135 miles from the Taconite State Trail near Tower to just south of International Falls, is well known as a winter snowmobile trail and can also be used for mountain biking in summer, though many areas are low and may be covered with water. Mountain bikers also use the old logging roads in the area. For information, call the International Falls Area Chamber of Commerce, **800-FALLS-MN.**

Boating
CANOEING

In addition to Voyageurs National Park and the Boundary Waters Canoe Area Wilderness on the eastern border of the national park, canoers may want to try canoe routes on the Bigfork, Littlefork, and Vermilion Rivers. All are state-designated canoe routes with campsites, access points, and parking sites. The Bigfork and Littlefork, which were used for major logging drives, flow north into Rainy River west of International Falls; the Vermilion extends north for 40 miles from Lake Vermilion to Crane Lake on the eastern edge of Voyageurs National Park. Low water in summer may hamper rapids negotiation. The **Bigfork** is an easy river to canoe, with several Class I rapids. Two waterfalls—Little American Falls near Craigville and Big Falls at the town of the same name—must be portaged. Small farms are interspersed among the heavily forested riverbanks, and fish and wildlife are abundant. The **Littlefork** is quiet, with cloudy water due to sediment deposit. There are Class I and II rapids in the upper part, with smooth stretches in between. The scenery varies from wilderness to areas with houses and farms. The **Vermilion** is the wildest and woolliest of the three, with dense forest surrounding most of it and rapids varying from Class I to IV. There are many portages, as necessary now as in the days when the Vermilion was part of the voyageur "highway." For maps of all three, contact the Dept. of Natural Resources, **500 Lafayette Rd., St. Paul, 55155; 888-MINNDNR** or **651-296-6157.**

Rentals and Tours

Anderson's, in business for several decades, does general outfitting and rents canoes, boats and motors, and camping equipment. Most cus-

Nelson's Resort offers a scenic backdrop for fishing at Crane Lake.

tomers head for the Boundary Waters Canoe Area Wilderness; some go into Voyageurs National Park. Anderson's is located **just south of Crane Lake; 800-777-7186.**

Fishing

This is prime fishing country, with big and small lakes as well as rivers just waiting to be fished. Fishing is good on the Vermilion River, with walleye, smallmouth bass, and occasionally rock bass found. See Fishing in Major Attractions as well.

Rentals and Tours

Many anglers hire guides. One of the best known is **Butch Eggen,** who, along with his wife and her family, operates Nelson's Resort (see Where to Stay). Eggen, who grew up in the area, says fishing guides not only teach people how to fish, but "you're making memories, a day they'll always remember. How many fish are killed may be irrelevant for some of our customers if you can show them an eagle's nest or a loon." Walleyes, Eggen admits, are "king of the Minnesota fishes, but we try to bring to light some of the alternative species, such as smallmouth bass." Eggen, who sometimes puts in 10-hour days during peak fishing season, often guides for women. "Women shouldn't

be intimidated about using a fishing guide," he adds. In one case, it's a woman who *is* the fishing guide— that's **Kathy Wilson,** owner of Arrowhead Lodge (see Where to Stay) on Lake Kabetogama and possibly the only woman in Minnesota who holds a master's guiding license from the U.S. Coast Guard.

Hiking

Even in this watery paradise, a hiker can get a good workout. There are many trails in the Superior National Forest, in addition to the state forest trails and the national park trails (see Hiking in Major Attractions). Many of the trails are multipurpose: the 13-mile Echo Lake Trail, northeast of Orr, is popular with hikers and hunters. In the works is a new multiuse trail from Lake Kabetogama to Ash River, a joint project of the local communities, the state Dept. of Natural Resources, and the federal government.

Orr Wetlands Walk

The 0.5-mile "bog walk," which begins just off the parking lot at the Orr Area Information Center, is like a trip to another world. The boardwalk, accessible to wheelchairs, first winds through shady, spooky bits, with upended tree roots along the boardwalk forming fantastic sculptures. Farther on, there are sunny stretches along the Pelican River. Wildlife and birds, including the namesake pelican, abound. The Orr Area Information Center is located on Hwy. 53 slightly south of Orr. Call for times of a naturalist-led tour; **800-357-9255.**

Tilson Bay Hiking Trail

Adjacent to Voyageurs National Park is a 1.3-mile trail along a rocky ridge that overlooks Rainy Lake. The trail, part of Koochiching State Forest, is 6.5 miles east of International Falls just off Hwy. 11. There is a parking area and fishing dock on the east side of Tilson Creek.

Hunting

Deer, black bear, and moose, and birds from ruffed grouse to all manner of waterfowl, draw hunters to the Voyageurs area. See information on hunting in this book's Introduction.

Skiing

CROSS-COUNTRY

Cross-country ski trails in the Voyageurs area will expand with the new multipurpose trail from Lake Kabetogama to Ash River (see Hiking). For other opportunities, contact Voyageurs National Park's visitor centers (see Getting There in Major Attractions). There are also ski trails at Grand Mound, west of International Falls. The 3.5-mile Echo Bay Trail is accessible from the Northern Lights Rd. in the town of Kabetogama.

Tilson Creek Trails

The main ski trail, approximately 10 miles long, varies in terrain from flat, open bog to steep ridges, all in Koochiching State Forest east of International Falls. The trailhead is just off Hwy. 11 on Tilson Creek next to Rainy Lake. The main trail is multilooped for those who like a shorter tour. It links with the 3-mile Tilson Creek East Trail, which connects with the main trail to Voyageurs National Park's Rainy Lake Visitor Center. There is parking at the visitor center. The park sponsors moonlight ski events in winter; check with the visitor center for dates. A map of the trails is available from the Dept. of Natural

Resources, **500 Lafayette Rd., St. Paul, 55155; 888-MINNDNR** or **651-296-6157.**

Snowmobiling

Snowmobiling is probably the most popular winter activity in the Voyageurs area. Groomed trails in addition to national park trails include the 135-mile Arrowhead State Trail (see Biking), from Tower to just south of International Falls, and several trails out of Orr, Crane Lake, and International Falls. Voyageurs Trail West, which extends to Bemidji, zips through International Falls. A map of area trails is in the International Falls tourism guide. For a copy of the guide or for snow conditions, call **800-FALLS-MN.** A comprehensive map of outdoor recreation opportunities (snowmobiling, hiking, cross-country skiing, camping, canoeing, and boat launching) in Koochiching County, for which International Falls is the county seat, is available from the Minnesota Travel Information Center in International Falls (see Services).

Seeing and Doing

Museums and Historic Sites

Grand Mound Center

The 25-foot prehistoric burial mound, near the conjunction of the Rainy and Bigfork Rivers, was constructed by the Laurel Indians (200 B.C.–A.D. 800) and the Blackduck Indians (A.D. 800–ca. 1400). The Grand Mound, the largest prehistoric structure in the Upper Midwest, is covered with ferns and trees and projects an air of tranquillity. Respect it as you would a modern cemetery. There are four smaller mounds nearby. The interpretive center has exhibits and programs. Hiking and cross-country ski trails take visitors past the mounds. Grand Mound is administered by the Minnesota Historical Society. Fee except for MHS members. Open Thurs.–Sun.; call for hours. Located **17 miles west of International Falls on Hwy. 11; 218-285-3332.**

Koochiching County Historical Museum and Bronko Nagurski Museum

The newly renovated historical museum has many interactive exhibits covering county history, from the geology to the first peoples to the logging and gold rush booms. Adjacent to the museum proper is the Bronko Nagurski Museum, devoted to the career of the Falls' own remarkable athlete, the late Nagurski. He played football for the University of Minnesota and later the Chicago Bears, and went on to a pro wrestling stint after he retired from football. The Bronk's uniforms, footballs, and other memorabilia fascinate football and history fans alike. Open Memorial Day–Labor Day, daily, 9:00 A.M.–5:00 P.M.; rest of the year, Mon.–Fri., 9:00 A.M.–5:00 P.M. Fee. **214 Sixth Ave., International Falls, 56649; 218-283-4316.**

Parks

Superior National Forest

Voyageurs National Park is adjoined by Superior National Forest, which covers much of Northeast Minnesota. The forest has a number of hiking and hunting trails, snowmobile and ski trails, and campsites. Information is also available on bird-watching, naturalist programs, and the forest itself. The closest forest office to the Voyageurs area is LaCroix Ranger District at Cook, **218-666-0020.**

Shopping

Birch-bark Canoes

Birch-bark canoe making, which American Indians did for eons, is nearly a lost art. Although some Minnesota Ojibwe still build the sleek white beauties, the only place producing them commercially in Minnesota seems to be the Hafeman Boat Works, on the Bigfork River. The canoe builder is Ray Boessel Jr., whose wife's grandfather started the business in 1921 because he needed transport. Boessel makes large canoes (from 13-foot solo canoes to the 26-foot "North" canoes) and small-scale models that are five to 10 feet long. Visitors are welcome and may even get to try paddling one of Boessel's canoes. If the door's open, Boessel says, come on in. In summer, he makes one full-size canoe per week. They don't come cheap, but in many ways they are priceless. The workshop located is 30 miles north of Deer

River on the south side of Hwy. 6. **59520 Hwy. 6, Bigfork, 56628; 218-743-3709** (evenings).

Tours

Boise Cascade Mill Tour

Paper making is big business in this part of the state, and it's *the* industry in International Falls. Tours of the mammoth mill last a little more than an hour (reservations required); there are occasional tours of the surrounding forest, and also a brochure for a self-guided forest tour. Tours are given June–Aug., Mon.–Fri., several times a day. **218-285-5011.**

Wildlife Viewing

Bear Feeding

Local logger Vince Shute started feeding black bears near Orr more than 50 years ago. He still visits his buddies, but the nonprofit American Bear Association has now taken over the feeding duties. Visitors watch from a viewing platform. The bears are fed Memorial Day–Labor Day, Tues.–Sun., 5:00 P.M.–dusk. Located **15 miles northwest of Orr on Pelican Lake; 800-357-9255.**

Where to Stay

Hotels, Motels, and Inns

Kettle Falls Hotel—$$$

Yes, it's tough getting to the remote location, but it's worth the effort, for the imposing white frame hotel has seen a lot of history. But it isn't just history that calls: the hotel is a wonderful place to relax on a summer's day, sipping lemonade on the wide veranda and eating a walleye sandwich. Built over a three-year period, from 1910 to 1913 and reputedly financed by Nellie Bly, the hotel first housed construction workers. Robert Williams bought the place in 1918 for a thousand bucks and four barrels of whiskey. If you can't stay in one of the hotel's 12 simple but charming rooms with shared baths (includes continental breakfast), do ask for a tour. The interior has fascinating period furniture and photos, etc., and the bar's warped floor makes you feel like you've been partying too long. Ask about the ghostly music some guests hear. In addition to the hotel with its rooms and restaurant, there are three lodges (call for lodge rates) with a total of 10 units, one of them handicapped-accessible. Five of the units have kitchens. The hotel is open year-round, except during periods when the ice is forming in fall or melting in spring. The hotel is accessible only by boat in summer and snowmobile in winter. There is a ferry service from Ash River, from Sunset Resort, twice daily, and also tour boats from Lake Kabetogama Visitor Center in Voyageurs National Park stop at the hotel. **10502 Gamma Rd., Ray, 56669; 888-KF-HOTEL or 218-374-4404.**

Other Accommodations

Houseboats—$$ to $$$$

Houseboating is a popular way to experience Voyageurs National Park. There are houseboat tie-up sites throughout the park. Novices are given extensive instruction. The boats come furnished with kitchen equipment, dishes and silverware, and pillows and blankets. Linens and towels can be brought along or rented. Fishing boats are included in the rental at some establishments. Extras that can be rented include hot tubs. The season is generally mid-May–early or mid-Oct., depending on the weather. Rates vary greatly, depending on the size of the boat, time of year, and length of time rented. Houseboat rental firms include the following. **Dougherty's Rainy Lake Houseboats, 2031 Town Rd. 488, International Falls, 56649; 800-554-9188 or 218-286-5391. Ebel's Minnesota Voyageur Houseboats, 10326 Ash River Trail, Orr, 55771; 800-253-5475 or 218-374-3571. Northernaire Floating Lodges** (on Rainy Lake), **2690 County Rd. 94, International Falls, 56649; 800-854-7958. Voyagaire Lodge and Houseboats, Dept. C96, Crane Lake, 55725; 800-882-6287.**

Resorts

Thunderbird Lodge—$$$ to $$$$

Get up early if you have an east-facing room at the Thunderbird Lodge and watch the sun rise gloriously over Rainy Lake. Thunderbird Lodge,

a sprawling complex, with 15 rooms and a big and very busy restaurant and bar in the lodge itself, plus 10 cabins (call for cabin rates), is a fixture on Rainy Lake. Rooms are comfortable, but not fancy. Thunderbird has a large marina and is directly across from Dougherty's Rainy Lake Houseboats. The lodge and the houseboat business are owned by the Williams and Dougherty families, in the restaurant business on Rainy Lake since 1918. Fishing is the main activity here, and fishing guides are available. Boats, canoes, and paddleboats can be rented. **2170 County Rd. 139, International Falls, 56649; 800-351-5133 or 218-286-3151.**

Arrowhead Lodge—$$$

Kathy Wilson, tired of life in the Twin Cities, bought this old but rock-solid logging camp in 1978 and turned it into a good-size resort that has a cozy feel. The 11 red-and-white cabins—clean and modern inside—resemble Swedish cabins. The red-painted log lodge has seven rooms upstairs that share baths, and a sweeping wraparound porch. From the rustic dining room, there are wonderful views of Lake Kabetogama. Wilson, who is probably the only female fishing guide in the state to have U.S. Coast Guard certification, guides fishing parties with advance reservation. And who says there is no free launch? The resort offers guests a free "get-acquainted" boat tour of the lake, with guides pointing out good fishing spots, plus hazards such as sand- and gravel bars. Children's activities are available. Open fishing opener–Oct. 1. **10473 Waltz Rd., Box RG, Ray, 56669; 218-875-2141.**

Ash Trail Lodge—$$$

Situated on the Ash River, between Lake Kabetogama and Namakan Lake, the resort has three luxurious new log cabins, all with fireplaces, in addition to the seven older ones. It's ideal for large families or groups; the largest cabin sleeps up to 26. The recently redone log lodge has a spacious restaurant and bar. There are three rooms in the lodge; in winter, the four-room carriage house can be rented; both share baths. There is a sheltered harbor, with private docks fronting most cabins. Meals are available and there are basic groceries for sale. Some cabins are open year-round. **10418 Ash River Trail, Orr, 55771; 800-777-4513** (reservations only) or **218-374-3131. Website: www.ashtraillodge.com.**

Burchell's Moosehorn Resort—call for rates
A nice choice for families, Moosehorn has been operated by the Burchell family since 1939. The resort is on Moosehorn Point on Lake Kabetogama, tucked away from the winds, making it ideal for kids playing on the beach or for beginning water-skiers. There are eight cabins, ranging from one to six bedrooms. The newest one, Valhalla, has four bedrooms, two wood-burning fireplaces, and a whirlpool. Jovial Alan Burchell and his wife, Miriam, are helpful hosts. Recreation equipment available includes fun bugs, a seacycle, playaks, canoes, and a combination pickleball/basketball court. What's pickleball? Ask Alan. Then again, just sit on the bench at the end of the dock and watch the colors of the evening sky. Some units are open in winter. **10434 Waltz Rd., Ray, 56669; 800-777-7968** or **218-875-3491. Website: www.moosehornresort.com.**

Nelson's Resort—call for rates
Surely the Norse gods don't go to Valhalla when they die, but to Nelson's. There is even a collection of Viking drinking horns in the dining room to make them feel at home. But everyone feels at home at Nelson's, as much for its spirit of summer as for its cozy and tidy yellow-trimmed cabins and variety of activities, both active and quiet. Can there be anything more relaxing than watching the sunset colors from a log bench that bears the inscription, "Uf da, it feels good to sit down"? John and Millie Nelson started the resort on Crane Lake in 1931 and passed it on to their daughter Goldie Pohlman and her children. The fourth generation is coming along nicely, nearly ready to greet the many folks that return to Nelson's year after year. It was Millie Nelson who laid out the resort, cleverly situating the cabins to fit the curves of the lakeshore so that each has a feeling of privacy, yet none is far from the main lodge. The 28 cabins are traditionally decorated and very comfortable. Millie was a jill-of-all-trades: she painted many of the pictures that grace many of the cabin walls and she started the resort garden that still provides nearly all of the vegetables for the delicious meals served in the restaurant. Chief gardener now is Jacque Eggen, her granddaughter. The garden theme spills over all of the resort, with bright flowers blooming everywhere. Nelson's has all the requisite resort activities—a sandy beach for swimming, a variety of equipment for water sports, a 3-mile hiking trail, indoor games such as Ping-Pong and pool, and—for the end of the day—a sauna. Nelson's staff and guides deal efficiently with all aspects of fishing, from boat and equipment rental to launch facilities for those who bring their own boats to providing guides who will help visitors fish and also fix them the legendary north-country shore lunch. Nelson's offers both American and Modified American plans and other packages. Open Fri. before fishing opener–end of Sept. **7632 Nelson Rd., Crane Lake, 55725; 800-433-0743** or **218-993-2295. Website: www.nelsonsresort.com.**

Watson's Harmony Beach Resort and Lodge—call for rates
At Harmony Beach, owned by Tim and Char Watson, choose from either a two-bedroom apartment in a new fourplex, a room in the lodge, or a cabin. Six of the 13 cabins are on the shore of Lake Kabetogama, with great views from the decks. The resort also has three wooded campsites, with water and electrical hookups. The fourplex units, new in 1998, share a hot tub, but each has its own kitchen and living and dining areas. The Watsons also offer outfitting for trips into Voyageurs National Park. There are complete and partial canoe and motorboat packages available. The lodge rooms and fourplex are open year-round. **10002 Gappa Rd., Ray, 56669; 218-875-2811.**

Camping

Superior National Forest Campgrounds—$
Lakeside campgrounds at **Lake Jeanette** and **Echo Lake,** both near Hwy. 116, are administered by the national forest. They have water and latrines, but no showers. There are 24 sites at Echo Lake

and 12 at Lake Jeanette. For information on recreational opportunities within the area, call the LaCroix Ranger District, **218-666-0020.**

Woodenfrog Campground—$

Woodenfrog, which has 59 sites, none with hookups, is a popular place on summer weekends, as it is right on the shore of Lake Kabetogama, on the edge of Voyageurs National Park. It's in the Kabetogama State Forest. No reservations are taken for the sites at this primitive campground. There are water spigots, but no showers—but then, who needs one with the lake so near? Naturalists from Voyageurs National Park give campfire programs on some evenings. To reach the campground, go north from Orr on Hwy. 53, turn right onto County Rd. 122, and follow signs for 6 miles. For information on other state forest campgrounds in the area, contact the Dept. of Natural Resouces, **500 Lafayette Rd., St. Paul, 55155; 888-MINNDNR** or **651-296-6157.**

Voyageurs National Park—free

There are 200 campsites, including those designated for houseboats, in Voyageurs National Park. They are first-come, first-served. Campsites have a place to put up a tent, a fire ring, a latrine, a picnic table, and (most often) a bear-proof locker in which to store food. Campsites are scattered throughout the park, often on tiny, rocky islands with a scrap of a sandy private beach. Occasionally, sites may be closed; check at the visitor centers to make sure they are open. For information, call the visitor centers (see Getting There in Major Attractions).

Where to Eat

Many of the resorts in the area, such as Nelson's, the Ash Trail Lodge, and the Thunderbird Lodge (see Where to Stay), offer excellent food and are open to the public.

Nelson's—$$ to $$$$

Go in the evening, and the wonderful collection of copper shines warmly in the light of the cozy restaurant at Nelson's. The venerable restaurant has maintained its quality for decades. The restaurant's menu remains substantially the same as in earlier years, and the Thurs.-night smorgasbord is still offered. The cooks take advantage of the wonderful vegetables and herbs grown right in Nelson's own garden. A dinner specialty is dry-aged Kansas City steaks. After you've eaten, sit by the fire and page through the Nelson scrapbooks for a fascinating look at how the resort grew—with photos of Minnesota governors galore! Open, as is the bar, to the public as well as guests, mid-May–Sept., daily, 6:30 A.M.–9:30 P.M. **7632 Nelson Rd., Crane Lake, 55725; 800-433-0743** or **218-993-2295.**

The Spot—$$ to $$$

Fire fighting is the theme in this International Falls mainstay, and the food is also hot stuff, though never too spicy for Minnesota palates. Prime ribs and ribs with the Spot's special barbecue sauce are the star items here, though the Spot offers a full range of dinner entrees; the Spot also has its own wine label, bottled in California. Happy family groups seem to be the norm at the friendly Spot. Three generations of volunteer-firefighter Olsons, starting in 1936, have guided the Spot. Current award-winning chef Rick Olson is the grandson of founders "Chink" and Isabelle Olson. The restaurant is spacious, with several rooms, a snug bar, and an outdoor patio. Everywhere is firefighter memorabilia—helmets converted to lights for the bar, two full-size fire trucks in front of the restaurant and several more scattered around the site, spotted dalmatian dogs, etc. Open Mon.–Sat., 5:00–10:00 P.M. Located at the **intersection of Hwy. 53 and 18th St. in International Falls; 218-283-2440.**

Grandma's Pantry—$ to $$$

Grandma's pancakes are bigger than most fish stories—the huge hotcakes can measure nearly a foot across—and they are good, too. Local folks and tourists alike fill up the homey cafe for the pancakes and omelets. Other specialties include wild rice soup and walleye. Open

Mon.–Fri., 6:00 A.M.–7:00 P.M., and Sat., 6:00–10:00 A.M. **2079 Spruce St., Ranier, 56668; 218-286-5584.**

Bait 'n Bite—$ to $$

If you need a hearty breakfast, a packed lunch, and bait for a day of fishing, this is the place—in fact, the sign in front of the solid log building says it humorously and best: "Eat here and get worms." The cafe part of the establishment, adjacent to the bait shop, is a pleasant place with walls of knotty pine, and it has won awards for cleanliness. The soups are homemade, and specials such as Swiss Mushroom Chicken are offered in the evening. Open in summer, daily; call for hours. Located on County Rd. 122 (also known as Gamma Rd.) 1 mile north of Hwy. 53. **9634 Gamma Rd., Lake Kabetogama, 56669; 218-875-2281.**

Services

The Falls area is well represented at the **International Falls Area Chamber of Commerce, 301 Second Ave., International Falls, 56649; 800-FALLS-MN** or **218-283-9400. Website: www.intlfalls.org.**

Nearby is the **Minnesota Travel Information Center, 200 Fourth St., International Falls, 56649, 218-285-7623,** which has information about the region and other parts of Minnesota.

Just outside the town of Orr is the **Orr Area Information Center,** which has plenty of details about Voyageurs National Park as well as local information. Don't miss strolling along the adjacent bog walk (see Hiking). **P.O. Box 236, 4429 Hwy. 53, Orr, 55771; 800-357-9255.**

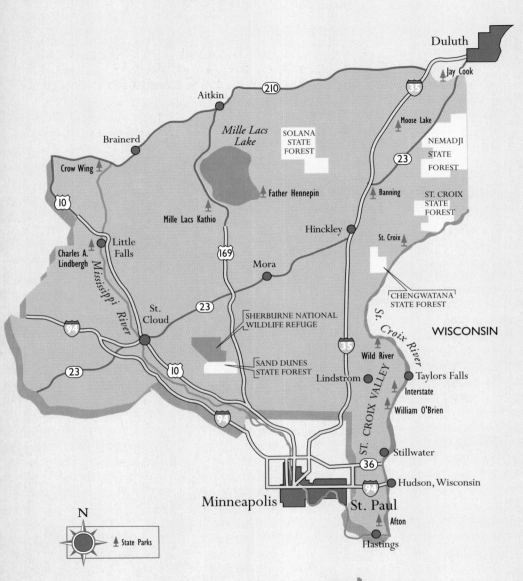

Duluth

Jay Cook

210

35

Aitkin

Mille Lacs Lake

SOLANA STATE FOREST

Moose Lake

NEMADJI STATE FOREST

23

Brainerd

Crow Wing

Father Hennepin

Banning

ST. CROIX STATE FOREST

10

Mille Lacs Kathio

Hinckley

St. Croix

Little Falls

Charles A. Lindbergh

Mississippi River

169

Mora

CHENGWATANA STATE FOREST

St. Cloud

23

SHERBURNE NATIONAL WILDLIFE REFUGE

St. Croix River

WISCONSIN

94

23

10

SAND DUNES STATE FOREST

35

Wild River

ST. CROIX VALLEY

Lindstrom

Taylors Falls

Interstate

94

William O'Brien

Stillwater

N

36

Minneapolis

St. Paul

Hudson, Wisconsin

94

Afton

State Parks

Hastings

East-Central Region

East-Central Region

The St. Croix River Valley at Interstate State Park. Copyright © Minnesota Office of Tourism. Used by permission.

Hinckley

Hinckley is midway between the Twin Cities and Duluth, and many people make it a ritual not just to take a rest at Hinckley, a historic lumber town, but specifically to stop on the east side of I-35 at Tobies for a caramel roll. Tobies started out small and seems to get bigger every time you visit. There is a casino east of Tobies, and restaurants west of I-35 are packed, too. Traffic is heavy on Sun. afternoons and early evenings, and you may want to avoid Hinckley then.

In addition to contemporary attractions such as the casino, and historic sites such as the North West Company fur post in Pine City and the Hinckley Fire Museum, the area around Hinckley and along I-35 has many recreational opportunities.

Hinckley is probably the best known of the towns in the area, but Pine City, Sandstone, and Mora—farther to the west—have attractions for tourists, too. In Mora, look for the 22-foot-high orange "Dala" horse in the Kanabec County Fairgrounds, south of downtown Mora on Hwy. 65. The Dala horses are a symbol of Sweden and an appropriate mascot for this Swedish-American community.

History

Logging began in Hinckley in 1869, and was the catalyst for European settlement, but prior to that there were several Ojibwe settlements in the area. Lumber and railroads were Hinckley's lifeblood, but it was the 1894 fire—the largest in Minnesota history—that etched its name deeply in state history books. Today Hinckley is the gateway to northern Minnesota and outdoor recreation.

Festivals and Events

Mora Vasaloppet
second Sun. in Feb.
Like the original Vasalopp cross-country ski race in Sweden, this one is a grueling trek for the nearly 2,000 skiers who attend. The two main races are 35 and 21 miles, but there is a shorter race, and also one for classical skiing, rather than skate-skiing. As in its sister race in Mora, Sweden, there are entrants from around the world, and blueberry soup to refresh tired athletes. Lots of spectators show up, too. Occasionally, lack of snow means the race is canceled. The finish line is in downtown Mora. **800-368-6672.**

Fall Gathering
mid-Sept.
This annual weekend festival at the North West Company fur post near Pine City usually attracts several thousand participants, who talk with costumed interpreters of both the fur trade and Ojibwe cultures, listen to live music, sample buffalo burgers, and take part in competitions, many of which, like the foot race and stone toss, are themselves historic. Free in the past, but call to see whether there is a fee. **320-629-6356.**

Outdoor Activities

Biking

Willard Munger Trail
The Willard Munger Trail is actually several mul-

tiple-use trails extending from Duluth to the Hinckley area. The main, paved portion, also called the Hinckley Fire Trail, follows the route of the train that saved the lives of many residents during the 1894 Hinckley fire and the Moose Lake–Cloquet fire of 1918. The paved trail extends for 70 miles and passes through Moose Lake State Park and near Banning State Park. There are parking lots at the north end of Hinckley, at Willow River, and at Moose Lake. For trail maps, contact the Dept. of Natural Resources, **500 Lafayette Rd., St. Paul, 55155, 800-766-6000** or **651-296-6157,** or the Munger Trail Towns Association, **218-485-8870.**

Boating

CANOEING

For maps of the rivers described below, contact the Dept. of Natural Resources, **500 Lafayette Rd., St. Paul, 55155; 800-766-6000 or 651-296-6157.**

Kettle River

During the great Hinckley fire of 1894, many Sandstone residents took cover in the Kettle River, but canoers and kayakers know the Kettle is one of the best white-water rivers in the region, with the rapids in Banning State Park (see Kayaking) ranging from Class II difficulty all the way to Class IV. In Pine County, the Kettle is classified as a state Wild and Scenic River. The river flows between wooded banks, with rocky cliffs seen along the Banning and lower Kettle rapids. The removal of a dam at Sandstone in 1995 has facilitated the flow of the river.

St. Croix River

The upper St. Croix is a virtual wilderness, its banks heavily wooded. Though generally easy to canoe, the St. Croix does have rapids to negotiate a few miles before the Kettle River joins it south of St. Croix State Park. There are numerous campsites and access points along the river. The river is designated a National Scenic Riverway, administered by the National Park Service. The Marshland Visitor Center for the upper river has a slide show, video, and exhibits on the

Getting There
Hinckley is about 75 miles north of the Twin Cities, right on I-35.

river ecology and other topics. The center has maps and camping information. Open Memorial Day–Labor Day, Thurs.–Mon., 8:30 A.M.–5:00 P.M.; May and Sept., Sat.–Sun., 8:30 A.M.–5:00 P.M. Located 12 miles east of Rock Creek. **Rte. 1, Box 134, Pine City, 55063; 320-629-2148.**

Snake River

The Snake River varies in difficulty from a calm stream to rapids of Class I to IV before it flows into the St. Croix River. Much of the river is very scenic, with some exposed sandstone bluffs. Granite outcrops and rolling hills provide proof of glacial activity.

KAYAKING

See the Kettle River in Canoeing.

Banning State Park

This wonderful state park can be overlooked by visitors hurrying to northern Minnesota, but it is well worth getting to know. The park is on the Kettle River, a beautiful, rushing river and one of the best white-water rivers in the state. Kayakers know it well. In fact, one of the park staff says visitors tend to come for two reasons: to kayak and to watch kayakers. And it's true that it's fascinating to watch kayakers decide how to shoot the rapids. The rapids in the river have descriptive names, such as Blueberry Slide, Mother's Delight, Dragon's Tooth, and Hell's Gate. The park is located at **Hwy. 23 and I-35, Sandstone, 55072; 320-245-2668.**

Fishing

Grindstone Lake near Sandstone is stocked annually with brown and rainbow trout yearlings. Other kinds of fish in Grindstone include lake trout, northern, large- and smallmouth bass, smelt, and herring. At 1,456-acre Sturgeon Lake, you'll find walleye, northern, largemouth bass, black crappies, rock bass, white sucker, and bluegill. Many other lakes in the county also offer good fishing. At Moose Lake State Park, there is a fishing pier; there are walleye, northern, and largemouth bass in both Moosehead and Echo Lakes (see Parks).

Hiking

There are plenty of hiking trails in the Hinckley area. See the Willard Munger Trail in Biking. In Banning State Park (see Kayaking), there is scenic and challenging hiking along the Kettle River, with plenty of rock formations to scramble over. Some of the cantilevered rocks look like rough-hewn versions of modern Finnish architecture. A 1.8-mile self-guided quarry trail goes past remnants of the quarry that was important in this area. There are 17 miles of hiking trails in all, plus 2 miles of trails for horseback riders and 1 mile of surfaced bike trail. Moose Lake State Park has 5 miles of hiking trails. The vast St. Croix State Park has 127 miles of hiking trails, with a 1.5-mile self-guided trail. See Parks.

Skiing

CROSS-COUNTRY

The state parks in the Hinckley area have groomed cross-country ski trails. In winter, 12 miles in Banning State Park are designated cross-country ski trails. In Moose Lake State Park, cross-country skiers have 7 miles of trails. Cross-country skiers have 11 miles of trails in St. Croix State Park. There is also skiing along the Willard Munger Trail (see Biking).

Snowmobiling

Pine County, which includes Hinckley and Pine River, has about 460 miles of groomed snowmobile trails, connecting with 1,200 miles of trails in adjoining areas. Banning State Park has 6 miles of trails for snowmobilers. In Moose Lake State Park, snowmobilers have 2 miles of trails. There are 80 miles of groomed snowmobile trails in St. Croix State Park, and a warming house to take the chill off. Nemadji State Forest has 68 miles of multipurpose trails, groomed for snowmobiles in winter. For information on trail conditions for snowmobiling or skiing, call **800-657-3700;** for

general information, contact the Hinckley Convention and Visitors Bureau, **800-996-4566.**

Seeing and Doing

Museums and Historic Sites

Hinckley Fire Museum

Even though it had been a hot, dry summer in Hinckley, no one was prepared for the Sept. 1, 1894, firestorm that killed 418 people in four hours, destroying six towns and consuming 400 square miles. Fireballs leaped more than 4 miles high and could be seen from as far away as Iowa. Despite these grim statistics, it is the individual tales—of both heroism and cowardice—told in the Hinckley Fire Museum that are the most affecting. One room in the museum is a re-created train depot office, where 25-year-old telegrapher Tommy Dunn was on duty as the fire began. A photo of Dunn shows a handsome young man with wavy dark hair, regular features, and a luxuriant mustache waxed into curls at each end. As the news of the fire spread, Tommy briefly left the office to tell the young woman who cared for his blind mother that he had tickets for them to leave on the "limited." That train, bound for Hinckley from Duluth, was heroically staffed by engineer Jim Root and his crew. Unable to turn around because of the fire, and swarmed with people trying to escape the flames, Root backed up the train through the flames and heat to the safety of Skunk Lake. Tommy Dunn, however, remained at his post. When the depot roof caught fire, everyone but Tommy ran. His last message was a poignant, "I think I stayed too long." His body was found the next day. Objects recovered from the fire, including china dolls, a once-white plate burned totally black, and a painted cream pitcher that survived unscathed, are easier to look at than the chilling record of the dead, with names, ages, and identifying characteristics, if they were known. Entry to the museum in the depot, rebuilt after the fire, includes a slide show and a look at the depot agent's apartment above the main depot. Open May 1–mid-Oct., daily, 10:00 A.M.–5:00 P.M. Fee. **106 Old Hwy. 61, Hinckley, 55037; 320-384-7338.**

North West Company Fur Post

History is easily absorbed during a visit to the North West Company Fur Post in Pine City. At the reconstructed wintering post, costumed living-history interpreters re-create the post's occupants, including John Sayer, director of the post, his company clerk, voyageurs, and Ojibwe Indians. The interpreters describe the post's life during the winter of 1804–1805 through a vivid "show and tell" of everyday objects in the living quarters and trading post located inside the palisaded enclosure, as well as outside in a birch-bark-covered wigwam. The post, on the Snake River, was used only a short time, then disappeared and was a cornfield until the 1960s, when Minnesota Historical Society archaeologists found evidence of the post. It was reconstructed with the help of Sayer's diary and opened in 1971. There is a trail along the river and there are picnic facilities. Open May–Labor Day, holiday Mon. and Tues.–Sat., 10:00 A.M.–5:00 P.M., and Sun., noon–5:00 P.M. Free. Exit I-35 at Pine City and follow County Rd. 7 for 1.5 miles to the post. **Box 51, Pine City, 55063; 612-629-6356.**

Parks

Banning State Park

A gem of a park, Banning is well known to kayakers (see Kayaking), but there is a bit of something for everyone—hikers and history buffs included. The park is located at **Hwy. 23 and I-35, Sandstone, 55072; 320-245-2668.**

Moose Lake State Park

Moose Lake State Park, one of the more recent state parks, was created in response to community requests for a recreation area. It is primarily a park for families who want to camp, swim, and fish. The sandy beach on the lake is nice for kids and there is a playground also. The park rents boats and canoes. Because the park is just off the interstate, it's a handy place for a cooling swim and a picnic for visitors headed still farther north. Located 0.25 mile east of I-35 on County Rd. 137 (take the Moose Lake exit). **4252 County Rd. 137, Moose Lake, 55767; 218-485-5420.**

St. Croix State Park

The St. Croix River was a conduit for meltwater from Lake Superior after the last glacial period, which left various soil types in the river valley, including a sand plain. The meltwater also swept debris from the Kettle River Valley, exposing sandstone and basalt. This action is evident at the Kettle River Highbanks in St. Croix State Park. The park administration is working to restore the unusual jack-pine barren area within the park. Eagles, bears, and timber wolves can be seen in the park, along with numerous wildflowers, including moccasin flowers and blazing stars. This huge recreation area (more than 34,000 acres), the largest in the system of state parks, has an unusual history. It is on land that was first cleared by logging and then abandoned by settlers who couldn't make a living out of the poor soil. In 1935, 18,000 acres were purchased to form the St. Croix Recreational Demonstration Area (RDA) to provide group camps for urban dwellers who wouldn't otherwise have a chance for a vacation outside the city. The Civilian Conservation Corps (CCC) and the Works Progress Administration (WPA) landscaped the area, built roads, and constructed the camps. The RDA became St. Croix State Park in 1943, but many of the buildings still stand and a number are on the National Register of Historic Places. In 1998 the entire park was declared a National Historic Landmark, a coveted designation. Interpretive signs describe the CCC workers and their lives. The park also has a lake with a swimming beach, and rents canoes and bikes. The park has 5.5 miles of surfaced bike trails. In addition, there are 21 miles of trails for mountain biking and 75 miles of trails for horseback riding. Located 15 miles east of Hinckley on Hwy. 48, then 5 miles south on County Rd. 22. **Rte. 3, Box 450, Hinckley, 55037; 320-384-6615.**

State Forests

Several state forests are in the Hinckley area. The two state forests north of St. Croix State Park—the **St. Croix** and **Nemadji State Forests**—both have a variety of recreational opportunities. The eastern, unpaved portion of the Willard

Munger Trail (see Biking) and also the Gandy Dancer Trail, a multipurpose trail that is in both Minnesota and Wisconsin, run through both forests. The St. Croix River forms the southeast boundary of the St. Croix Forest, and the Lower Tamarack River, along which there are several primitive campsites and a group horsecamp, winds through the forest. There are hiking, snowmobiling, and horseback riding trails. South of St. Croix State Park is the **Chengwatana State Forest,** bordered on the east by the St. Croix River. The Snake River flows through the forest. North of Hinckley, near Sturgeon Lake, is the smaller **General Andrews State Forest,** which has 9 miles of groomed and marked trails for snowmobiles, ATVs, and motorcycles. All four forests have campsites. For maps of the state forests, contact the Dept. of Natural Resources, **500 Lafayette Rd., St. Paul, 55155; 888-MINNDNR** or **651-296-6157.**

Tours

BOAT TOURS

Lady Savannah

A 65-foot replica of a paddle wheeler, the *Lady Savannah* offers sight-seeing as well as sight-seeing-and-meal cruises during summer on spring-fed Sturgeon Lake. Blue herons, osprey, eagles, loons, and lots of ducks may be seen during the cruise. Located **one block east of I-35 at the Sturgeon Lake exit (exit 209); 218-384-4908** or **218-372-4165.**

Wagering

Grand Casino Hinckley

In addition to thousands of slots, blackjack, bingo, and other games of chance, Grand Casino Hinckley has a children's activity center plus an arcade for teenagers. Grand Casino has restaurants, entertainment, and lodging in a hotel with 281 rooms; there is also an RV park. Open 24 hours. Located **east of I-35 at the Hinckley exit; 800-472-6321.**

Where to Stay

Hotels, Motels, and Inns

There are several chain motels in the Hinckley area, including the **Holiday Inn Express** in Hinckley, **800-558-0612** or **320-384-7171,** and **EconoLodge,** which is owned by Tobies (see Where to Eat), **800-55-ECONO** or **320-384-7451,** in addition to the hotel at Grand Casino (see Wagering). Ask at the tourist bureaus for other suggestions (see Services), including resorts.

Ann River Motel—$$

Swedish guests who come to the neat motel close by the Ann River outside of Mora must be pleasantly surprised to hear the owner, Roy Carlson, speaking Swedish to them. Carlson, who is Swedish American, and his wife, Sharon, have named the 23 units in the motel to each represent a different Swedish province, and decorated them with Carl Larsson prints and original art as well as some furniture made by Swedish-American craftspeople. The motel also stocks Swedish travel literature. Don't even think about turning up for the Vasaloppet cross-country ski race in Feb. without a reservation. Located at the intersection of Hwys. 65 and 23. **1819 S. Hwy. 65, Mora, 55051; 320-679-2972.**

Camping

State Forests—$

St. Croix State Forest has **Boulder Campground** (19 sites on Rock Lake) and a horsecamp on the Tamarack River (12 sites with no drinking water). The Chengwatana State Forest has the **Snake River Campground,** with 26 sites and canoe access to the river. For information on all, call **320-384-6146.**

State Parks—$

St. Croix State Park has a wide variety of accommodations. There are 211 drive-through sites, 42 with electricity, two backpack campsites, 10 canoe-in sites on both the Kettle and St. Croix Rivers, and four walk-in sites. In addition, there are 25 horsecamp sites, plus two two-story guest houses for groups and five summer-only housekeeping cabins that sleep two persons each. Tent campers predominate at **Banning State Park,** since only 11 of the 33 sites have electricity. There is one backpack campsite and also four canoe-in sites. **Moose Lake State Park** has 33 campsites, 20 with electricity, and also two walk-in campsites. For reservations at all state parks, call **The Connection, 800-246-CAMP** or **612-922-9000.**

Where to Eat

Tobies Restaurant—$ to $$$$

The original Tobies opened in downtown Hinckley in 1948, and the present owners bought it and moved it to the east side of the Hinckley exit off the interstate when it opened in 1966. Tobies has cheerful, friendly service and a casual atmosphere for travelers who want a break from the interstate. Known for its caramel and cinnamon rolls, Tobies also has a full menu in the coffee shop and restaurant. All the baked goods served with the meals are made by Tobies. There is often a line for the bakery goods during busy times. Open year-round, daily, 24 hours. Take exit 183 off I-35 in Hinckley. **320-384-6174.**

The Sportsman's Cafe—$ to $$

The Sportsman's in Mora is your typical small-town cafe, next to a bait shop and a block from a major intersection (Hwys. 65 and 23). What makes it memorable is the homemade pie. *Yesssss.* The rhubarb custard I ate one day consisted of tangy, tender chunks of rhubarb surrounded by velvety custard that had a lick of nutmeg in it. Most days, the cafe offers eight or 10 different kinds of pie. Try them all! Open year-round, daily, 24 hours. **67 Hwy. 65 N., Mora, 55051; 320-679-2322.**

Services

Hinckley Convention and Visitors Bureau, which moved to the east side of I-35 in the fall of 1998, has information on Hinckley and the surrounding area. **109 Tobie's Mill, Hinckley, 55037; 800-996-4566** or **320-384-0126.**

Mora Area Chamber of Commerce, 800-291-5792 or **320-679-5792.**

Mille Lacs and Aitkin

Mille Lacs is a lake, a band of Anishinabe (Ojibwe) Indians, and very nearly a state of mind. The lake itself is the second largest lake that is wholly within the state of Minnesota, second only to Red Lake. Its horizon seems endless. North of the lake, starting approximately at the busy little city of Aitkin, lies that idyllic country that Minnesotans simply refer to as "Up North." Near Mille Lacs, the countryside changes over to wilder, more forested land, with an increasing concentration of lakes and evergreens and far fewer farms. The area—Mille Lacs Lake in particular—draws serious anglers. The lake is ringed by resorts and is one of the last strongholds for small mom-and-pop cabins.

The communities around and near the lake—Onamia, Garrison, Isle, and, to a lesser degree, Aitkin—depend on tourism for their economic health. Aitkin, the largest town, with a population of 1,700, is the county seat of Aitkin County and the place where area residents go to shop, conduct business, and watch first-run movies in the art deco Rialto Theatre.

Located at the intersection of two major highways—169 and 210—Aitkin is a city with a sense of humor. Its visitor guide cites Aitkin's one stoplight as its most famous feature, notes that Aitkin has no parking meters, and claims that the distance from Aitkin to Lake Wobegon is 1,200 miles and 16 toll booths.

History

There is archaeological data showing that Mille Lacs has been inhabited for thousands of years, but it was the Dakota Indians who lived there when recorded history began. The Dakota inhabited the Mille Lacs area long before the Ojibwe (Anishinabe) moved in from the east. In 1679 Daniel Greysolon, Sieur Du Luth, planted the French flag in the large Dakota village called Izatys on the southwestern shore of the lake, and claimed it for France.

A year later, Father Louis Hennepin, a Recollect priest, and two companions were exploring the Mississippi River. "They were taken by Dakota Indians to a Dakota village at Kathio, and they stayed there about six months," says Jim Cummings, naturalist at Mille Lacs Kathio State Park. Du Luth returned to the Dakota village and Hennepin left with him. Hennepin later wrote a detailed account of his stay with the Dakota, including the hunting trip he took with a party that hunted buffalo from their canoes on the Rum River nearly where it meets the Mississippi near Anoka.

The Ojibwe and Dakota clashed often, and eventually the Ojibwe drove the Dakota out, primarily to southern Minnesota. According to Ojibwe historian William Warren, the decisive battle took place in 1750. The Mille Lacs Band of Ojibwe still lives on the western edge of the lake, on reservation land. Of late years, the band has seen its fortunes increase with the opening of a casino.

The fur trade flourished for a time here, with an American Fur Company post close to present-day Aitkin in the early 1800s. Lumbering replaced the fur trade as Aitkin's principal industry in the mid-1800s. To the west in the Cuyuna Iron Range, mining was carried out for several decades in the early 20th century. Tourism has been in the Mille Lacs area for decades; Izatys began as a small resort in 1922.

Major Attractions

Mille Lacs

Mille Lacs, which means "thousand lakes" in French, is indeed about as big as a thousand smaller lakes. The huge lake is about 200 square miles, with a surface area of approximately 132,000 acres. The lake, which would be nearly round if its east side weren't pushed in and flattened out, has about 80 miles of shoreline. It is relatively shallow, with an average depth of 20 feet; the deepest portion is approximately 42 feet. It is a notoriously dangerous place to be in a storm. Mille Lacs Lake has one outlet, the Rum River, which extends down to Anoka, where it meets the Mississippi River. Hwy. 169 runs along the west side of the lake, with a close-up view unobstructed by trees. In fact, the lake can look extremely bleak in gray weather, though—like any large body of water—it is extremely changeable and worth gazing at in all kinds of weather.

At the little town of Garrison, there is a rock concourse with a giant statue of a walleye on it. The fish is the symbol of the big draw on the lake. According to the Mille Lacs Area Tourism Council, 200,000–400,000 walleyes are caught in the lake each year. Mille Lacs is perhaps Minnesota's busiest fishing spot, winter and summer, day and night. A good share of the anglers are from the nearby Twin Cities. Many people fish from launches operated by resorts around the lake. Mille Lacs has its own website, with a wealth of information on fishing, lodging, etc., and a chat room that is absolutely filled with comments and

Getting There
Mille Lacs Lake is about one and a half hours north of the Twin Cities, on Hwy. 169; Aitkin is another half hour beyond the north end of the lake.

questions from anglers. Check it out. **Website: www.millelacslake.com.**

Rentals and Tours

Many resorts on the lake have launches for fishing, including **Izatys Golf and Yacht Club** in Onamia, **800-533-1728** or **320-532-3101; Eddy's Lake Mille Lacs Resort** in Onamia, which has half- and full-day launch trips daily, **320-532-3657; Twin Pines Resort and Motel** in Garrison, **800-450-4682** or **320-692-4413;** and **Fisher's Resort** in Isle, **320-684-2221,** which offers day and night fishing trips on its three launches. In addition, some of the sport shops in the area offer guide and launch service. The Mille Lacs Area Tourism Council (see Services) has a complete list. Many resorts and sports shops also rent ice-fishing houses and equipment. Most fish houses are heated and some can be used for overnight accommodations. The Mille Lacs Area Tourism Council has a complete list.

Closeup of beadwork at the Mille Lacs Indian Museum. Copyright © Minnesota Office of Tourism. Used by permission.

Festivals and Events

Mille Lacs Band PowWow

third weekend in Aug.

Sponsored by the Mille Lacs Band of Ojibwe, the powwow includes dance competitions, music, and drumming. The costumes are works of art. The powwow arena is north of the Grand Casino Mille Lacs (see Wagering), right beside the lake on the east side of Hwy. 169 in Onamia. Call the Mille Lacs Area Tourism Council (see Services).

Festival of Adventures/William Aitkin Fur Trade Rendezvous

mid-Sept.

Walk behind the Aitkin Depot and step into the past. Everywhere along the little Mud River are the sights and sounds of the Aitkin of 1790–1890, a century that saw the fur trade, the pine lumber camps, lively steamboat traffic on the Mississippi River, Ojibwe communities, and an influx of immigrants from Europe. They are all represented in this festival, their lives portrayed by costumed living-history interpreters who chat with visitors and demonstrate bygone skills, such as blacksmithing. Among the characters is William Aitkin, for whom Aitkin was named, who was the chief factor in the American Fur Company in the Aitkin area at one time. A temporary bridge spans the Ripple River (then called the Mud River) and leads visitors from one era to another. Period music, dancing and drumming by Ojibwe, and food are all part of the experience. Fee. The festival is held at the Depot Museum in Aitkin.

Camp the way your ancestors did, during the annual Festival of Adventures. Campers can reserve a spot, bring their own tepee or marquee, and participate in a living-history encampment. The camping is very basic—wood fires only, and no running water or electricity or indoor bathrooms here, but all basic needs are provided for. Participants are asked to dress in period clothing and take part in the historic nature of the festival. The Aitkin Area Chamber (see Services) has a packet of guidelines for first-time period campers. The campground is near the Aitkin Depot Museum. Call the Aitkin Area Chamber of Commerce (see Services).

Aitkin's World Famous Fish House Parade

Fri. after Thanksgiving

Along about Thanksgiving in Aitkin and other fishing strongholds, people start thinking about ice fishing. And in Aitkin, they don't just think about getting the fish house out on the ice, they parade them through the main street, in what seems to be the only fish house parade in the world. The ice-fishing houses, decorated with signs, slogans, and amusing paint jobs, are toted on top of ATVs. Entries have included a round fish house, a fish house owned by self-described "grumpy old women," and an antique fish house (circa 1947). Other floats, including outhouses, appear in the parade. Many of the fish houses wind up on Mille Lacs Lake just south of Aitkin, where "Frostbite Flats," a winter-only community of about 5,000 fish houses, blossoms on ice each year. For information, call **800-526-8342.**

Outdoor Activities

Biking

Soo Line Trail

The Soo Line Trail—114 miles in all—is under the jurisdiction of several counties and two states, and it has two spur trails. The portion of the trail from Onamia to Isle consists of two side-by-side tracks; one is paved. Farther north, sections in Aitkin County, including from McGregor to Palisade, are not paved and are primarily used by ATVs in summer and snowmobiles in winter. For information on the Onamia–Isle portion, call **888-350-2692;** for a map for the snowmobile portion of the trail, call the Aitkin Chamber of Commerce, **800-526-8342.**

Birding

Birders find the Aitkin/Mille Lacs area especially rewarding, as the number of state and federal land units provide good habitat and feeding material for both nesting and migrating birds. More than 200 species of birds have been sighted in the area. Visitors to Father Hennepin State Park may see hawks, ospreys, owls, and eagles.

Aspen stands provide good habitat for ruffed grouse. See Parks.

Rice Lake National Wildlife Refuge

In generations past, vast flocks of migrating birds passed over the sky like clouds. Today, this concentration of birds is a rare sight, but it can be seen each fall at Rice Lake, when about 150,000 ducks stop at the lake, usually during mid-Oct. In 1994, according to refuge officials, an astoundingly (and unusually) high number of ducks were estimated, 1.5 million. The refuge, created in 1935 by President Franklin Roosevelt, is also worth visiting at other times of the year. In addition to bird and wildlife observation, visitors can picnic and hike or cross-country ski along the trails. Binoculars and field guides are available on loan from the refuge headquarters. Free. Located off Hwy. 65, south of McGregor. The refuge headquarters is open during normal business hours, Mon.–Fri., 8:00 A.M.–4:30 P.M., but the refuge itself is always open. **Rte. 2, Box 67, McGregor, 55760; 218-768-2402.**

Boating

CANOEING

Mississippi River

Near Aitkin, the slow-moving Mississippi River is easy for beginners to canoe. There are many oxbows, with channels looping around islands in the river. The terrain is flat, as this area is the bed of Glacial Lakes Upham and Aitkin. For a map, contact the Dept. of Natural Resources, **500 Lafayette Rd., St. Paul, 55155; 888-MINNDNR or 651-296-6157.**

Ripple River

The Ripple, one of the state's longest rivers, is a pleasant place to canoe near Aitkin. The Aitkin Area Chamber of Commerce (see Services) has information on local recreational opportunities.

Rum River

The meandering Rum River, designated a State Wild and Scenic Riverway, has many Class I rapids, with some Class II occurring during high water. There are a number of rocky boulder beds,

which may be difficult for beginners to deal with. The river begins in Mille Lacs Lake and extends to Anoka, a distance of 145 miles. The upper river valley has perhaps the greatest number of prehistoric sites, including burial mounds, in Minnesota. The river travels through marshes, farmland, hardwood-covered bottomlands, and remnants of the great white and red pine forests. Campsites and accesses are noted on the map, which is available from the Dept. of Natural Resources, **500 Lafayette Rd., St. Paul, 55155; 888-MINNDNR or 651-296-6157.**

Diving

Lakes formed when the mines were abandoned in the Cuyuna Iron Range, 10 miles west of Aitkin and north of Mille Lacs, are now favored spots for scuba divers. For information, contact the Aitkin Area Chamber of Commerce (see Services).

Fishing

Walleye? Did someone say walleye? Yes, walleye and Mille Lacs are nearly synonymous (see Major Attractions). The lake, a famed "walleye factory," also contains big perch, muskies, pike, and smallmouth bass. Ice fishing is also big at Mille Lacs. If you drive around the lake in spring, summer, or fall, you'll spot clusters of ice-fishing houses. In winter, they are all out on the ice, approximately 5,000 of them. Most locals have their own, but anglers up for the day or several days can rent them also (see Major Attractions). Mille Lacs is not the only lake in the area with fish, however. Within a 10-mile radius of Aitkin alone there are 365 lakes, according to the chamber of commerce. Ask resorts and also the Aitkin Area Chamber of Commerce (see Services) for advice on where to fish. There is also good fishing in the Rum River, with northerns found near the source of the river and smallmouth bass throughout.

Golf

In addition to those listed below, there are courses in Deerwood, Garrison, Hill City, and McGregor/Palisade; call the tourism bureaus (see Services) for details.

Izatys Golf and Yacht Club

Located on the south shore of Mille Lacs Lake, and designed by the Dye Designs course architects, Izatys Sanctuary course is abloom with wildflowers in season. Ten holes have natural water hazards, and 13 of the 18 holes are doglegs. The 11th hole is 612 yards long (from the championship tees). A second 18-hole course, Black Brook, is scheduled to open in July 1999. Greens fees range from $35–$85; higher fees include a cart. Open mid-Apr.–Sept., 7:00 A.M.–dusk (Sanctuary) and 7:00 A.M.–5:00 P.M. (Black Brook). **800-533-1728.**

Ruttger's Bay Lake Resort

Golfing has been a part of northern Minnesota vacations since Ruttger's on Bay Lake put in the first resort course in 1921. That early course, which had oiled sand greens, has long since been upgraded. Now Ruttger's has 27 holes of golf—**The Lakes,** a championship course designed by Joel Goldstrand, is built around two natural lakes; water hazards added to the lakes mean that there is water to be admired (and avoided) on 10 of the 18 holes. Ruttger's also has a nine-hole course on Hwy. 6, northwest of Garrison. Greens fees for 18 holes are $38.50 Mon.–Fri. and $42.50 Sat.–Sun. Clubs can be rented. Open mid-Apr.–Oct., daily, dawn–dusk. **800-450-4545 or 218-678-2885.**

Hiking

State parks and the Rice Lake National Wildlife Refuge (see Birding) are among the best hiking

Aitkin's annual fish house parade. Photo courtesy of the Aitkin Area Chamber of Commerce: Carol Kukowski.

bets, along with the Soo Line Trail (see Biking). Mille Lacs Kathio State Park has 35 miles of hiking trails, with a 0.5-mile self-guided trail. There are 4 miles of hiking trails in Father Hennepin State Park, along the lakeshore and in the park interior. See Parks.

Hunting

Hunting is a big part of life for many people in the Mille Lacs area. Deer, bear, game birds, and ducks are the usual quarries. For more information, contact the Dept. of Natural Resources field office in Onamia, **320-532-3537.**

Skiing

CROSS-COUNTRY

There are numerous miles of cross-country trails in the area. Mille Lacs Kathio State Park has a fine system for all levels, with 19.6 miles of trails. In Father Hennepin State Park, local residents often ski on the 3 miles of ungroomed trails. See Parks. For information on other trails, contact the tourism bureaus (see Services).

Snowmobiling

The Aitkin/Mille Lacs area together have hundreds of miles of groomed snowmobile trails. Mille Lacs Kathio State Park has 19 miles of trails for snowmobilers, plus a sliding hill and a warming house. Contact the tourism bureaus (see Services) for details and reports on snow conditions.

Seeing and Doing

Art Galleries and Museums

Jaques Art Center

Francis Lee Jaques grew up in Aitkin, and there he learned to love and observe the outdoors well. He became a well-known artist, often drawing on his Minnesota roots. He painted many of the dioramas in the American Museum of Natural History in New York, and also the Bell Museum on the University of Minnesota campus. He is perhaps better known as an illustrator of many books, including those of his wife, Florence Page

Jaques, and famed naturalist Sigurd Olson (see the Ely chapter in the Northeast Region). Many of Jaques's works are powerful, stark woodcuts. The art center, which opened in 1996, is assembling some of Jaques's works, and also holds exhibits of other artists as well as offers classes. Open year-round, Tues.–Sat., 11:00 A.M.–4:00 P.M. Located in a 1911 Carnegie library in Aitkin. **121 Second St. NW, Aitkin, 56431; 218-927-2363.**

Museums and Historic Sites

Aitkin County Historical Society Museums

The Depot Museum, in the old Aitkin train depot, has an extensive collection depicting various phases in Aitkin history, including immigration, the part the Mississippi played in early transportation, and the changes wrought by the coming of the railroad in the 1870s. Adjacent to the Depot Museum is a Logging Museum. Living-history presentations are a popular part of the museums' programs. Located two blocks south of the stoplights in Aitkin. Open Wed. and Fri.–Sat., 10:00 A.M.–4:00 P.M. **P.O. Box 215, Aitkin, 65431; 218-927-3348.**

Ice fishing on Mille Lacs Lake. Copyright © Minnesota Office of Tourism. Used by permission.

Croft Mine Historical Park

The mine elevator rumbles and visitors have the deceptive sensation of descending hundreds of feet. When the door opens, they walk along an underground corridor, once a railroad track in the iron mine on the Cuyuna Iron Range in north-central Minnesota. Costumed "miners" explain the workings of the mine at various stations along the way. On the surface are mining machines, Cuyuna Iron Range discoverer Cuyler Adams's office, and other historic artifacts and buildings. The Croft Mine is now operated by the Minnesota Dept. of Natural Resources. Call for hours. Fee. Located in Crosby. For information, write the Crosby-Ironton Joint Powers Board, **Box 97, Ironton, 56455; 218-546-5466** or **218-546-5625.**

Mille Lacs Indian Museum

Thousands of years of history are retold at the beautiful museum, new in 1996. The building itself is part of the story: the stylized oak-leaf tile design around the outside of the cedar building is based on traditional design and created by the late Batiste Sam, who was well known for her beadwork. Inside, the museum tells the Ojibwe story from the time they migrated to Minnesota to the present day, using interactive displays, videos, and recordings. The Ojibwe daily life of 200 years ago throughout the seasons is explained in the Four Seasons Room, with dioramas and special lighting. The figures portraying the long-ago Ojibwe are plaster casts modeled on real people. One of them, Frank Sam, who is in the "summer" section of the room, is an elder of the Mille Lacs Band. Exhibits include a section on Ojibwe in the U.S. military service and also on dancing. The story of the origin of the jingle dresses worn in dance competitions fascinates visitors. If you are lucky, band artisans may be demonstrating traditional crafts, such as beadwork and birchbark basket making, or teaching them to people enrolled in the classes offered frequently. Special events at the museum include Ojibwe storytelling and tasting festivals of traditional foods. In the fall of 1999, a series of programs featuring members of other tribes—including Navaho and Ho-Chunk (formerly called Winnebago)—will be presented. The museum, although on the Mille Lacs Reservation, is operated by the Minnesota Historical Society. Open mid-Apr.–Labor Day, Mon.–Sat., 10:00 A.M.–6:00 P.M., and Sun., noon–6:00 P.M.; Labor Day–mid-Apr., Mon.–Sat., 10:00 A.M.–5:00 P.M., and Sun., noon–5:00 P.M. Fee. Located on the southwest shore of Mille Lacs Lake. **HCR 67, Box 195, Onamia, 56359; 320-532-3632.**

Parks

Father Hennepin State Park

The beautiful sand beach at Father Hennepin, one of the smaller state parks, is a major attraction of the park. The curving beach is a wonderful spot for kids, and also provides an excellent spot to watch the setting sun and its reflections on the lake. A playground is adjacent to the beach. There is a handicapped-accessible fishing pier on the lake as well as two boat ramps. Remnants of the pine forest, most of which was logged earlier, are in the park, along with hardwood trees. Located on the southeast shore of Mille Lacs Lake near Isle. **P.O. Box 397, Isle, 56342; 320-676-8763.**

Mille Lacs Kathio State Park

Mille Lacs Kathio can be enjoyed for many different reasons. The large park—fourth largest in the state system—has both superb recreational facilities and sites of great historic importance. For thousands of years, the area that is now the park was inhabited by a succession of American Indian communities, from the Old Copper Culture group to the Dakota to the Ojibwe who still live in the area today. Extensive archaeological digs in and near the park have revealed village sites, burial mounds, and habitation sites that are as old as 3,500 years, plus spearheads and artifacts believed to be 9,000 years old. More than 20 prehistoric sites are on the three lakes formed within the Rum River as it flows south out of Mille Lacs Lake. In one of these villages, the priest/explorer Louis Hennepin spent six months among the Dakota in 1680. The historic and recreational aspects of the park blend felicitously in programs under the direction of Jim Cummings, an anthropologist and former high school teacher who

has been the park naturalist since 1984. "What makes my job exciting is to connect people with their history," says Cummings. Of the canoe trips offered each summer to visitors, he says, "Visitors can paddle in the same kind of craft on the same river as Father Hennepin." In addition to the canoe trips, programs include campfire storytelling, climbing the 100-foot observation tower, walks to Petaga Point's 3,500-year-old "campsite," cross-country skiing by candlelight, snowshoe hikes, demonstrations of how arrowheads were made by flint knapping, and nature films. Canoes, skis, and snowshoes are provided for these activities by reservation. Many of the programs have size limits; reserve places early. The park has 25 miles of trails for horseback riding. Located 1 mile off Hwy. 169 on County Rd. 26. **15066 Kathio State Park Rd., Onamia, 56359; 320-532-3523.**

Scenic Drives

The 9.5-mile self-guided auto tour of Rice Lake National Wildlife Refuge is perhaps best driven in the fall, when the open fields turn gentle hues and trees that line the road on part of the drive meet overhead in a kaleidoscope of colors. Signs along the route explain historic sites, including a former CCC camp, an abandoned rail line, and American Indian burial mounds. See Birding.

Shopping

Butler's

Is this a department store, a museum, or a quilter's specialty shop? Whatever—as Minnesotans say. Housed in an enormous, high-ceilinged building that was once the Aitkin Opera House, Butler's has lots of items you didn't know you needed till you see them, such as checked oilcloth, cobbler's aprons, and penny candy. There is a display of Victorian artifacts, old license plates, farm implements, and an arrowhead collection in addition to clothing, and a huge selection of fabrics in the downstairs portion. Located 1 block north of the stoplight in Aitkin. Open Mon.–Fri., 9:00 A.M.–5:30 P.M., and Sat., 9:00 A.M.–5:00 P.M. **301 Minnesota Ave. N., Aitkin, 56431; 218-927-2185.**

Mille Lacs Indian Museum Trading Post

Don't miss the trading post if you want to buy

locally made Ojibwe crafts and also good-quality items from other tribal groups. Some of the artists who do the beadwork, birch-bark baskets, moccasins, and other items are well known for their traditional arts. There has been a trading post here beside the lake since 1925, and the recent refurbishing of it has kept the period charm, right down to the old-fashioned gas pumps in front of the white frame building. Open mid-Apr.–Labor Day, Mon.–Sat., 10:00 A.M.–6:00 P.M., and Sun., noon–6:00 P.M.; Labor Day–mid-Apr., Mon.–Sat., 10:00 A.M.–5:00 P.M., and Sun., noon–5:00 P.M. Located next to the Mille Lacs Indian Museum, on the southwest shore of Mille Lacs Lake (see Museums and Historic Sites). **HCR67, Box 195, Onamia, 56359; 320-532-3632.**

Wagering

Grand Casino Mille Lacs

The Mille Lacs Band of Ojibwe runs this huge casino, bustling with people who come to gamble at the slots, blackjack, and bingo tables and listen to the big-name entertainers. The casino has several restaurants and a child-care facility, plus a pool and hotel adjacent to the casino. Open 24 hours. Located **on Hwy. 169 on the west shore of Mille Lacs Lake north of Onamia; 800-626-5825.**

Wineries

Minnesota Wild Winery

The fruits and berries of northern Minnesota are used in making wines here. Visitors are welcome to taste before buying. Adjacent to the tasting room is a shop with other north-woods products, including syrups, jellies, honey, and wild rice. Open Mon.–Sat., 10:00 A.M.–5:00 P.M., and Sun., noon–5:00 P.M. Located **0.5 mile north of McGregor on Hwy. 65; 800-328-6731.**

Where to Stay

Resorts

Eddy's Lake Mille Lacs Resort—$$$ to $$$$

This resort, right on the west shore of Mille Lacs,

has large, nicely furnished rooms, all with a microwave, coffeemaker, and refrigerator. The 80 units include one suite with a wood-burning fireplace, one with a gas fireplace, and one with a Jacuzzi. The hotel has a pool and sauna. The resort has a 73-foot launch for fishing, with three trips daily, May 15–Oct. 15. **HCR67, Box 104, Onamia, 56359; 800-657-4704** or **320-532-3657.**

Izatys Golf and Yacht Club—$$$ to $$$$

Izatys is a sleek resort, with a multitude of activities, winter and summer, including a 120-slip marina, fishing with guides, swimming in the inviting outdoor pool, hiking trails, supervised children's programs, and an ice-skating rink. From 1922 until 1988, Izatys was a family resort but has since changed hands and expanded enormously. In addition to its current championship golf course, Izatys plans to open another 18-hole course by the year 2000 (see Golf). The accommodations include two-story beach villas, two-story cottages alongside the golf course, and townhomes on the lake. All have kitchens and some have fireplaces. Located on the south shore of Mille Lacs Lake, on Izatys Rd., off Hwy. 27 E. **40005 85th Ave., Onamia, 56359; 800-533-1728. Website: www.izatys.com.**

Ruttger's Bay Lake Resort—$$$ to $$$$

Such a deal—bed, board, and a boat for five bucks a week at Ruttger's Bay Lake Resort. But wait—that was in 1898, the year Minnesota's first resort was started, by Joe and Josie Ruttger. The fourth generation of Ruttgers is running the resort (and other Ruttger resorts in the state) and the prices are considerably higher, but times have changed and Ruttger's has changed with the times. You can do all of the traditional resort activities at Ruttger's, such as fishing, swimming from the 2,000-foot sandy beach, etc., but there are many other activities—including cooking classes, wine seminars, and windsurfing lessons. Ruttger's has 27 holes of golf (see Golf) and the grounds are filled with 50,000 blooming annuals and perennials. Accommodations range from log cabins with modern amenities to lake- or golf-side condominiums, villas, and lodge rooms. The log dining room in the main lodge was built in

Exterior of Mille Lacs Indian Museum. Photo courtesy of the Minnesota Historical Society.

1922. **Box 400, Deerwood, 56444; 800-450-4545. Website: www.ruttgers.com.**

Twin Pines Resort and Motel—$$ to $$$$

A good example of the Mille Lacs mom-and-pop resorts, the Twin Pines is close to the lake on the west shore. The mom and pop here—Linda and Bill Eno—came to the area after working in major hotel chains, and their experience shows. There are six rooms above the main building, including the St. Alban's Suite, a corner room with an outstanding view of the lake, a fireplace, a full kitchen, and a separate seating area. There are five cabins attached by carports and two completely separate cabins. Twin Pines has a swimming beach and a water trampoline, and rents wet-bikes. Fishing launch trips are available. Located on Hwy. 169, 1.5 miles south of Garrison. **HCR1, Box 35, Garrison, 56450; 800-450-4682 or 320-692-4413.**

Camping

Aitkin Campground—$

This is the best of both camping worlds. Aitkin Campground on the Mississippi River has a country feel to it, but it's within walking distance of downtown Aitkin. There are only seven campsites, six with electrical hookups. There is boat access to the river, drinking water, and an RV dump station. (There are also three other county campgrounds in Aitkin County.) Reservations by check; no credit cards. Contact the Aitkin County Land Dept., **209 Second St. NW, Aitkin, 56431; 218-927-7364.**

State Parks—$

Father Hennepin State Park has 103 drive-in sites, 41 with electricity and four of them handicapped-accessible. **Mille Lacs Kathio State Park** has 70 drive-in sites, 22 with electricity, three walk-in sites, a horsecamp with 10 sites, and five year-round camper cabins. For reservations at all state parks, call **The Connection, 800-246-CAMP** or **612-922-9000.**

Where to Eat

Some of the resorts (see Where to Stay), such as Ruttger's and Izatys, have restaurants serving excellent meals. The smaller resorts sometimes do not have food service.

Headquarters Lodge—$$ to $$$

Housed in one of the oldest buildings on the lakeshore, the Headquarters is a busy place known for its good food. The H.Q. specialty is walleye prepared several ways, including broiled and blackened. The Louisiana Gumbo Boat served in a ceramic boat is another favorite. The Headquarters also has steak, chicken, and seafood entrees. On Sundays in summer there is a smorgasbord, and in winter ethnic food is featured every few weeks. Open year-round, daily, 4:00–10:00 P.M. Located **on Hwy. 169 in Garrison; 320-692-4346.**

Zig's (Ruttger's Bay Lake Lodge)—$$ to $$$

"Zig" was an early Ruttger's employee who took tender care of the golf course. Now his name adorns the main Ruttger's restaurant. One dinner specialty is walleye, pan-fried with a potato crust, served over a mix of wild rice and orzo with cucumber relish. Lunch entrees include sandwiches and burgers, and among the brunch entrees is potato pancakes, served with applesauce, sausage, and maple syrup. Open Apr.–Oct., Mon.–Sat., 11:00 A.M.–11:00 P.M., and Sun., 9:00 A.M.–9:00 P.M.; Nov.–Mar., Thurs.–Sat., 5:00–9:00 P.M. **Box 400, Deerwood, 56444; 800-450-4545** or **218-534-2929** for current restaurant hours. **Website: www.ruttgers.com.**

Eddy's Waterfront Restaurant—$ to $$$

This casual restaurant, decorated with trophy fish and owned by the adjacent Lake Mille Lacs Resort, is a good place for a meal with a view. The menu includes homemade soup and chili and hamburger specials as well as walleye and other dinner entrees. Open Sun.–Thurs., 7:30 A.M.–9:00 P.M., and Fri.–Sat., 7:30 A.M.–10:00 P.M. Located **north of Onamia on Hwy. 169; 800-657-4704 or 320-532-3657.**

Twin Pines—$ to $$$

Dinner specials at Twin Pines are barbecue pork ribs, broasted chicken, and ham steak served in the cozy dining room, but the real claim to fame at Twin Pines is the all-day breakfast. Open year-round, daily, 7:00 A.M.–8:00 P.M.. Located on Hwy. 169, 1.5 miles south of Garrison. **HCR1, Box 35, Garrison, 56450; 800-450-4682 or 320-692-4413.**

Services

The **Aitkin Area Chamber of Commerce** has a wealth of information for tourists. Stop by and pick up some brochures or call the pleasant people who run it. Aitkin's website is among the most helpful around. Located **on Aitkin's main street, Second St. NW, between First Ave. NW and Minnesota Ave. N.; 800-526-8342 or 218-927-2316. Website: www.aitkin.com.**

Devoted exclusively to the Mille Lacs area, the **Mille Lacs Area Tourism Council** has a brochure chock full of information. P.O. **Box 362, Isle, 56342; 888-350-2692. Website: www.millelacs.com.**

St. Cloud and Little Falls

St. Cloud, just an hour to the northwest of the Twin Cities, is within commuting distance for school or work either from or to Minneapolis–St. Paul. While St. Cloud is not a tourist destination, it is worth a stop, if only to see the spectacular and inviting Munsinger and Clemens Gardens (see Gardens and Arboreta), which are among the highlights of the state.

Another reason not to just visit but to move to St. Cloud is a Harvard study that indicated that women in Stearns County live longer than anyone else in the country—an average of 83.5 years. St. Cloud has a population of nearly 50,000 and Little Falls, which is approximately 25 minutes north of St. Cloud, has more than 7,000. Both are on the Mississippi River. Little Falls draws tourists who come to see the boyhood home of aviator Charles Lindbergh.

History

The Woodland Culture Indians inhabited the area near the current cities of St. Cloud and Little Falls in prehistoric times. Their successors were first the Dakota and later the Ojibwe. In the late 1700s, there were fur-trading posts along the Mississippi; in 1805 Lieutenant Zebulon Pike journeyed to Little Falls and wrote that it was "a remarkable rapid in the river, opposite a high piny island." Extensive white settlement began after the Dakota relinquished rights to most of southern Minnesota in 1851.

Settlement began early in Little Falls, and in 1849 the Little Falls Mills and Land Company was formed, building a dam at the falls that served as a source of power. A later dam was constructed in 1887, and the era of big lumber began when the Pine Tree Lumber Company was started by Charles Weyerhaeuser and R. D. Musser.

The first large-scale German immigration to St. Cloud arrived in 1854, encouraged by missionary Father Francis X. Pierz. During World War I, the loyalty of St. Cloud's German Americans was called into question, and the Minnesota National Guard was activated to protect several railroad bridges against potential acts of sabotage, according to an article in the May 1998 issue of *Crossings,* a publication of the Stearns County Historical Society. St. Cloud and surrounding towns are still known as German Catholic strongholds.

Festivals and Events

Swayed Pines Folk Festival
late Apr.
Fans of folk music flock to St. John's University at Collegeville, north of St. Cloud, for a day of outdoor fiddling, demonstrations of such crafts as pottery, violin making, and woodworking, and evening performances by well-known folk musicians. **320-363-3249.**

Wheels, Wings and Water Festival

late June

Billed as one of the largest festivals in areas outside the Twin Cities, this four-day event has something for everyone, in venues all over St. Cloud. It features free concerts of both orchestral and popular music, a bike tour, an art fair, a parade, and children's activities. Call the St. Cloud Area Convention and Visitors Bureau (see Services).

Getting There

St. Cloud is about an hour north of the Twin Cities, via I-94 or U.S. Hwy. 10. Little Falls is another 25 or 30 minutes north of St. Cloud on U.S. Hwy. 10.

Outdoor Activities

Biking

The **Beaver Islands Trail** runs for 2.5 miles along the west bank of the Mississippi River in St. Cloud; call **320-255-7216** for details. St. Cloud also has bike trails in Whitney Park and along Clearwater Rd. The Lake Wobegon (a registered trademark) Regional Trail opened in 1998; call the St. Cloud Area Convention and Visitors Bureau (see Services) for information.

Birding

Sherburne National Wildlife Refuge

Bring your binoculars when you visit the refuge, stay in one spot for a while, and scan the fields, ponds, and trees for sandhill cranes, great horned owls, great blue herons, eaglets in their nest, and other wild creatures. The refuge is a vast place (31,000 acres) that keeps its secrets from those who try to rush through it. Stop at the headquarters for advice, then hike a trail. On weekends, volunteers are often on duty with spotting scopes to help visitors. Consult refuge authorities about when and where hunting, fishing, and biking are permitted. An 8-mile wildlife drive is open to vehicles late Apr.–end of Oct., during daylight hours. To reach the refuge, turn west on County Rd. 9 from U.S. Hwy. 169; the headquarters is 5.5 miles down the road. **17076 293rd Ave., Zimmerman, 55398; 612-389-3323.**

Boating

CANOEING

The St. Francis River, which runs through Sherburne National Wildlife Refuge, can be canoed, and there are several designated access points (see Birding).

Mississippi River

If you don't mind portaging around four dams between Little Falls and St. Cloud, canoeing on this stretch of the Mississippi can be pleasant. However, there are rapids before each dam, and canoers should be careful to portage well before the dams. The river is less wild below Little Falls, but there is still good fishing and plenty of wildlife to be seen, including a heron rookery atop a 60-foot bluff. There are campsites at Seven Islands between Little Falls and St. Cloud. South of Little Falls, Charles A. Lindbergh State Park has one canoe-in campsite on Pike Creek, which empties into the river. Below the town of Sartell, the riverbanks become very urban. For a map of the canoe route, contact the Dept. of Natural Resources, **500 Lafayette Rd., St. Paul, 55155; 800-766-6000 or 651-296-6157.**

Skiing

CROSS-COUNTRY

Lindbergh State Park (5.5 miles of trails—see Parks), St. Cloud city parks, and the Sherburne National Wildlife Refuge (see Birding) all have cross-country ski trails. The groomed trails at Camp Ripley, north of Little Falls, are open to the public on some Sun. during winter (see Museums and Historic Sites). Call the Camp Operations for details; **320-632-7346.**

Snowmobiling

There are more than 400 miles of groomed trails in the Little Falls area; call the chamber of commerce (see Services) for a guide.

Charles A. Lindbergh, Jr. House in Little Falls. Photo courtesy of the Minnesota Historical Society.

Seeing and Doing

Gardens and Arboreta

Munsinger Gardens and Clemens Rose Gardens

The Munsinger and Clemens Gardens together are surely one of the best, if not *the* best, gardens in the state. Parallel to one another, they provide visitors with totally different experiences. The Clemens Rose Gardens, a series of six connected gardens that include a garden with more than 1,200 rosebushes, an all-white garden, and a perennial garden, is formal in design and accented with cast-iron ornamentation, including a marvelous tiered fountain. It was donated to the city by Bill Clemens, a St. Cloud businessman whose late wife, Virginia, had been disabled by multiple sclerosis. The Clemenses lived across from the garden and Mrs. Clemens was able to look out and see the garden her husband dedicated to her. The origin of the Munsinger Gardens is not nearly so romantic. The gardens began as part of a park in 1915 and became a garden in the 1930s. The gardens, directly below the rose gardens and con-

nected by a walkway, are on the site of a sawmill right along the Mississippi River. Much less formal than the Clemens Gardens, the Munsinger Gardens are a marvelous haven, with huge mature trees, both shade- and sun-loving flowers, curving paths, a lily pond, gazebo, and swaying benches on which to sit and gaze at the rivers. All the plants in the garden are grown in the greenhouses here. Free. Both gardens open daily, sunrise–sunset. Located **between Michigan Ave. and 13th St. SE, and between Kilian Blvd. and the river in St. Cloud; 320-255-7238.**

Museums and Historic Sites

Charles A. Weyerhaeuser Memorial Museum

This gem of a museum operated by the Morrison County Historical Society is worth a visit to see the building and grounds alone; the exhibits on county history, displayed in light and airy rooms, are icing on the cake. Historical exhibits include the Mississippi River, lumbering, and ethnic settlement in the county. Fittingly, since Weyerhaeuser was a lumber baron, the museum is a paean to wood, as it is constructed with narrow wooden siding, interior and exterior wood shutters, and wood-paneled doors. The floors in the corridors are paved in slate. The three wings of the museum shelter a pretty paved courtyard with a fountain and gazebo. Prairie plants on the grounds are native to the county. Free. Open year-round, Tues.–Sat., 10:00 A.M.–5:00 P.M.; mid-May–mid-Oct., Sun., noon–5:00 P.M. **1600 Lindbergh Dr. S., Little Falls, 56345; 320-632-4007.**

Hill Monastic Manuscript Library

Located in St. John's University (see below), the manuscript library, begun in 1965, is the largest repository of microfilm copies of manuscripts, primarily medieval, in the world. More than 25 million pages from more than 90,000 volumes have been filmed. The public is welcome to visit and even to do research on the manuscripts. The catch is, nearly all are in medieval Latin. The library also has original manuscripts and books, including beautifully illuminated versions of the Book of Hours, many manuscript facsimiles, and also many books of interest to medieval scholars. A slide show introduces the library to visitors. A gift shop carries medieval reproductions and tapes and CDs of medieval music. There is a charge for copies of microfilmed manuscripts, but entrance to the library is free. The library is open Mon.–Fri., 8:00 A.M.–4:30 P.M.; the gift shop is open Mon.–Fri., 8:00 A.M.–4:30 P.M., Sat., 10:00 A.M.–4:30 P.M., and Sun., 11:30 A.M.–4:30 P.M. For directions, see St. John's University, below. **320-363-3514. Website: www.csbsju.edu/hmml.**

Lindbergh House

Charles A. Lindbergh, Jr., in 1927 the first person to fly the Atlantic Ocean alone, spent his boyhood here on the banks of the Mississippi. The farmhouse was mostly used in summers by the Lindbergh family. The house contains many family items; the adjacent interpretive center, operated by the Minnesota Historical Society, tells the story of Lindbergh's life. Open mid-May–Labor Day, Mon.–Sat., 10:00 A.M.–5:00 P.M., and Sun., noon–5:00 P.M.; Labor Day–late Oct., Sat., 10:00 A.M.–4:00 P.M., and Sun., noon–4:00 P.M. Fee. **1620 Lindbergh Dr. S., Little Falls, 56345; 320-632-3154.**

Minnesota Baseball Hall of Fame

Photographs and artifacts of state baseball history, from amateurs to the Minnesota Twins, can be seen in this exhibit, housed on the second level of the St. Cloud Civic Center (the Hall of Fame is hoping for a more permanent home). Open Mon.–Fri., 8:00 A.M.–4:30 P.M., and also at times when the Civic Center is open for evening or weekend events. Free (except when admission is charged for Civic Center programs). **10 Fourth Ave. S., St. Cloud, 56301; 320-255-7272.**

Minnesota Military Museum

The museum located at Camp Ripley, a National Guard training camp, showcases Minnesota's role in the state and national military, from the early days of Fort Snelling to the present. The museum includes a collection of small arms used by the military and an exhibit about frontier forts, including old Fort Ripley, on the site of the current Camp Ripley. Open late May–early Sept., Wed.–Sun., 10:00 A.M.–5:00 P.M.; closed national holidays. Free. Located **7 miles north of Little Falls on Hwy. 115; 320-632-6631, ext. 374.**

St. John's University

St. John's University—Minnesota's oldest continuous center of higher learning, founded in 1857—balances the old and the new in its campus a few miles northwest of St. Cloud. The most striking structure is the massive Abbey Church, designed by architect Marcel Breuer and finished in 1961. Breuer also designed many other buildings at St. John's, including part of St. John's Abbey. The Abbey building, where the monks live, is a quadrangular building, part dating to 1868. Somehow, Breuer's stark, strong lines coexist happily with the campus's older buildings, many built a century before the newcomers. On campus is the studio of Richard Bresnahan, a potter who uses local clay for his pottery. A brochure with a detailed, self-guided walking tour is available. Tours of the campus are also given daily in summer; assemble at the Sexton Commons. Exit at the Collegeville sign going north on I-35 from St. Cloud. **Collegeville, 56321; 320-363-2011.**

Stearns County Heritage Center

This handsome museum set in a nature center amid ponds and hiking paths has exhibits on the granite industry (St. Cloud is called the granite city), natural and pioneer history, and transportation, including the "Pan" automobile, made in St. Cloud by a charming scalawag named Samuel Pandolfo, who persuaded local businesspeople to support his automobile factory. The cars were just starting to come off the assembly line when Pandolfo was jailed for fraud. Later he was still welcomed back to the city. One part of town is still called "Pan town." Open June–Aug., Mon.–Sat., 10:00 A.M.–4:00 P.M., and Sun., noon–4:00 P.M.; Sept.–May, Tues.–Sat., 10:00 A.M.–4:00 P.M., and Sun., noon–4:00 P.M. Fee. **235 33rd Ave. S., St. Cloud, 56301; 320-253-8424.**

Parks

Charles A. Lindbergh State Park

This park was named for the father of the famous aviator, not "Lucky Lindy" himself. The 340-acre park is across from the Lindbergh family home, and the original acreage was given to the state by the Lindbergh family in 1931. The small park is bisected by meandering Pike Creek, which empties into the Mississippi River nearby; a rustic bridge near the parking lot provides access to the 6 miles of hiking trails (5.5 miles of cross-country ski trails in winter) on both sides of the creek. One branch of the historic Red River Ox Cart Trail passed near what is now the park, on the Mississippi's east bank. The park rents snowshoes and canoes. The Lindbergh House (see Museums and Historic Sites) is on park property but is operated by the Minnesota Historical Society. The park is located on the south side of Little Falls, off Lindbergh Dr. (County Rd. 52). **P.O. Box 364, Little Falls, 56345; 320-616-2525.**

Where to Stay

Both St. Cloud and Little Falls have familiar chain hotels and motels, plus some locally owned establishments, including resorts in the area. Request information on lodging from the visitors bureaus (see Services).

Bed-and-Breakfasts

Victorian Oaks Bed-and-Breakfast—$$$ to $$$$

This 1891 house adjacent to downtown is on the National Register of Historic Places. The three bedrooms are filled with antiques. A full breakfast is served in the dining room. **404 Ninth Ave. S., St. Cloud, 56301; 800-476-5035,** then enter **PIN 1404,** or **320-202-1404.**

Hotels, Motels, and Inns

Holiday Inn Hotel and Suites—$$$ to $$$$

This hotel has 257 rooms, including 43 two-room suites. Each room has an ironing board and iron, and most have hair dryers and reclining chairs. It's the pool and recreation complex that make this hotel stand out, however. There are two volleyball courts, two half-size basketball courts, two swimming pools, and two hot tubs, one big enough for 40 people. **755 S. 37th Ave., St. Cloud, 56301; 800-465-4329** or **320-253-9000.**

Camping

St. Cloud's and Little Falls' visitor bureaus (see Services) have information on camping, in addition to camping that is available at the state parks.

Charles A. Lindbergh State Park

The park has 38 drive-in sites, 15 with electricity, plus one backpack campsite and one canoe-in site. For reservations, call **The Connection, 800-246-CAMP** or **651-922-9000.**

Where to Eat

Anton's Fish and Whiskey—$ to $$$$

If Anton's seems a little off the beaten track, there's a historical reason for that—the log structure was a speakeasy during the 1920s. The sprawling, casual restaurant—with a log cabin interior—has an upstairs lounge, plus a gazebo and deck. Curious ducks and geese peer at diners through the floor-to-ceiling windows and honk loudly if visitors venture too close to their nests in spring. Featured entrees are steaks, walleye, and sometimes turtle. The bar carries about 60 scotches, with 40 single-malts. Open Mon.– Thurs., 11:00 A.M.–2:00 P.M., for lunch; Sun.– Thurs., 4:00–10:00 P.M., for dinner; and Fri. and Sat., 11:00 A.M.–11:00 P.M., for lunch and dinner. **2001 Frontage Rd. N., Waite Park (just outside St. Cloud), 56387; 320-253-3611.**

Maid-Rite—$

St. Cloud accountant Allen Anderson had such fond memories of eating Maid-Rite sandwiches—a bun filled with a quarter pound of loose, lean ground beef cooked with a secret seasoning—that he and his wife, Audrey, took over the St. Cloud franchise about a dozen years ago. The Maid-Rites were founded in 1926 in Muscatine, Iowa, and there's been a Maid-Rite in St. Cloud for more than 50 years. The Maid-Rite sandwiches are cooked in a special, slanted machine that drains the fat, so they aren't greasy, according to Audrey Anderson, who is also a teacher in addition to being the Maid-Rite maker. Over the years, Maid-Rite sandwiches have been mentioned by such diverse celebrities as Ronald Reagan and Garrison Keillor. There are other menu items, too, but some customers even have Maid-Rites for breakfast. Open Mon.–Fri., 9:00 A.M.–9:00 P.M.; Sat., 10:00 A.M.–9:00 P.M.; Sun.,

11:00 A.M.–8:00 P.M. The spanking-clean building, with its trademark red-and-white sign, is located just outside St. Cloud. **124 Second St. S. (Hwy. 23), Waite Park, 56387; 320-251-8895.**

Meeting Grounds—$

Try the hearty homemade soups and breads in made-to-order sandwiches at this pleasant restaurant in a historic downtown St. Cloud building, built in the late 1800s. Lots of students from nearby St. Cloud State University gravitate to the casual, comfortable restaurant. Leave room for dessert, too. Open Sun.–Thurs., 7:00 A.M.–11:00 P.M., and Fri.–Sat., 7:00 A.M.– midnight. **14 Fifth Ave. S., St. Cloud, 56303; 320-202-8880.**

Services

Little Falls Chamber of Commerce Convention and Visitors Bureau, 200 NW First St., Little Falls, 56345; 800-325-5916 or 320-632-5155.

   St. Cloud Area Convention and Visitors Bureau, 30 Sixth Ave. S., St. Cloud, 56301; 800-264-2940, ext. 129, or 320-656-3829. Website: www.stcloudcvb.com.

St. Croix Valley

The St. Croix Valley has been a travel destination for more than 100 years, and it continues to attract visitors who want to experience a bit of rural as well as wildish countryside close to urban areas. The river itself bears the designation of National Scenic Riverway, rather unusual for a river so close to a metropolitan area. Although the St. Croix National Scenic Riverway (which includes the Namekagon River) is 252 miles long, this chapter describes the St. Croix from Taylors Falls and St. Croix Falls in the north to the point where it flows into the Mississippi River 52 miles to the south. The scenery along the river and in its broad valley is at times spectacular and at other times pastoral; there are scattered reminders that the area was once a wilderness. The St. Croix Valley is still as much of a draw for visitors now as it was earlier for fur traders and loggers.

Though tourists like to think of the towns along the river as charming little villages—and some of them are—the larger towns have become booming bedroom communities for those who work in the Twin Cities. Stillwater and Hastings in Minnesota (and Hudson and River Falls in Wisconsin) are all fast-growing valley cities. Stillwater, once a logging boomtown, is now the main destination for those who visit the valley, and it is extremely crowded with bumper-to-bumper traffic on fall weekends. A controversial proposal to build a new bridge across the St. Croix to replace the old bridge in the heart of town is still pending; if a bridge is built outside Stillwater proper, some of the congestion may be relieved.

The valley is busy year-round, as cross-country skiers and snowmobilers take advantage of its close-to-the-city charms. You'll find dozens of bed-and-breakfasts and antiques stores, with half a dozen state parks to explore, ornate white riverboats looking like floating wedding cakes, and two excursion trains.

Both the Minnesota and Wisconsin sides are well worth exploring, though the Wisconsin side

is only touched on in this book. Hastings (and Prescott, Wisconsin) is on the southern end of the valley and is also a gateway to the Mississippi River. Marine-on-St. Croix is most people's idea of the perfect little village, and Afton is not far behind. A bit beyond the valley, but still close and linked by common heritage, are the Swedish-American towns of Lindstrom and Chisago City. At the northern end of the tourist region is Taylors Falls, another pretty village (on the Wisconsin side are Osceola and St. Croix Falls).

Recommended Reading

Afton Remembered (Afton Historical Society Press, 1996) by Edwin G. Robb, who has known the village since he was a child, provides an engaging look at this charming village on the St. Croix. *In the Land of Kichi Saga,* written and self-published by Theodore A. Norelius in 1973, is a detailed and colorful look at the life and inhabitants of the Swedish settlements near the St. Croix. The late Norelius, born in Lindstrom to a well-known Swedish-American family, was the editor of the *Chisago County Press* for years; he spent hours talking with author Vilhelm Moberg before Moberg wrote his famous books in the 1950s about Swedish immigrants, *The Emigrants, Unto a Good Land, The Settlers,* and *Last Letter Home* (Simon and Schuster).

History

The St. Croix Valley has seen human habitation for about 6,000 years, first by unknown ancestors of today's American Indians and later by the Dakota and Ojibwe. The first European explorer to see the valley was probably Daniel Greysolon, Sieur Du Luth, in 1680. In the 18th and 19th centuries, there were fur-trading posts along the river, with the Columbia Fur Trading Company establishing Fort Barbour at St. Croix Falls in 1825.

Settlement began after the Dakota and the Ojibwe Indians signed separate treaties with the U.S. government in 1837. The white-pine forests beckoned then, and logging soon became a thriving industry, with the logs floated down the river. Stillwater, one of Minnesota's oldest towns, began life as a logging town when four men started the Stillwater Lumber Company in 1843. The Dalles of the St. Croix were known for the huge logjams that built up between the basalt cliffs—the largest jam was a 7-mile pileup in 1886 near what is now Interstate State Park.

The Taylors Falls/Scandia/Chisago Lakes region of the St. Croix River Valley was one of the earliest areas of settlement for Swedish immigrants. The first Swedes came to the valley in the mid-1800s, with four families arriving at the Taylors Falls landing in 1851. The area still has a strong Swedish-American presence, though few of the residents speak Swedish today. The story of their hard struggle was told in Vilhelm Moberg's immigrant saga about the fictional characters of Karl Oskar and Kristina. The books were later made into two popular films, directed by Jan Troell and starring Liv Ullman and Max von Sydow. Though Moberg created these fictional characters, their story is not unlike that of the Swedish immigrants who settled the St. Croix Valley. The towns of the St. Croix Valley are now bedroom communities for many

Getting There

How to get to the valley depends on what part you want to see. Hwy. 95 runs along the river from Afton to Taylors Falls, though Hwy. 21 is closer to the river near Afton. (On the Wisconsin side, Hwy. 35 follows the river, although from Hudson south to Prescott, County Rd. F is closer.) Generally, the highway is closer to the river on the Minnesota side. To reach the southern part of the valley, drive east on I-94 from the Twin Cities. Taking Hwy. 36 east and turning north at Manning Trail gives you a shortcut to the northern part of the area covered in this chapter, and helps you avoid the Stillwater congestion. To reach the Swedish-American string of towns (see Tours), drive north on I-35 and take Hwy. 8 (a notoriously dangerous road, by the way), newly christened the Moberg Trail after author Vilhelm Moberg.

commuters to Twin Cities jobs. Tourism is now a major factor in the economy.

Major Attractions

St. Croix National Scenic Riverway

Look at the beautiful St. Croix River and thank the U.S. Congress of 1968 for protecting it for posterity. Designated a National Scenic Riverway and administered by the National Park Service, the riverway includes both the St. Croix and the Namekagon Rivers, a total of 252 miles. In summer, park rangers lead programs. The St. Croix River from St. Croix Falls (where a dam necessitates a portage) to where the Apple River joins the St. Croix is perhaps the best stretch for canoers. Farther downstream, there is heavy motorboat traffic. There are very few rapids in the river and it is calm for the most part. The National Scenic Riverway Visitor Centers all have maps, camping information, a list of canoe outfitters, slide shows and videos, and children's

Panoramic view of the St. Croix River. Photo courtesy of the Hudson, Wisconsin, Area Chamber of Commerce.

touch tables. Exhibits at the centers are on various topics related to the river and the area around it. Both are open year-round, daily, 9:00 A.M.–5:00 P.M. The **Headquarters Visitor Center** is located on the corner of Hamilton and Massachusetts Sts. in St. Croix Falls; **P.O. Box 708, St. Croix Falls, WI 54024; 715-483-3284.** The **Lower River Visitor Center** is in Stillwater at **117 S. Main St., Stillwater, 55082; 651-430-1938.**

Festivals and Events

Hot Air Affair
first full weekend in Feb.
Colorful hot-air balloons brighten up the winter landscape each Feb. in Hudson, Wisconsin. The weekend celebration includes launches and mass ascents of more than 40 hot-air balloons, a torchlight parade with marching kazoo bands, candlelight cross-country skiing, fireworks, and volleyball in the snow. The balloons fire up one evening and remain on the ground, looking like giant Chinese lanterns in the snow. The affair includes a chili cook-off and a pancake breakfast. The balloon launches take place Sat.–Sun., at 8:00 A.M. (weather permitting), at the J.T. Rock

School in Hudson, at 13th and Summer Sts. For information, call the Hudson Area Chamber of Commerce and Tourism Bureau (see Services).

Midsommar Dag
fourth Sat. in June
Is this Swedish heaven? No, it's Scandia on Midsommar Dag. There is dancing around the maypole at Gammelgården, the open-air museum (see Museums and Historic Sites), lots of singing, music, an exhibition of Dala painting (from the Swedish province of the same name), Swedish folk crafts, and a smorgasbord (reserve ahead). Wear a Swedish folk costume if you're lucky enough to have one. Visitors can help decorate the maypole at 10:00 A.M.; the program starts at 2:00 P.M. Located in Scandia, off Hwy. 97, at **20880 Olinda Trail, Scandia, 55073.** For information or reservations, contact the director, **9885 202 St. N., Forest Lake, 55025; 651-433-3430** or **651-433-5053.**

Lumberjack Days/Drum Beauty
mid-July
Stillwater's heritage is honored with this festival, which features a lumberjack show with log rolling, pole climbing, and other yesteryear skills. Among the events are a pie-baking contest, free

concerts from a barge floating in the St. Croix River, and fireworks. The festival includes the two-day Drum Beauty competition at Stillwater Junior High, in which drum and bugle corps compete. Most of the main festival events are in Stillwater's Lowell Park downtown. **651-430-2306. Website: www.lumberjackdays.com.**

Stillwater Antiquarian Book Fair
third Fri. and Sat. in Oct.

Stillwater, being the first officially designated book town in North America, is a fitting place for this huge book sale. Stillwater got the tongue-in-cheek "book town" designation several years ago, by proclamation of Richard Booth (you can call him King Richard, if you like), who started the book town concept with his huge bookstore in the tiny town of Hay-on-Wye in Wales. Two Stillwater bookstore owners asked for the honor of being named a book town and, lo, it was granted. More than 40 booksellers appear at this two-day event, at which mostly old or out-of-print books are sold. **651-430-0732.**

Taylors Falls Lighting Festival
last weekend in Nov.

The picture-postcard-pretty village of Taylors Falls, which has fewer than 800 residents, lights up in a blaze of holiday lights and events on Thanksgiving weekend. Several historic houses are open for visitors, and horse-drawn wagon rides are given. Call the Taylors Falls Chamber of Commerce, **651-465-6661.**

Outdoor Activities

Biking

Several of the state parks in the area have short bike trails—Afton has 4 miles; see Parks—and some communities and counties in the area also have them. Hastings has information on local bike paths through rolling terrain; contact the Hastings Chamber of Commerce for information (see Services). Hudson, Wisconsin, has a brochure detailing a 16-mile bike tour or a 32-mile auto tour; both routes start from Lakefront Park in Hudson. Afton Alps (see Skiing) has 7 miles of mountain

bike trails in the summer season, with bikes and helmets for rent. The Gandy Dancer Trail, a limestone-surfaced biking/hiking trail, begins at the intersection of Hwys. 35 and 8 in St. Croix Falls, Wisconsin.

Boating

CANOEING

Canoeing on the St. Croix River (see Major Attractions) is a popular summer and fall activity. Much of the river is calm and suitable for beginners and families.

Fishing

Area lakes and streams have good fishing. There is fishing for northern, walleye, bass, and brown trout in the St. Croix River in William O'Brien State Park; see Parks. Willow River State Park, Wisconsin, has five fishing stations that are handicapped-accessible; no motors are allowed on Little Falls Lake, which makes for peaceful fishing. The Kinnickinnic River, which flows through River Falls, Wisconsin, is regarded as one of the best trout streams in the entire upper Mississippi River basin. Both brown and brook trout are in the "Kinni," and they are there by natural reproduction, not by stocking. The river is 13.6 miles long, with nine access points from County Rd. J to where it meets the St. Croix. The season usually opens the first Sat. in May and continues until the last Sat. in Oct. For a map, call the River Falls Chamber of Commerce in Wisconsin, **715-425-2533** (see Services).

Balloon festival. Photo courtesy of the Hudson Hot Air Affair: Evalyn Peterson-Nerbonne.

Golf

There are many golf courses in the St. Croix Valley. The course at New Richmond is one that is highly regarded. Ask the tourism bureaus (see Services) for information on courses in the valley.

Hiking

You can't beat the variety of hiking trails found in the state parks on both sides of the St. Croix River Valley, including the rugged Ice Age Trail, which starts in St. Croix Falls, Wisconsin, in Interstate State Park. In Afton State Park there are 20 miles of hiking trails and a 0.75-mile self-guided hiking trail. Kinnickinnic State Park, Wisconsin, has 7 miles of hiking trails. Among the 35 miles of hiking trails in Wild River State Park are 2.7 miles of self-guided trails, including a pond trail and old logging roads with the ruts still visible. See Parks. Willow River State Park, Wisconsin, has about 10 miles of hiking trails, plus handicapped-accessible Hidden Ponds nature trail; located about 5 miles northeast of Hudson, Wisconsin; **715-386-5931.**

Skiing

CROSS-COUNTRY

The many state parks along the river, especially William O'Brien State Park (11.5 miles of trails and 10 miles for skate-skiing), have excellent cross-country ski trails. The warming house at O'Brien has a welcome wood fire; winter camping, with rustic toilets, is permitted in the park. In Afton State Park, there are 18 miles of trails for cross-country skiing and a sliding hill, plus a warming house. There are 35 miles of trails for cross-country skiers in Wild River State Park. Willow River State Park, Wisconsin, has 8 miles of cross-country ski trails and a sliding hill.

DOWNHILL

Afton Alps

Afton Alps is buzzing in winter, as it is one of the closest downhill ski areas to the Twin Cities. It has a vertical drop of 350 feet, with 40 runs served by 20 chair lifts, and a half pipe for snowboarders. The longest run is 3,000 feet.

There are four chalets and three rental shops, with snowboard as well as ski rentals. Located 15 miles east of St. Paul. **6600 Peller Ave. S., Hastings, 55033; 800-328-1328** or **651-436-5245.**

Wild Mountain

Wild Mountain, northwest of Taylors Falls, is a family-run ski area with 23 runs, four quad chair lifts, and a vertical drop of 300 feet. On Fri., there is late skiing until 3:00 A.M. Skiers and snowboarders share the runs. Located on Hwy. 16. **Box 235, Taylors Falls, 55084; 800-447-4958, 651-257-3550** (toll-free from the metro area), or **651-465-6315** (local calls). **Website: www.wildmountain.com.**

Swimming

Wild River

In summer, Wild River transforms from a ski hill (see Downhill Skiing) into a water park and alpine slide. Kids of all ages love it as a place to cool off on a hot summer day. The water slides range from tame to terrifying, and the alpine slide provides an exciting swoop down the hill. Adults who accompany kids may opt for going round and round in an inner tube on the Lazy River instead of a nearly straight shot down the Black Hole Speed Slide. The park also has Formula K Go-Karts. Located on Hwy. 16. **Box 235, Taylors Falls, 55084; 800-447-4958, 651-257-3550** (toll-free from the metro area), or **651-465-6315** (local calls). **Website: www.wildmountain.com.**

Seeing and Doing

Antiquing

The St. Croix Valley has dozens of antiques shops. Stillwater is perhaps the biggest draw for those seeking antiques, with more than a dozen antiques stores, mostly along Main St. One popular store is **Mulberry Point Antiques,** which has wares from 65 dealers on four levels. Open daily; call for hours. **270 N. Main St., Stillwater, 55082; 651-430-3630.** Many other towns, including Taylors Falls and Prescott and Osceola, Wisconsin, have thriving antiques businesses. Bench St. in Taylors Falls has several antiques shops, including **Newbery House, 418 Bench St., Taylors Falls, 55084; 651-465-6802.**

Art Galleries and Museums

Franconia Sculpture Park
Out on the wide prairie above the St. Croix River is a 14-acre sculpture garden in progress. Finished works of poured iron, plastic, hay, and other materials are displayed side by side with artists working on-site to create another sculpture for the garden. Artists from the area, other parts of the United States, and other countries have works in the unusual garden. Sculptors are in residence during the summer in the park, which was started by Fuller Cowles and John Hock. Free. Open daily, 10:00 A.M.–dusk. Located on Hwy. 8 near Taylors Falls. **20665 Lake Blvd., Shafer, 55074; 651-465-3701. Website: www.franconia.org.**

Phipps Center for the Arts
The Phipps Center in Hudson, Wisconsin, near the St. Croix River, is a sleek, modern showcase for the arts and art education. Series offered include musical theater presentations, musical performances, special events, and pipe-organ concerts played on the Phipps' Wurlitzer theater pipe organ, with its three manual consoles and 16 ranks of pipes. The Phipps also has three galleries for art exhibits featuring regional artists. The galleries are open year-round, Mon.–Fri., 9:00 A.M.–4:30 P.M., and Sat., 9:00 A.M.–noon. **109 Locust St., Hudson, WI 54016; 715-386-8409.**

Gardens and Arboreta

Squire House Gardens
It does your heart good to stop at these lovely gardens and peek in the shop. Squire House in the charming village of Afton has showplace gardens carved out in the lot next to the old house that serves as the shop and office. There are a sunken garden, a water garden, and paths winding among perennials. At one end is a traditional Swedish rail fence. Squire House sells plants and wonderful scented soaps and such, has special

programs on garden-related topics, and helps customers design their own gardens. Open Jan.–Mar., Thurs.–Sun., 10:00 A.M.–5:00 P.M.; Apr.–Dec., Tues.–Sun, 10:00 A.M.–5:00 P.M. **3390 St. Croix Trail S., Afton, 55001; 651-436-8080.**

Museums and Historic Sites

Afton Historical Society
This village museum located in an 1868 church building tells the story of the farming community that slowly became a resort over the years and now is beginning to become a small bedroom community for Twin Cities commuters. The museum has permanent exhibits on local history, agriculture, and war correspondent Ernie Pyle (who married a local girl). Open Memorial Day–mid-Oct., Wed.–Sun., 1:00–4:00 P.M.; mid-Oct.–Memorial Day, Wed.–Sat., 1:00–4:00 P.M. Located **in the old Afton Village Hall on Afton's main street, S. St. Croix Trail; 651-436-3500.**

Folsom House
The 1855 W.H.C. Folsom House, built in the Greek Revival style by a local pioneer civic leader and businessman and his wife, Mary Jane, is part of the Angel Hill neighborhood in Taylors Falls. The house, which is on the National Register of Historic Places, is owned by the Minnesota Historical Society and operated by the Taylors Falls Historical Society. Open Memorial Day–mid-Oct., daily, 1:00–4:30 P.M. Fee. **272 W. Government St., Taylors Falls, 55084; 651-465-3125.**

Gammelgården Museum
This open-air museum, which means "the old farm" in Swedish, consists of several log buildings that date from the early Swedish immigration to the Chisago Lakes area. Among them is the oldest Lutheran church building in Minnesota, an immigrant house circa 1855, a barn, and a parsonage. The museum also has a more recent *Stuga*—Swedish vacation cabin—and picnic area and playground. Special events at the museum include Midsommar Dag on the fourth Sat. in June (see Fesivals and Events) and the Lucia Fest on the Sun. closest to Dec. 13. Open mid-May–mid-Oct.,

Fri.–Sun., 1:00–4:00 P.M. Fee for groups. Located 35 miles north and a little east of St. Paul in Scandia, off Hwy. 97. **9885 202 St. N., Forest Lake, 55025; 651-433-3430** or **651-433-5053.**

Octagon House

This eight-sided, white frame house is a magnificent example of a building fad that was popular in the mid-1800s. The house was built by Judge Shaw Moffat and his wife, Nancy, who came to Hudson, Wisconsin, in 1854. Four generations of that family lived in the house; with its furnishing, the house epitomizes gracious living, Victorian style. The Moffats were a musical family and there are several instruments, including a piano, among the furnishings. In the children's room is a fascinating doll collection. The house, which is on the National Register of Historic Places, has features that many modern house owners envy, including lots of built-in closet space. The grounds, garden, and carriage house are also worth exploring. The house is owned and operated by the St. Croix County Historical Society. Open May–Oct., Tues.–Sat.; Nov.–Dec., some days; call for hours. **1004 Third St., Hudson, WI 54016; 715-386-2654.**

Octagon House. Photo courtesy of the Hudson, Wisconsin, Area Chamber of Commerce.

Washington County Historical Museum

This seasonal museum is housed in the sturdy stone "Warden's House," home to wardens at the state prison that is adjacent to the warden's house. The most notorious criminals incarcerated in the prison were Cole, Jim, and Bob Younger, who tried to rob the bank in Northfield along with Jesse and Frank James (see the Northfield chapter in the Southeast Region). The museum has exhibits on Stillwater's long history. Open May–Oct., Tues., Thurs., Sat., and Sun., 2:00–5:00 P.M.; also early Dec., for Christmas teas (call for hours). **602 N. Main St., Stillwater, 55082; 651-439-5956.**

Nature Centers

Carpenter Nature Center

What better way to spend a lovely fall day than to wander through this nature center, on the shore of the St. Croix River? The center, a 600-acre private, nonprofit preserve, was established by Thomas and Edna Carpenter, who lived in a limestone house on what is now Carpenter Nature Center land. The Carpenters, who were childless, created a foundation to protect their home and the land for others to enjoy. There are 15 miles of trails through wooded areas and restored prairie and oak savanna. A working apple orchard is part of the center, as are herb and flower gardens and nature exhibits. There are many special programs. Open year-round, daily, 8:00 A.M.–4:30 P.M. Free. Located northeast of Hastings on County Rd. 21. **12805 St. Croix Trail, Hastings, 55033; 651-437-4359.**

Parks

Afton State Park

Afton State Park on the St. Croix River is a multilevel park that gives a good workout to the many hikers who flock there. Ravines slice deeply into the park, making the terrain a challenge for skiers and hikers. In addition, the park has 4 miles of paved bike trails and 5 miles of trails for horseback riders. It is one of the closest state parks to the Twin Cities—only 40 minutes away—and gets many day users. The park has several kinds of territory: in addition to the wooded ravines, there are restored prairies and also portions of the original oak savanna. Exhibits in the interpretive center explain the park's various habitats. There is a lot of bird life in the park, particularly in spring when the warblers stop during their migration. Before it was designated as a park, the area was mostly farmland. To protect park environment, development has been kept to a minimum and the campground, beach, and interior of the park can only be reached on foot. Camping is limited to those who can pack or canoe in. Located 9 miles east from St. Paul on I-94, then 7 miles south on County Rd. 15, and 3 miles east on County Rd. 20. **6959 Peeler Ave. S., Hastings, 55033; 651-436-5391.**

Interstate State Park

As its name implies, there are two state parks of this name, one on either side of the St. Croix River, administered by Minnesota and Wisconsin separately. The river here is in a deep, rocky gorge and is very scenic. Sit on a rock high above the river and spot the little white paddle wheeler cruising up the river, and be transported back in time. Interstate has long been a popular spot.

"This is Minnesota's original tourist destination," says Park Manager Stephen Anderson. As long ago as the 1880s, tourists were coming to see the St. Croix Valley. The park itself was established in 1895, making it the second oldest state park in Minnesota. Interstate State Park on the Minnesota side is small by most state park standards, only about 300 acres, but, according to Anderson, "The unique thing is the diversity—it's pretty amazing." There are the glacial potholes, dense woods, the river floodplain, and the river valley itself. There are microclimates within the park due to different lighting conditions. The basalt cliffs were formed from volcanic activity 1.1 billion years ago. This was followed by the area being covered first by a sea, later by glaciers. The resulting glacial meltwaters also made changes in the landscape, chiefly the glacial potholes that are so fascinating to visitors. These potholes, the deepest of which, at 60 feet, is called "the bottomless pit," are the deepest potholes in the world. There are approximately 100 potholes

in the small space of 20 acres, the largest concentration in the world. There is a short, self-guided trail in the pothole area. Interstate has many rare and endangered species, such as the five-lined skink, which has a metallic blue tail. The skink, Anderson says, is apt to tail rock climbers, maybe looking for a handout. The park is full of wildflowers in the spring, and the trail up to Curtain Falls (closed in winter) brings hikers close to them. The 4 miles of hiking trails include some on either side of Hwy. 95. An excursion-boat landing is located within the park. A private firm rents canoes in the park. Located off U.S. Hwy. 8 (Hwy. 95) south of Taylors Falls. **P.O. Box 254, Taylors Falls, 55084; 651-465-5711.**

Twin to Minnesota's Interstate State Park across the St. Croix River, Wisconsin's Interstate State Park (the state's oldest) shares the same high cliffs and spectacular rock formations. Established in 1900, the park pays particular attention to its glacial history, with an Ice Age Interpretive Center. It is also the western terminus for the Ice Age Trail, a national and state scenic trail that follows the path of the last glacier and, when completed, will be 1,000 miles long, all in Wisconsin. The park has 1.7 miles of nature trails, 7.2 miles of hiking trails, and 10.6 miles of snowmobile trails. The entrance is located **just off Hwy. 35 in St. Croix Falls, Wisconsin; 715-483-3747. Website: www.iceagetrail.org.**

Kinnickinnic State Park

Dreaming of sugar-sand beaches? Don't save up for Florida—discover Wisconsin's Kinnickinnic State Park. Here the Kinnickinnic River flows into the St. Croix and forms a huge delta. It's great for swimming and sunning. Picnic tables and grills near the beach make it a perfect spot to spend the day. But there *is* the matter of the hill. Remember to take everything you need with you before you climb down the steep hill to the beach, because you won't want to climb up again in a hurry. The Kinnickinnic (fun to say, isn't it?) is a day-use park only, except for boat campers, who must have their own facilities. The river itself is a famous trout stream and there is a separate river parking lot far from the beach (see

Fishing). Located **9 miles south of Hudson, Wisconsin, off County Rd. F; 715-425-1129.**

Wild River State Park

Heavily wooded Wild River is one of Minnesota's largest parks, with nearly 7,000 acres and 18 miles of frontage along the St. Croix River. The river here is wide and tranquil, with a broad sandbar (with signs warning of drop-offs) near the remains of the old Nevers Dam. There are other signs of the park's past: a cemetery, two old town sites, the remains of two fur-trading posts. A year-round naturalist presents many programs geared for families, including searches for wildflower seeds to be used in replanting. In front of the visitor center is a garden of native plants that attract wildlife. The park has 18 miles of trails for horseback riders, and also rents canoes, skis, and snowshoes. The terrain is steep in places and the hiking trails can be a challenge. Located east of Cambridge. **39755 Park Trail, Center City, 55012; 651-583-2125 or 651-583-2925.**

William O'Brien State Park

This wonderful recreation area is just an hour from the Twin Cities. Before it was established in the 1940s, even that distance seemed a long way. Henry Hansen, professor emeritus of forestry at the University of Minnesota, was asked to help assess the area's suitability for a state park. The other man doing the assessment with him, Hansen says, remarked dubiously to him, "Do you think people would come this far to a park?" Yes, people really do come—in droves, sometimes. The park is equally popular in both winter and summer. Lake Alice has a swimming beach, canoe rental, and a campground nearby. The lake is connected to the St. Croix River, whose channels near the lake create several islands. The largest, Greenberg Island, is accessible by canoe and is a wildlife and wildflower haven. The park's different habitats result in a variety of animal and bird life. Along the 12 miles of hiking trails, visitors can see huge white pines that remain after the heyday of logging. The park has a visitor center with a year-round naturalist and excellent interpretive programs, including canoe floats, bike and ski tours, and special events. Located on Hwy. 95, 2 miles

north of Marine-on-St. Croix. **16821 O'Brien Trail N., Marine-on-St. Croix, 55047; 651-433-0500 or 651-433-0506.**

Shopping

Book Town

Stillwater is the place to go for used books. Now officially named a "book town" (see Festivals and Events), Stillwater boasts several bookstores, among them the unusual **Loome Theological Booksellers, 320 N. Fourth St., 651-430-1092,** and **St. Croix Antiquarian Booksellers, 232 S. Main St., 651-430-0732. Website: www.booktown.com.**

J. von Stern

Judy Stern designs and sells practical, stylish outdoor clothes, all made of natural materials. Stern's line includes vests, jackets, and hats made of tough canvas with deerhide trim. Her shop in Marine-on-St. Croix also features canoes; antler "art" in the form of lamps, chandeliers, etc.; snowshoes; rustic furniture; and original art. Stroll around town, too, when you stop—this is quite possibly Minnesota's most picturesque village. Open Wed.–Sun.; call for hours. **P.O. Box 42, Marine-on-St. Croix, 55047; 651-433-5700.**

St. Croix Outfitters

This four-level store, crammed to the rafters with outdoor equipment, skis, casual clothing, shoes, and moccasins, has been a Stillwater staple for half a century. Dick Slachta took it over from his dad in 1972 and it is still going strong. The store, adorned with beautiful pelts of fox, wolf, bear, beaver, and other animals, has many services for outdoor sports lovers, including skate sharpening, ski tune-ups, tennis racquet stringing, and cross-country ski rentals. Open year-round, Mon.–Fri., 9:00 A.M.–9:00 P.M.; Sat., 9:00 A.M.–6:00 P.M.; Sun., noon–6:00 P.M. **223 S. Main St., Stillwater, 55082; 651-439-4891.**

Sports

Kansas City Chiefs Football Camp

Each summer, National Football League fans get

a chance to watch the Kansas City Chiefs team practice and scrimmage other NFL teams at the team's summer camp, mid-July–mid-Aug. Practices are usually free. **800-4-KCC-KCC. Website: www.uwrf.edu/chiefs.**

Tours

Stillwater Trolley
The cute little red-and-yellow trolleys leave from Stillwater's waterfront and scoot all over town in an amusing narrated tour that explores the upper portion of the city, with its beautiful old homes. The trolley swooshes quickly downhill to the lower part of the city to finish the tour. Fee. Located at the Freight House Restaurant in downtown Stillwater, **400 Nelson St., Stillwater, 55082; 651-430-0352.**

AERIAL TOURS
Several businesses along the St. Croix offer hot-air balloon rides; check with the tourist bureaus (see Services).

BOAT TOURS
Afton Cruise Lines offers a public champagne-brunch cruise, May–Oct.; call for details, **651-436-8883. Andiamo Enterprises** has several boats that offer public and chartered cruises on the St. Croix out of Stillwater; **651-430-1234. Website: www.andiamo-ent.com.** The **Taylors Falls** *Princess* glides along the St. Croix River looking like a floating wedding cake. The paddle wheeler takes passengers on excursions past ancient rock formations with evocative names such as the Old Man of the Dalles and the Devil's Chair; the formations were "sculpted" as the glaciers retreated thousands of years ago. There are picnic cruises on Wed. evenings, dinner cruises in the fall, and Mother's Day brunch and dinner cruises. Tours given early May–mid-Oct., four times daily. The boat landing is located near the bridge in Taylors Falls on Hwy. 16. **Box 235, Taylors Falls, 55084; 800-447-4958, 651-257-3550** (toll-free from the metro area), or **651-465-6315** (local calls).

TRAIN TOURS
Minnesota Zephyr
The elegant *Zephyr* takes visitors back to the 1940s as well as on excursions outside of Stillwater. The lunch and dinner trains leave from the historic Stillwater Depot, chugging slowly along the track and back in a leisurely, three-hour journey, giving passengers plenty of time to get acquainted and eat a five-course meal with a choice of several entrees. There are five dining cars on the train, each decorated differently. **651-430-3000 or 800-992-6100. Website: www.minnesotazephyr.com.**

Osceola and St. Croix Valley Railway
The Scenic Osceola and St. Croix Valley Railway leaves from a renovated depot in Osceola, Wisconsin, and then takes a puff-and-toot trip through Wisconsin and into Minnesota and back. The 10- or 20-mile excursions are on diesel or steam trains. The trains and depot are a joint project of the Osceola Historical Society and the Minnesota Transportation Museum. Tours run Memorial Day–Oct., Sat.–Sun. and holidays. Located **on Depot St., off Hwy. 35, south of the railroad bridge; 800-711-2591 or 651-228-0263. Website: www.mtmuseum.org/railroad/oscv-location.html.**

WALKING TOURS
Most of the communities along the St. Croix Valley have historic districts that visitors enjoy strolling through. In **Hastings,** among the most intriguing buildings is the LeDuc-Simmons Mansion, built in Gothic Revival style in 1865, as well as the wonderful old courthouse and the main downtown street. (Hudson, Wisconsin, has a tour past many historic houses, including the Octagon House; see Museums and Historic Sites.) **Stillwater,** one of the oldest of the river towns, has many historic properties. **Taylors Falls** has the Folsom House and other buildings in the Angel Hill district, all on the National Register of Historic Places. Taylors Falls also has a short walking path, with benches beside the river, from Interstate State Park to downtown. Ask the tourism bureaus of these towns (see Services) for self-guided brochures of walking tours.

Swedish-American History Tours

Author Vilhelm Moberg made up the characters in his books about Swedish immigrants to the Midwest, but visiting Swedes seemed determined to know more about them. So, in self-defense, the town of Lindstrom put up statues of Karl Oskar and Kristina on the main street, and renovated an old house to represent the house in which they supposedly spent their last years. Moberg did research in the area in 1948 before writing the novels, riding from town to town on a bicycle borrowed from a local druggist. A statue of Moberg, bike at his side, is in Chisago City. Across the road from the fictional immigrants' house is the Glader Cemetery, the oldest Swedish pioneer cemetery in Minnesota, where many gravestones are in Swedish. In Chisago Lake Lutheran Church in Center City is a beautiful tapestry that traces the history of the church and community. If you go seeking these places, you'll be in good company: the king and queen of Sweden toured the area in 1996. Their guide was Helen Fosdick, who also guides lesser mortals, in groups or individually, in English or in Swedish. Fosdick, along with Alice and John Mortenson, operate the tour company. Fosdick is at **Box 671, Lindstrom, 55045; 651-257-4386.** The Mortensons can be reached at **651-257-2519.** A brochure for a self-guided tour of the Swedish-American sites is available from the Chisago Lakes Chamber of Commerce, **651-257-1177.**

Wineries

Alexis Bailly Vineyard

Out-of-staters are often surprised that Minnesota produces wine, and good wine at that. One taste of Alexis Bailly's seven wines will convince you. Nan Bailly, who keeps a vine cutter hanging from her belt, wanted to be a sportswriter until her dad started the vineyard, and she grew into the business. She learned wine making in France, and that influence shows. Her wry sense of humor is reflected in the slogan on the bottle labels: "[Minnesota] Where the grapes can suffer." Special events include the arrival of Bailly's Foch Nouveau the second weekend in Nov. and of the vintages during the first two weekends in June.

Tastings are offered June–Nov., Fri.–Sun., 11:00 A.M.–5:00 P.M. Located 1 mile south of Hastings off Hwy. 61 at 170th St. **18200 Kirby Ave., Hastings, 55033; 651-437-1413. Website: www.abvwines.com.**

Where to Stay

Bed-and-Breakfasts and Inns

Although the St. Croix Valley has its share of grand hostelries such as Stillwater's Lowell Inn and chain motels, it is the little inns and bed-and-breakfast establishments that are a big draw. There is an old jailhouse b-and-b in Taylors Falls, a lakeside farmhouse b-and-b in Osceola, Wisconsin, and an array of upscale Victorian b-and-bs in Stillwater (and Hudson, Wisconsin). Stillwater has a b-and-b association that sponsors an annual progressive tea and tours; **651-430-0359.** Also, 16 b-and-bs and inns throughout the valley are on display at a **Website: www.innsofthevalley.com.**

Arbor Inn—$$$$

The Arbor Inn's porch was just made for sitting and sipping a glass of lemonade in summer. The inn, built by a prominent Prescott family in 1902, has four rooms and friendly, folksy owners, Marv and Linda Kangas. The largest room has a woodburning fireplace and a private deck overlooking the St. Croix River. The Silhouette Room is well named, as Linda Kangas's collection of 85 silhouette pictures is on display. Three of the rooms have whirlpool baths and all have hand-pieced quilts on the beds. **434 N. Court St., Prescott, WI 54021; 888-262-1090.**

Baker Brewster Victorian Inn—$$$$

More than a century ago, a Baker married a Brewster and their union created the catchy name for this supremely comfy bed-and-breakfast in Hudson, Wisconsin. Current owners Dawn and Keith Kleinknecht were married in a bed-and-breakfast and were determined to have their own—the result is the Baker Brewster. The Kleinknechts' 1882-vintage Queen Anne Victorian retains the best aspects of Victoriana and suffuses them with sunlight and modern conveniences, such as whirlpool baths and computer modem connections. Each of the rooms has an individual character, from the light and airy flowered bower with its white iron bed to the staunchly patriotic red, white, and blue room that makes you feel like breaking out in a couple of verses of the *Star Spangled Banner*. The Kleinknechts are warm, witty hosts who manage to deftly combine the house's elegance with their own casual informality, a felicitous blend that puts guests instantly at ease. The Baker Brewster has begun offering mystery weekends in Jan. Located close to many of the St. Croix Valley's parks and attractions. **904 Vine St., Hudson, WI, 54016; 715-381-2895.**

The Historic Afton House—$$$ to $$$$

One of Minnesota's oldest inns, the Afton House—a tidy, white frame building—began its long career in 1867. Just a stone's throw from the St. Croix River, the charming little inn has 15 rooms, all decorated with a delicate country touch, with quilts and antiques abounding. Some rooms have four-poster beds, Jacuzzis, patios, and fireplaces, and all have private baths. Located in the heart of Afton and close enough to Selma's to skip down for a double-dip cone. **3291 S. St. Croix Trail, Afton, 55001; 651-436-8883.**

St. Croix River Inn—$$$ to $$$$

Notice that this is an inn, not a b-and-b. The difference is privacy, privacy, privacy. Husbands who run away screaming at the mention of staying in a bed-and-breakfast go docilely along when they learn they can have breakfast in their own room and lounge on their private patio or porch, watching the St. Croix River glide by. The inn has seven rooms, all with Jacuzzis and reproduction antiques. The decor is restrained but very pleasant, another point in its favor for reluctant husbands. All of this is in an 80-year-old stone house in Osceola, a Wisconsin river town that is beginning to be discovered by tourists. **305 River St., Osceola, WI 54020; 800-645-8820 or 715-294-4248.**

Thorwood and Rosewood Inns—$$$ to $$$$

Privacy, romance, and rubber duckies, too— Thorwood and Rosewood manage to combine all three in their superlative historic inns in Hastings. The 1880 mansions, both on the National Register of Historic Places, were rescued from undignified fates by Pam and Dick Thorsen. Pam, a serene hostess with an ex-journalist's lively curiosity, recounts that Thorwood, built in the French Empire style, was condemned and scheduled to be torn down when the Thorsens bought it. "We didn't have this planned; we believe in destiny. We always loved old buildings, and Dick and I are both preservationists at heart." The Thorsens redid the house one room at a time, and they did it magnificently, opening for business in 1983. Rosewood, built in the Queen Anne style, is a few blocks from Thorwood and opened in 1989. Thorwood is a bit more informal in atmosphere, although both houses are rife with creature comforts and pleasing extra touches, such as the rubber duckies in each bath and *The Shower Song Book* in showers. Many of the rooms have fireplaces, whirlpool baths, and handpainted touches by local artists. In the solarium, look for the painted fox lurking near the floor and the bird's nest with its nestlings in the bath. It would be difficult to pick a favorite room, but Mississippi Under the Stars, in Rosewood, is a strong contender. The suite has a private staircase leading to a Turkish delight, with a bed adorned with a paisley spread. A sprinkling of stars shine from the ceiling when the lights go down. It's a bath-lovers' paradise, with a double, teakwood-framed whirlpool, a round ceramic shower, and an antique soaking tub. There is also a reading alcove. Why would anyone ever want to leave? Guests are welcomed with a generous snack, breakfast is in the room or at small tables in the dining room, and dinner is served by reservation. Some of the 15 rooms have a two-night minimum stay on weekends. Special packages are available. **315 Pine St., Hastings, 55033; 651-437-3297.**

Hotels and Motels

Lumber Baron's Hotel—$$$$

Take the opulence of the Victorian era and graft on modern amenities, and you have the Lumber Baron's, yet another reason to go to Stillwater.

The Lumber Baron's rooms and suites are stately and comfortable, many decorated in the dark shades and rich fabrics that typify Victoriana. Rooms have views of the St. Croix or downtown Stillwater. Many of the units have canopy beds, gas fireplaces, balconies, and whirlpool baths. The hotel's lobby is striking and there is a 300-foot patio facing the river, a perfect place to relax with a drink and watch the river flow by. **101 Water St. S., Stillwater, 55082; 651-439-6000.**

Pines Motel—$$ to $$$

Small and clean and right in the heart of the St. Croix Valley, the Pines has been run by the same family in Taylors Falls for several decades. There are eight rooms, some with one bed and some with two. The Pines is convenient to recreation and shopping, and close to Taylors Falls' beloved Drive-In restaurant (see Where to Eat). **543 River St., Taylors Falls, 55084; 651-465-3422.**

Camping

In the **Lower St. Croix National Scenic Riverway,** the National Park Service has camping zones and also some specific campsites, most accessible only by boat or canoe. Contact the National Park Service Visitor Centers to find campground locations (see Major Attractions). For those who want more amenities, there are many state and private campgrounds near the river that have more facilities and can accommodate RVs.

State Parks—$

Afton has one canoe-in site and 24 backpack sites. Wild River has 96 drive-in sites, 17 with electricity, eight sites each for packing and canoeing in, two year-round camper cabins, and a guest house. Interstate in Minnesota has 37 campsites, 22 with electricity; Wisconsin's Interstate has 85 campsites; **715-482-5742.** William O'Brien has 124 sites, 61 with electricity, and two walk-in sites. Seven of the campsites are handicapped-accessible. There is one camper cabin. Willow River, Wisconsin, has 72 campsites, 19 with electricity; **715-386-5931.** For reservations in Minnesota state parks, call **The Connection, 800-246-CAMP** or **612-922-9000.**

Where to Eat

The St. Croix Valley is full of small cafes and restaurants. There are many other good choices in addition to those mentioned below. In Stillwater, **La Belle Vie** and the restaurants of the **Lowell Inn** in Stillwater are more upscale and formal than **Brine's** and **Savouries,** but all are popular. (The **Steamboat Inn** in Prescott, Wisconsin, is a local institution; also check out the eating places in Osceola.)

The Dock Cafe—$$ to $$$

Dine at the Dock for the best river view along the St. Croix. This Stillwater cafe has outdoor tables as well as indoor dining with sweeping views. The food is just as good as the view—with homemade soup (try the roasted garlic and spinach), pastas, walleye panfried in a cornmeal-and-garlic coating, Atlantic salmon, blackened catfish, and steak among the favorites. The cafe, which has restful, pared-down decor, is 12 years old. Open Mon.–Thurs., 11:00 A.M.–9:00 P.M.; Fri.–Sat., 11:00 A.M.–10:00 P.M.; Sun., 11:00 A.M.–8:00 P.M. Located in downtown Stillwater on the river. **425 E. Nelson St., Stillwater, 55082; 651-430-3770.**

Crabtree's Kitchen—$ to $$$

Someone described Crabtree's food as "rural yuppie," and owner Terry Bennett is satisfied with that. "We do everything the old-fashioned way here, but on weekends you see as many Harleys and Porsches as you do Chevrolets and Buicks," says Bennett, who—along with his wife, Bev, and son Wayne—has owned and operated the restaurant for the past 20 years. The restaurant was well established before the Bennetts bought it, and it celebrated its 50th anniversary in 1999. The Bennetts take care with the food: the turkeys are roasted whole for the turkey dinners and high-piled sandwiches; the desserts are home-baked, some from recipes as old as the restaurant; and the lutefisk is prepared on the premises. Lutefisk and Swedish apple pie with sour cream are two of the menu items that reflect the Swedish heritage of the area. In fact, the lutefisk—a love-it-or-hate-it dish—is served all during Dec. A local radio celebrity regularly extolls the strawberry shortcake. There is outdoor dining on the deck in season. The decor is a cross between cozy and kitschy, with license plates, old farm implements, and sassy signs about lutefisk on the walls. Open Apr.–Oct., Tues.–Fri., 11:00 A.M.–8:30 P.M.; Sat., 8:30 A.M.–8:30 P.M.; Sun., 8:30 A.M.–7:30 P.M.; Nov.–Mar., Tues.–Thurs., 11:00 A.M.–7:00 P.M.; Fri., 11:00 A.M.–8:00 P.M.; Sat., 9:00 A.M.–8:00 P.M.; Sun., 9:00 A.M.–7:00 P.M. Located on Hwy. 95 in the tiny village of Copas, north of Marine-on-St. Croix. **19713 Quinnell Ave. N., Scandia, 55047; 651-433-2455.**

The Drive-In—$ to $$

Go back to the '50s at the Drive-In at Taylors Falls. Homemade root beer and hand-packed burgers are on the menu, and carhops in poodle skirts serve you. But there are also veggie subs—this is the '50s, '90s-style. The Drive-In, which has been in the village since the '50s, is on Main St. in Taylors Falls. Look around; you may spot Kirby Puckett, former player for the Minnesota Twins baseball team, who is a regular customer. There is a miniature golf course and picnic tables behind the Drive-In. Open Memorial Day–Labor Day, daily, 11:00 A.M.–10:00 P.M.; Apr.–May and Labor Day—until leaf peepers go home, Sat.–Sun. (call for hours). Located **on Bench St. on the north end of Taylors Falls; 800-996-4448 or 651-465-7831.**

Rainbow Cafe—$ to $$

This is the place where Vilhelm Moberg's books on Swedish immigration began. The late Ted Norelius, editor of the local paper and descendant of Swedish immigrants himself, sat and chatted with Moberg by the hour in this cozy little cafe. Both men are gone now, but the cafe is still here, still dispensing homemade soups and pies, and still a nice place to stop for a bite to eat. Open Mon.–Sat., 7:00 A.M.–4:00 P.M.; Sun., 7:00 A.M.–2:00 P.M. **12715 Lake Blvd., Lindstrom, 55045; 651-257-5944.**

Coffeehouses, Sweets, and Treats

Coffee Talk—$

This is a coffee shop plus—coffee plus morning buns and other scrumptious baked goodies, plus magnetic poetry, plus a charming setting in the village of Taylors Falls. The light, airy space belies the fact that the building is of 1892 vintage. John Coffey (really, that's his name) opened the coffee shop in 1995. Open Sun.–Thurs., 7:00 A.M.–9:00 P.M.; Fri.–Sat., 7:00 A.M.–11:00 P.M. **479 Bench St., Taylors Falls, 55084; 651-465-6700.**

Eichten's Specialty Shop—$

Don't forget to stop at Eichten's for fresh cheese and lean buffalo meat from the herd around the back. Yes—really—there is a herd of buffalo here. Eichten's has lots of cheese varieties and sells other meats in addition to buffalo. Sandwiches are available from the counter. Open daily, 8:30 A.M.–6:00 P.M. Located between Center City and Taylors Falls on Hwy. 8. **16440 Lake Blvd., Center City, 55012; 651-257-1566.**

Services

Minnesota

Hastings Chamber of Commerce, 888-612-6122.

Scenic St. Croix Valley. Website: www.uwrf.edu/scvrta.

City of Stillwater Chamber of Commerce, 324 S. Main St., Stillwater, 55082; 651-439-4001. Website: www.stillwaterguide.com.

Stillwater Area Chamber of Commerce (includes the entire valley), **651-439-7700.**

Reach the **Taylors Falls Chamber of Commerce** by calling Wild Mountain, **800-447-4958** or **651-257-3550.**

Wisconsin

Hudson Area Chamber of Commerce and Tourism Bureau, 502 Second St., Hudson, WI 54016; 800-657-6775 or **715-386-8411.**

Osceola Chamber of Commerce, 715-755-3300.

Prescott Area Chamber of Commerce, 715-262-3284.

River Falls Chamber of Commerce, 715-425-2533.

Index

(*Note:* page numbers in italics indicate photographs.)

About the Author

Anne Gillespie Lewis is a third-generation Minnesotan who started asking questions as soon as she could talk and has never stopped. In 1967, after working as a sportswriter and assistant sports editor for the *Minnesota Daily* during her undergraduate years at the University of Minnesota, she talked herself into a job sportswriting for the *Minneapolis Star,* becoming one of few women sportswriters in the country.

Anne resigned from the *Star* for a summer stint working on a dairy farm above the Arctic Circle in Norway. She brought home an English husband and, after living in England for two years, they settled in her old home town, Minneapolis. They and their two children—now grown—have been

exploring Minnesota ever since. She and her family can't bear to pass a historical marker without stopping to read it.

A voracious reader, Anne speaks Norwegian pretty well and mangles French. She has driven dogsled teams, skied in the mountains of Norway, and taken her own fish off the hook once or twice. Her latest exploit is jumping through a hole in the ice into the frigid waters of a lake at a cross-country ski resort in northern Minnesota. A freelance writer—and, by avocation, a baker and gardener—Anne's travel and food stories have appeared in such magazines and newspapers as *Better Homes and Garden, Ladies' Home Journal, The Boston Globe, The Miami Herald,* and *The Denver Post.*